# Intercultural Communication: A Reader

Fifth Edition

LARRY A. SAMOVAR

San Diego State University

RICHARD E. PORTER

California State University,
Long Beach

Wadsworth Publishing Company
Belmont, California
A Division of Wadsworth, Inc.

Communications Editor: Kristine Clerkin
Editorial Assistant: Melissa Harris
Production Supervision: Miller/Scheier Associates
Designer: MaryEllen Podgorski; R. Kharibian
Copy Editor: Ruth Cottrell
Compositor: Graphic Typesetting Service
Cover: Stephen Osborn and Associates, Inc.

Printed in the United States of America

2 3 4 5 6 7 8 9 10—92 91 90 89 88

ISBN 0-534-08598-9

Library of Congress Cataloging in Publication Data

Intercultural communication: a reader / [Edited by]
  Larry A. Samovar, Richard E. Porter — 5th ed.

      p.      cm.
  Includes bibliographies and indexes.
  1. Intercultural communication.      I. Samovar,
  Larry A.      II. Porter, Richard E.
  HM258.I52  1988    303.4′    82—dc19      87-21461
                                              CIP
    ISBN 0-534-08598-9

# Contents

## Chapter 3　Nondominant Domestic Cultures　　119

## Chapter 4　Cultural Contexts　　173

**PART THREE**
**INTERCULTURAL INTERACTION:**
**TAKING PART IN INTERCULTURAL COMMUNICATION**　　215

## Chapter 5　Verbal Interaction　　218

## Chapter 6  Nonverbal Interaction  270

## PART FOUR
## INTERCULTURAL COMMUNICATION:
## BECOMING MORE EFFECTIVE  319

## Chapter 7  Communicating Interculturally  321

## Chapter 8  Ethical Considerations and Prospects for the Future  355

# Preface

The occasion of the fifth edition of our reader on intercultural communication is both pleasant and exciting because it indicates an ongoing acceptance of our ideas and views about intercultural communication among a wide variety of scholars and teachers in a field that has great personal meaning to us. We also are pleased that the intercultural communication field is continuing to grow and that we have helped shape and define that field. This latest edition represents our continuing attempt to refine our thoughts and feelings about the field and to share them with you.

As in the past, we intend this anthology to be for the general reader. Consequently, we have selected materials that are broadly based and comprehensive, which are suitable for both undergraduate and graduate students. Although the level of difficulty varies from article to article, we believe that, with only one or two exceptions, we have not gone beyond the difficulty level found in most texts for advanced undergraduate students. Twenty-three essays are new to this edition, eleven of which were prepared especially for this volume.

*Intercultural Communication: A Reader* is designed to meet three specific needs. The first comes from our belief that successful intercultural communication is a matter of the highest importance if humankind and society are to survive. This book, then, is designed to serve as a *basic anthology* for courses providing theoretical and practical knowledge about intercultural communication processes. Our intention is to make this book useful not only to students of communication theory, but also to readers seeking practical and immediately usable knowledge. Second, the book may be used as a *supplementary text* in existing service and basic communication skills courses and in interpersonal communication courses. Third, the book provides *resource material* for advanced courses in public speaking, communication theory, small group communication, organizational and business communication, and mass communication, as well as for courses in anthropology, sociology, social psychology, social welfare, business, and political science or international relations. It also may serve as a resource manual for people who find themselves in programs or situations involving intercultural communication.

The book is organized into four closely related parts. In Part One, "Intercultural Communication: An Introduction," the first chapter contains essays that examine the philosophical basis for intercultural communication and discuss what intercultural communication is, what it tries to accomplish, and the nature of intercultural communication. Parts Two, Three, and Four trace the intercultural communication experience by means of a topical sequence. Part Two, "Socio-Cultural Backgrounds: What We Bring to Intercultural Communication," examines the influences of socio-cultural factors on intercultural interaction. In this section, Chapter 2 deals with the understanding of international cultures while Chapter 3 explores nondominant domestic cultures, subcultures, and deviant subgroups. Chapter 4 continues with an exploration of the cultural contexts within which intercultural communication occurs. We believe that through an examination of the cultural differences in what we bring to our intercultural communication acts, we are better able to understand and to appreciate what goes on during the communication event itself. In Part Three, "Intercultural Interaction: Taking Part in Intercultural Communication," our analysis focuses on the problems of intercultural interaction. Chapter 5 in this section examines cultural differences in verbal interaction; Chapter 6 focuses on differences in nonverbal interaction. Part Four: "Intercultural Communication: Becoming More Effective," is concerned with improving intercultural communication. In Chapter 7 the readings offer the knowledge and experiences of successful intercultural communicators and practical suggestions for improving intercultural communication. Chapter 8, the final chapter, examines the ethical dimensions of intercultural communication, the future of intercultural communication, and possible directions for change and improvement.

This book continues to be the outcome of a joint venture. The ideas reflected in it and the decisions necessary for its development and preparation grew out of an association and a dialogue that have persisted for over twenty years. Both of us share a mutual concern that if the human race is to endure in the decades ahead—decades that will, in both time and space, bring all humans closer together in a global community—we must all be able to communicate with people from cultures far removed from our own.

We wish to express our appreciation to the many authors, professional associations, and publishers whose cooperation has helped make this book possible. In addition, various individuals have played a significant role in the development and completion of this project. Especially, we should like to thank Karin Peterson for her assistance in researching this edition. We wish to thank the following reviewers for their helpful suggestions: Gale S. Auletta, California State University, Hayward; Howard P. Holladay, California State University, Los Angeles; Albert M. Katz, University of Wisconsin, Superior; Dorothy K. Williamson-Ige, Indiana University Northwest.

Finally we are grateful to all the users of the fourth edition who contributed feedback from using the book in their courses.

Larry A. Samovar
Richard E. Porter

# PART ONE

## Intercultural Communication: An Introduction

*Precision of communication is important, more important than ever, in our era of hair-trigger balances, when a false or misunderstood word may create as much disaster as a sudden thoughtless act.*

*—James Thurber*

Intercultural communication, as we might rightly suspect, is not new. As long as people from different cultures have been encountering one another there has been intercultural communication. What is new, however, is the systematic study of exactly what happens when cross-cultural contacts and interaction take place—when the communication process involves people from different cultures.

Perhaps the knowledge that technology has produced the means of our own self-destruction has prompted this concern. Historically, intercultural communication, more often than not, has employed a rhetoric of force rather than reason. Maybe we are now seeking something other than traditional force. Or perhaps the reason for this new study is more pragmatic, brought about by our mobility, increased contact among cultures, and a widening world marketplace. Traditionally, intercultural communication took place among only an extremely small proportion of the world populace. Ministers of state and government, certain merchants, and a few tourists were the travelers and visitors to foreign lands. Until rather recently, we Americans had little contact with other cultures, even within our own country. The ghetto or barrio dwellers remained in the ghetto or barrio. If they did emerge, it was to serve the upper class, not to interact as equals. And those who made up the vast white middle America remained at home, rarely leaving their own county. This situation, of course, has changed markedly; we are now a mobile society among ever-increasing mobile societies.

This increased contact with other cultures, subcultures, and deviant subgroups makes it

1

imperative for us to make a concerted effort to get along with and understand people who are vastly different from ourselves. The ability, through increased awareness and understanding, to coexist peacefully with people who do not necessarily share our backgrounds, beliefs, values, or life styles can not only benefit us in our own neighborhoods but can also be a decisive factor in forestalling nuclear annihilation.

There remains a need to specify the nature of intercultural communication and to recognize the various viewpoints that see it somewhat differently. From what we have already said, you should suspect that there are a variety of ways in which the topic of intercultural communication can be explored. There are perspectives that look at intercultural communication from a mass media point of view. Scholars who follow this approach are concerned with issues such as international broadcasting, worldwide freedom of the press, the Western domination of information, and the use of modern electronic technologies for the instantaneous worldwide transmission of information. Other groups investigate international communication. Here the emphasis is on communication between nations and between governments. It is the communication of diplomacy and propaganda. Although both of these approaches are of great value, they are not the domain of this book. Our concern is with the more personal aspects of communication—what happens when people from different cultures interact face-to-face. Hence, we identify our approach as one that examines the *interpersonal dimensions* of intercultural communication. For this reason, the articles and essays we have selected for this collection have been selected because they focus on those variables of both culture and communication that come into play *during* the communication encounter—during the time that participants from different cultures are trying to share ideas, information, and feelings.

Inquiry into the nature of intercultural communication has raised many questions, but it has produced few theories and far fewer answers. Most of the inquiry has been associated with fields other than communication: primarily anthropology, international relations, social psychology, and socio- and psycholinguistics. Although the direction of research has been diverse, the knowledge has not been coordinated. Much that has emerged has been more a reaction to current socio-racial-ethnic concerns than an attempt to define and to explain intercultural communication. But, it is quite clear that knowledge of intercultural communication can aid in solving communication problems before they arise. School counselors who understand some of the reasons why the poor perceive schools as they do might be better able to treat young truants. Those who know that native Americans and Mexicans use eye contact in ways that differ from other Americans may be able to avert misunderstandings. In essence, what we are saying is that many problems can be avoided by understanding the components of intercultural communication.

# 1

# Approaches

We begin this exploration of intercultural communication with a series of diverse articles that (1) introduce the philosophy that underlies our concept of intercultural communication, (2) provide a general orientation and overview of intercultural communication, (3) theorize about the analysis of intercultural transactions, (4) provide insight into cultural differences, and (5) demonstrate the relationships between culture and perception. Our purpose at this point is to give you a sufficient introduction to the many wide and diverse dimensions of intercultural communication so that you will be able to approach the remainder of this volume with an appropriate frame of reference to make your further inquiry interesting, informative, and useful.

Dean C. Barnlund in "Communication in a Global Village" traces communication and transportation developments that have led to the apparent shrinking of the contemporary world and the emergence of the global community. He points out the ramifications of the global village in terms of the forms and kinds of interactions that necessarily accompany such a new community of people. Barnlund considers problems of meaning associated with cultural differences, interpersonal encounters, intercultural encounters, and the role of the "collective unconscious" in intercultural interactions.

In the next article, "Approaching Intercultural Communication," we introduce some of the *specific* topics and issues associated with the study of intercultural communication and present in rather broad terms what it involves. We start by defining and explaining the role of human communication. We then turn our attention to the specific areas of culture and communication and show how they interrelate to form the field of intercultural communication. By examining the major variables that affect intercultural communication, we better understand how it operates. By knowing at the outset of the book what the study of intercultural

3

communication entails, you should have a greater appreciation for the selections that follow.

Next, Michael Argyle provides us with a different overview of intercultural communication in "Intercultural Communication." He begins with the basic assumption that "many people have to communicate and work with members of other cultures." Because the differences that exist between these cultures have an impact on interpersonal interaction, Argyle believes that particular communication problems will arise. These problems can serve as an outline for the study of intercultural communication because they point out which areas of human interaction must be examined and understood before successful intercultural communication can occur. Argyle places these areas of difficulty into six categories: (1) language, including forms of polite usage; (2) nonverbal communication; (3) rules of social behavior, which include bribing and gift giving; (4) social relationships that govern family and work relationships; (5) motivation, which includes cultural concerns with achievement and face-saving; and (6) concepts and ideology involving ideas derived from religion and politics.

The importance of culture in human interaction is underscored by Edward T. Hall in his selection "Context and Meaning." The grand connection between culture and human communicative behavior is revealed when Hall demonstrates how culture provides a highly selective screen between people and their outside worlds. This cultural filter effectively designates what people attend to as well as what they choose to ignore. This link between culture and behavior is further illustrated through Hall's discussion of high- and low-context communication, in which he shows how people from different cultural backgrounds learn to concentrate on the unique aspects of their environments.

The ability of a person to understand the communicative behaviors of someone from a different culture requires a knowledge of that culture's value system. Myron Lustig introduces us to the concept of cultural values and gives us insight into how these values are shaped and how they are manifest within a culture in his article, "Value Differences in Intercultural Communication." Lustig contends that values are powerful unseen forces that provide a set of basic assumptions used by a culture to deal with its problems.

Examining the religion of a people gives us an excellent opportunity to continue our study of cultural values. In "Religion-caused Complications in Intercultural Communication," Reginald Smart contends that a knowledge of a culture's religion is crucial to understanding that culture because it deals with "ultimate values" that underlie all values and assumptions. The study of religious differences is, in fact, the study of differences in cultural values. To help us grasp these diversities, Smart divides religious orientations into two groups: the Mid-Eastern and Western group based on dualistic approaches to the notion of God and the Far Eastern groups based on a search for harmony and the presence of god in everything. By seeing the differences between these two major orientations and the effect they have on values and approaches to living, we can better understand the behavior of the people who follow these spiritual doctrines.

# Communication in a Global Village

## DEAN C. BARNLUND

*Nearing Autumn's close.*
*My neighbor—*
*How does he live, I wonder?*

—*Bashō*

These lines, written by one of the most cherished of *haiku* poets, express a timeless and universal curiosity in one's fellow man. When they were written, nearly three hundred years ago, the word "neighbor" referred to people very much like one's self—similar in dress, in diet, in custom, in language—who happened to live next door. Today relatively few people are surrounded by neighbors who are cultural replicas of themselves. Tomorrow we can expect to spend most of our lives in the company of neighbors who will speak in a different tongue, seek different values, move at a different pace, and interact according to a different script. Within no longer than a decade or two the probability of spending part of one's life in a foreign culture will exceed the probability a hundred years ago of ever leaving the town in which one was born. As our world is transformed our neighbors increasingly will be people whose life styles contrast sharply with our own.

The technological feasibility of such a global village is no longer in doubt. Only the precise date of its attainment is uncertain. The means already exist: in telecommunication systems linking the world by

satellite, in aircraft capable of moving people faster than the speed of sound, in computers which can disgorge facts more rapidly than men can formulate their questions. The methods for bringing people closer physically and electronically are clearly at hand. What is in doubt is whether the erosion of cultural boundaries through technology will bring the realization of a dream or a nightmare. Will a global village be a mere collection or a true community of men? Will its residents be neighbors capable of respecting and utilizing their differences, or clusters of strangers living in ghettos and united only in their antipathies for others?

Can we generate the new cultural attitudes required by our technological virtuosity? History is not very reassuring here. It has taken centuries to learn how to live harmoniously in the family, the tribe, the city state, and the nation. Each new stretching of human sensitivity and loyalty has taken generations to become firmly assimilated in the human psyche. And now we are forced into a quantum leap from the mutual suspicion and hostility that have marked the past relations between peoples into a world in which mutual respect and comprehension are requisite.

Even events of recent decades provide little basis for optimism. Increasing physical proximity has brought no millenium in human relations. If anything, it has appeared to intensify the divisions among people rather than to create a broader intimacy. Every new reduction in physical distance has made us more painfully aware of the psychic distance that divides people and has increased alarm over real or imagined differences. If today people occasionally choke on what seem to be indigestible differences between rich and poor, male and female, specialist and nonspecialist within cultures, what will happen tomorrow when people must assimilate and cope with still greater contrasts in life styles? Wider access to more people will be a doubtful victory if human beings find they have nothing to say to one another or cannot stand to listen to each other.

Time and space have long cushioned intercultural encounters, confining them to touristic ex-

From Dean C. Barnlund, *Public and Private Self in Japan and the United States* (Tokyo: Simul Press, Inc., 1975), pp. 3–24. Reprinted by permission of the publisher. Professor Barnlund teaches at San Francisco State University. Footnotes deleted.

changes. But this insulation is rapidly wearing thin. In the world of tomorrow we can expect to live—not merely vacation—in societies which seek different values and abide by different codes. There we will be surrounded by foreigners for long periods of time, working with others in the closest possible relationships. If people currently show little tolerance or talent for encounters with alien cultures, how can they learn to deal with constant and inescapable coexistence?

The temptation is to retreat to some pious hope or talismanic formula to carry us into the new age. "Meanwhile," as Edwin Reischauer reminds us, "we fail to do what we ourselves must do if 'one world' is ever to be achieved, and that is to develop the education, the skills and the attitudes that men must have if they are to build and maintain such a world. The time is short, and the needs are great. The task faces all men. But it is on the shoulders of people living in the strong countries of the world, such as Japan and the United States, that this burden falls with special weight and urgency."

Anyone who has truly struggled to comprehend another person—even those closest and most like himself—will appreciate the immensity of the challenge of intercultural communication. A greater exchange of people between nations, needed as that may be, carries with it no guarantee of increased cultural empathy; experience in other lands often does little but aggravate existing prejudices. Studying guidebooks or memorizing polite phrases similarly fails to explain differences in cultural perspectives. Programs of cultural enrichment, while they contribute to curiosity about other ways of life, do not cultivate the skills to function effectively in the cultures studied. Even concentrated exposure to a foreign language, valuable as it is, provides access to only one of the many codes that regulate daily affairs; human understanding is by no means guaranteed because conversants share the same dictionary. (Within the United States, where people inhabit a common territory and possess a common language, mutuality of meaning among Mexican-Americans, White Americans, Black-Americans, Indian-Americans—to say nothing of old and young, poor and rich, pro-establishment and anti-establishment cultures—is a sporadic and unreliable occurrence.) Useful as all these measures are for enlarging appreciation of diverse cultures, they fall short of what is needed for a global village to survive.

What seems most critical is to find ways of gaining entrance into the assumptive world of another culture, to identify the norms that govern face-to-face relations, and to equip people to function within a social system that is foreign but no longer incomprehensible. Without this kind of insight people are condemned to remain outsiders no matter how long they live in another country. Its institutions and its customs will be interpreted inevitably from the premises and through the medium of their own culture. Whether they notice something or overlook it, respect or ridicule it, express or conceal their reaction will be dictated by the logic of their own rather than the alien culture.

There are, of course, shelves and shelves of books on the cultures of the world. They cover the history, religion, political thought, music, sculpture, and industry of many nations. And they make fascinating and provocative reading. But only in the vaguest way do they suggest what it is that really distinguishes the behavior of a Samoan, a Congolese, a Japanese, or an American. Rarely do the descriptions of a political structure or religious faith explain precisely when and why certain topics are avoided or why specific gestures carry such radically different meanings according to the context in which they appear.

When former President Nixon and former Premier Sato met to discuss a growing problem concerning trade in textiles between Japan and the United States, Premier Sato announced that since they were on such good terms with each other the deliberations would be "three parts talk and seven parts 'haragei'." Translated literally, "haragei" means to communicate through the belly, that is to feel out intuitively rather than verbally state the precise position of each person.

Subscribing to this strategy—one that governs

many interpersonal exchanges in his culture—Premier Sato conveyed without verbal elaboration his comprehension of the plight of American textile firms threatened by accelerating exports of Japanese fabrics to the United States. President Nixon—similarly abiding by norms that govern interaction within his culture—took this comprehension of the American position to mean that new export quotas would be forthcoming shortly.

During the next few weeks both were shocked at the consequences of their meeting: Nixon was infuriated to learn that the new policies he expected were not forthcoming, and Sato was upset to find that he had unwittingly triggered a new wave of hostility toward his country. If prominent officials, surrounded by foreign advisers, can commit such grievous communicative blunders, the plight of the ordinary citizen may be suggested. Such intercultural collisions, forced upon the public consciousness by the grave consequences they carry and the extensive publicity they receive, only hint at the wider and more frequent confusions and hostilities that disrupt the negotiations of lesser officials, business executives, professionals and even visitors in foreign countries.

Every culture expresses its purposes and conducts its affairs through the medium of communication. Cultures exist primarily to create and preserve common systems of symbols by which their members can assign and exchange meanings. Unhappily, the distinctive rules that govern these symbol systems are far from obvious. About some of these codes, such as language, we have extensive knowledge. About others, such as gestures and facial codes, we have only rudimentary knowledge. On many others—rules governing topical appropriateness, customs regulating physical contact, time and space codes, strategies for the management of conflict—we have almost no systematic knowledge. To crash another culture with only the vaguest notion of its underlying dynamics reflects not only a provincial naïvete but a dangerous form of cultural arrogance.

It is differences in meaning, far more than mere differences in vocabulary, that isolate cultures, and that cause them to regard each other as strange or even barbaric. It is not too surprising that many cultures refer to themselves as "The People," relegating all other human beings to a subhuman form of life. To the person who drinks blood, the eating of meat is repulsive. Someone who conveys respect by standing is upset by someone who conveys it by sitting down; both may regard kneeling as absurd. Burying the dead may prompt tears in one society, smiles in another, and dancing in a third. If spitting on the street makes sense to some, it will appear bizarre that others carry their spit in their pocket; neither may quite appreciate someone who spits to express gratitude. The bullfight that constitutes an almost religious ritual for some seems a cruel and inhumane way of destroying a defenseless animal to others. Although staring is acceptable social behavior in some cultures, in others it is a thoughtless invasion of privacy. Privacy, itself, is without universal meaning.

Note that none of these acts involves an insurmountable linguistic challenge. The words that describe these acts—eating, spitting, showing respect, fighting, burying, and staring—are quite translatable into most languages. The issue is more conceptual than linguistic; each society places events in its own cultural frame and it is these frames that bestow the unique meaning and differentiated response they produce.

As we move or are driven toward a global village and increasingly frequent cultural contact, we need more than simply greater factual knowledge of each other. We need, more specifically, to identify what might be called the "rulebooks of meaning" that distinguish one culture from another. For to grasp the way in which other cultures perceive the world, and the assumptions and values that are the foundation of these perceptions, is to gain access to the experience of other human beings. Access to the world view and the communicative style of other cultures may not only enlarge our own way of experiencing the world but enable us to maintain constructive relationships with societies that operate according to a different logic than our own.

# SOURCES OF MEANING

To survive, psychologically as well as physically, human beings must inhabit a world that is relatively free of ambiguity and is reasonably predictable. Some sort of structure must be placed upon the endless profusion of incoming signals. The infant, born into a world of flashing, hissing, moving images, soon learns to adapt by resolving this chaos into toys and tables, dogs and parents. Even adults who have had their vision or hearing restored through surgery describe the world as a frightening and sometimes unbearable experience; only after days of effort are they able to transform blurs and noises into meaningful and therefore manageable experiences.

It is commonplace to talk as if the world "has" meaning, to ask what "is" the meaning of a phrase, a gesture, a painting, a contract. Yet when thought about, it is clear that events are devoid of meaning until someone assigns it to them. There is no appropriate response to a bow or a handshake, a shout or a whisper, until it is interpreted. A drop of water and the color red have no meaning, they simply exist. The aim of human perception is to make the world intelligible so that it can be managed successfully; the attribution of meaning is a prerequisite to and preparation for action.

People are never passive receivers, merely absorbing events of obvious significance, but are active in assigning meaning to sensation. What any event acquires in the way of meaning appears to reflect a transaction between what is there to be seen or heard, and what the interpreter brings to it in the way of past experience and prevailing motive. Thus the attribution of meanings is always a creative process by which the raw data of sensation are transformed to fit the aims of the observer.

The diversity of reactions that can be triggered by a single experience—meeting a stranger, negotiating a contract, attending a textile conference—is immense. Each observer is forced to see it through his own eyes, interpret it in the light of his own values, fit it to the requirements of his own circumstances. As a consequence, every object and message is seen by every observer from a somewhat different perspective. Each person will note some features and neglect others. Each will accept some relations among the facts and deny others. Each will arrive at some conclusion, tentative or certain, as the sounds and forms resolve into a "temple" or "barn," a "compliment" or "insult."

Provide a group of people with a set of photographs, even quite simple and ordinary photographs, and note how diverse are the meanings they provoke. Afterward they will recall and forget different pictures, they will also assign quite distinctive meanings to those they do remember. Some will recall the mood of a picture, others the actions; some the appearance and others the attitudes of persons portrayed. Often the observers cannot agree upon even the most "objective" details—the number of people, the precise location and identity of simple objects. A difference in frame of mind—fatigue, hunger, excitement, anger—will change dramatically what they report they have "seen."

It should not be surprising that people raised in different families, exposed to different events, praised and punished for different reasons, should come to view the world so differently. As George Kelly has noted, people see the world through templates which force them to construe events in unique ways. These patterns or grids which we fit over the realities of the world are cut from our own experience and values, and they predispose us to certain interpretations. Industrialist and farmer do not see the "same" land; husband and wife do not plan for the "same" child; doctor and patient do not discuss the "same" disease; borrower and creditor do not negotiate the "same" mortgage; daughter and daughter-in-law do not react to the "same" mother.

The world each person creates for himself is a distinctive world, not the same world others occupy. Each fashions from every incident whatever meanings fit his own private biases. These biases, taken together, constitute what has been called the "assumptive world of the individual." The world each person gets inside his head is the only world he knows. And it is this symbolic world, not the real world, that he talks about, argues about, laughs about, fights about.

## Interpersonal Encounters

Every communication, interpersonal or intercultural, is a transaction between these private worlds. As people talk they search for symbols that will enable them to share their experience and converge upon a common meaning. This process, often long and sometimes painful, makes it possible finally to reconcile apparent or real differences between them. Various words are used to describe this moment. When it involves an integration of facts or ideas, it is usually called an "agreement"; when it involves sharing a mood or feeling, it is referred to as "empathy" or "rapport." But "understanding" is a broad enough term to cover both possibilities; in either case it identifies the achievement of a common meaning.

If understanding is a measure of communicative success, a simple formula—which might be called the *Interpersonal Equation*—may clarify the major factors that contribute to its achievement:

*Interpersonal Understanding = f (Similarity of Perceptual Orientations, Similarity of Belief Systems, Similarity of Communicative Styles)*

That is, "Interpersonal Understanding" is a function of or dependent upon the degree of "Similarity of Perceptual Orientations," "Similarity of Systems of Belief," and "Similarity in Communicative Styles." Each of these terms requires some elaboration.

"Similarity in Perceptual Orientations" refers to a person's prevailing approach to reality and the degree of flexibility he manifests in organizing it. Some people can scan the world broadly, searching for diversity of experience, preferring the novel and unpredictable. They may be drawn to new foods, new music, new ways of thinking. Others seem to scan the world more narrowly, searching to confirm past experience, preferring the known and predictable. They secure satisfaction from old friends, traditional art forms, familiar life styles. The former have a high tolerance for novelty; the latter a low tolerance for novelty.

It is a balance between these tendencies, of course, that characterizes most people. Within the same person attraction to the unfamiliar and the familiar coexist. Which prevails at any given moment is at least partly a matter of circumstance: when secure, people may widen their perceptual field, accommodate new ideas or actions; when they feel insecure they may narrow their perceptual field to protect existing assumptions from the threat of new beliefs or life styles. The balance may be struck in still other ways: some people like to live in a stable physical setting with everything in its proper place, but welcome new emotional or intellectual challenges; others enjoy living in a chaotic and disordered environment but would rather avoid exposing themselves to novel or challenging ideas.

People differ also in the degree to which their perceptions are flexible or rigid. Some react with curiosity and delight to unpredictable and uncategorizable events. Others are disturbed or uncomfortable in the presence of the confusing and complex. There are people who show a high degree of tolerance for ambiguity; others manifest a low tolerance for ambiguity. When confronted with the complications and confusions that surround many daily events, the former tend to avoid immediate closure and delay judgment while the latter seek immediate closure and evaluation. Those with little tolerance for ambiguity tend to respond categorically, that is, by reference to the class names for things (businessmen, radicals, hippies, foreigners) rather than to their unique and differentiating features.

It would be reasonable to expect that individuals who approach reality similarly might understand each other easily, and laboratory research confirms this conclusion: people with similar perceptual styles attract one another, understand each other better, work more efficiently together and with greater satisfaction than those whose perceptual orientations differ.

"Similarity in Systems of Belief" refers not to the way people view the world, but to the conclusions they draw from their experience. Everyone develops a variety of opinions toward divorce, poverty, religion, television, sex, and social customs. When belief and disbelief systems coincide, people are likely to understand and appreciate each other better. Research done by Donn Byrne and replicated by the author demonstrates how powerfully human beings are drawn to those who hold the same beliefs and how sharply they are repelled by those who do not.

Subjects in these experiments were given questionnaires requesting their opinions on twenty-six topics. After completing the forms, each was asked to rank the thirteen most important and least important topics. Later each person was given four forms, ostensibly filled out by people in another group but actually filled out to show varying degrees of agreement with their own answers, and invited to choose among them with regard to their attractiveness as associates. The results were clear: people most preferred to talk with those whose attitudes duplicated their own exactly, next chose those who agreed with them on all important issues, next chose those with similar views on unimportant issues, and finally and reluctantly chose those who disagreed with them completely. It appears that most people most of the time find satisfying relationships easiest to achieve with someone who shares their own hierarchy of beliefs. This, of course, converts many human encounters into rituals of ratification, each person looking to the other only to obtain endorsement and applause for his own beliefs. It is, however, what is often meant by "interpersonal understanding."

Does the same principle hold true for "Similarity of Communicative Styles"? To a large extent, yes. But not completely. By "communicative style" is meant the topics people prefer to discuss, their favorite forms of interaction—ritual, repartee, argument, self-disclosure—and the depth of involvement they demand of each other. It includes the extent to which communicants rely upon the same channels—vocal, verbal, physical—for con-

veying information, and the extent to which they are tuned to the same level of meaning, that is, to the factual or emotional content of messages. The use of a common vocabulary and even preference for similar metaphors may help people to understand each other.

But some complementarity in conversational style may also help. Talkative people may prefer quiet partners, the more aggressive may enjoy the less aggressive, those who seek affection may be drawn to the more affection-giving, simply because both can find the greatest mutual satisfaction when interpersonal styles mesh. Even this sort of complementarity, however, may reflect a case of similarity in definitions of each other's conversational role.

This hypothesis, too, has drawn the interest of communicologists. One investigator found that people paired to work on common tasks were much more effective if their communicative styles were similar than if they were dissimilar. Another social scientist found that teachers tended to give higher grades on tests to students whose verbal styles matched their own than to students who gave equally valid answers but did not phrase them as their instructors might. To establish common meanings seems to require that conversants share a common vocabulary and compatible ways of expressing ideas and feelings.

It must be emphasized that perceptual orientations, systems of belief, and communicative styles do not exist or operate independently. They overlap and affect each other. They combine in complex ways to determine behavior. What a person says is influenced by what he believes and what he believes, in turn, by what he sees. His perceptions and beliefs are themselves partly a product of his manner of communicating with others. The terms that compose the Interpersonal Equation constitute not three isolated but three interdependent variables. They provide three perspectives to use in the analysis of communicative acts.

The Interpersonal Equation suggests there is an underlying narcissistic bias in human societies that draws similar people together. Each seeks to find in the other a reflection of himself, someone who views the world as he does, who interprets it as he does, and who expresses himself in a similar way. It is not surprising, then, that artists should be drawn to artists, radicals to radicals, Jews to Jews—or Japanese to Japanese and Americans to Americans.

The opposite seems equally true: people tend to avoid those who challenge their assumptions, who dismiss their beliefs, and who communicate in strange and unintelligible ways. When one reviews history, whether he examines crises within or between cultures, he finds people have consistently shielded themselves, segregated themselves, even fortified themselves, against wide differences in modes of perception or expression (in many cases, indeed, have persecuted and conquered the infidel and afterwards substituted their own cultural ways for the offending ones). Intercultural defensiveness appears to be only a counterpart of interpersonal defensiveness in the face of uncomprehended or incomprehensible differences.

## INTERCULTURAL
## ENCOUNTERS

Every culture attempts to create a "universe of discourse" for its members, a way in which people can interpret their experience and convey it to one another. Without a common system of codifying sensations, life would be absurd and all efforts to share meanings doomed to failure. This universe of discourse—one of the most precious of all cultural legacies—is transmitted to each generation in part consciously and in part unconsciously. Parents and teachers give explicit instruction in it by praising or criticizing certain ways of dressing, of thinking, of gesturing, of responding to the acts of others. But the most significant aspects of any cultural code may be conveyed implicitly, not by rule or lesson but through modelling behavior. The child is surrounded by others who, through the mere consistency of their actions as males and females, mothers and fathers, salesclerks and policemen, display what is appropriate behavior. Thus the grammar of any culture is sent and received largely unconsciously, making one's own cultural assump-

tions and biases difficult to recognize. They seem so obviously right that they require no explanation.

In *The Open and Closed Mind*, Milton Rokeach poses the problem of cultural understanding in its simplest form, but one that can readily demonstrate the complications of communication between cultures. It is called the "Denny Doodlebug Problem." Readers are given all the rules that govern his culture: Denny is an animal that always faces North, and can move only by jumping; he can jump large distances or small distances, but can change direction only after jumping four times in any direction; he can jump North, South, East or West, but not diagonally. Upon concluding a jump his master places some food three feet directly West of him. Surveying the situation, Denny concludes he must jump four times to reach the food. No more or less. And he is right. All the reader has to do is explain the circumstances that make his conclusion correct.

The large majority of people who attempt this problem fail to solve it, despite the fact that they are given all the rules that control behavior in this culture. If there is difficulty in getting inside the simplistic world of Denny Doodlebug—where the cultural code has already been broken and handed to us—imagine the complexity of comprehending behavior in societies where codes have not yet been deciphered. And where even those who obey these codes are only vaguely aware and can rarely describe the underlying sources of their own actions.

If two people, both of whom spring from a single culture, must often shout to be heard across the void that separates their private worlds, one can begin to appreciate the distance to be overcome when people of different cultural identities attempt to talk. Even with the most patient dedication to seeking a common terminology, it is surprising that people of alien cultures are able to hear each other at all. And the peoples of Japan and the United States would appear to constitute a particularly dramatic test of the ability to cross an intercultural divide. Consider the disparity between them.

Here is Japan, a tiny island nation with a minimum of resources, buffeted by periodic disasters, overcrowded with people, isolated by physical fact and cultural choice, nurtured in Shinto and Buddhist religions, permeated by a deep respect for nature, nonmaterialist in philosophy, intuitive in thought, hierarchical in social structure. Eschewing the explicit, the monumental, the bold and boisterous, it expresses its sensuality in the form of impeccable gardens, simple rural temples, asymmetrical flower arrangements, a theater unparalleled for containment of feeling, an art and literature remarkable for their delicacy, and crafts noted for their honest and earthy character. Its people, among the most homogeneous of men, are modest and apologetic in manner, communicate in an ambiguous and evocative language, are engrossed in interpersonal rituals and prefer inner serenity to influencing others. They occupy unpretentious buildings of wood and paper and live in cities laid out as casually as farm villages. Suddenly from these rice paddies emerges an industrial giant, surpassing rival nations with decades of industrial experience, greater resources, and a larger reserve of technicians. Its labor, working longer, harder and more frantically than any in the world, builds the earth's largest city, constructs some of its ugliest buildings, promotes the most garish and insistent advertising anywhere, and pollutes its air and water beyond the imagination.

And here is the United States, an immense country, sparsely settled, richly endowed, tied through waves of immigrants to the heritage of Europe, yet forced to subdue nature and find fresh solutions to the problems of survival. Steeped in the Judeo-Christian tradition, schooled in European abstract and analytic thought, it is materialist and experimental in outlook, philosophically pragmatic, politically equalitarian, economically competitive, its raw individualism sometimes tempered by a humanitarian concern for others. Its cities are studies in geometry along whose avenues rise shafts of steel and glass subdivided into separate cubicles for separate activities and separate people. Its popular arts are characterized by the hugeness of Cinemascope, the spontaneity of jazz, the earthy loudness of rock; in its fine arts the experimental, striking, and monumental often stifle the more

subtle revelation. The people, a smorgasbord of races, religions, dialects, and nationalities, are turned expressively outward, impatient with rituals and rules, casual and flippant, gifted in logic and argument, approachable and direct yet given to flamboyant and exaggerated assertion. They are curious about one another, open and helpful, yet display a missionary zeal for changing one another. Suddenly this nation whose power and confidence have placed it in a dominant position in the world intellectually and politically, whose style of life has permeated the planet, finds itself uncertain of its direction, doubts its own premises and values, questions its motives and materialism, and engages in an orgy of self criticism.

It is when people nurtured in such different psychological worlds meet that differences in cultural perspectives and communicative codes may sabotage efforts to understand one another. Repeated collisions between a foreigner and the members of a contrasting culture often produce what is called "culture shock." It is a feeling of helplessness, even of terror or anger, that accompanies working in an alien society. One feels trapped in an absurd and indecipherable nightmare.

It is as if some hostile leprechaun had gotten into the works and as a cosmic caper rewired the connections that hold society together. Not only do the actions of others no longer make sense, but it is impossible even to express one's own intentions clearly. "Yes" comes out meaning "No." A wave of the hand means "come," or it may mean "go." Formality may be regarded as childish, or as a devious form of flattery. Statements of fact may be heard as statements of conceit. Arriving early, or arriving late, embarrasses or impresses. "Suggestions" may be treated as "ultimatums," or precisely the opposite. Failure to stand at the proper moment, or failure to sit, may be insulting. The compliment intended to express gratitude instead conveys a sense of distance. A smile signifies disappointment rather than pleasure.

If the crises that follow such intercultural encounters are sufficiently dramatic or the communicants unusually sensitive, they may recognize the source of their trouble. If there is patience and constructive intention the confusion can sometimes be clarified. But more often the foreigner, without knowing it, leaves behind him a trail of frustration, mistrust, and even hatred *of which he is totally unaware*. Neither he nor his associates recognize that their difficulty springs from sources deep within the rhetoric of their own societies. Each sees himself as acting in ways that are thoroughly sensible, honest and considerate. And—given the rules governing his own universe of discourse—each is. Unfortunately, there are few cultural universals, and the degree of overlap in communicative codes is always less than perfect. Experience can be transmitted with fidelity only when the unique properties of each code are recognized and respected, or where the motivation and means exist to bring them into some sort of alignment.

## THE COLLECTIVE UNCONSCIOUS

Among the greatest insights of this modern age are two that bear a curious affinity to each other. The first, evolving from the efforts of psychologists, particularly Sigmund Freud, revealed the existence of an "individual unconscious." The acts of human beings were found to spring from motives of which they were often vaguely or completely unaware. Their unique perceptions of events arose not from the facts outside their skins but from unrecognized assumptions inside them. When, through intensive analysis, they obtained some insight into these assumptions, they became free to develop other ways of seeing and acting which contributed to their greater flexibility in coping with reality.

The second of these generative ideas, flowing from the work of anthropologists, particularly Margaret Mead and Ruth Benedict, postulated a parallel idea in the existence of a "cultural unconscious." Students of primitive cultures began to see that there was nothing divine or absolute about cultural norms. Every society had its own way of viewing the universe, and each developed from its premises a coherent set of rules of behavior. Each tended to be blindly committed to its own style of

life and regarded all others as evil. The fortunate person who was able to master the art of living in foreign cultures often learned that his own mode of life was only one among many. With this insight he became free to choose from among cultural values those that seemed to best fit his peculiar circumstances.

Cultural norms so completely surround people, so permeate thought and action, that few ever recognize the assumptions on which their lives and their sanity rest. As one observer put it, if birds were suddenly endowed with scientific curiosity they might examine many things, but the sky itself would be overlooked as a suitable subject; if fish were to become curious about the world, it would never occur to them to begin by investigating water. For birds and fish would take the sky and sea for granted, unaware of their profound influence because they comprise the medium for every act. Human beings, in a similar way, occupy a symbolic universe governed by codes that are unconsciously acquired and automatically employed. So much so that they rarely notice that the ways they interpret and talk about events are distinctively different from the ways people conduct their affairs in other cultures.

As long as people remain blind to the sources of their meanings, they are imprisoned within them. These cultural frames of reference are no less confining simply because they cannot be seen or touched. Whether it is an individual neurosis that keeps an individual out of contact with his neighbors, or a collective neurosis that separates neighbors of different cultures, both are forms of blindness that limit what can be experienced and what can be learned from others.

It would seem that everywhere people would desire to break out of the boundaries of their own experiential worlds. Their ability to react sensitively to a wider spectrum of events and peoples requires an overcoming of such cultural parochialism. But, in fact, few attain this broader vision. Some, of course, have little opportunity for wider cultural experience, though this condition should change as the movement of people accelerates. Others do not try to widen their experience because they prefer the old and familiar, seek from their affairs only further confirmation of the correctness of their own values. Still others recoil from such experiences because they feel it dangerous to probe too deeply into the personal or cultural unconscious. Exposure may reveal how tenuous and arbitrary many cultural norms are; such exposure might force people to acquire new bases for interpreting events. And even for the many who do seek actively to enlarge the variety of human beings with whom they are capable of communicating there are still difficulties.

Cultural myopia persists not merely because of inertia and habit, but chiefly because it is so difficult to overcome. One acquires a personality and a culture in childhood, long before he is capable of comprehending either of them. To survive, each person masters the perceptual orientations, cognitive biases, and communicative habits of his own culture. But once mastered, objective assessment of these same processes is awkward since the same mechanisms that are being evaluated must be used in making the evaluations. Once a child learns Japanese or English or Navaho, the categories and grammar of each language predispose him to perceive and think in certain ways, and discourage him from doing so in other ways. When he attempts to discover why he sees or thinks as he does, he uses the same techniques he is trying to identify. Once one becomes an Indian, an Ibo, or a Frenchman— or even a priest or scientist—it is difficult to extricate oneself from that mooring long enough to find out what one truly is or wants.

Fortunately, there may be a way around this paradox. Or promise of a way around it. It is to expose the culturally distinctive ways various peoples construe events and seek to identify the conventions that connect what is seen with what is thought with what is said. Once this cultural grammar is assimilated and the rules that govern the exchange of meanings are known, they can be shared and learned by those who choose to work and live in alien cultures.

When people within a culture face an insurmountable problem they turn to friends, neighbors, associates, for help. To them they explain their predicament, often in distinctive personal ways. Through talking it out, however, there often emerge new ways of looking at the problem, fresh incentive to attack it, and alternative solutions to it. This sort of interpersonal exploration is often successful within a culture for people share at least the same communicative style even if they do not agree completely in their perceptions or beliefs.

When people communicate between cultures, where communicative rules as well as the substance of experience differs, the problems multiply. But so, too, do the number of interpretations and alternatives. If it is true that the more people differ the harder it is for them to understand each other, it is equally true that the more they differ the more they have to teach and learn from each other. To do so, of course, there must be mutual respect and sufficient curiosity to overcome the frustrations that occur as they flounder from one misunderstanding to another. Yet the task of coming to grips with differences in communicative styles—between or within cultures—is prerequisite to all other types of mutuality.

# Approaching Intercultural Communication

RICHARD E. PORTER
LARRY A. SAMOVAR

In the decades of the 1960s and 1970s, numerous events had profound effects on the world and humankind. Rapid and wide-ranging improvements in forms of transportation and communication caused the world to shrink in a figurative sense; we entered the era of the global village. Our mobility improved until distances no longer mattered. Jet airplanes can put us anywhere within hours. This newfound mobility is not exclusively ours; people around the world are on the move. International tradesmen, foreign students, diplomats, and especially tourists are moving in and out of an assortment of cultures—cultures that often appear unfamiliar, alien, and at times mysterious. Additional cultural contact also has emerged through the influx of refugees into the United States. People from Vietnam, Cambodia, Laos, Cuba, and Haiti, to name just a few countries, have entered the United States and are trying to adjust to life in their new homes. As these people try to assimilate into this culture, we will have many opportunities for intercultural contacts in our daily lives.

This original essay appeared in print for the first time in the third edition. All rights reserved. Permission to reprint must be obtained from the publisher and the authors. Professor Porter teaches in the Speech Communication Department at California State University, Long Beach. Professor Samovar teaches in the Speech Communication Department, San Diego State University.

While this global phenomenon was taking place, there was also a kind of cultural revolution within our own boundaries. Domestic events made us focus our attention upon new and often demanding cultures, subcultures, and deviant subgroups. Blacks, Chicanos, women, homosexuals, the poor, the Weatherman underground, the Symbionese Liberation Army, the drug culture, youth, and countless other groups became highly visible and vocal, and they disturbed many of us. Frequently, their communicative behaviors seemed strange, even bizarre, and failed to meet our normal expectations.

This attention to minority subcommunities made us realize that intercultural contact not only is inevitable but often is unsuccessful. We discovered, in short, that intercultural communication is difficult. Even when the natural barrier of language is overcome, we can still fail to understand and to be understood. These failures, both in the international arena and on the domestic scene, give rise to the marriage of culture and communication and to the recognition of intercultural communication as a field of study. Inherent in this fusion is the idea that intercultural communication entails the investigation of culture and the difficulties of communicating across cultural boundaries.

*Intercultural communication* occurs whenever a message producer is a member of one culture and a message receiver is a member of another. Our discussion, therefore, will deal with intercultural communication and point out the relationships among communication, culture, and intercultural communication.

## COMMUNICATION

To understand intercultural interaction we must first understand human communication. Understanding human communication means knowing something about what happens during an encounter, why it happens, what can happen, the effects of what happens, and finally what we can do to influence and maximize the results of that event.

## Understanding and Defining Communication

We begin with a basic assumption that communication has something to do with human behavior and the satisfaction of a need to interact with other human beings. Almost everyone needs social contact with other people, and this need is met through the exchange of messages that serve as bridges to unite otherwise isolated individuals. Messages come into being through human behavior. When we talk, we obviously are behaving, but when we wave, smile, frown, walk, shake our heads, or gesture, we also are behaving. Frequently these actions are messages; they are used to communicate something to someone else.

Before these behaviors can be called messages, they must meet two requirements. First, they must be observed by someone, and second, they must elicit meaning. In other words, any behavior to which meaning is given is a message.

If we examine this last statement for a moment we can see several implications. First, the word *any* tells us that both verbal and nonverbal behaviors may function as messages. Verbal messages consist of spoken or written words (speaking and writing are word-producing behaviors) while nonverbal messages consist of the entire remaining repertory of behaviors.

Second, behavior may be either conscious or unconscious. We occasionally do something without being aware of it. This is especially true of nonverbal behavior. Habits such as fingernail biting, toe tapping, leg jiggling, head shaking, staring, and smiling, for instance, occur many times without conscious awareness. Even such things as slouching in a chair, chewing gum, or adjusting glasses are frequently unconscious behaviors. And since a message consists of behaviors to which meaning may be attributed, we must acknowledge the possibility of producing messages unknowingly.

A third implication of behavior-message is that we frequently behave unintentionally. For instance, if we are embarrassed we may blush or speak with vocal disfluencies. We do not intend to blush or to stammer, but we do so anyway. Again, these unintentional behaviors become messages if someone sees them and gives meaning to them.

With this concept of conscious-unconscious, intentional-unintentional behavior relationships, we are ready to formulate a definition of communication. Here, *communication* is defined as that which happens whenever meaning is attributed to behavior or to the residue of behavior. When someone observes our behavior or its residue and gives meaning to it, communication has taken place regardless of whether our behavior was conscious or unconscious, intentional or unintentional. If we think about this for a moment, we must realize that it is impossible for us not to behave. The very act of being is a form of behavior. And if behavior has communication potential, then it is also impossible for us not to communicate; in other words, *we cannot not communicate*.

The notion of behavior residue mentioned in our definition refers to those things that remain as a record of our actions. For instance, this article is a behavior residue resulting from certain behaviors; as the authors we had to think, write, and type. Another example of behavior residue might be the odor of cigar smoke lingering in an elevator after the cigar smoker has departed. Smoking the cigar was the behavior; the odor is the residue. The meaning you give to that smell is a reflection of your past experiences and attitudes toward cigars, smoking, smoking in public elevators, and, perhaps, people who smoke cigars.

Our approach to communication has focused on the attribution of meaning to behavior. Attribution means that we take meaning that we already have and give it to behavior we observe in our environment. We might imagine that somewhere in each of our brains is a meaning reservoir in which we have stored all of the meanings we possess. These various meanings have developed throughout our lifetimes as a result of our culture acting upon us as well as the result of our individual experiences within that culture. Meaning is relative to each of us because each of us is a unique human being with a unique background and experiences.

When we encounter a behavior in our environment we each dip into our individual, unique meaning reservoirs and select the meaning we believe is most likely to be most appropriate for the behavior encountered and the social context in which it occurred. Usually this works quite well, but at other times it fails and we misinterpret a message—we attribute the wrong meaning to the behavior we have observed.

Our definition of communication has been general, thus far, in order to accommodate the many circumstances under which communication may occur. We now are going to propose a modified definition that assumes a conscious intention to communicate yet realizes that unconscious and unintentional behavior may complicate communication situations. Our definition also will specify the ingredients of communication and some of the dynamics present in communication.

## The Ingredients of Communication

Before we examine the ingredients of communication, we must have a definition that specifies the ingredients and their relationships. As our purpose in studying intercultural communication is to develop communication skills to apply with conscious intent, our working definition of communication specifies intentional communication. *Communication* is now defined as a dynamic transactional behavior-affecting process in which sources and receivers intentionally code their behavior to produce messages that they transmit through a channel in order to induce or elicit particular attitudes or behaviors. Communication is complete only when the intended message recipient perceives the coded behavior, attributes meaning to it, and is affected by it. In these transactions must be included all conscious or unconscious, intentional or unintentional, verbal, nonverbal, and contextual stimuli that act as cues to both the source and the receiver about the quality and credibility of the message.

This definition allows us to identify eight specific ingredients of communication within the context of intentional communication. First is the *source*. A source is a person who has a need to communicate. This need may range from a social desire for recognition as an individual to the desire to share information with others or to influence the attitudes and behaviors of one or more others. The source's wish to communicate is a desire to share an internal state of being with another human being. Communication, then, really is concerned with the sharing of internal states of being with varying degrees of intention to influence the information, attitudes, and behaviors of others.

Internal states of being cannot be shared directly, however. We must rely on symbolic representations of our internal states. This brings us to the second ingredient, *encoding*. Encoding is an internal activity in which verbal and nonverbal behaviors are selected and arranged according to the rules of grammar and syntax applicable to the language being used to create a message.

The result of encoding behavior is a *message*. A message is a set of verbal and/or nonverbal symbols that represent a source's particular state of being at a particular moment in time and space. Although encoding is an internal act that produces a message, a message is external to the source; the message is what must pass between a source and a receiver if the source is to influence the receiver.

Messages must have a means by which they move from source to receiver. The fourth communication ingredient is the *channel* that provides the connection between source and receiver. A channel is the physical means by which the message moves between source and receiver.

The fifth ingredient is the *receiver*. Receivers are the people who intercept messages and as a consequence become linked to the message source. Receivers may be those intended by the source or they may be others who, by whatever circumstance, come in contact with the message once it has entered the channel.

Receivers have problems with messages not unlike the problems sources have with internal states of being. Messages usually impinge on receivers in the form of light waves and sound waves although they may be in forms that stimulate any of the senses. Whatever the form of sensory stimulation, receivers must convert these energies into meaningful experiences.

Converting external energies into a meaningful experience is the sixth ingredient, called *decoding*. It is akin to the source's act of encoding, as it also is an internal activity. Decoding is the internal processing of a message and the attribution of meaning to the source's behaviors that represent the source's internal state of being.

The seventh ingredient we need to consider is *receiver response*. This is most easily thought of as what a receiver decides to do about the message. Response may vary along a minimum-maximum dimension. Minimum response is the receiver's decision to ignore or to do nothing about the message. Maximum response, in contrast, is an immediate overt physical act of possibly violent proportion. If communication has been somewhat successful, the response of the receiver, to some degree, will resemble that desired by the source who created the response-eliciting message.

The final ingredient we consider is *feedback*. This is information available to a source that permits qualitative judgments about communication effectiveness in order to adjust and adapt to an ongoing situation. Although feedback and response are not the same thing, they are clearly related. Response is what the receiver decides to do about the message while feedback is information about communication effectiveness. They are related because receiver response is a normal source of feedback.

The eight ingredients just discussed are only a partial list of the factors that function during a communication event. In addition to these elements, when we conceive of communication as a process there are several other characteristics that help us understand how communication actually works.

First, communication is *dynamic*. It is an ongoing, ever-changing activity. As participants in communication we constantly are affected by other people's messages and, as a consequence, we undergo continual change. Each of us in our daily life meets and interacts with people and these people exert some influence over us. Each time we are influenced we are changed in some way, which means that as we go through life we do so as continually changing individuals—dynamic persons.

A second characteristic of communication is that it is *interactive*. Communication must take place between a source and a receiver. This implies two or more people who bring to a communication event their own unique backgrounds and experiences that serve as a backdrop for communicative interaction. Interaction also implies a reciprocal situation in which each party attempts to influence the other. That is, each party simultaneously creates messages designed to elicit specific responses from the other.

Third, communication is *irreversible*. Once we have said something and someone has received and decoded the message, we cannot retrieve it. This circumstance is sometimes called "putting your foot in your mouth." The point is that because of the process nature of communication, once a receiver has been affected by a message, that result cannot be called back. The source may send other messages in attempts to modify the effect, but it cannot be eliminated. This frequently is a problem when we unconsciously or unintentionally send a message to someone. We may affect them adversely and not even know it. Then during future interaction we may wonder why that someone is reacting to us in an unusual way.

Fourth, communication takes place in both a *physical* and a *social* context. When we interact with someone it is not in isolation but within specific physical surroundings and under a set of specific social dynamics. Physical surroundings include specific physical objects such as furniture, window coverings, floor coverings, lighting, noise levels, acoustics, vegetation, presence or absence of physical clutter, as well as competing messages. Many aspects of the physical environment can and do affect communication—the comfort or discomfort of a chair, the color of the walls, or total atmosphere of a room are but a few. Also affecting communication is the symbolic meaning of the physical surroundings—a kind of nonverbal communication. To illustrate, recall briefly the Paris Peace Talks in which much time was spent in deciding on a table shape acceptable to all parties. While this may seem trivial, it was very important to the negotiators because a table with equal sides symbolically represented an equality of all parties at the table. The South Vietnamese did not want to give this recognition to the Viet Cong any more than North Vietnam wished to give this recognition to the United States.

Social context defines the social relationships that exist between source and receiver. In our American culture we tend to be somewhat cavalier toward social hierarchies and pay much less attention to them than do people in other cultures. Nevertheless, such differences as teacher-student, employer-employee, parent-child, Admiral-Seaman, senator-citizen, friend-enemy, physician-patient, and judge-attorney affect the communication process. And, quite frequently, the physical surroundings help define the social context. The employer may sit behind a desk while the employee stands before the desk to receive an admonition. Or, in the courtroom, the judge sits elevated facing the courtroom, jurors, and attorneys, indicating the social superiority of the judge relative to the other officers of the court. The attorneys sit side by side indicating a social equality between accuser and accused until such time as the jury of peers renders a verdict.

No matter what the social context, it will have some effect on communication. The form of language used, the respect or lack of respect shown one another, the time of day, personal moods, who speaks to whom and in what order, and the degree of nervousness or confidence people express are but a few of the ways in which the social context can affect communication.

At this point, we should see clearly that human communication does not take place in a social vacuum. Rather, communication is an intricate matrix of interacting social acts that occur in a complex social environment. This social environment reflects the way people live, how they come to interact with and get along in their world. This social environment is culture, and if we truly are to understand communication, we also must understand culture.

## CULTURE

When we begin to consider culture, we are concerned with the way people live because culture is the form or pattern for living. People learn to think, feel, believe, and strive for what their culture considers proper. Language habits, friendships, eating habits, communication practices, social acts, economic and political activities, and technology all follow the patterns of culture. If people speak Tagalog, shun members of another race, eat snakes, avoid wine, live in communal housing, bury their dead, talk on the telephone, or rocket to the moon, it is because they have been born into or at least reared in a culture that contains these elements. What people do, how they act, and how they live and communicate are both responses to and functions of their culture.

Culture is an intriguing concept. Formally defined, *culture* is the deposit of knowledge, experiences, beliefs, values, attitudes, meanings, hierarchies, religion, timing, roles, spatial relations, concepts of the universe, and material objects and possessions acquired by a large group of people in the course of generations through individual and group striving. Culture manifests itself in patterns of language and in forms of activity and behavior that act as models for both the common adaptive acts and the styles of communication that enable people to live in a society within a given geographic environment at a given state of technical development at a particular moment in time. Culture also specifies and is defined by the nature of material things that play an essential role in common life. Such things as houses, instruments and machines used in industry and agriculture, forms of transportation, and instruments of war provide a material foundation for social life. Culture is persistent, enduring, and omnipresent; it includes all of the behavioral reinforcements received during the course of a lifetime. Culture also dictates the form and structure of our physical realm, and it encompasses and specifies the social environment permeating our lives. The effect of culture on our lives is largely unrealized. Perhaps a way to understand cultural influences is by way of analogy with electronic computers: As we program computers to do what they do, our culture to a great extent programs us to do what we do and to be what we are. Our culture affects us in a deterministic manner from conception to death—and even after death in terms of funeral rites.

Culture and communication are inseparable because culture not only dictates who talks with whom, about what, and how the communication proceeds, it also helps to determine how people encode messages, the meanings they have for messages, and the conditions and circumstances under which various messages may or may not be sent, noticed, or interpreted. In fact, our entire repertory of communicative behaviors is dependent largely on the culture in which we have been raised. Culture, consequently, is the foundation of communication. And, when cultures vary, communication practices also vary.

## Subcultures and Subgroups

A *subculture* is a racial, ethnic, regional, economic, or social community exhibiting characteristic patterns of behavior sufficient to distinguish it from others within an embracing culture or society. Subcultures in the United States include, for example, Oriental Americans, Polish Americans, Jews, the urban poor, Hare Krishnas, and the Mafia.

Another important societal element that does not meet criteria necessary to be called a subculture, but nevertheless poses similar communication problems, is the *deviant subgroup*. Included among the deviant subgroups are gays, pimps and prostitutes, the drug community, youth gangs, religious cults, and revolutionary organizations. These subgroups are products of the dominant culture, but their group existence has not persisted long enough nor developed a sufficiently wide enough pattern of deviant behaviors to qualify as a culture or subculture. The main distinguishing feature of subgroups is that their values, attitudes, and behavior or elements of their behavior are at odds

with the majority community. Subgroups exist within a community that is displeased with them, generally disagrees with them, and has difficulty understanding and communicating with them. But, from the point of view of commuication, these subgroups can be considered as if they are subcultures.

Each subculture or subgroup is a social entity that, although a part of the dominant main culture, is unique and provides its members with a set of experiences, backgrounds, social values, and expectations that may not be found elsewhere in the dominant culture. Hence, communication between people who appear similar may not be easy because in reality they are members of very different subcultures or subgroups and their experiential backgrounds are so different they may be unable to relate meaningfully.

## INTERCULTURAL COMMUNICATION

In all respects, everything so far said about communication applies to intercultural communication. The functions and relationships between the components of communication obviously apply. But what especially characterizes intercultural communication is that sources and receivers come from different cultures. This alone is sufficient to identify a unique form of communicative interaction that must take into account the role and function of culture in the communication process. In this section, intercultural communication will first be defined and discussed through the perspective of a model and then its various forms will be shown.

## Intercultural Communication Model

Intercultural communication occurs whenever a message producer is a member of one culture and a message receiver is a member of another. In this circumstance, we immediately are faced with the problems inherent in a situation where a message encoded in one culture must be decoded in another. As we have already seen, culture shapes the individual communicator. It largely is responsible for the entire repertory of communicative behaviors and meanings each person possesses. Consequently, those repertories possessed by two people from different cultures will be very different, which can lead to all sorts of difficulties. But, through the study and understanding of intercultural communication, we can reduce or nearly eliminate these difficulties.

The influence of culture on the individual and the problems of encoding and decoding messages across cultures are illustrated in Figure 1. Three cultures are represented in this model by three distinct geometric shapes. Cultures A and B are relatively similar to one another and they are represented by a square and an irregular octagon that is nearly square. Culture C is quite different from cultures A and B. This greater difference is represented both by the circular shape of culture C and its physical distance from cultures A and B.

Within each culture is another shape somewhat similar to the shape of the culture. This represents an individual who has been shaped by the culture. The shape of the individual is slightly different from that of the influencing culture. This suggests two things. First, there are other affecting influences besides culture that help shape the individual. And, second, although culture is a dominant shaping force on an individual, people vary to some extent from each other within any culture.

Message encoding and decoding across cultures is illustrated by a series of arrows connecting them. These arrows indicate the transmission of messages between cultures. When a message leaves the culture in which it was encoded, it contains the meaning intended by the encoder. This is represented by the arrows leaving a culture containing the same pattern as that within the individual encoder. When a message reaches the culture where it is to be decoded, it undergoes a transformation in which the influence of the decoding culture becomes a part of the message meaning. The meaning content of the original message becomes modified during the decoding phase of intercultural communication because the culturally different repertory of communicative behaviors and meanings possessed by the decoder does not contain the same cultural meanings possessed by the encoder.

The degree to which culture influences intercultural communication situations is a function of the dissimilarity between the cultures. This is indicated in the model by the degree of pattern change shown in the message arrows. The change between cultures A and B is much less than the change between cultures A and C and between cultures B and C. This is due to the greater similarity of cultures A and B. The repertory of communicative behaviors and meanings is similar and the decoding effort therefore produces results more nearly like those intended in the original message encoding. But since culture C is represented as being vastly different from cultures A and B, the decoding also is vastly different and more nearly represents the pattern of culture C.

The model suggests that there can be wide variation in cultural differences during intercultural communication. This is due in part to circumstances. Intercultural communication takes place in a wide variety of situations that range from interactions between people in whom cultural differences are extreme to interactions between people who are members of the same dominant culture and whose differences are reflected by membership in different subcultures or subgroups. If we think of differences varying along a minimum-maximum dimension (see Figure 2), the amount of difference between two cultural groups can be seen to depend on the comparative social uniqueness of the two groups. Although this scale is crude, it permits us to examine an intercultural communication act and gain insight into the effect of cultural differences. In order to understand this scale, we will look at some of the examples of cultural differences positioned along the scale.

The first example represents a maximum difference—differences between Asian and Western cultures. This is typified in a conversation between two farmers, one from a communal farm on the outskirts of Beijing and the other from a large mechanized wheat and corn farm near Des Moines. In this example, we find the greatest number of

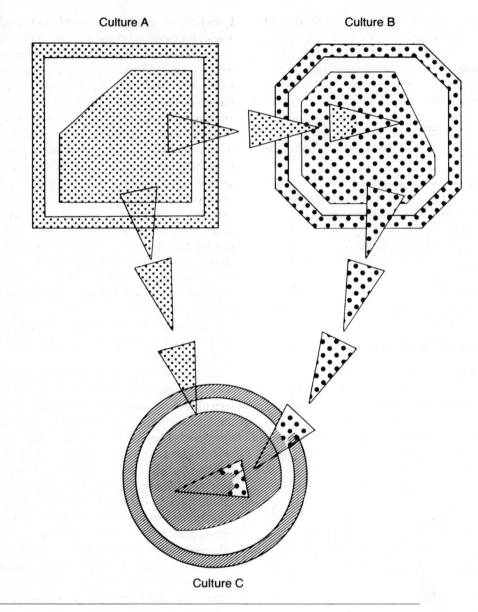

Culture A

Culture B

Culture C

**Figure 1** Model of Intercultural Communication

cultural factors subject to variation. Physical appearance, religion, philosophy, social attitudes, language, heritage, basic concepts of self and the universe, and degree of technological development are among the cultural factors that differ sharply. We also must recognize that these two far-

mers share the commonality of farming and a rural life style. In some aspects of cultural patterns they may be more closely related to each other than they are to members of their own cultures who live in a large urban metropolis. In other words, across some cultural dimensions, the Iowa farmer may

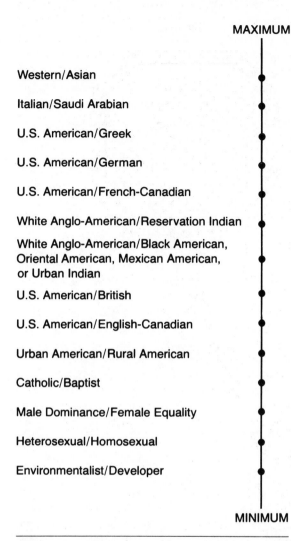

MAXIMUM

Western/Asian

Italian/Saudi Arabian

U.S. American/Greek

U.S. American/German

U.S. American/French-Canadian

White Anglo-American/Reservation Indian

White Anglo-American/Black American,
Oriental American, Mexican American,
or Urban Indian

U.S. American/British

U.S. American/English-Canadian

Urban American/Rural American

Catholic/Baptist

Male Dominance/Female Equality

Heterosexual/Homosexual

Environmentalist/Developer

MINIMUM

**Figure 2** Arrangement of Compared Cultures, Subcultures, and Subgroups along a Scale of Minimum to Maximum Socio-cultural Differences

losophies lie in ancient Greece, and most Americans and Germans share the Christian religion.

Examples near the minimal end of the scale are characterized in two ways. First are variations found between members of separate but similar cultures—for instance, between U.S. Americans and English-Canadians. The difference is less than that found between American and German cultures, between American and Greek cultures, or even between American and British cultures but greater than that generally found within a single culture. Second, minimal differences may be seen between subcultures or deviant subgroups of the same dominant culture. Socio-cultural differences can be found between members of the Catholic church and members of the Baptist church, between members of the Sierra Club and advocates of offshore oil drilling, between middle-class Americans and the urban poor, between mainstream Americans and the homosexual community, or between male dominance advocates and female equality advocates.

In any of these examples—comparisons between separate but similar cultures or between subcultures or subgroups—members of each cultural group share much more in common than compared groups in the examples at the maximum end of the scale. They probably speak the same language, share the same general religion, attend the same schools, and inhabit the same geographical area. Yet, these groups are still somewhat culturally different; they do not share the same experiences nor do they share the same perceptions. They see the world differently. Their life styles may be different, and their beliefs, values, and attitudes are not all the same. Because of their cultural similarity, they differ primarily in limited aspects of their social perceptions.

Social perception is the process by which we attach meanings to the social objects and events we encounter in our environments and is an extremely important aspect of communication. Culture conditions and structures our perceptual processes in such a way that we develop culturally determined perceptual sets. These perceptual sets not only influence which stimuli reach our awareness,

share more in common with the Chinese farmer than with a New York City stockbroker.

An example closer to the center of the scale is the difference between American culture and German culture. Less variation is found—physical characteristics are similar, and the English language is derived in part from German and its ancestor languages. The roots of German and American phi-

but more important, they have a great influence on the judgmental aspect of perception—the attachment of meaning to these stimuli. It is our contention that *intercultural communication* can best be understood as *cultural variance in the perception of social objects and events*. The barriers to communication caused by this perceptual variance can best be lowered by a knowledge and understanding of cultural factors that are subject to variance, coupled with an honest and sincere desire to communicate successfully across cultural boundaries.

A sincere desire for effective communication is critical because a successful exchange may be hampered not only by cultural variations but also by unfriendly or hostile attitudes. Problems of racial and ethnic prejudice can inhibit communication between cultures and races. If these problems are present, no amount of cultural knowledge or communication skill will make the encounter a pleasant one. Our major concern then is with those situations where there are cultural differences in the encoding and decoding of verbal and nonverbal messages during intercultural interaction and the problems inherent in the varying situations.

## CULTURE AND COMMUNICATION

The link between culture and communication is crucial to understanding intercultural communication because it is through the influence of culture that people learn to communicate. A Korean, an Egyptian, or an American learns to communicate like other Koreans, Egyptians, or Americans. Their behavior can convey meaning because it is learned and shared; it is cultural. People view their world through categories, concepts, and labels that are products of their culture.

Cultural similarity in perception makes the sharing of meaning possible. The ways in which we communicate, the circumstances of our communication, the language and language style we use, and our nonverbal behaviors are all primarily a response to and a function of our culture. Communication is cultural. And, as cultures differ from one another, the communication practices and behaviors of the individuals reared in those cultures also will vary.

Culture is an all-encompassing form or pattern for living. It is complex, abstract, and pervasive. Numerous aspects of culture help to determine communicative behavior. These socio-cultural elements are diverse and cover a wide range of human social activity. For the sake of simplicity and to put some limitation on our discussion, we will examine a few of the socio-cultural elements associated with *perception*, *verbal processes*, and *nonverbal processes*.

These socio-cultural elements are the constituent parts of intercultural communication. When we combine them, as we do when we communicate, they are like the components of a stereo system—each one relates to and needs the other. In our discussion, the elements will be separated in order to identify and discuss them. In actuality, however, they do not exist in isolation nor do they function alone. They all form a complex matrix of interacting elements that operate together to constitute the complex phenomenon called intercultural communication.

## Perception

In its simplest sense, perception is the internal process by which we select, evaluate, and organize stimuli from the external environment. In other words, perception is the way in which we convert the physical energies of our environment into meaningful experience. A number of corollary issues arise out of this definition that help explain the relationship between perception and culture. It is generally believed that people behave as they do because of the ways in which they perceive the world, and that these behaviors are learned as part of their cultural experience. Whether in judging beauty or describing snow, we respond to stimuli as we do primarily because our culture has taught us to do so. We tend to notice, reflect on, and respond to those elements in our environment that are important to us. In the United States we might respond principally to a thing's size and cost while to the Japanese, color might be the important criterion. Culture tends to determine which are the important criteria of perception.

Intercultural communication can best be understood as cultural variance in the perception of social objects and events. A central tenet of this position is that minor problems in communication often are exaggerated by these perceptual differences. To understand others' worlds and actions, we must try to understand their perceptual frames of reference. We must learn to understand how they perceive the world. In the ideal intercultural encounter we would hope for many overlapping experiences and a commonality of perceptions. The nature of culture, however, tends to introduce us to dissimilar experiences, and hence, to varied perceptions of the external world.

Three major socio-cultural elements have a direct and major influence on the meanings we develop for our percepts. These elements are our *belief/value/attitude-systems*, our *world view*, and our *social organization*. When these three elements influence our perceptions and the meanings we develop for them, they are affecting our individual, subjective aspects of meanings. We all may see the same social entity and agree upon what it is in objective terms, but what the object or event means to us individually may differ considerably. Both a Saudi Arabian and an American would agree in the objective sense that a particular person is a woman. But they most likely would disagree completely on what a woman is in a social sense. Each of the three major socio-cultural elements will be considered individually to show how they affect perception.

**Belief/Value/Attitude-Systems.** *Beliefs*, in a general sense, can be viewed as individually held subjective probabilities that some object or event possesses certain characteristics. A belief involves a link between the belief object and the characteristics that distinguish it. The degree to which we believe that an event or an object possesses certain characteristics reflects the level of our subjective probability and, consequently, the depth or intensity of our belief. That is, the more certain we are in a belief, the greater is the intensity of that belief.

Culture plays an important role in belief formation. Whether we accept the *New York Times*, the Bible, the entrails of a goat, tea leaves, the visions induced by peyote, or the changes specified in the Taoist *I Ching* as sources of knowledge and beliefs depends on our cultural backgrounds and experiences. In matters of intercultural communication there are no rights or wrongs as far as beliefs are concerned. If someone believes that voices in the wind can guide one's behavior along the proper path, we cannot throw up our hands and declare the belief wrong; we must be able to recognize and to deal with that belief if we wish to obtain satisfactory and successful communication.

*Values* are the evaluative aspect of our belief/value/attitude-systems. Evaluative dimensions include qualities such as usefulness, goodness, aesthetics, need-satisfaction ability, and pleasure production. Although each of us has a unique set of values, there also are values that tend to permeate a culture. These are called *cultural values*.

Cultural values usually are derived from the larger philosophical issues that are part of a culture's milieu. These values generally are normative in that they inform a member of a culture what is good and bad, right and wrong, true and false, positive and negative, and so on. Cultural values define what is worth dying for, what is worth protecting, what frightens people and their social systems, what are considered proper subjects for study and ridicule, and what types of events lead individuals to group solidarity. Cultural values also specify which behaviors are important and which should be avoided within a culture. Cultural values are a set of organized rules for making choices and reducing conflicts within a given society.

Values express themselves within a culture by prescribing behaviors that members of the culture are expected to perform. These are called *normative values*. Thus, Catholics are supposed to attend Mass, motorists are supposed to stop at stop signs, and workers in our culture are supposed to arrive at work at the designated time. Most people follow normative behaviors; a few do not. Failure to do so may be met with either informal or codified sanctions. Thus the Catholic who avoids Mass may receive a visit from the priest, the driver who runs a stop sign may receive a traffic ticket, and the employee who is tardy may be fired. Normative behavior also extends itself into everyday manners and becomes a guide to individual and group behavior that minimizes or prevents harm to individual sensitivities within cultural groups.

Beliefs and values contribute to the development and content of our *attitudes*. We may define an attitude formally as a learned tendency to respond in a consistent manner with respect to a given object of orientation. Attitudes are learned within a cultural context. Whatever cultural environment surrounds us helps shape and form our attitudes, our readiness to respond, and ultimately our behavior.

The cultural bias of belief/value/attitude-systems can be seen in the example of bullfighting. Many North Americans believe that cruelty to animals is wrong and that the systematic wearing down and killing of a bull is an example of that cruelty. Consequently, many North Americans view bullfighting within a negative attitude frame and will actively avoid attending bullfights or even viewing them on television. Some even campaign to have bullfights banned. To most Latin Americans, however, bullfighting is a contest of courage between man and beast. It is evaluated positively, and the triumph of the matador is not seen as cruelty to animals but as the exercise of courage, skill, and physical agility. In this cultural context, to witness a bullfight is to witness one of life's finer moments when man again demonstrates his dominance over the beast. This mastery of the bull even has metaphorical overtones of good triumphing over evil.

**World View.** This cultural element, though abstract in concept and description, is one of the most important elements found in the perceptual aspects of intercultural communication. World view deals with a culture's orientation toward such things as God, humanity, nature, the universe, and the other philosophical issues that are concerned with the concept of being. In short, our world view helps us locate our place and rank in the universe.

Because world view is so complex, it is often difficult to isolate during an intercultural interaction. In this examination, we seek to understand its substance and its elusiveness.

World view issues are timeless and represent the most fundamental basis of a culture. A Catholic surely has a different world view than does a Moslem, Hindu, Jew, Taoist, or atheist. The way in which native American Indians view the individual's place in nature differs sharply from the middle-class Euro-American's view. Native Americans have a world view that places them at one with nature. They perceive a balanced relationship between man and the environment, a partnership of equality and respect. In other words, middle-class Euro-Americans have a human-centered picture of the world. Because of their profound belief that humans are supreme and are apart from nature, they treat the universe as theirs—a place to carry out their desires and wishes through the power of science and technology.

World view influences a culture at a very deep and profound level. Its effects often are quite subtle and not revealed in such obvious and often superficial ways as dress, gestures, and vocabulary. Think of a culture's world view as being analogous to a pebble tossed into a pond. Just as the pebble causes ripples that spread and reverberate over the entire surface of the pond, world view spreads itself over a culture and permeates every facet of it. World view influences beliefs, values, attitudes, uses of time, and many other aspects of culture. In many subtle and often not obvious ways, it is a powerful influence in intercultural communication because as a member of a culture, each communicator's world view is so deeply imbedded in the psyche that it is taken completely for granted, and the communicators each assume automatically that everyone else views the world as they do.

**Social Organization.** The manner in which a culture organizes itself and its institutions also affects how members of the culture perceive the world and how they communicate. It might be helpful to look briefly at two of the dominant social units found in a culture.

The *family*, although it is the smallest social organization in a culture, is one of the most influential. Families set the stage for a child's development during the formative periods of life. The family presents the child with a wide range of cultural influences that affect almost everything from a child's first attitudes to the selection of toys. The family also guides the child's acquisition of language. Skills from vocabulary building to dialects are the purview of the family. Even the amount of emphasis placed on language is governed by the family. The family also offers and withholds approval, support, rewards, and punishments, which have a marked effect on the values children develop and the goals they pursue. If, for example, children by observation and communication learn that silence is paramount in their culture, as it is in Japan, they will reflect that aspect of culture in their behavior and bring it to intercultural settings.

The *school* is another social organization that is important. By definition and history, schools are endowed with a major portion of the responsibility for passing on and maintaining a culture. They are a community's basic link with its past as well as its taskmaster for the future. Schools maintain a culture by relating to new members what has happened, what was important, and what one as a member of the culture must know. Schools may teach geography or wood carving, mathematics or nature lore; they may stress revolution based on peace or predicated on violence. Or they may relate a particular culturally accepted version of history. But whatever is taught in a school is determined by the culture in which that school exists. Recognition of this fact has motivated some black communities in the United States to open storefront alternative schools that stress black power and "black is beautiful." These concerns are strictly a part of the black cultural experience and are not found as integrated components of the dominant U.S. culture's school functions.

Having shown the importance of perceptual systems to our understanding of culture and intercultural communication, we next turn our attention to verbal processes.

## Verbal Processes

Verbal processes include not only how we talk to each other but also the internal activities of thinking and meaning development for the words we use. These processes (*verbal language* and *patterns of thought*) are vitally related to perception and the attachment and expression of meaning.

**Verbal Language.** Any discussion of language in intercultural settings must include an investigation of language issues in general before dealing with specific problems of foreign language, language translation, and the argot and vernacular of subcultures and subgroups. Here, in our introduction to the various dimensions of culture, we will look at verbal language as it relates to our understanding of culture.

In the most basic sense, language is an organized, generally agreed upon, learned symbol system used to represent human experiences within a geographic or cultural community. Each culture places its own individual imprint on word symbols. Objects, events, experiences, and feelings have a particular label or name solely because a community of people have arbitrarily decided to so name them. Thus, because language is an inexact system of symbolically representing reality, the meanings for words are subject to a wide variety of interpretations.

Language is the primary vehicle by which a culture transmits its beliefs, values, and norms. Language gives people a means of interacting with other members of their culture and a means of thinking. Thus, language serves both as a mechanism for communication and as a guide to social reality. Language influences perceptions and transmits and helps pattern thoughts.

**Patterns of Thought.** The mental processes, forms of reasoning, and approaches to problem solution prevalent in a community are another major component of culture. Unless they have had experiences with people from other cultures who follow different patterns of thought, most people assume everyone thinks in much the same way. But we should be aware that there are cultural differences in aspects of thinking. These differences can be clarified and related to intercultural communication by making a general comparison between Western and Eastern patterns of thought. In most Western thought there is an assumption of a direct relationship between mental concepts and the concrete world of reality. This orientation places great stock in logical considerations and rationality. There is a belief that truth is out there somewhere, that it can be discovered by following the correct logical sequences. One need only turn over the right rock and it will be there. The Eastern view, best illustrated by Taoist thought, holds that problems are solved quite differently. To begin with, people are not granted instant rationality. Truth is not found by active searching and the application of Aristotelian modes of reasoning. On the contrary, one must wait, and if truth is to be known it will make itself apparent. The major difference in these two views is in the area of activity. To the Western mind, human activity is paramount and ultimately will lead to the discovery of truth. In the Taoist tradition, truth is the active agent, and if it is to be known it will be through the activity of truth making itself apparent.

A culture's thought patterns affect the way individuals in that culture communicate, which in turn will affect the way each person responds to individuals from another culture. We cannot expect everyone to employ the same patterns of thinking, but understanding that many patterns exist and learning to accommodate them will facilitate our intercultural communication.

## Nonverbal Processes

Verbal processes are the primary means for the exchange of thoughts and ideas, but closely related nonverbal processes often can overshadow them. Although there is not complete agreement as to what constitutes the province and domain of nonverbal processes, most authorities agree that the following topics must be included: gestures, facial expressions, eye contact and gaze, posture and movement, touching, dress, objects and artifacts, silence, space, time, and paralanguage. As we turn to the nonverbal processes relevant to intercultural communication, we will consider three aspects: *nonverbal behavior* that functions as a silent form of language, *concepts of time*, and the *use and organization of space*.

**Nonverbal Behavior.** It would be foolish for us to try to examine all of the elements that constitute nonverbal behavior because of the tremendous range of activity that constitutes this form of human activity. An example or two should enable us to visualize how nonverbal issues fit into the overall scheme of intercultural understanding. Touch as a form of communication can demonstrate how nonverbal communication is a product of culture. In Germany, women as well as men shake hands at the outset of every social encounter; in the United States, women seldom shake hands. In Thailand, people do not touch in public, and to touch someone on the head is a major social transgression. You can imagine the problems that could arise if one did not understand some of the variances.

Another illustrative example is eye contact. In the United States we are encouraged to maintain good eye contact when we communicate. In Japan eye contact often is not important. And in some American Indian tribes young children are taught that eye contact with an elder is a sign of disrespect. A white school teacher working on an Indian reservation was not aware of this and thought her students were not interested in school because they never looked at her.

As a component of culture, nonverbal expression has much in common with language. Both are coding systems that are learned and passed on as part of cultural experience. Just as we learn that the word *stop* can mean to halt or to cease, we also have learned that an arm held up in the air with the palm facing another person frequently means the same thing. Because most nonverbal communication is culturally based, what it symbolizes often is a case of what a culture has transmitted to its members. The nonverbal symbol for suicide, for example, varies among cultures. In the United States it is a finger pointed at the temple, in Japan it is a hand thrust into the stomach, and in New Guinea, it is symbolized by a hand on the neck. Both nonverbal symbols and the responses they generate are part of cultural experience—what is passed from generation to generation. Every symbol takes on significance because of one's past experience with it. Culture influences and directs those experiences, and is, therefore, a major contributor to how we send, receive, and respond to these nonverbal symbols.

**Concept of Time.** A culture's concept of time is its philosophy toward the past, present, and future, and the importance or lack of importance it places on time. Most Western cultures think of time in lineal-spatial terms. We are timebound and well aware of the past, present, and future. In contrast, the Hopi Indians pay very little attention to time. They believe that each thing—whether a person, plant, or animal—has its own time system.

Even within the dominant American culture we find groups that have learned to perceive time in ways that appear strange to many outsiders. Mexican-Americans frequently speak of Chicano time when their timing varies from the predominant Anglo concept. And blacks often use what is referred to as BPT (black people's time) or hang-loose time—maintaining that priority belongs to what is happening at that instant.

Time, like other components of culture, serves to underscore a basic theme of this book—vast differences exist between diverse cultures, and those differences affect communication.

**Use of Space.** The way in which people use space as a part of interpersonal communication is called *proxemics*. It involves not only the distance between people engaged in conversation but also their physical orientation. We all most likely have some familiarity with the fact that Arabs and Latins tend to interact physically closer together than do North Americans. What is important is to realize that people of different cultures do have different ways in which they relate to one another spatially and that when talking to someone from another culture we must expect what in our culture would

be violations of our personal space and be prepared to continue our interaction without reacting adversely. We may experience feelings that are difficult to handle; we may believe that the other person is overbearing, boorish, or even making unacceptable sexual advances when indeed the other person's movements are only manifestations of his or her cultural learning about how to use space.

Physical orientation is also culturally influenced, and it helps to define social relationships. North Americans prefer to sit where they are face to face or at right angles to one another. We seldom seek side-by-side arrangements. Chinese, however, often prefer and feel more comfortable in a side-by-side arrangement and may feel uncomfortable when placed in a face-to-face situation.

We also tend to define social hierarchies through our nonverbal use of space. Sitting behind a desk while speaking with someone who is standing is usually a sign of a superior-subordinate relationship with the socially superior person seated. This same behavior, however, can also be used to convey disapproval, disrespect, or insult if one violates cultural norms. Misunderstandings easily occur in intercultural settings when two people, each acting according to the dictates of his or her cultures, violate each other's expectations. If we were to remain seated when expected to rise, we could easily violate a cultural norm and insult our host or guest unknowingly.

How we organize space also is a function of our culture. Our homes, for instance, nonverbally preserve our cultural beliefs and values. South American house designs are extremely private with only a door opening directly onto the street and everything else behind walls. North Americans are used to large unwalled front yards with windows looking into the house allowing passersby to see what goes on inside. In South America, a North American is liable to feel excluded and wonder about what goes on behind all those closed doors.

## SUMMARY

In many respects the relationship between culture and communication is reciprocal. They affect and influence each other. What we talk about, how we talk about it, what we see, attend to, or ignore, how we think, and what we think about are influenced by our culture. In turn, what we talk about, how we talk about it, and what we see help shape, define, and perpetuate our culture. One cannot exist without the other. One cannot change without causing change in the other.

We have suggested that the chief problem associated with intercultural communication is error in social perception brought about by cultural variations that affect the perceptual process. The attribution of meaning to messages is in many respects influenced by the culture of the message decoder. When the message being interpreted was encoded in another culture, the cultural influences and experiences that produced that message may have been entirely different from the cultural influences and experiences that are being drawn upon to decode the message. Consequently, grave errors in meaning may arise that are neither intended nor really the fault of the communicators. These errors are the result of people with entirely different backgrounds being unable to understand one another accurately.

The approach we have taken also is based on a fundamental assumption: The parties to intercultural communication must have an honest and sincere desire to communicate and seek mutual understanding. This assumption requires favorable attitudes on the part of intercultural communicators and an elimination of superior-inferior relationships based on membership in particular cultures, races, or ethnic groups. Unless this basic assumption has been satisfied, our theory of cultural variance in social perception will not produce improvement in intercultural communication.

We have discussed several socio-cultural variables that are major sources of communication difficulty. Although they were discussed in isolation, we cannot allow ourselves to conclude that they are unrelated. They all are related in a matrix of cultural complexities. For successful intercultural communication, we must be aware of these cultural factors affecting communication in both our own culture and in the culture of the other party. We need to understand not only cultural differences but also cultural similarities. While understanding differences will help us determine sources of potential problems, understanding similarities may help us become closer to one another.

# Intercultural Communication

## MICHAEL ARGYLE

## INTRODUCTION

Many people have to communicate and work with members of other cultures, and social skills training is now being given to some of these who are about to work abroad. Intercultural communication (ICC) is necessary for several kinds of people:

1. Tourists are probably the largest category, though they stay for the shortest periods and need to master only a few simple situations—meals, travel, shopping, taxis, etc. To a large extent they are shielded from the local culture by the international hotel culture.

2. Business, governmental, and university visitors, on short business trips, have to cope with a wider range of problems, but are often accommodated in hotels or somewhere similar, and looked after by other expatriates. They, too, are somewhat shielded from the local culture; they rarely learn the language and are given a great deal of help.

3. Businessmen, or others on longer visits of up to five years, students who stay from one to three years, and members of the Peace Corps and Voluntary Service Overseas who stay for two years. This is much more demanding, involving living in a house or apartment, coping with many aspects of the local culture and learning at least some of the language.

From Stephen Bochner (ed.), *Cultures in Contact: Studies in Cross-Cultural Interaction* (Oxford: Permagon Press, 1982), pp. 61–79. Reprinted by permission of the publisher and the author. Mr. Argyle is a reader in Social Psychology in the Department of Experimental Psychology at Oxford University.

4. Immigration may take place as a deliberate move, or as a gradual process while a visit becomes extended. This requires mastery of the new culture, as well as changes of attitude and self-image.

5. Those who stay at home may meet visitors from abroad, and may need to work effectively with them. They may also have to deal with refugees, those from other racial groups and other social classes. However, these contacts are usually limited to meals and work settings.

A number of category schemes have been produced to describe the main modes of response of visitors to different cultures. The principal alternatives are: (1) detached observers, who avoid involvement; (2) reluctant and cautious participants in the local culture; (3) enthusiastic participants, some of whom come to reject their original culture; and (4) settlers (Brein and David 1971).

How can intercultural effectiveness be assessed? An important minimal criterion is whether an individual manages to complete the planned tour or whether he packs up and returns home early. For some British firms as many as 60 percent of those posted to Africa or the Middle East fail to complete their tours, at great costs to the firms. For those who succeed in staying the course there are several possible indices of success:

1. Subjective ratings of comfort and satisfaction with life in the other culture (e.g., Gudykunst, Hammer and Wiseman 1977).

2. Ratings by members of the host culture of the acceptability or competence of the visitor (e.g., Collett 1971).

3. Ratings by the field supervisor of an individual's effectiveness at the job, as has been used in Peace Corps studies. The effectiveness of salesmen could be measured objectively, and this applies to a number of other occupational roles.

4. Performance in role-played intercultural group tasks, as used by Chemers et al. (1966).

Hammer, Gudykunst and Wiseman (1978) analyzed ratings by returned visitors to other cultures and found that they recognized three dimensions of intercultural competence (ICC): (a) ability to deal with psychological stress, (b) ability to communicate effectively, and (c) ability to establish interpersonal relations.

Competent performance as a visitor to another culture, or in dealing with members of another culture, can be regarded as a social skill, analogous to the skills of teaching, interviewing, and the rest. ICC is different in that a wide range of situations and types of performance are involved, together with a variety of goals. Intercultural skills may include some quite new skills, where quite different situations or rules are involved, such as bargaining, or special formal occasions. It may be necessary to perform familiar skills in a modified style, e.g., a more authoritarian kind of supervision, or more intimate social relationships. There are often a number of themes or modes of interaction in a culture, which are common to a wide range of situations. I suggest that these themes can be the most useful focus of training for ICC. In the next section we shall examine the main themes of this kind.

There is a special phenomenon here which has no clear equivalent among other social skills, i.e., "culture shock." Oberg (1960) used this term to refer to the state of acute anxiety produced by unfamiliar social norms and social signals. Others have extended the notion to include the fatigue of constant adaptation, the sense of loss of familiar food, companions, etc., rejection of the host population or rejection by it, confusion of values or identity, discomfort at violation of values, and a feeling of incompetence at dealing with the environment (Taft 1977).

Some degree of culture shock is common among those living abroad for the first time, especially in a very different culture, and it may last six months or longer. Those going abroad for a limited period, like a year, show a U-shaped pattern of discomfort: in the first stage they are elated, enjoy the sights, and are well looked after. In the second stage they have to cope with domestic life, and things get more difficult; they keep to the company of expatriates and are in some degree of culture shock. In the third phase they have learned to cope better and

are looking forward to returning home. There may be problems when they do return home, and many people experience problems of re-entry, due for example to a loss of status, or a less exciting life (Brein and David 1971).

Another special problem for ICC is how far a visitor should accommodate to local styles of behavior. It is the general experience of Europeans and Americans in Africa and Third World countries generally, that they are *not* expected to wear local clothes or engage in exotic greetings. There seems to be a definite "role of the visitor" to which one is expected to conform. Rather greater accommodation to local ways is expected of those who stay for longer periods, and this may include mastering the language. In the United States, on the other hand, much greater conformity is expected, probably as a result of the long history of assimilating immigrants. Where total conformity is not required, it is still expected that visitors shall show a positive attitude towards the local culture, that one should not complain or criticize, like the so-called "whingeing Pom" in Australia. There may be a temptation to keep to hotels, clubs, and cantonment, but this will lead to isolation from the local community. Bochner, McLeod and Linn (1977) found that foreign students usually had friends both from their home country and the local one—the latter were needed to help them cope with the culture.

In this article I shall examine some of the areas of difference between cultures, which can give rise to communication problems. Any successful form of social skills training (SST) for ICC should take account of these differences. Then I shall discuss the main forms of training which have been developed for this purpose.

## CULTURAL DIFFERENCES IN SOCIAL INTERACTION

### Language

This is one of the most important differences between many cultures, and one of the greatest barriers. The person who has learned a language quite well can still make serious mistakes, as with the Dutchman on a ship who was asked if he was a good sailor and replied indignantly that he was not a sailor but a manager.

Several studies have shown that language fluency is a necessary condition for the adjustment of foreign students in the United States, though there is also evidence that confidence in the use of language regardless of ability is just as important (Gullahorn and Gullahorn 1966). Often there are variations in accent, dialect, or grammar—as in Black American English, or in the actual language used—as in multilingual communities. An individual may indicate a positive or negative attitude to another by shifting towards a more similar or less similar speech style (Giles and Powesland 1975). Visitors to another culture should be aware of the impression they are creating by the speech style which they use. While efforts to speak the language are usually well received, this is not always so; the French dislike the inaccurate use of their language. Taylor and Simard (1975) found that lack of interaction between English and French Canadians was less due to lack of language skills than to attitudes; language helped to preserve ethnic identity.

Most cultures have a number of forms of polite usage, which may be misleading. These may take the form of exaggeration or modesty. Americans ask questions which are really orders or requests ("Would you like to . . . ?"). In every culture, in many situations, there are special forms of words, or types of conversation, which are thought to be appropriate—to ask a girl for a date, to disagree with someone at a committee, to introduce people to each other, and so on. Americans prefer directness, but Mexicans regard openness as a form of weakness or treachery, and think one should not allow the outside world to penetrate their thoughts. Frankness by Peace Corps volunteers in the Philippines leads to disruption of smooth social relationships (Brein and David 1971).

There are cultural differences in the sequential structure of conversations. The nearly universal question–answer sequence is not found in some African cultures where information is precious and not readily given away (Goody 1978). In Asian countries the word "no" is rarely used, so that "yes"

can mean "no" or "perhaps." Saying "no" would lead to loss of face by the other, so indirect methods of conveying the message may be used, such as serving a banana (an unsuitable object) with tea to indicate that a marriage was unacceptable (Cleveland, Mangone, and Adams 1960). The episode structure of conversations varies a lot: Arabs and others have a "run-in" period of informal chat for about half an hour before getting down to business.

Some of these differences are due to different use of nonverbal signals. Erickson (1976) found that White Americans interviewing Blacks often thought the interviewee wasn't attending or understanding, and kept rewording questions in simpler and simpler forms. In several cultures "thank you" is signalled nonverbally; in China this is done at meals by rapping lightly on the table.

## Nonverbal Communication (NVC)

It is now known that NVC plays several essential parts in social interaction—communicating attitudes to others, e.g., of like-dislike, expressing emotions, and in supporting speech by elaborating on utterances, providing feedback from listeners, and managing synchronizing. Although nonverbal signals are used in similar ways in all cultures, there are also differences and these can easily produce misunderstanding (Argyle 1975). Triandis, Vassiliou, and Nassiakou (1968) observed that friendly criticism may be interpreted as hatred, and very positive attitudes as neutral, by someone from another culture. Several studies have found that if people from culture A are trained to use the nonverbal signals of culture B (gaze, distance, etc.), they will be liked more by members of the second culture (e.g., Collett 1971).

The face is the most important source of NVC. Similar basic emotional expressions are found in all cultures, and are at least partially innate. However, Chan (1979) has found that the Chinese express anger and disgust by narrowing the eyes, the reverse of that found in the United States. There are also different display rules, prescribing when these expressions may be shown, where one may laugh,

**Table 1** Accuracy of Recognition of Nonverbal Cues for Emotions and Interpersonal Attitudes by English, Italian, and Japanese, Expressed in Percentages

| Judges | Performers | | | |
|---|---|---|---|---|
| | English | Italian | Japanese | Average |
| English | 60.5 | 55 | 36 | 50 |
| Italian | 52 | 61.5 | 29 | 47 |
| Japanese | 54 | 56 | 43 | 51 |
| Average | 56 | 57 | 36 | |

From Shimoda, Argyle, and Ricci Bitti 1978.

cry, and so on (Ekman, Friesen, and Ellsworth 1972). We carried out an experiment on the intercultural communication of interpersonal attitudes, in which judges decoded videotapes, the main cues being face and voice. As Table 1 shows, Japanese subjects found it easier to decode British and Italian than Japanese performers, probably because Japanese display rules forbid use of negative facial expressions (Shimoda, Argyle, and Ricci Bitti 1978). This shows that the Japanese are indeed relatively "inscrutable," but it is not yet known whether they make use of alternative channels, such as posture, for transmitting information normally conveyed by the face. There are also some variations of facial expression within cultures, between different regions and social classes. Seaford (1975) reports the use of a "pursed smile" facial dialect in the state of Virginia.

Gaze also is used in a similar way in all cultures but the amount of gaze varies quite widely. Watson (1970) studied the gaze of pairs of students from different countries. The highest levels of gaze were shown by Arabs and Latin Americans, the lowest by Indians and northern Europeans. When people from different cultures met, if the other had a low level of gaze he was seen as not paying attention, impolite, or dishonest, while too much gaze was seen as disrespectful, threatening, or insulting. Some cultures have special rules about gaze, such as not

looking at certain parts of the body, or at certain people. Gaze may have a special meaning, as when old ladies with squints are believed to have the evil eye (Argyle and Cook 1976).

Spatial behavior varies between cultures. Watson and Graves (1966) confirmed earlier observations that Arabs stand much closer than Americans (or western Europeans), and found that they also adopt a more directly facing orientation. When an Arab and an American meet it would be expected that the American would move backwards, turning, in a backwards spiral, closely followed by the Arab. An elaborate set of rules about distance is found in India, prescribing exactly how closely members of each caste may approach other castes. There are also rules for spatial behavior in different situations—far greater crowding is allowed in lifts and buses, football matches, and parties. There are other cultural differences in the use of space. Americans establish temporary territorial rights in public places, but Arabs do not consider that people have such rights, e.g., to the seat they are sitting on.

Bodily contact is widely practiced in some cultures, but allowed only under very restricted conditions in others. "Contact" cultures include Arab, Latin American, south European, and some African cultures, and they also have high levels of gaze. In non-contact cultures, bodily contact is confined to the family, apart from greeting and parting, and various professional actions, like those of actors and tailors. Bodily contact outside these settings is taboo, and a source of considerable anxiety.

Gestures, bodily movements, and posture vary widely between cultures. There are few if any universal gestures. Some gestures are used in one culture, not in others; there are probably more gestures in Italy than anywhere else; and the same gesture can have quite different meanings in different cultures. For example the V-sign, showing the back of the hand, which is a rude sign in Britain, simply means "2" in Greece. The pursed hand means a question in Italy, "good" in Greece, and "fear" in northern Europe (Morris et al. 1979). Many gestures are distinctive to a particular culture or cultural area and it is possible to construct "gesture dictionaries" giving the local meanings of such gestures (e.g., Saitz and Cervenka 1972). Graham and Argyle (1975) found that Italian subjects could communicate spatial information (complicated shapes) more readily when able to use their hands; for British subjects adding the hands made less difference. Greeting is performed in a great variety of ways, including the Japanese bowing, the Indian placing of the hands together, and more exotic performances in pre-industrial societies (Krout 1942). Disagreement is signalled by a head-shake in Western countries, but a head-toss in Greece and southern Italy. Some cultures use special postures; where furniture is uncommon, various kinds of squatting, kneeling, or leaning on spears are common (Hewes 1957).

Nonverbal aspects of vocalization vary between cultures. Arabs speak loudly and give the impression of shouting. Americans speak louder than Europeans and give the impression of assertiveness. Speech style, especially accent, varies within cultures, and is an important clue to social class. The Japanese use the sound "hai" a lot, meaning literally "yes" but usually indicating understanding rather than agreement.

## Rules

The existence of different rules in another culture is one of the main areas of difficulty in ICC. As we showed earlier, rules arise to regulate behavior so that goals can be attained and needs satisfied. Systems of rules create behavior patterns which are functional, but different sets of rules can emerge to do the same job. Here are some examples:

**"Bribery."** In many parts of the world it is normal to pay a commission to civil servants, salesmen, or professional people who have performed a service, although they are already receiving a salary. Sometimes there is a regular fee, e.g., 1–3 percent of sales. This is regarded locally as a perfectly normal exchange of gifts, but in Europe and North America it is often illegal and unethical. Various devices are resorted to in overseas sales, such as paying a "sales commission" to an intermediary who uses some of the money for a bribe.

**"Nepotism."** In Africa and other countries people are expected to help their relatives, and this is the local equivalent of social welfare. Sometimes relatives have contributed to an individual's education; when he gets a good job as a result they expect some return. If he is a civil servant or manager, such favors are regarded by others as nepotism and greatly disapproved of. In fact there are usually local rules which limit the forms which these favors can take.

**Gifts.** In all cultures it is necessary to present relatives, friends, or work colleagues with gifts on certain occasions, but the rules vary greatly. The Japanese spend a great deal of money on gifts, which must be bought from standard gift shops so that their value can be ascertained and a gift of the same value returned. The gift is not opened in the presence of the giver and a small token present is given immediately, in return (Morsbach 1977).

**Buying and Selling.** There are several alternate sets of rules here—barter, bargaining, fixed-price sales, and auction. In cultures where bargaining is used it is normal to establish a relationship first, perhaps while drinking tea, and there are conventions about how the bargaining should proceed.

**Eating and Drinking.** One of the main problems is that there are rules in all cultures about what may not be eaten or drunk, especially certain kinds of meat—pork, beef, dog, etc., and alcohol. There may be very strong sanctions for breaking these rules, for example for consuming alcohol in some Arab countries. There are rules about how the eating is performed—knife and fork, chopstick, right hand, etc.; and there are extensive rules about table manners—when to start eating, how much to leave, how to obtain or refuse a second helping, and so on.

**Rules about Time.** How late is "late"? This varies greatly. In Britain and North America one may be 5 minutes late for a business appointment, but not 15 and certainly not 30 minutes late, which is perfectly normal in Arab countries. On the other hand in Britain it is correct to be 5–15 minutes late for an invitation to dinner. An Italian might arrive 2 hours late, an Ethiopian later, and a Javanese not at all—he had accepted only to prevent his host losing face (Cleveland, Mangone, and Adams 1960). A meal in Russia at a restaurant normally takes at least 3 hours. In Nigeria it may take several days to wait one's turn at a government office, so professional "waiters" do it for you.

**Seating Guests.** In Britain, in middle-class circles at least, there are rules about seating people at table, when there are 6, 8, or other numbers present. In the United States there appear to be no such rules, and British visitors are commonly surprised to see familiar rules broken. In China the tables are circular and the seating rules are different again, and similar to the British though the most important person faces the door. In Japan different seating positions in a room have different status. There may also be rules about who should talk to whom, as in the "Boston switch"—hostess talks to person on her right during first course, switches to person on her left for the next course, and everyone else pairs off accordingly.

**Rules Based on Ideas.** Sometimes the rules of another culture are quite incomprehensible until one understands the ideas behind them. In Moslem countries there are strict rules based on religious ideas, such as fasting during Ramadan, saying prayers five times each day, and giving one-fortieth of one's money as alms (Roberts 1979). In order to visit some kinds of Australian Aboriginals it is necessary to sit at the edge of their land and wait to be invited further: To move closer would be regarded as an invasion of territory. It is necessary for them to have smoking fires (without chimneys) for religious reasons, despite possible danger to the health of those inside (O'Brien and Plooij 1977).

In addition to different rules for the same or similar situations, there may also be new situations. Black American youths play the "dozens" (ritual insulting of the other's mother), other Americans go on picnics, Chinese families go to pay respect to their ancestors, Oxford dons drink port and take a special form of dessert. There may be special ceremonies connected with engagement, marriage, childbirth, and other rites of passage.

Cultures also vary in the extent to which behavior is a function of situations, as a result of their rules and other properties. Argyle, Shimoda, and Little (1978) found that Japanese were more influenced by situations, while the British behaved more consistently, i.e., as a function of personality. This means that it is more difficult to infer the properties of personality from instances of behavior for the Japanese.

Within cultures in developing countries there are often two sets of rules and ideas, corresponding to Traditional and Modern attitudes. Inkeles (1969) found similar patterns of modernization in different countries, centered round independence from parental authority, concern with time, involvement in civil affairs, and openness to new experience. Dawson, Whitney, and Lan (1971) devised T–M scales, of which some of the core concepts were attitudes to parental authority, gift-giving, and the role of women. Modernism is highly correlated with education and social class.

In some cases it is essential for the visitor to conform to rules, for example in matters of eating and drinking. In other cases the rules may be in conflict with his own values, the practice of his home organization, or the laws of his own country, as in the case of "bribery." There may be no straightforward solution to these problems, but it is at least necessary to recognize what the local rules are, and the ideas behind them, rather than simply condemning them as wrong.

## Social Relationships

The pattern of social relationships at work in the family, and with friends, takes a somewhat different form in different cultures, and different skills are needed to handle these relationships. Surveys by Triandis, Vassiliou, and Nassiakou (1968) and other research workers have shown that relationships vary along the same dimensions in all cultures—in-group/out-group, status, intimacy, and hostility or competition.

### FAMILY RELATIONSHIPS

In developing countries the family is more important than in developed countries. A wider range of relatives are actively related to; relationships are closer and greater demands are made. These include helping to pay for education, helping to get jobs, and helping when in trouble. Foa and Chemers (1967) point out that in traditional societies the family is the most important source of relationships, and many different role-relationships are distinguished, but relative few outside the family. Throughout Africa and the Middle East the family takes a similar form—marriage is arranged as a contract between families, and money is paid for the bride, kinship is traced through the father and male relatives, and polygyny is accepted (Roberts 1979). In China great respect is paid to older generations: Parents are respected, large financial contributions are made to the family by unmarried children who have left home, regular visits are paid to the graves of ancestors. The family itself may take varied forms, such as having more than one wife, or a wife and concubines. The way in which different relations are grouped as similar varies: Distinctions may be based primarily on age, generation, consanguinity, or sex (Tzeng and Landis 1979). Sex roles vary: In the Arab world women traditionally do not work or drive cars, but spend most of their time at home. The reverse operates in countries like Israel, China, and Poland where women do nearly all the same jobs as men. Patterns of sexual behavior vary—promiscuity may be normal, or virginity greatly prized; businessmen visiting parts of the East are sometimes embarrassed by being offered girls as part of the hospitality. Cultures vary from complete promiscuity before and after marriage to a complete taboo on sex outside marriage (Murdoch 1949). Goody (1976) has shown that there is great control over premarital sexual behavior in societies which have advanced agriculture, where marriage is linked with property (especially land) transactions so that it is necessary to control unsuitable sexual attachments. Americans, and to a lesser extent Europeans, mix work and family life, and receive business visitors into the home; Japanese and Arabs do not.

### SUPERVISION OF GROUPS

In most of the world outside Europe and North America, there is greater social distance between ranks, more deference and obedience, and a generally more authoritarian social structure. Subordinates do not speak freely in front of more senior people, and less use is made of face-to-face discussion. Melikian (1959) found that Egyptian Arabs, whether Moslem or Christian, had higher scores on authoritarianism than Americans. While the democratic–persuasive type is most effective in the United States and Europe, this is not the case elsewhere. In India the authoritarian style has been found to be more effective; in China there was no difference and in Japan authoritarian-led groups did best with a difficult task (Mann 1980). In Japan the teachers and superiors at work adopt an Oyabun–Koyun relationship, involving a paternalistic care for subordinates.

### GROUPS

Ethnographic studies have shown that groups have more power over their members in a number of cultures—in Japan, China, Israel, and Russia, for example. The individual is subordinated more to the group, and a high degree of conformity is expected. America and Europe are thought to be more individualistic, and social psychological experiments have shown relatively low levels of conformity in Germany and France. It has also been found that conformity pressures are stronger in the cultures where conformity is greatest. In Japan group decisions are traditionally carried out by a kind of acquiescence to the will of the group, without voting. In some cultures there is great stress on co-operation rather than competition in groups, e.g., in the Israeli kibbutz, Mexican villages, and among Australian aboriginals (Mann 1980).

## CASTES AND CLASSES

In all cultures there are hierarchical divisions of status and horizontal divisions of inclusion and exclusion. The hierarchical divisions may take the form of social classes, which can be recognized by clothes, accent as in Britain, or other ways. There may be ethnic groups which have their places in the hierarchy, as in the United States; or there may be immutable castes, as in India. This creates special problems for visitors in India: European visitors are relatively rich and clean, and so appear to be of high caste, but also eat meat even with the left hand and drink alcohol like untouchables, so a special visitor caste, of *videshis,* has been created. However, visitors to ashrams who adopt the costume of holy men do not fit this caste and cause great offense to the Indians (Wujastyk 1980). The horizontal divisions between different tribes or classes are also of great importance. In Africa it may be necessary to make up work groups from members of the same tribe, and it would be disastrous to appoint a leader from another tribe. Similar clan divisions are of course found in Scotland, and also in China (Hsu 1963). In-group versus out-group distinctions can take varied forms. Studies of helping behavior have found that fellow countrymen are usually given more help than visitors, but in Greece tourists are treated like family and friends (Triandis, Vassiliou, and Nassiakou 1968).

## Motivation

Several forms of motivation have been found to differ on average between cultures. This means that typical members of another culture are pursuing different goals, and are gratified by different rewards. Sometimes the causes of these motivational differences can be found in other features of a culture. For example, societies which are constantly at war with their neighbors encourage aggressiveness in their young males (Zigler and Child 1969).

### ACHIEVEMENT MOTIVATION

McClelland (1961) found that cultures differed in the level of achievement motivation, as measured by the popularity of children's stories with achievement themes; the high need for achievement (n.Ach) countries had higher rates of economic growth, and this may be due in part to the motivational difference. The United States over the last century has been high in n.Ach; underdeveloped countries have been lower. McClelland and Winter (1969) ran a training course for Indian managers, in which the latter role-played high n.Ach managers. The result was that they increased the size and turnover of their enterprises after attending the course. There is of course a wide range of individual differences within a culture, but it is worth realizing that in some areas individuals are likely to work hard to take risks in order to earn more money, improve their status, and to build up the enterprise in which they work. While in other areas people expect to be rewarded on the basis of the social position of their family or clan, not their own efforts.

### ASSERTIVENESS

Assertiveness or dominance versus submissiveness is one of the main dimensions along which social behavior varies. In the United States social skills training has concentrated on assertiveness, presumably reflecting a widespread approval of and desire to acquire assertive behavior. This interest in assertiveness is strong among American women, as part of the women's movement. It has also been suggested that the absence of universally accepted rules makes it necessary to stand up for your rights rather frequently.

Americans are perceived as assertive in other parts of the world. However, there are some cultures, e.g., China and parts of Indonesia, where assertiveness is not valued, and submissiveness and the maintenance of pleasant social relations are valued more (Noesjirwan 1978). In Britain candidates for social skills training are more interested in making friends. Furnham (1979) found that European white nurses in South Africa were the most assertive, followed by Africans and Indians.

## EXTRAVERSION

Surveys using extraversion questionnaires show that Americans and Canadians are more extraverted than the British (e.g., Eysenck and Eysenck 1969). What exactly this means in terms of social behavior is rather unclear. It is commonly observed that Americans are good at the early stages of a relationship, where the British can be shy and awkward. In the United States the peer group plays an important part in the life of children and adolescents; and among adults great value is placed on informal relationships (Riesman, Glazer, and Denney 1955).

In the East great value is placed on maintaining good social relationships, so that assertiveness and disagreement are avoided, or at least confined to members of the same family, clan or group.

## FACE

It is well known that in Japan, and to a lesser extent other parts of the Far East, maintaining face is of great importance. Special skills are required to make sure that others do not lose face. Foa, Mitchell, and Lekhyananda (1969) found that students from the Far East who experienced failure in an experimental task withdrew from the source of the failure message. In negotiations it may be necessary to make token concessions before the other side can give way. Great care must be taken at meetings over disagreeing or criticizing, and competitive situations should be avoided.

## VALUES

These are broader, more abstract goals, the general states of affairs which are regarded as desirable. Triandis, Malpass, and Davidson (1972) studied twenty values by asking for the antecedents and consequences of eleven concepts. In parts of India they found that status and glory were valued most, whilst wealth was not valued (being associated with arrogance and fear of thieves), nor was courage or power. The Greeks valued punishment (which was associated with justice) and power. The Japanese valued serenity and aesthetic satisfaction, and disvalued ignorance, deviation, and loneliness. Szalay and Maday (cited by Triandis, Malpass, and Davidson 1972) found that Americans rated *love* and *friendship* as their most important life concerns, *health* as 5th: Koreans ranked these values as 12th, 14th, and 19th. Triandis (1971) found that "work" was regarded as a good thing in moderately difficult environments where economic development was rapid, but it was rated less favorably in easy or difficult environments.

## Concepts and Ideology

Certain aspects of life in another culture may be incomprehensible without an understanding of the underlying ideas. Some of these ideas are carried by language, and knowing a language deepens understanding of the culture. The words in a language reflect and provide labels for the cognitive categories used in the culture to divide up the world. The color spectrum is divided up in different ways, and the color words reflect this in different cultures (Berlin and Kay 1969).

The same is true of every other aspect of the physical and social world, so that knowledge of the language provides knowledge of the culture. Translation of words may lead to changes of emotional association—the Australian word "Pom" doesn't only mean "British immigrant" but has negative and joking associations as well. Words in one language and culture may have complex meanings which are difficult to translate, as with the Israeli Chutzpah ( = "outrageous cheek," such as exporting tulips to

Holland), Russian versus Western concepts of "freedom" and "democracy," and the Japanese concept of the Oyabum–Koyum relationship.

There may be misunderstanding due to differences in thinking. Sharma (1971) notes how Western observers have criticized Indian peasants for their passivity and general lack of the "Protestant ethic," despite having produced a great increase in productivity by adapting to the Green Revolution. African languages are often short of words for geometrical shapes, so that it is difficult to communicate about spatial problems. Some words or ideas may be taboo, e.g., discussion of family planning (Awa 1979).

Some of the differences in rules which were discussed above can be explained in terms of the ideas behind them, as in the cases of "bribery" and "nepotism." Attitudes to business practices are greatly affected by ideas and ideology. Marxists will not discuss "profits"; Moslems used to regard "interest" as sinful. Surprisingly the stricter forms of Protestantism have been most compatible with capitalism and gave rise to the "Protestant ethic" (Argyle 1972).

## Training Methods

**Language Learning.** There are many cultures where visitors, especially short-term visitors, can get by quite well without learning the language. On the other hand this probably means that they are cut off from communicating with the majority of the native population, and that they do not come to understand fully those features of the culture which are conveyed by language. Language learning can be greatly assisted by the use of a language laboratory, and by textbooks like Leech and Svartlik's *A Communicative Grammar of English,* which provide detailed information on the everyday informal use of language.

**Use of Educational Methods.** Despite the use of more active methods of SST in other areas, for ICC reading and lectures are currently the most widely used methods. The most sophisticated approach here has been the development of Culture Assimilators. Critical-incident surveys have been carried out on occasions when Americans have gotten into difficulty in Thailand, Greece, etc., and a standard set of difficult episodes has been written, for example:

*One day a Thai administrator of middle academic rank kept two of his assistants about an hour from an appointment. The assistants, although very angry, did not show it while they waited. When the administrator walked in at last, he acted as if he were not late. He made no apology or explanation. After he was settled in his office, he called his assistants in and they all began working on the business for which the administrator had set the meeting (Brislin and Pedersen [1976] pp. 90–91).*

Several explanations were offered, of which the correct one is:

*In Thailand, subordinates are required to be polite to their superiors, no matter what happens, nor what their rank may be (ibid., p. 92).*

and further information is added.

These episodes are put together in a tutor-text, which students work through by themselves (Fiedler et al. 1971).

There have been a number of follow-up studies of the use of culture assimilators, showing modest improvements in handling mixed cultural groups in laboratory settings, and in one case in a field setting. However, not very much field assessment has been done, the effects of training have not been very striking, and the subjects used have all been of high motivation and intelligence (Brislin and Pedersen 1976).

A similar method is the use of case studies. These are widely used for management training in international firms, the cases being based on typical managerial problems in the other culture. They play an important part in two-week courses, using educational methods. It is common to include wives and children in such courses, with special materials for them too (DiStephano 1979).

Educational methods can probably make a valuable contribution to cross-cultural training, since there is always a lot to learn about another culture.

However, as with other skills, it is necessary to combine such intellectual learning with actual practice of the skills involved.

**Role-Playing.** Several types of role-playing have been used for ICC, though it has not been the usual form of training. One approach is to train people in laboratory situations in the skills or modes of communication of a second culture, using videotape playback. Collett (1971) trained Englishmen in the nonverbal communication styles of Arabs, and found that those trained in this way were liked better by Arabs than were members of a control group.

The American Peace Corps has used simulation techniques to train their members. Trainees have been sent to work on an American Indian reservation, for example. Area simulation sites were constructed to train members for different locations, e.g., one in Hawaii for Southeast Asian volunteers, complete with water buffaloes. However, it is reported that these rather expensive procedures have not been very successful, and they have been replaced by training in the second culture itself (Brislin and Pedersen 1976).

**Interaction with Members of the Other Culture.** In the intercultural communication workshop trainees go through a number of exercises with members of the other culture, and use is made of role-playing and the study of critical incidents (Alther 1975). This looks like a very powerful method, but no follow-up results are available. At Farnham Castle in Britain the training courses include meetings with members of the other culture, and with recently returned expatriates.

When people arrive in a new culture they are frequently helped both by native members of the culture, and by expatriates. Bochner, McLeod, and Lin (1977) found that foreign students in Hawaii usually had friends of both kinds, who could help them in different ways.

**Combined Approaches.** We have seen that each of the methods described has some merits, and it seems very likely that a combination of methods would be the most effective. This might include some language instruction, learning about the other culture, role-playing, and interaction with native members of the culture. Gudykunst, Hammer, and Wiseman (1977) used a combination of several methods, though not including any language teaching, in a three-day course, and found that this led to higher reported levels of satisfaction for Naval personnel posted to Japan.

Guthrie (1966) describes one of the training schemes used by the Peace Corps, for those going to the Philippines. The training included: (1) basic linguistics, so that trainees could pick up local dialects quickly; later this was replaced by teaching specific dialects; (2) lectures by experts on different aspects of the Philippines culture; (3) physical and survival training at the Puerto Rican jungle camp; as noted earlier this was later replaced by training in the culture itself.

## CONCLUSIONS

A very large number of people go abroad to work in other cultures; some of them fail to complete their mission and others are ineffective, because of difficulties of intercultural communication.

Difficulties of social interaction and communication arise in several main areas: (1) language, including forms of polite usage; (2) nonverbal communication: uses of facial expression, gesture, proximity, touch, etc.; (3) rules of social situations, e.g., for bribing, gifts, and eating; (4) social relationships, within the family, at work, between members of different groups; (5) motivation, e.g., achievement motivation and for face-saving; (6) concepts and ideology, e.g., ideas derived from religion and politics.

Several kinds of training for ICC have been found to be successful, especially in combination. These include language-learning, educational methods, role-playing, and interaction with members of the other culture.

## REFERENCES

Alther, G. L. (1975) "Human relations training and foreign students," *Readings in Intercultural*

*Communication,* Vol. 1 (Edited by Hoopes, D.) Intercultural Communications Network of the Regional Council for International Education, Pittsburgh.

Argyle, M. (1972) *The Social Psychology of Work.* Penguin Books, Harmondsworth.

Argyle, M. (1975) *Bodily Communication.* Methuen, London.

Argyle, M. and Cook, M. (1976) *Gaze and Mutual Gaze.* Cambridge University Press, Cambridge.

Argyle, M., Shimoda, K. and Little, B. (1978) "Variance due to persons and situations in England and Japan," *British Journal of Social and Clinical Psychology,* 17, 335–7.

Awa, N. E. (1979) "Ethnocentric bias in developmental research," *Handbook of Intercultural Communication* (Edited by Asante, M. K., Newmark, E, and Blake, C. A.). Sage Publications, Beverly Hills, Calif.

Berlin, B. and Kay, P. (1969) *Basic Color Terms.* University of California Press, Berkeley, Calif.

Bochner, S., McLeod, B. M. and Lin, A. (1977) "Friendship patterns of overseas students: A functional model," *International Journal of Psychology,* 12, 277–94.

Brein, M. and David, K. H. (1971) "Intercultural communication and the adjustment of the sojourner," *Psychological Bulletin,* 76, 215–30.

Brislin, R. W. and Pedersen, P. (1976) *Cross-Cultural Orientation Programs.* Gardner Press, New York.

Chan, J. (1979) *The Facial Expressions of Chinese and Americans.* Unpublished Ph.D. thesis, South Eastern University, Louisiana.

Chemers, M. M., Fiedler, F. E., Lekhyananda, D., and Stolurow, L. M. (1966) "Some effects of cultural training on leadership in heterocultural task groups," *International Journal of Psychology,* 1, 301–14.

Cleveland, H., Mangone, G. J. and Adams, J. G. (1960) *The Overseas Americans.* McGraw-Hill, New York.

Collett, P. (1971) "On training Englishmen in the non-verbal behaviour of Arabs: An experiment in intercultural communication," *International Journal of Psychology,* 6, 209–15.

Dawson, J., Whitney, R. E. and Lan, R. T. S. (1971) "Scaling Chinese traditional–modern attitudes and the GSR measurement of 'important' versus 'unimportant' Chinese concepts," *Journal of Cross-Cultural Psychology,* 2, 1–27.

Distephano, J. J. (1979) "Case methods in international management training," *Handbook of Intercultural Communication* (Edited by Asante, M. K., Newmark, E. and Blake, C. A.). Sage Publications, Beverly Hills, Calif.

Ekman, P., Friesen, W. V. and Ellsworth, P. (1972) *Emotion in the Human Face: Guidelines for Research and a Review of Findings.* Pergamon Press, New York.

Erickson, F. (1976) "Talking down and giving reasons: Hyper-explanation and listening behavior in inter-social situations." Paper presented at the Ontario Institute for the Study of Education Conference, Toronto.

Eysenck, H. J. and Eysenck, S. B. G. (1969) *Personality Structure and Measurement.* Routledge & Kegan Paul, London.

Fiedler, F. E., Mitchell, R. and Triandis, H. C. (1971) "The culture assimilator: An approach to cross-cultural training," *Journal of Applied Psychology,* 55, 95–102.

Foa, U. and Chemers, M. (1967) "The significance of role behavior differentiation for cross-cultural interaction training," *International Journal of Psychology,* 2, 45–57.

Foa, U. G., Mitchell, T. R. and Lekhyananda, D. (1969) "Cultural differences in reaction to failure," *International Journal of Psychology,* 4, 21–6.

Furnham, A. (1979) "Assertiveness in three cultures: Multidimensionality and cultural differences," *Journal of Clinical Psychology,* 35, 522–7.

Giles, H. and Powesland, P. F. (1975) *Speech Style and Social Evaluation.* Academic Press, London.

Goody, E. N. (1978) "Towards a theory of questions," *Questions and Politeness* (Edited by Goody, E. N.). Cambridge University Press, Cambridge.

Goody, J. (1976) *Production and Reproduction.* Cambridge University Press, Cambridge.

Graham, J. A. and Argyle, M. (1975) "A cross-cultural study of the communication of extra-verbal meaning by gestures," *International Journal of Psychology,* 10, 57–67.

Gudykunst, W. B., Hammer, M. R. and Wiseman, R. L. (1977) "An analysis of an integrated approach to cross-cultural training," *International Journal of Intercultural Relations,* 1, 99–110.

Gullahorn, J. E. and Gullahorn, J. T. (1966) "American students abroad: Professional versus personal development," *The Annals of the American Academy of Political and Social Science,* 368, 43–59.

Guthrie, G. M. (1966) "Cultural preparation for the Philippines," *Cultural Frontiers of the Peace Corps* (Edited by Textor, R. B.). M.I.T. Press, Cambridge, Mass.

Hammer, M. R., Gudykunst, W. B. and Wiseman, R. L. (1978) "Dimensions of intercultural effectiveness: An exploratory study," *International Journal of Intercultural Relations,* 2, 382–93.

Hewes, G. (1957) "The anthropology of posture," *Scientific American,* 196, 123–32.

Hsu, F. L. K. (1963) *Caste, Clan and Club.* Van Nostrand, Princeton, N.J.

Inkeles, A. (1969) "Making men modern: On the causes and consequences of individual change in six developing countries," *American Journal of Sociology,* 75, 208–25.

Krout, M. H. (1942) *Introduction to Social Psychology.* Harper & Row, New York.

Leech, G. and Svartlik, J. (1975) *A Communicative Grammar of English.* Longman, London.

Mann, L. (1980) "Cross cultural studies of small groups," *Handbook of Cross-cultural Psychology,* Vol. 5 (Edited by Triandis, H.). Allyn & Bacon, Boston.

McClelland, D. C. (1961) *The Achieving Society.* Van Nostrand, Princeton, N.J.

McClelland, D. C. and Winter, D. G. (1969) *Motivating Economic Achievement.* Free Press, New York.

Melikian, L. H. (1959) "Authoritarianism and its correlation in the Egyptian culture and in the United States," *Journal of Social Issues,* 15 (3), 58–68.

Morris, D., Collett, P., Marsh, P. and O'Shaughnessy, M. (1979) *Gestures: Their Origins and Distribution.* Cape, London.

Morsbach, H. (1977) "The psychological importance of ritualized gift exchange in modern Japan," *Annals of the New York Academy of Sciences,* 293, 98–113.

Murdoch, G. P. (1949) *Social Structure.* Macmillan, New York.

Noesjirwan, J. (1978) "A rule-based analysis of cultural differences in social behaviour: Indonesia and Australia," *International Journal of Psychology,* 13, 305–16.

Oberg, K. (1960) "Cultural shock: Adjustment to new cultural environments," *Practical Anthropology,* 7, 177–82.

O'Brien, G. E. and Plooij, D. (1977) "Development of culture training manuals for medical workers with Pitjantjatjara Aboriginals," *Journal of Applied Psychology,* 62, 499–505.

Riesman, D., Glazer, N. and Denney, R. (1955) *The Lonely Crowd: A Study of the Changing American Character.* Doubleday, New York.

Roberts, G. O. (1979) "Terramedian value systems and their significance," *Handbook of Intercultural Communication* (Edited by Asante, M. K., Newman, E. and Blake, C. A.). Sage Publications, Beverly Hills, Calif.

Saitz, R. L. and Cervenka, E. J. (1972) *Handbook of Gestures: Colombia and the United States.* Mouton, The Hague.

Seaford, H. W. (1975) "Facial expression dialect: An example," *Organization of Behavior in Face-to-Face Interaction* (Edited by Kendon, A., Harris, R. M. and Key, M. R.). Mouton, The Hague.

Sharma, H. (1971) "Green revolution in India: A prelude to a red one?" Unpublished paper (cited by Awa, 1979).

Shimoda, K., Argyle, M. and Ricci Bitti, P. (1978) "The intercultural recognition of emotional expressions by three national groups—English, Italian, and Japanese," *European Journal of Social Psychology,* 8, 169–79.

Taft, R. (1977) "Coping with unfamiliar cultures," *Studies in Cross-cultural Psychology,* Vol. 1 (Edited by Warren, N.). Academic Press, London.

Taylor, D. M. and Simard, L. M. (1975) "Social interaction in a bilingual setting," *Canadian Psychological Review,* 16, 240–54.

Triandis, H. (1971) "Work and leisure in cross-cultural perspective," *Theories of Cognitive Consistency: A Sourcebook* (Edited by Abelson, R. P. et
al.). Rand McNally, Chicago.

Triandis, H. (1972) *The Analysis of Subjective Culture.* Wiley, New York.

Triandis, H., Malpass, R. S. and Davidson, A. R. (1972)
"Cross-cultural psychology," *Biennial Review of
Anthropology,* 24, 1–84.

Triandis, H. C., Vassiliou, V. and Nassiakou, M. (1968)
"Three cross-cultural studies of subjective culture," *Journal of Personality and Social Psychology,* 8, (Monograph Supplement), Part 2, pp.
1–42.

Tzeng, O. C. S. and Landis, D. (1979) "A multidimensional scaling methodology for cross-
cultural research in communication," *Handbook
of Intercultural Communication* (Edited by
Asante, M. K., Newmark, E. and Blake, C. A.). Sage
Publications, Beverly Hills, Calif.

Watson, O. M. (1970) *Proxemic Behavior: A Cross-
cultural Study.* Mouton, The Hague.

Watson, O. M. and Graves, T. D. (1966) "Quantitative
research in proxemic behavior," *American
Anthropologist,* 68, 971–85.

Wujastyk, D. (1980) "Causing a scandal in Poona,"
*The Times* (London), 24 April, p. 14.

Zigler, E. and Child, I. L. (1969) "Socialization," *The
Handbook of Social Psychology,* Vol. 3 (Edited
by Lindzey, G. and Aronson, E.). Addison-Wesley,
Reading, Mass.

# Context and Meaning

## EDWARD T. HALL

One of the functions of culture is to provide a highly selective screen between man and the outside
world. In its many forms, culture therefore designates what we pay attention to and what we
ignore.[1] This screening function provides structure
for the world and protects the nervous system from
"information overload."[2] Information overload is a
technical term applied to information processing
systems. It describes a situation in which the system
breaks down when it cannot properly handle the
huge volume of information to which it is subjected. Any mother who is trying to cope with the
demands of small children, run a house, enjoy her
husband, and carry on even a modest social life
knows that there are times when everything happens at once and the world seems to be closing in
on her. She is experiencing the same information
overload that afflicts business managers, administrators, physicians, attorneys, and air controllers.
Institutions such as stock exchanges, libraries, and
telephone systems also go through times when the
demands on the system (inputs) exceed capacity.
People can handle the crunch through delegating
and establishing priorities; while institutional solutions are less obvious, the high-context rule seems
to apply. That is, the only way to increase informa-
tion-handling capacity without increasing the mass
and complexity of the system is to program the
memory of the system so that less information is
required to activate the system, i.e., make it more

From Edward T. Hall, *Beyond Culture* (Garden City, N.Y.:
Doubleday & Company, 1976), pp. 85–103. Copyright © 1976
by Edward T. Hall. Reprinted by permission of Doubleday &
Company, Inc. and The Lescher Agency. Professor Hall
teaches at Northwestern University.

like the couple that has been married for thirty-five years. The solution to the problem of coping with increased complexity and greater demands on the system seems to lie in the preprogramming of the individual or organization. This is done by means of the "contexting" process. . . .

The importance of the role of context is widely recognized in the communication fields, yet the process is rarely described adequately, or if it is, the insights gained are not acted upon. Before dealing with context as a way of handling information overload, let me describe how I envisage the contexting process, which is an emergent function; i.e., we are just discovering what it is and how it works. Closely related to the high–low-context continuum is the degree to which one is aware of the selective screen that one places between himself and the outside world.[3] As one moves from the low to the high side of the scale, awareness of the selective process increases. Therefore, what one pays attention to, context, and information overload are all functionally related.

In the fifties, the United States government spent millions of dollars developing systems for machine translation of Russian and other languages. After years of effort on the part of some of the most talented linguists in the country, it was finally concluded that the only reliable, and ultimately the fastest, translator is a human being deeply conversant not only with the language but with the subject as well. The computers could spew out yards of print-out but they meant very little. The words and some of the grammar were all there, but the sense was distorted. That the project failed was not due to lack of application, time, money, or talent, but for other reasons, which are central to the theme of this [article].

The problem lies not in the linguistic code but in the context, which carries varying proportions of the meaning. Without context, the code is incomplete since it encompasses only part of the message. This should become clear if one remembers that the spoken language is an abstraction of an event that happened, might have happened, or is being planned. As any writer knows, an event is usually infinitely more complex and rich than the language used to describe it. Moreover, the writing system is an abstraction of the spoken system and is in effect a reminder system of what somebody said or could have said. In the process of abstracting, as contrasted with measuring, people take in some things and unconsciously ignore others. This is what intelligence is: paying attention to the right things. The linear quality of a language inevitably results in accentuating some things at the expense of others. Two languages provide interesting contrasts. In English, when a man says, "It rained last night," there is no way of knowing how he arrived at that conclusion, or if he is even telling the truth, whereas a Hopi cannot talk about rain at all without signifying the nature of his relatedness to the event—firsthand experience, inference, or hearsay. This is a point made by the linguist Whorf[4] thirty years ago. However, selective attention and emphasis are not restricted to language but are characteristic of the rest of culture as well.

The rules governing what one perceives and [what one] is blind to in the course of living are not simple; at least five sets of disparate categories of events must be taken into account. These are: the subject or activity, the situation, one's status in a social system, past experience, and culture. The patterns governing juggling these five dimensions are learned early in life and are mostly taken for granted. The "subject" or topic one is engaged in has a great deal to do with what one does and does not attend. People working in the "hard" sciences, chemistry and physics, which deal with the physical world, are able to attend and integrate a considerably higher proportion of significant events observed than scientists working with living systems. The physical scientist has fewer variables to deal with; his abstractions are closer to the real events; and context is of less importance. This characterization is, of course, oversimplified. But it is important to remember that the laws governing the physical world, while relatively simple compared to those governing human behavior, may seem complex to the layman, while the complexity of language appears simple to the physicist, who, like everyone else, has been talking all his life. In these terms it is all too easy for the person who is in full command of a particular behavioral system, such as language, to confuse what he can *do* with a given system, with the unstated rules governing the way the system operates. The conceptual model I am using takes into account not only what one takes in and screens out but what one does not know about a given system even though one has mastered that system. The two are *not* the same. Michael Polanyi[5] stated this principle quite elegantly when he said, "The structure of a machine cannot be defined in terms of the laws which it harnesses."

What man chooses to take in, either consciously or unconsciously, is what gives structure and meaning to his world. Furthermore, what he perceives is "what he intends to do about it." Setting aside the other four dimensions (situation, status, past experience, and culture), theoretically it would be possible to arrange all of man's activities along a continuum ranging from those in which a very high proportion of the events influencing the outcome were consciously considered to those in which a much smaller number were considered. In the United States, interpersonal relations are frequently at the low end of the scale. Everyone has had the experience of thinking that he was making a good impression only to learn later that he was not. At times like these, we are paying attention to the wrong things or screening out behavior we should be observing. A common fault of teachers and professors is that they pay more attention to their subject matter than they do to the students, who frequently pay too much attention to the professor and not enough to the subject.

The "situation" also determines what one consciously takes in and leaves out. In an American court of law, the attorneys, the judge, and the jury are compelled by custom and legal practice to pay attention only to what is legally part of the record. Context, by design, carries very little weight. Contrast this with a situation in which an employee is trying to decipher the boss's behavior—whether he is pleased or not, and if he is going to grant a raise. Every little clue is a story in itself, as is the employee's knowledge of behavior in the past.

One's status in a social system also affects what must be attended. People at the top pay attention to different things from those at the middle or the bottom of the system. In order to survive, all organizations, whatever their size, have to develop techniques not only for replacing their leader but for switching the new leader's perceptions from the internal concerns he focused on when he was at the lower and middle levels to a type of global view that enables the head man or woman to chart the course for the institution.

The far-reaching consequences of what is attended can be illustrated by a characteristic fault in Western thinking that dates back to the philosophers of ancient Greece. Our way of thinking is quite arbitrary and causes us to look at ideas rather than events—a most serious shortcoming. Also, linearity can get in the way of mutual understanding and divert people needlessly along irrelevant tangents. The processes I am describing are particularly common in the social sciences; although the younger scientists in these fields are gradually beginning to accept the fact that when someone is talking about events on one level this does not mean that he has failed to take into account the many other events on different levels. It is just that one can talk about only a single aspect of something at any moment (illustrating the linear characteristic of language).

The results of this syndrome (of having to take multiple levels into account when using a single-level system) are reflected in a remark made by one of our most brilliant and least appreciated thinkers in modern psychiatry, H. S. Sullivan,[6] when he observed that as he composed his articles, lectures, and books the person he was writing to (whom he projected in his mind's eye) was a cross between an imbecile and a bitterly paranoid critic. What a waste. And so confusing to the reader who wants to find out what the man is really trying to say.

In less complex and fast-moving times, the problem of mutual understanding was not as difficult, because most transactions were conducted with people well known to the speaker or writer, people with similar backgrounds. It is important for conversationalists in any situation—regardless of the area of discourse (love, business, science)—

to get to know each other well enough so that they realize what each person is and is not taking into account. This is crucial. Yet few are willing to make the very real effort—life simply moves too fast—which may explain some of the alienation one sees in the world today.

Programming of the sort I am alluding to takes place in all normal human transactions as well as those of many higher mammals. It constitutes the unmeasurable part of communication. This brings us to the point where it is possible to discuss context in relation to meaning, because what one pays attention to or does not attend is largely a matter of context. Remember, contexting is also an important way of handling the very great complexity of human transactions so that the system does not bog down in information overload.

Like a number of my colleagues, I have observed that meaning and context are inextricably bound up with each other. While a linguistic code can be analyzed on some levels independent of context (which is what the machine translation project tried to accomplish), *in real life the code, the context, and the meaning can only be seen as different aspects of a single event.* What is unfeasible is to measure one side of the equation and not the others.[7]

Earlier, I said that high-context messages are placed at one end and low-context messages at the other end of a continuum. A high-context (HC) communication or message is one in which most of the information is either in the physical context or internalized in the person, while very little is in the coded, explicit, transmitted part of the message. A low-context (LC) communication is just the opposite; i.e., the mass of the information is vested in the explicit code. Twins who have grown up together can and do communicate more economically (HC) than two lawyers in a courtroom during a trial (LC), a mathematician programming a computer, two politicians drafting legislation, two administrators writing a regulation, or a child trying to explain to his mother why he got into a fight.

Although no culture exists exclusively at one end of the scale, some are high while others are low. American culture, while not on the bottom, is toward the lower end of the scale. We are still considerably above the German-Swiss, the Germans, and the Scandinavians in the amount of contexting needed in everyday life. While complex, multi-institutional cultures (those that are technologically advanced) might be thought of as inevitably LC, this is not always true. China, the possessor of a great and complex culture, is on the high-context end of the scale.

One notices this particularly in the written language of China, which is thirty-five hundred years old and has changed very little in the past three thousand years. This common written language is a unifying force tying together half a billion Chinese, Koreans, Japanese, and even some of the Vietnamese who speak Chinese. The need for context is experienced when looking up words in a Chinese dictionary. To use a Chinese dictionary, the reader must know the significance of 214 radicals (there are no counterparts for radicals in the Indo-European languages). For example, to find the word for star one must know that it appears under the sun radical. To be literate in Chinese, one has to be conversant with Chinese history. In addition, the spoken pronunciation system must be known, because there are four tones and a change of tone means a change of meaning; whereas in English, French, German, Spanish, Italian, etc., the reader need not know how to pronounce the language in order to read it. Another interesting sidelight on the Chinese orthography is that it is also an art form.[8] To my knowledge, no low-context communication system has ever been an art form. Good art is always high-context; bad art, low-context. This is one reason why good art persists and art that releases its message all at once does not.

The level of context determines everything about the nature of the communication and is the foundation on which all subsequent behavior rests (including symbolic behavior). Recent studies in sociolinguistics have demonstrated how context-dependent the language code really is. There is an excellent example of this in the work of the linguist Bernstein,[9] who has identified what he terms "restricted" (HC) and "elaborated" (LC) codes in which vocabulary, syntax, and sounds are all altered: In the restricted code of intimacy in the home, words and sentences collapse and are shortened. This even applies to the phonemic structure of the language. The individual sounds begin to merge, as does the vocabulary, whereas in the highly articulated, highly specific, elaborated code of the classroom, law, or diplomacy, more accurate distinctions are made on all levels. Furthermore, the code that one uses signals and is consistent with the situation. A shifting of code signals a shift in everything else that is to follow. "Talking down" to someone is low-contexting him—telling him more than he needs to know. This can be done quite subtly simply by shifting from the restricted end of the code toward the elaborated forms of discourse.

From the practical viewpoint of communications strategy, one must decide how much time to invest in contexting another person. A certain amount of this is always necessary, so that the information that makes up the explicit portions of the message is neither inadequate nor excessive. One reason most bureaucrats are so difficult to deal with is that they write for each other and are insensitive to the contexting needs of the public. The written regulations are usually highly technical on the one hand, while providing little information on the other. That is, they are a mixture of different codes or else there is incongruity between the code and the people to whom it is addressed. Modern management methods, for which management consultants are largely responsible, are less successful than they should be, because in an attempt to make everything explicit (low-contexting again) they frequently fail in their recommendations to take into account what people already know. This is a common fault of the consultant, because few consultants take the time (and few clients will pay for the time) to become completely contexted in the many complexities of the business.

There is a relationship between the worldwide activism of the sixties and where a given culture is situated on the context scale, because some are more vulnerable than others. HC actions are by definition rooted in the past, slow to change, and highly stable. Commenting on the need for the stabilizing effect of the past, anthropologist Loren Eiseley[10] takes an anti-activist position and points out how vulnerable our own culture is:

*Their world (the world of the activist), therefore, becomes increasingly the violent, unpredictable world of the first men simply because, in lacking faith in the past, one is inevitably forsaking all that enables man to be a planning animal. For man's story,[11] in brief, is essentially that of a creature who has abandoned* instinct *and replaced it with cultural tradition and the hard-won increments of contemplative thought. The lessons of the past have been found to be a reasonably secure construction for proceeding against an unknown future.[12]*

Actually, activism is possible at any point in the HC–LC continuum, but it seems to have less direction or focus and becomes less predictable and more threatening to institutions in LC systems. Most HC systems, however, can absorb activism without being shaken to their foundations.

In LC systems, demonstrations are viewed as the last, most desperate act in a series of escalating events. Riots and demonstrations in the United States, particularly those involving blacks,[13] are a message, a plea, a scream of anguish and anger for the larger society to *do something.* In China (an HC culture), the Red Guard riots apparently had an entirely different significance. They were promulgated from the top of the social order, not the bottom. They were also a communication from top to bottom: first, to produce a show of strength by Mao Tse-tung; second, to give pause to the opposition and shake things up at the middle levels—a way of mobilizing society, not destroying it. Chinese friends with whom I have spoken about these riots took them much less seriously than I did. I was, of course, looking at them from the point of view of one reared in a low-context culture, where such riots can have disastrous effects on the society at large.

Wherever one looks, the influence of the subtle hand of contexting can be detected. We have just spoken of the effects of riots on high- and low-context political systems, but what about day-to-day matters of perception? On the physiological level of color perception, one sees the power of the brain's need to perceive and adjust everything in terms of context. As any interior designer knows, a powerful painting, print, or wall hanging can change the perceived color of the furnishings around it. The color psychologist Faber Birren[14] demonstrated experimentally that the perceived shade of a color depends upon the color context in which it occurs. He did this by systematically varying the color of the background surrounding different color samples.

Some of the most impressive demonstrations of the brain's ability to supply the missing information—the function of contexting—are the experiments of Edwin Land, inventor of the Land camera. Working in color photography using a single red filter, he developed a process that is simple, but the explanation for it is not. Until Land's experiments, it was believed that color prints could be made only by superimposing transparent images of three separate photographs made with the primary colors—red, blue, and yellow. Land made his color photographs with two images: a black-and-white image to give light and shadow, and a single, *red* filter for color. When these two images were projected, superimposed on a screen, even though red was the only color, they were perceived in full color with all the shades and gradations of a three-color photograph![15] Even more remarkable is the fact that the objects used were deliberately chosen to provide no cues as to their color. To be sure that his viewers didn't unconsciously project color, Land photographed spools of plastic and wood and geometric objects whose color would be unknown to the viewer. How the eye and the visual centers of the brain function to achieve this remarkable feat of internal contexting is still only partially understood. But the actual stimulus does only part of the job.

Contexting probably involves at least two entirely different but interrelated processes—one inside the organism and the other outside. The first takes place in the brain and is a function of either past experience (programmed, internalized contexting)

or the structure of the nervous system (innate contexting), or both. External contexting comprises the situation and/or setting in which an event occurs (situational and/or environmental contexting).[16]

One example of the growing interest in the relationship of external context to behavior is the widespread interest and concern about our public-housing disasters. Pruitt-Igoe Homes in St. Louis is only one example. This $26-million fiasco imposed on poor blacks is now almost completely abandoned. All but a few buildings have been dynamited, because nobody wants to live there.

Objections and defects in high-rise public housing for poor families are legion: Mothers can't supervise their children; there are usually no community service agencies nearby and no stores or markets; and quite often there is no access to any public transportation system. There are no recreation centers for teenagers and few places for young children to play. In any budget crunch, the first thing to be cut is maintenance and then the disintegration process starts; elevators and hallways turn into death traps. The case against high-rise housing for low-income families is complex and underscores the growing recognition that environments are not behaviorally neutral.

Although situational and environmental context has only recently been systematically studied, environmental effects have been known to be a factor in behavior for years. Such men as the industrialist Pullman[17] made statements that sounded very advanced at the time. He believed that if workers were supplied with clean, airy, well-built homes in pleasant surroundings, this would exert a positive influence on their health and general sense of well-being and would make them more productive as well. Pullman was not wrong in his analysis. He simply did not live up to his stated ideals. The main street of his company town, where supervisors lived, was everything he talked about. But his workers were still poorly housed. Being isolated in a company town in close proximity to the plush homes of managers made their inadequate living conditions more obvious by way of contrast, and the workers finally embarked on a violent strike.

There were many other human, economic, and political needs, which Pullman had not taken into account, that led to worker dissatisfaction. Pullman's professed idealism backfired. Few were aware of the conditions under which his laborers actually lived and worked, so that the damage done to the budding but fragile environmentalist position was incalculable and gave ammunition to the "hard-nosed," "practical" types whose minds were focused on the bottom-line figures of profit and loss.

Quite often, the influence of either programmed contexting (experience) or innate contexting (which is built in) is brushed aside. Consider the individual's spatial needs and his feelings about certain spaces. For example, I have known women who needed a room to be alone in, whose husbands did not share this particular need, and they brushed aside their wives' feelings, dismissing them as childish. Women who have this experience should not let my talking about it raise their blood pressure. For it is very hard for someone who does not share an unstated, informal need with another person to experience that need as tangible and valid. Among people of northern European heritage, the only generally accepted proxemic needs are those associated with status. However, status is linked to the ego. Therefore, while people accept that the person at the top gets a large office, whenever the subject of spatial needs surfaces it is likely to be treated as a form of narcissism. The status and organizational aspects are recognized while internal needs are not.

Yet, people have spatial needs independent of status. Some people can't work unless they are in the midst of a lot of hubbub. Others can't work unless they are behind closed doors, cut off from auditory and visual distractions. Some are extraordinarily sensitive to their environments, as though they had tentacles from the body reaching out and touching everything. Others are impervious to environmental impact. It is these differences, when and if they are understood at all, that cause trouble for architects. Their primary concern is with aesthetics, and what I am talking about lies underneath aesthetics, at a much more basic level.

As often happens, today's problems are being solved in terms of yesterday's understanding. With few exceptions, most thinking on the man-environment relationship fails to make the man-environment (M-E) transaction specific, to say nothing of taking it into account. The sophisticated architect pays lip service to the M-E relationship and then goes right on with what he was going to do anyway, demonstrating once more that people's needs, cultural as well as individual—needing a room of one's own—are not seen as real. Only the building is real! (This is extension transference again.)

Of course, the process is much more complex than most people think. Until quite recently, this whole relationship had been unexplored.[18] Perhaps those who eschewed it did so because they unconsciously and intuitively recognized its complexity. Besides, it is much easier to deal with such simple facts as a balance sheet or the exterior design of a building. Anyone who begins to investigate context and contexting soon discovers that much of what is examined, even though it occurs before his eyes, is altered in its significance by many hidden factors. Support for research into these matters is picayune. What has to be studied is not only very subtle but is thought to be too fine-grained, or even trivial, to warrant serious consideration.

One hospital administrator once threw me out of his office because I wanted to study the effects of space on patients in his hospital. Not only was he not interested in the literature, which was then considerable, but he thought I was a nut to even suggest such a study. To complicate things further, proxemics research requires an inordinate amount of time. For every distance that people use, there are at least five major categories of variables that influence what is perceived as either correct or improper. Take the matter of "intrusion distance" (the distance one has to maintain from two people who are already talking in order to get attention but not intrude). How great this distance is and how long one must wait before moving in depends on: what is going on (activity), your status, your relationship in a social system (husband and wife or boss and subordinate), the emotional state of the parties, the urgency of the needs of the individual who must intrude, etc.

Despite this new information, research in the social and biological sciences has turned away from context. In fact, attempts are often made to consciously exclude context. Fortunately, there are a few exceptions, men and women who have been willing to swim against the main currents of psychological thought.

One of these is Roger Barker, who summarized twenty-five years of observations in a small Kansas town in his book *Ecological Psychology*.[19] Starting a generation ago, Barker and his students moved into the town and recorded the behavior of the citizens in a wide variety of situations and settings such as classrooms, drugstores, Sunday-school classes, basketball games, baseball games, club meetings, business offices, bars, and hangouts. Barker discovered that much of people's behavior is situation-dependent (under control of the setting), to a much greater degree than had been supposed. In fact, as a psychologist, he challenged many of the central and important tenets of his own field. In his words:

*The view is not uncommon among psychologists that the environment of behavior is a relatively unstructured, passive, probabilistic arena of objects and events upon which man behaves in accordance with the programming he carries about within himself. . . . When we look at the environment of behavior as a phenomenon worthy of investigation for itself, and not as an instrument for unraveling the behavior-relevant programming within persons, the situation is quite different. From this viewpoint the environment is seen to consist of highly structured, improbable arrangements of objects and events which* coerce *behavior in accordance with their own dynamic patterning. . . . We found . . . that we could predict some aspects of children's behavior more adequately from knowledge of the behavior characteristics of the drugstores, arithmetic classes, and basketball games they inhabited than from knowledge of the behavior tendencies of particular children. . . . (emphasis added) (p. 4)*

Later Barker states,

*The theory and data support the view that the environment in terms of behavior settings is much more than a source of random inputs to its inhabitants, or of inputs arranged in fixed array and flow patterns. They indicate, rather, that the environment provides inputs with controls that regulate the inputs in accordance with the systemic requirements of the environment, on the one hand, and in accordance with the behavior attributes of its human components, on the other. This means that the same environmental unit provides different inputs to different persons, and different inputs to the same person if his behavior changes; and it means, further, that the whole program of the environment's inputs changes if its own ecological properties change; if it becomes more or less populous, for example. (p. 205)[20]*

Barker demonstrates that in studying man *it is impossible to separate the individual from the environment in which he functions.* Much of the work of the transactional psychologists Ames, Ittelson, and Kilpatrick,[21] as well as my earlier work,[22] leads to the same conclusion.

In summary, regardless of where one looks, one discovers that a universal feature of information systems is that meaning (what the receiver is expected to do) is made up of: the communication, the background and preprogrammed responses of the recipient, and the situation. (We call these last two the internal and external context.)

Therefore, what the receiver actually perceives is important in understanding the nature of context. Remember that what an organism perceives is influenced in four ways—by status, activity, setting, and experience. But in man one must add another crucial dimension: *culture.*

Any transaction can be characterized as high-, low-, or middle-context [Figure 1]. HC transactions feature preprogrammed information that is in the receiver and in the setting, with only minimal information in the transmitted message. LC transactions are the reverse. Most of the information must be in the transmitted message in order to make up

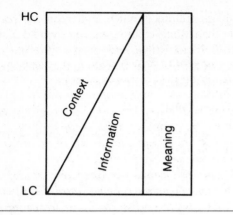

**Figure 1**

for what is missing in the context (both internal and external).

In general, HC communication, in contrast to LC, is economical, fast, efficient, and satisfying; however, time must be devoted to programming. If this programming does not take place, the communication is incomplete.

HC communications are frequently used as art forms. They act as a unifying, cohesive force, are long-lived, and are slow to change. LC communications do not unify; however, they can be changed easily and rapidly. This is why evolution by extension is so incredibly fast; extensions in their initial stages of development are low-context. To qualify this statement somewhat, some extension systems are higher on the context scale than others. A system of defense rocketry can be out of date before it is in place and is therefore very low-context. Church architecture, however, was for hundreds of years firmly rooted in the past and was the material focus for preserving religious beliefs and ideas. Even today, most churches are still quite traditional in design. One wonders if it is possible to develop strategies for balancing two apparently contradictory needs: the need to adapt and change (by moving in the low-context direction) and the need for stability (high-context). History is replete with examples of nations and institutions that failed to adapt by holding on to high-context modes too long. The instability of low-context systems, how-

ever, on the present-day scale is quite new to mankind. And furthermore, there is no reservoir of experience to show us how to deal with change at this rate.

Extensions that now make up most of man's world are for the most part low-context. The question is, how long can man stand the tension between himself and his extensions? This is what *Future Shock*[23] and *Understanding Media*[24] are all about. Take a single example, the automobile, which completely altered the American scene in all its dimensions—exploded communities, shredded the fabric of relationships, switched the rural-urban balance, changed our sex mores and churchgoing habits, altered our cities, crime, education, warfare, health, funerals. (One undertaker recently experimented with drive-in viewing of the corpse!) In summary:

*The screens that one imposes between oneself and reality constitute one of the ways in which reality is structured.*

*Awareness of that structure is necessary if one is to control behavior with any semblance of rationality. Such awareness is associated with the low-context end of the scale.*

*Yet there is a price that must be paid for awareness—instability; obsolescence, and change at a rate that may become impossible to handle and result in information overload.*

*Therefore, as things become more complex, as they inevitably must with fast-evolving, low-context systems, it eventually becomes necessary to turn life and institutions around and move toward the greater stability of the high-context part of the scale as a way of dealing with information overload.*

### NOTES

1. *The Hidden Dimension* discusses this quality of culture in more detail.

2. Meier (1963)

3. Man also imposes a selective screen between the

conscious part of his mind and the unconscious part. Sullivan (1947) and Freud (1933)

4. Whorf (1956)

5. Polanyi (1968)

6. Sullivan (1947)

7. The linguist Noam Chomsky (1968) and his followers have tried to deal with the contexting feature of language by eliminating context and going to so-called "deep structure." The results are interesting but end up evading the main issues of communication and to an even greater extent stress ideas at the expense of what is actually going on.

8. For further information on Chinese, see Wang (1973).

9. Bernstein (1964)

10. Eiseley (1969)

11. I do not agree with Eiseley's generalizing about all of mankind, because activism, like everything else, has to be taken in context. As we will see, LC cultures appear to be more vulnerable to violent perturbations than HC cultures.

12. Saul Bellow's (1974) article on the role of literature in a setting of changing times is also relevant to this discussion. Bellow makes the point that for some time now there has been a conscious effort on the part of avant-garde Western intellectuals to obliterate the past. "Karl Marx felt in history the tradition of all dead generations weighing like a nightmare on the brain of the living. Nietzsche speaks movingly of 'it was,' and Joyce's Stephen Dedalus also defines history as a 'nightmare from which we are trying to awaken.'" Bellow points out, however, that there is a paradox that must be met, for to do away with history is to destroy one's own part in the historical process. It is reasonably certain, however, that what these men were trying to do was to redefine context in order to reduce its influence on men's actions. Simply to do away with the past would lead to an incredibly unstable society, as we shall see.

13. Black culture is much higher on the context scale than white culture, and one would assume from our model that riots do not have the same meaning for blacks as they do to the white society in which the blacks are imbedded.

14. Birren (1961)

15. For further details on this fascinating set of experiments, see Land (1959).

16. These distinctions are completely arbitrary and are for the convenience of the writer and the reader. They do not necessarily occur in nature. The inside-outside dichotomy has been struck down many times, not only by the perceptual transactionalists (Kilpatrick, 1961) following in Dewey's footsteps but in my own writings as well. Within the brain, experience (culture) acts on the structure of the brain to produce mind. It makes little difference *how* the brain is modified; what is important is that modification does take place and is apparently continuous.

17. Buder (1967)

18. See Hall (1966a) for a comprehensive treatment of man's relationship to the spaces he builds as well as a bibliography on the subject.

19. Barker (1968) and Barker and Schoggen (1973)

20. The interested reader will find it worthwhile to consult Barker's works directly.

21. Kilpatrick (1961)

22. Hall (1966a)

23. Toffler (1970)

24. McLuhan (1964)

## BIBLIOGRAPHY

Barker, Roger G. *Ecological Psychology.* Stanford, Calif.: Stanford University Press, 1968.
———, and Schoggen, Phil. *Qualities of Community Life.* San Francisco: Jossey-Bass, 1973.

Bellow, Saul. "Machines and Story Books," *Harper's Magazine*, Vol. 249, pp. 48–54, August 1974.

Bernstein, Basil. "Elaborated and Restricted Codes: Their Social Origins and Some Consequences." In John J. Gumperz and Dell Hymes (eds.). The Ethnography of Communication, *American Anthropologist,* Vol. 66, No. 6, Part II, pp. 55–69, 1964.

Birren, Faber. *Color, Form and Space*. New York: Reinhold, 1961.

Buder, Stanley. "The Model Town of Pullman: Town Planning and Social Control in the Gilded Age," *Journal of the American Institute of Planners*, Vol. 33, No. 1, pp. 2–10, January 1967.

Chomsky, Noam. *Language and Mind*. New York: Harcourt, Brace & World, Inc., 1968.

Eiseley, L. "Activism and the Rejection of History," *Science*, Vol. 165, p. 129, July 11, 1969.

Freud, Sigmund. *New Introductory Lectures on Psychoanalysis*. New York: W. W. Norton & Company, Inc. 1933.

Hall, Edward T. "Art, Space and the Human Experience." In Gyorgy Kepes (ed.). *Arts of the Environment*. New York: George Braziller, Inc., 1972.

———. *The Hidden Dimension*. Garden City, N.Y.: Doubleday, 1966(a).

———. "Human Needs and Inhuman Cities." In *The Fitness of Man's Environment, Smithsonian Annual II*. Washington, D.C.: Smithsonian Institution Press, 1968. Reprinted in *Ekistics*, Vol. 27, No. 160, March 1969.

Kilpatrick, F. P. *Explorations in Transactional Psychology* (contains articles by Adelbert Ames, Hadley Cantril, William Ittelson, and F. P. Kilpatrick). New York: New York University Press, 1961.

McLuhan, Marshall. *Understanding Media*. New York: McGraw-Hill, 1964.

Meier, Richard. "Information Input Overload: Features of Growth in Communications-Oriented Institutions," *Libri* (Copenhagen), Vol. 13, No. 1, pp. 1–44, 1963.

Polanyi, M. "Life's Irreducible Structure," *Science,* Vol. 160, pp. 1308–12, June 21, 1968.

Sullivan, Harry Stack. *Conceptions of Modern Psychiatry*. New York: William Alanson White Psychiatric Foundation, 1947.

Toffler, Alvin. *Future Shock*. New York: Bantam Books, 1970.

Wang, William. "The Chinese Language," *Scientific American*, Vol. 228, No. 2, February 1973.

Whorf, Benjamin Lee. *Language, Thought, and Reality*. New York: The Technology Press of M.I.T. and John Wiley, 1956.

# Value Differences in Intercultural Communication

MYRON W. LUSTIG

Nearly twenty-five hundred years ago, the Greek historian Herodotus, whom Cicero called "The Father of History," related a story about Darius, the first monarch of the great Persian empire. Darius became King of Persia (now Iran) in 521 B.C., and he ruled a vast empire that, for a time, included most of the known world, including southeastern Europe, northern Africa, India, southern Russia, and the Middle East. Darius, so the story goes,

*... sent for the Greeks at his court to ask them their price for devouring the corpses of their ancestors. They replied that no price would be high enough. Thereupon the Persian king summoned the representatives of an Indian tribe which habitually practiced the custom from which the Greeks shrank, and asked them through the interpreter, in the presence of the Greeks, at what price they would burn the corpses of their ancestors. The Indians cried aloud and besought the king not even to mention such a horror. From these circumstances the historian drew the following notable moral for human guidance: If all existing customs could somewhere be set before all men in order that they might select the most beautiful for themselves, every nation would choose out, after the most searching scrutiny, the customs they had already practiced (Gomperz 1901, pp. 403–404).*

In the preceding passage, Herodotus described what today is called *ethnocentrism,* which is the belief that the customs, practices, and values of one's own culture (or group, society, tribe, et cetera) are superior to those of other cultures. Ethnocentrism is a learned belief in cultural superiority. Although ethnocentrism can be a major source of problems in intercultural communication episodes, it is present in all cultures and serves a useful purpose by maintaining order and cultural stability. After all, cultural practices would not survive, and the cultures themselves would disintegrate, if the members did not believe that *their* values and customs were superior to the alternatives.

A culture's value system is regarded as superior by that culture's members precisely because it is rarely, if ever, "changed, challenged, questioned, or even seen" (Laing 1972, p. 106). As with Isaac Newton's falling apple, which led to the discovery of the physical laws of thermodynamics, only the most perceptive people pay attention to the commonplace world around them. Most people remain oblivious to the unseen forces that govern cultural behaviors, like fish who are unaware of the water that surrounds them. The tendency for most people to be "blind to the obvious" has led Ichheiser (1970) to declare that "nothing evades our attention as persistently as that which is taken for granted" (p. 8).

This article is about the "taken-for-granteds" of human cultures. It deals with the unseen forces— the cultural values—that underlie cultural behaviors and decisions. These unseen forces are very important because they include both the cultural assumptions about what the world is and the collective judgments about what it should be. These impressions about what constitutes a good or bad world, in turn, influence the kinds of experiences that are sought and the interpretations that are made of everyday events.

## WHAT ARE VALUES?

Cultures can exist only because their members follow predictable behavior patterns. Tasks such as eating, sleeping, dressing, working, playing, and relating socially are so predictable and commonplace within a culture that they pass nearly unnoticed. In the United States, freeways clog during rush hours, lunch is usually over by 1:30 P.M., gifts brought by dinner guests are usually opened in the presence of the guests, and toilet flushing dramatically increases during the televised commercials of the annual Super Bowl. In Italy, lunch hasn't even begun by 1:30 P.M., and soccer is more popular than American football. In Malaysia, gifts are never opened in front of the giver; doing so is considered bad manners.

These predictable behavior patterns, which are stable over time and which lead to roughly similar behaviors across similar situations, are based upon a form of mental programming called *values*. Values are what people regard as good or bad, beautiful or ugly, clean or dirty, valuable or worthless, right or wrong, kind or cruel, just or unjust, and appropriate or inappropriate. Despite their importance in the control of cultural behaviors, values can't be seen, heard, tasted, or experienced because values are not available for direct investigation, although the consequences of particular values—human behaviors, or what people say and do—are readily observable. Values are inside people, in their minds. They are a way of thinking about the world, of orienting oneself to it. Values, therefore, are mental programs that govern specific behavior choices.

Some aspects of this mental programming are, of course, unique to each specific individual. Even within a single culture, no two people are programmed identically, and these ideosyncratic personality differences separate the individual members of a culture. Comparing across cultures, some mental programs are shared by all humanity and are essentially universal, or *etic* (Pike 1967). A mother's concern for her newborn infant, for example, reflects a biological program that exists across all known cultures and that is a part of our common genetic inheritance. In addition to those portions of our mental programs that are unique or universally held, there are mental programs that are widely shared, but only by members of a particular group or culture. Termed *emic* (Pike 1967), these collective programs can be understood only within the

context of a particular culture, and they include cultural differences in the preferred degree of social equality, the importance of group harmony, the degree to which emotional displays are permitted, the value ascribed to assertiveness, and the like.

As you can see, *value* and *culture* are inextricably linked. Each can be understood only in terms of the other because values form the basis for cultural differences. In a sense, a culture's values provide the basic set of standards and assumptions that guide thought and action. By providing its members with shared beliefs and assumptions about the "right" and "proper" ways of behaving, cultures provide the context within which individual values develop (Lee 1948).

## HOW CULTURAL VALUES FORM

Cultures invent, discover, or develop specific values as a result of two forces that affect the culture as a whole: *environmental adaptations* and *historical factors*. Environmental adaptations refer to the need for the culture to accommodate specific external constraints such as harsh weather, the availability or unavailability of certain foods and other raw materials, and biological forces such as life expectancy and fertility rates, which influence the culture's ability to sustain itself. Historical factors refer to the unique experiences within cultures that have become a part of the collective mental programming. Wars, inheritance rules, economic developments, prior experiences, legislative acts, and the allocation of power to specific individuals are all historical events that influence the formation of cultural values.

As an example of environmental and historical forces that influence the formation of cultural values, Singer (1987) described the effects of population, religion, resource availability, and life expectancy on the formation of certain cultural values within Ireland and India during the late nineteenth century. In Ireland, the population was large relative to the available food, and severe food shortages were not uncommon. Therefore, a pressing need existed to reduce the size of the population. Because the Irish were predominantly Catholic, artificial methods of birth control were unacceptable. Given the negative cultural value associated with birth control and the problems with overpopulation and a lack of food, a cultural value evolved that women ought not to marry before the age of about thirty. The population was reduced, of course, by delaying marriages.

India, at about the same time, also had harsh economic conditions, but the average life expectancy was about twenty-eight years, and nearly half of the children died before age five. Given that reality, a cultural value evolved that the preferred age for an Indian woman to marry was around twelve or thirteen. That way, all available childbearing years were available for procreation, thus increasing the chances for the survival of Indian society.

Singer (1987) suggested that these extreme cultural adaptations were not made consciously. Rather, the cultures were faced with the need to adapt to their environments, and had they not succeeded, they might have perished.

*Every group is confronted with environmental realities of one sort or another. Every group must deal with those realities in one way or another, or it will perish. Some groups may not adapt as well as others. There is no rule that says every group must survive. Throughout history many have not (Singer 1987, p. 168).*

Once formed, a culture's basic values have to be transmitted from one generation to another. The primary agents for transmitting these values are parents, but the entire folklore of a culture provides an unrelenting message about the preferred ways of thinking, feeling, perceiving, and acting in relation to problems with which the culture must cope. Most of these core values are programmed at a very early age. North Americans, for example, value achievement, practicality, material comfort, freedom, and individuality. These values are not so much consciously taught as unconsciously experienced as a byproduct of day-to-day activities.

## DIMENSIONS OF VALUES

Cultural values can differ in a variety of ways. Thus any description of value differences requires a listing of the ways in which cultures could potentially differ. One such description of values has been provided by Rokeach (1968, 1971, 1973, 1975, 1979). In his extensive writings, Rokeach said that cultures develop values about broad modes of conduct and about end-states of existence—means and ends. Table 1 provides a listing of these two kinds of values.

The values referring to broad modes of conduct, called *instrumental values,* include honesty, love, obedience, ambitiousness, and independence. The listing of instrumental values is further subdivided into those with a moral focus and those concerned with competence or self-actualization. *Moral values* are most closely related to interpersonal communication and include such modes of conduct as being cheerful, helpful, loving, and honest with others. *Competence values* are related to an individual's personality and include such modes of conduct as being ambitious, imaginative, logical, and self-controlled.

The values referring to end-states of existence, called *terminal values,* include freedom, a comfortable life, wisdom, a world at peace, and true friendship. Like the instrumental values, the listing of terminal values is further subdivided into those with a social or interpersonal focus and those with a personal focus. Terminal values with a social focus include a world at peace, social recognition, and true friendship. Terminal values with a personal focus include freedom, happiness, and salvation.

Another taxonomy of the dimensions along which cultures differ has been provided by Hofstede (1980). Hofstede (1980) has assembled some impressive data concerning cultural differences in work-related value orientations. Recent evidence suggests that Hofstede's dimensions are applicable not only to work-related values but to cultural values generally (Forgas and Bond 1985; Hofstede and Bond 1984). Using survey data gathered from more than 116,000 respondents in 40 countries, Hofstede (1980) described four dimensions along which cultural value

**Table 1** Rokeach's Instrumental and Terminal Values

*Instrumental Values*

Ambitious (hard working, aspiring)
Broad-minded (open-minded)
Capable (competent, effective)
Cheerful (lighthearted, joyful)
Clean (neat, tidy)
Courageous (standing up for your beliefs)
Forgiving (willing to pardon others)
Helpful (working for the welfare of others)
Honest (sincere, truthful)
Imaginative (daring, creative)
Independent (self-reliant, self-sufficient)
Intellectual (intelligent, reflective)
Logical (consistent, rational)
Loving (affectionate, tender)
Obedient (dutiful, respectful)
Polite (courteous, well mannered)
Responsible (dependable, reliable)
Self-controlled (restrained, self-disciplined)

*Terminal Values*

A comfortable life (a prosperous life)
An exciting life (a stimulating, active life)
A sense of accomplishment (lasting contribution)
A world at peace (free from war and conflict)
A world of beauty (beauty of nature and the arts)
Equality (brotherhood, equal opportunity for all)
Family security (taking care of loved ones)
Freedom (independence, free choice)
Happiness (contentedness)
Inner harmony (freedom from inner conflict)
Mature love (sexual and spiritual intimacy)
National security (protection from attack)
Pleasure (an enjoyable, leisurely life)
Salvation (saved, eternal life)
Self-respect (self-esteem)
Social recognition (respect, admiration)
True friendship (close companionship)
Wisdom (a mature understanding of life)

systems can be ordered: power distance, uncertainty avoidance, individualism-collectivism, and masculinity-femininity. Table 2 provides a ranking of the forty countries on each of the four dimensions.

*Power distance* indicates the degree to which the culture believes that institutional and organizational power should be distributed unequally.

Cultures with a small power distance, such as Austria, Denmark, Israel, and New Zealand, believe in minimizing social or class inequalities, reducing hierarchical organizational structures, and using power only for legitimate purposes. Cultures with a large power distance, such as Mexico, the Philippines, Venezuela, and India, believe in a social order in which each person has a rightful and protected place, that hierarchy presumes existential inequality, and that the legitimacy of the purposes desired by the power holder is irrelevant.

*Uncertainty avoidance* indicates the degree to which the culture feels threatened by ambiguous situations and tries to avoid uncertainty by establishing more structure. Cultures with weak uncertainty avoidance, including Great Britain, Hong Kong, Ireland, and Sweden, believe in the reduction of rules, the acceptance of dissent, a willingness to take risks in life, and tolerance for deviation from expected behaviors. Cultures with strong uncertainty avoidance, including Greece, Belgium, Japan, and Portugal, have high levels of anxiety and aggressiveness that create a strong inner urge to work hard, the need for extensive rules and regulations, a desire for consensus about goals, and a craving for certainty and security.

*Individualism-collectivism* indicates the degree to which a culture relies upon and has allegiance to the self or the group. Cultures with an individualist orientation, such as the United States, Australia, Netherlands, and Belgium, believe that people are only supposed to take care of themselves and, perhaps, their immediate families such that autonomy, independence, privacy, and an "I" consciousness are the ideal. Cultures with a collectivist orientation, such as Venezuela, Thailand, Pakistan, and Peru, expect their in-groups to take care of them, in exchange for which they feel an absolute loyalty to the group. Consequently, collectivist cultures believe in obligations to the group, dependence of the individual on organizations and institutions, a "we" consciousness, and an emphasis on belongingness.

*Masculinity-femininity* indicates the degree to which a culture values "masculine" behaviors such as assertiveness and the acquisition of wealth or

**Table 2** Ranking of Forty Countries on Hofstede's Four Dimensions of Values*

| | Power Distance | Uncertainty Avoidance | Individualism | Masculinity |
|---|---|---|---|---|
| Argentina | 25 | 10 | 23 | 18 |
| Australia | 29 | 27 | 2 | 14 |
| Austria | 40 | 19 | 18 | 2 |
| Belgium | 12 | 3 | 8 | 20 |
| Brazil | 7 | 16 | 25 | 23 |
| Canada | 27 | 31 | 4 | 21 |
| Chile | 15 | 8 | 33 | 34 |
| Colombia | 10 | 14 | 39 | 11 |
| Denmark | 38 | 39 | 9 | 37 |
| Finland | 33 | 24 | 17 | 35 |
| France | 9 | 7 | 11 | 29 |
| Germany | 30 | 21 | 15 | 9 |
| Great Britain | 31 | 35 | 3 | 8 |
| Greece | 17 | 1 | 27 | 16 |
| Hong Kong | 8 | 37 | 32 | 17 |
| India | 4 | 34 | 21 | 19 |
| Iran | 18 | 23 | 24 | 28 |
| Ireland | 36 | 36 | 12 | 7 |
| Israel | 39 | 13 | 19 | 25 |
| Italy | 23 | 17 | 7 | 4 |
| Japan | 22 | 4 | 22 | 1 |
| Mexico | 2 | 12 | 29 | 6 |
| Netherlands | 28 | 26 | 5 | 38 |
| New Zealand | 37 | 30 | 6 | 15 |
| Norway | 34 | 28 | 13 | 39 |
| Pakistan | 21 | 18 | 38 | 22 |
| Peru | 13 | 7 | 37 | 31 |
| Philippines | 1 | 33 | 28 | 10 |
| Portugal | 16 | 2 | 30 | 33 |
| Singapore | 6 | 40 | 34 | 24 |
| South Africa | 24 | 29 | 16 | 12 |
| Spain | 20 | 9 | 20 | 30 |
| Sweden | 35 | 38 | 10 | 40 |
| Switzerland | 32 | 25 | 14 | 5 |
| Taiwan | 19 | 20 | 36 | 27 |
| Thailand | 14 | 22 | 35 | 32 |
| Turkey | 11 | 11 | 26 | 26 |
| U.S.A. | 26 | 32 | 1 | 13 |
| Venezuela | 3 | 15 | 40 | 3 |
| Yugoslavia | 5 | 5 | 31 | 36 |

*A low ranking (e.g., 3) indicates a high rating on that dimension.

Adapted from Geert Hofstede, *Culture's Consequences: International Differences in Work-Related Values* (Beverly Hills, Calif.: Sage Publications, 1980), p. 315.

"feminine" behaviors such as caring for others and the quality of life. Cultures with a masculine orientation, including Japan, Austria, Italy, and Mexico, believe in performance, achievement, ambition, the acquisition of material goods, and ostentatious manliness. Cultures with a feminine orientation, including Austria, Norway, Portugal, and Venezuela, believe in the quality of life, service to others, equality between the sexes, nurturing roles, and sympathy for the unfortunate.

It is instructive to examine Table 2 in order to determine how citizens of the United States differ from their nearest cultural neighbors. The United States is just below the midpoint on power distance, does not avoid uncertainty, is extremely individualistic, and is somewhat masculine in its value orientations. Canada has a pattern of values that is very similar to that of the United States, but Mexico differs from the United States on all dimensions except masculinity. The ethnocentric tendency to regard the values of one's own culture as superior to others suggests that the United States and Mexico will sometimes differ on what each country regards as appropriate. For instance, many American college students, given their high regard for individualism, consider it appropriate to live hundreds of miles from home if doing so will allow them to pursue the best education. Many Mexican college students, on the other hand, have refused educational opportunities that required them to live far away from their homes and families because their collectivist orientation places group relationships before individual achievement.

## WHEN VALUES CLASH

Normally, one's values lead to consistent expectations about potential courses of action. The value system provides a generalized plan

*. . . that can perhaps best be likened to a map or architect's blueprint. Only that part of the map or blueprint that is immediately relevant is consulted, and the rest is ignored for the moment. Different subsets of the map or blueprint are acti-*

*vated in different social situations (Rokeach 1973, p. 14).*

Sometimes, however, components of the internal blueprint—the value system—may conflict, or cultural differences in value orientations may create disagreements. At an individual level, a person may feel a conflict about being polite versus being honest, or being ambitious versus being helpful. When two people are from different cultures, value differences may hinder the achievement of rational agreement on important issues. As Nadler, Nadler, and Broome (1985) have suggested, "In an intercultural negotiation context, certain values may influence what interactants bring to the conflict, the process of negotiation, and eventually modes of conflict resolution" (p. 89).

Etzioni (1968) has argued that there is no such thing as a truly "rational" decision, as virtually all cultural decisions presume an agreement on fundamental values that were acquired without specific intent or even conscious awareness. For instance, some cultures have a system of patronage in which gifts are given to public officials in return for assistance. Such gifts are both expected and accepted by members of that culture as the proper way of doing things. Therefore, any "rational" attempts to approach such governmental bureaucracies would include the giving of such gifts as a natural and proper component of the interaction. Other cultures, including that of the United States, object to such patronage and consider the gifts to be illegal payoffs. As with other examples of ethnocentrism, all cultures consider their own customs to be preferable to any others.

For encounters within a single culture, such value differences rarely collide. However, when members of two or more cultures communicate, differences in values greatly increase the likelihood of misunderstandings. When a young Peruvian woman applied for employment with a well-known company in the United States, she attached twenty dollars to her application. To her, the money was given because it was the only polite thing to do. To have done otherwise, she believed, would have been as rude as refusing to shake hands in the initial greeting ritual. The American employer, of course, was angered by what he perceived to be an attempt at bribery.

Of course, shared values don't guarantee the absence of conflict. Many conflicts between cultures occur precisely because there is agreement on the value and importance of certain scarce resources but disagreement about who should control them. Nevertheless, value differences are often behind intercultural disagreements.

## CONCLUSION

Values are powerful unseen forces that are collectively shared within a culture. Values provide a pattern of basic assumptions that are used by the culture to cope with its problems. It is hoped that an awareness of and sensitivity to cultural value differences will help to promote intercultural understanding and will help to make attempts at intercultural communication more successful.

## REFERENCES

Etzioni, A. (1968). *The Active Society.* New York: Free Press.

Forgas, J. P. and M. H. Bond. (1985). "Cultural Influences on the Perception of Interaction Episodes." *Personality and Social Psychology Bulletin,* 11:75–88.

Gomperz, T. (1901). *Greek Thinkers: A History of Ancient Philosophy, Vol. 1* (L. Magnus, trans.). New York: Charles Scribner's Sons.

Hofstede, G. and M. H. Bond. (1984). "Hofstede's Culture Dimensions: An Independent Validation Using Rokeach's Value Survey." *Journal of Cross-Cultural Psychology,* 15:417–433.

Hofstede, G. (1980). *Culture's Consequences: International Differences in Work-Related Values.* Beverly Hills, Calif.: Sage Publications.

Ichheiser, G. (1970). *Appearances and Realities: Misunderstandings in Human Relations.* San Francisco: Jossey-Bass.

Laing, R. D. (1972). *The Politics of the Family and Other Essays.* New York: Vintage Books.

Nadler, L. B., M. K. Nadler, and B. J. Broome. (1985). "Culture and the Management of Conflict Systems." In W. B. Gudykunst, L. P. Stewart, and S. Ting-Toomey (eds.), *Communication, Culture, and Organizational Processes.* Beverly Hills, Calif.: Sage Publications, 1985, 87–113.

Pike, Kenneth L. (1967). *Language in Relation to a Unified Theory of Human Behavior,* 2nd ed. The Hague: Mouton.

Rokeach, M. (1979). "Value Theory and Communication Research: Review and Commentary." In D. Nimmo (ed.), *Communication Yearbook 3.* New Brunswick, N.J.: Transaction, 395–405.

Rokeach, M. (1975). "Long-Term Value Change Initiated by Computer Feedback." *Journal of Personality and Social Psychology,* 32:467–476.

Rokeach, M. (1973). *The Nature of Human Values.* New York: Free Press.

Rokeach, M. (1971). "Long-Range Experimental Modification of Values, Attitudes, and Behavior." *American Psychologist,* 26:453–459.

Rokeach, M. (1968). "A Theory of Organization and Change within Value–Attitude Systems." *Journal of Social Issues,* 24:13–33.

Singer, Marshall R. (1987). *Intercultural Communication: A Perceptual Approach.* Englewood Cliffs, N.J.: Prentice-Hall.

# Religion-Caused Complications in Intercultural Communication

## REGINALD SMART

## WHY RELIGION COMPLICATES

Religion is probably the least acknowledged but the most powerful complicator of communication between persons of different cultures. The preceding statement makes immediate sense if we step back from our own attitude toward religion and look at the term's broad meaning as an *individual's ultimate concern* (Tillich 1959). It might be expected that one person's ultimate concern should also be the ultimate complicator when he or she tries to communicate with someone who does not share that concern. The ultimate concerns of those who affirm the Judeo–Christian–Moslem heritage *are* radically different from those nurtured in the benign religious traditions of the Far East. Indeed, so deep and pervasive is the influence of religion on cultural patterns (and particularly on values) that even the most secularized Westerner or Far Easterner unconsciously carries extensive remnants of the particular religious heritage that permeates his or her culture.

Even persons who completely reject all religion are influenced by it. In an age where secular thought is popular among the intelligentsia, acknowledging the religious roots of anything—from literary allusions like "the salt of the earth" to the scientific drive for mastery of the natural world—is unpopular. If you're an Eastern secularist, acknowledging the religious origins of concern for good manners, group obligations, and harmony is also unpopular. The simple fact is this: The final sanctions behind most cultural norms are religious, for the cultural norms are seen as the means toward the ultimate fulfillment of life itself. And although religious explanations may not be attached to them, the cultural norms are still treated as seriously as if eternal joy or damnation hinged upon them.

Examples of religion causing difficulties in intercultural communication are not hard to find. The most obvious are those situations in which primitive people are affronted by someone who unknowingly trespasses on sacred ground or otherwise exhibits "sacrilegious" behavior or speech. The careless use of the names for deity is an equal affront to devout Jews, Christians, and Moslems. And how frustrated is the Far Easterner when her acceptance of a misfortune is interpreted as apathy; for example, "She can't have loved him if she's so calm about his death."

I recall vividly the occasion in 1956 when a servant's infant was having a third set of convulsions. Her family refused to allow me to take Minah and her little Azziz to the hospital. I felt callous and torn as I walked away from their refusal of help: "If he lives or dies, it is the will of Allah." There was no way I could communicate with the mother at that moment. It was made impossible not only by *her* religious beliefs, which dictated acceptance, but by *mine,* which dictated action.

Another example is the "one-downmanship" that can characterize the Japanese in a negotiation situation. The statement, "If you would honor this poor person's suggestion," can put a Westerner badly off balance. The latter is inflated and made to feel superior if he or she accepts this self-deprecation, yet in so doing he or she feels a little guilty. Is it possible that the slightly guilty feeling goes back to those words, "Blessed are the humble . . ." rather than the dominant? Does that feeling of guilt predispose the Westerner to agree to "this poor person's suggestion"? For each of us, religious assumptions and traditions determine, and confuse, the "objective" issues. This article is thus written out of a profound conviction that we ignore *at our peril* the religious dimension of interactions with other cultures.

## TWO MAJOR GROUPS OF RELIGIONS (RELIGIOUS TRADITIONS)

How can we manageably think about the diverse faiths of humankind? Surely this task is beyond our interest in the current subject? Not so. With only minor distortion, it is possible to group the world's major religions into two divisions—those who see the ultimate good in terms of *harmonization* and those who see it in terms of *transformation*. The traditions of Hinduism, Shintoism, Buddhism, Confucianism, and Taoism see harmony as the Way, whereas Jews, Christians, and Moslems see divine grace as the desired end, whether in this life or the next. The development of these two groups can be traced in the histories of several individuals in very specific socio-historic circumstances. Out of each individual's struggle with his situation came the beliefs and ethics that inspire and inform the lives of his disciples to this day. Consequently, we shall review those two sets of religious founders and their concomitant ethics, and we shall demonstrate how their beliefs still flourish in the behavior of our contemporaries around the globe.

Of course, religions existed long before any of those leaders just mentioned came along, but today more than 90 percent of the world falls into the sphere of influence of one of these two categories. If one counts the most nominal adherents of these two groups, each group consists of about 45 percent of the world's population, which topped 5 billion in 1986. There are currently 600 million Moslems, and they belong to the fastest-growing major group, dominating much of Asia and Africa. Communists make up the largest group of nonbelievers. Religions based on nature still characterize many of the more indigenous populations of Africa, the Americas, and Australasia.

In all the religions of the Far East, deity is *immanent*—that is, "in things," which means that deity is all mixed up with every aspect of life: the good, the bad; the ugly, the beautiful; the happy, the sad. It isn't just that God *knows* about these things; it's that god *is* these things. That's the key notion of religion in the Far East: Everything (and everybody) is god. That idea represents the basic view of almost half the human race—namely, most of China, India, and the smaller Far Eastern countries.

In the Middle East (the place from which all Western religions came), however, we find the origins of the other major group of religious tradition. In this group, the key notion is that deity is *transcendent*—that is, beyond all limitations—and thus deserves to be spelled with a capital G—as God. From the Hebrews to Jesus of Nazareth to Mohammed there runs a clear line of development and a shared tradition: These religions are basically of the same type; all adherents believe in one, absolute ruler, who started this whole universe, determines the details of its continuance, keeps it going, and will eventually bring to an end all things and all human life. As a result, within that tradition, you begin a service of worship with something like the hymn:

*Praise to the Lord, the Almighty the King of Creation;*
*Oh my soul, phrase Him, for He is your health and salvation; . . .*

To put this description another way: The Western tradition starts with a *dualism*. It starts with God *out there* everything else *here*. Between these two places there is a great gulf. Everything else is alienated from God. Things don't work the way God meant them to in the first place; something went wrong.

In the Far East it's quite different: Religion starts with us human beings—the way we are in our family, in our neighborhood, in our town, *and* farther away in an adjacent valley—and how we relate to others and the world around us. There is an awareness of *us* that comes first, and religion enters the scene as a way of explaining (and maybe improving) what happens among people and even within each person.

In Hinduism and Buddhism, the chief interest is in explaining what happens inside each of us: Why do I feel a certain way as a child? Another way as a parent? Another way when I am middle aged? And yet another way when I approach death? Understanding these questions is the essence of these two religions. You might say, "That sounds like psychology," and you'd be right: A psychological orientation is the dominant quality of the two great South Asian (Indian) religions—Hinduism and Buddhism.

The North Asian religious tradition started not with the individual, but with the group. Why and how do some groups of people get along? Why are groups sometimes torn apart? Why is it nice or nasty to be part of a group? The father of that kind of thinking is Confucius. The origin of Confucianism, the building upon it, and the refining of it took place in China. (Huston Smith claims that the three great civilizations of the world made their prime contributions to mankind as follows: an understanding of nature by Western civilization, an understanding of personality by Indian civilization, and an understanding of human society by Chinese civilization.) You might well categorize the North Asian religious tradition as social ethics.

The information in this article to date can be summarized as follows: In the Western tradition, God determines all things; in the Eastern tradition, god is an idea that comes into the picture when you happen to think you need it. As a result, in the Western tradition, the finest description we can give of *man* is that he is "made in the image of God." The Western tradition has the notion: "The *best* that you find in people is a reflection of God, while the rest of our behavior is a distortion of what God meant to be." In the Eastern tradition, god is made in the image of man; in other words: Sometimes I feel angry enough to kill someone, so there are killer gods; sometimes I am very lustful, so there are lustful gods of both sexes; sometimes I want to take care of people, so there are strongly nurturing gods; and so it goes. All ideas about God or gods came

from what people knew or experienced in themselves. These two schools of thought embrace radically different ways of thinking about what we are as human beings.

What people believe they *should* do is equally different in the two major groups. In the West, you believe you have to obey God. As a result of this belief, there is structure, particularly in the way you worship. Ethnocentric Westerners look for a regular time of worship in the East and find none; they look for congregations and find none. Westerners take their categories and expect to find them elsewhere and do not. Eastern religions just don't operate that way. They do not have formal structures for correct behavior as we do. In the East, the custom is rather to search oneself and society for the insights, the skills, and the strengths needed to lead to their ultimate good, both as individuals and as groups.

## THE WESTERN TRADITION: ABSOLUTIST RELIGIONS

Let us first seek the shared tradition of these absolutist Western religions—Judaism, Christianity, and Islam—the religions that see God "out there" and man "down here." They can also be called *dualistic religions* because they see two separate parts to reality—God and creation. Westerners who call themselves *humanist* in preference to *religious* have been strongly influenced, *not* by Eastern thought, but by nineteenth-century philosophy. At that time a key notion was that God was a hypothesis developed to explain what people did not know. It follows from the "God-of-the-gaps" theory that, as we reduce the gaps in our knowledge, we have less and less need for God. This theory leads, said Nietzsche, to the "death" of "God" as a living concept in our minds. Religion, according to this theory, was a source of strength for those people who needed a source outside of themselves (preachers would later claim "there are no atheists in the trenches"). Nietzsche claimed seriously that we were then entering an age where supermen no longer needed religion as it existed.

What is this tradition that influences all of us in

the West? There is no better way to answer this question than to review some of the "men of faith" who are most revered in this tradition. Descriptions of a few of them follow.

Around 1700 B.C. lived a man named *Abraham*. He and his wife Sarah always wanted to have children but were unable to do so. When Abraham was ninety-nine and Sarah about ten years younger, Abraham had a vision. God told Abraham that Sarah would have a son and that his descendants would rule the earth. Abraham could scarcely believe it, but he agreed to God's covenant and Sarah became pregnant. They had a son and they were awed by this miracle. As the boy grew, Abraham had another vision, in which he was confronted with the worst command he could ever have imagined—the sacrifice of his son Isaac. In obedience to that vision he took his son Isaac to a hilltop where they prepared a pile of wood on which to burn the offering to God. Isaac asked where the sacrificial lamb was. His father replied in a tearful whisper that God had commanded that Isaac be the sacrifice. Abraham knew that the same God who had promised him countless descendants now required the sacrifice of the son who was the very means of fulfilling that promise. It did not make sense, but it was God's demand. In complete obedience he sharpened his knife and was raising it to cut Isaac's throat when the voice of God came again and told him to stop. God did not want Isaac's life. He wanted Abraham's blind obedience. It was a test.

The story of Abraham and Isaac is the one that Christians, Jews, and Muslims all tell when they want to explain what they mean by *faith*. This story is the model of what it means to be a believer in their terms; they are ready to destroy even the thing they value most whether or not they understand the reason. Questioning God's will is not part of these three religions, which I call the Western tradition. We must start with Abraham's blind faith if we are to understand them.

Next we have Abraham's grandson, *Jacob*. He was very bright. The texts on genetics used in agricultural schools often have a story about Jacob in the preface because he was the first person to dis-cover some of the laws of genetics. The story goes that as a young man he married into a family with large flocks and herds. His father-in-law was delighted by Jacob's proposition that he would care for the animals with no compensation except that he would get the striped and spotted calves and kids—ones considered inferior. Fifteen years later when the animals were herded from distant valleys, almost all of them were striped or spotted, and therefore Jacob's. He had cheated his father-in-law out of his entire fortune—by selective breeding. Jacob was now rich but in danger of his life at the hand of his very irate father-in-law. Consequently he took his wife, children, and concubines away and they lived as wanderers for years, with no settled abode but increasing wealth and many dependent families who helped tend the thousands of animals. One day Jacob's scouts brought the news that he was trapped in a valley in such a way that he must confront his brother, whom he had cheated out of his share of the family inheritance when both were teenagers. He arranged matters so that all his people went before him—as gifts—to this angry brother. Finally, he sent even his immediate family over the river— to make sure his brother was not bent on vengeance, leaving open the possibility of a last-minute escape for himself. The night before Jacob was to meet his brother and in sight of his brother's camp he had a dream, a vision of God, and he agreed to be God's man. God changed Jacob's name to Israel, and *his* descendants have been at odds with *his brother's* descendants ever since, for these two men were the progenitors of the Jews and the Arabs. Israel henceforth obeyed Yahweh in the absolute way of his grandfather to carry on God's wishes on earth. It was not the goodness of the man which led God to choose him but his absolute obedience.

Centuries later these people became a kingdom headed by *David*. David believed himself chosen by God to be their leader. He had a strong appreciation for beautiful women. One day he saw Bathsheba. He asked who she was and learned that she was the wife of one of his generals. David ordered General Uriah's subordinates to desert the general the next time they were in battle, which would leave

David free to marry the desirable widow. Soon after he did so, she bore David a son. Then one day a wild, bearded, dirty man-of-God named Elisha appeared in the court. This religious man asked for a hearing about "an injustice," and he told David how a poor man with only one lamb to his name had been robbed even of that lamb by his wealthy landlord. David shouted in righteous indignation and demanded to know the identity of the man, saying he should be killed. In the hushed court Elisha quietly said that David was the guilty man. David was touched to the quick, and rather than destroying the man for his insolence, David repented. God told David he would be forgiven, but for a price. David's son died as punishment, but David became an even greater servant of Yahweh, and because of this event he was even more admired as a hero of the Faith.

## Christianity

*Jesus of Nazareth* was of the same line. A carpenter by trade, a descendent of David, living in a despised corner of Israel, he became sure he was uniquely chosen by God to preach about the nature of God's reign—on earth and beyond time. He was completely obedient to his "Father's" will, and he consequently ran afoul of the authority of both the Jewish religious leaders and the Roman secular powers. Rather than do good works in the provinces, he risked his life by confronting these authorities—and dying for it—in absolute certainty that he was God's specially chosen one. Subsequently his disciples became equally convinced and followed his example of selfless martyrdom.

In later centuries great "men of faith" in this Western tradition were equally blind in their obedience to their demanding God—regardless of the price. In obedience to God's command, the young *Francis* rejected the pleas of his wealthy father and discarded his clothes right in court, saying that God demanded he give up "all"; to this day his followers wear a simple, brown cloth. In obedience to God's command, *Phillip of Spain* traveled to Rome—on his knees. In obedience to God's command, Martin Luther stood boldly against the enraged powers of the Pope, in whose service he was a priest, defiantly saying "Here stand I, I can do no other."

## Islam

Of this same line was another Semite (racially the same as Abraham, Jacob, David, and Jesus), called *Mohammed.* In Mecca, Saudi Arabia, this ordinary but religious-minded young man was born into a leading tribe in A.D. 571. He knew and reviewed the stories just presented, and he knew that some of Jesus' followers taught that he was not only a man but also God in human flesh. Mohammed married, not for beauty but for money, a woman with an extensive trading business who was 15 years older. He was initially in charge of her trading activities, but as he approached forty, he became more and more preoccupied with religious and ethical matters. Mecca seemed to him to be the essence of decadence. He thought that Allah (an Arabic variant of the Jewish word for God) in fact wanted none of what he saw around him—none of the drunkenness; none of the prostitution; none of the idol worship (of 396 deities); none of the abuse of children, women, and debtors. For nearly 20 years he spent extended periods in the desert thinking about how God must react to this horrendous scene. Then one day while he was in the desert he had a vision. He was visiting a cave near the base of Mount Hira, a huge barren rock that erupted from the desert a few miles north of Mecca, to which he went regularly because there he felt the presence of Allah. But on this occasion he heard a voice commanding him to "Cry!" The command was given thrice. Terrified, he asked what he should cry. He raced home and found a supportive wife who told him he was not mad. She did tell him she thought he had become a prophet. He heard the voice when he went again, and it commanded:

*Recite thou in the name of thy Lord who
    created;—*
*Created man from Clots of Blood:—*
*Recite thou! For thy Lord is the most Beneficent,*
*Who hath taught the use of the pen:—*
*Hath taught man that which he knoweth not. . . .*

*Your compatriot erreth not, nor is he led astray,*
*Neither speaketh he from mere impulse.*
*The* Koran *is no other than a revelation revealed*
*to him:*
*One terrible in power taught it him.*
*Endued with wisdom. . . .*

According to Moslem belief, everything in the resultant *Koran,* every word, was written down *as it was said.* This belief gives it an advantage over all other religious writings, which were subjected to oral repetition for years and even centuries before being written. Hence the Moslems revere their holy book as superior to and even correcting the holy books of the Jews and Christians, which went through various editing processes, including the exclusion of those sections judged as "uninspired." To make the point acutely, the Koran is seen as the verbatim transcript of God's own words, the actual words spoken by the archangel Gabriel. The outcome was that all of the Koran was given to Mohammed in a period of two months, and it was written immediately. It included rules covering every situation in daily Arabian life. It was indeed a complete law book. It is still a law book, used as *the* law in Indonesia, Saudi Arabia, and Iran.

The merchant Mohammed now became a religious teacher. His reception was hostile because monotheism undermined a lively trade in idols, deprived men of their hedonistic life style, and demanded justice that threatened the privileged. Some listened, and those who did shared the prophet's rejection and persecution. But Mohammed would not be quiet; God had commanded him to "Cry" and he would do so whatever the cost.

Eventually, his life threatened, he escaped from Mecca to a city now called Medina 200 miles to the north. This flight—the Hegira—is remembered as the turning point in world history. It happened in A.D. 622—the year from which Moslems date their calendar. It is celebrated annually in forty days of fasting from sunrise to sunset, called *Ramadan.* The greatest act of piety is to journey to Mecca and retrace Mohammed's path in that flight.

The prophet Mohammed's new city accepted his teachings and believed that the Koran was of Allah and that Allah's will was for all to live as the Koran directed. Mohammed developed the statesmanlike qualities needed in a leader, took over the city, and overwhelmed Mecca and eventually the whole of Saudi Arabia. In twenty-five years, this religious visionary became the ruler of the whole Arab world. When he died his successors (known as Caliphs) were responsible for making sure that all was done in accord with Allah's gift of the Koran through "the last of the prophets," Mohammed.

A number of elements lend tremendous power to the Koran's teachings. The most important is the clear picture of heaven and hell.

*After this sort will we recompense the*
*transgressors.*
*They shall make their bed in Hell, and above*
*them shall be coverings of fire! . . .*
*And the inmates of the fire shall cry to the inmates*
*of Paradise: "pour upon us some water!" . . .*

*Oh! how wretched shall be the people of the left*
*hand!*
*Amid pestilential winds and in scalding water,*
*And in the shadow of a black smoke,*
*Not cool, and horrid to behold. . . .*
*Then ye, O ye the erring, the gainsaying,*
*Shall surely eat of the tree Ez-Zakkoum. . . .*

*It is a tree which cometh up from the bottom of*
*Hell;*
*Its fruit is as it were heads of Satans;*
*And, lo! the damned shall surely eat of it and fill*
*their bellies with it:*
*Then shall they have, thereon, a mixture of boil-*
*ing water. . . .*

*Verily the tree of Ez-Zakkoum*
*Shall be the sinner's food:*
*Like dregs of oil shall it boil up in their bellies,*
*Like the boiling of scalding water.*
*"—Seize ye him, and drag him into the mid-fire;*
*Then pour on his head of the tormenting boiling*
*water.*
*"—'Taste this:' for thou forsooth art the mighty,*
*the honorable!*
*Lo! this is that of which ye doubted."*

*But the pious shall be in a secure place,*

*Amid gardens and fountains,*
*Clothed in silk and richest robes, facing one*
    *another....*

*On inwrought couches*
*Reclining on them face to face:*
*Aye-blooming youths go round about to them*
*With goblets and ewers and a cup of flowing*
    *wine;*
*Their brows ache not from it, nor fails the sense:*
*And with such fruits as shall please them best,*
*And with flesh of such birds as they shall long for:*
*And theirs shall be the Houris, with large dark*
    *eyes, like pearls hidden in their shells,*
*In recompense for their labors past....*
*Of a rare creation have we created the Houris,*
*And we have made them ever virgins,*
*Dear to their spouses, of equal age with them.*

That is the picture of *man's* heaven. Yet one of the interesting things is that the great changes Mohammed brought about in the Arab world benefited women and children more than anyone else. The Koran spelled out very clear laws of inheritance. Before the Koran the eldest male child got everything. Under Koranic Law, every child gets something. At the time of his vision, girls were often buried alive at birth because they were not wanted—a practice forbidden by the Koran. The preceding description is the heaven to which nothing in this life can compare. Moslems believe this absolutely, without a single question or qualification. In the wider picture, the growth of Islam today is impressive. It outdistances all other faiths.

### What the Western Tradition Says about Human Nature

We must not conclude this quick overview of Western religious tradition without a clear picture of where it leads. As sure as day follows night, certain things follow *about man.* Man is not just alienated from God; man is the image of God. Man has enormous responsibility to *do* what God wants, to bring about what God wants here and now. As a result, in obedience to the all-powerful God, man invents things, explores the universe, colonizes, kills Indi-

ans, finds a cure for polio, goes to the moon, and so on. None of these actions make sense in themselves unless you are guided by the dual notion that you have (a) a *right* and (b) an *obligation* to do them. Followers of the other religions think that none of those things lead to any long-lasting good. The objective evidence might be that man has produced some good and much evil. Science has created environmental problems with its acidification of the soil, the re-emergence of buried wastes, and the reduction of the protective ozone layer—as we obeyed God in subduing nature. We thus became alienated from nature and our total environment through our belief in our right and obligation to control it.

It is no great leap from these religious perspectives to the broad cultural values of the West noted by Kluckhohn and others who have built on her work. The self as unique and beyond valuation; human nature as fallen potentiality; nature and time as purposive; these all derive from the great themes of Western religious tradition and constitute a "short-hand" way for the non-Westerner to begin to enter our frame of reference.

It would be an oversight to fail to recall the debt owed to Islam by Westerners in general. The Renaissance would have been less than a half-birth but for the Moslems. They preserved and used Greek thought and learning. In philosophy, science, and mathematics, this learning was enshrined in the world's first university, the El-Haram, in Cairo. It was transmitted to the "new" universities the Moslems built in Spain at Toledo and Salamanca. Islam was a great impetus to Western science and mathematics and to the father of Catholic philosophy, Thomas Aquinas. Moslem scholars preserved what we have built upon in this century. They preserved it against the hordes of Northern Europe who would have destroyed it all unknowingly!

### THE FAR EASTERN TRADITION: THE BENIGN RELIGIONS

How are Westerners to enter the frame of reference of the Far Easterners? The answer, to continue the central thesis of this article, is to gain some appreciation of the Far Eastern religious tradition.

The major difficulties for a Westerner who looks at these very alien religious perspectives derive from that Westerner's ethnocentrism. Nowhere is the temptation so great to use *one's own* perspective in *viewing* another. Nowhere is the temptation so great to use *one's own* perspective in *judging* another. Aged 27, with a long-term interest in "other" religions, I went to live in Singapore. I sought every possible contact with Buddhists, Hindus, and Confucianists. The Buddhist temples were often run down, almost always deserted, and the buddhas (statues of Buddha) all seemed obese and apathetic amidst the emaciated, suffering Singapore slumdwellers. Hindu teachers were easier to find, amidst voluptuous statuary, bright flowers, and suppliants poor and rich. Yet answers to my questions about ethical norms, individual welfare, and social responsibility seemed to me "evasive and irrational" at best and, finally, "sub-Christian." My view was *determined* by the religious perspective I used to evaluate "them." Somehow we must avoid using Western categories and conclusions in approaching Far Easterners; otherwise we remain forever inside our world and outside theirs. *Can* we hope to be other than "objective," "rational," "individualistic," and "ethical" as we approach them?

As a means to entering this other world, it can be useful to remember some very basic differences.

1. *Monotheism versus pantheism* (One God versus god-is-everything): The early Christian missionaries saw followers of the Far Eastern religions as heathens who worshipped many idols. They misinterpreted what the figures were and the followers' relation to them. The outcome was that the missionaries labeled such people "uncivilized pagans." Today we realize that the Far Eastern traditions never limited deity to a single place or form. Deity was believed to be in every place and in every form.

2. *Dualistic versus monistic:* Western religions all see the world as split into two—the way it was intended to be versus the way it is, the norms of what is good and desirable versus the fallen nature

of man and the idea of sin. In the Far East, none of these words is used; sin does not exist. This fact creates great difficulty for those of us who come from the Western tradition. In the Far East, everything is benign; nothing is really worth worrying about. The normal way Far Easterners respond to any important issue is to smile. For many Westerners this smile is the most difficult thing to deal with because it isn't just on the surface; it goes deep, deep, deep into the whole of their being and the whole of their thought structure. To them, the best response to anything in life is indeed a smile, because it keeps things nice and *nothing* that we Westerners are concerned about is going to matter very much in the long run. That concept is very, very difficult for us. (Note that even the "opposites" of the Yin and Yang symbols aren't really opposite. Not only does each give form to the other, lacking meaning without it, but also at the very heart of each is some of its "opposite.")

3. *Absolute versus relative:* In the Middle-Eastern religions, ethics is a matter of what is absolutely desirable, and we label it as "right." In the Far Eastern religions, everything is always relative to the situation. Tell me about fads and I'll tell you what *might* be best. It all depends . . . say these relativists.

4. *Teleological versus cyclical:* In the Western tradition, everything is seen as headed somewhere. In Western religion we are headed toward the Kingdom of God, distorted by non-Christian Greek concepts into the idea of heaven. (Jesus himself was completely dominated by the thought of the Kingdom of God or the reign of the Supreme Being.) In any form, such thoughts lead to an end *(telos)* in two ways—the end of human life and the end of individual life. At the end there will be an apocalyptic time for all mankind, and there will be an accounting and a payoff in the form of life after death or resurrection of the body for the individual. Later Islamic and Christian traditions focus on the first; Jewish and Christian sacred writings stress the second. But in the Far East, life is circular. Reincarnation means to be put again into physical form and involves the notion that your essence will be put

into another physical form after you die, on and on, without end (except in the Buddhist concept of Nirvana).

**5. Sacred versus secular:** In Western religions there is a strong emphasis on some things being sacred, belonging to God and, to religion; some things are so special you should treat them with awe and reverence. In the Eastern tradition, the place where you will find the absolute,* where you will find supreme goodness,* and where you will find your greatest happiness* (that for which you were born), may be in the most ordinary things of your whole existence. The sphere of what is desirable is in everything, in the whole world, not just in special places or acts called *sacred*.

The thing about the Eastern religious tradition that attracts Westerners is that it deals with and stresses (indeed often seems limited to) the here and now. It is not a matter of "pie in the sky when you die," it is very much oriented to life here and now. The fact that it seems to require no great sacrifices and could even accompany indulgence makes it very attractive to lots of us. Consequently many people think the Far Eastern way is easy. It is not. It is far more difficult than Western religions. Thus most of the people in the Far East have not achieved what you read about in texts on Far Eastern religions.

The Far Eastern tradition has two great strands, and one of them is mainly Chinese. It says you will get where you want to be by arranging society the right way. The other group says you will get where you want to be through getting in touch with yourself. (The latter is very much part of the twenty-year-old self-realization movement in the United States.) I have to be me, to fulfill my potential—this is a Westernized version of Hinduism. It is interesting that such thought is now an important strand of many of the most successful Christian groups in the United States. If you look carefully at their preaching, it says: "You are fantastic. You have a right to be successful and to enjoy it. And if you're

---

*These phrases are all Western ones that do not really fit Eastern thought.

frustrated because you don't have something, don't put up with that frustration; go for it. You've got a right to it." It is true that in Hinduism a number of ways lead to happiness, but none is without a price, as is sometimes promised in the United States.

## Hinduism

Hinduism seems to have begun around 1500 B.C. when the Aryans invaded India and combined their culture with the existing Dravidian culture of India. (This migration also explains the wide range of color and features so noticeable as one moves around the subcontinent.) The oldest scriptures, the *Vedas,* were begun around 1000 B.C.

In a nutshell, Hinduism regards the multiplicity of gods and goddesses in its pantheon as manifestations of the one divine spirit, Brahman. (It also accepts Jesus as a major manifestation.) Hindus hold that spiritual peace and happiness come through discipline (physical and mental), which improves a spirit's next rebirth.

Hinduism says you can have what you want. The chief issue is not *whether* you *can* have what you want, but how to *know* what you want so you can try to get it. It says there are four options: Liberation, Duty, Pleasure, and Worldly Success (evidenced by wealth, power, recognition, or heightened self-esteem). The latter two do not last. You can be on top of the recording world in 1986, a has-been in 1987, and forgotten in 1990. Worse than being precarious, both Pleasure and Success demand more of the same in greater amounts. When you think you have gotten all you wanted, you find something more that you want. (Everybody who has been successful [or satiated] confirms that.) Neither of these appetites can ever be fully satisfied, maybe because these things are "too small for the heart's eternal trust," as Huston Smith puts it. These two wants are labeled by Hindus as "The Paths of Desire." The two other goals are *probably* more productive, but the Hindus say you *can* get "there" by the pursuit of Pleasure or Success.

The third goal is Duty—the urge to give to the

human community. You might do so as a teacher, a doctor, a police officer, or in any of a myriad ways. Many women give to the human community by being good wives and mothers; that is a possible route.

Finally there is Liberation, the goal of goals. Liberation means to have three things to an infinite degree: being, awareness, and joy.

By *joy,* Hindus mean that positive sense within yourself which is bigger than any physical pain, any frustrated desires, any boredom. Some readers have known fleeting moments like this, when they could say: "There's every reason I should feel awful today, yet *I feel fabulous!*" For most of us, such moments are very brief. Nevertheless you can probably relate to that experience.

The idea of *awareness* is to get beyond ignorance, beyond an inability to understand. For many of us, learning has become a fanaticism: I look at the nebula in the Sword of Orion and I want to know *all* about it. There's no end to such questioning, but we feel high when we get beyond some parts of our ignorance.

*Being* is the most basic of these three. It is a matter of living fully, of being satisfied in the sense that, regardless of the results, one is maximizing one's whole being at that moment. It is the moment one feels really alive, quite apart from whether one accomplishes anything. I usually define *being* as the antithesis of most middle-aged people, who are too often "the tombstones of unlived lives." Lots of young people are like this, only partly "with it" in spite of the endless wonders of life. Those who are really "into" *being* can say, as a friend wrote to me, "This has been a really good year, probably the best year of my life. I have known the whole range of human experience in 1982." She was not saying it was what we would normally call a "good" year, but simply a year in which she had felt completely alive. That's the idea of *being.*

After deciding one wants "Liberation" beyond Pleasure, Success, or Duty, the Hindu then confronts the question: How do you get an endless sense of being, awareness, and joy? Here we find a word we've all heard—*yoga.* It means *way* in Sanskrit, the language of classical Indian writings.

## The Four Major Ways (or Yoga)

The first way is *Jana Yoga.* It means to find happiness through knowledge. You "get it together" in your head. Alan Watts and Shirley MacLaine are two Westerners who have worked very hard at understanding by reflecting deeply and persistently on the nature of themselves and the ultimate. In *Out on a Limb,* Shirley MacLaine reports such side effects of her absorption as being unaware of cold and a meeting with a princess she had known "before" (several hundred years before, in fact). She is to be taken seriously, and what she reports is the product of her extensive, lifelong search. Jana Yoga is said to be the hardest, yet the shortest, route to Liberation, by realizing one's fill of being, awareness, and joy.

Most of us who believe our convictions are "'true" are claiming that what our *words* symbolize is the same as what is "there." But our symbols are always terribly limited. The difficulty in having complete "faith" in any symbolization of reality (such as saying "I believe Jesus was the Son of God") is that it amounts to making an absolute out of something that is not absolute and, thereby, according to the Old Testament, committing the number one sin of the monotheists—idolatry. The user of Jana Yoga acknowledges this in the prayer:

*O Lord, forgive three sins that are due to my human limitations:*
*Thou art everywhere, but I worship you here;*
*Thou art without form, but I worship you in these forms;*
*Thou needest no praise, yet I offer you these prayers and salutations.*
*Lord, forgive three sins that are due to my human limitations.*

The second way is *Bhakti Yoga.* It says the way to get to Liberation is through your emotions. (As you read this, you may be tempted to label this one "hedonism," but please don't do so.) I think of the wife of a federal judge with four children, ages three through twelve. To her, everything is beautiful and all people are beautiful. All she wants is to love them all and have them all love her. This is not phony, but real: She spreads this feeling everywhere. She thinks lovingly and talks about being loving all the time. She expresses it all the time in acts, in music, and in poetry. She goes out of her way endlessly for others and everybody adores her. She is a wonderful human who is going the route of Bhakti Yoga—the emotional route.

The third way is *Karma Yoga.* It is used by those with an active bent. The best examples are some executives, great craftspeople, great artists, and a man like John F. Kennedy. Such people say "There is something I must *do;* I am going to *change* things. I am going to *achieve* something. I am going to *make* something of my life." They live their total lives this way. Yet few, even in this achievement-oriented society, have had the experience of being 100 percent immersed in a particular activity for several days. The nearest one comes is probably during the panic to write a term paper. But that is not to be equated with doing something you *love* with your whole heart and being—something that shuts out everything else in your world for several days. The latter is what we are talking about with Karma Yoga. Many Hindus would see a fanatical American, family-abusing workaholic living his work day and night and taking a vacation only once in a decade going the route of Karma Yoga. Karma Yoga uses *work* as a means of "getting it together."

The fourth way is *Raja Yoga*—the royal way—which is best thought of as getting "there" through meditation. The most common examples of this in the United States are those persons involved in Transcendental Meditation (TM). TM has become extremely popular in the United States, and research has demonstrated its extraordinary power to influence others and to change the total psycho-physical system of a meditator, even to the point of being able to levitate (float in the air). Most of us know very little about yoga except to associate it with exercises and breathing. In Raja Yoga you *start* by controlling your body or having complete awareness of your body, i.e., by exercises or focused breathing. But as the relaxation and trance level advance, all such awareness of oneself slips away, and the demands of the body are left behind.

**Stages of Life.** Whichever of the four routes one takes, it is basic to Hinduism that you live at the appropriate stage of your life. (It is interesting that the Western tradition has very little tradition of marking "the seasons of a man's life," as a recent study report has been called. Hitherto "development" was considered something you grew beyond, as you "matured.") The stages identified by Hindus are those of student, householder, retireer and possibly, *sunyassin.* The fourth means one who knows neither hate nor love of anything—a stage akin to Nirvana. The most important thing to know about Hinduism is that there may be many paths but there is one God. Hindus use the image of us all climbing a mountain. It is possible to climb any side, and each is different, but the pathways merge at the top.

## Buddhism

We now move to *Gautama,* an Indian who grew beyond the Hinduism of his day (the fifth century B.C.). He saw Hinduism as oversimplified in the figures of mythological personages in the *Ramayana* (the Hindu's epic equivalent of the *Odyssey* about a princess stolen by the Sri Lankans and retrieved only after many exploits). In India today it is these figures that most impress foreign visitors to any shrine. The voluptuousness of the woman has to be seen to be believed, while the stains left by men seeking "oneness" with such goddesses are all too obvious. This is no distortion of the way many have practiced Hinduism. Such abuses of the thousand-year teachings were the kind that worried the prince Gautama, who was to become the Enlightened One, the Buddha.

He was very protected as he grew up, but when he went beyond his pampered life in the palace in his late twenties, the realities of the world threw him into a state of shock. He was appalled at human suffering and the fact that the world was not "good" for most people as he had always believed it to be. Choosing the ascetic way of meditation, he left his beautiful wife and child to find an isolated spot for such pursuit. He sought to purify the Hindu tradition, first in himself and then in his followers, as he and they tried all the paths to no avail. What he sought eluded him. But after six years, a great event that lifted him into the ranks of the handful of religious geniuses in human history occurred. In the *Pali* (Buddhist) scriptures, it is described as The Great Awakening. When asked in later years who he was: "A god?" "An angel?" "A saint?", his answer was: "I am awake." These are words used to answer the question: Who are you? How do you now have such powers? Simply, "I am the man who woke up."

Getting beyond the legends that have grown around this great religious innovator, it seems that his life was radically changed at this time and for the wonderful forty-five years thereafter. Nine of every twelve months were spent teaching, preaching, counseling, and comforting the distressed, for more than twelve hours every day. He lived effortlessly now, and the following are the central themes he taught. In protest against the dominant aspects of the Hinduism of his day, his religion was devoid (a) of authority (he rejected Brahminism and its promulgation of caste), (b) of ritual, and (c) of speculation (no metaphysics, no supernatural, no life after death, no "spiritual realities"). It was the antithesis of indulgence for it required great self-effort out of the belief that you are not bound by your "fate." On the other hand, what he taught *was* empirical, scientific, pragmatic, therapeutic, psychological, democratic, and personal.

His analysis of life was put forward as the four Noble Truths:

1. Life is out of joint.

2. The cause of life's dislocation is the drive for private fulfillment.

3. That disease *can* be cured by overcoming the egoistic drive; there is hope.

4. The way is by the Eightfold Path.

The steps in this Eightfold Path are right knowledge, right hoping, right speech, right behavior, right occupation, right effort, right thought, and right absorption. We cannot but be impressed by the noble norms by which, 2,500 years ago, this man defined "right behavior": sexual moderation; no stealing, lying, or alcohol; and no killing of anything at all (thus their vegetarian diet). In brief, Gautama taught that rigid moral and spiritual discipline helps end striving, and the resulting state of Enlightenment frees the spirit of rebirth.

Within 300 years of his death, his teachings dominated the whole of Asia, due mainly to one Buddhist, the great King Asoka (272–232 B.C.), whose compassionate rule is a marked contrast to most in the ancient worlds. But even as Buddhism spread, it split into two quite different forms—Theravada (in Thailand and Burma today) and Mahayana (in Tibet, China, Mongolia, Korea, and Japan today). India quickly forgot its prophet-son, and what we know as Indonesia, Malaysia, and Pakistan are now staunchly Moslem. The Theravada form follows Gautama's teachings faithfully, and in Thailand and Burma a large proportion of the populace spends a period of life as monks. In its Mahayana form, the old habits of ritual, superstition, and petitionary prayer are dominant. The variant best known to Westerns is Zen.

*Zen* characterizes that semantic sophistication which acknowledges that words and reason always fall short of the reality they strive to encompass. While all artists and saints agree with this as *a* truth, Zen Buddhism makes this *central* to its way of attaining enlightenment. By spending hours mediating on a "problem" or "koan," such as "What is the sound of one hand clapping?", its followers are taught that reason is limited. They may not dismiss this as absurd, but they must surrender their reason to another mode (akin to intuition) by which "reality" can be grasped more accurately. The goal is to engender such discontent with our mental habits that we get beyond the prison they constitute. The resultant state is called *satori*. After seven years of such training in Kyoto, one Westerner said "It is not a parapsychic state, in my experience. But I wake up every morning to a world which seems so beautiful I can hardly stand it." With that comes a sense of connectedness with all persons and all things. And finally there is a sense of everything being in the smallest acts. In this state one gets beyond all opposites such as good and evil, pleasure and pain, to that place Gautama described, with such wonderful simplicity, as being "awake." It is strange indeed that Buddhism took the Zen form in Japan, whose home-grown religion was and remains Shinto. That very ancient nature worship has always been closely linked to the very creation and existence of the Japanese as a people, and it is in contrast to Zen's rejection of the supernatural and its individualism. Yet the Eastern mind is untroubled by what Westerners insist on seeing as "contradictions"; how hard it is for us to get beyond "either-or" to "both-and."

To Western minds, the confluence of Buddhism with the existing Chinese philosophies of Confucius and Lao Tse is easier to comprehend than the transformation into Zen. Harmony is a central value in Confucius, Lao Tse, and Gautama. During the two centuries from 100 B.C. to A.D. 100, we see Mahayana Buddhism developing its distinctive qualities that combine the story of Gautama's compassionate life with natural harmony and filial piety (reverence for ancestors).

*Lao Tse* (born 604 B.C.) taught a quietist religion of living in the way *(Tao)* of nature. This Tao is the underlying principle of all that is; it is the path *to* ultimate reality; it is the way the universe functions; it is the way man should live. What is natural is spontaneous and glorious: We are naturally good and beautiful when we are in tune with the universe. This "way" is usually an expression of apparent opposites, but all opposites are limited views of complementarities—the "opposites" that complete each other and make a whole. The best visual expression of this is the way a circle is made up of two parts, the *yang* and the *yin*. At the heart of each is a nucleus of the other. There are tensions between the parts, but they are necessary to each other. Relativity becomes a key concept in this thinking.

Obviously such Taoist thought was akin to Gautama's, but so was the philosophy of *Confucius* (551–479 B.C.). Confucius was troubled by the anarchy of his chaotic, brutal society and asked himself why it should be the way it was. His answers, written in the *Analects,* have been (for 2,500 years) and remain the most significant determinant of the Chinese way of life. He taught that people get along best not by force, or by love, or by reason, or by accident, but by the development and maintenance of a *deliberate* tradition of social harmony. Thus he came to the rules for exercising the responsibilities we have in our basic relationships—between ruler and subject, father and son, husband and wife, friend and friend, brother and brother. Mutual benevolence is the key virtue that should dominate both parties (called *Jen*). This benevolence must be more than an outward show; it must permeate the total person *(Chuntzu)*, making one comfortably free of violence, vulgarity, or awkwardness and considerate regardless of cost to self. It is important to behave appropriately (with *Li*), especially as befits another's status, such as being older or male. Control of others should be by reason of greater virtue *(Te)* rather than by greater power. The greatest arts are not those of war but those of peace *(Wen)*, which should occupy the wise man. His basic formula was:

*If there be righteousness in the heart,*
*    there will be beauty in character.*
*If there be beauty in the character,*
*    there will be harmony in the home.*
*If there be harmony in the home,*
*    there will be order in the nation.*
*If there be order in the nation,*
*    there will be peace in the world.*

It is easy to see how these teachings reinforced the hallowed Chinese practice of ancestor worship by providing a moral basis for all relationships. It is not surprising that it has outlived all of China's changes and all incursions upon her life—for 2,500 years. It is also not surprising that Chinese so often harbor the pride that they were already "civilized" more than 1,000 years before the rest of us gave up a nomadic, brutalizing existence.

## CONCLUSION

The next time you meet a member of another culture, consider that person's religious heritage. If possible, check your hunch as to what it is. (The Pakistani may *look* like the Indian and speak English with the same accent, but underneath they are radically different, for the former is almost bound to be Moslem while the other is very probably a Hindu.) Then keep in mind the broad contrasts we have first mentioned. A summary of these contrasts follows.

The West Asian religious tradition started with a dualism: man confronted by the other. The East Asian religious tradition started with us, our awareness of our own being, focusing on the individual in the south of Asia and on the group in the north. The tradition in the West produced a monotheistic, judgmental, and goal-oriented life. In the East the result was a pantheistic, benign, and passive acceptance of cyclical existence.

In the Western tradition, deity determines everything; in the Eastern tradition, concepts of deity come into the picture only as and when needed by man or society.

In the West, God is an historic, objective reality, determining or even entering historical events. In the East, gods are mythical figures, known through great legends akin to the myths of the Greeks and Romans.

In the West, man sees himself as a reflection of God—made in His image, but flawed. In the East, man sees gods who unabashedly reflect aspects of ourselves and man is able to live free of a sense of sin (such as caring and lust).

In the West, man is called upon to obey specific injunctions, and there is structure in worship, theology, and ethics. In the East, man searches himself and social history for the insights, skills, and strength to be what leads to his good, both immediately and in the bigger perspective.

In the West, *the* issue is felicity beyond this life. In the East, the issue is harmonizing with whatever is given, within oneself and the world. One is driven to change even as the other quietly "accepts."

In both cases, it is easy to distort by selective appropriation of *some* elements—in the West, leading to fundamentalism; in the East, leading to self-indulgence.

Religion is a rich resource in our quest for inter-cultural understanding. Its ramifications influence every aspect of a culture. It is at our peril that we ignore a communicator's religious heritage. It is easy to dismiss the religious tradition of another, asking what it could possibly have to do with communicating except if they be devotees. Surely the Indian one meets is more likely to be a hedonist than a Hindu, and the Chinese a communist than a Confucian? Surely the Western European is more likely to be utilitarian than Christian, secular rather than saintly. The answer is that ideas live long and die slowly, that "deep culture" survives much of the ebb and flow of events and innovation. Each of us is socialized into values very similar to those of our forebears in recent *centuries*.

This is the reason Hofstede's study of IBM executives worldwide displayed such diversity among 55 cultural groups of employees who have all become part of IBM corporate culture. Those whose religious traditions seek harmony value the group over the individual and are generally more at ease with ambiguity. Those whose religious traditions are profoundly rooted in history are deeply concerned with success, achievement, and "direction." It matters little that the Age of Reason started in the seventeenth century or that Nietzsche proclaimed the death of God and the day of superman a full century ago: The assumptions of an all-powerful other still pervade Western life. It matters no more that China had its Communist Revolution and Japan its Modernization periods this century: The values of Confucius and Tao abide almost as fresh as if 2,000 years had never passed.

The pragmatic value of an awareness of these two dichotomous streams of religious thought is that they still dominate the lives of most who are socialized in their sphere of influence, and thus they provide initial stereotypes from which we can build our understanding of the individual we meet anywhere in the global village.

## SUGGESTED READINGS

Chacour, Elias. *Blood Brothers: A Palestinian Struggles for Reconciliation in the Middle East.* Grand Rapids, MI: Zondervan, 1984. In this moving autobiography a Palestinian priest expresses the commonalities among Christians, Jews, and Moslems, as well as the tension. This book is a contemporary and exciting introduction to the significance and shared roots of these three traditions.

Cragg, Kenneth. *The Call of the Minaret*. New York: Oxford University Press, 1956. An evangelical Christian writes out of deep appreciation for another religious tradition, analyzing contemporary Middle East issues.

Hesse, Hermann. *Siddhartha*. New York: New Directions, 1951. This great German author has fictionalized the spirited quest of an Indian not unlike Buddha, including periods of sensuality and financial success, the loss of the love of a son, and the final "becoming one with all things" as he poles a ferry across a river in his old age. In Western thought forms, it captures something of what "enlightenment" means.

MacLaine, Shirley. *Out on a Limb*. New York: Bantam, 1983. "A stunningly honest, engrossing account of an intimate journey inward" by a serious celebrity. It reports a Western woman's successes in using the Hindu way to fulfillment during her forties. Seemingly outrageous, it helps us into a non-Western mind set.

Smith, Huston. *The Religions of Man*. New York: Harper and Row, 1959. Devout followers of every faith comment that "this man understands *my* faith." Hinduism, Buddhism, Confucianism, Taoism, Islam, Judaism, and Christianity are each explained simply and vividly in a style that respects the sensitivities of each.

Tillich, Paul. *Theology of Culture*. New York: Oxford University Press, 1959. This leader of twentieth century theological thought considered religion to be the very essence of any culture—not *a* religion, but religion *per se*. Few thinkers have matched his ability to link all aspects of human experience, as seen by every discipline, from every corner of history and throughout the globe.

Watts, Alan W. *Psychotherapy East and West*. New York: Random House, 1963. The foremost Western expositor of Zen here argues that Western counseling and Zen use almost the same method to free people of their problems. He relates all the major strands of both psychotherapy and Far Eastern thought.

Wu Cheng En. *Monkey*. New York: Grove Press, 1958. Translated by Arthur Waley. This seventh century Chinese epic tells the adventurous and hilarious story of the most profane "angel" and how he helps a Chinese Buddhist priest make a pilgrimage to India. The spirit is profoundly true to the Buddha yet the book is easy reading for all ages. It is a classic both as literature and in its exposition of both the Mahayana and Hinyana traditions of Buddhist thought and life.

## CONCEPTS AND QUESTIONS
## FOR CHAPTER 1

**1.** How does the concept of a global village affect your view of international relations and your ability to relate to world events?

**2.** What does Barnlund mean by the "collective unconscious" and how does it relate to intercultural communication?

**3.** In what ways are intercultural communication and communication alike? In what ways are they different?

**4.** What is meant by social perception and how does it relate to intercultural communication?

**5.** What is the relationship between culture and perception?

**6.** What are the six categories of intercultural communication difficulties discussed by Argyle? How do cultural differences within these areas affect intercultural communication?

**7.** How does Hall's discussion of high- and low-context communication relate to Singer's analysis of the twelve premises of intercultural perception?

**8.** What is meant by the term "cultural value"? How are these values manifest within a given culture?

**9.** How do the two major religious orientations differ? What effect could these differences have on intercultural communication?

**10.** How would someone from an extremely different cultural background respond on a first visit to your city? To your home?

## SUGGESTED READINGS

Asante, M. K., E. Newmark, and C. A. Blake, eds. *Handbook of Intercultural Communication*. Beverly Hills, Calif.: Sage Publications, 1979. This collection of 25 original essays is a review of theoretical and methodological findings in the field of intercultural communication. The book is divided into six parts: theoretical considerations, conceptual frameworks, issues in intercultural communication, general problems with data, research in specific cultures, and practical applications. Each of these parts contain well-written selections that introduce the reader to some of the main issues and topics of intercultural communication.

Brislin, R. W. *Cross-Cultural Encounters: Face-to-Face Interaction*. New York: Pergamon Press, 1981. The major purpose of this book is to examine the commonalities in the experiences of diverse people: experiences that can, according to Brislin, improve intergroup interaction. Among other topics, the book covers the influence of history on behavior, individual attitudes, traits and skills, thought and attribution processes, and membership and reference groups.

Casse, P. *Training for the Cross-Cultural Mind*. Washington, D.C.: Society for Intercultural Education, Training, and Research, 1979. This book is based on the premise that everything we say and do is cultural. By emphasizing commonality among human beings, Casse is unsurprisingly optimistic in his outlook toward the intercultural experience and believes it can be a rewarding one if properly managed or handled.

Condon, J. C. and F. Yousef. *An Introduction to Intercultural Communication*. New York: Bobbs-Merrill, 1975. This book serves as an introduction to the field of intercultural communication. The authors write in a casual manner that makes the book very readable. The book examines essential ingredients of intercultural communication such as values, language, nonverbal behaviors, and social organization.

Dodd, C. H. *Dynamics of Intercultural Communication*. Dubuque, Iowa: William C. Brown Publishers, 1982. This book is a basic text in intercultural communication. The author's main theme is that the impact of culture becomes especially obvious when people from different cultures interact. Dodd looks at various components of culture such as belief systems, credibility, language, and nonverbal communication.

Ehrenhaus, P. "Attribution Theory: Implications for intercultural communication" in M. Burgoon, ed. *Communication Yearbook*, 6. Beverly Hills, Calif.: Sage Publications, 1982, pp. 721–734. The author presents an excellent overview of several issues in the attribution literature as they apply to the study of intercultural communication. The chapter is divided into an examination and discussion of Heider's causal analysis, a discussion of attribution theory in intercultural literature, the uses of this theory in intercultural interaction, and implications of the attribution process for intercultural training.

Furnham, A. and N. Alibhai, "Value differences in foreign students," *International Journal of Intercul-*

tural Relations 9 (1985), 365–375. This study discovers that a number of differences that occur among foreign students are based on their cultures' traditional values and affluence. Results from the Rokeach Valley survey are interpreted in terms of cultural and economic differences and are related specifically to sojourner adjustment literature.

Ganst, F. C. and E. Morbeck, eds. Ideas of Culture. New York: Holt, Rinehart & Winston, 1976. This collection of 38 essays examines culture from a variety of perspectives. It explores the nature of culture, culture as symbols, social order as culture, the patterns of culture, and many other dimensions that help explain the role of culture in our daily lives.

Glenn, E. S. and C. G. Glenn. Man and Mankind: Conflict and Communication between Cultures. Norwood, N.J.: Ablex, 1981. In this volume the authors introduce a new theoretical model for communication analysis embodying a cognitive approach to cultural contact. The model not only defines an overall methodology of the acquisition and storage of information, it also determines the cognitive "styles" of various cultures and subcultures, links them to their attendant communication processes, and predicts areas of conflict.

Gudykunst, W. B. and S. J. Halsall. "The application of a theory of contraculture to intercultural communication: Searching for isomorphic processes" in D. Nimmo, ed., Communication Yearbook 4. New Brunswick, N.J.: Transaction, 1980, pp. 427–436. This paper addresses itself to one of the major problems plaguing the field of intercultural communication—the lack of overarching theoretical perspectives. The authors agree that there is a need for such frameworks, but they suggest that new perspectives do not always have to be developed from scratch. Specifically, the authors use a "theory" of contraculture generated from the prison literature to integrate the diverse findings of sojourner adjustment research.

Hofstede, G. Culture's Consequences: International Differences in Work Related Values. Beverly Hills, Calif.: Sage Publications, 1984. This book explores the differences in thinking and social action that exist between members of four different modern nations as they apply to four work related values—power distance, uncertainty avoidance, individualism, and masculinity. The data for this investigation came from two massive surveys that generated more than 116,000 questionnaires. What that survey shows is that culture does indeed influence a person's perception of work related values.

Hvitfeldt, C. "Picture perception and interpretation among preliterate adults." Passage: A Journal of Refugee Education, 1 (1985), 27–30. The author presents an intriguing discussion of some of the difficulties that arise when a modern literate society uses its symbolic conventions to communicate with traditional groups of people.

Knepler, H. and M. Knepler. Crossing Cultures. New York: Macmillan Publishing Company, 1983. This collection of readings focuses on the many ways in which men and women live in different cultures and co-cultures. The selections discuss the origins of that diversity as well as its consequences in particular examples of encounters between people of differing life styles.

Munroe, R. H., R. L. Munroe, and B. B. Whiting, eds. Handbook of Cross-Cultural Human Development. New York: Garland, 1980. This volume consists of 26 chapters that focus on the influences culture can have on human development. The editors note that cross-cultural research may help "unpackage" the mechanisms underlying the operation of globally defined environmental variables and may distinguish what seems to be universally true of development from what is malleable in varying environments.

Oddou, G., and M. Mendenall. "Person perception in cross-cultural settings: A review of cross-cultural and related cognitive literature." International Journal of Intercultural Relations 8 (1984), 77–96. This article gives a comprehensive review of the studies and literature concerning person perception in a cross-cultural setting. Because there has been little common theory-driven research, the authors determine that cross-cultural research in those areas reviewed suffers from a lack of unity. Finally, they present potentially contributive cognitive theories and concepts.

Oliver, R. T. Culture and Communication. Springfield, Ill.: Charles C Thomas, 1962. An excellent approach to an understanding of rhetorical systems in different cultures appears in this volume. Oliver analyzes how differences in Oriental and Western cultures call for different "logics" and strategies of persuasion.

Prosser, M. H. The Cultural Dialogue: An Introduction to Intercultural Communication. Boston: Houghton Mifflin Company, 1978. This text serves as an excellent introduction to the field of intercultural communication. Prosser examines the basic components of communication and intercultural communication.

Renwick, G. W. "Intercultural communication—state-of-the-art study" in N. C. Jain, ed., *International and Intercultural Communication Annual,* vol. 5. Falls Church, Va.: Speech Communication Association, 1979, pp. 92–100. This essay describes the purpose, methods, and products of a three-year comprehensive study designed to describe and assess the current status of the field of intercultural communication. The study involved three surveys gathering data on 700 individuals, 500 organizations, and 3,000 courses and training programs in the field.

Rich, A. *Interracial Communication.* New York: Harper & Row, 1974. This well-written and well-researched book describes various interracial interaction situations and explores possible reasons for the problems that occur when people from different races attempt to communicate.

Sarbaugh, L. E. "A systematic framework for analyzing intercultural communication" in N. C. Jain, ed., *International and Intercultural Communication Annual,* vol. 5. Falls Church, Va.: Speech Communication Association, 1979, pp. 11–22. This article presents a systematic conceptualization for understanding and analyzing intercultural and intracultural communication. The author proposes establishing levels of interculturalness rather than thinking of intercultural and intracultural as discrete categories of communication.

Sarbaugh, L. E. *Intercultural Communication.* Rochelle Park, N.J.: Hayden Books, 1979. This text seeks to serve as an introduction to the study of intercultural communication. The author attempts to answer two important questions: First, what is the difference, if any, between what we label intercultural and what we label intracultural? Second, how do we communicate differently in each of these situations?

Segall, M. H. *Cross-Cultural Psychology: Human Behavior in Global Perspective.* Monterey, Calif.: Brooks/Cole, 1979. This excellent text covers such vital areas as perception, cognition, and personality. These and other topics are all treated in a cultural setting. The major thesis is that human behavior is primarily of cultural original.

Smith, A. G., ed. *Communication and Culture.* New York: Holt, Rinehart & Winston, 1966. This classic text is a comprehensive volume that contains the efforts of many distinguished scholars in the field of communication. Especially useful is the paradigm for arranging the readings because it helps to clarify the relationships between various components of the communication process.

Szalay, L.B. "Intercultural communication—A process model." *International Journal of Intercultural Relations* 5 (1981), 133–146. This article presents an intercultural model that emphasizes the importance of adapting communication content to the cultural meanings and frames of reference of one's audience. Examples demonstrate the nature and depth of the meaning differences that need to be bridged. The potential of free word associations to reveal cultural meanings is illustrated through examples.

## ADDITIONAL READINGS

Abe, H. and R. L. Wiseman. "A cross-cultural confirmation of the dimensions of intercultural effectiveness." *International Journal of Intercultural Relations* 7 (1983), 53–68.

Althen, G., ed. *Learning across Cultures: Intercultural Communication and International Education Exchange.* Washington, D.C.: National Association for Foreign Student Affairs, 1981.

Bochner, S., ed. *Cultures in Contact: Studies in Cross-Cultural Interaction.* Oxford: Pergamon, 1982.

Brislin, R. W. "Cross-cultural research in psychology." *Annual Review of Psychology* 34 (1983), 363–400.

Burgoon, M., J. Dillard, N. Doran, and M. Miller. "Cultural and situational influences of the process of persuasive strategy selection." *International Journal of Intercultural Relations* 6 (1982), 85–100.

Casmir, F. L. "Phenomenology and Hereneutics: Evolving approaches to the study of intercultural and international communication." *International Journal of Intercultural Relations* 7 (1983), 309–324.

Casmir, F. L., ed. *Intercultural and International Communication.* Washington, D.C.: University Press of America, 1978.

Doob, L. W. "The inconclusive struggles of cross-cultural psychology." *Journal of Cross-Cultural Psychology* 11 (1980), 59–73.

Dubbs, P. J. and D. D. Whatney. *Cultural Contexts: Making Anthropology Personal.* Boston: Allyn & Bacon, 1980.

Endler, N. S., and D. Magnusson. "Toward an international psychology of personality." *Psychological Bulletin* 83 (1976), 956–974.

Gans, E. *The End of Culture*. Berkeley, Calif.: University of California Press, 1985.

Gardner, G. H. "Cross-cultural communication." *Journal of Social Psychology* 58 (1962), 241–256.

Geertz, D. *The Interpretation of Culture*. New York: Basic Books, 1973.

Gudykunst, W. B., ed. *Intercultural Communication Theory: Current Perspectives*. Beverly Hills, Calif.: Sage Publications, 1983.

Gudykunst, W. B. and T. Nishida. "Constructing a theory of intercultural communication: The promise and paradox." *Speech Education: Journal of the Communication Association of the Pacific* 7 (1978), 13–25.

Hall, E. T. *Beyond Culture*. Garden City, N.Y.: Doubleday/Anchor Books, 1976.

Hall, E. T. *The Hidden Dimension*. New York: Doubleday, 1966.

Hammet, M. P. and R. W. Brislin, eds. *Research in Culture Learning*. Honolulu: The University of Hawaii Press, 1980.

Hori, T. "Culture and personality: Standpoints of cultural anthropology." *Japanese Psychological Review* 23 (1980), 382–391.

Hui, C. H. "Locus of control: A review of cross-cultural research." *International Journal of Intercultural Relations* 6 (1982), 301–323.

Hymes, D. "The anthropology of communication" in F. E. X. Dance, ed. *Human Communication Theory*. New York: Holt, Rinehart & Winston, 1967.

LaBarre, W. *Culture in Context*. Durham, N.C.: Duke University Press, 1980.

Marsella, A., R. G. Tharp, and T. Ciboronski. *Perspectives on Cross-Cultural Psychology*. New York: Academic Press, 1979.

Matthews, E. *Culture Clash*. Chicago: Intercultural Press, 1982.

Nishida, H. and T. Nishida. "Values and intercultural communication." *Communication: The Journal of the Communication Association of the Pacific* 10 (1981), 50–58.

Rogers, E. M. *Diffusion of Innovations*. New York: Free Press, 1983.

Rohrlic, R. E. "Toward a unified conception of intercultural communication: An integrated systems approach." *International Journal of Intercultural Relations* 7 (1983), 191–210.

Saral, T. B. "Intercultural communication theory and research: An overview of challenges and opportunities" in D. Nimmo, ed., *Communication Yearbook* 3. New Brunswick, N.J.: Transaction, 1979, 395–405.

Smith, E. C., and L. B. Luce, eds. *Toward Internationalism: Readings in Cross-Cultural Communication*. Rowley, Mass.: Newbury House, 1979.

Trimillos, R. E. "One formalized transmission of culture." *East-West Culture Learning Institute* 9 (1983).

Warwick, D. "The politics and ethics of cross-cultural research" in H. Triandis and W. Lambert, eds. *Handbook of Cross-Cultural Psychology, Perspectives,* vol. 1.

Webb, H. "Cross-cultural awareness: A framework for interaction." *Personnel and Guidance Journal* 61 (1983), 498–500.

# PART TWO

## Socio-Cultural Backgrounds: What We Bring to Intercultural Communication

*All persons are puzzles until at last we find in some word or act the key to the man, to the woman; straightway all their past words and actions lie in light before us.*

*—Emerson*

One of the most important aspects of human communication is the fact that the experiential backgrounds participants bring to a communication experience will affect their behavior during the encounter. Psychologists A. H. Hastorf and H. Cantril underscore this issue when they note that each person acts according to the personal uniqueness he or she brings to the occasion. Think about those countless situations when you and some friends shared an experience and found that there were major differences in your reactions. What you deemed dull your companions found exciting; what you considered pointless they found meaningful. The messages being received were the same for all participants; yet, because each of you has a unique personality and background, you experienced a variety of feelings, sensations, and responses. Each of you brought different backgrounds to the event and as a result attributed individual meanings to the shared experience. In short, the event meant what it did to you because of your own unique past history.

We contend that in order to understand any communication encounter you must appreciate the idea that there is much more to communication than the mere analysis of messages. Messages and the responses you make to them are products of your unique past experiences. And it is this uniqueness of experience that greatly contributes to the "immutable barriers in nature" between each individual's thoughts.

Individual past experience takes on added significance when we introduce the many dimensions of culture. Individuals are influenced not only by personal experiences but by their culture as well. As we suggested in Part One, culture refers to those cumulative deposits of knowledge, values, and behaviors acquired by a large group of people and passed on from one generation to the next. In this sense, culture, in both conscious and unconscious ways, not only teaches you how to think and what to think about, it also dictates such values as what is attractive and what is ugly. In addition, culture teaches you such things as how close to stand next to strangers and even the various ways you can display your anger. When you are interacting with others and become disturbed by their actions you can, for instance, cry, become physically violent, shout, or remain silent. Each of these behaviors, depending on your culture, is a manifestation of what you have learned; it is culturally influenced. These cultural influences affect your ways of perceiving and acting; they contain the societal experiences and values that are passed from generation to generation. Because these behaviors are so much a part of your thinking, you might forget they vary from culture to culture. This is why a person from Japan, for example, might remain silent if disturbed by someone's actions while an Israeli or an Italian would more likely verbalize such displeasure.

Whatever the culture, you can better understand your behavior and the reactions of others if you realize that what you are hearing and seeing is a reflection of that culture. As you might predict, this understanding is greatly facilitated when your cultural experiences are similar to those of the people you are interacting with. Conversely, when different and diverse backgrounds are brought to a communication encounter, it is often difficult to share internal states and feelings. In this section we focus on those difficulties by examining some of the experiences and perceptual backgrounds found in a variety of foreign cultures as well as those found in several American subcommunities.

# 2

# International Cultures

Communication between members of international cultures poses one of the most perplexing intercultural communication problems. How we are to understand others when they come from different sections of our global village is a most difficult question. We need only to look around the world at any particular moment in time to find disagreement, strife, and fighting. The locations may change, but the problems persist. Nations become prominent in the news, and what happens within them and between them directly affects the entire world. Although few of us are directly involved with these countries, we may be in contact with students from them who are studying in the United States. They may be our classmates or our students.

To help us better understand people from other cultures and the diverse personalities they can produce, and to give us a perspective from which we may be able to learn how to interact with those with whom we do come in contact, this chapter offers articles that will introduce us to five different international cultures.

In the last twenty years, Japan has become a major force in the international economic area. Its products and its culture are now seen around the world. Therefore, it behooves students of intercultural communication to understand this unique group of people. Elaine Haglund contributes to that understanding by examining important cultural characteristics of the Japanese people in "Japan: Cultural Consideration." Among other topics, she explains (1) the importance of the Japanese emphasis upon group solidarity, (2) Confucianism, (3) the Japanese sense of obligation, and (4) why respect for authority is crucial. She also discusses some of the cultural contradictions that outsiders often misinterpret.

While China contains more than one-fourth of the earth's population, it still remains one of the most isolated and misunderstood countries in the world. In recent years, however, the "sleeping giant" has started to stir, and the people of China and the United States are having more and more contact. Often cultural differences have kept this contact from being successful and rewarding. We suggest that an awareness of these differences can help facilitate improved intercultural communication. Some of these major differences are considered by Douglas P. Murrary in his "Face-to-Face: American and Chinese Interactions." His list of dissimilarities includes differences between open and closed societies, levels of politeness, and variations in thought, time, and language.

In most instances, understanding the behavior of people in other cultures is extremely difficult when our experiences are far removed from their life styles in that culture. Our reactions to the people of Saudi Arabia are one of the best examples of distorted and confused perceptions. We often see them as "primitive Bedouins" or as "indulgent millionaires." Myron Lustig, in "Cultural and Communication Patterns of Saudi Arabians," seeks to clarify our images of this culture by explaining such topics as the role of the Islamic religion in Saudi life. He also discusses the main values of that culture and how it uses verbal and nonverbal communication.

Nemi C. Jain shifts our attention to the Indian subcontinent as he provides a glimpse of Hindu culture in his article "Some Basic Cultural Patterns of India." Here he examines what it means to be Hindu and discusses how the Hindu tradition contributes to the culture of India and provides a basis for the perceptual frames of reference common to India.

In the last article, "'... So Near the United States,'" John Condon focuses on communication between Mexicans and Americans. Condon analyzes the cultural relations between Americans and Mexicans, concentrating on differences in how they perceive things in the context of working relationships.

# Japan: Cultural Considerations

ELAINE HAGLUND

*These are the best people so far discovered, and it seems to me that among the unbelievers, no people can be found to excel them.*

—*St. Francis Xavier's* Report on Japan

The Japanese people have historically shown themselves to be human counterparts of their volcanic island setting; just as the thermal land on which they live, the Japanese have demonstrated a dynamic ability to erupt and renew themselves, as evidenced by their national experience during the Meiji Restoration and post-World War II recovery years.

It has been suggested that the Japanese have traditionally been very much aware that they were different from the rest of the world, a factor that has led to considerable national homogeneity and to an in-group cohesiveness (Bieda 1970). Japan's awareness of its being a relative orphan of the mainland is reflected somewhat in the fact that the people often regard their country as an island-nation *(shimaguni),* rather than just an island *(shima)* or only a nation *(kuni).* The tradition of isolation in Japan is both culturally and geographically abetted. During the Tokugawa Era (1603–1867), every effort was made to seal her culture from the rest of the world, from the divergent influences which would occur through cross-fertilization of ideas. And generally, the Japanese have not felt greatly threatened

From *International Journal of Intercultural Relations* 8 (1984), 61–76. Reprinted by permission of the publisher and the author. Dr. Haglund teaches in the Department of Educational Psychology and Administration at California State University, Long Beach.

by external military forces; part of this feeling of security comes from absence of land borders, which affords an island-nation a basic immunity from land invasion and international conflicts and concerns. Domestically, too, Japan has not known significant conflicts of interest, due to her high degree of homogeneity, ethnically and culturally. Furthermore, linguistically Japan represents perhaps less diversity than any other nation of comparable size. One explanation may be that the enigmatic nature of the written language, perhaps more complex than the Chinese script, has hardly been conducive to the cross-national spreading of the language. For this reason, the Japanese have historically been linguistic isolates, and the impact is currently being felt. There has been little effort to learn the major neighbor languages such as Russian or Chinese (not even during the occupation in the 1930s). Only since the Meiji Restoration has English, as the international *lingua franca,* been considered a second-language necessity for educated citizens. Even with a pervasive program of English instruction in the schools and industries, communication with other countries has remained a difficult barrier for Japan. According to some authorities, this lack of a non-international language facility, as a vestige of the self-imposed policy of isolationism, may handicap the range of effectiveness of Japan's international efforts.

Additional evidence of homogeneity is expressed through the standardization of house building and house arrangements. In Japan, especially in rural Japan, there is one kind of insulation that helps to decrease the discomfort of cold floors. There is a mat, the *tatami,* which covers all floors of most rural houses. It is uniform in length and breadth (roughly 3 feet by 6 feet) and therefore is used as a unit of measure in the plans for houses.[1] The methods of Western house building are so thoroughly individualistic, by comparison, that the significance of this "mat module" may be missed. What this kind of standardization means is that virtually all elements of the entire building can also be standardized and made interchangeable with other buildings.

Education has long been a highly revered institution in Japan, as evidenced by the existence of *samurai* (knight) schools in feudalistic Japan. Indeed, today the country enjoys the reputation of having one of the highest, if not the highest, literacy rates in the world. As a result, Japan is reputed to be one of the most well-read societies. Because education is so highly regarded, it has been a very significant force in effecting and perpetuating uniformity, conformity, and, in a sense, isolation.

But education has also been responsible for having introduced the borrowed ideas from other countries, practices that the government has found not only acceptable, but necessary and valuable for national development and reform. Therefore, education and the homogeneous nature of Japan have served both to compound isolationism and also to have facilitated an assimilation and refinement of new ideas throughout the whole society. Ideas were able to be introduced and rapidly initiated over a widespread area. In the nineteenth century, America's Commodore Perry forced Japan to open its doors to the world; and the Meiji Restoration followed with a policy of Westernization, one which encouraged aggressive pursuit of ideas and technologies from all over Europe and North America. The process was of such a rapid and fervent nature that it almost appears that Japan, in a generation, wished to compensate for its 250 years of isolation. In *The Structure and Operation of the Japanese Economy* (1970), Bieda writes that, at this time, highest priority was assigned to economic development. The Meiji leaders wanted economic growth for the sake of military defense against the possible onslaught of European colonialism. Relatively widespread education was established, a process that helped to prepare the people for the absorption of new ideas. In the words of John Whitney Hall and Richard Beardsley (1965, p. 387), the Japanese nation "entered the world community of nations as learner, rather than instructor"; it was a process that served to strengthen the country's identity, rather than to fragment it. Indeed, Japan has what some have dubbed as a plastic ability to assimilate foreign "know-how." As one can glean from the following list of influences, Japan is unique in that the country does not fall easily into either a Western or into an Eastern group of nations.

From China in the seventh century, Japan adopted the Chinese laws, customs, method of writing, Buddhism, and Confucianism. Shintoism easily accommodated to Buddhism, for the animist and ancestor gods became gods to help Buddha save humankind.

Portugal and Spain, in the sixteenth century, introduced trade, Christianity, printing, and rifles, although trade and Christianity were banished ideas in the Tokugawa period which was to follow.

In the nineteenth century, the Meiji Restoration patterned itself after the European Industrial Revolution and modeled its education and political structure on the Western prototypes.

It is a well-known phenomenon that Japan has historically been a borrow-culture; but a copy-culture, it is not. The Japanese tend to improve upon each imitation, for they ingeniously make an idea go further. The Japanese genius for borrowing has more recently revealed itself in transistorized, computerized electronics and precision lenses and instruments. In effect, Japan could actually be considered a seminal culture; the originality involved here is the innovation that the Japanese attach to nearly every loan that comes their way. As Kinhide Mushakoji writes in *The Japan Annual of International Affairs* (1963–64, p. 80),

*Western models serve as a kind of generalized phenomenon of* seiyo kabure *which was actually the imitation of external customs in one's own manner. These models were usually sought to be built on the principle of* saicho hotan—*adoption of foreign strong points to supplement Japanese weak points.*

Indeed, this unique readiness to accept new ideas does not preclude loyalty to certain indigenous aspects such as Japanese food and traditional clothing. In fact, the very quality of receptiveness perhaps indicates a confidence in how secure, deep, and sturdy certain values are, for new patterns are not perceived as threatening or corrosive to established mores (Hall and Beardsley 1965). Modern

Japan has even been portrayed as an acrobat who has never had to perform without a safety net beneath him or her; if daring advances failed, the traditions of Japan were always there to protect and rescue (Guillain 1970). Japan has greatly profited by its role as learner or borrower, for the nation has been enriched by the confluence of many streams of thoughts and habits. For instance, *Kanji,* the written language, derives from Chinese script, but Japan developed *Kata-kana* and *Hiragana* by simplifying the Chinese characters, thereby providing for adaptation to the spoken Japanese language. The people have tended to adopt ideas as means to the ends of utility and expediency. But Mushakoji suggests that the importing also has been done in terms of an exotic quest for new stimuli, a curiosity for that which is foreign (1963–64). Hall and Beardsley also support this thesis; the word, *hakurai,* apparently means "imported from the West," but it tended to carry along with it the attitude that anything foreign was good. This suggestion is viable and consistent, for historically, nearly every foreign contact that Japan has had has heightened the culture.

It is noteworthy here that the rulers of Japan, not the citizens, have traditionally promoted the foreign-culture learning which has led to the new movements in the country. This is not true of development in the West, as represented by the Renaissance and the Industrial Revolution which had their roots in the common people. The Japanese have not been consistently exposed to national rulers who were exceptionally ruthless and tyrannical. In fact, the "Divine Right of Kings" element is relatively atypical in the Japanese experience. This may be due, in part, to the influence of Mencius, the Chinese sage, who believed that a leader's responsibility was to ensure peace of mind to his followers so that they, in turn, would be free to do good. It was incumbent upon a leader to look at his people as limbs of a body, and the citizenry would subsequently view the leader as its heart; in effect, a *noblesse oblige* was invoked. The benevolence from above has assured the relative propriety and Confucian obeisance from below and has propagated the success of a system based on deference to vertical authority.

In the twentieth century, the presence of the Allied Forces Occupation in Japan caused a major transformation from the suppressive military regime during the late 1930s and 1940s. The total and unquestioned acceptance of constitutional government ironically tended to reflect Japan's background of obedience to higher command rather than its short historical trend toward democratization of legal and other institutions that was evident in the 1920s, with the cabinet of Prime Minister Hara. Witness the fact that within three years of the end of World War II, seven million people were organized into unions. Honor toward one's conquerors, as part of the Confucian ethic, was a stoic reaction, a behavior not easily overcome.

The question arises in some critics' minds as to whether democracy is just another ceiling-lamp security or, if indeed the people have really internalized the principles of democracy. Have the people been thoroughly socialized to the ideas, or have just the structures been democratized? Some pessimists suggest that only the skill, and not the soul, has been adopted. However, it must be remembered that Japan has had a long tradition of making decisions based upon group consensus—a different form of democracy from the Western mode but nonetheless participatory in nature. However, despite this point, many experts proffer that Japan's ready adjustment to the Occupation Forces was totally compatible with the Confucian ethic of obedience to exalted power and with the Buddhist virtue of passive acceptance of destiny, rather than an active modification of it.

Japanese industry has capitalized on the tradition of Confucian discipline. Routine, assembly line jobs are not considered as abhorrent to the Japanese as they might be to the Westerner who derives meaning from initiative and self-assertiveness. Unlike his or her Western counterpart, a Japanese person may well find significant freedom in regimentation. For instance, the essence of Japanese art, poetry, the tea ceremony, gardening, and flower arranging is based in this adulation of punctilious form. The prescription seems to be to understate the essence or to eliminate the nonessential; in other words, less is more. Black and white brush painting (sumie)

and the poetry of *Haiku* (17 syllables) and *Tanka* (31 syllables) are generated from definite restrictions and rules of expression; and the assiduously pruned gardens and the formalized placing of stones also reflect the obedience to regulations. The Japanese appear to believe that greatness is achieved through self-restraint and restriction. Perfunctory tasks can be liberating in that a degree of freedom is found in limitations.

In regard to Buddhist fatalism, people are expected to be agile in response to an altered situation; it is anticipated that they will accommodate themselves to the external realities; they learn to live in a current change, for change is considered the one absolute truth. People are to surrender according to the direction of the forces at the time. As might be expected, Japanese poetry reflects the transitory nature of life; themes are usually centered in natural objects passing through various seasonal changes and through life–death cycles. But change is not conceived as being caused by the will of the people; rather, environmental demands or daily ordeals dictate the behavior of the people. Such logic justifies the aggressive war effort: Why reprehend individuals for the war if they could not be divorced from the dynamics of the period? After all, increased land domains were a need and a pressure of the time. Such resignation to the trends of the time also helps explain why there was not resistance to the Occupation.

In the people's attempt to justify this, they compare themselves to water in that they consider themselves able to take any shape according to the container. As an example of this quality of supple acceptance, one is reminded of the successful adjustment Japan made when the Meiji Restoration brought it into the international community, thereby having unshackled the country from its long Tokugawa isolation of over 250 years. It took only a relatively short time for the nation to relinquish its former feudalistic structure and to position itself among the economic leaders of the world scene. This is a notable shift when one considers that in the traditional pattern of Japanese society, the merchant and trader were members of a denigrated class. Among the warrior and landed gentry, there was utter scorn for money; disdain for money-making was one of the fundamentals found in the code of honor. At the top of the social hierarchy were the fief-holders, followed by the warriors; beneath them were the peasantry, then the artisans, and last of all, the tradesmen. As a result, commercial morality during the Tokugawa period had become as maligned as the commercial class itself. But by 1917, Japan had significantly advanced its economic prowess, a development that had taken less than 50 years to accomplish. More recently, of course, Japan has even accepted for itself an identity of middle-class materialism. The public now aspires to own the esteemed "3 Cs": a car, a cooler (air conditioner), and a color television; and to this list one could add the camera, calculator, and computer. Indeed, this relatively recent national image of a financially successful middle class represents a cultural adaptation of considerable magnitude.

The Japanese people's ability to accept change was further manifested in the post–World War II years when they were ordered to make major modifications, such as the abolition of emperor worship. On a lesser scale, one may point to the people's willingness to operationalize and follow MacArthur's request to change the system employed in identifying house addresses. This situational shift involved switching to the Western "logical" plan of identifying spatially consecutive building lots. However, with the departure of the American forces, the country reverted to its prior arrangement. For the Japanese, the American format had been a non sequitur; the pattern more familiar to them involved numerals which were assigned according to the temporal order in which buildings had been constructed. The positive side of this ability to adjust is obviously flexibility, a characteristic vital to the people's survival. For instance, the catastrophe of World War II left 5 million people dead, 8 billion homeless, 5 million repatriates penniless, and half of the territory lost; yet the country made a remarkably rapid recovery, partly by having borrowed and compliantly modified practices from the West.

Robert Guillain remarks that the adoption of Western ideas has meant a bi-civilized people, for Japan has binary forms of everything: "two ways of life, two hotel systems, two different ways of cooking, two architectures, two ways of dressing, two styles of painting, two kinds of music, two theaters, two cinemas" (Guillain 1970, p. 332). And one might include two calendars, two types of courtship patterns, two kinds of marriage ceremonies, ad infinitum. Indeed, the people have become a mass-consumption society, as in the West; in fact, in some people's minds, they are simply an "almond-eyed America." This bifurcation—East-West or tradition-modernity—actually coexists compatibly; the two extremes are often juxtaposed and reciprocally interacting. However, in the urban areas, the thrust is definitely toward the Western pattern. The people's tolerance of overcrowded urban conditions further attests to their inordinate ability to cope. Most Japanese city dwellers live in exiguous quarters which makes private life extremely public; however, the people have learned to live with the unpleasant realities of their densely populated setting—such as the notorious overcrowding on trains and the extreme congestion of traffic.

Another example of "copability" concerns Japan's adjustment to the weather. Despite the severe holocausts of earthquakes, typhoons, and the wide ranges in temperature and humidity, the people are not unduly alarmed by the misfortunes which are often wrought by nature. The Japanese live in a land where earthquakes, wind, flood, and fire have repeatedly decimated their world of wood and paper. The methods and materials employed in house building are palpable examples of the Japanese ability to adjust to the environment.[2] Statistics indicate that there are annually more than 2,000 earthquakes in Japan. (When the earth began to rock, some people used to say that the great subterranean fish on which their world rested was waking up and beginning to wiggle about.) But the fires which often ensue from the more destructive earthquakes are somehow not regarded as overwhelmingly devastating as they might be in the West. It is almost as if the people's spirit accepts these disasters, perhaps as an opportunity for cleansing and renewing themselves and their buildings; this belief is immeasurably encouraged by the Buddhist doctrine of reincarnation in which it is believed that brittle flesh and blood can only achieve immortality through regeneration.

Perhaps this facet of pliancy in the Japanese is also partially related to their not coveting any fixed, resolute ideologies. Hall and Beardsley suggest that the people display "persistent inquisitiveness and flexibility in the face of new and demonstrably superior intellectual systems" (1965, p. 387). One Japanese person explained this by way of an analogy to the *furoshiki*, a wrapping cloth, used for carrying virtually everything and anything of small size. American logic can be figuratively thought of as a suitcase, an encasement which is square and has finite limits. Japanese mentality is conceived in terms of a *furoshiki*, a soft cloth which can be folded flexibly to accommodate the contents and also be put into the pocket when not needed.

To explore the *furoshiki* logic further, it is said that the Japanese are born dialecticians; they believe that existence is contradiction. However, these contradictions are not really conceived in terms of the stumbling blocks represented by the Kantian antinomies or the theories of Western dualism; they are simply necessary elements for existence. Every single object in the universe holds two opposing, mutually supplementing elements, standing against each other, as in finite and infinite, life and death. Even book titles of sociological descriptions of Japan indicate the contradictory nature of Japan, such as Quentin Crew's *Japan: A Portrait in Paradox* or *The Chrysanthemum and the Sword* by Ruth Benedict, both written as so many other volumes, to explain what may appear to a Westerner as a conundrum of dichotomies. The recurring themes in these books represent the many antitheses involved in Japan's culture: the temerity and brutality of Nanking or the cycles of fervent xenophobia, as contrasted with the delicate art expressions, the gracious hospitality, and the timorous diffidence of the people.

Perhaps because of Japan's compatibility with contradiction, the people have not outlined complex formulations of philosophy; to a Japanese, Spinoza's *Ethics* might look like a geometry book with axioms, propositions, definitions, and proofs. Indeed,

no dogmatic, crystallized theory can tolerate contradiction. Consequently the Japanese have only general policies, not fixed principles, by which to think. To a Westerner, accustomed to established guidelines of philosophic approaches, the Japanese appear to be lost in a lacuna of incoherence.

Hajime Nakamura explains the lack of systematic, theoretical ideologies as a matter of the inadequacy of the language to express complex ideas: "The Japanese language is, generally speaking, very poor in imaginative words based on abstract and universal ideas" (1964, p. 557). It is apparently as Benjamin Whorf has suggested: Language is more than just a medium of expressing thought; it is, in fact, a major element in the formation of thought. If the Japanese, then, are not doctrinaire in their approach to life, it must be pointed out that they do have profound sentimentality of feeling. Since the eighth century, Japan has had a superb literature and exquisite fine arts with the most delicate touch of sensitivity. There have been countless numbers of metaphysical treatises of inspiring depth. But there have been no broad categories of thought; there has been no *Republic,* no *Bible,* no *Summa Theologica,* no *Ethics.* The Japanese intellectuals, the *interi,* as they call themselves, do not necessarily indulge in thought for thought's sake, as Europeans have tended to do. Such "idleness" is considered a luxury and an evasion of reality; the idea for them is there to be lived, if necessary to be died for. Again, as Nakamura (1964) has suggested, the nature of the Japanese language may not lend itself to deliberate, structured ways of thinking. This may be due, in part, to the fact that in Japanese the fundamental division is infinite; present, past, and future do not exist as they do in Western tongues. The language seems to be based upon moods. Not time, but the element of probability and the relation of the speaker to the one spoken to dominate the character of the language. As a result, it is a language full of allusion, suggestion, mood, and association of endless poetic nuance and possibility; it is also a language rich in a hierarchy of honorifics with para-language gestures such as the bow. But it is not a language particularly amenable to abstract thinking. Even today, as Japan becomes more and more scientifically, technologically oriented, the people have been forced to borrow appropriate terms from languages that are more precise and "rational."

Some Westerners observe that the Japanese have a dualistic approach to problem solving. Japanese people appear to spend considerable time on the development of an idea in an idealistic and emotional sense without actually following through in an operational way. Obviously, this is simply another cross-cultural misinterpretation, or else Japan would not have made the remarkable strides that it has in its recent history. It is simply a different approach to problems, perhaps one mixed with the *kimochi* of the Japanese. *Kimochi* is best translated as a type of mien, an inner feeling, an intuition that has grown out of Buddhism.

Japan's version of Zen-Buddhism is described as transcendental and noumenal metaphysics, based on the senses, intuition, and meditation. There is no holy writ; nor does Buddha survive as a guide to conduct.[3] Zen-Buddhists have no real concept of a God in the Western sense, one who transcends earthly life; because of this, Christian missionaries were handicapped in their goals of converting the people. Because Zen-Buddhism is centered in the liberation of the self and in self-enlightenment, a Zen-Buddhist may only vaguely understand the exhortations of "Love thy neighbor as thyself" or "I am my brother's keeper," at least, not much beyond one's immediate social milieu.

There is, in Japan, a structural morality, rather than an individual code of ethics. Sin or guilt as an impulse-control mechanism is not as prominent as it is in the West; rather, there is the factor of shame, based on losing face with one's associates (although admittedly, Japanese experience both shame and guilt, just as Westerners experience both guilt and shame). Anyone involved in some ignominious act can be expected to suffer from feelings of reproach, due to the opprobrium exacted by his or her social censors—the members of one's social group or work enterprise. Subtle training for this deeply embedded set of mores begins very early in a child's life. Children who are still too young for "shame" can nonetheless be taught to avoid being embarrassed

to avoid the world's laughing at them (Benedict 1946).[4] A gradual series of restraints are introduced at home and in school, but the serious concerns of preparing for patterns of adult life do not really commence until a child has been in school two or three years. At about age eight, incisive pressure is exerted upon a child to subordinate his or her own will to the ever-increasing realm of duties-to-others. Moral imperatives, then, are generated from the people who surround a person. This aspect of Japanese life accounts for the pattern of labor unions in Japanese industry. Membership of many unions is limited to the work force of a single enterprise or firm. Therefore, strongly entrenched among the wage and salary earners is the idea of "enterprise consciousness," in contrast to occupation or class consciousness. This social mechanism supports strong identification with and loyalty to the employer and to one's immediate work group. One speaks from a position within the vertical society, in terms of his or her social nexus where one's individuality is sublimated; it is a commitment to collectivities and to member-mindedness, dependent on the vagaries of the time. According to linguistic pundits, the essence of this "I am we" formula is captured in the intransitive verb of *ameru,* which means "to depend and presume upon another's benevolence" (Doi 1962). Related to this are Buddhist teachings which tend to conceive of the individual as part of the total cosmos rather than as a unique individual in the Christian sense.

Emphasis on the social grouping gives priority to the rights of the group above those of the participating individual members. Indeed, in the Japanese language there exists no word for *privacy.* Even individual birthdays, except for the first one, have traditionally gone uncelebrated; the fact that these personal occasions have not been observed, until more recently, is somewhat indicative of the group submersion behavior. Ceremonies in Japan tend toward age or gender rituals. For example, November 15th is the nationally designated day for *Shichi-go-san* when parents take their seven-, five-, or three-year-old children to visit a shrine. Similarly, Boys' Day (May 15) and Girls' Day (March 3) are special holidays which direct attention to childhood gender roles, not to one particular child. Another group pattern is the formation of *donen,* groups of males of the same age; the *donen* arrangement is an extremely important fraternal identity with friends who sometimes become closer to one another than they do to their wives. But within this group ethic, there is a strong sense of obligation which undergirds the "we feeling," based upon the three main principles of the Confucian code of *Kou* (filial piety), *giri* (duty), and *on* (obligation). For instance, one becomes socialized to the need to do something for another to whom one feels *on* or *giri.* These duties and obligations run deeper than the gratitude Western children feel toward their parents, and although less rigid today, these aspects continue to play a very significant part in Japanese life. The *oyakobun* relationship (*oya,* senior—*ko,* junior) extends throughout the academic, political, and business world in the form of *batsu;* the *batsu* represents a patronage network which allows young people a support base with which to face society as a young adult. Indeed, an influential and beneficent *oya* is often responsible for the very success of his *ko,* or his protégé, and this bond tends to obligate the young person to an endless pledge of loyalties and respect to his senior benefactor. It follows, then, that one of the most cherished national epics is "The 47 Ronin," a heroic story concerning the eulogized warlord, the paragon of probity. The tale involves the warrior's struggle to maintain face and to discharge his social obligations on the basis of *quid pro quo.* Because the story centers around these two cardinal facets which govern Japanese life, the people readily identify with it; consequently, the tale has enjoyed immense popularity, indicating perhaps that the enduring legends of a culture may serve as master keys to increased understanding of people within a given society.

The Japanese language and mode of expression correspond to the tradition of group identity. For example, in the vernacular the first and second person is sometimes omitted, therefore reducing the possibilities for attributing actions to a specific performer. In Japan, even when venturing an opinion or expressing a personal feeling, one is gambling; if what is communicated appears ludicrous or inappropriate to others, there is cause for the speaker to suffer the dreaded loss of face.

Dependence upon the group, then, offers the Japanese a sense of security, as well as a collective identity, but such allegiance to the group does not inspire an individual to be personally assertive or to take direct responsibility for one's actions. This situation, of course, is all integral to the cultural matrix of self-negation which Westerners, as products of rugged individualism, find difficult to understand. However, the West's propensity toward self-reliance and Japan's penchant for group-mindedness both need to be put into the perspective of cultural relativism. In the West, assertive, competitive behavior which shows little concern for the welfare of the group can be viewed, even by Westerners, as aggressive self-interest or egoism. Whereas in Japan, there is pervasive acceptance of the principle that states that a wise man does not speak, for "It is the shallow water which makes the noise."

As indicated above, Confucianism involves a vast yoke of structure, starting with filial piety, continuing with the duty to the group, and culminating with loyalty to the state. In view of employees' responsiveness to the paternalism existent in the huge cartels of modern Japanese industry, some say Confucianism is represented atavistically in a twentieth century version, that of corporate allegiance. Again, related to this security of group identification is the semantic pattern, for it is said that as a language group speaks and assigns meaning, so it is as a culture. There seems to be little idiomatic evidence that refers to the dignity and equality of people or their freedom to pursue excellence as individuals. As a Japanese friend once said, "In the West, because two thinking people can easily identify themselves by their mutual respect for the dignity of a man, they can, therefore, realize the society of man. In our language, there is not even the vocabulary to express that concept." In a further spirit of national deprecation, he sorrowfully added that because his culture lacked the consciousness for individualism, Japan's history had "no beautiful flowers" as in Greece's heroic triumvirate of Socrates, Plato, and Aristotle. Be that as it may, it cannot be denied that these "I-less" people have indeed had a history of high-quality culture.

It is revealing to analyze the language further, for it tends to articulate the bimodal aspects of the East and the West. Whereas the West has customarily tended toward the concept of free will—an individual as a self-propelling source of acts—and toward the Leibnitz control of the environment, the East has been considered as more apt to adjust passively to outside forces. In effect, this dichotomy reflects the venerable, enduring extremes of *Eindringlichkeit* (dramatic penetration) found in the Dionysian type societies and the *Einführung* (serene acceptance) seen in the Apollonian type cultures. The lists of expressions in Table 1 somewhat represent the differing views of traditional Japan and those of the West (although each item is not necessarily juxtaposed in exact equivalence to its counterpart).

In the West, Bacon and most of those who have followed him wished to conquer nature in a Promethean fashion. Western people have sought to manipulate their environment in order to benefit economically and technologically. But Japan has historically tried to harmonize itself, integrate rather than intervene, with nature. It has been said that European culture reflected nature while Japanese culture imitated it; the one seeks to express itself, the other to express nature, but unfortunately, Japan's Shinto sense of communion with nature is fast dissipating. The lovely panoramas of the Old Tokkaido Road, made famous by the exacting wood block prints of the esteemed Hiroshige, are now scenes of odious, polluting effluence. And just as with all other developed countries, the pernicious arms of industry stretch far beyond their own national boundaries.

Japan's rapid and successful industrialization is today a subject of very intense interest to the world. This small island-nation, within the last 100 years, has demonstrated remarkable energy and ineffable innovation. In the mid-nineteenth century, Japan drew its period of isolationism to a close, and presently is the Asian country, nonpareil, to have developed an industrial, urban, middle-class society that in many ways is similar to Western industrial cul-

**Table 1** Expressions Representative of the Differing Views of the East and West

| *The East* | *The West* |
| --- | --- |
| What is possible depends upon the circumstances. | All things are possible. |
| One does not make the wind but is blown by it. | Where there is a will, there is a way. |
|  | I am the captain of my soul, captain of my fate. |
|  | The word *impossible* is only in the dictionary of fools. |
| The greatness of a person may be measured by one's humility, not by one's assertiveness. "Quiet waters run deep." | It's the squeaky wheel that gets the oil. |
|  | You have to blow your own horn. |
|  | Faint heart never won fair maiden. |
|  | Nice guys finish last. |
| The nail that stands above the board gets nailed down. | He travels the fastest who travels alone. |
|  | Two roads diverged in a wood<br>And I—I took the one less traveled by<br>And that has made all the difference |
|  | If a man does not keep pace with his companions, perhaps it is because he hears a different drummer. |

tures. In doing so, Japan has de-emphasized individualistic spirit—an aspect that has normally characterized Western industrial development. Japan, so limited in size with only a minimum of arable land, has managed to create an economic structure, the magnitude of which is marked by its exceptionally high overall GNP and its astonishingly fast rate of growth. The nation's record of economic success suggests that the characteristics commonly associated with industrialization are not those necessarily exclusive or essential to economic development. In fact, the traditional value Japan places upon honor of authority, compliant, fatalistic behavior, group identity and solidarity, discipline, and obligation—may well combine to serve as an alternate model to national development. Indeed, if Japan is successful in maintaining a reasonable balance between its traditional and emergent values, it would not be too surprising if the twenty-first century were in fact to be Japan's. If so, according to Herman Kahn, a Japan observer, "the 'new Mediterranean' (the Northeast Pacific Basin) ... might well be ... the creative center of the post-industrial culture and civilization" (1970, p. 145).

## NOTES

1. The *tatami* is about 2 or 3 inches thick and is composed of straw which is covered by a woven matting. This mat provides one explanation for the custom of leaving street shoes in the entry: Under the pressure of leather soles or wooden clogs, the mat would become shredded rather rapidly. The Japanese mat is probably one of the most versatile pieces of architectural equipment ever devised. It serves as floor insulation, as carpet, and as a sitting pad.

2. It is curious that wood was so universally employed as a building material, for lumber was not always that readily available. The reason for the use of wood rested in the concept of the house as a special kind of shelter. Wood and paper were not thought of as a separation from nature; rather, they were considered to be in communion with nature and they afforded sun- and moonlight in the home. Indeed, some structures were so attuned to the earth that they almost appeared to have grown out of it. Faced with the problem of making the houses stable and of designing in harmony with nature, the Japanese concentrated the weight of the house not in the ground, as in the West, but in the roof where the load of tile or thatch and massive beams kept the structure in place on its underpinning. In a gale, the house could sway and creak perilously, much like a loaded fruit tree, without being blown down. It should be noted here that stone has been used in Japan for building, but usually only for defense purposes in the massive castles which have served as fortifications.

3. Zen-Buddhism is only one of the three major forms of Buddhism in Japan. Amida-Buddhism (Jodo and Jodo-shin) and the Nichiren-Buddhism both teach a standard of conduct according to a holy writ and neither emphasizes meditation or metaphysics.

4. However, it is necessary to add that maximum willfulness, freedom, and indulgence are allowed to infants and small children in Japan. This is strikingly true for boys. In comparison to most child-rearing practices in the United States, Japan's infant feeding and sleeping patterns are considered very permissive. Indeed, a familiar belief is that the children know no shame *(haji);* that is why they are so happy. This privileged period of ease is not experienced again until late maturity when one is finally relieved of the many pressing personal obligations to others.

## REFERENCES

Benedict, R. *The Chrysanthemum and the Sword.* Boston: Houghton-Mifflin Company, 1946, p. 288.

Bieda, K. *The Structure and Operation of the Japanese Economy.* Sydney: John Wiley and Sons, Australasia Pty., Ltd., 1970.

Crewe, Q. *Japan, Portrait of Paradox.* New York: Thomas Nelson, 1962.

Doi, L. "Amaé": A Key Concept for Understanding Japanese Personality Structure," in R. J. Smith and R. K. Beardsley (eds.), *Japanese Culture, Its Development and Characteristics.* (Chicago: Aldine Publishing Company, 1962), p. 132.

Guillain, R. *The Japanese Challenge,* translated from French by P. O'Brian. Philadelphia: J. B. Lippincott & Company, 1970.

Hall, J. W., and R. Beardsley. *Twelve Doors to Japan.* New York: McGraw-Hill, 1965.

Kahn, H. *The Emerging Japanese Superstate: Challenge and Response.* (Englewood Cliffs, N.J.: Prentice-Hall, Inc., 1970), p. 145.

Mushakoji, K. "From Fear of Dependence to Fear of Independence." *The Japan Annual of International Affairs,* 1963–64, 80.

Nakumura, H. *Ways of Thinking of Eastern Peoples: India, China, Tibet, Japan.* (Honolulu: East West Center Press, 1964), p. 557.

# Face-to-Face: American and Chinese Interactions

DOUGLAS P. MURRAY

We found during a recent stay in China that some of our most memorable interactions with Chinese never happened.[1] Curtains were pulled to eat behind, to drive behind, even to view the Yangzi Gorges behind. Served lunch in the aft dining room of the "East is Red #48" river boat from Chongqing to Wuhan, we and forty-odd other foreigners routinely had a wall of cloth pulled over the panoramic windows that would otherwise have framed some of the world's most spectacular scenery. Our initial befuddlement at this seeming madness dissolved quickly as we realized once again that the purpose was not to impede us but to *protect* us—from the mass of Chinese faces outside pressed against the panes to watch our gaggle of brightly attired aliens using chopsticks. (As it was, the curtains were not seamless, and the steady stare of Chinese passengers, one eye at a time, could usually be spotted at the blowing edges.) We were being shielded from rudeness, not from the scenery; we were being "helped," not hindered. But one man's sweet is another man's sour, and the interactions of Americans and Chinese remain bittersweet, largely because each understands so little about the motivations of the other.

## THE CONTEXT OF CONTACT

The protective screen on the Yangzi was only one vivid reminder that the two cultures and political

From Robert A. Kapp (ed.), *Communicating with China* (Chicago: Intercultural Press, 1983), pp. 9–27. Reprinted by permission of the publisher and the author. Dr. Murray is president of the China Institute in America, Inc.

systems approach each other from very different perspectives and seek communication from different premises about social relations. Chinese, for example, traditionally have not cast their nets of civic concern very widely; but those clearly within one's net (family, friends, colleagues, clients) receive all possible protection, nurture, and support—and foreign guests receive far more than most. Americans define social responsibilities much more broadly, but we assume they primarily involve regulating our *own* behavior, and worry about others within our purview largely when they are clearly in trouble. Victor Li, in *Law Without Lawyers,* provides a metaphor of the contrasting views of law that applies equally to the wider realm of social order. Americans generally allow each other to walk freely toward the cliff, reluctant to interfere until someone falls off the edge of crime or major deviance, at which point the power of civic or state institutions is rushed to the scene (at least ideally). For Chinese, Li observes, the cliff doesn't exist, being replaced by a long gradual slope; every step people take down the slope toward danger is (again, ideally) countered by supportive hands that try to push them back up to the straight and narrow. Prevention, not cure or punishment, is the primary goal, including prevention of embarrassment and loss of face. Chinese expect support and protection; Americans often resent it. . . .

Our interactions are not, however, a simple extension of our vastly different cultures and politics. While reflecting both, they also vary independently—with time, place, age, education, language skills, and certainly with personality. After 1971, the contacts renewed with such enthusiasm through Ping-Pong were a study in formal hospitality, decorum, and mutual acceptance. But since 1978 or so, with frenetic speed, our cultural, economic, academic, and tourist encounters have assumed a more open, warts-and-all quality, due in large part to the domestic relaxation within China that probably will (but might not) continue. The greater directness, even bluntness, that we find when traveling south from Peking through China's "mediterranean" provinces is paralleled by Chinese encounters with the hectic rough-and-tumble of New York after the more

easy-going hospitality of San Francisco and/or the Midwest. China's urban elite, with whom we customarily interact, present a very different face than do the worker and peasant masses whom we see largely from a distance. Foreigners who speak Chinese can find China equally, perhaps even more, puzzling than do those who must travel under the protective wing of English-speaking guides, though for different and more complex reasons; and in our quest to fathom and communicate with Chinese society our encounters with China's English-speaking (the "modern" elite) can be as misleading as they are rewarding. Any sampling of letters from the hundreds of Americans working in the PRC demonstrates that China remains a massive Rorschach test that can evoke the full range of our longtime love-hate sentiments toward things Chinese. There is no consistent pattern to the interactions of Americans and Chinese, just as neither country has a uniform culture. But there are parameters that help in understanding those variations. The way we extend or avoid socially protective nets is a particularly useful frame of reference for understanding Sino-American communication.

## PROTECTION AND PARANOIA

All too often, when Chinese hosts cast a protective net "in friendship," Americans try to free themselves from it;[2] and when American hosts extend a hand in greeting, with little or no protective net attached, Chinese wonder about the sincerity of this "friendship" and even grow anxious about their sustained well-being.[3] Consequently, as any period of residence in China soon demonstrates, Chinese and Americans develop—along with mutual enjoyment and friendship—varying degrees of paranoia that can put even the most routine behavior under suspicion.

One explanation, of course, is that even paranoids have real enemies, as Henry Kissinger occasionally reminds us. China's governance involves both the overt system of public institutions with whose members we interact rather easily and the more shadowy system of political and security organs whose work usually is "not open" *(bugongkai)* yet imposes constraints on all manner of dealings with foreigners. A fundamental concern with national security and political rectitude both reflects and reinforces cultural resistance to alien influence; official Chinese "regulations" and "directives," both acknowledged and denied, form a backdrop to apparently spontaneous behavior. Chinese students and teachers *are* periodically reminded to deal with foreign residents only with caution, if at all. There *are* signs near every Chinese city reading "foreigners not permitted beyond this point," just as there are research facilities and industries in the United States that PRC Chinese (and others from socialist states) cannot freely visit. Telephonic eavesdropping is not an unknown practice in either country. The assumption of foreigners resident in China that their mail is regularly reviewed is probably fair enough in many cases, and Chinese scholars in the United States are hardly oblivious to the occasional invigilation of our government. While it is unlikely that, as one student in China claimed, "we Americans are constantly being followed," it would be naive to argue that such incidents never happen.

Despite the ubiquitous registration *(dengji)* system for Chinese entering foreigners' hotels and dormitories, Americans generally are quite innocent about the possible risks they pose to their Chinese friends and associates and are immensely distressed when confronted with them. But few Chinese, including those who seem most relaxed and straightforward, ever lose sight of the potential hazards or the extent to which they are "protected" in their associations with us. There are just enough "real" problems and constraints to keep a true paranoid of either nationality quite content, often to the great embarrassment of hosts in China and the United States who themselves have no wish or reason to express anything other than gracious hospitality.

A second element breeding suspicion is our inadequate understanding of the interactions among Chinese themselves. Like most foreigners, Americans are remarkably quick to see Chinese behavior as aimed specially at them, when in fact they simply are sharing in local culture. How many of us realize that the offensive "registration" of our Chinese guests

is only an extension of the system to which *everyone* normally is subjected when visiting Chinese offices? We are eager for home hospitality, to see how our friends and acquaintances "really live"; yet entertainment almost invariably is provided formally, in clubs or restaurants. We satisfy ourselves with the explanation that Chinese living quarters are small, humble, and thus probably embarrassing to our potential hosts. While the explanation is usually true, it does not touch the heart of the matter: that home hospitality is rare among the Chinese and usually reserved for the very closest of friends and most special of occasions. One American teacher in China recently was astounded to learn from a Chinese woman who accepted her invitation that it was the first time in twenty years her guest had dined at a colleague's home. Similarly: Why, despite endless visits to institutions and agencies, do we see only comfortable reception halls and common rooms, and never the offices of working staff? Why do foreign experts, hired by a Chinese institution, spend the bulk of their time in their hotel and feel so isolated from the hum of academic life? Perhaps because only the most senior Chinese professors and administrators have their own offices, while faculty members normally work at home, coming in only one or two days a week to lecture. We don't see the "work place" because so often there isn't any.

Given this context for communication across cultures, even the purest motives and most gracious practices can yield ambiguous interpretations. The need to decipher the codes of "hospitality," "protection," and "interference" could be the largest single challenge in our cultural interactions. In this respect, the directness and informality of most Americans give our Chinese counterparts a great advantage in reading our intentions. We tend to do for others only what we would do for ourselves (with a little gilding, perhaps) and, after initial courtesy, quickly "tell it like it is." . . .

Americans, however, have a much harder time fathoming the meanings of China's double-edged hospitality. When barriers arise within an otherwise warm reception and our seemingly reasonable requests are blocked, *our* gorge also rises, for a variety of reasons: (1) eager to learn and explore, we assume a right to learn more about Chinese society than we know even about our own (I, for one, haven't visited a U.S. farm, factory, or courtroom since I left grammar school); (2) few of us comprehend how basic and hence embarrassing are the Chinese standards of material life we yearn to sample; (3) few Chinese will voluntarily explain the likely difficulties of such sampling, especially if the reasons might seem unpleasant; and (4) the Chinese sense of personal responsibility for a guest's welfare is stronger than we can fully grasp. Repeated urgings that visitors be chauffeured even short distances have yielded the most sinister interpretations, since the common statement that "you might get lost" seems patently ridiculous. A direct (and honest) explanation that there *is* crime in the city, that traffic *can* be extremely hazardous, and that the "responsible persons" *could* be severely criticized if anything untoward happened is usually avoided, leaving Americans to read between the lines, often erroneously.

Meals in special restaurants and dining rooms become a symbol of the wish to isolate us from the people, from Chinese reality. A simple explanation that "people's" restaurants are crowded beyond our probable tolerance, dirty by Western standards, and serve generally unpalatable food would be painful in the giving, though not as painful as the humiliation of letting honored guests be so badly served or be the objects of public curiosity. But we then suspect that our Chinese hosts intend to shield us from learning about their society. Is all this generous hospitality meant simply to divert our attention from those other things we really want to do? . . .

## THE POLLYANNA SYNDROME

These unhappy suspicions usually develop only *after* real contact has begun—after we're actually caught up in China's protective net or after the Chinese are actually in the United States looking for one. They become salient largely because both sides have been so predisposed to think the very best, to make each other's virtues larger than life. . . . For Americans

meeting Chinese young people today, it is hard to miss their underlying hope that our social problems and "spiritual crises" are not as serious as the media make out: that American ingenuity, science, and even power really can be part of China's, and perhaps their personal salvation. With mutual expectations so high, reality easily becomes suspect.

One reflection of these Pollyanna tendencies is the familiar pattern of "out-politeing" each other, the fear of offending that so often shields both parties from candid talk and brass tacks. The euphoria of a lively dinner or warm discussion yields next morning to a realization that nothing much was learned or accomplished. The excessive courtesy—Chinese in origin and so attractive to us—is *not* uniformly apparent among Chinese themselves, and foreigners resident in China are often shocked by the pervasive "rudeness." The eagerly helpful, friendly, courteous, and kind responses of friends and service personnel can quickly be eclipsed by the sullen indifference of people encountered in less personal settings. But courtesy usually is offered so compellingly to "foreign friends" that we actually can end up wildly misinformed. . . .

Caught up in a gracious reception, Americans new to China frequently find it difficult to press a line of questioning or to probe issues being dealt with circumspectly by their hosts. Appearing to doubt or question what one is told seems simply rude in the prevailing atmosphere. Yet this serves only to reinforce problems of communication. Within Chinese conversational style is a tendency to respond in terms of expectations, goals, even models rather than with mundane facts. Courtesy prompts *good* answers, not just technically accurate ones, and one strains to assume that what *should* be, *is,* or at least soon will be. Question: "Will your university have a Chinese language program for foreign students this summer?" Answer: "Yes." "How many students will you have?" "One hundred." But further questioning reveals that the institution simply has decided in *principle* to have a course, that no dates have been set, no students have yet applied, and no arrangements with foreign institutions made. For purposes of the question, however, a plan had become a concrete reality.

American scholars visiting China for a few weeks ask repeatedly about birth rates in the localities they visit and are impressed by the apparent success of population control efforts that the accumulated answers suggest. Only by accident toward the end of their stay do they realize that, in most cases, the figures given them were the *targets* for last year and this. Actual data had not yet been compiled, but the presumption of correspondence between goals and reality was strong enough to justify using the target figures. Probably not a conscious attempt to deceive, but a form of deception nevertheless to which the reluctance of foreign guests to probe too deeply made them accomplices. Yet, when persistence finally does uncover the "truth," our suspicions are heightened, not allayed. Why aren't we given a "straight answer" in the first place?

## COMMUNICATION AND CONCEPTS

Our problems of mutual comprehension stem not only from cultural norms, but from more particular traits of thought and communication. The indirection that permeates Chinese speech, even in English translation, can be particularly disconcerting to Americans. "Perhaps" and "maybe" are cultural stock-in-trade. "Maybe I will come with you" usually means "I'm coming." "Perhaps it is too far for you to walk" means "There's no way I'll let you walk." When something is "inconvenient," it most likely is impossible. But more than verbal indirection is at work here. The absence of a categorical statement implies that "perhaps" some room for discussion remains; and, in any case, a subsequent reversal will not represent a clear backing-down. Despite the firm signal that conditional speech often implies, negotiation is never totally foreclosed and dignity is maintained, at the expense of American patience. . . .

Phrases that Western visitors and residents in China must learn to live with are "we'll consider it" *(kaolu)* and "we'll study it" *(yanjiu)*. These common responses to requests seem the ultimate in hedging and avoiding potentially difficult issues. But they also reflect the pervasive need in China to consult with higher-level colleagues before making

decisions. Forgetting the foibles of our own bureaucratism, and unaware that routine tasks of communication at home can be major chores in the PRC, Americans quickly become frustrated by the need to consider-and-study even the apparently simplest appeals. We are dealing here with the way the *system* works, not only with verbal styles; but the difference is often hard to discern in our discourse with Chinese culture.

Other aspects of China's style also challenge our comprehension and patience. The sense of time, for example. Not until one has tried for several hours to dial a phone number before getting through, or in despair has taken a cab three miles to deliver the message, can one "know" what it means for things to take *time*; one phone (if any) per office, very few private lines, whole apartment buildings with one or two communal phones where messages can be left *if* someone answers. If one knows the informal network—who works or lives near whom and can serve as an intermediary—then things go faster; but it takes still more time to learn each informal network. Perhaps as a result, Chinese don't seem comfortable doing business by telephone, which for them is essentially a vehicle for communicating information or arranging future face-to-face sessions, not for discussing or resolving problems. . . . The frustrations Americans feel in the absence of full and complete replies to our inquiries arise so often because we assume China's patterns of communication are like our own. Yet we can hardly expect an entire cultural system to revise its sense of time and process just because we enter it. . . .

Problems of comprehension are compounded by the common American personality that delights in action, in "making things happen," and in the private ego-satisfaction that results even without monetary or institutional rewards. We often create projects, offer assistance, or propose cooperation in large part because "we get a kick out of it." In response, our Chinese associates, more practically minded, wonder what we're really after—what we have left unsaid. Their concern has roots in the history of American philanthropy in China and Chinese presumptions that our recently renewed "friendship" implies practical benefits. Surely our *intentions* are to help China, but since our motivation is often simply self-interest, suspicion can be the eventual outcome, for understandable reasons on both sides.

If the first Chinese priority is to learn the useful, the way to do it is not primarily by inductive analysis, but by emulation, by studying the successful experience of others. The PRC has made maximum use of this traditional approach; designation of model communes, model factories, model teachers, model workers has been paramount in the official reward system, and "Learn from . . ." campaigns are continually employed for pedagogy and political mobilization alike. While hardly alien to us, the reliance on "models" in China's civic life seems to the average Western visitor greatly overdone, rather like an adult Boy Scout camp or Sunday school. And it can involve direct consequences for us. One American student at a large Chinese university didn't know whether to laugh or cry when he discovered that several weeks previously he had been chosen "model foreigner"; the institution's Foreign Affairs Office had advised everyone in his department to observe him, to emulate his diligence, and to learn from his example how a foreigner ought to behave in Chinese society. (After his discovery, he decided to sloppy-up a bit, just to clear his good name with his Western friends; he also surmised that some *negative* models must also have been selected among his peers!)

Innumerable writers and foreign visitors have noted the concern with "face" and "respect" that pervades Chinese culture. This concern may well be the glue that has held this ancient civilization together, reflecting the primacy of human relations (or "human feelings"—*renqing*) in Chinese values. It would not normally occur to Americans to include in the text of solemn international treaties, academic exchange agreements or dinnertime toasts a vow to "respect" the other party. Yet it is commonplace in our dealings with Chinese, and we seem to relish it, both because it is China's equivalent of apple pie and motherhood and because we rather admire this virtue so often obscured at home. But this call for "respect" can be a cultural trap for Americans. One often *insists* on respect when its loss is feared, when the grounds for deserving it

are either weak or unlikely to be understood. Chinese needs for respect often appear as defense mechanisms against possible criticism of conditions they believe we might *not* respect in our own society. A preemptive assurance of mutual respect is a superb diplomatic asset when foreigners later violate "Chinese customs" by taking "inappropriate" photographs, breaking the extremely early curfews in college dorms, visiting apparently innocuous places that technically are "not open," or expressing complaints so candidly as to cause embarrassment to a Chinese host. If the salience of "respect" in Chinese culture is admirable, it is also a mine-field for Americans not familiar with the insecurities underlying it and the diverse circumstances in which it can be invoked.

## ON BEING ALIEN

One could write endlessly (as others have) about the characteristics of Chinese culture and behavior, and their differences with the West. But our concern here is the aggregate consequences for our interactions: namely, a profound sense among most Chinese that we are, indeed, alien. Our not being Chinese justifies intense curiosity about us, the most special treatment, and, of course, selective emulation. Few if any long-term foreign residents of China, despite their acculturation and abiding love of the country, admit to being fully accepted, to being considered "non-foreign." There is great import in the old and probably true story of the missionary who, in good local dialect, asks a Chinese peasant directions to the next village. Getting only stoney silence, he walks away, only to overhear the peasant say to his friend, "Funny, it almost sounded like he was asking how to get to the next village." Having once assumed the tale apocryphal (though instructive), I learned better recently when driving along the Fujian coast and stopping in a small town to take a photo. It was only seconds before the inevitable mob of faces gathered to affix the dispassionate stares that all foreigners must live with. Trying as usual to unfreeze the tableau, I offered the front row some friendly wisecracks in Chinese, producing the equally usual smiles and *bonhommie*. Turning to snap the picture that was my purpose, I heard the middle-aged man at my left ear solemnly assure the group, "No, he's not a foreigner; he speaks Chinese!" Though I might have felt honored by this instant admission to Chinese civilization (perhaps as a Uighur from Xinjiang?), his logic clearly was different; nothing could be foreign and Chinese at the same time. Seeming in one respect Chinese, I could not possibly also be foreign. An either-or, black-and-white proposition that allows little room for degrees of acculturation or diversity.

Although this psychic distance is well reflected in the special tourist amenities noted earlier, it is most clearly expressed in the new foreigner "clubs," cocktail lounges (replete with pop-bands) and game rooms featuring pinball and Space Invader machines now appearing in China's major hotels. Both the thoughtfulness and commercial good sense of making foreigners feel at home can be appreciated; but the reproduction of our presumed natural habitat within an environment so extremely dissimilar is jarring—especially considering how little effort seems devoted to assuring either our easy access to *Chinese* social institutions or Chinese access to our special enclaves within the PRC. Above and beyond the linguistic and cultural barriers to the latter course, the sharp separation of East and West seems more natural and instinctive to Chinese hosts than do imaginative efforts to blur the boundaries and encourage genuinely relaxed interchange. In this respect, cultural preferences, economic realities, and official policy are mutually supportive—despite the irony that China is now busily replicating the "foreign concessions" that were a primary target of its Revolution.

In the end, it seems, the most supportive and protective net that China knows how to provide in her own land is the one that permits foreigners to live separate if not equal, to be treated very well but from a distance. Like the wider Chinese society it reflects, this pattern is not likely to change in a big hurry. Americans and Chinese will continue to communicate, face to face, across a cultural gap of sizable proportions. Perhaps that is what makes real communication, when it does occur, so very rewarding.

## NOTES

1. Much has happened in China since this was written late in 1981, but has much changed? A brief "spiritual pollution" campaign gave way to rapid economic and incipient political reforms, followed by student demonstrations, the resignation of Party General Secretary Hu Yaobang (January 1987), and another tightening of Party discipline aimed at curbing "all-out westernization." Throughout, a steady rise in living standards was reflected in improved housing and communications, more colorful styles, and a general lightening of the public mood. Tens of thousands of Chinese went abroad to study, and foreigners gained easier access to Chinese society—noting a more sophisticated and gentle touch from those charged with handling them. Yet despite all this, I doubt that the underlying patterns of Chinese culture have changed at all; the determinants of "Chinese and American interactions" described in the article might be less *evident* to visitors today, but they are no less influential.

2. At 4:30 A.M., a full hour before the end of an overnight train ride, I was helpfully awakened by the steward so that "you can wash your face." No one had told me to wash my face in almost forty years, and I rejected this solicitous concern out of hand!

3. Many Americans were distressed in the early years of U.S.-PRC exchange to see Chinese delegations cordoned off by State Department security officers; how many realized that they represented *protection* fervently requested by the Chinese, not isolation imposed by the U.S. hosts? Women university students in China apologize for leaving their foreign roommate alone for a night because a Chinese friend's roommate will be away and needs their company; being alone is a frightening prospect.

# Cultural and Communication Patterns of Saudi Arabians

MYRON W. LUSTIG

For most Americans, impressions of Saudi Arabia are based on distorted media images. Saudi Arabians have been alternatively characterized as primitive Bedouins and as indulgent millionaires. Though both of these stereotypes are obviously inaccurate, Americans are often unable to obtain a more accurate portrayal of members of that country. Saudi Arabia's central role in global affairs requires an understanding of its cultural and communication patterns that is more accurate than distorted media stereotypes and more detailed than a glorified travelog or a simplified guide on customary business practices.

## CULTURAL PATTERNS

The most pervasive influence on Saudi Arabian life is Wahhabism, which is a strict interpretation of the Islamic religion. Wahhabism is similar in many respects to Puritanism, with its strict codes of behavior that govern all aspects of social life. For instance, the consumption of pork and alcoholic beverages is prohibited; prayer is required five times daily, and modesty is expected of women in both dress and demeanor. The Shari'ah, which is the comprehensive code of conduct that guides the life of all practicing Moslems, prescribes appropriate practices concerning marriage, divorce, childrearing, and most

This essay was written especially for this fifth edition. All rights reserved. Permission to reprint must be obtained from the publisher and the author. Dr. Lustig teaches at San Diego State University.

other instances of social conduct. While the prescriptions of the Shari'ah are followed by all who believe in Islam, in Saudi Arabia they are interpreted more strictly than in other Islamic countries.

Westerners often have difficulty in understanding the pervasiveness of Islam on all aspects of everyday life. The influence of Islam is analogous to the effects of Catholicism in medieval Europe or the Amish religion on its present-day adherents. In each of these examples, the laws, norms, behaviors, and world views are dictated by the tenets of the religion. The profound belief in the will of God results, in each instance, in a cultural belief in fatalism and religiocentrism. Among Saudi Arabians, phrases such as *Insha'allah* (God willing), *Maktoob* (It is written), and *La illah il-allah* (There is no God but Allah) are commonly heard in conversations and reflect the belief that one can make plans but not promises.

Closely related to the cultural influence of Islam is Arab nationalism. Indeed, the late King Ibn Saud, who founded the Kingdom of Saudi Arabia in 1932, said that Islam and Arab nationalism are the two most important forces in his life. This statement suggests the deeply powerful value of Arab nationalism in Saudi Arabia's psychological, social, and political processes. However, although religion, language, heritage, and economic considerations unite Saudi Arabia with most of the Arab world, differences in geography, history, and political ideology make Saudi Arabia more moderate and more politically conservative than many of the other Arab nations.

The cultural values most relevant to Saudi Arabians are similar to those that are important in many other Middle Eastern countries: conservatism, courage, family devotion, fatalism, group harmony, honor, hospitality, male dominance, nationalism, other-orientedness, patience, piety, pride, self-respect, sexual modesty, status, and traditionalism. Men, in particular, are expected to bring honor upon themselves and their households while avoiding shame. The subordination of one's individual needs to those of the family and the community are common themes used to explain or justify behaviors. Even the governmental structures at the highest levels are characterized by extended kinship patterns that encourage dependence upon and devotion to the group.

## COMMUNICATION PATTERNS

The influence of Islam on all aspects of Arabic life is especially evident in Saudi Arabian communication patterns. Arabic is regarded as a sacred language, and the Koran is universally regarded as the most artistically perfect Arabic that has ever been created. Consequently, children are taught to read by rote memorization of the Koran, and the Koran is also the primary sourcebook for information on appropriate Arabic grammar and style.

The Koran forbids the visual depiction of living beings. Consequently, verbal artistry, particularly in poetry and literature, has developed as the major art form. Even ordinary conversations are regarded as vehicles for eloquence and aesthetic expression.

### Verbal Patterns

Verbal language patterns that emphasize creative artistry by using rhetorical devices such as repetition, metaphor, and simile are highly valued. In part because of the poetic influence of the Koran, the form, meter, and rhythms of the Arabic language have a persuasive and almost irresistible influence on its users. At times, the words used to describe an experience are more important than the experience itself, for the rhythms of the language can produce a magical, captivating, and hypnotic state on its users.

There is a tendency for Arabic speakers to chain seemingly unrelated ideas together by using parallel linguistic constructions, conjunctions, and other grammatical forms. Westerners, who are more familiar with linear reasoning patterns, find it difficult to locate the main idea in Saudi Arabians' messages. Alternatively, Saudi Arabians often fault Westerners for their insensitivity to linguistic artistry.

Among Saudi Arabians, as with other Arabic speakers, words often function as a substitute for actions. This is particularly true if the actions involve conflict or violence. For example, verbal threats and flamboyant language are common, but these displays of overassertion and exaggeration are usually intended to channel the aggression and thereby diffuse it, thus preventing actual violence. Essentially, verbal aggression often functions as a psychological release and not as an actual intention.

### Paralinguistic Patterns

Paralinguistic patterns, which are qualities of the voice such as vocal pitch, rhythm, intonation, and inflection, often convey a message in addition to that provided on the verbal channel. In Arabic, the intonation pattern is such that many of the individual words in the sentence are stressed. A flat intonation pattern is used in declarative sentences. The intonation pattern for Arabic exclamatory sentences is much stronger and more emotional than that which is common to English speakers. The higher pitch range of Arabic speakers also conveys a more emotional tone than does English when spoken by a native speaker.

As the emotional meanings conveyed by paralinguistic patterns are usually "taken for granted" by native language users, they can be the cause of considerable intercultural misunderstandings when they fail to conform to preconceived expectations. For instance, when speaking to an American in English, a Saudi Arabian will usually transfer his native intonation patterns without being aware that he has done so. Consequently, the Saudi Arabian paralinguistic patterns may result in unwarranted negative impressions. The American may incorrectly perceive that the Saudi Arabian is excited or angry when in fact he is not. Questions by the Saudi that merely seek information may sound accusing. The monotonous tone of declarative sentences may be perceived as demonstrating apathy or a lack of interest. Vocal stress and intonation differences may result in a perception of aggressiveness or abrasiveness when only polite conversation is intended. Conversely, the Saudi Arabian may incorrectly interpret certain behaviors of the American speaker as an expression of calmness and pleasantness when anger or annoyance is being conveyed. Similarly, a statement that seems to be a firm assertion to the American speaker may sound weak and doubtful to the Saudi Arabian.

## Nonverbal Patterns

Nonverbal communication patterns of Saudi Arabians have much in common with those of Americans. For instance, the hand held over the heart symbolizes *sincerity,* the thumb-forefinger circle signifies *OK,* and tapping the side of the forehead means *thinking.* Though many nonverbal behaviors are similar to those of English speakers, Saudi Arabian gestures that are not identical to those common among Americans include the chin flick *(disinterest),* a forefinger placed on the side of nose *(dislike of idea),* an upward toss of the head *(no),* and a downward tug of the lower eyelid *(incredulity).*

In social conversations, Saudi Arabians stand slightly closer to one another than Americans do. They gesture frequently and often touch one another while talking. Both the speaker and the listener engage in mutual eye gaze almost continuously. By watching for changes in the pupils of the eyes, they are gathering information about changes in mood or emotional response, as the pupils dilate (i.e., enlarge) when a person is relaxed and shows an increased level of interest in something or someone.

A communication pattern that frequently occurs in Saudi Arabian interactions is the elaborate and extended introduction ritual that is characterized by excessive politeness and attention to social etiquette. Handshakes often extend for several minutes, and a very stylized exchange of polite questions and blessings can continue almost indefinitely. "Welcome," "How do you do," "May Allah bless you," "How is your family," "How do you feel," "We pray you are well," "We are honored to have you with us" are all forms of the introduction ritual. The greeting ritual reflects the value placed on community allegiance and group harmony. Before serious discussions can even begin, Arabian coffee is usually served with a ceremony as complex as a formal Japanese tea ceremony. The coffee is much more than a gesture of hospitality and social eti-

quette. To refuse the coffee is regarded as an insult as it deprives the host of an opportunity to be hospitable and therefore honorable.

Saudi Arabians often fault Americans for their inattention to polite social rituals before entering into task-oriented discussions. In business dealings, in particular, Americans are expected to socialize first in an effort to develop trust, friendship, and acceptance. This interpersonal dimension, which is extremely important to the Saudi Arabians, is a prerequisite to doing business. Indeed, Saudi Arabians sometimes feel insulted if Americans attempt to become task-oriented too quickly. They prefer to engage in "small talk" before starting business conversations because this demonstrates to them that the Americans believe the discussion is worth their time.

The importance of Saudi Arabia in the world's economic affairs requires a thorough understanding of the cultural and communication patterns common to members of that country. Westerners who intend to interact with Saudi Arabians would benefit from some rudimentary training in common Arabic phrases because attempts at speaking Arabic are invaluable in establishing a favorable social climate. The influence of religion on cultural expectations, the importance of linguistic artistry in both oral and written expressions, and the desire for involvement in elaborate social rituals are all important components of the Saudi Arabian world view. The difference between Western and Arab logic patterns suggests that there is a significant potential for major intercultural communication problems to occur.

One must be cautious in accepting any firm conclusions about Saudi Arabia, however, as rapid societal changes and economic forces are having a major influence in the country, particularly on the newly emerging middle class. Nevertheless, despite the Saudis' exposure to modern political and social trends, social customs continue to be tempered by traditional Saudi Arabian values.

# Some Basic Cultural Patterns of India

NEMI C. JAIN

Why study basic cultural patterns of India? To many Americans, the word *India* brings to mind a wonderland peopled with snake charmers, bearded and turbaned giants, Ganges bathers, *dhoti*-clad peasants, and lumbering elephants—all parading past, with the Taj Mahal serving as the backdrop.[1] But if this is all that India is about, then why has the United States given more than $10 billion in loans, grants, and agricultural products since India's independence from British rule in 1947? Why is there so much concern in the halls of Congress, in the mass media, and in the corridors of the United Nations over the question of whether India will "make it"? In short, why the persistent anxiety, concern, and interest about a country and people who reside far away from American shores, not just in miles but in culture, language, habits of thought and life?[2]

The desire to find answers to these questions—and the very existence of the questions themselves—is one of the characteristics that distinguishes this generation from all others that have gone before. No major country lies farther away in miles from the United States than does India. It is becoming increasingly obvious, however, that "no man is an island" and that actions in one part of the globe cause reactions in many other countries of the world. India is a most suitable culture for study because her preeminence (along with Communist China) in Asia and her leadership role among nations of the Third World point toward her importance in international affairs. More importantly, India's cultural tradition provides an instructive contrast to American cultural patterns.[3]

Indian culture has a long continuous history that extends over 5,000 years. Very early, India evolved a distinctive culture and religion, Hinduism, which was modified and adjusted as it came into contact with outside elements. In spirit, however, India has maintained the essential unity of the indigenous doctrines and ideas of Hinduism. It is this characteristic of Indian culture that has enabled it to withstand many vicissitudes and to continue to mold the lives of millions of people in India and abroad.[4]

Like any other culture, the Indian culture is complex and consists of many interrelated beliefs, values, norms, social systems, and material cultural elements. In spite of the multi-ethnic, multi-lingual, and highly stratified nature of contemporary Indian society, India is united by a set of basic cultural patterns that are widely shared among the Hindus who comprise about 80 percent of India's population of over 650 million. The major aim of this article is to outline some of these basic cultural patterns that have persisted over the thousands of years of Indian history, patterns that continue to influence many aspects of Indian social institutions and that affect communication and thought patterns of millions of Hindus in India and abroad. More specifically, this article will describe briefly the following interrelated categories of basic cultural patterns of India: (1) world view, (2) reincarnation, (3) *Dharma,* (4) caste system, and (5) spirit of tolerance.

Each of these categories includes several specific cultural beliefs, values, and norms that are closely interrelated. Each cultural pattern represents a continuum, and within the same culture, variations of the pattern normally occur. Contradictions among cultural patterns are probably universal throughout societies. Despite internal variations and contradictions, there is an overall integration to the patterns of Hindu Indian culture. It is possible to simplify its description by isolating the various cultural patterns and considering them one at a time.

## WORLD VIEW

One of the unique characteristics of Indian culture is its world view involving the Hindu concepts of *Brahman* and *Atman.* In Hinduism, the Supreme Being is the impersonal *Brahman,* a philosophical Absolute, serenely blissful, beyond all limitations either ethical or metaphysical. *Brahman* is the supreme reality. The basic Hindu view of God involves infinite being, infinite consciousness, and infinite bliss. The chief attributes to be linked with *Brahman* are *sat, chit,* and *ananda;* God is being, awareness, and bliss. Even these words cannot claim to describe him literally, however, for the meanings they carry for people are radically unlike the senses in which they apply to God.[5]

The Hindu conception of the universe is essentially cyclic. Hinduism does not believe in an absolute beginning or end of the universe but maintains that creation, existence, and destruction are endless processes ever repeating. This does not preclude a belief in the creation or end of a particular universe. This present world, for example, had a beginning and will have an end; but it is a mere link in the endless chain of universes that preceded it and are yet to succeed it. This world was created by *Brahman* and after a definite period will be destroyed and replaced by another world that will suffer a similar fate.[6]

According to Hinduism, the *Brahman* is in a sense the very world itself, including both living and nonliving aspects of the universe. Hinduism recognizes the relationship between living and nonliving parts of the universe. It emphasizes the need for understanding the nature of relationships among human beings, other living organisms, and nonliving creations of God, including mountains, rivers, and other aspects of the physical universe. Hinduism lays considerable emphasis on the value of all created life, including animals, birds, and trees. It is indeed interesting to note that the gods of the Hindu pantheon are associated with animals. *Shiva,* who has *Nandi* or the Bull as his mount *(vahana),* is regarded as the Lord of animals, *Pasupathi.* Likewise, *Vishnu* has the Serpent and *Garuda; Brahma,* the Swan; *Indra,* the Elephant; *Surya* (Sun God), the Horse; *Durga,* the Lion; *Ganesha,* the Rat; and *Muruga,* the Peacock. Among the ten principal incarnations *(avataras)* of Lord *Vishnu,* three—*Matsya* (the Fish), *Kurma* (the Tortoise), and *Varaha* (the Boar)—are in animal forms, while the fourth, *Narasimha,* is in a form that is half man and half lion. According to Hindu beliefs, the Buddha's former births were also in animal forms. The Hindus have naturally invested the animals with an element of divinity. This association of gods with the animal world is indicative of a healthy attitude toward nature. The same association is true of mountains, rivers, and trees, which have more than an ordinary significance in Indian life—many are considered sacred and holy. In short, Indian culture takes into its fold all nature. Hinduism emphasizes the importance of harmony among human beings, other living organisms, and the physical creations of the universe.[7]

In Hinduism, *Brahman* is also conceived of as the Supreme Soul of the universe. Every living soul is a part of the *Brahman,* a particular manifestation of the *Brahman.* These particular manifestations, individual souls, seem to change from generation to generation, but actually only the unimportant, outer details change—a body, a face, a name, a different condition or status in life. The *Brahman,* however, veiled behind these deceptive "realities," is continuous and indestructible. This hidden self or *Atman* is a reservoir of being that never dies, is never exhausted, and is without limit in awareness and bliss. *Atman* is the infinite center of every life. Body, personality, and *Atman* together comprise a human being.[8]

A Hindu cannot believe in the *Brahman* without believing also in a firm bond among all people, since they are all manifestations of the *Brahman.* Furthermore, a Hindu cannot really believe in any individual as a distinct and separate person, because Hinduism contends that each individual is only a tiny part of the whole universe, which is the *Brahman.*[9]

The eternal *Atman* is usually buried under the almost impenetrable mass of distractions, false ideas, and self-regarding impulses that compose one's surface being. The aim of human life is to cleanse the dross from one's being to the point where its infinite center, the eternal *Atman,* will be fully manifest.[10]

What kind of world do we have? Hinduism answers: (1) a multiple world that includes innumerable galaxies horizontally, innumerable tiers vertically, and innumerable cycles temporally; (2) a moral world in which the law of *Karma* never wavers; (3) a middle world that will never in itself replace the supreme as destination for the human spirit; (4) a world that is *maya,* deceptively tricky in that its multiplicity, materiality, and welter of dualities appear ultimate whereas these are in fact provisional only; (5) a training ground that can advance human beings toward the Highest; (6) a world that is *lila,* the play of the divine in its cosmic dance, untiring, unending, resistless, but ultimately gentle, with a grace born of infinite vitality.[11]

## REINCARNATION

The Hindu belief in reincarnation affirms that individual souls enter the world, by God's power, and pass through a sequence of bodies or life cycles. On the subhuman level, the passage is through a series of increasingly complex bodies until at last a human one is attained. Up to this point, the soul's growth is virtually automatic. With the soul's graduation into a human body, this automatic, escalator mode of ascent comes to an end. The soul's assignment to this exalted habitation is evidence that it has reached self-consciousness, and with this estate come freedom, responsibility, and effort. Now the individual soul, as a human being, is fully responsible for its behavior through the doctrine of *Karma*—the moral law of cause and effect. The present condition of each individual life is a product of what one did in the previous life; and one's present acts, thoughts, and decisions are determining one's future states.[12]

This concept of *Karma* and the completely moral universe it implies carries two important psychological corollaries. First, it commits the Hindu who understands it to complete personal responsibility. Each individual is wholly responsible for his or her present condition and will have exactly the future

he or she is now creating. Conversely, the idea of a moral universe closes the door to all appeals to chance or accident. In this world there is no chance or accident. *Karma* decrees that every decision must have its determinate consequences, but the decisions themselves are, in the last analysis, freely arrived at. Or, to approach the matter from the other direction, the consequences of a person's past decisions condition his or her present lot, as a card player is dealt a particular hand but is left free to play that hand in a number of ways. This means that the carrier of a soul, a human being, as it threads its course through innumerable human bodies, is guided by its choice, these in turn being decided by what the soul wants at each particular stage of its pilgrimage.[13]

Never during its pilgrimage is the individual soul completely adrift and alone. From start to finish its nucleus is the *Atman.* Underlying its whirlpool of transient feelings, emotions, and delusions is the self-luminous, abiding point of God himself. Although he is buried too deep in the soul to be noticeable, he is the sole ground of a person's being and awareness. God alone energizes the surface self in all that it does; in the end it is his radiance that melts the soul's thick cap that at first hides his glory almost completely but becomes at last a pure capacity for God. After reaching this level of purity, the individual soul passes into complete identification with God.[14] This state for an individual soul is called *Moksha* or *Nirvana*—when the soul is free from the process of reincarnation or transmigration and has merged with the *Brahman,* from whence it originated in the first place.

According to Hinduism, the aim of life is the gradual revelation in one's human existence of the eternal within oneself. The general progress is governed by the law of *Karma* or moral causation. The Hindu religion does not believe in a God who from his judgment seat weighs each case separately and decides on its merits. He does not administer justice from without, enhancing or remitting punishment according to his will. God is *in* each individual, and so the law of *Karma* is organic to human nature. Every moment each person is on trial, and every honest effort will do him or her good in this eternal endeavor. The character that each individual builds will continue into the future until he or she realizes oneness with God.[15]

## DHARMA

The concept of *Dharma* is another unique feature of Hinduism and Indian culture. *Dharma* refers to a code of conduct that guides the life of a person both as an individual and as a member of society. It includes ideals and purposes, influences and institutions that shape the character of a person. It is the law of right living, the observance of which secures the double object of happiness on earth and salvation. The life of a Hindu is regulated in a very detailed manner by the laws of *Dharma*. Personal habits, social and family ties, fasts and feasts, and actions are all conditioned by it.[16]

*Dharma* is the binding law that accounts for the cohesion in the social system throughout the history of Indian society. Since *Dharma* is trans-individual, no social contract proves necessary; harmony is achieved when everyone "follows" his or her own *Dharma*. *Dharma* is a code of conduct supported by the general conscience of the people. It is not subjective in the sense that the conscience of the individual imposes it, nor external in the sense that the law enforces it. It is the system of conduct that the general opinion or spirit of the people supports. *Dharma* does not force people into virtue but trains them for it. It is not a fixed code of mechanical rules but a living spirit that grows and moves in response to the development of the society.[17]

*Dharma* has two sides that are interdependent: the individual and the social. The conscience of the individual requires a guide, and one must be taught the way to realize one's purpose and to live according to spirit and not sense. The interests of society require equal attention. *Dharma,* on the social level, is that which holds together all living beings in a harmonious order. Virtue is conduct contributing to social welfare, and vice is its opposite. It is frequently insisted that the highest virtue consists in doing to others as you would be done by. Both the individual and the social virtues are included in what are called *nitya karmas,* or obligatory duties, which are cleanliness or *saucam,* good behavior and manners or *acharam,* social service or *panchamahyajnas,* and prayer and worship or *sandhyavandanam.* The *varnashrama dharma,* which deals with the caste system and the stages of the individual life, develops the detail about *Dharma* at the individual and social level.[18]

The concept of *Dharma* at the individual level recognizes four stages in each person's life. In the first stage of *Brahmacharya* (student phase), the obligations of temperance, sobriety, chastity, and social service are firmly established in the minds of the young. All have to pass through this discipline, irrespective of caste, class, wealth, or poverty. In the second stage of *Grahastha* or householder, the individual undertakes the obligations of family life, becoming a member of a social body and accepting its rights and obligations. Self-support, thrift, and hospitality are enjoined in this stage. Caste rules are relevant only to this stage. At this stage, the individual's energies and interests turn naturally outward. There are three fronts for satisfying human wants at this stage: one's family, one's vocation, and the community to which one belongs. Normally the person will be interested in all three. This is the time for satisfying the first three human wants: pleasure through the family primarily, success through the vocation, and duty through one's responsibilities as a citizen.[19]

In the third stage of *Vanaprastha* (retirement) the individual is required to check his or her attachment to worldly possessions, suppress all the conceits bred in through the accidents of the second stage (such as pride of birth or property, individual genius, or good luck), and cultivate a spirit of renunciation. It is the time for working out a philosophy into oneself, the time of transcending the senses to find and dwell at one with the timeless reality that underlies the dream of life in this natural world. Beyond retirement the final stage in which the goal is actually reached is the state of the *sannyas,* a disinterested servant of humanity who finds peace in the strength of spirit. A state of perfect harmony with the Eternal is reached, and the education of the human spirit terminates.[20]

## CASTE SYSTEM

The caste system is a unique feature of Indian culture. The caste rules relate to the social functions of individuals. According to Hinduism, a person's nature can be developed only by a concentration of one's personality at a particular point in the social order. Since human beings show one or the other of the three aspects of mental life (thought, feelings, and action) in a greater degree, the *dvijas* or the twice-born are distinguished into the three classes of men of thought, men of feeling, and men of action. Those in whom no one quality is particularly developed are the *Sudras.* The four castes correspond to the intellectual, militant, industrial, and unskilled workers, who are all members of one organic whole.[21]

Accordingly, Indian society has been divided into the fourfold classification of castes, hierarchically from higher to lower castes: (1) *Brahmins*—priests or seers who have such duties as that of teaching, preaching, assisting in the sacrificial processes, giving alms, and receiving gifts; (2) *Kashtryas*—protectors of life and treasure, identified with the administrative or the ruling classes; (3) *Vaisyas*—cultivators, traders, businesspeople, and herders; and (4) *Sudras*—artisan specialists such as carpenters, blacksmiths, and laborers. In the course of time, there developed a fifth group, ranked so low as to be considered outside and beneath the caste system itself. The members of this fifth "casteless" group are variously referred to as "Untouchables," "outcastes," "Scheduled Castes," or (by Gandhi) *Harijans,* "children of God." People in this group inherit the kinds of work that in India are considered least desirable, such as scavenging, slaughtering animals, leather tanning, and sweeping the streets and footpaths.[22]

Although the caste system began as a straightforward, functional division of Indian society, it was later misinterpreted by priests as permanent and immutable as the word of God. Accordingly, the caste system was justified in terms of the "immutable and inborn" qualities of individuals, the unchangeable result of "actions in previous incarnations" and the unalterable basis of Hindu religion.[23]

The particular caste a person belongs to is determined by birth. Each caste has its appropriate status, rights, and duties. There are detailed rules about communication and contact among people of different castes. A caste has considerable influence on the way of life of its members. Most important relations of life, above all marriage, take place within the caste. Castes have great power over their members. To break caste is to cut oneself off from one's group, which means from family, from friends, and from all of those who live in the same way. One who cuts oneself off has no hope of being adopted by another group—not only is ostracized by one's own group but will not be accepted even by a lower caste.[24] Thus, the caste is a major "significant other" influence in the Indian culture and continues to affect the day-to-day lives of millions of Hindus, especially in villages and small towns.

## SPIRIT OF TOLERANCE

An outstanding feature of Indian culture is its tradition of tolerance. Indian culture, because of the influence of Hinduism, believes in universal toleration and accepts all religions as true. Indian culture is comprehensive and suits the needs of everyone, irrespective of caste, creed, color, or sex. It has universal appeal and makes room for all. It has the modesty to admit the propriety of other points of view. This idea has been beautifully developed in the Jaina theory of *Syadvada* or the theory of *may be.* According to this theory no absolute affirmation or denial is possible. As all knowledge is probable and relative, the other person's point of view is as true as one's own. In other words, it suggests that one must show restraint in making judgments—a very healthy principle. One must know that one's judgments are true only partially and can by no means be regarded as true in absolute terms. This understanding and spirit of tolerance have been largely responsible for the advancement of Indian culture. This attitude has helped to bring together the divergent races with different languages and religious persuasions under a common culture.[25]

This brief exposition of Indian culture has shown its highly pluralistic and dynamic qualities. Through the examination of world view, reincarnation, *Dharma,* the caste system, and the spirit of tolerance, Indian culture has been seen to embody such basic values as synthesis *(samanvaya),* desire to know the truth *(satyajijnasa),* nonviolence *(ahimsa),* and above all the attitude of toleration. This view of Indian culture has further explained the role and influence of Hindu thought as it is manifest in Indian culture and has shown that the two are inseparable. What India needs is to realize herself, to broaden her spiritual heritage, not to rest upon the foundation already nobly erected by her own saints and scholars, but to continue along the same inspiring lines.[26]

## NOTES

1. Fersh, Seymour. *India and South Asia.* (New York: Macmillan, 1965), p. 1.

2. Fersh, pp. 1–3.

3. Fersh, p. 3.

4. Sreenivasa Murthy, H. V., and S. U. Kamath, *Studies in Indian Culture.* (Bombay: Asia Publishing House, 1973), pp. 4–5.

5. Smith, Huston. *The Religions of Man.* (New York: Harper & Row, 1958), p. 72.

6. Thomas, P. *Hindu Religion, Customs and Manners,* 3rd ed. (Bombay: D. B. Taraporevala Sons & Co., 1956), p. 1.

7. Murthy and Kamath, pp. 7–8.

8. Smith, pp. 27–28.

9. Katz, Elizabeth. *India in Pictures.* (New York: Sterling Publishing, 1969), pp. 36–37.

10. Smith, pp. 27–28.

11. Smith, p. 85.

12. Smith, p. 76.

13. Smith, p. 77.

14. Smith, p. 79.

15. Radhakrishnan, S. *Indian Religions.* (New Delhi: Vision Books Private Ltd., 1979), pp. 52–53.

16. Radhakrishnan, pp. 70–71.

17. Radhakrishnan, p. 61.

18. Radhakrishnan, p. 62.

19. Smith, p. 62.

20. Smith, pp. 62–63.

21. Radhakrishnan, pp. 63–64.

22. Chopra, S. N. *India: An Area Study.* (New Delhi: Vikas Publishing House Private Ltd., 1977), pp. 26–27.

23. Chopra, pp. 27–28.

24. Fersh, pp. 17–21.

25. Murthy and Kamath, p. 5.

26. Murthy and Kamath, p. 8.

# "... So Near the United States": Notes on Communication between Mexicans and North Americans

JOHN CONDON

"Poor Mexico," said Porfirio Diaz, "so far from God, so near the United States." In the years since Mexico's last pre-Revolutionary president said these words the nations on both sides of the border have been greatly altered. Some might speculate on the resulting changes in Mexico's proximity to the Lord, but none would deny that geographically and commercially Mexico has never been so near the United States. The cultural distance, however, is something else, for in many respects the cultural gaps between these societies are as great as ever. Thus when President Kennedy said during his highly successful visit to Mexico in 1962 that "geography has made us neighbors, tradition has made us friends," many Mexicans thought it more accurate to say that "geography has made us close but tradition has made us more distant than ever."

Not that there has been any shortage of contact between people of these two cultures. The fifteen hundred mile border that spans the continent is crossed in both directions by more people than any other international border on the globe. These include millions of tourists annually who venture south into Mexico to make up more than 80 percent

From *The Bridge,* Spring 1980. Reprinted by permission of the publisher. John Condon has taught at Northwestern University and the International Christian University in Tokyo. He is currently a communication consultant in San Diego, California.

of that nation's primary source of revenue, tourism. It also includes the countless numbers of workers, both legally admitted and undocumented, business people, students and tourists, too, who cross from Mexico into the United States. Quite apart from this daily traffic, the cultural presence of each society is to be found across the border. The capital city of Mexico is that nation's, and soon the world's, largest metropolis; but the second largest number of Mexicans reside in Los Angeles. And it is worth recalling that scarcely a century and a half ago half of the land that had been Mexico became a part of the United States, a fact remembered more in Mexico than north of the border. Intercultural contact is hardly a phenomenon of the jet age.

Information about and from each society has never been greater than one finds today. Studies show that the average Mexico City daily newspaper contains a greater percentage of news about the United States than the average *New York Times* reports about all the rest of the world combined. North American foods, fashions, products, and loan words are enough in evidence in the cities of Mexico to make the casual visitor overlook some significant differences in values and beliefs. Indeed, many veteran observers of relations between Mexicans and North Americans believe that the increase in superficial similarities actually contributes to culture-based misunderstandings.

Insights into contrasting cultural assumptions and styles of communication cannot be gained without an appreciation of the history and geography of the two societies. One quickly learns that where there are intersections, such as the major river that marks a good part of the border or the major war that literally gave shape to each nation, the interpretations and even the names are different in each society. The name "America" itself is one that many Mexicans feel should not be limited to the United States of America alone, particularly since culturally the "anglo" culture is a minority among the nations of the Americas. "North America" and "North American" may be more appreciated.

North Americans trace their history from the time of the first English settlers. The people already living on the continent possessed no great cities or monuments to rival anything in Europe, and they held little interest for the European colonists so long as they could be displaced and their land cultivated. The North American Indian has remained excluded from the shaping of the dominant culture of the new nation just as he had been excluded from the land. With political independence and the continuous arrival of immigrants, largely from Northern Europe, the nation took shape in a steady westward pattern. The outlook was to the future, to new land and new opportunities. The spirit was of optimism.

When the Spanish soldiers arrived in Mexico in the sixteenth century they found cities and temples of civilizations that had flourished for thousands of years. In what some have called a holy crusade, the Spanish attempted to destroy the old societies and reconstruct a new order on top. In religion, in language, in marriage, there was a fusion of Indian and European which was totally different from the pattern in the United States. While Cortés is no hero in Mexico—there are no statues of him anywhere in the country—the fusion of European and native American cultures is a source of great pride, not only in Mexico but extending throughout the Latin American republics. This is the spirit of *la raza* which serves in part to give a sense of identification with other Latin Americans and a sense of separateness from those of the anglo world.

There are other contrasts to be noted as well. The land that became the United States was for the most part hospitable and, for much of the country's history, seemingly endless. Less than a fifth of the land in Mexico, in contrast, is arable.

The images which the people on each side of the border hold of the other differ. Mexico's image of the United States was to a great extent shaped in Europe, formed at a time when European writers had little good to say about the anglo-American world. Even today when Mexicans speak of the ideals of freedom and democracy, their inspiration is more likely to be French than North American. The rivalry between England and Spain, compounded by the religious hostility between Protestants and Catholics, influenced in a comparable way the North American's image of Mexico.

Finally, by way of introduction, we should note that regional differences are pronounced and of importance in understanding the people of Mexico. Social and economic differences vary considerably, and even in language, with perhaps 150 different languages still spoken in the country, there are truly "many Mexicos." Thus it is not surprising that for years there has been a serious interest among Mexicans to find "the Mexican." Some say this search for identity began even before the Conquest, for the sixteenth century Spaniard was himself unsure of his identity: he arrived in Mexico less than 25 years after driving out the last of the Moors from his own homeland.

An early Adlerian analysis of "the Mexican" by Samuel Ramos found the essence of the Mexican national character in the *pelado,* "the plucked one," at the bottom of the pecking order. While the Ramos thesis has been considered over the years, some of the same themes of doubt and frustration and of a tragic outlook on life continue in contemporary Mexican interpretations.

The history of relations between the United States and Mexico has not been one of understanding and cooperation, though many persons on both sides of the border are working toward those ends. Even under the best of conditions and with the best of intentions, Mexicans and North Americans working together sometimes feel confused, irritated, distrustful. The causes lie not within either culture but rather can be best understood interculturally. Here are four perspectives.

## INDIVIDUALISM

In the North American value system are three central and interrelated assumptions about human beings. These are (1) that people, apart from social and educational influences, are basically the same; (2) that each person should be judged on his or her own individual merits; and (3) that these "merits," including a person's worth and character, are revealed through the person's actions. Values of equality and independence, constitutional rights, laws and social programs arise from these assumptions. Because a person's actions are regarded as so important, it is the comparison of accomplishments—Mr. X compared to Mr. X's father, or X five years ago compared to X today, or X compared to Y and Z—that provides a chief means of judging or even knowing a person.

In Mexico it is the uniqueness of the individual which is valued, a quality which is assumed to reside within each person and which is not necessarily evident through actions or achievements. That inner quality which represents the dignity of each person must be protected at all costs. Any action or remark that may be interpreted as a slight to the person's dignity is to be regarded as a grave provocation. Also, as every person is part of a larger family grouping, one cannot be regarded as a completely isolated individual.

This contrast, which is sometimes expressed as the distinction between "individualism" in the case of the North American, and "individuality" in the case of the Mexican, frequently leads to misunderstandings in intercultural encounters ranging from small talk to philosophical arguments.

Where a Mexican will talk about a person's inner qualities in terms of the person's soul or spirit *(alma* or *espíritu),* North Americans are likely to feel uncomfortable using such words to talk about people. They may regard such talk as vague or sentimental, the words seeming to describe something invisible and hence unknowable, or at the very least "too personal." The unwillingness to talk in this way only confirms the view held by many Mexicans that North Americans are insensitive. "Americans are corpses," said one Mexican.

Even questions about the family of a person one does not know well may discomfit many North Americans, since asking about a person's parents or brothers or sisters may also seem too personal. "I just don't know the person well enough to ask about his family," a North American might say, while the Mexican may see things just the opposite: "If I don't ask about the person's family, how will I really know him?"

The family forms a much less important part of an individual's frame of reference in the United States than is usually the case in Mexico. Neighbors, friends, or associates, even some abstract "average Ameri-

can," may be the basis for the comparison needed in evaluating oneself or others. "Keeping up with the Joneses" may be important in New York or Chicago, but keeping up with one's brother-in-law is more important in Mexico City. In the same way, the Mexican depends upon relatives or close friends to help "arrange things" if there is a problem, or to provide a loan. While this is by no means rare in the United States, the dominant values in the culture favor institutions which are seen as both efficient and fair.

So it is that tensions may arise between Mexicans and North Americans over what seems to be a conflict between trusting particular individuals or trusting abstract principles. In a business enterprise, the North American manager is likely to view the organization and its processes as primary, with the role of specific people being more or less supportive of that system. People can be replaced if need be; nobody is indispensable. When one places emphasis on a person's spirit or views an organization as if it were a family, however, then it seems just as clear that nobody can be exactly replaced by any other person.

Both North Americans and Mexicans may speak of the need to "respect" another person, but here too the meanings of the word respect (or *respeto)* differ somewhat across the cultures. In a study of associations with this word conducted in the United States and Mexico, it was found that North Americans regarded "respect" as bound up with the values of equality, fair play and the democratic spirit. There were no emotional overtones. One respects others as one might respect the law. For Mexicans, however, "respect" was found to be an emotionally charged word involving pressures of power, possible threat and often a love-hate relationship. The meaning of respect arises from powerful human relationships such as between father and son or *patrón* and *péon,* not a system of principles to which individuals voluntarily commit themselves.

## STRAIGHT TALK

Last year the leaders of both the United States and France visited Mexico. A prominent writer for the distinguished Mexican daily, *Excelsior,* commented on their visits and on the words they spoke. Interpreting the impressions they made on Mexicans, the writer alluded to cultural differences. President Carter was seen as following the anglo-saxon values of his culture as he spoke bluntly of realities. President Giscard d'Estaing, as a product of a cultural tradition which was more familiar to that of Mexico, spoke in a style far more grand, and if his words were in some way further from realities they were at least more beautiful. When all was said and done and the two leaders returned to their capitals, the writer concluded, the world had been little changed as a result of their visits but the French leader's words had at least made his Mexican listeners feel better for a while.

The ceremonial speaking of heads of state actually shows fewer differences between Mexican and North American styles than do routine conversations. It is not simply that two styles, plain and fancy, contrast; rather, persons from each culture will form judgments about the personality and character of the other as a result. The Mexican is far more likely to flatter, tease or otherwise attempt to charm another than is the North American whose culture has taught him to distrust or poke fun at anyone who "really lays it on."

Often the problem is heightened when there is a difference in the sex, status, or age of the two persons in conversation. Mexicans may want to maximize those differences while North Americans often make a great effort to minimize them. North Americans may at present be most sensitive to the way in which a businessman talks to a businesswoman, lest he be accused of "sexism," but the same values apply to "making too much" of one's age or status. Thus the very style which is called for in one culture may be regarded as quite uncalled for in the other culture. North Americans are often suspicious of one who seems effusive in praise; they are also likely to make light of one who seems too enamored of titles. Mexicans, on the other hand, value one who has the wit and charm to impress another. Nor are titles or other indications of one's status, age, or ability to be slighted. The owner of an auto repair shop may defer to a mechanic who

is older and more experienced as *maestro;* doctors, lawyers and other professional people will take their titles seriously. To make light of them is to challenge one's dignity.

## THE TRUTH

During the world congress held in Mexico for the International Women's Year, some first time visitors experienced the kind of problem that many North Americans have long complained about in Mexico. The visitors would be told one thing only to discover that what they were told seemed to bear no resemblance to the facts. A delegate who would ask where a meeting was being held might be given clear directions, but upon reaching the destination she would find no such meeting. "It was not that the Mexicans were unfriendly or unhelpful—just wrong!" North American managers working with Mexicans have sometimes voiced similar complaints: An employee says something is finished when in fact it has not even been begun.

Rogelio Díaz-Guerrero, head of the psychology department at the National University of Mexico and a foremost interpreter of Mexican behavior patterns, offers this explanation. There are two kinds of "realities" which must be distinguished, objective and interpersonal. Some cultures tend to treat everything in terms of the objective sort of reality; this is characteristic of the United States. Other cultures tend to treat things in terms of interpersonal relations, and this is true of Mexico. This distinction, we may note, bears some resemblance to the distinction made by the *Excelsior* columnist.

Viewed from the Mexican perspective, a visitor asks somebody for information which that person doesn't know. But wanting to make the visitor happy and enjoy a few pleasant moments together, the Mexican who was asked does his best to say something so that for a short while the visitor is made happy. It is not that Mexicans have a monopoly on telling another person what that person wants to hear: Perhaps in all cultures the truth is sometimes altered slightly to soften the impact of a harsh word or to show deference to one's superior. It is the range of situations in which this occurs in Mexico and the relatively sharper contrast of "truth-telling" standards in U.S.-Mexican encounters that is so notable.

In value, if not always in fact, North Americans have given special importance to telling the truth. The clearest object lessons in the lives of the nation's two legendary heroes, Washington and Lincoln, concern honesty, while the presidents who have been most held in disrepute, Harding and Nixon, are held up to scorn because of their dishonesty.

Francisco Gonzales Pineda has written at length about lying. Starting from premises to those offered by Samuel Ramos mentioned earlier, including the idealization of manliness of the *pelado,* Gonzalez Pineda says that a Mexican must be able to lie if he is to be able to live without complete demoralization. He says that general recognition of this has made the lie in Mexico almost an institution. He describes variations of lies in different regions of Mexico, including the capital in which he says the use of the lie is socially acceptable in all its forms. He contrasts the Mexican style of lie to that which is used by North Americans. In the United States the lie is little used aggressively or defensively or to express fantasy. The more common form of defense is the expression of the incomplete truth or an evasion of truth. There are stereotyped expressions which are purposefully ambiguous and impersonal, so lacking in emotional content that they do not conflict with the emotional state of the liar.

Whether or not one supports the interpretation of Gonzalez Pineda, an examination of difficulties between North Americans and Mexicans is to be found in the broad area of matching words, deeds and intentions. The North American in a daily routine has a much narrower range of what he considers permissible than is found in similar situations in Mexico.

## TIME

If a culture is known by the words exported, as one theory has it, then Mexico may be best known as the land of *mañana*. Differences in the treatment of time may not be the most serious source of mis-understanding between people of the two cultures but it is surely the most often mentioned. Several issues are actually grouped under the general label of "time."

In Edward Hall's influential writings on time across culture, he has distinguished between "mono-chronic" (M-time) and "polychronic" (P-time) treatments of time; these correspond to the North American and Mexican modes respectively. M-time values take care of "one thing at a time." Time is lineal, segmented. (American football is a very "M-time" game.) It may not be that time is money but M-time treats it that way, with measured precision. M-time people like neat scheduling of appointments and are easily distracted and often very distressed by interruptions.

In contrast, P-time is characterized by many things happening at once, and with a much "looser" notion of what is "on time" or "late." Interruptions are routine, delays to be expected. Thus it is not so much that putting things off until *mañana* is valued, as some Mexican stereotypes would have it, but that human activities are not expected to proceed like clock-work. It should be noted in this regard that the North American treatment of time appears to be the more unusual on a world scale. This writer discovered that even in Japan, a culture not known for its imprecision or indolence, U.S. business people were seen by Japanese colleagues as much too time-bound, driven by schedules and deadlines which in turn thwarted an easy development of human relationships.

North Americans express special irritation when Mexicans seem to give them less than their undivided attention. When a young woman bank teller, awaiting her superior's approval for a check to be cashed, files her nails and talks on the phone to her boyfriend, or when one's taxi driver stops en route to pick up a friend who seems to be going in the same direction, North Americans become very upset. North Americans interpret such behavior as showing a lack of respect and a lack of "professionalism," but the reason may lie more in the culturally different treatment of time.

Newly arrived residents seem to learn quickly to adjust their mental clocks to *la hora Mexicana* when it comes to anticipating the arrival of Mexican guests at a party; an invitation for 8:00 may produce guests by 9:00 or 10:00. What takes more adjusting is the notion that visitors may be going to another party first and yet another party afterwards. For many North Americans this diminishes the importance attached to their party, much as the teller's action diminishes the respect shown the customer. The counterpart of this, Mexicans' irritation with the North American time sense, is in their dismay over an invitation to a party which states in advance the time when the party will be over. This or subtler indications of the time to terminate a meeting before it has even gotten underway serve as further proof that Americans are slaves to the clock and don't really know how to enjoy themselves.

The identification of common problem areas in communication across cultures is always incomplete; there are always other interpretations and, since culture is a whole, the selection of "factors" or "themes" is never completely shown in its entire context. Nevertheless, a common effort to appreciate differences across cultures is essential, particularly in the relations between people of the United States and Mexico.

It is not an exaggeration to say that if North Americans cannot learn to communicate more effectively with Mexicans, our capacity to function in cultures elsewhere in the world will be doubted. Many of the well-springs of Mexican culture flow freely elsewhere, not only in other Latin American states but in such distant lands as the Philippines.

## CONCEPTS AND QUESTIONS FOR CHAPTER 2

**1.** What cultural variables in Japanese culture might affect intercultural communication between Japanese and Americans most seriously?

**2.** How might Japanese respect for authority contribute to difficulties in intercultural communication?

**3.** What conclusions can be reached about cultural influence on intercultural communication with the People's Republic of China?

**4.** What are some of the characteristics of the People's Republic of China that affect intercultural communication?

**5.** What would be different about communicating with someone who lives in the People's Republic of China? How does this factor differ from the patterns of intercultural communication discussed earlier in this chapter?

**6.** How might cultural differences in Arabic and North American friendliness behaviors affect intercultural communication?

**7.** What are the basic differences in the role of religion in Arabic and North American cultures? How can these differences affect intercultural interactions?

**8.** What unique perspectives of world view are inherent in the Hindu culture of India?

**9.** How might the Hindu perspective of the universe and of humankind's role in the universe affect intercultural communication between Indians and North Americans?

**10.** How do differences in thought patterns affect intercultural communication?

**11.** In what areas of interaction are there major problems between Mexicans and North American cultures? How can these differences affect intercultural interactions?

**12.** How do North American and Mexican views of individualism differ? How might these differences affect intercultural communication?

## SUGGESTED READINGS

Almaney, A. J. and A. J. Alwan. *Communicating with the Arabs: A Handbook for the Business Executive.* Prospect Heights, Ill.: Waveland Press, 1982. The aim of this book is to "enable the businessman to develop a better understanding of the Arabs." Specifically, the authors focus on the fundamental forces that play a major role in influencing Arab thought and actions. Although the book is intended primarily for the businessperson, it can be used profitably by others interested in intercultural communication.

Bauer, W. *China and the Search for Happiness: Recurring Themes in Four Thousand Years of Chinese Cultural History.* New York: Seabury Press, 1976. This impressive volume traces the sources of Chinese culture over the last 4,000 years. The impact of history, religion, and government is treated in great detail.

Delgado, M. "Hispanic cultural values: Implications for groups." *Small Group Behavior* 12 (1981), 69–80. This article presents a brief overview of the literature on Hispanic groups, describes a conceptual framework for examining value orientations within the Hispanic culture, and presents a series of recommendations for group leaders interested in developing Hispanic groups.

Diaz-Guerrero, R. *The Psychology of the Mexican: Culture and Personality.* Austin: University of Texas Press, 1967. In an effort to understand and describe the behavior of the Mexican, Diaz-Guerrero looks at the relationship between culture and personality. He examines concepts such as family structure, interpersonal relationships, motivation, values, respect, and status.

Fallows, J. "The Japanese are different from you and me." *The Atlantic Monthly* (September 1986), 35–41. This article outlines various differences between the Japanese and Americans in a delightful manner. Politics, pornography, racism, and other topics are discussed.

Hingley, R. *The Russian Mind.* Woodbury, N.Y.: The Bodley Head, 1977. This book attempts to look at the Russian personality, character, and mentality. Hingley focuses on the Russian as a person, not on Russia as a country. He is concerned with how Russians show emotion and with their attitudes, values, and behavior. In addition, some chapters examine communication systems and group consciousness.

Lenero-Otero, L., ed. *Beyond the Nuclear Family Model: Cross-Cultural Perspective.* Beverly Hills, Calif.: Sage Publications, 1977. This book is concerned with the concept of the nuclear family in a variety of countries. A special feature of this collection is the series of articles comparing various families across selected cultures.

Neuliep, J. W. and V. Hazelton, Jr. "A cross-cultural comparison of Japanese and American persuasive strategy selection." *International Journal of Intercultural Relations* 9 (1985), 389–404. The authors reveal that Japanese and American cultures differ significantly in the selection of compliance-gaining messages. In addition, the Marwell and Schmitt typology and the Schenck-Hamlin, Wiseman, and Georgacarakos typology are compared to one another, and the strengths and weaknesses of spontaneous elicitation procedures versus checklist procedures are examined.

Nomura, N. and D. Barnlund. "Patterns of interpersonal criticism in Japan and the United States." *International Journal of Intercultural Relations* 7 (1983), 1–18. Preliminary interviews were conducted to look at patterns of interpersonal criticism in Japan and the United States. An Interpersonal Criticism Questionnaire examined sources of dissatisfaction, the status of communication partners, and modes of giving criticism. The results showed a significant difference between the cultures but no significant difference between the sexes. Both cultures favored expressing dissatisfaction directly. The Japanese expressed criticism passively and Americans more actively. The Japanese adapted messages to the person involved, while the Americans adapted messages to the reasons behind the provocations.

Reischauer, E. O. *The Japanese.* Cambridge, Mass.: Harvard University Press, 1972. This book contains a picture of the background culture and values of Japan. Reischauer concentrates on the social organization, values, political system, and international relationships of the Japanese.

Roberts, G. O. *Afro-Arab Fraternity: The Roots of Terramedia.* Beverly Hills, Calif.: Sage Publications, 1980. Roberts discusses the Middle East and Africa as a single unit, focusing on its geography, history, religion, social structures, and ethnic orientations in order to understand the common postcolonial problem faced by the countries in this region of the world.

Ross, S. R., ed. *Views across the Border: The U.S. and Mexico.* Albuquerque: University of New Mexico Press, 1978. Ross has collected 17 essays that explore the U.S.-Mexican border area in terms of psychology, politics, culture, migration, social class, and personality development.

Stein, H. F. "Adversary symbiosis and complementary group dissociation: An analysis of the U.S./U.S.S.R. conflict." *International Journal of Intercultural Relations* 6 (1982), 55–83. This article examines the psychological basis of the reciprocal stereotyping that governs U.S./Soviet perceptions of each other. It explores the influence of American and Russo-Soviet national psychology and cultural history on present perceptions, expectations, and attitudes.

Wolfson, K. and W. Barnett Pearce. "A cross-cultural comparison of the implications of self-disclosure on conversational logics." *Communication Quarterly* 31 (1983), 249–255. The differences in cultural acts are difficult to describe without using the perspective of one's own culture. "Transcultural concepts" are designed to avoid the ethnocentric attitude. The transcultural concept of "logical force" is discussed between North American and Chinese subjects.

## ADDITIONAL READINGS

Barnlund, D. C. "Intercultural encounters: The management of compliments by Japanese and Americans." *Journal of Cross-Cultural Psychology* 16 (1985), 9–26.

Bond, M., K. Leung, and W. Kwok Choi. "How does cultural collectivism operate? The impact of task and maintenance contributions of reward distribution." *Journal of Cross-Cultural Psychology* 13 (1982), 186–200.

Bruneau, T., R. E. Cambra, and D. W. Klopf, "Communication apprehension: Its incidence in Guam and elsewhere." *Communication* 9 (1980), 46–51.

Bush, R. and J. Townsend. *One Peoples Republic of China: A Basic Handbook.* New York: Learning Resources in International Studies, 1982.

Chan, M. K. M. and D. W. Lee. "Chinatown Chinese: A linguistic and historical reevaluation." *Amerasia Journal* 8 (1981), 111–131.

Condon, J. C. *With Respect to the Japanese.* Yarmouth, Me.: Intercultural Press, 1984.

Goldberg, H. "Introduction: Culture and ethnicity in the study of Israeli society." *Ethnic Groups* 1 (1977), 163–186.

Heisey, D. R. "A Swedish approach to international communication." *Topics in Culture Learning,* vol. 2. Honolulu: East-West Center, 1974, 41–49.

Helm, C. "The German concept of order: The social and physical setting." *Journal of Popular Culture* 13 (1979), 67–80.

Kamikawa, I. M. "Elderly: A Pacific/Asian perspective." *Aging* (July/August 1981), 2–9.

Kaufman, M. "Reporting from Africa." *The Bridge: A Review of Cultural Affairs and International Training* (Spring 1981), 10–11, 39–40.

Kitzinger, S. *Women as Mothers: How They See Themselves in Different Cultures.* New York: Random House, 1979.

Korzenny, F. and K. Neuendorf. "The perceived reality of television and aggressive predispositions among children in Mexico." *International Journal of Intercultural Relations* 7 (1983), 33–51.

Kreger, R. O., L. A. Wood, and T. Beam. "Are the rules of address universal?" *Journal of Cross-Cultural Psychology* 15 (1984), 259–272.

Liebman, S. *Exploring the Latin American Mind.* Chicago: Nelson-Hall, 1976.

Marsella, A. J., D. Kinzie, and P. Gordon. "Ethnic variations in the expression of depression." *Journal of Cross-Cultural Psychology* 4 (1973), 435–458.

Mason, A. *Ports of Entry: Ethnic Impressions.* New York: Harcourt Brace Jovanovich, 1984.

Mernissi, F. *Beyond the Veil: Male-Female Dynamics in a Modern Muslim Society.* New York: John Wiley, 1975.

Patai, R. *The Arab Mind.* New York: Scribner's Sons, 1973.

Penner, L. A. and T. Any. "A comparison of American and Vietnamese value systems." *Journal of Social Psychology* 101 (1977), 187–204.

Pratt, W. F. *Privacy in Britain.* London: Lewisburg Bucknell University Press, 1979.

Reynolds, B. K. "A cross-cultural study of values of Germans and Americans." *International Journal of Intercultural Relations* 8 (1984), 269–278.

Rohrlich, B. L. "Contrasting rules: Eastern and Western European women." *International Journal of Intercultural Relations* 3 (1979), 487–496.

Rorer, B. A. and R. C. Ziller. "Iconic communication values among American and Polish students." *Journal of Cross-Cultural Psychology* 13 (1982), 352–361.

Rowland, D. *Japanese Business Etiquette: A Practical Guide to Success with the Japanese.* New York: Warner Books, Inc., 1985.

Schumacher, H. E. and G. M. Guthrie. "Culture and counseling in the Philippines." *International Journal of Intercultural Relations* 10 (1984), 241–253.

Shumpei, K. "Some principles governing the thought and behavior of Japanese." *Journal of Japanese Studies* 8 (1982), 5–17.

Shuter, R. "Initial interaction in interracial and intraracial interactions." *Journal of Social Psychology* (1982), 22–28.

Smith, H. *The Russians.* New York: Ballantine Books, 1976.

Tefft, S. K., ed. *Secrecy: A Cross-Cultural Perspective.* New York: Human Sciences Press, 1980.

Ting-Toomey, S. "Japanese communication patterns: Insider versus the outsider perspective." *World Communication* 15 (1986), 113–126.

Wright, P. "Doing business in Islamic markets." *Harvard Business Review* 59 (1981), 34–66.

# 3

# Nondominant Domestic Cultures

In Chapter 2 we focused on international cultures, that is, cultures which exist beyond the immediate borders of the United States. There are also numerous nondominant cultures, subcultures, and deviant subgroups of various religious, economic, ethnic, age, and racial compositions within U.S. society itself, however, that often bring alien and diverse experiences to a communication encounter. Because these social communities are much more visible than foreign cultures, Americans often take their presence for granted. Yet, if you do not understand the unique experiences of these groups, you can encounter serious communication problems. The articles in this chapter, therefore, will examine some of the cultural experiences inherent in a few of the nondominant communities in the United States. Admittedly there are many more of these social communities than the ones included in our analysis. Our selection, however, was based on three considerations. First, limited space and the necessity for efficiency prohibited a long list of subcultures and subgroups. Second, we decided to include those social communities that are often in conflict with the larger society. And third, we wanted to emphasize the subcultures and subgroups that you are likely to interact with. To this end, we selected some of the major subcommunities of the United States.

Edith A. Folb in "Who's Got the Room at the Top?" discusses the concept of *intra*cultural communication. This is communication between members of the same dominant culture who hold slightly differing values. Folb sees the crucial characteristics of this form of communication as the interrelationships of power, dominance, and nondominance as they are manifest in the particular cultures. She carefully examines these variables as they apply to blacks, native Americans, Chicanos, women, the aged, the physically challenged, and other groups that have been "caste marked and more often negatively identified when it comes to issues of power, dominance, and social control."

119

The next article looks at "style" as a form of intercultural communication. Style is the *way* in which individuals express an attitude about themselves and their culture. Blacks, like other cultural groups, have a style that says something about their view of the environment in which they live. Their style "is more self-conscious, more assertive, more aggressive, and more focused on the individual than is the style of the larger society of which blacks are part." These are just some of the differences between black and white styles. Thomas Kochman examines these differences in detail by looking at how both groups communicate their styles in casual, everyday contexts and on the playing field in "Black Style in Communication." By understanding these differences we may be able to appreciate the axiom that "different is not better or worse, but only different."

The U.S. population is becoming older. For the first time in history, more than half of the population is over 35 years of age. As this trend continues, new social problems emerge that must be solved to prevent an age versus youth division in our society. Carl W. Carmichael, in his essay "Intercultural Perspectives of Aging," asserts that aging presents both a communication and a cultural problem because the aging process is related to the beliefs, attitudes, and stereotypes about aging found within the culture and to the interaction patterns prevalent in the culture. Carmichael then examines these aspects of the U.S. culture and compares them to these aspects of the Japanese culture. Since the increasing age of the population is a new cultural experience for the United States, the culture must adapt and develop processes to accommodate the increasing proportion of its elderly members.

In recent years it has become apparent that disabled persons are a co-culture in our society. While there are approximately 11 million disabled Americans between the ages of 16 and 64, they often find themselves either cut off from or misunderstood by the dominant culture. The next essay by Dawn Braithwaite looks at some of the reasons for this isolation in "Viewing Persons with Disabilities As a Culture." More specifically, she examines how disabled persons view their communication relationships with able-bodied persons. Braithwaite interviewed fifty-seven physically disabled adults, and she learned that they go through a process of redefinition. She found that redefinition involves four steps: (1) redefinition of the disabled as members of a "new" culture; (2) redefinition of self by the disabled; (3) redefinition of disability for the disabled; and (4) redefinition of disability for the dominant culture. By becoming familiar with these steps, we can improve our communication with members of the disabled co-culture.

Recently much attention has been paid to a social community previously taken for granted. Because women are so much a part of one's perceptual field, and hence part of one's daily life, it was seldom conceived that the experience of being female was a viable area of investigation. The resurgence of feminism in the last decade has, however, prompted a re-examination of what it means to be a member of that particular social community. And particularly how that community might be different from the male-dominated community.

One of the major differences between these two communities is how they communicate. These differences, and some of the reasons behind them, are the major concern of the article by Judy C. Pearson, "Gender and Communication." She points out how gender and communication are related. Pearson also traces how gender differences begin to be formed very early in life and treats verbal and nonverbal patterns of communication in detail. Pearson also examines the problems created by variations in communication and perception. Stereotyping and male bias are examples of some of the more common problems impeding gender communication.

Randall E. Majors in his monograph "The Nonverbal Elements of a Gay Culture," offers innumerable insights into the cultural experience of the homosexual. There can be little doubt that in recent years the gay culture has emerged as one of the most vocal and visible groups on the American scene. It has, as do most co-cultures, special patterns of communication. Majors investigates the nonverbal dimensions of these patterns. He has selected nonverbal communication as it relates to the gay neighborhood, gay social institutions, gay symbology, gay costumery, and gay "cruising" behavior. From this specific perspective, we can gain some insight into both the experiences and communication styles of the gay community.

# Who's Got the Room at the Top? Issues of Dominance and Nondominance in Intracultural Communication

EDITH A. FOLB

"If a phenomenon is important, it is perceived, and, being perceived, it is labeled." So notes Nathan Kantrowitz, sociologist and student of language behavior. Nowhere is Kantrowitz's observation more apparent than in that realm of communication studies concerned with the correlates and connections between culture and communication—what the editors of this text have termed "intercultural communication." Our contemporary technology has brought us into both literal and voyeuristic contact with diverse cultures and customs, from the Stone Age Tasaday to the computer age Japanese. Our domestic liberation movements, moreover, have forced upon our consciousness the existence and needs of a multiplicity of groups within our own nation. So, the phenomenon of culture-linked communication is pervasively before us. And, as scholars concerned with culture and communication, we have tried to identify and characterize what we see. This attempt to "label the goods," as it were, has generated a profusion of semantic labels and categories—international communication, cross-cultural communication, intercultural communica-

This original essay appeared in print for the first time in the third edition. All rights reserved. Permission to reprint must be obtained from the publisher and the author. Professor Folb teaches at San Francisco State University.

tion, intracultural communication, trans-racial communication, interracial communication, interethnic communication. What we perceive to be important, we label.

Some may chide us for our penchant for classifications—an example of Aristotelian excessiveness, they may say. However, I see it as a genuine attempt to understand what we do individually and collectively, what we focus on within the field of communication studies. I believe this effort to characterize what we do serves a useful function: It continually prods us to examine and expand our vision of what culture-linked communication is, and, at the same time, it helps us bring into sharper focus the dimensions and differences within this area of study. As Samovar and Porter (1982) remind us, "There is still a great need to specify the nature of intercultural communication and to recognize various viewpoints that see the phenomenon somewhat differently" (p. 2). It is my intention in this essay to attempt what the editors of this text suggest, to look at the correlates and connections between culture and communication from a different point of view, one that examines the properties and issues of dominance and nondominance in communicative exchange. The essay is speculative and sometimes polemical. And the focus of my interest and discussion is the realm of intracultural communication.

## THE CONCEPT OF INTRACULTURAL COMMUNICATION

The label "intracultural communication" is not unknown within the field of communication studies, although it is one that has not been widely used. Sitaram and Cogdell (1976) have identified intracultural communication as "the type of communication that takes place between members of the same dominant culture, but with slightly differing values" (p. 28). They go on to explain that there are groups ("subcultures") within the dominant culture who hold a minimal number of values that differ from the mainstream, as well as from other subgroups. These differences are not sufficient to

identify them as separate cultures, but diverse enough to set them apart from each other and the culture at large. "Communication between members of such subcultures is *intracultural communication*" (Sitaram and Cogdell, 1976, p. 28).

In another vein, Sarbaugh (1979) sees intracultural communication as an indicator of the degree of cultural experience shared (or not shared) by two people—the more culturally homogeneous the participants, the greater the level of "intraculturalness" surrounding the communicative act. For Sitaram and Cogdell, then, intracultural communication is a phenomenon that operates within a given culture among its members; for Sarbaugh, it is a measure of homogeneity that well may transcend country or culture.

Like Sitaram and Cogdell, I see intracultural communication as a phenomenon that functions within a single, designated culture. However, like Sarbaugh, I am concerned with the particular variables within that context that importantly influence the degree and kind of cultural homogeneity or heterogeneity that can and does exist among members of the culture. Furthermore, the variables of particular interest to me are those that illuminate and underscore the interrelationship of power, dominance, and nondominance in a particular culture.[1] Finally, I believe that the concept of hierarchy, as it functions within a culture, has a deep impact on matters of power, dominance, and nondominance and, therefore, on both the form and content of intracultural communication.

As a backdrop for the discussion of dominance and nondominance in an intracultural context, I would like to formulate a frame of reference within which to view the discussion.

## A FRAME OF REFERENCE FOR INTRACULTURAL COMMUNICATION

### Society and Culture

Thomas Hobbes, the seventeenth century political philosopher, left us an intriguing legacy in his work, *Leviathan*. He posited a hypothetical starting point for humankind's march to political and social organization. He called it "the state of nature." In this presocietal state, the biggest club ruled. Kill or be killed was the prevailing modus operandi. Somewhere along the evolutionary road, our ancestors began to recognize a need to change their ways—if any of them were to survive for very long. The principle of enlightened self-interest became the name of the game. Our forebears, however grudgingly, began to curb their inclination to kill, maim, steal, or otherwise aggress upon others and joined together for mutual survival and benefit. The move was one of expediency, not altruism. "Do unto others as you would have them do unto you," whatever its religious import, is a reiteration of the principle of enlightened self-interest.

So, this aggregate of beings came together in order to survive, and, in coming together, gave up certain base instincts, drives, and predilections. "Society" was formed. Those who may scoff at this postulated state of nature need only remember back to the United States' final pullout from Vietnam. The media showed us, in all too brutal detail, the rapidity with which a society disintegrates and we return to the force of the club.

But let us continue with the telling of humankind's tale. It was not sufficient merely to form society; it must be maintained. Controls must be established to ensure its stability. Thus, the social contract was enacted. It was, indeed, the social contract that ensured mutual support, protection, welfare, and survival for the society's members.

However, social maintenance and control did not ensure the perpetuation of the society as an intact entity, carrying along its cumulative and collective experiences, knowledge, beliefs, attitudes, the emergent relationship of self to other, to the group, to the universe, to matters of time and space. That is, it did not ensure the perpetuation of society's accoutrements—its culture. Institutions and structures were needed to house, as it were, the trappings of culture. So, culture was not only embodied in the precepts passed on from one generation to another, but also in the artifacts created by society to safeguard its culture. Looked at in a different light, culture is both a blueprint for con-

tinued societal survival as well as the pervasive cement that holds the social mosaic together. Culture daily tells us and shows us how to be in the universe, and it informs future generations how to be.[2]

From the moment we begin life in this world, we are instructed in the cultural ways that govern and hold together our society, ways that ensure its perpetuation. Indeed, the social contract that binds us to our society and our culture from the moment of birth is neither of our own choice nor of our own design. For example, we are labeled by others almost immediately—John, Sandra, Pearl, David. Our genders are determined at once and we are, accordingly, swaddled in appropriate colors and treated in appropriate ways.[3]

As we grow from infancy to childhood, the socialization process is stepped up and we rapidly internalize the rules of appropriate and inappropriate societal behavior. Religion, education, recreation, health care, and many other cultural institutions reinforce our learning, shape and regulate our behavior and thought so they are orderly and comprehensible to other members of our society. Through the socialization process the human animal is transformed into the social animal. Thus, society is maintained through instruction and indoctrination in the ways of the culture.

But the question that pricks and puzzles the mind is: Whose culture is passed on? Whose social order is maintained? Whose beliefs and values are deemed appropriate? Whose norms, mores, and folkways are invoked?

## Hierarchy, Power, and Dominance

In most societies, as we know them, there is a hierarchy of status and power. By its very nature, hierarchy implies an ordering process, a sense of the evaluative marketing of those being ordered. Our own vernacular vocabulary abounds with references to hierarchy and concomitant status and power: "top dog," "top banana," "king pin," "king of the mountain."

High status and attendant power may be accorded to those among us who are seen or believed to be great warriors or hunters, those invested with magical, divine, or special powers, those who are deemed wise, or those who are in possession of important, valued, and/or vital societal resources and goods. Of course, power and high status are not necessarily—or even usually— accorded to these specially designated members of the society in some automatic fashion. Power, control, and subsequent high status are often forcibly wrested from others and forcibly maintained. Not everyone abides by the social contract, and strong-arm rule often prevails, as conquered, colonized, and enslaved people know too well.

Whatever the basis for determining the hierarchy, the fact of its existence in a society assures the evolution and continued presence of a power elite—those at the top of the social hierarchy who accrue and possess what the society deems valuable or vital. And, in turn, the presence of a power elite ensures an asymmetrical relationship among the members of the society. In fact, power is often defined as the ability to get others to do what you want and the resources to force them to do your bidding if they resist—the asymmetrical relationship in its extreme form.

But the perpetuation of the power elite through force is not the most effective or efficient way of ensuring one's position at the top of the hierarchy. It is considerably more effective to institute, encourage, and/or perpetuate those aspects of culture—knowledge, experiences, beliefs, values, patterns of social organization, artifacts—that subtly and manifestly reinforce and ensure the continuation of the power elite and its asymmetrical relationship within the society. Though we may dismiss Nazism as a malignant ideology, we should attend to the fact that Hitler well understood the maintenance of the power elite through the manipulation and control of culture—culture as propaganda.

Though I would not imply that all power elites maintain themselves in such an overtly manipulative way, I would at least suggest that the powerful in many societies—our own included—go to great lengths to maintain their positions of power and what those positions bring them. And to that end, they support, reinforce, and, indeed, create those particular cultural precepts and artifacts that are likely to guarantee their continued power. To the extent that the culture reflects implicitly or expressly the needs and desires of the power elite to sustain itself, it becomes a vehicle for propaganda. Thus, cultural precepts and artifacts that govern such matters as social organization and behavior, values, beliefs, and the like can often be seen as rules and institutions that sustain the few at the expense of the many.

So, we come back to the question of whose rules, whose culture? I would suggest that when we in communication studies refer to the "dominant culture" we are, in fact, not talking about numbers. That is why the label "minorities" is misleading when we refer to cultural groups within the larger society. Blacks in South Africa and women in the United States are not numerical minorities—but they are not members of the power elite either. In fact, when we talk about the concept of dominant culture, we are really talking about power—those who *dominate* culture, those who historically or traditionally have had the most persistent and far-reaching impact on culture, on what we think and say, on what we believe and do in our society. We are talking about the culture of the minority and, by extension, the structures and institutions (social, political, economic, legal, religious, and so on) that maintain the power of this minority. Finally, we are talking about rules of appropriate and inappropriate behavior, thought, speech, and action for the many that preserve power for the few. Dominant culture, therefore, significantly reflects the precepts and artifacts of those who dominate culture and is not necessarily, or even usually, a reference to numbers, but to power.

So, coming full circle, I would suggest that our socialization process, our social introduction to this aggregate of people who form society, is an introduction to a rule-governed milieu of asymmetrical societal organization and relationship, and the communicative behaviors and practices found there are likewise asymmetrical in nature. As the witticism goes, "All men (perhaps even women) are created equal—some are just more equal than others."

Given this frame of reference, I would now like to explore some definitions and concepts that, I believe, emerge from this perspective. It is my hope that the discussion will provide the reader with another way to look at intracultural communication.

## A NOMENCLATURE FOR INTRACULTURAL COMMUNICATION

### The Concept of Nondominance

As already indicated, I view intracultural communication as a phenomenon that operates within a given cultural context. However, my particular focus, as suggested, is not a focus on numbers but an attention to dominance, nondominance, and power in the cultural setting. That is, how do nondominant groups intersect and interact with the dominant culture membership (with those who enact the precepts and support the institutions and systems of the power elite)? For purposes of discussion and analysis, I will take most of my examples from the geopolitical configuration called the United States.

By "nondominant groups" I mean those constellations of people who have not historically or traditionally had continued access to or influence upon or within the dominant culture's (that is, those who dominate culture) social, political, legal, economic, and/or religious structures and institutions. Nondominant groups include people of color, women, gays, the physically challenged,[4] and the aged, to name some of the most prominent. I use the expression "nondominant" to characterize these people because, as suggested, I am referring to power and dominance, not numbers and dominance. Within the United States, those most likely to hold and control positions of real—not token—power and those who have the greatest potential ease of access to power and high status are still generally white, male, able-bodied, heterosexual, and youthful in appearance if not in age.[5]

Nondominant people are also those who, in varying degrees and various ways, have been "invisible" within the society of which they are a part and at the same time bear a visible caste mark. Furthermore, it is this mark of caste identity that is often consciously or habitually assigned low or negative status by members of the dominant culture.

The dimensions of invisibility and marked visibility are keen indicators of the status hierarchy in a given society. In his book, *The Invisible Man*, Ralph Ellison instructs us in the lesson that nondominant people—in this instance, black people—are figuratively "invisible." They are seen by the dominant culture as no one, nobody and therefore go unacknowledged and importantly unperceived.[6] Furthermore, nondominant peoples are often relegated to object status rather than human status. They are viewed as persons of "no consequence," literally and metaphorically. Expressions such as, "If you've seen one, you've seen them all"; "They all look alike to me"; "If you put a bag over their heads, it doesn't matter who you screw" attest to this level of invisibility and dehumanization of nondominant peoples, such as people of color or women. Indeed, one need only look at the dominant culture's slang repertory for a single nondominant group, women, to see the extent of this object status: "tail," "piece of ass," "side of beef," "hole," "gash," "slit," and so on.

At the same time that nondominant peoples are socially invisible, they are often visibly caste marked. Though we tend to think of caste in terms, say, of East Indian culture, we can clearly apply the concept to our own culture. One of the important dimensions of a caste system is that it is hereditary—you are born into a given caste and are usually marked for life as a member. In fact, we are all born into a caste, we are all caste marked. Indeed, some of us are doubly or multiply caste marked. In the United States, the most visible marks of caste relate to gender, race, age, and the degree to which one is able-bodied.

As East Indians do, we too assign low to high status and privilege to our people. The fact that this assignment of status and privilege may be active or passive, conscious or unconscious, malicious or unthinking does not detract from the reality of the act. And one of the major determinants of status, position, and caste marking relates back to who has historically or traditionally had access to or influence upon or within the power elite and its concomitant structures and institutions. So, historically blacks, native Americans, Chicanos, women, the old, the physically challenged have at best been neutrally caste marked and more often negatively identified when it comes to issues of power, dominance, and social control.[7]

Low status has been assigned to those people whom society views as somehow "stigmatized." Indeed, we have labels to identify such stigmatization: "deviant," "handicapped," "abnormal," "substandard," "different"—that is, different from those who dominate. As already suggested, it is the white, male, heterosexual, able-bodied, youthful person who both sets the standards for caste marking and is the human yardstick by which people within the United States are importantly measured and accordingly treated. As Porter and Samovar (1976) remind us, "We [in the United States] have generally viewed racial minorities as less than equal; they have been viewed as second class members of society—not quite as good as the white majority—and treated as such. . . . Blacks, Mexican-Americans, Indians, and Orientals are still subject to prejudice and discrimination and treated in many respects as colonized subjects" (p. 11). I would add to this list of colonized, low status subjects women, the physically challenged, and the aged. Again, our language is a telling repository for illuminating status as it relates to subordination in the social hierarchy: "Stay in your place," "Don't get out of line," "Know your place," "A woman's place is chained to the bed and the stove," "Know your station in life," are just a few sample phrases.

It is inevitable that nondominant peoples will experience, indeed be subjected to and suffer from, varying degrees of fear, denial, and self-hatred of their caste marking. Frantz Fanon's (1963) characterization of the "colonized native"—the oppressed native who has so internalized the power elite's perception of the norm that he or she not only serves and speaks for the colonial elite but is often more critical and oppressive of her or his caste than is the colonial—reveals this depth of self-hatred and denial.

In a parallel vein, the concept of "passing" which relates to a person of color attempting to "pass for" white, is a statement of self-denial. Implicit in the act of passing is the acceptance, if not the belief, that "white is right" in this society, and the closer one can come to the likeness of the privileged caste, the more desirable and comfortable one's station in life will be. So, people of color have passed for white—just as Jews have passed for Gentile or gay males and females have passed for straight, always with the fear of being discovered "for what they are." Physical impairment, too, has been a mark of shame in this country for those so challenged. Even so powerful a figure as F.D.R. refused to be photographed in any way that would picture him to be a "cripple."

If the act of passing is a denial of one's caste, the process of "coming out of the closet" is a conscious acceptance of one's caste. It is an important political and personal statement of power, a vivid metaphor that literally marks a rite of passage. Perhaps, the most striking acknowledgement of one's caste marking in our society relates to sexual preference. For a gay male or lesbian to admit their respective sexual preferences is for them to consciously take on an identity that our society has deemed abnormal and deviant—when measured against the society's standard of what is appropriate. They become, quite literally, marked people. In an important way, most of our domestic liberation movements are devoted to having their membership come out of the closet. That is, these movements seek not only to have their people heard and empowered by the power elite, but to have them reclaim and assert their identity and honor their caste. Liberation movement slogans tell the story of positive identification with one's caste: "Black is beautiful," "brown power," "Sisterhood is powerful," "gay pride," "I am an Indian and proud of it."

The nature and disposition of the social hierarchy in a given society, such as the United States, is reflected not only in the caste structure, but also in the class structure and the role prescriptions and expectations surrounding caste and class. Although the power structure in the United States is a complex and multileveled phenomenon, its predominant, generating force is economic. That is, the power elite is an elite that controls the material resources and goods in this country as well as the means and manner of production and distribution. Though one of our national fictions is that the United States is a classless society, we have, in fact, a well-established class structure based largely on economic power and control. When we talk of lower, middle, and upper classes in this country, we are not usually talking about birth or origins, but about power and control over material resources, and the attendant wealth, privilege, and high status.

There is even a kind of status distinction made within the upper-class society in this country that again relates to wealth and power, but in a temporal rather than a quantitative way—how long one has had wealth, power, and high-class status. So, distinctions are made between the old rich (the Harrimans, the Gores, the Pews) and the new rich (the Hunt family, Norton Simon, and their like).

Class, then, is intimately bound up with matters of caste. Not all, or even most, members of our society have the opportunity—let alone the caste credentials—to get a "piece of the action." It is no accident of nature that many of the nondominant peoples in this country are also poor peoples. Nor is it surprising that nondominant groups have been historically the unpaid, low paid, and/or enslaved work force for the economic power elite.

Finally, role prescriptions are linked to both matters of status and expectations in terms of one's perceived status, class, and caste. A role can be defined simply as a set of behaviors. The set of behaviors we ascribe to a given role is culture-bound and indicative of what has been designated as appropriate within the culture vis-à-vis that role. They are prescriptive, not descriptive, behaviors. We hold certain behavioral expectations for certain roles. It is a mark of just how culture-bound and prescriptive these roles are when someone is perceived to behave inappropriately—for example, the mother who gives up custody of her children in

order to pursue her career; she has "stepped out of line."

Furthermore, we see certain roles as appropriate or inappropriate to a given caste. Though another of our national myths—the Horatio Alger myth—tells us that there is room at the top for the industrious, bright go-getter, the truth of the matter is that there is room at the top if you are appropriately caste marked (that is, are white, male, able-bodied, and so on). The resistance, even outright hostility, nondominant peoples have encountered when they aspire to or claim certain occupational roles, for example, is a mark of the power elite's reluctance to relinquish those positions that have been traditionally associated with privileged status and high caste and class ranking. Though, in recent years, there has been much talk about a woman Vice-President of the United States, it has remained just talk. For that matter, there has not been a black Vice-President or a Hispanic or a Jew. The thought of the Presidency being held by most nondominant peoples is still "unspeakable."

The cultural prescription to keep nondominant peoples "in their place" is reinforced by and reinforces what I refer to as the "subterranean self"—the culture-bound collection of prejudices, stereotypes, values, and beliefs that each of us embraces and employs to justify our world view and the place of people in that world. It is, after all, our subterranean selves that provide fuel to fire the normative in our lives—what roles people ought and ought not to perform, what and why certain individuals are ill- or well-equipped to carry out certain roles, and our righteously stated rationalizations for keeping people in their places as we see them. Again, it should be remembered that those who dominate the culture reinforce and tacitly or openly encourage the perpetuation of those cultural prejudices, stereotypes, values, and beliefs that maintain the status quo, that is, the asymmetrical nature of the social hierarchy. Those who doubt the fervent desire of the power elite to maintain things as they are need only ponder the intense and prolonged resistance to the Equal Rights Amendment. If women are already "equal," why not make their equality a matter of record?

The foregoing discussion has been an attempt to illuminate the meaning of nondominance and the position of the nondominant person within our society. By relating status in the social hierarchy to matters of caste, class, and role, it has been my intention to highlight what it means to be a nondominant person within a culture that is dominated by the cultural precepts and artifacts of a power elite. It has also been my intention to suggest that the concept of "dominant culture" is something of a fiction, as we in communication studies traditionally use it. Given my perspective, it is more accurate to talk about those who dominate a culture rather than a dominant culture per se. Finally, I have attempted to point out that cultural dominance is not necessarily, or even usually, a matter of the numbers of people in a given society, but of those who have real power in a society.

## Geopolitics

The viewpoint being developed in this essay highlights still another facet of dominance and nondominance as it relates to society and the culture it generates and sustains—namely, the geopolitical facet. The United States is not merely a territory with certain designated boundaries—a geographical entity—it is a geopolitical configuration. It is a country whose history reflects the clear-cut interrelationship of geography, politics, economics, and the domination and control of people. For example, the westward movement and the subsequent takeover of the Indian nations and chunks of Mexico were justified by our doctrine of Manifest Destiny, not unlike the way Hitler's expansionism was justified by the Nazi doctrine of "geopolitik." It is no accident that the doctrine of Manifest Destiny coincides with the rapid growth and development of U.S. industrialization. The U.S. power elite wanted more land in which to expand and grow economically, so it created a rationalization to secure it.

Perhaps nowhere is a dominant culture's (those who dominate culture) ethnocentrism more apparent than in the missionary-like work carried on by its members—whether it be to "civilize" the na-

tives (that is, to impose the conquerors' cultural baggage on them), to "educate them in the ways of the white man," or to "Americanize" them. Indeed, the very term *America* is a geopolitical label as we use it. It presumes that those who inhabit the United States are the center of the Western hemisphere, indeed its only residents.[8] Identifying ourselves as "Americans" and our geopolitical entity as "America," in light of the peoples who live to the north and south of our borders speaks to both our economic dominance in this hemisphere and our ethnocentrism.

Identifying the United States in geopolitical terms is to identify it as a conqueror and controller of other peoples, and suggests both the probability of nondominant groups of people within that territory as well as a polarized, even hostile relationship between these groups and those who dominate culture. What Rich and Ogawa (1982) have pointed out in their model of interracial communication is applicable to most nondominant peoples: "As long as a power relationship exists between cultures where one has subdued and dominated the other ... hostility, tension and strain are introduced into the communicative situation" (p. 46). Not only were the Indian nations[9] and parts of Mexico conquered and brought under the colonial rule of the United States, but in its industrial expansionism, the United States physically enslaved black Africans to work on the farms and plantations of the South. It also economically enslaved large numbers of East European immigrants, Chinese, Irish, Hispanics (and more recently, Southeast Asians) in its factories, on its railroads, in its mines and fields through low wages and long work hours. It coopted the cottage industries of the home and brought women and children into the factories under abysmal conditions and the lowest of wages.

Indeed, many of the nondominant peoples in this country today are the very same ones whom the powerful have historically colonized, enslaved, disenfranchised, dispossessed, discounted, and relegated to poverty and low caste and class status. So, the asymmetrical relationship between the conquerer and the conquered continues uninterrupted. Although the form of oppression may change through time, the fact of oppression—and coexistent nondominance—remains.

It has been my desire throughout this essay to speculate about the complex ways in which society, culture, position, and place in the societal hierarchy affect and are affected by the matters of dominance, power, and social control. To this end, I have chosen to identify and characterize configurations of people within a society not only along a cultural axis but along a socio-economic and a geopolitical axis as well. I have tried to reexamine some of the concepts and definitions employed in discussions of culture-linked communication in a different light. And I have chosen the issues and conditions surrounding dominance and nondominance as points of departure and return. As I said at the beginning of this essay, the content is speculative, exploratory, and, hopefully, provocative. Above all, it is intended to encourage dialogue and exchange about the conditions and constraints surrounding intracultural communication.

## NOTES

1. See Folb (1980) for another perspective on the intersection of power, dominance, and nondominance as they operate within a discrete microcultural group, the world of the black ghetto teenager.

2. For a fascinating account of how and what kind of culture is transmitted from person to person, see Margaret Mead's *Culture and Commitment* (1970).

3. Mary Ritchie Key's book, *Male/Female Language* (1975), provides an informative discussion of the ways in which females and males are catalogued, characterized, and compartmentalized by our language. She illuminates its effects on how we perceive ourselves, as well as discussing how others perceive us through the prism of language.

4. The semantic marker "physically challenged" is used in lieu of other, more traditional labels such as "handicapped," "physically disabled," or "physically impaired," because it is a designation perferred by many so challenged. It is seen as a positive, rather than a negative, mark of identification.

5. In a country as youth conscious as our own, advanced age is seen as a liability, not as a mark of honor and wisdom as it is in other cultures. Whatever other reservations people had about Ronald Reagan's political aspirations in 1980, the one most discussed was his age. His political handlers went to great lengths—as did Reagan himself—to "prove" he was young in spirit and energy if not in years. It was important that he align himself as closely as possible with the positive mark of youth we champion and admire in this country.

6. It is no mere coincidence that a common thread binds together the domestic liberation movements in this country. It is the demand to be seen, heard, and empowered.

7. See Nancy Henley's *Body Politics* (1977) for a provocative look at the interplay of the variables power, dominance, and sex as they affect nonverbal communication.

8. The current bumper sticker, "Get the United States Out of North America," is a pointed reference to our hemispheric self-centeredness.

9. Neither the label "Indian" nor the label "native American" adequately identifies those people who inhabited the North American continent before the European conquest of this territory. Both reflect the point of view of the labeler, not those so labeled. That is why many who fought for the label "native American" now discount it as not significantly different from "Indian."

## BIBLIOGRAPHY

Fanon, Frantz. *Wretched of the Earth*. New York: Grove Press, Inc., 1963.

Folb, Edith A. *Runnin' Down Some Lines: The Language and Culture of Black Teenagers*. Cambridge: Harvard University Press, 1980.

Porter, Richard E. and Larry A. Samovar. "Communicating Interculturally." In *Intercultural Communication: A Reader*, 2nd ed., ed. Larry A. Samovar and Richard E. Porter. Belmont, Calif.: Wadsworth, 1976.

Rich, Andrea L., and Dennis M. Ogawa. "Intercultural and Interracial Communication: An Analytical Approach." In *Intercultural Communication: A Reader*, 3rd ed., ed. Larry A. Samovar and Richard E. Porter. Belmont, Calif.: Wadsworth, 1982.

Samovar, Larry A. and Richard E. Porter, eds. *Inter-cultural Communication: A Reader*, 3rd ed. Belmont, Calif.: Wadsworth, 1982.

Sarbaugh, L. E. *Intercultural Communication*. Rochelle Park, N.J.: Hayden Book Co., 1979.

Sitaram, K. S., and Roy T. Cogdell. *Foundations of Intercultural Communication*. Columbus, Ohio: Charles E. Merrill, 1976.

# Black Style in Communication

THOMAS KOCHMAN

Style is an attitude that individuals within a culture express through their choice of cultural form—blacks prefer cultural forms that do not restrict their expressive capacities—and the way they choose to express themselves within a given form. By these standards, black style is more self-conscious, more expressive, more expansive, more colorful, more intense, more assertive, more aggressive, and more focused on the individual than is the style of the larger society of which blacks are part.

Style pervades every aspect of life, from how one is born to how one is buried. Every way in which the style of one group differs from that of another group is not only noticeable and recognizable; it is a difference that can evoke admiration and imitation or hostility and conflict.

Blacks have evoked the admiration of the larger society in the performing arts: in music, dance, the theater, and on the playing fields, where they also "perform." Their everyday attire and ways of walking, standing, talking, greeting, and so forth produce more mixed reactions. The schoolroom and the work place are of central importance to the functioning of American society, and there we find the greatest problems. . . .

## BODY LANGUAGE

The way a person stands, leans, or moves can communicate intent. . . . During an argument between

From Thomas Kochman, *Black and White Styles in Conflict in Communication* (Chicago: University of Chicago Press, 1981), pp. 130–152. Reprinted by permission of the publisher and author. Professor Kochman teaches at the University of Illinois, Chicago Circle Campus.

blacks, a change in position may well indicate a preparation for physical combat. . . . More basically, even the simplest use of the body expresses cultural style. There is a difference between the way blacks and whites walk. As Paul Harrison says, "Rather than simply walk, we *move:* the swaying swagger of the hips and the bouncing, bopping head-shoulder motion associated with *bopping* are derived from a strong rhythmic mode of walking" (1972, p. 73).

This "strong rhythmic mode of walking" has direct links to black dancing, which "is not so much the steps but what you do going from step to step. It's the rubato [rhythmic flexibility] of the black body" (Alvin Ailey, quoted in Saal 1980, p. 64). On the dance floor, when the underlying rhythm is let loose, the movement can become an explosive and daring statement of individual style: "a testament, in form and substance, of our peoples' power sensibility." When young black men *bop* down the street, their gait communicates the same power idea—an image designed to "give notice of one's intentions to harmonize whatever is necessary for one's survival" (Harrison 1972, pp. 67, 73). In walking, as in all other matters, style is of the essence. Kenneth Johnson has written, "*Where* the young black male is going is not as important as *how* he gets there. . . . The means are more important than the end" (1971, p. 19).

Black greetings are also stylized to convey forceful expression or exhibition, whether the greeting is an embrace, "giving skin," the black-power handshake, or the more extended and elaborate hand, elbow, and hip movements called *dapping* (Cooke 1972, pp. 33–43).

## DRESS

Obviously the fundamental purpose of clothes is to cover the body. Beyond this, groups differ in their style of dress and their view of what constitutes appropriate wear on different types of occasion. Blacks regard clothing as a way to make the most powerful statement about themselves that they can. Harrison observes that "the attitude of a garment, in texture and color, is ritualistically assembled to

create the most potent image that one's Nommo [life force] can conjure. The image—sharp, mean, bad—is designated to harmonize the threat of any force that might question one's humanity; its effectiveness is validated by the community's affirmative response" (1972, p. 32). On the street, the effectiveness of one's appearance is validated by the greater personal space accorded young men who are powerfully well dressed. Edith Folb reports that streetwise black teenagers in Los Angeles tend to adopt a "hands-off policy" toward those dudes who are *clean.* Even hardheads—"those who are into physical fireworks [violence] rather than costuming"—give them grudging admiration and respect. One teenager put it this way: "Dude dress nice, stay clean, brother maybe think twice 'fore he mess 'im up" (Folb 1980, p. 111).

The respect and admiration that blacks receive from their peers for the vital imagery of their costume often contrasts markedly with the reception they get from whites in official settings such as school. There whites tend to adopt a strictly utilitarian attitude toward clothing. Hats are outer wear, designed to protect the head from the cold as sunglasses are designed to shield the eyes from the sun. Once indoors, whites expect outer wear to be removed. But blacks consider hats and sunglasses *(shades)* artistic adornments, like jewelry, calculated to "effect a magical attitude," one that is neither motivated by nor responsive to white notions of pure utility (Harrison 1972, p. 33). When whites insist that once inside blacks remove their hats and sunglasses, the latter balk, for this would create an entirely different image from the one that they took great care to prepare that morning—a preparation that took into account the various places in which their costume would be worn. Much conflict between black students and white school officials occurs because of their different attitudes toward clothing.

## "I'M ON, DADDY, I'M ON."

The black's method of combining movement and dress to activate powerful and expressive imagery is in itself a performance, even if the individual is about to do no more than walk down the block. The professional performer is especially aware of this situation. As Sammy Davis, Jr., said, "as soon as I go out the front door of my house in the morning, I'm on, Daddy, I'm on" (quoted in Messinger, Sampson, and Towne 1962, pp. 98–99). Often the stylized routines of the professional performer continue until, and sometimes include, the moment the performance itself begins.

J. P. ("Jellyroll") Morton has described the type of ritual that each jazz piano player back in the twenties went through before playing a note on the keyboard. As reported by Harrison, the ritual included

*the stroll from the café's doorway with a certain gait, through the audience and over to the piano, the tucking of the overcoat inside out to expose the red lining, the folding of the coat, placing it carefully on top of the piano, cane and hat on top of coat, and then, with calculated exaction, the suspending of the hands over the keyboard at the proper angle to allow the diamond rings to reflect the light and sparkle, just for a moment, before striking the keyboard to make one's own note. One's own signature completed the harmony of the ritual (Harrison 1972, p. 33).*

It is characteristic of black performers in general to view their entire time in front of the public as performance time. Muhammad Ali clearly does so, using whatever time he gets in front of the television cameras to display his verbal power—his boasting and bragging ("campaigning") or ring verse ("Feats of Clay")—which is all of a piece with his powerful performance in the ring, his boxing skill and showboating ("The Ali Shuffle"). Baseball player Reggie Jackson extends and accentuates the vitality of his individual image by managing to be alone on the field during the playing of the national anthem, which ritually occurs after the teams have had their warmup practice and returned to the dugout. Jackson arranges this easily and inconspicuously: As Allen Harris has commented, he simply does not return to the dugout with his teammates after the warm-up.

## INDIVIDUAL STYLE

… The performer's individual power is acknowledged by the audience's immediate and ongoing confirmation of the intensity of the image that is being created. This functions as the response but also as a further call to the performer to generate an even more powerful image. As Roger Abrahams has said (1976, p. 9), the performer's task "is not to make a thing but to bring about an experience in which not only his creative energies but the vitality of others may find expression." Thus the black performer's role is not just to demonstrate but also to instigate: to have the power of the created image function as an invocation (call) that serves, as Harrison puts it, "to galvanize the collective unconscious" from which the performer and the audience together draw spiritual sustenance (1972, p. 157).

Black performers, however, want the powerful images they generate to be indisputably their own. Often their nicknames reflect their success in achieving this status. Professional basketball player Lloyd Free got his nickname "World" from his playground teammates when they saw him turn 360° in the air one day and slam-dunk the ball on the way down (Elderkin 1979, p. 17). Walt Frazier got his nickname "Clyde" from the movie *Bonnie and Clyde*, not only because he wears flamboyant clothes but also because of his daring style of play, "stealing balls, gambling all the time, and dribbling behind my back to escape pursuers" (Frazier and Berkow 1974, pp. 20–21).

The performer who tries unsuccessfully to perfect an individual style or is thought to be performing in someone else's style is regarded much less highly. Indeed, such people are usually treated with scorn or indifference. That is why black performers who are relative newcomers to the public scene tend to resent and resist comparisons with established black performers. When George McGinnis first came into the National Basketball Association from the rival American Basketball Association, he said, "People compare me with Connie Hawkins or Elgin Baylor but I think I have my own style" (in Lamb 1975, p. 36). And when a white television sports announcer interviewed a young black fighter after his bout and compared his fighting style with Muhammad Ali's, Greg Page protested, "There was only one Muhammad Ali. Let there be only one Greg Page."

Baseball player William Mays Aikins, named after the illustrious Willie Mays, has expressed displeasure over the constant reference and comparison to Mays, caused by the similarity of their names, which has made it more difficult for him to create his own public identity. His problem was reinforced when he joined his new team and his old number was not available. One of the few numbers available, and the one he finally chose, was the same number that Willie Mays had worn. He chose the number with some hesitation. "I don't want people to think I'm trying to copy Mays. I just want to be known for myself and my own accomplishments" (in Eldridge 1980, p. 18).

The emphasis on developing one's own style also helps to explain why one does not see in the black community the kind of public imitation of star performers that one finds in the white community, which welcomes "Beatlemania" and duplicate Elvis Presleys. No blacks with talent would be content simply to copy the style of other performers, no matter how famous, in lieu of developing a style of their own. To do so would signify to other blacks a lack of individual resourcefulness, imagination, and pride.

It would also be regarded as a presumption of another individual's ability, since blacks generally acknowledge performers, as artists, to be sole proprietors of the images they create through stylistic performance. To copy them would be an infringement of individual entitlement. For individuals to copy the performances of others and attempt to pass them off as their own would be an even worse violation. This is why blacks bristle at the very thought of white performers over the years getting the credit and reaping the benefits for simply reproducing styles that individual black performers originated and developed.

Of course blacks would be equally displeased to have their individual performance style or image co-opted by other blacks. All black performers want clear and undisputed entitlement to the image that they have personally developed and are publicly claiming for themselves. They do not always get it, however, since disputes occasionally arise among blacks over who has the greater right to a particular image, style, or title. One less than serious example of such a dispute was partially instigated and reported by sports reporter Don Pierson, in his effort to drum up additional interest in the 1979 Super Bowl confrontation between the Dallas Cowboys and the Pittsburgh Steelers. Pierson told Dallas linebacker "Hollywood" Henderson that the Steelers' lineman L. C. Greenwood had said Henderson had stolen Greenwood's nickname. This would also imply that Henderson had co-opted the "Hollywood" image that he had been publicly flaunting. Henderson's response was to defend his own greater entitlement to the "Hollywood" label, while discrediting Greenwood's: "L. C. Greenwood? L. C. Greenwood? I never heard anybody call him Hollywood. They must call him Hollywood in Pittsburgh in practice. They call me Hollywood everywhere." (Pierson 1976, sec. 6, p. 2).

Henderson's playful put-down of Greenwood ("They must call him Hollywood . . . in practice") indicates the "jive" nature of the dispute. On the other hand, for Greenwood's accusation to function even as a playful provocation indicates the seriousness with which blacks typically regard attempts to co-opt their individual public style. . . . This is not to imply that young black performers do not or should not incorporate stylistic features of established black performers in developing their own performance style. They do, in a time-honored tradition in the black community. But when they do, it is important to give proper credit to the source and then not to take on so much of another performer's style as to become a mere copy. Sugar Ray Leonard's fighting styles and skills—especially the quick hands—are clearly reminiscent of Sugar Ray Robinson. And there would have to be some stylistic similarity between the two for Leonard even to consider using the same nickname. But Leonard also has a distinctive style and has been quite open in acknowledging his indebtedness to the influence of Robinson and other established fighters. Blacks would regard Leonard's assumption of the nickname "Sugar Ray" not as an improper attempt to co-opt Robinson's fighting style and image but, rather, as a tribute. . . .

## CONSTRAINTS ON
## PERFORMANCE STYLE

Black style, like other styles, is learned very early in life. The young black male bopping down the street, practicing the style he is still developing, tests his success—as both Folb (1980, p. 111) and Harrison (1972, pp. 32, 73) have noted—by whether his peers pay proper respect to his movement and his attire ("Dude dress nice . . . brother think twice").

Although black performers strive to develop their own style within the larger framework of black style, for their style to be accepted by their peers it must succeed, that is, be "together." An attempt to manifest style in performance without regard to the totality of the context, purpose, or nature of the event invites disapproval, even ridicule. Harrison (1972, p. 33) reports that a young, gifted black singing group from San Francisco repelled the audience at Harlem's Apollo theater despite the vigor of imagination they brought to their songs and choreography, because their costumes—net tank shirts, bell-bottomed levis, and sandals, the trappings of hippiedom—were inappropriate.

## PERFORMANCE STYLE IN
## SPORTS

In other contexts the same standards for stylistic acceptance apply. For example, it would not be a matter for admiration how high a basketball player leaped, or how long he was able to suspend himself in mid-air, if on freeing himself for the shot he missed the basket. Ken Johnson gave me an example of a black card player who, at a critical point in the game, threw a card down from his hand with a great flourish, only to discover that it was the wrong card. This mental lapse immediately canceled whatever credit for style he might have gained from others had he thrown the right card down. As Johnson put it, "his

manner of throwing the card down was nullified by his having thrown the wrong card down." Edwin McDowell cites a black Pittsburgh Steeler who, thinking he had reached the end zone, "spiked" the football ten yards short of the goal line. Another player, after catching a pass and thinking himself in the clear, stopped running and started prancing with the ball while he was still twenty yards short of the end zone, only to lose the ball when an opposing player hit him from behind (McDowell 1976, p. 16). Muhammad Ali introduced his famous "Ali Shuffle" in his first fight with Frazier, which he lost. When stylistic expression is not accompanied by a successful execution, the result is humiliating, because the audience regards a performer as having laid claim to greater expertise than he can demonstrate. As the saying in the black community goes, "everything must come together" (Holt 1972a, p. 60). To the extent that everything has not come together, black style cannot succeed.

## Conflicting Styles on the
## Field and Court

Basketball players Julius Erving ("Doctor J") and John Havlicek epitomize black and white styles of playing basketball. Jeff Greenfield has contrasted the two:

*Erving has the capacity to make legends come true; leaping from the foul line and slam-dunking the ball on his way down; going up for a layup, pulling the ball to his body and throwing it under and up the other side of the rim, defying gravity and probability with moves and jumps. Havlicek. . . brings the ball downcourt, weaving left, then right, looking for a path. He swings the ball to a teammate, cuts behind a pick, takes the pass and releases the shot in a flicker of time. It looks plain, unvarnished. But there are not half a dozen players in the league who can see such possibilities for a free shot, then get that shot off as quickly and efficiently as Havlicek. . . .*

*"White" ball then, is the basketball of patience and method. "Black" ball is the basketball of electric self-expression (Greenfeld 1975, p. 248).*

Greenfield's apt description of some of the differences between white and black ball playing makes it clear that one can expect to see conflict as well as conflicting styles on the field and court. This conflict has occurred, although it has lessened as white coaches learn to work with their black players and some white players who also "play black." The differences in style, however, are not so easily resolved, because they are based on differences in cultural attitudes—attitudes not only about expressiveness but also about competition, winning and losing, and even (perhaps especially) about the nature and definition of individuality within the context of team play.

## The Team

The traditional white conception of a sports team is that of a group working together toward one goal—to win and, moreover, to accomplish their plays in the most efficient, economical, and cooperative manner possible. Underlying this concept is an assumption about the process of accommodation: the extent to which individuals are expected to adapt themselves to fit within the team's framework and the extent to which the team's management can or will adapt to the individuality of any given player. There are also accepted limitations on the extent to which individuals can shape or define their activity or role on the team. . . .

## Expressive Play and Showboating

Into this highly structured and tightly managed team framework comes the black athlete and player, guided by cultural norms that not only sanction but promote, encourage, even demand that individuals "do their thing" or "showboat." As Holt puts it, it is "the only way one can present the person/self in a manner worthy of that self" (1972a, p. 60).

The black athlete, then, adds elements of performance style—vitality and individuality—to the team's shared goal of winning the game. Black players improvise, adding to the play some personal routine or maneuver that will make the play more dramatic and individually distinctive. Black players seek to go beyond the mechanics or technical aspects of play, intending to perform not simply proficiently but with flair. Blacks "prance and dance" for the sake of art and style as well as the sake of the game. White players might also be allowed to prance and dance on the playing field, but only for the sake of the game, as when they are working their way toward the end zone. Black players are more conscious of the powerful statement they are making when they execute such maneuvers on the field. They also show their independent concern with artful showmanship during official pauses within the game, as in the end zone after a touchdown has been scored, which McDowell has called the "Touchdown Follies,"

*. . .that brief interim after a score when the ball carrier goes into anything from a leadfooted buck-and-wing to something that would pass muster on the stage of Radio City Music Hall.*

*As football fans know by now, Touchdown Follies come in all shapes, sizes, and descriptions— not just the dances listed above but one-act plays culminating in melodramatically spiking the ball into the turf or letting it dribble down one's back in a tantalizing, controlled descent (McDowell 1976, p. 16).*

The Touchdown Follies occur after the points have been made. But more often than not, blacks also demonstrate their showmanship while making the point. In basketball, they do not simply lay the ball in for an uncontested basket. That would be too prosaic. Rather, with the ball in both hands, they leap as high as they can and slam it through the hoop (Greenfield 1975, p. 170). The height of the leap is functional, since it increases the players' chances of making the basket. At the same time, it is electrifying, and thereby gains credit for the player from his peers for having performed with style. As Greenfield says, "when you jump in the air, fake a shot, bring the ball back to your body, and throw up a shot, all without coming back down, you have proven your worth in uncontestable fashion" (1975, p. 170).

The dual goal is clear: not only to make the point but to project the most powerful image possible while making it. If either objective is not met, blacks will not regard the performance as successful. This is why they occasionally make the execution of a simple task more difficult, thereby turning its achievement into a more powerful statement. On the other hand, they often realize the same effect by making exceedingly difficult tasks look simple. Julius Erving does this when he appears to be making a simple, straightforward move in getting off the mark past his opponent, until one discovers that he has covered the distance from the foul line to the basket in one step, while more mortal players need to take two. Professional basketball player Darryl Dawkins carried the idea of power behind the slam-dunk to its logical limit when he shattered the backboard while slam-dunking the basketball in a few games during the 1979–80 season. He also carried to the limit the idea that such powerful slam-dunks are functional. He made the baskets and scored the points, so strictly speaking, they were functional, but at the expense of another phase of the game: the need to maintain continuity of play.

Showboating, as the word itself implies, is entertainment, and the use of showboating within the framework of a competitive event like basketball or football is an extension of the black cultural view that contests are a form of entertainment and that competition provides the atmosphere in which performers can best perform (Abrahams 1970, p. 42). For blacks every game has a dual purpose: to win and dominate one's opponent, to be sure, but also to showboat, to demonstrate individual skill and style simultaneously. Depending on the score or the team standing, one element or the other is likely to surface. When one team is well ahead in the game and the outcome clearly decided, black players consider it show time. Harold Thomas, one of my students and a former basketball player, put it this way: "The showboating, or razzle-dazzle display, would begin only when the team was well ahead by twenty-five points or so, and rather than simply go ahead and win by sixty, we would start to showboat to entertain the crowd."

Within the framework of competition, black performers often use an opponent to highlight their own superior abilities and to showboat. In his prime,

Muhammad Ali would demonstrate his dominance in the ring and then use his opponent to demonstrate his showmanship. The Harlem Globetrotters regularly use an opposing team as a foil to contrast their own showboating ability. The black pattern, then, is this: Once the outcome of a game is clear, the adversary no longer needs to be vanquished. But the adversary can serve a further role, contributing to the crowd's entertainment. It may not make an opponent happier to find himself being used to help a superior player show off, but it does keep the crowd in the stadium. White players have no other option, once the outcome has been decided, than to make their behavior appear as though the outcome were still in doubt. The game becomes a charade—what white players call "going through the motions." And it is at this point that the crowd, with five minutes of game time still remaining, begins to file out.

Blacks also consider it permissible for players on the losing team to showboat. Once the outcome has been decided, individual members of the losing team can also do their thing. "Hollywood" Henderson was thus not at all reluctant to flash his "Hollywood" smile and his "number one" sign when the television camera zoomed in on him during a game, even though Dallas was losing. Unfortunately for Henderson, this act cost him his job with the Dallas team. White coaches might tolerate showboating when the team is winning, but not when it is losing. The reason the Cowboy management gave for Henderson's dismissal was "lack of concentration."

## Conflict and Confluence

If an athletic team is to be run like an army, ideally consisting of "interchangeable parts," with players given no latitude to define their individual roles, what does the traditionally minded coach do with a player who insists on doing his own thing? If efficient accomplishment of a task is the goal and an athlete makes extra and seemingly unnecessary moves, doesn't this challenge authority and interfere with discipline? And how do white players, asked to subordinate *their* individuality to the team effort, look upon black players who use every opportunity to draw attention to themselves on the court by magnifying aspects of their performance that clearly serve ends other than scoring or winning? One might reasonably expect that the first reaction of such a coach would be to tighten the rules and that the first reaction of the white players would be to retaliate against the exhibitionistic black player to get him to curtail this kind of behavior. This has been the case.

Some white coaches have tried to solve what they see as problems created by black style by simply cracking down on the players. One such instance occurred at a midwestern university. The black football players responded by filing a list of grievances with the school administration against their white football coach, accusing him of racial discrimination. Among their grievances was the charge that the coach tried to keep them from showing emotion on the playing field. The specific instance cited occurred at the end of a practice session when blacks were doing a lot of congratulatory hand slapping. The coach called the team together and, according to the allegation, told the players to "keep those goddamn gestures at home" (Hersh and Berler 1980, p. 125).

In addition to cracking down, white coaches and sports officials added rules prohibiting certain kinds of behavior. The usual reason for adding or changing a rule is to keep one team from having an unfair advantage. In the 1942–43 season, George Mikan, a white player on the DePaul University basketball team, "batted a dozen Kentucky shots away from the basket by out-and-out goaltending. There was no rule against goaltending then, but it became illegal as soon as Kentucky's coach Adolph Rupp got the attention of the rule makers" (Enright 1980, p. 50). Mikan was much taller than any other player on any other team. Eliminating goaltending was necessary to give other teams a more equal opportunity against teams with very tall players.

But how can one explain the rule that penalizes spiking the football in the end zone during college games? The player who does this is not threatening to gain an advantage—play itself is officially in a state of pause. Showboating, the Touchdown Follies, cannot affect the conduct of the game or the score. Thus the rule that penalizes spiking the football could have been designed only to curb black expressiveness, to repress what whites see as immodest, unrestrained, and self-congratulatory gloating over one's own achievement. Professional football rules still allow spiking the football in the end zone after a touchdown has been made, but nowhere else. Consequently several black players have seen their entire run for a critical first down cancelled because, in their exuberance over their success, they spiked the football to punctuate their achievement.

Blacks are not, however, so limited that they cannot counter repression in one area with expression in another. As Ken Johnson told me, "if they outlaw spiking the football on scoring a touchdown, blacks will just dance more, and that's all right, because I'd rather see them dance. If they outlaw touchdown dances, blacks will come up with something else." Anthony Carter of the University of Michigan came up with "something else" equally thrilling after he scored one of his team's winning touchdowns in the 1981 Rose Bowl game. A friend of mine watching a telecast saw him "leap like a ballet dancer into the waiting arms of a black teammate, after which they hugged and danced around a little in front of the goal post." . . .

In contact sports like football and basketball, whites have regarded black showboating as crowing or gloating over the defeat of an adversary, which they consider poor sportsmanship. Thus, when one black football player had just scored a touchdown and was prancing about the end zone with the football raised in his hand—the Touchdown Follies were just getting started—a white player from the opposing team ran by and knocked the football out of his hand.

Bob Cousy, former Boston Celtics basketball superstar, displayed a similar reaction to black showboating near the end of a game in which the New York Knickerbockers had pulled well ahead of the Celtics. With the game in hand, "Sweetwater" Clifton of the Knickerbockers considered it show time and started to do some of his former Harlem Globetrotter tricks with the basketball. Cousy viewed Sweetwater's antics as an attempt to humiliate him and his teammates, notwithstanding the fact that Sweetwater was obviously playing to the crowd. Consequently, Cousy got even with Sweetwater by confronting him and embarrassing him with a slick basketball maneuver of his own.

The differences in the way blacks and whites approach basketball, football, and other competitive sports account for these confrontations. Whites view competitive sports exclusively in terms of winning and losing. Blacks view competing in sports in terms of dominating the field, being the best, and performing in a show. To whites, showboating within a game is directed only against one's opponent rather than, as blacks intend it, toward the crowd in the stands.

There are other reasons underlying the hostile reaction of whites to black style. One is that whites view many of the moves that blacks make for style to be irrelevant to the concepts of "team" and "winning." They are considered extraneous to the concept of efficiency, which requires that only simple, straight-forward, and necessary moves be made. In terms of economy and winning, therefore, extra maneuvers can be regarded as at least wasteful and extravagant. At worst, individual style can be regarded as subversive, a threat to the white team concept, because an athlete who does his own thing implies that he is no longer properly subordinating himself to the complete authority of the coach.

This subordination, especially in the area of role definition, is the kind of accommodation that white coaches and players alike consider necessary to developing and maintaining a cohesive team and a concentrated effort. It is necessary to them because of the systems-oriented approach that traditional white coaches and managers use to define and govern individual and team play. They attempt to anticipate the various situations that might arise during the course of the game and to develop set plays in advance to cover each type of situation. This approach also leads players to produce lines of play for which set procedures have been established and to avoid lines of play that require individual initiative and improvisation. In setting up a tightly structured game plan beforehand, whites hope to increase their control over the course of the game. In doing so they

sacrifice what they consider incidental and negotiable, but which blacks consider basic and non-negotiable, namely, spontaneity: being able to move and act as impulse, feelings, and intuition direct. Former New York high school star Bill Spivey said, "Cats from the street have their own rhythm when they play. It's not a matter of somebody setting you up and you shooting. You *feel* the shot. When a coach holds you back, you lose the feel and it isn't fun anymore" (in Greenfield 1975, p. 171). . . .

I would also describe the coach-dominated white style of play as machine-like, characterized by mechanical repetition and interchangeable parts, although it is definitely also warlike in its exclusive focus on winning. Black emphasis on style and showmanship, on the artistic side of play and on individuality, constitutes both a threat and an antidote to this traditional white view.

The greater acceptance of black playing style today is in part a result of its commercial success. The fans not only want to see a winner; they also want to be entertained, and what and whom they pay to see has great influence with the front office. Coaches have become believers, too, because nothing succeeds like success, and blacks have demonstrated without question that their more individualistic style of play makes a team more effective. . . .

There is clearly a possibility for blending the best of white and black playing styles into a winning combination. The whites' need for players to accept certain roles for the good of the team and the blacks' need for the team to organize itself around the special talents of individual players can, when combined, produce both greater individual satisfaction and team success. The Chicago Bears are certainly no worse a team when they throw the football to Walter Payton out in the flat and help him demonstrate his brilliant broken-field running ability. Nor are the Philadelphia 76ers any worse a team when the other players clear the lane to allow Julius Erving to go one-on-one against his opponent. As Lloyd Free says, "I'm as much a team player as anybody, but let me tell you something. There are times when every team needs a great one-on-one player that it can give the ball to in a clutch situation who will get them the basket" (in Elderkin 1980b, p. 16). . . .

There does not indeed appear to be any reason why individual skill and style cannot be incorporated at the planning stage into a winning team strategy on the court and field, as it has in dance, theater, instrumental groups, and even, as we saw earlier in this article, on the street. For the black performer, skill and style—the integral components of doing your own thing—are symbiotic. They draw upon and reinforce each other and combine to enable performers to make the most powerful statement of which they are capable. To encourage stylistic expression within a team effort, to plan and build around it, is thus to bring out the best in the individual black player and performer.

# Intercultural Perspectives of Aging

CARL W. CARMICHAEL

In the United States, concern for older people has grown considerably during the last two decades. Evidence of this concern ranges from the emergence of more than 200 departments of gerontology in institutions of higher education to the passing of hundreds of congressional bills and the creation of numerous government programs to aid the elderly. Yet all of this attention has barely put a dent in the problems of growing old in a youth-oriented culture.

Of course, problems of aging have been prevalent in virtually every society. Whereas the nature of those problems and the treatment of the aged vary widely from culture to culture, the fact that this subpopulation is viewed as a *problem* does not vary. In keeping with the theme of this book, we discuss three aspects of aging. First, we look at how communication relates to aging in several important ways; second, although people normally think of aging as something that happens to an individual, we show that it is very much a cultural phenomenon; and third, we point out that the intercultural aspects of aging are interesting and useful areas of study for the communication scholar.

## COMMUNICATION ASPECTS OF AGING

The field of gerontology has focused on a particular population subgroup, and it has used a "social prob-

This essay was written especially for this fifth edition. All rights reserved. Permission to reprint must be obtained from the publisher and the author. Professor Carmichael teaches at the University of Oregon.

lem" orientation. The study of aging and the problems of the aged have necessarily been an interdisciplinary venture. Unfortunately, until recently, communication has not been included as one of the traditional subdisciplines. However, the kind of knowledge and the kind of perspective found in communication studies would obviously be useful in dealing with this social problem. Certainly, one can argue that any social problem or cultural phenomenon cannot be fully understood unless one studies the communication systems that relate to it. But, more specifically, many of the problems of the aged are communication problems, and they should be studied as such.[1]

The relevance and the value of communication to aging begins at the very heart of how the field of communication has defined itself. Two of the major conceptual aspects of communication are: (1) information processing and (2) human interaction—interpersonally or through the media. Many of the traditionally studied problems of aging relate to one of these aspects, and an analysis from this communication perspective leads to new areas of study that have great potential in gerontological theory development.

## Information Processing

Communication—whatever the setting, the level, or the type—inherently involves the processing of information. The individual human organism encodes, decodes, packages, distorts, and relays information, as do the group, the business organization, the social system, and the culture. Some of the oldest and most researched theories of aging relate to information processing.

Recent research on changes in memory function as a result of aging has led to a re-evaluation of widely held beliefs previously confirmed by earlier research.[2] Similarly, the deterioration of intelligence was always assumed to be a normal function of aging, but this assumption is now controversial thanks to recent findings and improved research techniques.[3] Questions relating to linguistic function or language facility are now being asked by gerontologists.[4] The processing of nonverbal cues

has been the focus of two papers delivered at recent national meetings of the Gerontological Society and the Speech Communication Association.[5]

One of the most serious communication problems faced by older people is the reduction of information to process because of age-related sensory losses. Under normal conditions of aging, older people can expect noticeable decreases in the sensory abilities—hearing, vision, touch, and smells.[6] Furthermore, some abnormal conditions that severely impair one's health are age-related, and they result in serious communication problems. For example, strokes often damage the speech centers in the brain; arteriosclerosis can reduce the oxygen supply to the brain and thus affect the information processing functions. Surely the communication process is significantly affected when any of these normal or pathological changes in information processing occur. How the process is affected and how improvements can be made are socially relevant research questions for the communicologist.

## Human Interaction

While the field of communication, in its broadest sense, can include the study of computer systems and even animal behavior, the bulk of the research and writing has been focused on human interaction. Most current definitions of communication contain the concept of interaction (transaction, linking, and so on), and most communicologists are primarily, if not exclusively, concerned with interaction on the human level. In our coursework and in our research, we have studied every type of setting—from the classroom to the business conference room—and every size of group—the dyad, the triad, the small group, the assembly, the social system. Yet almost none of this tremendous accumulation of knowledge relates specifically to older people.

There is no reason to believe that the basic, human need to communicate—to interact with other human beings for socializing, decision making, or whatever—should change with age. Older people are subject to the same communication anxieties, the same communication needs, the same communication dependencies, and the same communication problems in relationships as younger people are, and their needs occur in the same kinds of settings—from the family (perhaps now a redefined unit for them) to the classroom. Some older people use the media more than younger people do, and some even use it as a substitute for dwindling interpersonal communication.[7]

## CULTURAL ASPECTS OF AGING

There are times when everyone feels very much alone; we are born, struggle for survival, and go to our graves alone. Yet while that feeling may be justified, the reality is that we do not and cannot live in a social vacuum in this complex, interpersonally interdependent culture. Our lives are inextricably interwoven with many other individuals and institutions. We cannot escape the rules, the laws, the social conditioning, the media—the basic socialization process of our culture.

The aging process may appear at first to be a uniquely individual experience, but that is simply not the case. The aging process is very much related to such cultural phenomena as attitudes toward aging, beliefs about aging, and stereotypes of aging found within the culture. Also, the aging individual is greatly affected by cultural mechanisms and policies that determine such daily needs as health care and employment. Mandatory retirement is an example of a formalized policy that demonstrates that integrating older people into the mainstream of society is not a cultural goal.

### Attitudes

In recent years numerous studies have been conducted to discover what the attitudes of our culture are toward older people and the aging process. I myself have reviewed nearly 300 such studies.[8] The subjects in these studies ranged in age from the very young (preschoolers) to the very elderly (those in their nineties). While the findings are far too diverse to relate in detail here, one general conclusion prevails: From the teenage years on, the atti-

tudes of people in our culture toward growing old are fairly negative. They don't begin that way, as many of the studies with younger children reveal, but something in our culture changes our attitudes to negative ones around the age of puberty. Communicologists must now seek to learn how these attitudes are communicated, what factors reinforce them, and how they can be changed.

The phenomenon at issue here should be of great concern to us. Although the concept of attitude has been difficult to define, it usually refers to some kind of a cognitive evaluation. An attitude is how we feel about something, how much we like or don't like something. Unquestionably, how we *feel* about older people and the aging process—the prevailing attitudes toward aging in our culture—relates to how we *treat* our elderly, as well as to how we are affected by the aging process ourselves as individuals.

### Beliefs

A broad set of beliefs, or misbeliefs, about aging exists in our culture. Cultural communication, from generation to generation, has perpetuated myths of aging that have become so widely accepted they are all but impossible to change, even in the face of recent scientific evidence to the contrary. Consider a few salient examples and check your own beliefs in each case:

When people get old, they can expect increased memory loss.

You can't teach an old dog new tricks.

Intelligence declines in old age.

One of the worst problems in old age is loneliness.

People become more religious when they grow old.

Older people have no interest in sex.

The list could go on; however, these examples are typical of beliefs that are not only widely accepted in our culture but have been disputed by recent gerontological research. Some findings have even received popular coverage in the media, such as the CBS Special, "Sex after Sixty." Yet, such false beliefs are so firmly grounded in the American culture that change does not come easily, and many older people are quite directly affected by them. In fact, one could argue quite legitimately that one of the worst problems our culture imposes on its aging members is this false set of beliefs. Psychologically induced states of "oldness" may occur as a result of the self-fulfilling prophecy phenomenon and a belief system that abounds with myths, or at least half-truths, that are more applicable to the very elderly years than they are at the relatively younger ages of 60 or 62 when the word *old* becomes appropriate in our culture. It is quite possible that many older people have aged prematurely by adopting the age-related characteristics they have come to believe must exist after a certain age.

## Stereotyping

In some ways, the stereotyping process is a necessary evil. On the positive side, it enables communication efficiency in the sense that communication about a person or a group of people can be simplified by identifying the group in terms of its most basic, widely believed characteristics. One might argue that whether or not those beliefs are accurate is irrelevant as long as they come from the belief system of the communication receivers. Yet, this process, by its very nature, invites inaccuracy. So, on the negative side, people who are stereotyped are identified *only* in terms of those common-denominator characteristics that are believed, but are not necessarily true, and that relate to a whole category of people, but not necessarily to an individual.

Stereotyping requires cooperation on a cultural level. When an actor portrays an old man, he turns to the most convenient symbols of "oldmanness" his culture provides: white hair, stooped posture, a cane, a hearing aid, and a harsh, raspy voice. Note that the culture provides these symbols and, therefore, the actor is able to communicate the image of this character efficiently to an audience from that culture.

The problem for older people in this regard is obvious. Negative stereotypes, or at least inaccurate ones, are perpetuated by this process. The image that younger people have of their elders, the image that older people have of themselves, is affected by the stereotypes we see through the media and elsewhere. The burning question, of course, is who is at fault? Is the actor guilty of perpetuating a negative image? Or does he merely reflect cultural beliefs that just happen to be inaccurate and negative? When Carol Burnett plays her famous crotchety old woman role, should she be faulted for portraying characteristics that are unduly negative and not true of most older women? Or should she be commended for cleverly choosing characteristics that are true of at least some older women and hilariously funny to most of her viewers?

While those questions may be unanswerable, at least we must consider the problems produced for older people by the stereotyping process. The stereotypes of aging come from a cultural belief system that is highly inaccurate. That these images can sometimes be portrayed as funny by a comedian is no solace for one who tries to age gracefully in a culture that sees the aging person as ugly, wrinkled, stooped, deranged, decrepit, slow, sexless, and crotchety.

## Integration Not a Cultural Goal

Unquestionably, the United States has not been successful in integrating the elderly into the mainstream of American culture. As individuals, we may feel great compassion for the plight of our elderly and advocate strongly that people should remain in active roles and be a viable part of our culture as long as they live; but as a society we have acted collectively to make it difficult for this integration to take place. In fact, many of our cultural policies are unmistakably intended to militate against the integration of the aged into the mainstream of society.

The most blatant example of such a policy is mandatory retirement. In our culture one's occupation often becomes one's identity. "What do you do?" is an almost rote conversation opener in the United States because we evaluate others in terms of their occupational roles. One's job is also a major social outlet. For many people, most of their primary social affiliations are occupationally related, whether they are the breadwinners or the breadwinners' spouses. The typical person in our culture depends on the workplace to meet the normal needs of affiliation and social attachment. The loss of one's job can be a devastating disruption in the fulfillment of these needs. Such is the case when workers reach retirement age and discover they are no longer part of the social system at the office or the mill.

This article is not the place to debate the complicated issues relating to retirement. In fact, the problem is not retirement *per se* but the fact that retirement is mandatory at a given age. The point here is that mandatory retirement is a government-imposed, cultural mechanism, the intent of which is to remove people above a certain age from the job market. In our culture, when someone is removed from the job market, he or she is well on the way to being removed from the mainstream of society. Thus the goal in the United States seems to be to eliminate older people from the active roles that contribute to society rather than attempt to integrate them into the culture. Interestingly enough, we find considerable cultural variance on this issue. For example, the oriental cultures, though practices are rapidly changing in recent years, have a long history and tradition of utilizing the resources of its older citizens and integrating them more fully into the culture than do Western cultures.[9] This issue is just one of many that invites intercultural comparisons.

## INTERCULTURAL ASPECTS OF AGING

Gerontologists have long been aware of the usefulness of comparing cultures in the study of aging. The International Association of Gerontology, founded in 1950, sponsors an international congress every three years. One of the most significant publications on the intercultural aspects of aging, *International Handbook on Aging: Contemporary Developments and Research*, contains articles on 28 different countries. These articles reveal such demographic information about the elderly as population proportions and life expectancies, and they review the major programs, social services, medical care systems, and so on for the aged in each of these major cultures.[10] A noteworthy observation from this book is that, although the study of aging has experienced a golden age in the United States in the last 15 years, research in other cultures is not being done primarily by Americans. The list of contributors to the *International Handbook* shows that most research is being conducted by people from their own cultures and represents a variety of disciplines—none of which is communication.

Cross-cultural comparisons have enabled us to explore significant gerontological phenomena that necessarily go beyond cultural boundaries. Some areas that have been compared include demographic characteristics, treatment of the aged—both physically and mentally—roles and statuses of older people, types of programs available for the aged, and relationships among aspects of the aging process and numerous cultural characteristics such as socioeconomic factors, educational policies, social policies and values, and social conditions. One major reseach effort in intercultural aspects of aging resulted in the observation that many age-related phenomena are interwoven with factors of modernization.[11] Such cross-cultural research has also led to the conclusion that there is a relationship between the numbers and proportions of older people in modernizing societies and the development of study, analysis, and education about aging.[12]

## Intercultural Comparisons

We could choose any of the 28 countries included in the *International Handbook* to exemplify the usefulness of cross-cultural comparisons in the area of communication and aging. In the interest of brevity, we will select only one.

Numerous types of comparisons have been made between Japan and the United States in the postwar years, but only recently, beginning in the mid-1970's, have we found gerontologists from the United States studying aging in Japan. Our research on aging in Japan is so recent that drawing conclusions is premature, but we cannot help but be intrigued by the fact that we are getting two distinctly different viewpoints about what it is like to become old in Japan.[13]

The catalyst in this discussion is Erdman Palmore's book, *The Honorable Elders*.[14] From beginning to end, the posture of this book is a very positive one, as the title indicates. After spending a sabbatical leave at the Gerontological Institute in Tokyo, Palmore came to the conclusion that there is much the United States can learn from Japan in the area of aging—that the old Confucian-related beliefs of giving great respect to the elderly and allowing them to grow old with dignity still persists and that there are only minor problems connected with aging in Japan.

Briefly, Palmore focuses on two major issues: (1) that the aged enjoy a high status in Japan and (2) that the Japanese elderly are well integrated into the social networks of their culture. He supports these notions with statistics from the prime minister's office, by personal observations of behavior, and by cultural studies. Palmore states that the high status of the aged in Japan is evidenced by (1) the honorific language used in speaking to or about the elderly; (2) family traditions in the household—elders being served first, getting special seats, walking in front, or being first in the bath; and, (3) public declarations of respect for the aged—specifically referring to the 1963 National Law for Welfare of the Elders, which states that:

*The Elders shall be loved and respected as those who have for many years contributed toward the development of society, and a wholesome and peaceful life shall be guaranteed to them. In accordance with their desire and ability, the elders shall be given opportunities to engage in suitable work or to participate in social activities.*

Palmore also notes the Japanese annual national holiday in September devoted to respecting the elders in the family.

Palmore's second major issue is the integration of the aged in Japanese society. He focuses on three levels of social integration—in the family, in the work force, and in the community—and he concludes that "Japan is an exception to the general rule that industrialization causes a sharp decline in status and integration of the aged" and that "Japan demonstrates that the aged need not suffer from prejudice and discrimination in modern society."

However, a considerably different perspective can be seen in the writings of other scholars.[15] Douglas Sparks conducted a study that focused mostly on retirement problems in Japan—certainly an area worth considering since retirement is one of the major adjustment problems for the aged in modern industrial societies.[16] Sparks argues that retirement is an especially serious problem in Japan. It usually occurs at age 55, or 20 years short of one's statistical life expectancy, which has increased dramatically from 45 years before World War II to 75 years today. Pension systems are grossly inadequate, according to Sparks. Some companies give a lump sum equivalent to two or three years' salary, hardly enough to sustain the retiree for 20 years. Public pension plans pay only a few hundred dollars a year, and benefits do not begin until age 60 (65 if employed). Therefore, the Japanese retiree must depend on the family for support or get another job, but postretirement jobs, as Sparks points out, typically mean a significant decline in status and responsibility.

David Plath explores the problems of aging in Japan from a broader sociological perspective.[17] He describes the cultural shifts from the Meiji Age (1868–1912), when Japan was becoming a modern nation, to the era between the world wars when the vertical society prevailed and when the Confucian values of paternalism and great respect for the elderly returned, to the postwar era of becoming a modern industrialized state—with its problems for the elderly. Plath's analysis includes such deeply imbedded cultural phenomena as (1) the concept of *obasute* (pronounced oh-boss-tay), literally meaning "discarding granny," death before dependence in old age; (2) the high suicide rate among the elderly in Japan—both statistically and in terms of the belief systems; (3) the discrepancy between the attitudes of younger people toward the care of the aged and the views expressed by the aged themselves; (4) the financial plight of the aged in Japan; and (5) the advent of nursing homes as a solution.

This more negative picture portrayed by Sparks and Plath is confirmed by my own research, conducted in Japan in 1976 and 1978, and by a prominent Japanese gerontologist, Daisaku Maeda, in a more recent publication.[18] I learned from interviews with housewives in Hiroshima, Osaka, and Tokyo that respect for elders in Japan has decreased considerably in recent decades. Lack of respect for the elderly was expressed frequently as the reason for the 1963 legislation and the special holiday in September to honor the old people in the family. Maeda agrees with Plath's conclusions, quoting from them throughout his article, but he presents a slightly more positive picture on some sociological dimensions; he cites surveys indicating that 80 percent of Japanese elders are "satisfied" with their lives and circumstances.

The marked contrast between the two discrepant positions represented by Palmore and Plath may actually reveal a discrepancy that currently exists in the Japanese culture between the reality of the problems of aging in contemporary Japan and deeply rooted cultural beliefs that survive through tradition. It would be extremely interesting to analyze this social problem in the communication classroom. Since any problem that can be characterized as social will find its expression in the communication systems of the culture within which it is found, a study of these communication systems should reveal the nature and extent of the social problem. This method of finding the extent of the problem may be especially important in cultures where the social problem may be a negative reflection on the culture or where the problem is in conflict with religious or ethnic belief systems within the culture. The latter may be the case in Japan in considering the problems of aging.

One interesting example of a socially significant theme that can be traced in the literature and communication systems is the concept of *obasute*. Plath and others who have studied this concept have traced it to the sixth century. A mountain west of Tokyo is named *obasute*; according to legend, old people are sent there, never to return. Throughout these many centuries, this Japanese legend has been repressed by the Confucian dictates of respect and honor for the aged, which are the opposite of *obasute*. In the 1950's *obasute* emerged as a theme in a widely read short story by Niwa Fumio; its descriptive title has been translated as "The Hateful Age."[19] Students may ask why this story was so popular, or why this theme found its way into other stories in the popular media, including "The Oak Mountain Song," some award winning movies within the last couple of years, and a No drama titled "Obasute."[20] What can we conclude from the current popularity, in the communication media, of a theme that depicts old age as despicable and its solution as abandonment? Should we believe the Confucian expressions of respect and honor for the elderly that are gathered in polite interviews, or should we listen to the statements of the people in the communication systems of the culture?

## SOME CONCLUSIONS

Our culture has chosen to ignore many of the normal communication needs of our older citizens. After retirement, social contacts decrease. For some, this process is a slow one that begins at retirement and continues through the young-old years (60 to 72), but for others the change occurs abruptly at retirement because most of their friendships were job related. Through the middle-old years (72 to 80), most older people experience the deaths of their closest friends and, perhaps, their spouses. Then, ultimately, in the old-old years (80 and older), most old people experience considerable aloneness or, worse yet, institutionalization—a cultural mechanism to care for the infirmed elderly that has been described by some as inhumane.

Some of the needs of older people get widespread attention, especially the medical and economic needs. But our culture has not shown any concern for the communication needs of the elderly. The major communication mechanisms that our culture provides for the older person are the media, but how much of the content of the media is geared to the older audience?

It may well be that many older people in our culture are communication starved. Many may experience a state of communication deprivation that is affecting other aspects of their lives, including such social psychological phenomena as life satisfaction, self-esteem, or even the will to live. If so, as a culture we have not responded to this problem.

Cross-cultural comparisons show that the United States may have one of the worst records for integrating the aging population into the mainstream of its culture. This problem is very much a *communication* problem. It could be solved in part by changing the retirement system and allowing at least part-time employment for older people. Perhaps some assistance could come in the form of increased educational opportunities for the aged, or more organizations for them to join, or even more attention in the media. But the problem isn't just one of employment, or education, or clubs. On a cultural level, we must change our attitudes, beliefs, stereotypes, values, and the public policies that affect the aged. Such change begins on the individual level, but it eventually permeates the communication systems of the whole culture.

## NOTES

1. For a more elaborate discussion of this point, see Carl W. Carmichael, "Communication and gerontology: Interfacing disciplines," *Western Speech Communication*, XL, Spring 1976, pp. 121–129.

2. For example, see Jack Adamowicz, "Visual short-term memory and aging," *Journal of Gerontology* 31 (1976), 39–46.

3. For example, see Paul Baltes and K. W. Schaie, "Aging and IQ: The myth of the twilight years," *Psychology Today*, March 1974, pp. 35–40.

4. For example, see Frain Pearson, *Language Facility and Aging,* Ph.D. Dissertation, University of Oregon, 1976.

5. Carl W. Carmichael, Jean McGee, and Melissa Barker, "Nonverbal communication and the aged," paper presented at annual conference of The Gerontological Society, San Diego, Calif., 1980; and, Carl W. Carmichael, "Nonverbal aspects of aging," paper presented at annual conference of Speech Communication Association, Chicago, 1986.

6. For literature reviews on individual senses, see James Birren and K. W. Schaie, *Handbook of the Psychology of Aging* (New York: Van Nostrand Rinehold, 1977).

7. For example, see Marshall J. Graney, "Media use as a substitute activity in old age," *Journal of Gerontology* 29 (1974), pp. 322–327.

8. Carl W. Carmichael, "Attitudes toward aging throughout the life span," *Journal of the Communication Association of the Pacific* VIII, August 1979, pp. 129–151.

9. Erdman Palmore, "The status and integration of the aged in Japanese society," *Journal of Gerontology* 30 (1975), pp. 199–208; and Erdman Palmore, "What can the USA learn from Japan about aging?" *The Gerontologist* (February 1975), pp. 64–67.

10. Erdman Palmore (ed.), *International Handbook on Aging: Contemporary Developments and Research* (Westport, Conn.: Greenwood Press, 1980).

11. Donald Cowgill and Lowell Holmes (eds.), *Aging and Modernization* (New York: Appleton-Century-Crofts, 1972); and Donald Cowgill, "Aging and modernization: A revision of the theory," in J. Gubrium, *Late Life* (Springfield, Ill.: Charles C. Thomas, 1974).

12. Donald Cowgill and R. A. Orgren, "The international development of academic gerontology," in H. Sterns, *Promoting the Growth of Gerontology in Higher Education* (Belmont, Calif.: Wadsworth, 1979).

13. For a summary of areas appropriate for comparison, see Aaron Lipman, "Conference on the potential for Japanese-American cross-national research on aging," *The Gerontologist* (June 1975), pp. 248–253. Contrasting perspectives also can be seen by comparing such articles as Merle Broberg. Dolores Melching, and Daisaku Maeda, "Planning for the elderly in Japan," *The Gerontologist* (June 1975), pp. 242–247; Michael P. Mealey, "Twilight years in the land of the rising sun," *Modern Healthcare* (June 1975), pp. 52–58; and, Daisaku Maeda, "Growth of old people's clubs 'n Japan," *The Gerontologist* (June 1975), pp. 254–25c.

14. Erdman Palmore, *The Honorable Elders* (Durham, N.C.: Duke University Press, 1975).

15. Carl W. Carmichael, "Aging in Japan and America: A communication perspective," *Journal of the Association of the Pacific*, VII, Fall 1978.

16. Douglas Sparks, "The still rebirth: Retirement and role discontinuity," in David W. Plath, *Adult Episodes in Japan* (Leiden, The Netherlands: E. J. Brill, 1975), pp. 64–74.

17. David W. Plath, "Japan: The after years," in Cowgill and Holmes, *Aging and Modernization*, pp. 133–150.

**18.** Daisaku Maeda, "Japan," in Palmore, *International Handbook on Aging: Contemporary Developments and Research*, pp. 251–270.

**19.** Niwa Fumio, "The hateful age (Iyagarase no nenrei)," translated by Ivan Morris, in Morris, *Modern Japanese Stories: An Anthology* (Rutland, Vt. and Tokyo: Charles H. Tuttle Publishing Co., 1962), p. 340.

**20.** Ito Sei, "On 'The Oak Mountain Song,'" *Japan Quarterly* IV (April-June 1957), pp. 233–235.

# Viewing Persons with Disabilities as a Culture

DAWN O. BRAITHWAITE

Johnathan is an articulate, intelligent, thirty-five year old man who has used a wheelchair since he became a paraplegic when he was twenty years old.[1] He recalls taking an able-bodied woman out to dinner at a nice restaurant. When the waitress came to take their order, she patronizingly asked his date, "And what would *he* like to eat for dinner?" At the end of the meal the waitress presented Jonathan's date with the check and thanked her for her patronage. Although it may be hard to believe the insensitivity of the waitress, this incident is not an isolated one. Rather, such an experience is a common one for persons with disabilities.

There has been a growing interest in the important area of health communication among communication scholars, with a core of researchers looking at communication between able-bodied persons and those with disabilities. Disabled persons are becoming an increasingly large and active minority in our culture due to (1) an increase in the number of persons who live long enough to develop disabilities and (2) advances in medical technology that allow those with disabilities to survive their illnesses and injuries. In the past disabled persons were kept out of public view, but today they are mainstreaming into all facets of modern society. All of us have or will have contact with persons with disabilities of some kind, and many of us will find family, friends, coworkers, or even ourselves part

This essay was written especially for this fifth edition. All rights reserved. Permission to reprint must be obtained from the publisher and the author. Ms. Braithwaite teaches at the University of Minnesota, Morris.

of the disabled culture. Says Marie, a college student who became a quadraplegic after diving into a swimming pool, "I knew there were disabled people around, but I never thought this would happen to me. I never even knew a disabled person before I became one. If before this happened, I saw a person in a wheelchair, I would have been uncomfortable and not known what to say."

The purpose of this essay is to discuss several aspects of communication between able-bodied and disabled individuals as an intercultural communication phenomenon. To better understand communication between able-bodied and disabled persons, we must view disabled persons as a *culture* (Emry and Wiseman 1985). That is, we must recognize that persons with disabilities develop certain unique communicative characteristics that are not shared by the majority of able-bodied individuals in U.S. society.

This essay presents research findings from a series of interviews with persons who have visible physical disabilities. First, we introduce the communication problems that can arise between persons in the able-bodied culture and those in the disabled culture. Second, we discuss some problems with the way research into communication between able-bodied and disabled persons has been conducted. Third, we present results from the interviews. These results show persons with disabilities engaged in a process whereby they critique the prevailing stereotypes of the disabled held by the able-bodied and engage in a process that we call *redefinition*. Finally, we discuss the importance of these findings for both scholars and students of intercultural communication.

## COMMUNICATION BETWEEN ABLE-BODIED AND DISABLED PERSONS

Persons with disabilities seek to overcome the barriers associated with physical disability because disability affects all areas of an individual's life: behavioral, economic, and social. When we attempt to understand the effects of disability, we must differentiate between disability and handicap. Many aspects of disability put limitations on an individual because one or more of the key life functions, such as self-care, mobility, communication, socialization, and employment, is interrupted. Disabilities are often compensated for or overcome through assisting devices, such as wheelchairs or canes, or through training. Disabilities become handicaps when the disability interacts with the physical or social environment to impede a person in some aspect of his or her life (Athelstan and Crewe 1985). For example, a disabled individual who is paraplegic can function in the environment with wheelchairs and curb cuts, but he or she is handicapped when buildings and/or public transportation are not accessible to wheelchairs. When the society is willing and/or able to help, disabled persons have the ability to achieve increasingly independent lives.

Many physical barriers associated with disabilities can be detected and corrected, but the social barriers resulting from disabilities are much more insidious. Nowhere are the barriers more apparent than in the communication between able-bodied persons and persons with disabilities. When able-bodied and disabled persons interact, the general, stereotypical communication problem that is present in all new relationships is heightened, and both persons behave in even more constrained and less spontaneous ways, acting overly self-conscious, self-controlled, and rigid because they feel uncomfortable and uncertain (Belgrave and Mills 1981; Weinberg 1978). While the able-bodied person may communicate verbal acceptance to the person with the disability, his or her nonverbal behavior may communicate rejection and avoidance (Thompson 1982). For example, the able-bodied person may speak with the disabled person, but stand at a greater distance than usual, avoid eye contact, and cut the conversation short. Disability becomes a handicap, then, for persons with disabilities when they interact with able-bodied persons and experience discomfort when communicating; this feeling blocks the normal development of a relationship between them.

Most able-bodied persons readily recognize that what we have just described is representative of their own communication experiences with disabled persons. Able-bodied persons often find themselves in the situation of not knowing what is expected of them or how to act; they have been taught both to "help the handicapped" and to "treat all persons equally." For example, should we help a person with a disability open a door or should we help them up if they fall? Many able-bodied persons have offered help only to be rebuffed by the person with the disability. Able-bodied persons greatly fear saying the wrong thing, such as "See you later!" to a blind person or "Why don't you run by the store on your way home?" to a paraplegic. It is easier to avoid situations where we might have to talk with a disabled person rather than face discomfort and uncertainty.

Persons with disabilities find these situations equally uncomfortable and are well aware of the discomfort of the able-bodied person. They are able to describe both the verbal and nonverbal signals of discomfort and avoidance that able-bodied persons portray (Braithwaite, Emry, and Wiseman 1984). Persons with disabilities report that when they meet able-bodied persons, they want to get the discomfort "out of the way," and they want the able-bodied person to see them as a "person like anyone else," rather than focus solely on the disability (Braithwaite 1985).

## PROBLEMS WITH THE PRESENT RESEARCH

When we review the research in the area of communication between able-bodied and disabled persons, three problems come to the forefront. First, very little is known about the communication behavior of disabled persons. A few researchers have studied disabled persons' communication, but most of them study able-bodied persons' reactions to disabled persons (most of these researchers are themselves able-bodied). Second, most researchers talk *about* persons with disabilities, not *with* them. Disabled persons are rarely represented in the studies; when they are, the disabled person is most often "played," for example, by an able-bodied person in a wheelchair. Third, and most significantly, the research is usually conducted from the perspective of the able-bodied person; that is, what can persons with disabilities *do* to make able-bodied persons feel more comfortable. It does not take into consideration the effects on the person with the disability. Therefore, we have what may be called an *ethnocentric bias* in the research, which focuses on able-bodied/disabled communication from the perspective of the able-bodied majority, ignoring the perspective of the disabled minority.

We shall discuss the results of an ongoing study that obtains the perspectives of disabled persons concerning their communication with able-bodied persons. To date, fifty-seven in-depth interviews have been conducted with physically disabled adults about their communication with able-bodied persons in the early stages of relationships. Here we are concerned with understanding human behavior from the disabled person's own frame of reference. This concern is particularly important in the area of communication between able-bodied and disabled persons and, as we have said, previous research has been conducted from the perspective of able-bodied persons; disabled persons have not participated in these studies. Doing research by talking directly to the person with the disability helps to bring out information important to the individual, rather than simply getting the disabled person's reaction to what is on the researcher's mind. This research represents a unique departure from what other researchers have been doing because the focus is on the perspective of the disabled minority.

## PROCESS OF REDEFINITION

When discussing their communication with able-bodied persons, disabled persons' responses often deal with what we call *redefinition*. That is, in their communication with able-bodied persons and among themselves, disabled persons engage in a process whereby they critique the prevailing stereotypes held by the able-bodied and create new definitions: (1) of the disabled as members of a "new" culture; (2) of self by the disabled; (3) of disability for the disabled; and (4) of disability for the dominant culture.

## Redefinition of the Disabled As Members of a "New" Culture

Persons with disabilities report seeing themselves as a minority or a culture. For some of the subjects, this definition crosses disability lines; that is, their definition of *disabled* includes all persons who have disabilities. For others, the definition is not as broad and includes only other persons with the same type of disability. Most persons with disabilities, however, do define themselves as part of a culture. Says one person:

*It's (being disabled) like West Side Story. Tony and Maria; white and Puerto Rican. They were afraid of each other; ignorant of each others' cultures. People are people.*

According to another man:

*First of all, I belong to a subculture because of the way I have to deal with things being in the medical system, welfare. There is the subculture. . .I keep one foot in the able-bodied culture and one foot in my own culture. One of the reasons I do that is so that I don't go nuts.*

Membership in the disabled culture has several similarities to membership in other cultures. Many of the persons interviewed likened their own experiences to those of other cultures, particularly to blacks and women. When comparing the disabled to both blacks and women, we find several similarities. The oppression is biologically based, at least for those who have been disabled since birth; one is a member of the culture by being born with cerebral palsy or spina bifida, for example. As such, the condition is unalterable; the disability will be part of them throughout their lifetime.

For those persons who are not born with a disability, membership in the culture can be a process that emerges over time. For some, the process is a slow one, as in the case of a person with a degen-erative disease that may develop over many years and gradually become more and more severe. If a person has a sudden-onset disability, such as breaking one's neck in an accident and waking up a quadraplegic, the movement from a member of the dominant culture—"normal person"—to the minority culture—disabled person—may happen in a matter of seconds. This sudden transition to membership in the disabled culture presents many challenges of readjustment in all facets of an individual's life, especially in communication relationships with others.

## Redefinition of Self by the Disabled

How one redefines oneself, then, from normal or able-bodied to disabled, is a process of redefinition of self. While blacks struggle for identity in white society and women struggle for identity in a male-dominated society, the disabled struggle for identity in an able-bodied world. One recurring theme from the participants in this study is "I am a person like anyone else" (if disabled since birth) or "I'm basically the same person I always was" (if a sudden-onset disability). The person who is born with a disability learns the process of becoming identified as "fully human" while still living as a person with a disability. The individual who is disabled later in life, Goffman (1963) contends, goes through a process of redefinition of self. For example, the subjects born with disabilities make such statements as, "I am not different from anyone else as far as I am concerned" or "Disability does not mean an incomplete character." Persons whose disabilities happened later say "You're the same person you were. You just can't do the same things you did before." One man put it this way:

*If anyone refers to me as an amputee, that is guaranteed to get me madder than hell! I don't deny the leg amputation, but I am me. I am a whole person. One.*

During the redefinition process, individuals come to terms with both positive and negative ramifications of disability. Some subjects report that "disability is like slavery to me." In contrast, one woman reports:

*I find myself telling people that this has been the worst thing that has happened to me. It has also been one of the best things. It forced to me examine what I felt about myself. . .confidence is grounded in me, not in other people. As a woman, not as dependent on clothes, measurements, but what's inside me.*

One man expresses his new-found relationship to other people when he says, "I'm more interdependent than I was. I'm much more aware of that now." This process of redefinition is evident in what those interviewed have to say.

## Redefinition of Disability for the Disabled

A third category of redefinition occurs as persons with disabilities redefine both disability and its associated characteristics. For example, in redefining disability itself, one man said, "People will say, 'Thank god I'm not handicapped.' And I'll say, 'Let's see, how tall are you? Tell me how you get something off that shelf up there!' " This perspective is centered on the view of the disability as a characteristic of the person rather than the person himself; it recognizes disability as situational rather than inherent or grounded in the person. In this view, everyone is disabled to some extent: by race, gender, height, or physical abilities, for example.

Redefinition of disability can be seen in the use of language. Says one subject who objected to the label *handicapped person*: "Persons with a handicapping condition. You emphasize that person's identity and then you do something about the condition." This statement ties into viewing one's self as a person first. Research reveals movement from the term *handicapped* to *disability* or *disabled*, although a wide variety of terms are used by these subjects to talk about the self. Another change in language has been the avoidance of phrases such

as "polio victim" or "arthritis sufferer." Again the emphasis is on the person, not the disability. "I am a person whose arms and legs do not function very well," says one subject who had polio as a child.

There have also been changes in the terms that refer to able-bodied persons. Says one man:

*You talk about the able-bodied. I will talk about the nonhandicapped. . .It's a different kind of mode. In Michigan they've got it in the law: "temporarily able-bodied."*

It is common for the persons interviewed to refer to the majority in terms of the minority: "nondisabled" or "nonhandicapped," rather than "able-bodied" or "normal." More than the change in terminology, the phrase "temporarily able-bodied" or TABS serves to remind able-bodied persons that no one is immune from disability. The persons interviewed also used TABS as a humorous reference term for the able-bodied as well. "Everyone is a TAB." This view jokingly intimates, "I just got mine earlier than you. . .just you wait!"

In addition to redefining disability, the disabled also redefine "assisting devices":

*Now, there were two girls about eight playing and I was in my shorts. And I'll play games with them and say, "which is my good leg?" And that gets them to thinking. Well, this one (pats artificial leg) is not nearly as old as the other one!*

Says another subject:

*Do you know what a cane is? It's a portable railing! The essence of a wheelchair is a seat and wheels. Now, I don't know that a tricycle is not doing the exact same thing.*

Again, in these examples, the problem is not the disability or the assisting device, such as a cane, but how one views the disability or the assisting device. These assisting devices take on a different meaning for the persons using them. Subjects expressed frustration with persons who played with their wheelchairs: "This chair is not a toy, it is part of me. When you touch my chair, you are touching me." One woman, a business executive, expanded on this by saying, "I don't know why people who push my chair feel compelled to make car sounds as they do it."

## Redefinition of Disability for the Dominant Culture

Along with the redefinitions that concern culture, self, and disability comes an effort to try to change society's view of the disabled and disability. Persons with disabilities are attempting to change the view of themselves as helpless, as victims, or merely sick. One man says:

*People do not consider you, they consider the chair first. I was in a store with my purchases on my lap and money on my lap. The clerk looked at my companion and said, "Cash or charge?"*

This incident with the clerk is a story that has been voiced by every person interviewed in some form or another, just as it happened to Jonathan at the restaurant with his date. One woman who has multiple sclerosis and uses a wheelchair told of her husband accompanying her while she was shopping for lingerie. When they were in front of the lingerie counter, she asked for what she wanted, and the clerk repeatedly talked only to her husband saying, "And what size does she want?" The woman told her the size and the clerk looked at the husband and said, "and what color?" Persons with disabilities recognize that able-bodied persons often see them as disabled first and persons second (if at all), and they expressed a need to change this view. Says a man who has muscular dystrophy:

*I do not believe in those goddamned telethons . . .they're horrible, absolutely horrible. They get into the self-pity, you know, and disabled folk do not need that. Hit people in terms of their attitudes and then try to deal with and process their feelings. And the telethons just go for the heart and leave it there.*

Most of the subjects indicate they see themselves as educators or ambassadors for all persons with disabilities. All indicate they will answer questions put to them about their disabilities, as long as they determine the other "really wants to know, to learn." One man suggests a solution:

*What I am concerned with is anything that can do away with the "us" versus "them" distinction. Well, you and I are anatomically different, but we're two human beings! And at the point we can sit down and communicate eyeball to eyeball. . .the quicker you do that, the better!*

Individually and collectively, persons with disabilities do identify themselves as part of a culture. They are involved in a process of redefinition of disability, both for themselves and for the able-bodied.

## CONCLUSIONS

This research justifies the usefulness of viewing disability from an intercultural perspective. Persons with disabilities do see themselves as members of a culture, and viewing communication between able-bodied and disabled persons from this perspective sheds new light on the communication problems that exist. Emry and Wiseman (1985) argue that intercultural training should be the focus in our perceptions of self and others: They call for unfreezing old attitudes about disability and refreezing new ones. Clearly, from these findings, that is exactly what persons with disabilities are doing, both for themselves and for others.

Of the fifty-seven persons with disabilities interviewed, only a small percentage had any sort of education or training concerning communication, during or after rehabilitation, that would prepare them for changes in their communication relationships due to their disabilities. Such education seems especially critical for those who experience sudden-onset disabilities because their self-concepts and all of their relationships undergo sudden, radical changes. Intercultural communication scholars have the relevant background and experience for this kind of research and training, and they can help make this transition from majority to minority an easier one.

As for able-bodied persons who communicate with disabled persons, this intercultural perspective leads to the following suggestions:

*Don't assume* that persons with disabilities cannot speak for themselves or do things for themselves. *Do assume* they can do something unless they communicate otherwise.

*Don't force* your help on persons with disabilities. *Do let* them tell you if they want something, what they want, and when they want it. If a person with a disability refuses your help, don't go ahead and help anyway.

*Don't avoid* communication with persons who have disabilities simply because you are uncomfortable or unsure. *Do remember* they probably feel the same way you do.

*Do* treat persons with disabilities as *persons first*, recognizing that you are not dealing with a disabled person but with a *person* who has a disability.

## NOTE

1. The names of all the subjects have been changed to protect their privacy.

## BIBLIOGRAPHY

Athelstan, G. and N. Crewe. Social and Psychological Aspects of Physical Disabilities. University of Minnesota, Extension Services, 1985.

Belgrave, F. Z. and J. Mills. "Effect upon Desire for Social Interaction with a Physically Disabled Person of Mentioning the Disability in Different Contexts," *Journal of Applied Social Psychology* 11(1), 44–57, 1981.

Braithwaite, D. O. "Impression Management and Redefinition of Self by Persons with Disabilities." Paper presented at the annual meeting of the Speech Communication Association, Denver, 1985.

Braithwaite, D. O., R. A. Emry, and R. L. Wiseman. "Able-bodied and Disablebodied Persons' Communication: The Disabled Persons' Perspective." ERIC ED 264 622, 1984.

Emry, R. A. and R. L. Wiseman. "An Intercultural Understanding of Able-bodied and Disabled Persons' Communication." Paper presented at the annual meeting of the Speech Communication Association, Denver, CO, 1985.

Goffman, E. *Stigma*. Englewood Cliffs, NJ: Prentice Hall, 1963.

Thompson, T. L. "Disclosure As a Disability-Management Strategy: A Review and Conclusions," *Communication Quarterly* 30, 196–202, 1982.

Weinberg, N. "Modifying Social Stereotypes of the Physically Disabled," *Rehabilitation Counseling Bulletin* 22(2), 114–124, 1978.

# Gender and Communication: Sex Is More Than a Three-Letter Word

JUDY C. PEARSON

Are men or women more likely to use the words, *puce, aquamarine, ecru,* and *mauve?* If a speaker discussed carburetors, pistons, overhead cams, and cylinders, would you guess that the speaker was male or female? Is the chief executive officer of a Fortune 500 company more likely to be a man or a woman? In almost any organization, are men or women more likely to have jobs as secretaries? Every day we make observations and predictions about people's sex on the basis of their communicative behaviors and the roles they have in our culture. Sex and communication is not a topic with which you are unfamiliar, although you may not realize that a great deal of theorizing and research has gone into this topic.

While an interest in the relationship between sex and communication may be traced to the beginning of this century (Stopes 1908), the past 15 years have produced the bulk of the research on *gender* and communication. The relationships among women, men, and communication are complex and bear careful scrutiny. This essay is concerned with some of the issues that allow us to conclude that "sex is more than a three-letter word" in the field of communication.

This essay was prepared especially for this fifth edition. All rights reserved. Permission to reprint must be obtained from the publisher and the author. Ms. Pearson is a Professor of Interpersonal Communication at Ohio University, Athens, Ohio.

## HOW ARE SEX, GENDER, AND COMMUNICATION RELATED?

To understand how sex, gender, and communication are related, we must understand the history of the research in this area. The term *sex* is used to refer to biological differences between people. Before the mid-1970s, studies in communication that considered sex differences simply categorized people on the basis of their biological differences and observed differences in communicative behavior. For example, we observed that women smile more frequently than do men (Argyle 1975), that men speak more loudly than do women (Market, Prebor, and Brandt 1972), that women are more likely to be observed or watched than are men (Argyle and Williams 1969), and that men are more likely to interrupt others than are women (Zimmerman and West 1975). Our use of the word *gender* is deliberate and important for our discussion.

In 1974, Sandra Bem created a new conceptualization of sex, as far as roles are concerned. Before this time, people were categorized on masculinity and femininity measures as being more or less of each of these measures. In other words, masculinity was placed at one end of the continuum and femininity was placed at the other end, as illustrated in Figure 1. An individual, through a series of questions, is categorized as masculine or feminine or somewhere in between. We should note that the more masculine one indicated that he or she was, the less feminine he or she was. An individual could not be high in both masculinity and femininity or low in both categories.

Masculinity                                    Femininity

**Figure 1**

In private conversations, Bem explained that she felt limited by this conceptualization of masculinity and femininity. She perceived of herself as possessing a number of masculine traits *and* a number of feminine traits. In other words, she felt that she should score high in both masculinity and femininity. Instead, when she was categorized, her score indicated that she was somewhere between masculine and feminine and was thus viewed as neither feminine nor masculine.

Bem (1974) created a new way to conceive of and measure sex roles in the Bem Sex Role Inventory. She suggested that masculinity and femininity are separate dimensions and that one might be high in masculinity and low in femininity (masculine), low in masculinity and high in femininity (feminine), high in masculinity and high in femininity (androgynous), or low in masculinity and low in femininity (undifferentiated). This view is depicted in Figure 2.

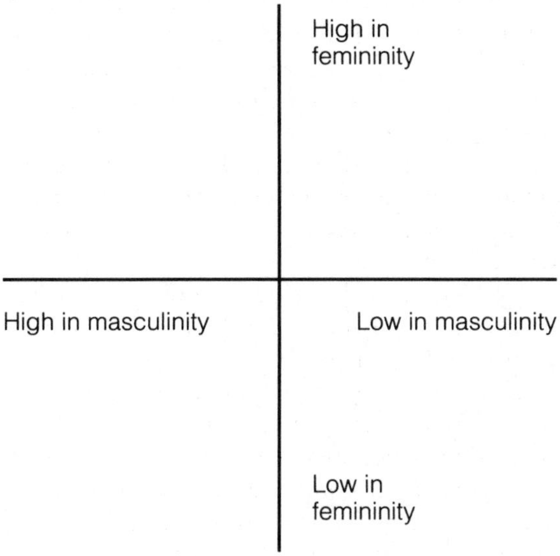

High in femininity

High in masculinity        Low in masculinity

Low in femininity

**Figure 2**

Although Bem's change may appear to be a fairly simplistic one, it radically altered the way women's and men's roles were categorized. At first, women and men were viewed as different because of biological traits alone. Then they could be categorized as masculine, feminine, or in between. Finally, Bem suggested that people should be categorized on the extent to which they internalize society's standards for masculine and feminine behaviors. Thus a biological male may be highly feminine or a biological female may be very masculine. When sex roles became a psychological, rather than a physical, variable, we began to talk about gender rather than sex. Sex still refers to biological differences between people; gender refers to internalized predispositions to masculine and feminine roles. As you will see, understanding the difference between sex and gender is critical for our understanding of gender and communication.

## Communication Creates Gender

Communication is related to gender in two ways. First, to a large extent, *communication creates gender.* How does communication create gender? Our communicative exchanges tell us what our roles are, and they encourage or discourage us from internalizing predispositions relating to masculinity or femininity.

Early theorists like William James, Charles Cooley, John Dewey, and I. A. Thomas all contributed to a theory that George Herbert Mead (1934) originated. That theory—symbolic interactionism—has important implications for us. Mead felt that people were actors, not reactors. He suggested that people develop through three stages.

The *preparatory stage* includes the stage in which infants imitate others by mirroring. The toddler may wash a surface, put on mommy's or daddy's shoes, or pat the dog. The child does not necessarily understand the imitated acts.

In the *play stage,* the child actually plays the roles of others. She may pretend to be mommy, daddy, the postal carrier, a fire fighter, a nurse, or a doctor. Each role is played *independently;* the behaviors are not integrated into a single set of role behaviors. In other words, the child does not play a superwoman who is a mother, a wife, a runner, an airplane pilot, a writer, and a teacher.

In the *game stage,* the child responds simultaneously in a generalized way to several others. The child generalizes a composite role by considering all others' definitions of self. The person thus develops a unified role from which he or she sees the self. This perception is the overall way that other people see the individual. People unify their self-concepts by internalizing this composite view. This self-picture emerges from years of symbolically interacting, or communicating, with others.

Your integrated self will tend toward the behaviors others encourage you to perform and will tend away from behaviors that others discourage you from performing. From birth, men and women are treated differently because of their genitalia. We dress male and female babies in different kinds and colors of clothing. Parents respond differently to male and female infants (Bell and Carver 1980). We describe male and female babies with different adjectives: boy are strong, solid, and independent, whereas girls are loving, cute, and sweet. People describe identical behavior on the part of infants differently if they are told the infant is a boy or a girl (Condry and Condry 1976). Preschool children observe commercials and cartoons on television, listen to stories, and play with toys that depict "appropriate" sex roles. In many ways, people are treated differently because of their sex.

## Communicative Behavior Is Related to Gender

A second way that communication and gender are related is that our specific use of verbal and nonverbal codes is highly related to gender. You know that different roles invite different languages. For example, terms like *bits, RAM, ROM, motherboard, modem, memory, monitor, hard disk, CPT, CRT,* and *CPU,* are common in the language about computers. Similarly, words like *coma, carcinoma, cardiovascular, chemotherapy, colostomy,* and *capillary* are common in the language of medicine.

Masculine and feminine individuals use different languages, and they put their words together differently. Maybe you never thought about the fact that sex roles place people in different subcultures. Psychological gender roles also place people in separate subcultures just as sex, race, and age do. All subcultures create special languages. Adolescents, for instance, purposefully talk in ways that their parents do not understand. ("Cool" and "neat" are replaced by "tubular," "grody to the max," "I'm so sure," and "mega-hard," which in turn are supplanted by "rad" and "wick.")

Masculine and feminine people similarly establish their own ways of talking as a result of being members of separate subcultures. Why do subcultures establish separate languages? We can offer at least two reasons: (1) A special language is developed to conduct the subculture's function or business and (2) a special language allows a subculture to symbolize its identity as a subculture. Feminine people may be more likely to know color terms such as *ecru* and *mauve* because they use these terms in their work, just as masculine people may use terms related to motors and engines in their work. Furthermore, feminine individuals may overuse adjectives to demonstrate that they are part of a feminine subgroup; masculine individuals may rely upon four-letter swear words to demonstrate their subculture.

A caveat is in order. Even when subcultures develop separate languages, their members often understand the language of the other subculture. They may even use the alternative language in their own subculture. For example, we may associate traditional four-letter swear words with masculine individuals, but feminine individuals understand these terms and sometimes use them as well—but in the exclusive company of other feminine persons. Masculine individuals may not touch each other in a caring way in mixed company, but they certainly rely on hugging, stroking, and touching on the football field.

Similarly, people may feel free to engage in out-of-role behavior when they are within the safety of an established relationship, but they will not engage in out-of-role behavior in the company of mere acquaintances and strangers. Dindia, Fitzpatrick, and Williamson (1986), for instance, showed that wives are likely to behave in a submissive manner with males other than their husbands whereas they behave in a dominant way with their spouses.

What are a few of the differences between the two subcultures? Bonaguro and Pearson (1986) determined that feminine individuals are more animated than masculine individuals and those with undifferentiated identities, and that feminine types are more relaxed than are androgynous and masculine types. Feminine individuals are less argumentative than are masculine individuals (Rancer and Dierks-Stewart 1983). Feminine types are likely to be relational, while masculine types are apt to be goal-oriented (Serafini and Pearson 1983). The feminine individual is generally higher than her masculine counterpart in empathy, caring, and nurturing (McMillan, Clifton, McGrath, and Gale 1977). Finally, feminine females report that they disclose personal information about themselves less frequently than do androgynous females, whereas masculine men have lower disclosure scores than do androgynous men (Greenblatt, Hasenauer, and Freimuth 1980). (For a comprehensive review of gender and sex differences in communication behaviors, see Pearson 1985).

## WHAT PROBLEMS EXIST?

As you might guess, the subject of gender and communication is in upheaval. There are at least three problems that account for our difficulty in coming to grips with effective and appropriate communication across these subcultures. First, most people still assume that sex and gender are synonyms. Second, we often confuse our *perceptions* of behavior with actual behavior. Third, both communication and U.S. culture have a masculine bias.

### Sex and Gender Are Presumed to Be Synonymous

The first problem is that while sex and gender are highly related (men are more likely to be masculine than are women, and women are more likely to be feminine than are men), they are not identical. Furthermore, a great number of people are androgynous (possess both male and female qualities) or undifferentiated (possess neither male nor female qualities). The concepts of sex and gender were never identical, and the two have become increasingly disparate in recent times. Let us consider the impact that recent changes have made on the concepts of sex and gender.

Our world and the roles of women and men in it are undergoing rapid change, but our interactions do not acknowledge these changes. To a great extent, we tend to live in the past. We behave on the basis of the naturalistic fallacy: What is (or has been) is what should be. For example, if you ask someone in Iowa how farming should be done, he or she will tell you that it should be done on relatively small plots of land owned by individual families. If you ask someone in New York who should control the major networks, he or she will tell you it should be persons trained in telecommunications and broadcast journalism. But family farms are nearly a thing of the past, and NBC and ABC are owned, operated, and controlled by large multinational corporations.

Our world has changed, and this change makes it impossible for us to know everyone we must deal with. More and more often we communicate with people on some basis other than an interpersonal one, such as on the basis of cultural and sociological information, and we categorize people simplistically on the basis of surface or demographic cues (biological sex) rather than on the basis of unique and idiosyncratic personal characteristics, including their gender role (knowing them interpersonally).

In days gone by, people often communicated only with members of their own communities and families. People knew a great deal about those with whom they interacted. They would know that one should not talk about sex with one's aunt, that one should hug one's grandparents, and that one should treat one's teachers with respect. People seldom traveled to other cities, states, and nations. Today such travel is commonplace. People are called upon to interact quickly with strangers and acquaintances in a wide variety of new settings.

We make errors in our assessments of other people in brief encounters for a variety of reasons. For instance, we may rely upon implicit personality theory, which suggests that our own experiences and assumptions about human nature are shared by others. For example, one may assume that everyone has a high achievement motivation and competes to win, not understanding that many people develop a fear of success. We may make the fundamental attribution error, which is underestimating situational influences on behavior and attributing behavior to internal personal characteristics alone. As an example, one may assume that a bartender is cold and closed-mouthed, not recognizing that her job description and her negative past experiences with others in bars dictate such behavior.

In our interactions with women and men, we are most likely to err, however, on the basis of four other errors in person perception. First, when we stereotype, we assume, for example, that all men are cold and unfeeling. Second, when we rely upon social roles, we assume, for example, that all mothers are nurturing. Third, when we make logical errors (assume that because a person has one characteristic, he or she will have other characteristics that "go together"), we assume, for example, that women who dress like "ladies" will also talk like them. Fourth, when we engage in wishful thinking (seeing others as we would like them to be rather than as they are), we assume, for example, that our husbands will be like our fathers.

## Perceptions of Behavior Are Confused with Actual Behavior

The second problem is that we often confuse our perceptions of behavior with actual behavior. In other words, we may view a given behavior of a woman as negative, but we may judge the same behavior to be positive when a man exhibits it. For instance, a businesswoman may be labeled "aggressive, pushy, and argumentative," whereas her male counterpart who exhibits the same behavior may be viewed as "ambitious, assertive, and independent." Countless studies have demonstrated that when women and men engage in identical behavior, the behavior is devalued for the woman. For example, Goldberg (1968), in a classic study, demonstrated that when an essay was attributed to either a woman or a man, the same essay was given a higher grade when respondents believed it was written by a man and a lower grade when respondents believed it was written by a woman. Furthermore, both women and men demonstrated their prejudice toward women.

One reason that we confuse perceptions of behaviors with actual behaviors comes from the lit-

erature on gender and communication itself. In all areas of inquiry, we must ask the question that Whitney Houston made famous in her song, "How will I know?" In the area of social science, and especially in the area of gender and communication, this question is particularly critical. Social science research can rely on self-perceptions, perceptions of others, or on actual observed behavior. In some cases, researchers have relied upon the perceptions of others to determine how women and men communicate. For instance, people may be asked if they believe that women or men speak more often. Although relatively recent behavioral research suggests that men talk more than women (Swacker 1975), most people, when asked, guess that women talk more than men. Similarly, in research on whether masculine or feminine managers are viewed as more successful, researchers often times asked subordinates and others in the work environment for their opinions. Although these perceptions may be valuable, they may also be value-laden, relying more on stereotypes than on actual observations.

Some research on gender and communication has relied upon individual's self-reports or self-perceptions. People have reported on their own communicative behaviors, but as we have learned recently, our self-reports may be based more on our notions of the ideal, or on a perfect example, than on our actual behaviors (Hample 1984; Pavitt and Haight 1986). Or, we may be responding on the basis of social desirability. In addition, we may forget how we actually behaved because of the passage of time (Sulloway and Christensen 1983).

Recently, some research has turned to indices of actual behavior. In other words, we have begun to measure people's actual communicative behaviors to determine the extent to which women and men communicate differently or similarly. Although these research reports are fewer in number than are the studies that have relied upon self-perceptions or self-report data, they suggest that the differences between women and men may be fewer than we once believed, that they may be based on factors other than sex as we have suggested, and that the rationale offered for the differences may be different from what we originally posited.

For example, if one asks most people if women or men exhibit more hostility and use more profanity and expletives, they would probably guess men. However Staley (1978) tested that common-sense view. She asked students between the ages of 18 and 47 to complete a questionnaire that listed a series of emotional situations. In each case, she asked the respondents to report the expletive they would use, to report the expletive they predicted a member of the opposite sex would use, and to define each expletive they provided. Surprisingly, she found that men and women averaged about the same number of expletives per questionnaire. She did find a great difference in predicted responses, however. Men predicted the use of far fewer expletives for women, and women predicted the use of far more expletives for men. Both women and men judged the use of expletives by women as weaker than males' use, even when the terms were identical. Staley thus demonstrated that women and men may be more alike than different on the usage of expletives; nonetheless, people still perceive of women's and men's behavior as being different.

None of these methods of learning about gender and communication is inherently superior to the others, but we should note that each one provides us with different answers. Sometimes we want to know how an individual perceives of himself or herself. In some cases, we may find others' perceptions of people important. Often we want to determine actual behavior. We always want to make sure that our means of making assessments is consistent with our research goal. Perhaps more importantly we want to ensure that people do not confuse their perceptions of behaviors with actual behaviors.

## Our Culture and Our Communication Evidence a Masculine Bias

The third problem that is relevant to gender and communication is that both communication and our culture have a male bias. Our culture and our communication exhibit masculinity. An increasing amount of research demonstrates that the symbols we use to communicate are man-made. The language that we use was created primarily by men, for men. The words we have available reflect male experiences and they encourage male domination.

Kramarae (1981) proposed that female/male communication can be best understood in terms of the muted group theory. This theory suggests that women are a muted (or silenced) group because of their exclusion from the creation of human symbols. Basically, she explains that males perceive the world and then create symbols to represent their experiences. Because women's experiences are different, and because women are not allowed to create an alternative set of symbols, women are muted. Eventually, women learn to use the male symbols, but the symbols are useful only insofar as women are willing to see the world through "male eyes."

What are some obvious examples of man-made words? We might consider the language of business. Although the business world may be viewed as an area that is open to both women and men, when you listen carefully you find that it is primarily a "male club." Many business cliches, for example, come straight from sports—a decidedly male activity. If you want to be successful, you have to "keep your eye on the ball," be a "boy wonder," "keep your head down," be a "team player," be a "pinch hitter," and "tackle the job." What do you avoid? You don't want to be "in the penalty box," "under fire," "under the gun," "in the cellar," be a "disqualified player," have a "jock mentality," or be "caught with your pants down."

We can also build the argument that language is male-dominated when we deal with so-called generic pronouns. When we talk about people in general, which pronoun do we choose? Most people use the male form to refer to both men and women. We use "he," "his," and "him" to refer to men *and* to refer to both men and women. We use "she" and "her" to refer to women, but we do not use these words to refer to both women and men. Why is it that the latter terms are not equally appropriate?

Language does not serve all of its users equally well. Women are left out far more often than men, but both men and women find that language limits the expression of their experiences. Students of gender and communication have created *sexlets,* which are "sniglets" about male and female experiences for which our language has no single words. The following examples are made-up "words" that are not currently in everyday use. First, suggestions from the women: "Sexpectations": when a man takes a woman out for a nice dinner, maybe a movie, and then expects sex at the end of the evening; and "PMS'ed off": the frustration a woman feels with male friends who always claim that when a woman is angry, she must be expecting her period. The men suggested: "Chronoloneliness": how one male felt when he had not seen his girlfriend for a long time; and "condomnesia": when you finally get your girlfriend ready for the big moment, she asks if you have protection, and you must admit that you forgot.

Our research has been similarly flawed in that it has encouraged a masculine bias. The U.S. culture, as we have observed, is one that exhibits masculinity. In other words, male values, attitudes, and perspectives dominate. Our government, our industry, and most of our public organizations are headed by men. Even our private associations, including friendships and family life, are dominated by men. As a result the investigations of women in male-dominated cultures have been, at the very least, biased. Wood, McMahan, and Stacks (1984) observe:

> ... the contexts for the bulk of study on women's communication are invariably male contexts: task groups, businesses, organizations. The tendency to study masculine activities and environments, then, achieves two outcomes. First, it constitutes an implicit argument for the importance of masculine issues, enterprises, and settings and a corresponding argument for the unimportance of feminine concerns, activities, and contexts. Second, it distorts descriptions, assessment, and understanding of women's communication by consistently observing it in alien environments (p. 41).

The social settings of our inquiries, then, have encouraged the continuation of a male-dominated social order. Deaux (1984) observes, "Some tasks may not be neutral arenas in which to test possible differences" (p. 107). We should be wise to heed the words of Kramarae (1981), who observed "Social scientific research is not impersonal, apolitical, and factual, but interpretive" (p. vi).

## HOW CAN WE SOLVE THE PROBLEMS OF COMMUNICATION AND GENDER?

Can we solve the problems we face in the area of communication and gender? We can if we are willing to engage in three practices. First, we must separate our perceptions of ourselves and of other people from the behaviors that we, or they, exhibit. Second, we need to view sex and gender as distinctly different constructs. Third, we need to understand the role of the masculine culture and the way it shapes both our perceptions and our behaviors.

### Separate Perceptions of Behaviors from Actual Behaviors

We must recognize that people's perceptions of another person's behavior may vary dramatically. At the very minimum, we must understand how our own attitudes, values, and perceptions intervene when we observe, predict, and evaluate the behavior of others.

The area of organizational communication provides an example. Within the past decade, researchers have begun to examine the role of women as leaders and managers. In general, in organizational research, we tend to use outcome variables such as productivity to determine the influence of independent variables such as information availability, upward and downward communication, and openness. However, when we investigate the influence of sex roles in the organization, we use people's *perceptions* of women in their positions. For instance, we do not study whether productivity increases or decreases when women serve as managers; instead we ask employees whether they prefer to work for a man or a woman. Given the current state of affairs, it is not difficult to guess which sex they prefer.

Research on communication and sex is no better. Too often we assume that masculine communication is standard. In other words, we begin with a masculine model of communication and then we look at women's communication to see how it differs from that model. Or, we study women's communication in clearly masculine contexts such as the masculine workplace. We also assume that women's behaviors determine their effectiveness. In other words, we don't take into account that women are often devalued simply because they are women. The most competent woman may be viewed negatively simply because she is a woman.

### View Sex and Gender as Distinctive Constructs

Second, we need to view sex and gender as distinctly different constructs. We are in the midst of a paradigmatic shift concerning sex and gender. Intercultural communication students are familiar with the notion of "passing," in which members of lower status groups sometimes attempt to pass as members of higher status groups. For instance, light-skinned blacks sometimes attempt to pass as white. In the same way, many women in contemporary society have attempted to pass as men. A number of successful female managers have done so by adopting masculine characteristics. Similarly, female graduate students often try to outperform their male counterparts. In the professional ranks, too, including medicine and law, women are regularly more masculine in their behavior than are the men with whom they work.

There are now more dual-career couples in our society than there are single-career couples. While some of us applaud the fact that women now have opportunities to work outside the home as well as within it, we should recognize what is occurring. To a large extent, dual-career marriages are made up of two masculine individuals. Biologically, the marriages include a man and a woman, but behaviorally, the marriages include two masculine types.

Changes in our social groupings encourage us to consider sex and gender as separate constructs.

We cannot assume that women are feminine or that men are masculine. In some instances, just the opposite is the case.

### Understand the Role of the Masculine Culture

Third, we need to understand the role of the masculine culture and how it shapes both our perceptions and our behaviors. Men are in charge of our culture, and masculine values and traits are generally viewed as superior to feminine values and traits. When women pass as men, they gain momentary success in the workplace at low-level positions, but they may never become CEOs of Fortune 500 companies. Furthermore, they may lose far more by discarding their feminine side than they gain in the workplace. Masculine behaviors have been shown to lead to physical destruction and disabilities. For example, heart attacks, strokes, and many forms of cancer are more prevalent in men than in women. As women have gained opportunities to compete with men, their rates of death from these diseases have increased. We must understand the inherent sexism that defines the U.S. culture and the values that are associated with the masculine perspective. Furthermore, we must consider whether we wish to continue the status quo.

### SUMMARY

This essay has discussed some of the theorizing and research that has gone on in the area of communication and gender. You have seen how gender and communication are related, the problems that occur in considering sex, gender, and communication, and how we might solve some of those problems in our everyday interactions as well as in our research. At this point, we hope you agree that, in communication, sex is more than a three-letter word.

### BIBLIOGRAPHY

Argyle, M. *Bodily Communication*. New York: International Universities Press, 1975.

Argyle, M., and M. Williams. "Observer or Observed? A Reversible Perspective in Person Perception." *Sociometry* 32 (1969), 396–412.

Bell, N. J., and W. Carver. "A Reevaluation of Gender Label Effects: Expectant Mothers' Responses to Infants." *Child Development* 51 (1980), 925–927.

Bem, S. "The Measurement of Psychological Androgyny." *Journal of Consulting and Clinical Psychology* 42 (1974), 155–162.

Bonaguro, E. W., and J. C. Pearson. *The Relationship between Communicator Style, Argumentativeness, and Gender.* Paper presented to the Speech Communication Association, Chicago, IL, November 1986.

Condry, J., and S. Condry. "Sex Differences: A Study of the Eye of the Beholder." *Child Development* 47 (1976), 812–819.

Deaux, K. "From Individual Differences to Social Categories." *American Psychologist* (1984), 105–116.

Dindia, K., M. A. Fitzpatrick, and R. Williamson. *Communication and Control in Spouse Versus Stranger Interaction.* Paper presented to the Speech Communication Association, Chicago, IL, November 1986.

Goldberg, P. "Are Women Prejudiced against Women?" *Transaction* 6 (1968), 28.

Greenblatt, L., J. Hasenauer, and V. Freimuth. "Psychological Sex Type and Androgyny in a Study of Communication Variables." *Human Communication Research* 6 (1980), 117–129.

Hample, D. "On the Use of Self-Reports." *Journal of the American Forensic Association* 20 (1984), 140–153.

Kramarae, C. *Women and Men Speaking.* Rowley, MA: Newbury House Publishers, 1981.

Markel, N., L. Prebor, and J. Brandt. "Biosocial Factors in Dyadic Communication: Sex and Speaking Intensity." *Journal of Personality and Social Responsibility* 23 (1972), 686–690.

McMillan, J., A. K. Clifton, D. McGrath, and W. S. Gale. "Women's Language: Uncertainty or Interpersonal Sensitivity and Emotionality?" *Sex Roles* 3 (1977), 545–559.

Mead, G. H. *Mind, Self, and Society.* Chicago: University of Chicago Press, 1934.

Pavitt, C., and L. Haight. "Implicit Theories of Communicative Competence: Situational and Competence Level Differences in Judgments of Prototype and Target." *Communication Monographs* 53 (1986), 221–235.

Pearson, J. C. *Gender and Communication.* Dubuque, IA: William C. Brown Company, 1985.

Rancer, A., and K. Dierks-Stewart. "The Influence of Sex and Sex-Role Orientation on Trait Argumentativeness." *The Journal of Personality Assessment* 49 (1985), 61–70.

Serafini, D., and J. Pearson. "Leadership Behavior and Sex Role Socialization: Two Sides of the Same Coin." *The Southern Speech Communication Journal* 49 (1984), 396–405.

Staley, C. "Male-Female Use of Expletives: A Heck of a Difference in Expectations." *Anthropological Literature* 20 (1978), 367–380.

Stopes, C. C. *The Sphere of "Man": In relation to That of "Woman" in the Constitution.* London: T. Fisher Unwin, 1908.

Sulloway, M., and A. Christensen. "Couples and Families As Participant Observers of Their Interaction." *Advances in Family Intervention, Assessment, and Theory* 3 (1983), 119–160.

Swacker, M. "The Sex of the Speaker As a Sociolinguistic Variable." In *Language and Sex: Difference and Dominance*, ed. B. Thorne and N. Henley. (Rowley, MA: Newbury House Publishers, 1975) 76–83.

Wood, J. T., E. M. McMahan, and D. W. Stacks. "Research on Women's Communication: Critical Assessment and Recommendations." In *Feminist Visions: Toward a Transformation of the Liberal Arts Curriculum*, ed. D. L. Fowlkes and C. S. McClure. (University, AL: The University of Alabama Press, 1984) 31–41.

Zimmerman, D., and C. West. "Sex Roles, Interruptions and Silences in Conversation." In *Language and Sex: Difference and Dominance*, ed. B. Thorne and N. Henley (Rowley, MA: Newbury House Publishers, 1975) 105–129.

# The Nonverbal Elements of a Gay Culture

RANDALL E. MAJORS

A gay culture that is unique in the history of homo-sexuality is emerging in the United States. Its roots are being discovered in the works and lives of art-ists, writers, thinkers, and political characters who are noted for their homosexual inclinations.[1] These people, whether in their actual works or in their symbolic importance, serve as the heroes of a cul-tural awareness. In its modern form, the gay culture consists of people from all walks of life whose iden-tity concepts, political behaviors, and life styles cre-ate a cultural reality. As more people "come out of the closet," identify themselves as gay, and join with others to work and live as openly gay people, a gay culture takes shape and becomes stronger with each passing year.

One useful way to analyze gay people and their life styles is to observe the nonverbal elements by which they construct a culture. Lesbians and gay men, hereafter considered together as gay people, are forging a unique community in the midst of the U.S. melting pot. They are creating social institu-tions, exercising political power, and solidifying a unique sense of identity–often under repressive and even dangerous conditions. Following is an analysis of five major nonverbal elements of the American gay culture: gay neighborhoods, gay meeting places, gay symbols, gay costumes, and gay meeting behav-iors. These nonverbal behaviors demonstrate the vibrancy and joy that a new culture offers.

This essay was prepared especially for this fifth edition. All rights reserved. Permission to reprint must be obtained from the publisher and the author. Professor Majors teaches at California State University, Hayward.

## GAY NEIGHBORHOODS

Most cultural groups feel a need to mark out a home turf, and gays are no exception. The acquisition of territory fulfills several needs. First, a gay person's sense of identity is reinforced if there is a home base[2]—a special place that is somehow imbued with "gayness." When a neighborhood becomes the home of many gay people, the ground is created for a feeling of belonging and sharing with others. Signs of gayness, whether overt symbols such as rainbow flags or the mere presence of gay people on the street, create the feeling that a certain territory is special to the group and full of the group's unique values. Gay neighborhoods reinforce individual identity by focusing on activities and events for members of the group. Celebrations of group unity and pride, demonstrations of group creativity and accomplishment, and services for individual mem-ber's needs are more easily managed when centralized.

How do you know when a neighborhood is gay? A general rule of thumb is: "enough gay people in a neighborhood and it becomes a gay neighbor-hood." There is usually nothing overt like a drive to paint the streetlamps lavender, but many factors converge to give a gay character to an area. The most subtle cue is the presence of gay people as they take up residence in a district. Usually word spreads that a certain area is starting to look attrac-tive to gay members. There is often a move to gen-trify older, cheaper sections of a city and build a new neighborhood out of the leftovers of the rush to the suburbs. Gay businesses, meaning those operated by or catering to gay people, often develop once enough gays are in an area. Eventually, the label *gay neighborhood* is placed on an area, and the transformation is complete. The Castro in San Francisco, Greenwich Village in New York, New Town in Chicago, the Westheimer district in Houston, and West Hollywood or Silver Lake—commonly called "Boy's Town"—in Los Angeles are examples of emergent gay neighborhoods in cities across the United States.

A second need fulfilled by the gay neighborhood is the creation of a meeting ground. Gay people can recognize and meet each other more easily when a higher density of gays is established. When alienation and isolation are major problems in the psychology of a group, as is the case with gay people, the need for a meeting ground is very important. Merely knowing that there is a specific place where other gay people live and work and play does much to anchor the psychological aspect of gayness in a tangible, physical reality.

A critical purpose for gay neighborhoods is that of physical and psychological safety. Most subcultures usually feel persecution and oppression from the larger, more homogeneous culture. For gay people, physical safety is a very real concern. Incidences of homophobic assaults and/or harassment are common in most U.S. cities.[3] Some safeguards can be mounted by centralizing gay activities. Large numbers of gay people living in proximity create a deterrent to violence, which may take the form of actual street patrols or be simply an informal awareness of the need to take extra precautions and to be on the alert to help other group members in distress. A sense of psychological safety follows these physical measures. Group consciousness raising on neighborhood safety and training in safety practices create a sense of group cohesion. The security inspired by the group creates a psychic comfort that offsets the paranoia that can be engendered by alienation and individual isolation.

A final significant factor of gay neighborhoods is the reality of political clout. In the context of grassroots democracy in the United States, a predominantly gay population in an area can lead to political power. The concerns of gay people are taken more seriously by politicians and elected officials representing an area when voters can be registered and gotten to the polls during elections. In many areas, openly gay candidates represent gay constituencies directly and voice their concerns in ever-widening forums. The impact of this kind of representation extends to other institutions as well: police departments, social welfare agencies, schools, churches, and businesses. When a group centralizes its energy, its members can bring pressure to bear on other cultural institutions, asking for or demanding attention to the unique needs of the group. Since U.S.

culture is particularly amenable to cultural diversity, gay neighborhoods are effective agents for the acceptance of gay people by the dominant culture. The gay rights movement, which attempts to secure housing, employment, and legal protection for gay people, finds its greatest support in the sense of community created by gay neighborhoods.

## GAY MEETING PLACES

On a smaller scale than the neighborhood, specific meeting places fulfill many social needs of gay people. The need for affiliation—to make friends, to share recreations, to find life partners, or merely to while away the time—is a strong drive in any group of people. Many gay people suffer from an isolation caused by their rejection by other people or by their own fear of being discovered as belonging to the group. This fear leads to difficulty in identifying and meeting other gay people, who would help to create a sense of dignity and caring. Gay meeting places serve the vital function of helping gay people recognize and find each other so that this affiliation need can be met.

Various institutions and businesses cater to gay clientele. In smaller towns and cities, a single business may be the only public meeting place for gay people. In larger cities, the choice is much wider. An elaborate array of bars, clubs, social groups, churches, service agencies, stores, restaurants, and the like become meeting places for the gay population.

The gay bar is often the most prominent meeting place since it is an economically feasible business to operate. In a rural setting, a bar may feature gay hours on weekends and be the only meeting place for gay people within hundreds of miles. In politically repressive environments, gay bars are often underground establishments that survive despite police harassment and occasional raids. Only thirty years ago in the United States, for instance, gay bars were consistently raided, and patrons who were arrested had their names published in newspapers, which often jeopardized their careers and family lives.

A gay bar is often the first public experience of gayness for a gay person. This early imprinting is carried through the gay culture, and a bar serves as a central focus in gay life for many people. Beyond the personal need of meeting people for potential relationships, a gay bar also serves the functions of entertainment and social activity. Bars offer a wide range of services suited to gay people: movies, holiday celebrations, dancing, costume parties, live entertainment, free meals, shops, and meeting places for social groups. The uniquely gay forms of entertainment such as drag shows and disco dancing were common in gay bars before spreading into the general culture. Bars can become a very central part of an individual's social life by sponsoring athletic teams, social charities, community service, and social events as well as serving as a meeting place.

For many reasons—a high rate of alcoholism among urban gay males being a prominent one—bars are not a satisfactory social outlet for some gay people. With the spread of the fatal venereal disease Acquired Immune Deficiency Syndrome (AIDS), the use of bars for meeting sexual partners has declined dramatically as gay people turn to more permanent relationships or to celibacy. Affiliation needs are still strong despite these dangers, however, and alternative social institutions that meet these needs are arising. In large urban areas where gay culture is more widely developed, meeting places include athletic organizations that sponsor teams and tournaments in all types of sports; dancing and leisure activity clubs that sponsor various recreations such as country-and-western dances, ballet, yoga, bridge, and hiking; religious groups such as Dignity (Roman Catholic), Integrity (Episcopal), and the Metropolitan Community Church (MCC), which was founded by the Rev. Troy Perry specifically to minister to gay people; volunteer agencies such as the AIDS Foundation; and professional concern groups such as the Golden Gate Business Association of San Francisco or the Gay Rights Task Force. Taken together, these groups compose a fabric of culture that pervades a gay person's life. In a metropolitan area, it is possible for a gay person to deal only with gay people and yet lead a full social and professional life.

## GAY SYMBOLS

Gay culture is replete with symbols. These artifacts spring up anew and constantly evolve as the culture moves from a personal and individual experience to a more complex public phenomenon. Any cultural group develops public expressions of group ideas and values, and the gay world has been quite creative in symbol making given its relatively brief history.

The most visible category is found in the names of gay establishments. Gay bars, bookstores, restaurants, and social groups are often caught between wanting to be recognized and patronized by gay people and not wanting to incur broad public hostility. This dilemma was particularly troublesome in the past when the threat of social consequences was greater than it is today. In earlier days, gay bars—the only major form of gay establishment—went by code words such as "blue" or "other," as in the Blue Parrot, the Blue Goose, the Other Bar, and Another Place. Since the liberalization of gay culture after the 1960s, the names of gay establishments have blossomed. The general trend is still to identify the place as gay through affiliation (Our Place or His 'n' Hers), humor (the White Swallow or Uncle Charlies'), high drama (the Elephant Walk or Backstreet), sexual suggestion (Ripples, Cheeks, or Rocks), and the extremely popular strategy of hypermasculinization for gay meeting places (the Ramrod, Ambush, Manhandlers, the Mine Shaft, the Stud, Boots, the Locker Room, or the Silver Bullet).

Gay restaurants and nonpornographic bookstores usually reflect more subdued names, drawing upon cleverness or historical associations: Dos Hermanos, Women and Children First, Diana's, the Oscar Wilde Memorial Bookstore, and Walt Whitman Bookstore. More commonly, gay establishments employ such general naming trends as location, ownership, or identification of product/service as do their heterosexual counterparts. The increasing tendency of businesses to target and cater to gay markets strengthens the sense of gay cultural growth and diversity.

A second set of gay symbols serves to identify members of the gay culture. In the past, such nonverbal cues were so popular as to become mythic: the arched eyebrow of Regency England, the green carnation of Oscar Wilde's day, and the "green shirt on Thursday" signal of mid-century America. A large repertoire of identifying characteristics has arisen in recent years. These characteristics make it possible not only to recognize other gay people but also to focus on particular interests. In the sexually promiscuous period of the 1970s, popular identifying symbols were a ring of keys in the rear pocket, either left or right depending upon one's sexual passivity or aggressiveness, and colored handkerchiefs in a rear pocket coded to desired types of sexual activity. Political sentiments are commonly expressed through buttons such as the "No on 64" campaign against the LaRouche initiative in California in 1986. The pink triangle as a political adornment recalls the persecution and annihilation of gay people in Nazi Germany. The lambda symbol, which refers to the ancient Greeks, conjures up classical images of gay freedom of expression. Stud earrings for men are gay symbols in some places, although such adornment is often used simply for the expression of general countercultural attitudes. The rainbow and the unicorn, mythic symbols associated with supernatural potency, are also common signals of gay enchantment, fairy magic, and spiritual uniqueness.

A final set of gay symbols comprises commonplace images in advertising, literature, theater, and film. The general heterosexual culture controls these media forms to a large extent, and the imprint of the dominant culture looms large in the symbology used. The representations of gay people in these media take on the expectations and assumptions of the straight majority. The results are stereotypes that oversimplify gay people and their values and do not represent the wide variety of people who belong to the gay culture. Because these stereotypes are generally unattractive, they are studiously avoided and resisted by large segments of the gay culture. Various authors have addressed the problem of heterosexual bias in film and literature.[4] Some progress is being made in depicting gay people more sympathetically and realistically, but advances are slow.

The rise of an active gay market for literature has done much to broaden the literary treatment of gay people. A positive, symbolic reality is created through gay characters, gay heroes, and stories that help gay people deal with the important issues of family, relationship, and social responsibility. This market is constantly threatened by harsh economic realities, however, and gay literature is not as well developed as it might be. To an even greater degree, the depiction of gay people in films is limited by economic risk and high costs of production. This lack is offset in most metropolitan areas by a thriving gay theater that features gay characters and settings. The gay theater is a well-supported art form.

Advertising has done more than any other means to promulgate gay symbols U.S. culture. Much widely quoted research suggests that gay people have large and disposable incomes. Since money-making is the issue in advertising, the incentive to develop uniquely gay forms of advertising is greater than the incentive to advance in the arts. Gay people become popular target markets for various products: tobacco, body care products, clothing, alcohol, entertainment, and consumer goods that fit gay life styles and trends.

Typical gay-directed advertising includes appeals based on male bonding and homoerotic art. Appeals to male bonding, such as those common in tobacco and alcohol ads, are attractive to both straight and gay men because they stimulate the bonding need that is a part of both cultures. Homoerotic art is widely used in clothing and body care product ads. Male and female bodies are displayed for their physical and sexual appeal. This eroticizing of the body may be directed at both women and men, and it may strike at the subconscious homosexual urge in all people.

Within the gay culture, advertising has made dramatic advances in the past ten years. This advance is due to the rise of gay-related businesses and products. Advertising aimed at gays appears most obviously in the media specifically directed at gay markets, such as gay magazines and newspapers, and in gay neighborhoods. Products and services for gays are generally publicized by the same means as are products for their straight counterparts. Product identification, economy, direct sexual appeal, and claims of exclusivity are common appeals. With the rise of sexual cuing in advertising for the general public through double entendre, sexual punning, subliminal seduction, and erotic art, it may be that advertising aimed at gays is only following suit in its emphasis on sexual appeal.

Significant to gay male culture is the hypermasculinization of these sexual appeals. Gigantically developed bodies and perfected masculine beauty are used in all aspects of advertising for products and service for gay people. Products that span the range from greeting cards to billboards for travel service to bars to hotels to restaurants and clothing stores tingle to the images of Hot 'n' Hunky Hamburgers, Hard On Leather, and the Brothel Hotel or its crosstown rival, the Anxious Arms. This trend toward idealizing masculine beauty is criticized as distorting and stereotyping—and just as bad as heterosexist misconceptions. These public symbols do evidence, however, an unwillingness or inability to deal with the broad range of human diversity in gay culture in terms of manners, appearance, and taste. Gay people are far more average and normal than the images that appear in public media suggest.

## GAY COSTUMES

One of the most obvious aspects of the emergent gay culture is its use of clothing. As with the other elements of gay culture, gay dress cannot be considered exclusive; not all gay people dress alike, nor does one have to dress a certain way to demonstrate being gay. There are common tendencies in dress behaviors, however, that can be used to identify modes and specifics of costumes that help create the fabric of a gay identity and culture.

The most obvious of these forms is the hypermasculinized stereotypes popularized by entertainment groups such as the Village People, whose name itself is a reference to a gay neighborhood. The mythic characters of the cowboy, the military man, the policeman, and the construction worker are central to the dress mythology of gay people, who assume the cultural powers of these characters when they don the magical clothing. As research in the

psychology of dress indicates, the external trappings are outward manifestations of internal processes. The deeper motives of hypermasculinized dress are the expressions of dominance, violence, power, and aggression that are part and parcel of the extremism of heterosexual masculine identity in U.S. culture. By assuming these roles, gay people outdo heterosexuals in being macho men or, even more recently, macho women. As attractive as these images may be, the disadvantages of phony role-playing and shallow cloning go hand-in-hand with these images.

In contrast to the mythic clothing trend in gay culture is a tendency toward "haute couture." A significant theme among some gay people is the pursuit of the novel: the latest trend, the newest fashion, the coming thing. This pursuit leads to innovation in interior design, the arts, and entertainment as well as in matters of dress. The popularity of designer styles that emphasize color, texture, line, and creativity demonstrate a strong aesthetic sensitivity in gay people. This trend goes so far as to include elements of high drama or even the camp "drag" rituals of cross dressing.

Because dress is such a powerful signal of personal values, cultural institutions can grow up along demarcation lines of clothing styles. Gay culture can be divided in terms of clothing into such units as the leather crowd, the designer disco crowd, the jocks, the urban cowboys, and the drag set. Needless to say, these groups do not mingle much, nor do their definitions and self-perceptions of gayness, beauty, or masculinity coincide. In fact, a descending order of exclusivity exists among these groups. "Leather bars" often exclude those wearing cologne or Lacoste shirts, disco bars often exclude those in drag attire, and drag bars usually let anybody in. Clearly a continuum exists as to how seriously dress is integrated into personal identity. Among the people in the hypermasculinized extreme, dress is taken very seriously. This group is where one usually sees the symbols of sexual activity such as handkerchiefs and keys. Among those in the drag extreme, dress is seen as theater—as a way of exploring the unknown depths of personal identity, particularly its feminine side.

Other motives beyond deep psychological expression are involved in the way gay people dress. Clothing serves as an identifying signal for recognition of gay people as well as a general estimate of values and attitudes. In short, it serves as a barometer of estimated relationship potential. A general attitude of casualness in dress, common among gay people, also communicates a certain rebelliousness toward heterosexual standards of dress. A common reactionary ritual among gay men, for example, is wearing blue jeans or leather to a conventional situation like the opera. A tremendous sense of freedom from external societal pressures is created by a refusal to dress "properly." This freedom from convention is paramount in the psychology of the coming out process, and experimentation with new dress behaviors is often a part of the formation of gay identity. This use of dress to express political and social revolutionary attitudes has a long history, and gay people are squarely in the tradition of the decline of aristocratic styles after the French Revolution, the people's uniform of the Chinese Revolution, and the wearing of trousers by women in the United States after the Sexual Revolution of the 1960s.

*Costumes* is the best descriptive term for the function of dress in aiding people to act out new roles and ways of being. What begins as fantasy and mythology gradually becomes fused into a shared reality—a culture. Thus dress is a powerful force for expressing an individual's sexuality, personal identity, and values. As a nonverbal indicator of culture, costumes are a significant element of gay culture.

## GAY MEETING BEHAVIOR

A final element of nonverbal communication in the gay culture is the vast set of behaviors by which gay people recognize and meet one another. In the more sexually active days before the concern about AIDS, this type of behavior was commonly called *cruising*. Currently, sexual signaling is far less common, and cruising has evolved into more standard meeting behaviors for identifying potential partners for relationships.

An extensive body of research has catalogued and described the verbal and nonverbal aspects of cruising, whether in specific contexts or as the initial phase of relationship development.[5] Gay people meet each other in various contexts: in public situations such as on the street or in a bus, in the workplace, in gay meeting places, and in the social contexts of friends and acquaintances. Within each context, a different set of adaptive behaviors is employed by which gay people recognize someone else as gay and determine the potential for establishing a relationship. These behaviors include such nonverbal signaling as frequency and length of interaction, posture, proximity, eye contact, eye movement and facial gestures, touch, affect displays, and paralinguistic signals. The constraints of each situation and the personal styles of the communicators allow for great differences in the effectiveness of these behaviors and ease with which they are displayed.

Cruising serves several purposes besides the recognition of other gay people. Most importantly, cruising is an expression of pride and joy in being gay. By observing other people closely and by appreciating the beauty of potential same-sex partners, gay people communicate their openness and willingness to interact. Being gay is often compared to belonging to a universal fraternity or sorority. Gay people are generally friendly and open to meeting other gay people in social contexts because of their common experiences of rejection and isolation. Cruising is the means by which gay people communicate their gayness and bridge the gap between stranger and newfound friend.

Cruising has become an integral part of gay culture because it is such a commonplace behavior. Without skill in cruising—newcomers to gay life often complain of their lack of comfort or ease with cruising—a gay person can have a difficult time in finding an easy path into the mainstream of gay culture. While cruising has a distinctly sexual overtone, the sexual side of cruising is often a charade. Often the goals of cruising are no more than friendship, companionship, or conversation. In this sense, cruising becomes an art form or an entertainment. Much as the art of conversation was the convention of a more genteel cultural age, gay cruising is the commonly accepted precursor to gay social interaction. The sexual element, transmitted by double meaning, clever punning, or blatant nonverbal signals, remains a part of cruising in even the most innocent of circumstances. As a quintessential gay behavior, cruising has replaced the bitchy camp of an early generation of gay people.[6]

Gay meeting behavior, or cruising, is an expression of solidarity within the gay culture. The more gay people see themselves as part of the culture—the more open they are—the more comfortable and tolerant they are of the social rituals that bind the culture together. Gay culture seems to be preeminently social due to the constant forging of new social groups and new relationships. This need to meet other gay people may be grounded in the freedom from, or absence of, the more common interaction patterns of heterosexuals, such as marriage and the nuclear family. Gay people build their families from friends and permanent partners as well as from their parents and siblings, and the family circle is usually open to newcomers.

The unique factor in gay cruising, and the one that distinguishes it from heterosexual cruising, is the level of practice and refinement the process receives. All cultures have rituals of introduction, recognition, assessment, meeting, and negotiation of new relationships. In the gay culture, the courtship ritual or friendship ritual of cruising is elaborately refined. While heterosexuals may use similar techniques in forming and developing relationships, gay people are especially self-conscious about the centrality of these signals to the perpetuation of their culture. There is a sense of adventure and discovery in being sexual outlaws, and cruising is the shared message of commitment to the gay life style.[7]

## CONCLUSION

The five nonverbal elements of gay culture discussed here comprise only a small part of what might be called gay culture. Other elements have been widely discussed elsewhere: literature, the gay press, religion, politics, art, theater, and relationships. Gay culture is a marvelous and whirling phenomenon. It is driven and buffeted by the energies of much intense feeling and creative effort. Centuries of cultural repression that condemned gay people to disgrace or persecution have been turned upside down in a brief period of time. The results of this turbulence have the potential for both renaissance and cataclysm. Internalized fear and hatred of repression is balanced by the incredible joy and idealism of liberation. Through the celebration of its unique life style, gay culture promises to make a great contribution to the history of sexuality and to the rights of the individual. Whether it fulfills this promise or succumbs to the pressures that face any creative attempt remains to be seen.

## NOTES

1. Several good reviews of famous homosexuals include the following: Barbara Grier and Coletta Reid, *Lesbian Lives* (Oakland, CA: Diana Press, 1976); Noel I. Garde, *Jonathan to Gide: The Homosexual in History* (New York: Nosbooks, 1969); and A. L. Rowse, *The Homosexual in History* (Metuchen, NY: Scarecrow Press, 1975).

2. An excellent analysis of the role of the Castro in gay culture appears in Frances FitzGerald, *Cities on a Hill* (New York: Simon and Schuster, 1986).

3. A discussion of violence against gay people and its effects appear in Dennis Altman, *The Homosexualization of America: The Americanization of Homosexuality* (New York: St. Martin's Press, 1982), p. 100–101.

4. The treatment of gay people in literature is discussed in George-Michel Sarotte, *Like a Brother, Like a Lover* (New York: Doubleday, 1978); Ian Young (ed.), *The Male Homosexual in Literature: A Bibliography* (Metuchen, NY: Scarecrow Press, 1975); and Roger Austen, *Playing the Game: The Homosexual Novel in America* (Indianapolis: Bobbs-Merrill Press, 1977). Gay people in films are discussed in Parker Tyler, *Screening the Sexes: Homosexuality in the Movies* (New York: Holt, Rinehart, and Winston, 1972), and Vito Russo, *The Celluloid Closet: Lesbians and Gay Men in American Film* (New York: Harper and Row, 1980).

5. Sexual cruising behaviors are discussed in Laud Humphreys, *Tearoom Trade: Impersonal Sex in Public Places* (New York: Aldine Press, 1975), and Jerry Corzine and Richard Kirby, "Cruising the Truckers: Sexual

Encounters in a Highway Rest Area," *Urban Life* 6:2 (1977), pp. 171–192.

6. Camp is discussed in Susan Sontag, "Notes on Camp," *Against Interpretation* (New York: Dell, 1969). For a dictionary of camp language, see Bruce Rodgers, *The Queen's Vernacular: A Gay Lexicon* (New York: Simon and Schuster, 1972).

7. Altman discusses cruising in *The Homosexualization of America,* p. 176.

## CONCEPTS AND QUESTIONS FOR CHAPTER 3

**1.** Can you think of other subcultures that fall into Folb's category of nondominant groups?

**2.** How do you suppose someone from a foreign culture would respond to one of our subcultures? Be specific.

**3.** What purpose does *style* serve as a means of expression?

**4.** How might a lack of understanding of *style* and its role in expression affect intercultural communication?

**5.** What does Carmichael mean when he suggests that integration of the elderly is not a cultural goal in the United States?

**6.** How does becoming disabled change a person's communication patterns?

**7.** What effect does sex have upon communication?

**8.** How does growing up female affect one's perceptions and ultimately one's communication behaviors?

**9.** What function does nonverbal gay behavior serve?

**10.** In what ways have gay people adopted specific nonverbal behaviors that signify the manifestation of their cultural orientation?

**11.** Do you believe that subcultures seeking to practice their own ways of life ought to be permitted that freedom?

**12.** In what different ways have racial and ethnic minorities been treated in the United States?

**13.** Why does the history of a culture or subculture offer us insight into its communication behaviors?

## SUGGESTED READINGS

Bahr, H. M. *Skid Row: An Introduction to Disaffiliation.* New York: Oxford University Press, 1973. This book deals with homeless skid row dwellers as a subculture. It presents a detailed profile of the skid row individual and looks at the social organizations, both formal and informal, that are found on skid row.

Blubaugh, J. A. and D. L. Pennington. *Crossing Difference: Interracial Communication.* New York: Charles Merrill, 1976. This short book is an introduction to the dynamics of interracial communication. The authors examine topics such as racism, power, language, nonverbal behavior, beliefs, and values.

Christensen, K. M. "Conceptual sign language as a bridge between English and Spanish." *American Annals of the Deaf,* 130 (1985), 244–249. The author addresses the unique communication problems facing a deaf child from a non-English-speaking family. This trilingual approach utilizes Conceptual Sign Language as a communicative bridge for the deaf child, his Spanish-speaking family, and the English-speaking signers at school. Direct observations of these linguistic phenomena are described.

Coles, R. *Eskimos, Chicanos, and Indians.* New York: Little, Brown, 1977. In this interesting and stimulating book, Coles looks at three cultures through the eyes of children. By talking to children and studying their drawings and paintings, he is able to gather valuable insight into these three co-cultures living within the United States.

Eubanks, E. E. "A study of perceptions of Black and White teachers in de facto segregated high schools." *Education,* 95 (1974), 51–57. Eubanks studied 97 teachers from six de facto segregated high schools, examining perceptions of job satisfaction, teacher-student relations, school status, attributes for success as a teacher, and opinions about the behavioral, emotional, and social characteristics of students.

Hess, B. "Stereotypes of the aged," *Journal of Communication,* 24 (1974), 76–85. Hess has reviewed the stereotypes of the aged and compared them to the real world so we can better understand the myth and the reality of being old. Hess also explains the factors that contribute to the stereotypes.

Kephart, W. M. *Extraordinary Groups: The Sociology of Unconventional Life-Styles.* New York: St. Martin's Press, 1982. This book is a collection of seven essays that focus on extraordinary groups. Kephart believes that a knowledge of these groups helps one understand subcultural diversity. The seven groups are the gypsies, the Old Order Amish, the Oneida Community, the Father Divine Movement, the Shakers, the Mormons, and the Hutterites.

Lampe, P. E. "Ethnicity and crime: Perceptual differences among Blacks, Mexican Americans, and Anglos." *International Journal of Intercultural Relations,* 8 (1984), 357–372. This study speculates that significant differences exist among three ethnic groups in their perceptions of the seriousness of crimes, personally threatening crimes, the perceptions of most crimes in their cities, and the imputation of responsibility for crimes. Differing perceptions of surrounding criminal activity were evidenced by members of all three ethnic groups.

Lowney, J., R. W. Winslow, and V. Winslow. *Deviant Reality: Alternative World Views.* Boston: Allyn & Bacon, 1981. This collection of essays presents firsthand accounts of deviant subcultures such as nudists, alcoholics, prostitutes, and lesbians.

Luhman, R. and S. Gilman. *Race and Ethnic Relations: The Social and Political Experience of Minority Groups.* Belmont, Calif.: Wadsworth, 1980. This book gives an excellent view of minorities in the United States, detailing social and political experiences, social stratification, reactions to majority pressures, and the impact of pluralism.

Rosen, P. *The Neglected Dimension: Ethnicity in American Life.* Notre Dame: University of Notre Dame Press, 1980. This volume is designed to "afford students opportunities to learn more about the nature of their own heritage and to study the contributions of the cultural heritage of other ethnic groups." The rationale behind this book is that ethnicity is a neglected aspect of the study of American culture, and that to understand that culture one must study behavior associated with belonging to an ethnic group.

## ADDITIONAL READINGS

Belt, A., and W. Weinberg. *Homosexualities: A Study of Diversity among Men and Women.* New York: Simon and Schuster, 1978.

Borisoff, D. and L. Merrill. *The Power to Communicate: Gender Differences As Barriers.* Prospect Heights, Ill.: Waveland Press, 1985.

Briggs, N., and M. Pinola. "Contemporary American women: Conflict in roles and self concept." *The Journal of the Communication Association of the Pacific* 8 (1979), 165–174.

Clark, A. J., L. A. Weiman, and K. A. Paschall. "A preliminary report of an investigation of unwillingness to communicate among physically handicapped persons." *The Journal of the Communication Association of the Pacific* 12 (1983), 155–160.

Cogdell, R. and S. Wilson. *Black Communication in White Society.* Saratoga: Century 21, 1980.

Donaldson, J. "Changing attitudes toward handicapped persons: A review and analysis of research." *Exceptional Children* 46 (1980), 504–514.

Ferrante, R. D. "Social posturing in homosexual men." *Et Cetera* 42 (1985), 376–380.

Jensen, G. E., J. H. Stauss, and V. W. Harris. "Crime, delinquency, and the American Indian." *Human Organization* 36 (1977), 252–257.

Joseph, H. "Gay male and lesbian relationships." In E. D. Macklin and R. H. Rubin, eds. *Contemporary Families and Alternative Lifestyles.* Beverly Hills, Calif.: Sage Publications, 1983.

Kitano, H. H. I. *Japanese Americans: The Evolution of a Subculture.* Englewood Cliffs, N.J.: Prentice-Hall, 1969.

McLemore, S. D. *Racial and Ethnic Relations in America.* Boston: Allyn & Bacon, 1983.

McNeely, R. L., and J. L. Colen, eds. *Aging and Minority Groups.* Beverly Hills, Calif.: Sage Publications, 1983.

Merry, S. E. "Racial integration in an urban neighborhood: The social organization of strangers." *Human Organization* 39 (1980), 59–69.

Pearson, J. C. *Gender and Communication.* Dubuque: Wm. C. Brown, Publishers, 1985.

Putnam, L. "In search of gender: A critique of communication and sex roles research." *Women's Studies in Communication* 5 (1982), 1–9.

Shanas, E. and M. B. Sussman. *Family, Bureaucracy, and the Elderly.* Durham, N.C.: Duke University Press, 1977.

Shearer, A. *Disability: Whose Handicap?* Oxford: Basil Blackwell Publishers, Ltd., 1984.

Shuter, R. "Initial interaction of American Blacks and Whites in interracial and intraracial dyads." *Journal of Social Psychology* 117 (1982), 45–52.

Shuter, R. and J. Miller. "An exploratory study of pain expression styles among Blacks and Whites." *International Journal of Intercultural Relations* 6 (1982), 281–290.

Staiano, K. V. "Ethnicity as process: The creation of an Afro-American identity." *Ethnicity* 7 (1980), 27–33.

Tajfel, H., ed. *Social Identity and Intergroup Relations.* Cambridge: Cambridge University Press, 1982.

Thompson, T. L. "The development of communication skills in physically handicapped children." *Human Communication Research* 7 (1981), 312–324.

Thompson, T. L. "You can't play marbles—you have a wooden hand: Communication with the handicapped." *Communication Quarterly* 30 (1982), 108–115.

Walum, R. L. *The Dynamics of Sex and Gender: A Sociological Perspective.* Boston: Houghton Mifflin, 1981.

Welford, A. T. "Social skill and aging: Principles and problems." *International Journal of Aging and Human Development* 17 (1983), 1–5.

# 4

# Cultural Contexts

Communication does not occur in a vacuum. All communication takes place in a social setting or environment. We call this the context because the setting is never neutral; it always has some impact on the communication event by influencing how the participants behave. We have all learned culturally appropriate patterns of communicative behavior for the various social contexts in which we normally find ourselves. But, as in other aspects of intercultural communication, the patterns of behavior appropriate to various social contexts differ from culture to culture. Problems, therefore, sometimes arise when we find ourselves in strange contexts without an internalized set of rules to govern our behavior, or when we are interacting with someone who has internalized a different set of rules.

The growth of international business during the last twenty years has been startling. Overseas transactions that were millions of dollars are now billions of dollars. In addition, the international business community has experienced a more profound change—business has become multinational and organizational units include participants from a variety of cultures. In fact, the multinational organization has become a subtopic of study within the fields of intercultural and organizational communication. Successful businesspeople functioning in international business and world markets must learn about approaches to business practices that may be vastly different from their own or those they studied in school.

As this economic growth has taken place and as international business has become mostly multinational, the businessperson no longer has the luxury of dealing with people who possess the same background and experiences. In this global economy, one's clients, peers, subordinates, and even supervisors are frequently from a different country and culture. Approaches to business differ significantly from culture to culture. Such aspects as gift giving, cheating, methods of negotiation, decision making, policy formulation, management structure, and patterns of communication are subject to cultural variation. Some of these communication differences as they operate in multinational/multicultural organizations are the subject of our first essay by Fathi S. Yousef, "Human Resource Management: Aspects of Intercultural Relations in U.S. Organizations." His concern is with the way cultural differences become evident in the way personnel are treated and by the way the treatment affects their productivity. More specifically, he analyzes the verbal and nonverbal dimensions involved in peer group relations and supervisor-employee interactions in the multinational/multicultural business context.

The Japanese approach to business and multinational organizations is one of special interest, not only because of the financial impact the Japanese have had on the world economy, but also because of the unique ways in which they perceive the business context and the consequent implications for communication within multinational organizations. Lea P. Stewart, in her article "Japanese and American Management: Participative Decision Making," examines Japanese and American management processes and their differing styles of decision making and conferencing through an analysis and description of their nature and characteristics. She concludes with an observation that although Japanese companies are highly successful, we must first wonder whether we want to measure success in terms similar to those used by Japanese society before we start a wholesale application of Japanese management to U.S. corporations.

The next article, "Japanese Social Experience and Concept of Groups," focuses on the Far East. Dolores and Robert Cathcart explore how a culture's view of a specific concept can influence behavior. In this case, the concept is the Japanese view of groups. If one's experience with groups changes from culture to culture, then it follows that each culture might well bring a different way of acting to a group situation. The Cathcarts investigate this issue when they compare Japanese concepts of groups with those found in the United

States. Their essay clearly illustrates the importance of what each of us brings to communication.

In recent years there has been a steady increase in the number of people who have found themselves having to negotiate with individuals from cultures other than their own. What has happened is rather simple; as economics and politics became more international, so did the need to negotiate with foreign cultures. What many negotiators found, however, was that success in the domestic arena did not always translate into success in the international context. In fact, in many instances relying on traditional techniques often produced added problems. As a way of overcoming some of these problems and improving international negotiations, we offer "International Negotiation" by Glen Fisher. It is Fisher's belief that the negotiator should begin by examining how the "national character" of a culture might affect the negotiation session. Fisher offers a list of those characteristics that demand attention. They are the self-image, values, styles of logic, reasoning, and style of persuasion of the culture with which the negotiator will meet. Admittedly, no single article can make one become a successful international negotiator, but this one does, however, highlight a number of concepts that ought to be considered when bargaining and negotiating with other cultures.

A completely different yet significant intercultural context is the courtroom. Wayne A. Beach, in his article, "Organizing Courtroom Contexts: International Resolutions to Intercultural Problems," explores courtrooms and their culture to determine how "fair and impartial treatment" can be a part of the legal process when defendants need interpreters to function as mediators between the defendant and the judges, lawyers, and jurors. Relying on transcribed segments of video-recorded court proceedings, Beach looks at traditional notions of differences between cultures and how these differences produce problems for Spanish-speaking defendants.

The classroom environment is one of those settings that specifically influences intercultural interaction. The rules, assumptions, values, customs, practices, and procedures of a given culture strongly affect the conduct of classroom activity. While many people naively believe that all classrooms are pretty much alike, Janis F. Andersen and Robert Powell take the position that learning environments are different from culture to culture and that they alter the communication patterns of people within those environments. To support this assertion they highlight intercultural differences in classroom settings, teacher-student relationships, nonverbal behaviors, what is taught, and how it is taught in their article, "Cultural Influences on Educational Processes."

# Human Resource Management: Aspects of Intercultural Relations in U.S. Organizations

FATHI S. YOUSEF

## INTRODUCTION

In White Plains, New York, after the fourth meeting in ten days, Bill Jones thinks that prospects for the West German deal he has been working on are dim. Hans Hoppe, the West German, seems formal, cool, and distant. When they meet, despite Bill's attempts at informality and friendliness ("Hi, Hans"), the response is still a short, quiet, "Good morning, Mr. Jones." Actually, Mr. Hoppe is quite interested in the deal. Bill's assumptions, which are beginning to affect his dealings, emanate from the conditioned and emphasized U.S. dislike and distrust of formality.

In Anaheim, California, in an entertainment park, Mark Fletcher, the Supervisor of Admissions, notices that the line is getting longer and not moving fast enough at the window of the new clerk from Taiwan, Mary Cheng. Mark notices that Mary doesn't use the electronic machine to check credit cards but uses the "lost and stolen" book instead. Mary says that something is wrong with the electronic checking machine. Mark examines the machine and shows Mary how to use it. A bit later, Mark finds that Mary still refers to the "lost and stolen" book instead of using the machine. Mark thinks the new clerk is obstinate and incompetent. Mary is embar-

This essay was prepared especially for this fifth edition. All rights reserved. Permission to reprint must be obtained from the publisher and the author. Fathi S. Yousef teaches at California State University, Long Beach.

rassed and thinks that Mark, her new, white, male, older supervisor will "lose face" if she says she doesn't understand his explanation.

And in St. Paul, Minnesota, in a computer firm, Ali Omar, a young Indonesian engineer, is surprised and confused when he asks Sam Stanford, the unit manager, a question and Sam says, "I don't know. I think you should ask Ralph in marketing about that." Ali is frustrated and disappointed. He expects the manager to be the expert who provides answers to all questions from subordinates. Sam, however, believes that his role is to help his employees discover ways to solve problems on their own. Sam's behavior reflects the North American managerial belief that providing answers discourages employees' initiative, creativity, and ultimately, their productivity.

Like the country's population, the composition of the work force in North American organizations has been changing rapidly. A major influx of foreign-born professional, technical, and semi-skilled personnel is swelling the ranks of white- and blue-collar workers. According to census data and projections, before the year 2000 the majority of the population of California, the most populous state in the Union, will no longer be white nor necessarily English speaking. In 1986 Hispanics were 25 percent of the state's population, Asians 15 percent, blacks 7 percent, and one of every five persons was foreign-born (Crawford 1986). Again, in California, "Some firms literally would have to pack it in if their foreign-born engineers—not to speak of their production-line workers—decided to leave the country en masse. In some Silicon Valley companies, the percentage of engineers from other countries is as high as 30 percent and their contribution to the success of the industry is immeasurable" (Cessaris 1986, p. 59). Obviously, the methods of dealing with and training multinational/multicultural work forces are very important; they affect the productivity and success of many organizations in the United States, whether their concerns are tourism or space, medical services or entertainment, computer research or market analysis. In this article, we present, illustrate, and examine some aspects of the roles of cultural values and their impact on personnel behavior

and productivity. We also discuss the impact of different national, ethnic, and cultural backgrounds in different organizations in relation to employee effectiveness, performance, obligations, and expectations.

## CASES FROM U.S. BUSINESSES

### Case 1: The Research and Development Department

With a degree in computer science and a couple of patented inventions, Park Lee Kim, a South Korean immigrant, has joined the research team of a major midwestern organization. After a few months, his North American research associates are quite unhappy with him.

In group projects and meetings, the researchers discuss their work and ask for feedback. They exchange, evaluate, and rank ideas. In the discussions, they frequently tear ideas apart. In these sessions, Park Lee Kim rarely contributes anything although his colleagues know he is bright and full of ideas. The group thinks Kim is aloof and arrogant. Yet he does go to his colleagues individually and asks for feedback on his projects.

The group members don't know what to make of Kim. At meetings, they think he is distant and self-centered. And, when he goes around discussing his projects with them individually, they think he is insecure and lacks self-confidence.

### Case 2: The Construction Firm

Ali Seif and Hussein Shahbaz are Iranian-born-and-raised U.S. citizens. They both have graduate degrees and are professional engineers. They both work for a major construction company in California. And, they are both considered highly competent and productive. Their managers find them respectful and cooperative in executing directives. Their performance evaluations, however, show that they have a problem getting along with their colleagues. The situation is such that some employees refuse to work with or for them.

176    Chapter 4 Cultural Contexts

Their North American colleagues find Ali and Hussein too authoritarian and aggressive. The male employees say Ali and Hussein are offensive. In conversations, they stand too close and they seem to stare. The female employees agree and say Ali and Hussein seem to be constantly undressing them with their eyes. A woman engineer in the group would have nothing to do with them and complained to senior management about remarks she overheard Ali and Hussein make about the make-up and dress of some women engineers.

## Case 3: The U.S. Subsidiary

"Roy" Takahashi and "Fred" Nishiyama are two senior management representatives from the head Tokyo office of a Japanese-American business concern in Wisconsin. They have just interviewed Brian Wills for the position of District Sales Supervisor, and they are surprised that Brian has been recommended to them by Fred Boylan, the Division Sales Manager. In the five years since his graduation, Brian has changed jobs three times, albeit with three salary increases. Now he is considering a fourth move.

"Roy" and "Fred" are also concerned about their secretarial pool. Friday afternoon, "Roy" mentioned to Mary Sampson, the pool's manager, that there was a lot of work in the "in" baskets that needed to be processed so the company could meet its deadlines. Yet, on Monday morning the work was still in the "in" baskets. Apparently no one had worked over the weekend.

## Case 4: The Pharmaceutical Lab

Le Roy Morgan, a black American in his early twenties, grew up in Arkansas and earned a degree in microbiology from a small state college in Arkansas. He is a new employee, on probation, with a pharmaceutical firm in Colorado. Le Roy was hired under the company's Affirmative Action Program.

Although Le Roy does his work efficiently from a technical standpoint, Sean Morris, his supervisor, who is a white Southerner, says that Le Roy is rather shifty and unreliable. Many of his white fellow workers say the same thing. He rarely looks others in the eye, and his handshake is not firm. He is certainly not like the black athletic stars they see on television.

## CONFLICTING VALUES

The cases presented here reflect aspects of the changing work environment in many North American organizations, where intercultural relations and global interdependence are becoming a more pronounced fact of corporate life. For example, "An American architectural-engineering firm is building three hotels in Saudi Arabia. The room modules for the hotels—right down to the soap dishes in the bathrooms—will be made in Brazil. The labor to build the hotels is coming from South Korea, and we Americans are doing the construction management, the information side. That's a model we will see a lot in the future" (Naisbitt 1982, p.67). Such work situations, in addition to the changing work force in U.S. organizations, clearly require a new, strong emphasis on the intercultural dimension in corporate employee and management training programs. In the four cases presented here, personnel problems have to do with conflicting value systems, not professional expertise or technical competence.

In Case 1, the strained and unsatisfactory relationship between the North American scientists and their South Korean colleague is due to different underlying value systems and the way these systems are reflected in behaviors on the job. Open discussions where ideas are torn apart in group meetings represent alien, insensitive, and unacceptable behavior to South Koreans and other members of what have been referred to as high-context, traditional, or collectivist societies (Hall 1977; Yousef 1985; Hofstede 1986). Actually, the issues of formality and saving-face are of such importance to members of these societies that learning and sensitivity training groups are considered taboo (Cox and Cooper 1977; Copeland and Griggs 1985). Thus, while Park Lee Kim discusses his projects and seeks input from his colleagues individually, he does not open-up in group settings. To him, his behavior is considerate and mindful of the feelings of his colleagues, while to them, Park Lee Kim seems uninvolved and self-centered. In addition, in individual interactions, Park Lee Kim rarely gives negative feedback or expresses disagreement with his colleagues. To them, he seems to care more about maintaining formal harmony than he cares about work. And, what seems to him like respectful and sensitive demeanor in his interactions with his colleagues is frequently considered insecurity and lack of self-confidence.

In Case 2, the professional competence of the Iranian engineers is not in question. Their managers find them respectful and reliable. Both men like clear directives and follow them, and they willingly accept authority. In turn, in relating to their North American employees and colleagues, they are authoritarian. Their manner frequently creates misunderstandings and hard feelings because, in North American value systems, equality, independence, and individualism rank high as opposed to the emphasis on hierarchical relations, interdependence, and the group in traditional societies (Sadler 1970; Hofstede 1980). The relationship between the engineers and their colleagues is also marked by different perceptions and cultural expectations. Ali and Hussein tend to violate North American territorial needs or comfort zones in dealing with their colleagues (Hall 1966; Sommer 1966; Yousef and Briggs 1975). In interpersonal relations, when the two engineers try to be friendly and come close to their male North American colleagues for an exchange of pleasantries or a serious discussion, their behavior is spatially too close by North American standards; it is unpleasantly aggressive and pushy. In such situations, the North American frequently backs up a little to maintain a comfortable personal space. As this behavior is going on, both parties develop, frequently unintentionally, negative views of and reactions to each other. The sense of discomfort is augmented by the long eye contact, with raised eyelids, that Ali and Hussein, like most Middle Easterners, Southern Europeans, and Latin Americans, maintain when they talk. That discomfort often creates a disruptive escalation of competitiveness that interferes with the ordinary give and take in North American transactions (Watson 1970; Scheflen 1973).

As to Ali and Hussein's female colleagues, aspects of the men's nonverbal behavior are also objectionable. The complaint that they seem to be undressing the women with their eyes is based on North American visual mores. The women feel that Ali and Hussein are ill-mannered. They seem to "really look at them—their eyes, hair, nose, lips, breasts, hips, legs, thighs, knees, ankles, feet, clothes, hairdo, even their walk" (Hall and Hall 1971, p. 140). It is the unfamiliar, unconsciously learned way in which both Ali and Hussein use their eyes that makes North American women feel self-conscious and look away.

In terms of verbal comments on and reactions to appearance and dress, Ali and Hussein reflect a cultural preoccupation with status, roles, and their manifestations. Particularly, in relation to women, the North American "doing orientation" that emphasizes comfort and practicality is frequently contrasted with aspects of the "being orientation" that places a high premium on formality, modesty, and the expectation and obligations of one's sex, place, and position in society (Peristiany 1965; Yousef 1974; Yousef 1985). The men and women who are made-up and dressed casually or formally by North American standards may present images that contrast with Ali and Hussein's notions about appearance at work, where the emphasis is usually more on conservative dress than on fashion.

Different cultural expectations and work values are again evident in Case 3. The Japanese managers are surprised that the recommended candidate for an important position is someone who has changed jobs several times in five years. Specialized and/or lateral career moves to different organizations are not valued in Japanese business thinking (Ouchi 1981). Whereas in North American culture Brian's moves reflect advancement and success, as shown by his salary increases, to the Japanese and other members of traditional societies, Brian's behavior reflects unreliability and lack of loyalty. The Japanese managers regard his candidacy with wariness and suspicion, while Jack Fletcher, the Division Sales Manager, is surprised that Brian's record of achievement doesn't guarantee him a job offer.

Conflicting values are again reflected in the concern and disappointment of the Japanese managers when the North American employees don't come on their own over the weekend to process the work in the "in" baskets. Compared to the Japanese and other members of traditional societies, North American employees draw the lines between their work and personal lives more clearly. In emergencies, they are called upon to help and they do so, with overtime pay or compensatory time off for nonexempt employees and no immediate reward for exempt employees. Otherwise, an individual's work takes a secondary position to one's personal life. Also, compared to Japan, North America has a low-context culture. When the Japanese manager, as is the case in high-context cultures, mentions or hints on Friday afternoon that there is a lot of work in the "in" baskets, the North American is not likely to understand that the intent is for the task to be attended to over the weekend. Messages in low-context cultures are usually articulated frequently, directly, and clearly (Hall 1977; Yousef 1978).

In Case 4, the issue centers around ethnicity and ethnocentrism. There are no complaints about Le Roy's job performance. Negative impressions about Le Roy are based upon average, U.S., white, middle-class assumptions about trustworthiness and reliability. He doesn't act like camera-conscious stars. Le Roy doesn't present one with a firm handshake and a straight look in the eye. When he talks with his supervisor and fellow workers, they feel as if he doesn't care about them or listen to them. On the other hand, at the same time Le Roy feels he is being scrutinized by his supervisors and fellow workers (Lafrance and Mayo 1976; Hickson III and Stacks 1986).

Differences in the eye behavior of Le Roy and his supervisor and fellow workers when they talk with each other may frequently reinforce and/or sustain their suspicions of each other and may be part of the explanation of some ethnic stereotypical reactions. Yet, growing up in North America, both parties, black and white, like other ethnic groups in the country, develop and are affected and conditioned to a large extent by their familial and environmental repertoire of ethnic nonverbal communication patterns that range from differing body

postures and gestures to eye behaviors and smiles (Birdwhistill 1970; Yousef 1976).

Because of space limitations, the discussion of the cases presented here is deliberately caricatural in order to highlight the points; for the subject itself is quite complex. For instance, one of the important questions that has not been addressed is the role of language in the verbal and nonverbal interactions presented (for example, Yousef 1968; Hofstede 1986). However, the importance and impact of value systems and ethnic behavior patterns on the issues raised cannot be overemphasized. They affect organizational productivity, personnel relations, and employee effectiveness. "Cultural norms, especially in North America, encourage managers to blind themselves to gender, race, and ethnicity, and to only see people as individuals and judge them according to their professional skills. This approach causes problems because it confuses recognition with judgment. Recognition occurs when a manager realizes that people from different cultural groups behave differently and that difference affects their relationship to the organization. People from one ethnic group are not inherently any better or worse (judgment) than those from another group; they are simply different. To ignore cultural differences is unproductive. Judging colleagues and clients based on membership in particular groups fosters prejudice—a prejudgment based on group rather than individual characteristics. *Judging* cultural differences as good or bad can lead to inappropriate, offensive, racist, sexist, ethnocentric attitudes and behaviors. *Recognizing* differences does not. Choosing not to see cultural diversity limits our ability to manage it—that is, to minimize the problems it causes while maximizing the advantages it allows" (Adler 1986, pp. 77–78).

## CULTURAL AWARENESS

The development of an intercultural dimension in training programs for U.S. organizations may seem like a forbidding task. A meaningful program, however, need *not* include the teaching of the value systems and behavior patterns of all the ethnic groups in an organization. In an effective program, the emphasis is on the dominant values and behavior expectations of the ethnic group present. The content should identify and address personal and group views on work and productivity in terms of the different elements of cultural value systems such as self, age, sex, the family, society, nature, the supernatural, and so on (for example, Condon and Yousef 1975 and 1986). Identifying the clarifying such notions and values will help the participants realize that their behaviors are ethnic and culture-bound—not universal.

After a major four-year study of the responses of 1,000 middle and upper-middle managers to a 56 point questionnaire, a prominent researcher cites the following example.

*The British company was feeling pleased. One of its upper-middle managers was due to go to Bangkok, so they had sent him for three days' instruction on Thailand. Surely he must have learned a lot and would be much more able to deal with the people he would meet out there.*

*But would he really? If a British company were to ask me how best to prepare this manager for Thailand, I would say: organize a workshop for him on the United Kingdom. He would then become more aware of his own culture, his own biases, filters and assumptions. In recognizing more about himself as the alien figure, he would be better able to interact with his new hosts (Laurent, 1983, p. 31).*

Training programs that address, clarify, and focus on the *value systems of the participants* help them to realize that different views, feelings of obligation, and expectations regarding colleagues at work, family members at home, people in the community, and society in general are, to a large extent, the results of one's own cultural conditioning. Whether the individual is in management or labor, issues about interpersonal relations and work productivity, commitment, stereotypes, and ethics are influenced by one's ethnic and cultural views about self and others. And, when understanding, objectivity, and rationality increase in an organization, emotionalism,

**Table 1** Misleading Assumptions in a Multicultural World

| *Common and Misleading Assumptions* | | *Less Common and More Appropriate Assumptions* | |
|---|---|---|---|
| Homogeneity | *The Melting Pot Myth.* We are all the same. | Heterogeneity | The *Image of Cultural Pluralism.* We are not all the same; there are many culturally different groups in society. |
| Similarity | The myth that they are all just like me. | Similarity and Differences | *They are not just like me.* Many people are culturally different from me. Most people have both cultural similarities and differences compared to me. |
| Parochialism | *The Only-One-Way Myth.* Our way is the only way. We do not recognize any other way of living, working, or doing things. | Equifinality | *Our way is not the only way.* There are many culturally distinct ways of reaching the same goal or of living one's life. |
| Ethnocentrism | *The One-Best-Way Myth.* Our way is the best way. All other ways are inferior versions of our way. | Cultural contingency | *Our way is one possible way.* There are many other different and equally good ways to reach the same goal. The best way is contingent on the culture of the people involved (Adler 1983, p. 486). |

biases, and hasty judgments decrease. Internal communication and interactions improve, and healthier relations develop with clients and the surrounding environment.

The intercultural dimension in employee or management training programs is not an attempt to change the value systems of the participants. It is a vehicle that helps to increase organizational effectiveness and productivity. A meaningful program helps the participants understand, accept, and relate to diversity and cultural plurality in the work force. An effective program provides the participants with mirrors that reflect their personal and societal views and biases and, in the process, helps them to avoid and maybe get rid of some cultural myths, as Table 1 shows.

# REFERENCES

Adler, N. "Domestic Multiculturalism: Cross-Cultural Management in the Public Sector." In *Handbook of Organization Management*, ed. W. Eddy. (New York: Marcel Dekker, Inc., 1983), 481–499.

Adler, N. *International Dimensions of Organizational Behavior.* Boston: Kent, 1986.

Birdwhistell, R. *Kinesics and Context.* Philadelphia: University of Pennsylvania Press, 1970.

Cessaris, A. "When Employees Don't Spell Well." *Training and Development Journal* 40, (10) (1986), 59–61.

Condon, J., and F. Yousef. *An Introduction to Intercultural Communication.* New York: Macmillan, 1975 and 1986.

Copeland, L., and L. Griggs. *Going International.* New York: Random House, 1985.

Cox, C., and C. Cooper. "Developing Organizational Development Skills in Japan and in the United Kingdom: An Experimental Approach." *International Studies of Management and Organization* 6, (1977), 72–83.

Crawford, B. "Intercultural Concepts As Integral to the Community College Curricula." Paper presented at the annual Internatioanl Communication Association Conference, Chicago, 1986.

Hall, E. *The Hidden Dimension.* New York: Doubleday, 1966.

Hall, E. *Beyond Culture.* Garden City, N.Y.: Anchor, 1977.

Hall, E., and M. Hall. "The Sounds of Silence." *Playboy* 18 (6) (1971), 138–140, 148, 204, 206.

Hickson III, M., and D. Stacks. *Nonverbal Communication Studies and Applications.* Dubuque, Iowa: Wm C. Brown, 1985.

Hofstede, G. *Culture's Consequences: International Differences in Work-Related Values.* Beverly Hills, Calif.: Sage Publications, 1980.

Hofstede, G. "Cultural Differences in Teaching and Learning." *International Journal of Intercultural Relations* 10 (3) (1986), 301–320.

Lafrance, M., and C. Mayo. "Racial Differences in Gaze Behavior during Conversations: Two Systematic Observational Studies." *Journal of Personality and Social Psychology* 33 (1976), 547–552.

Laurent, A. "Management Style a Matter of Nationality." *Management Review* 4 (1983), 31.

Naisbitt, J. *Megatrends.* New York: Warner, 1982.

Ouchi, W. *Theory Z.* New York: Avon, 1981.

Peristiany, J., ed. *Honor and Shame: The Values of the Mediterranean.* London: Weiderfield and Nicolson, 1965.

Sadler, P. "Leadership Style, Confidence in Management, and Job Satisfaction." *The Journal of Applied Behavioral Science* 6 (1) (1970), 3–19.

Scheflon, A. *Communicational Structure: Analysis of a Psychotherapy Transaction.* Bloomington, Indiana: Indiana University Press, 1973.

Sommer, R. "Man's Proximate Environment." *Journal of Social Issues* 22 (10) (1966), 59–70.

Watson, D. *Proxemic Behavior: A Cross-Cultural Study.* The Hague: Monton, 1970.

Yousef, F. "Cross-Cultural Testing: An Aspect of the Resistance Reaction." *Language Learning* 18 (3 and 4) (1968), 227–234.

Yousef, F. "Cross-Cultural Communication: Aspects of Contrastive Social Values between North Americans and Middle Easterners." *Human Organization* 33 (4) (1974), 383–387.

Yousef, F. "Nonverbal Behavior: Some Intricate and Diverse Dimensions in Intercultural Communication." In L. Samovar and R. Porter (eds.), *Intercultural Communication: A Reader* 2nd ed., L. Samovar and R. Porter. Belmont, Calif.: Wadsworth, 1976, 230–235.

Yousef, F. "Communication Patterns: Some Aspects of Nonverbal Behavior in Intercultural Communication." In E. Ross (ed.), *Interethnic Communication*, Athens, Georgia: The University of Georgia Press, 1978, 49–62.

Yousef, F. "North Americans in the Middle East: Aspects of the Roles of Friendliness, Religion, and Women in Cross-Cultural Relations." In L. Samovar and R. Porter (eds.), *Intercultural Communication: A Reader*, 4th ed., ed. L. Samovar and R. Porter. Belmont, Calif.: Wadsworth, 1985, 78–85.

Yousef, F. and N. Briggs. "The Multinational Business Organization: A Schema for the Training of Overseas Personnel in Communication." In *International and Intercultural Communication Annual* 2 (1975), 74–85.

# Japanese and American Management: Participative Decision Making

LEA P. STEWART

In recent years, Japanese management techniques have been proclaimed by both scholars and lay authors as the salvation of American business. Perhaps because of popular books such as *Theory Z* by William Ouchi (1981) and *The Art of Japanese Management* by Richard Tanner Pascale and Anthony G. Athos (1981), it seems that everyone has heard of the wonders of Japanese management. According to Ouchi, corporations such as Hewlett-Packard, Eli Lilly, and Dayton-Hudson are using his Theory Z approach to management. Given the glowing success stories described by Ouchi and others, it would seem that American industry could profit from the widespread application of these techniques. This may or may not be true. The danger lies in applying techniques based on Japanese management without critically examining them. This is easy to do because, as one searches for information on this approach, one finds that the vast majority of articles portray the Japanese system in a favorable light. Yet, there are some authors who criticize, or at least express concern about, Japanese management techniques. This paper will review some of these articles to provide a more balanced look at an approach to management that everyone seems to be talking about.

The differences between U.S. and Japanese man-

This original essay appeared in print for the first time in the fourth edition. All rights reserved. Permission to reprint must be obtained from the publisher and the author. Professor Stewart teaches at Rutgers University.

**Table 1**

|  | United States | Japan |
|---|---|---|
| Employment | Short term, market oriented | Long term, career oriented |
| Management values | Openness and accountability | Harmony and consensus |
| Management style | Action oriented, short term horizons | Perfectionism in long term, paralysis in short term |
| Work values | Individual responsibility | Collective responsibility |
| Control processes | Formalized and explicit | Not formalized, implicit |
| Learning systems | External consultants and universities | Internal consultants and company training |

agement are summarized in Table 1 adapted from McMillan (1980).

Americans and Japanese live in quite different conceptual worlds. Whereas Americans regard responsible individuality as a virtue and view lack of autonomy as a constraint, the Japanese regard individuality as evidence of immaturity, and autonomy as the freedom to comply with one's obligations and duties (Fox 1977). According to Fox, the "traditional Japanese male employee is born into an intricate web of obligations and relationships" in which ridicule is unbearable and the ideal is to "blend selflessly into a system of 'other-directedness'" (p. 77). This socially committed male is chosen from the graduating class of one of the best universities to become a manager in a Japanese company for life. As a Japanese manager who abhors unpleasant face-to-face confrontations and discord, he will manage through a system of apparent consensus building (Tsurumi 1978).

This consensus building system, the *ringi* system, is one of the most talked about virtues of the Japanese system. There is evidence, however, that this system is not dedicated to true consensus. Fox (1977) describes the *ringi* system as a process in which a proposal prepared by middle management is circulated to affected units of the organization for review, revision, and approval. When each unit has attached its approval seal to the proposal, it goes to the appropriate higher level authority for final approval and implementation. Although the system involves numerous group meetings and much delay, once final approval is granted, the organization moves surprisingly quickly to implement it. Fox claims that this system should be labeled "consensual understanding" instead of decision making by consensus. According to Fox:

*It is not uncommon for the* ringisho *to be merely the formalization of a suggestion from higher management which has had the benefit of considerable prior discussion before being drafted. Apparently, not many* ringisho *are drastically revised en route to the top or vetoed when they get there. And considerable discretion is retained by management to prescribe in detail when and by whom they will be implemented.* (pp. 79–80)

Although Fox believes the *ringi* system is not true decision making by consensus, he does believe the system nurtures commitment and, thus, "recalls the work of Lewin, Maier, Coch and French, and Likert who demonstrated the effectiveness of participative decision making in American organizations long ago" (p. 85). Krauss (1973) sees many parallels between the management styles of successful U.S. companies dedicated to participative decision making and the Japanese system. Tsurumi (1978) takes a more critical view and characterizes the decision-making process inside Japanese corporations as "personality-based." He claims that "the art of consensus-building is to sell ideas and decisions to others" (p. 60). This criticism echoes the claims of American critics who have challenged participative decision making. Often American employees are allowed only limited participation (see French et al. for a classic application of participation in a manufacturing plant), or are allowed to participate in making only insignificant decisions. Participation is often used to make an employee *feel* that he or she is taking part in the decision-making process even if the employee's input does not actually have an effect on the process.

Pascale (1978) reinforces the similarity in decision-making style between American and Japanese managers in an extensive study of communication practices in U.S. and Japanese corporations. Pascale found that managers in Japanese firms engage in over 30 percent more face-to-face contacts each day than do managers in U.S. firms. In addition, compared to U.S. managers, Japanese managers score themselves higher on decision quality and substantially higher on implementation quality. Yet, there is no significant difference in the style of decision making used by Japanese and U.S. managers. Japanese managers do not use a consultative decision-making process more often than do American managers. Pascale argues that the Japanese manager's tendency to use more face-to-face contacts is more efficient because the Japanese language does not lend itself to mechanical word processing and most written communication has to be done by hand, which is a lengthy process. In addition, face-to-face communication is encouraged by the crowded Japanese work setting in which many levels of the hierarchy are located in the same open work space. Thus, the nature of the Japanese language and of the work setting may be the major determinants of the Japanese manager's communication style. This face-to-face style, in turn, leads to higher perceived decision quality and higher perceived implementation quality.

The dominance of face-to-face communication may account for the perception that there is more openness about major decisions in Japanese firms and "more desire to explore and learn together" (McMillan 1980). While Japanese managers are not actually using a consultative decision-making style, they are talking to their workers a great deal. This increased face-to-face contact is interpreted by observers of the system as openness. Systematic research into the content of these face-to-face interactions is needed to determine if Japanese managers are being "open" with their subordinates or merely answering questions and giving advice.

No matter how decisions are actually made within Japanese corporations, there is no doubt that Japanese companies are highly successful. McMillan attributes the phenomenal success of Japanese industry to high productivity due to the "best technology-oriented hardware, which combines the newest processes available, an emphasis on quality control and cost-volume relationships, and, where necessary, automation and robot technology" (p. 28)—in essence, machines. McMillan argues that the Japanese have invested a great deal in developing and maintaining advanced hardware systems and are reaping the benefits of this technology. Fox (1977), on the other hand, takes a more human approach to the success of the Japanese system. He claims that the Japanese system has accomplished so much due to "dedicated, self-sacrificing workers, spurred by a sense of urgency" (p. 80). Supposedly these workers are rewarded by lifetime employment, but this is not actually the case.

Permanent employment (the *nenko* system) operates mainly in the larger Japanese firms and applies to a minority of Japanese workers (Oh 1976). It is reserved for male employees in government and large businesses (Drucker 1978). The limitation of the *nenko* system and its benefits to perhaps 30 percent of the nonagricultural Japanese labor force, according to Oh, "appears to be essential to the continued survival of the *nenko* system, and is probably its greatest cost to Japanese society" (p. 15). The benefits of the *nenko* system, however, are not limitless for those who are covered by it. Although a manager can expect yearly raises and bonuses since wages are based at least partly upon seniority, lifetime employment for most managers ends at age 55, pensions rarely exceed two or three years of salary, and government social security benefits are nominal (Fox 1977). To keep this system in operation and to assure a flexible supply of workers, the Japanese system considers 20 to 30 percent of its workers as "temporary" (Fox 1977). Women, by definition, are temporary employees (Drucker 1978) and are "consistently discriminated against with regard to pay, benefits, and opportunity for advancement" (Fox 1977, p. 79). Even Ouchi (1981) admits that "Type Z organizations have a tendency to be sexist and racist" (p. 77).

To avoid the stigma of becoming a temporary worker or a manual laborer, Japanese children are pressured at increasingly younger and younger ages to learn enough to be admitted to the most prestigious schools. According to Drucker (1978), since "career opportunities are dependent almost entirely on educational attainment" (p. 33), the pressure starts with the child's application to nursery school. As the pressure is becoming more intense, Drucker notes, the suicide rate among teenagers and even preteens is reaching alarming proportions. Perhaps partly because of this pressure, young people in Japan are starting to defect from the traditional values (Fox 1977). Although McMillan (1980) discounts its effect, he notes that "a growing minority of young people are impatient with the career employment system and the age-related wage practice" (p. 29). Oh (1976) claims that management tends to cultivate these grievances among younger workers to keep them from unifying with older workers to oppose management. Whether or not these grievances will become strong enough to challenge traditional management practices remains to be seen.

After careful examination, Japanese management appears to be a system of contradictions. Managers spend a great deal of time in face-to-face communication with workers, but they do not use consultative decision making more than American managers. The *ringi* system gives the appearance of consensus-seeking, but it is actually more of an information dissemination system. The Japanese are rewarded for their educational attainments, so they are pressured into starting on the path toward the best schools at increasingly earlier ages.

"Permanent" employment ends at age 55. Undoubtedly, the Japanese system has produced successful corporations, but, as Sethi (1973) notes, "Do we want to measure success in terms similar to those used by the Japanese society?" (p. 14). This question must be answered before we start the wholesale application of Japanese management to U.S. corporations.

## REFERENCES

Drucker, P. F. "The price of success: Japan revisited." *Across the Board*, 1978, 15 (8), 28–35.

Fox, W. M. "Japanese management: Tradition under strain." *Business Horizons*, 1977, 20 (4), 76–85.

French, J. R. P.; Ross, I. C.; Kirby, S.; Nelson, J. R.; and Smyth, P. "Employee participation in a program of industrial change." *Personnel*, 1958, 35 (6), 16–29. Reprinted in Redding, W. C., and Sanborn, G. A. (eds.), *Business and Industrial Communication*. New York: Harper & Row, 1964, 372–387.

Krauss, W. P. "Will success spoil Japanese management?" *Columbia Journal of World Business*, 1973, 8 (4), 26–30.

McMillan, C. "Is Japanese management really so different?" *Business Quarterly*, 1980, 45 (3), 26–31.

Oh, T. K. "Japanese management—A critical review." *Academy of Management Review*, 1976, 1, 14–25.

Ouchi, W. G. *Theory Z.* New York: Avon Books, 1981.

Pascale, R. T. "Communication and decision making across cultures: Japanese and American comparisons." *Administrative Science Quarterly*, 1978, 23, 91–110.

Pascale, R. T., and Athos, A. G. *The Art of Japanese Management*. New York: Warner Books, 1981.

Sethi, S. P. "Drawbacks of Japanese management." *Business Week*, November 24, 1973, 12–13.

"The profit in breaking Japanese traditions." *Business Week*, February 14, 1977, 51.

Tsurumi, Y. "The best of times and the worst of times: Japanese management in America." *Columbia Journal of World Business*, 1978, 13 (2), 56–61.

# Japanese Social Experience and Concept of Groups

DOLORES CATHCART
ROBERT CATHCART

*Deru kugi wa utareru* ("the nail that sticks up is hit") is a well-known saying in Japan. Japanese children hear it continually from parents and teachers. It reflects an important cultural attitude. Japanese are fond of the saying because it suggests their abhorrence of egocentricity and their wish to avoid being singled out for praise or blame. More importantly, this saying reminds them of the pain experienced when one fails to blend harmoniously into a group. It is this great desire to lose oneself within the confines of a group that is most characteristic of the Japanese.

If we were to place Japanese concepts of self and group at one end of a continuum it would be possible to produce an almost perfect paradigm by placing American concepts at the other. This remarkable polarity in cultural variation makes the study of Japanese groups useful to those interested in intercultural communication.[1] In both cultures we find a similar social phenomenon, highly developed group activity, but the contrasting perceptions of group dynamics are so disparate they bring into sharp focus the divergent social values of Japanese and Americans. Understanding these cultural variances in perception and values can help us cross communication barriers, and more importantly, help us understand how our American concepts of group are cultural variants rather than universal theories. In other words, the ethnocentrism of American theories of group dynamics may emerge more clearly as we examine Japanese concepts standing in polar opposition to our own.

## I

An American would most likely begin the examination of "group" by defining or categorizing groups. Questions would be asked like, "What is a group?" "Can two persons be a group?" "What are the main differences between a small group and a large group?" These questions reflect Western thought patterns and would represent one end of the cultural continuum. The Japanese would not begin in this manner. Groups are not defined, they simply "are." They are the "natural" or normal milieu in which human interaction takes place. There is no counterpart in Japan to that American thought process which produces long essays and collections of experimental data on "how best to define a group." Such attempts at defining and categorizing are typical of Western attitudes and values.

Another American approach to groups is to consider *the role of the individual* in the group. On this continuum the American position is represented by the attitude that the individual is the more important part of the group. In American culture each person is perceived of as having a unique identity, a "self" separate from but influenced by the other members of a group and by group norms. This leads to the view that a group is a *collection* of individuals in which a person has a great deal of freedom to choose individual roles or even to remain apart from the group if he so chooses. This belief carries with it the assumption that the individual can function, in theory at least, independent of the group, guided by a duty to self and obligated to do that which he sees as morally right no matter what course the group follows.

The Japanese view of "no-self" stands in opposition to this. In Japan it is believed society is composed of on-going groups in which individual

This original essay appeared in print for the first time in the second edition. All rights reserved. Permission to reprint must be obtained from the publisher and the authors. Dolores Cathcart is a freelance writer. Robert Cathcart teaches at Queens College of the City of New York. This joint project grew out of a research sabbatical spent in Japan.

identity is submerged. The Japanese approach to the group role is to perceive of oneself as an integral part of the whole. Sociologist Yoshiharu Matsumoto explains:

*The individual does not interact as an individual but as a son in a parent-child relationship, as an apprentice in a master-apprentice relationship, or as a worker in an employer-employee relationship. Furthermore, the playing of the role of son, apprentice, student, or worker persists twenty-four hours a day. There is no clear-cut demarcation between work and home life.*[2]

The identification through group rather than self can be observed in ordinary interactions. When Japanese family members converse, they address one another not by using their given names but by using names that denote the person's group functions. A daughter-in-law named Reiko will be called by a name that denotes her place in the family rather than "Reiko," which designates her individually. Should a father in a family die and be replaced by the eldest son as head of the family, the son would then be called "father" even by his own mother.

Groups in Japan are permanent and determinate. Individuals are temporary and have no existence, in theory, outside the group. This outlook does not negate the important functions and contributions of individuals within groups but it does subordinate the "self" to the group. Individual fulfillment of self is attained through finding and maintaining one's place within the group. If the group is successful, so is each part of it.

The American concept of individual responsibility based on a belief in individual morality stands in sharp contrast to the Japanese concept of *group* morality and ultimate group responsibility. The Japanese see all decisions and actions as the product of group consensus. The individual is not held morally responsible for such decisions. When a person commits a wrongful act, it is the group that is embarrassed and, in the final analysis, responsible for the misdeed. It is commonly accepted in Japanese law and practice that the group should

make amends and pay damages resulting from individual misconduct. This embodiment of group can be carried to the point where, in extreme circumstances, those persons at the top of the group hierarchy feel constrained to answer for the misdeeds of individual group members by committing *hara-kiri* (suicide) in order to erase the blot on the group's honor. This act of *hara-kiri* reflects a total denial of self and a complete loyalty to the group.

The Japanese is relieved of the typical American moral struggle wherein each person must continually weigh the duty to self and individual rights against obligations to the group. On the other hand, the Japanese cannot escape tremendous anxiety produced by having to ensure that every thought and act enhances the group. As Kawashima Takeoyoshi states it,

*There is no place for the concept of the individual as an independent entity equal to other individuals. In (Japanese) culture, the social order consists of social obligations, which are defined not in specific determinate terms, but in diffuse, indeterminate terms. . . . The indeterminateness of social obligations—hence the lack of concepts of equality and independent individual—does not allow the existence of [individual] "right" as the counterpart of social obligations.*[3]

Americans seldom feel an all-consuming loyalty to one group. As a result, America has been called a nation of "joiners." There is a tendency to be on the lookout for new groups to join which can fulfill one's personal desires as well as provide a place for meeting social obligations. Americans readily form groups, dissolve them, and go on to form new groups. The motivation is the individual search for identity.

Japanese cannot imagine this kind of "joining." A person in Japan is part of particular groups because that is the way society is structured, and the individual does not believe he can "go it alone." To leave a group in Japan is to lose one's identity, and it decreases the chances of finding fulfillment. Leaving a group is not a matter of individual choice just as joining a group is not. In Japan necessary group transitions such as leaving the university to join a company are circumscribed by elaborate rituals constructed to serve group needs rather than individual desires.

## II

The perceptual patterns and value systems that produce this extreme identification with group rather than self can be traced to the central role of family as a model for all Japanese interpersonal relationships. As in the West, the family is the primary group and is the place where most attitudes and values are learned. Unlike the nuclear family of the West, which functions primarily to protect the offspring while preparing them to leave and assume a role in the larger society (where it is expected they will replicate the family with another nuclear family), "the Japanese family is conceived of as existing from the past and into the future, unceasingly, independent of birth and death of its members."[4]

In Japan, the family does not prepare the child to leave it and enter the social order; the family, itself, is perceived as the *basis of all social order*. Within the family the child learns the intricate rituals and linguistic nuances that influence the Japanese personality and that are operative in all relationships in and outside the family. That is, the Japanese *replicate* the family group structure and process throughout their society.

The Japanese word for family is *ie*, which literally means "the house" or "the household." The use of the term *ie* emphasizes the organizational and functional aspects of family. Each household consists of the head of the house and all persons, whether related by blood or not, who share in the social and economic life of the family. This relationship is designated *keifu*, which means "bond" and which refers to the maintenance and continuance of the family as an institution. This is in contrast to the kinship that binds the Western family through blood and inheritance. Although strictly patrilinear in structure, the Japanese family can be headed by a member with no blood relationship to the other family members. This is possible through the traditional practice of "adoption." For example, if there is no son to take over as the head of the house, a family adopts a suitable "son" and he immediately takes on the role of the eldest son, with all the rights and privileges entailed and with all the duties and obligations that a son born to the position would have. After adoption, he would no longer "exist" as a son in the family he left and he could never return to or make claims in his blood family. His name is literally erased from that family's records. He takes a new name and his former name and "self" disappear.

The ancient feudal household consisting of a lord and all his retainers, peasants, warriors, and craftsmen was considered *ie*, or family. In this arrangement the line between kin and non-kin is blurred, and loyalty and contribution to the group becomes the bond (*keifu*) that unifies and distinguishes the family. In modern Japan, this concept of *ritual kinship* prepares a person to enter a group outside the family or household. When a Japanese is chosen to work for a company or organization he sees himself as being *adopted into a family* and he carries with him the same kinds of loyalties and methods of interpersonal relationships that he has learned in his (*ie*) family.

An important characteristic of the Japanese family is the way in which it fosters and perpetuates *dependency*. This dependency produces "indebtedness" or *on*, which in turn governs interpersonal relationships. A Japanese child, like an American one, learns at a very young age that he must rely on others. Unlike American families, the Japanese family purposefully *fosters* dependency as the child matures. Dependency, in Japan, is considered a natural and desirable trait capable of producing warm human relationships. (See the following discussion of *amae*.) In America, on the other hand, dependency is considered a limitation on individual growth and fulfillment, and so the family and school teach the child to become *self-reliant*.

A Japanese, even as an adult, never escapes dependency. All his life he depends on others, and all his life he must seek to repay his indebtedness to those who have cared for him by providing for those beneath him. This is what is meant by on.

On should be viewed as part of group structure and not as a relationship between two persons only. Everyone in a group *is at the same time* an *on*-receiver and an *on*-giver. Each member of the group is indebted to all those above him on whom he has had to depend, and in turn he must repay this indebtedness by giving assistance to all those below him who are dependent on him. On works to bind persons to the group, for if they left the group they would have no way of repaying the indebtedness incurred while a member of the group. It also functions as a means of linking all persons in the group in an unending chain of indebtedness and obligation.

While the *on* relationship might appear to be a typical pecking order hierarchy to the Westerner, it is a hierarchy of a very different quality. It is based on the natural dependency inherent in human relationships rather than on inherent individual qualities or attributes that enable some human beings to assume superior positions to others. On requires that the Japanese see himself as fitting into a hierarchy—a hierarchy that exists in every group of which he is a member.

The very strong personal relationships characteristic of this vertical dyadic order are fostered by the *oyabun-kobun* relationship, a companion dimension that exists along with *on*. The *oyabun* is a father, boss, or patron who protects and provides for the son, employee, or student in return for his service and loyalty. Again, this is a part of the two-way dependency relationship. Every boss or group leader recognizes his dependence on those below him. Without their undivided loyalty he could not function. He is acutely aware of the double dimension of this dependency because he has had to serve a long period as a follower or *kobun*, working his way up the hierarchy. He has reached his position at the top by faithfully serving his *oyabun* who in turn has protected him and provided for him. Each *oyabun* has one or more *kobun* whom he looks after much as a father looks after his chil-

dren. The more loyal and devoted the "children," the more he succeeds and the better he can care for them. In the Japanese business world the *oyabun* finds work for his *kobun*, places them where they are best suited, provides for them when they are out of work, and accepts responsibility for personal problems they have on and off the job. In turn, *kobun* must heed his advice, defend him, and depend on him for help. "Everyone gets some sort of reward for submitting to an *oyabun*; consequently followers remain faithful to their *oyabun* during difficult times in a way they never would for a man who has used sheer power to subordinate them."[5]

The *oyabun-kobun* relationship makes for a unique structure in Japanese groups, one not found in American groups, where relationships are dependent on changing role functions and where the ideal group is one in which every person is considered equal to every other, free to participate as he chooses. Relationships with a Japanese group are vertical: something like a chain, each person being a link in the chain. Each member has a direct relationship with the person above (one's *oyabun*) and the person or several persons directly below (one's *kobun*). Interaction is usually with one person at a time and never with more than one above. The *kobun* does not go over the head of his superior or *oyabun*. Indeed, it would be unnecessary ever to do so, because the *oyabun* would never make a decision without considering the needs, interests, and desires of the *kobun*.

On and *oyabun-kobun* stress dependency and loyalty of superior and inferior in the vertical hierarchy of Japanese society. Without some balance, however, these concepts would produce a highly factionalized system with little or no regard for the interests of the whole. The group or collective, to be strongly united, must demand a mutual regard or loyalty to something larger than one's faction or *oyabun-kobun* link. In Western societies the normal tendency toward factionalism is counterbalanced by individualism and by the individual's acceptance of a universalist ethic. An American, for example, might be a Republican or

Democrat but he has a duty to all other American citizens that supersedes or at least holds in check excessive loyalty to his chosen party. Oftentimes this is stated as one's duty to be a "good neighbor" or a "good Christian" and this requires the American to be helpful or understanding of others even though they may be members of competing organizations or factions.

Japanese adhere to no such universalist ethic. Instead, the Japanese have internalized the concept of *giri*, which serves a similar function in checking factionalism. *Giri* controls the horizontal relationships in this vertically organized society.

It is difficult to produce an easily understood translation of or definition of *giri*. The term is widely used in Japan and can be found in almost every discussion of Japanese behavior. John W. Hall and Richard K. Beardsley, in their book, *Twelve Doors to Japan*, offer the following explanation of *giri*:

*To some Japanese,* giri *is the blanket term for obligation between persons in actual situations as contrasted with a universalistic ethic of duty. Others see* giri *as the form of obligation to the group without superiority on one side and inferiority on the other as in the* on *relationship. In either case,* giri *connotes obligation and as such sets the tone of relationship toward specifiable other persons. . . . One can recognize the inevitable tensions between* giri *and* ninjo. . . . Ninjo *refers to what one would like to do as a human being and equally to what one finds distasteful or abhorrent out of personal sentiment;* giri *pertains to what one must do or avoid doing because of status or group membership.*[6]

*Giri* implies the self-discipline that must be used to repress or channel personal desires and feelings. One may not like, personally, the older members of the group or think they are particularly wise or competent, but one must show affection and humbleness toward them for the sake of the group. In this way the selfish impulses of an individual or faction are held in check, not out of a desire to be polite or to avoid confrontation but rather through an obligation not to embarrass the group by causing any member to lose face.

*Giri* is well-suited to this society, which produces lifelong relationships. Japanese spend most of every day in close proximity with the other members of their group, and without *giri* such an intense interaction over such an extended period of time would be impossible to bear. The highly ritualized mode of interpersonal relationships developed to accommodate *giri* prevents incidences that could produce hostility. It is not difficult to understand that American notions of group participation, such as "group communication should be characterized by frank, open, and candid statements expressing individual personal feelings, wishes, and dislikes," would be the antithesis of the Japanese concept of *giri*.

Family traditions, the concepts of *on, oyabun-kobun,* and *giri* confine the individual Japanese within a fixed group, keeping him there all his life, and effectively cut him off from other groups. He naturally grows more and more dependent on his group and more distrustful of anyone "outside." In fact, the Japanese are often callously indifferent (although always polite) to anyone outside their own group.

It is difficult for a Westerner to imagine a culture that so totally submerges the individual within the group. There is a tendency for Westerners to account for what they see by attributing subjugation of self to political and economic pressures that force or coerce submission to authority. Such an explanation does not fit Japanese culture nor can it account for the widespread satisfaction the Japanese feel for their way of life. A *Japanese* explanation of this behavior is offered by the psychiatrist, L. Takeo Doi. He maintains that the Japanese desire for group identity can be found in the concept of *amae*. There is no English equivalent of the word *amae* or *ameru* (the verb form), but it can be translated to mean to depend on or presume upon another's love, or it can mean lovable, or it can even mean "spoiled" as in the case of a child spoiled by too much affection. It can also mean "sweet" as in the sweet warmth of a mother's love.

According to Doi, "it (*amae*) carries a positive connotation related to the sweet and warm dependency that a child feels when surrounded by his parents and other loving kin."[7] Doi believes that the Japanese carry this notion with them both consciously and unconsciously throughout life, continually seeking this dependency status in all activities. This, he feels, would account for their desire to constantly subordinate themselves in a group. Each Japanese is attempting to recreate in each group that state of sweet bliss he first experienced in his family. Doi finds the concept of *amae* so pervasive, he claims that "*Amae* might be the very factor that distinguishes Japanese people from other nations. . . ."[8]

## III

The ability of the Japanese people to maintain their basic value system and to readily adapt their cultural concepts to new and changing situations is one of the more intriguing aspects of Japanese studies. Nowhere is this more apparent than in the Japanese re-creation of the Western industrial corporation as the twentieth-century counterpart of the feudal system family.

Today, Japan is a modern industrial giant absorbed in a technological race with other industrial nations. Her cities are overcrowded, polluted, fast-paced, and impersonal. To the casual observer, a Japanese city is like any other "big city" in the world: surrounded with huge factories populated by persons isolated from the rural regions, living in an impersonal atmosphere, bent on material acquisition. But anyone who lives in Japan knows how persistently the concepts of *on*, *giri*, and *amae* remain central to Japanese life. For example, the big corporation occupies a central position in modern Japan, not only as a producer of economic strength and goods, but as the system in which the Japanese maintain their traditional values. Chie Nakane, in an excellent sociological study called *Japanese Society*, argues that the corporate group is the unit that forms the basis for modern Japanese society.[9] Suzuki and Mitsubishi have replaced the feudal family, but the structure has remained the same.

In feudal Japan, and it is important to recall that the Japanese feudal era extended well into the nineteenth century, the family household—composed of the lord and his retainers, warriors, peasants, and craftsmen—was the basic social unit or group. The codes of behavior, loyalty, and honor that served the household then have been transformed in essentially the same form to the modern version of the *ie*, the corporate group. It also is organized in a strict hierarchical order. Seniority determines rank, and merit plays an insignificant part in the advancement of an employee. The *oyabun-kobun* concept governs company-employee interaction. Once a person enters employment with a company he becomes an integral part of that corporate community and usually remains with it the rest of his life. The new employee is indebted to all those above him and he repays *on* through his obligation to all those who come after him or are below him. He is totally dependent on his company and he finds pleasure and satisfaction in this institutionalization of *amae*. Unlike the American company, which is considered primarily a place of employment *apart* from one's family, religious, and social groups, the company in Japan is intimately involved in each member's life. It is the center of the individual's social and economic life. Off-work hours are spent with one's fellow employees, vacations are taken at the company-owned retreat, health services and counseling are provided, even family matters like marriage and divorce are the concern of the company. The worker becomes emotionally involved with the company group, and group duty or *giri* governs his life.

*Kaisha*, meaning "company" or "enterprise," has become a familiar word in modern Japan. *Kaisha*, superimposed on *ie*, has become the symbol of group consciousness. Nakane describes the importance of his "new" group:

Kaisha *does not mean that individuals are bound by contractual relationships into a corporate enterprise, while still thinking of themselves as separate entities; rather kaisha is "my" or "our" company, the community to which one belongs primarily, and which is all-important in one's life. Thus in most cases the company provides the whole social existence of a person, has authority over all aspects of his life; he is deeply involved in the association.*[10]

In less than one hundred years Japan has moved from a feudal, agrarian society to become a major industrial power. The startling changes necessitated by this quick transition have come about without markedly disrupting the basic patterns of human interactions or altering the fundamental group value orientations. The Japanese have had the ability to accept and absorb methods and ideas from Western culture and yet keep their traditional ritual and ethic. It is clear that the concept binding each Japanese to his group has served to preserve these ancient patterns.

## NOTES

1. See Richard E. Porter and Larry A. Samovar, "Approaching Intercultural Communication," in *Intercultural Communication: A Reader*, 3rd. ed., Larry A Samovar and Richard E. Porter (Belmont, Calif.: Wadsworth, 1982), p. 35.

2. Yoshiharu Matsumoto, "Contemporary Japan: The Individual and the Group," *Transactions of the American Philosophical Society*, 50:1 (January 1960), p. 60.

3. Kawashima Takeoyoshi, "The Status of the Individual in the Notion of the Law, Right, and Social Order in Japan," in *The Japanese Mind*, ed. Charles A. Moore (Honolulu: University Press of Hawaii, 1967), p. 274.

4. Kizaemon Ariga, "The Family in Japan," *Marriage and Family Living*, 16:4 (1954), p. 362.

5. John W. Hall and Richard K. Beardsley, *Twelve Doors to Japan* (New York: McGraw-Hill, 1965), p. 84.

6. Ibid., p. 94.

7. L. Takeo Doi, "Amae: A Key Concept for Understanding Japanese Culture," in *Japanese Culture: Its Development and Characteristics*, ed. Robert J. Smith and Richard K. Beardsley (New York: Aldine, 1962), p. 132.

8. Ibid, p. 133.

9. Chie Nakane, *Japanese Society* (Berkeley: Center for Japanese and Korean Studies, 1970).

10. Ibid., pp. 3–4.

# International Negotiation

## GLEN FISHER

For a variety of technical and research reasons, the term "national character" has not enjoyed the highest reputation among social scientists. But it might actually serve the negotiator's purposes better, for it can call attention both to the patterns of personality that negotiators tend to exhibit as products of their own society and to the collective concerns and outlooks that give a nation a distinctive "character" and outlook in international relationships.

We start by recalling the anthropological proposition that patterns of personality do exist for groups that share a common culture, that in the process of being socialized in a given society, the individual picks up the knowledge, the ideas, the beliefs and values, the phobias and anxieties of the group. Some of this is taught explicitly; most of it is absorbed subconsciously. Americans come to value time and efficiency, to place emphasis on the individual and individual achievement, and to love statistics. The Japanese as easily come to place emphasis on the group, to value and honor complex sets of obligations, to feel comfortable communicating in silence, and to recognize the virtues exemplified by the legendary forty-seven *ronin*. Mexicans learn to treat time less frenetically, to value human response and close personal relationships, and to more stoically accept fate than their northern neighbors. And the French present variations from American themes by differentiating more carefully between their public and private worlds, by seeing themselves as people

of thought and reason, and by taking history more seriously. If one makes such comparisons on the basis of statistical averages or probability rather than as rigid formulas for understanding individual counterparts, the validity is more apparent.

In comparing national character, it must be recognized that fundamental belief systems can carry deep emotional charge and be highly resistant to change. The psychology of the many conflicts in the Middle East demonstrates this. Even outlooks on life and death are affected by culture. A few years ago a group of psychiatrists compared notes on their experience in Egypt and Israel during and after the October war. They found that there were widely differing patterns in public response to battlefield deaths. The Israelis were more shaken and more likely to take that factor into account in their policy debate.

How "rational" or "irrational" a society's beliefs are has little to do with their effectiveness as factors in perception and motivation of action. The counsel of the psychological anthropologist applies: While people may be alike in basic human qualities, they do not necessarily think alike. Even if sophisticated international negotiators could do so because of their immersion in an internationalized culture, their clients would still reflect the special emotional and cognitive patterns of their respective societies. It is this reality that makes international negotiation such a special art.

For the purposes of negotiation, it is useful to recognize the areas in which the possibility of national character contrasts needs to be explored. These include matters of national images, values and assumptions which affect the substance of negotiation, and styles of reasoning. Therefore, discussion will be organized around several lead questions:

### 1. How do national self-images and images of the other party affect negotiation?

No other set of psychological factors was mentioned as frequently by persons who contributed to this study as the perceptions their counterparts held of their country's international position or of their special qualities as a nation. The context usually was

From Glen Fisher, *International Negotiation: A Cross-Cultural Perspective* (Chicago: Intercultural Press, Inc., 1980), pp. 37–52. Reprinted by permission of the author and publisher. Glen Fisher is an Adjunct Professor of International Policy Studies at the Monterey Institute of International Studies.

negotiation with the United States, of course, so therefore perceptions of the United States and of U.S. intentions were next most often noted. Interviewees who became still more analytical included American self-perceptions and American images of the other, recognizing that such images are often carried more out of awareness than American negotiators recognize.

French self-images seemed to stand out especially as a factor in negotiation. Their preoccupation with French culture and the French language would be familiar to the reader. Projection of French culture is almost a priority consideration in French foreign policy. They see nothing wrong with French cultural imperialism. . . . The French hold an acute consciousness of history—from the French point of view—and with this the glory of France as a unique force in Western civilization.

It follows that the French tend to perceive themselves as holding a special position in the international arena. France is not simply another European country—it is France. The country has a mystique that is part of the French soul. Its policy-makers do not need to apologize for taking actions that they see to be strictly in France's self interest. They do not hesitate in being the exception. One person noted that he could not imagine a French leader's self-image allowing him to say, as President Kennedy did at the Berlin Wall, "Ich bin ein Berliner."

In its uniqueness France has seen itself playing such special international roles as being a bridge between China and the West or having a special mentor relationship with the developing world. The French sense of close alliance with the United States runs deep and they usually do expect to extend close cooperation, but they do not hold U.S. leadership in awe. Stanley Hoffman notes that they expect the United States, like France, to act in its self-interest, and are not impressed by American declarations of altruistic motives. The French appreciated Marshall Plan assistance, but do not now see that this has left an obligation on their part. Where their self-image may suffer from less than complete assurance is in the realm of technological accomplishment. As this stands out as a standard of prestige in contemporary world affairs, the French

apparently feel some anxiety that they might be vulnerable—although they would rather be judged by other standards of civilization.

For Mexico, matters of national identity could hardly differ more. History is their problem rather than a source of assurance. Throughout their independence, the United States has been the overpowering reality and the mirror by which Mexico was always seen to have a lower national stature. While a blend of distinguished Indian tradition and a far-reaching social revolution have provided a satisfying distinctness to the Mexican sense of self, the consciousness of being "so far from God and so close to the United States" has molded many self-perceptions. Perhaps most important, awareness of the reciprocal image that Americans hold of Mexico and Mexicans, combined with a sense of having been cavalierly used, has heightened the defensive sensitivity to further dignity-shattering actions on the part of the colossus to the north.

One observer noted that the maximum time that even a friendly Mexican could spend with an American without bringing up some aspect of what the United States has done to Mexico is about two hours. However this might be, in virtually every negotiation, interaction has been complicated by sensitivity to their perceived dependent relationship with the United States and their long memory of patronizing and demeaning actions taken by the United States as a government, by American companies, and by Americans as individuals. Even after Americans think that they have taken this into account, they find they have not appreciated the depth and emotional charge of the outlook. Nor do they appreciate how subtly their own perceptions have become ingrained. The result is that they unwittingly display still more behavior that can be taken as patronizing or as discounting the Mexican's worth. Even President Carter's apparently honest attempt to be informally friendly and talk as an equal backfired when he joked about "Montezuma's revenge" in remarks made during his 1979 visit to Mexico. A construction company's boast regarding the efficiency of a new fence being constructed along the border or tactics used in policing illegal immigrants can set off instant public indignation in Mexico.

How closely a Mexican identifies with the United States can be a delicate matter, although less so in cities like Monterrey and the business sections of border communities. A Binational Center director noted that in dealing with his board of directors, he had to be sure that he did not force his cooperating Mexican members too far and too often out on a limb with their fellow citizens by expecting them to defend the Center against criticism or by making it appear that they were serving the American director instead of the other way around.

It is also reported, however, that some Mexicans have learned that this imbalance is not necessarily to their disadvantage. Americans, they find, are sensitive to being called insensitive. Therefore it is useful, especially in business agreements, to play the position of the weaker partner in negotiation, of the side that needs special consideration for being disadvantaged, even to be able to flatter the stronger partner's capacity to provide extra help. Where this approach crosses the line from being a sincerely felt position to calculated tactics is not easily determined. . . .

But the basic Mexican outlook is that they do not want to be beholden to the United States more than is absolutely necessary. The fact that AID and the Peace Corps have never been accepted there, as they have in other parts of Latin America, or that any private philanthropy that appears as patronizing is rejected, demonstrates the wariness. This outlook is more than a problem of poor versus rich; it is a matter of interpreting why the rich are rich and the poor are poor. From the way that history is taught in the Mexican classroom to the memory of expropriating the petroleum companies (1938), through a revolution in which privilege was denounced, to the political persuasions of university students—the United States has been held up as the source of Mexican misfortune. It takes a lot of reasonableness to override this pervasive pattern of perceptions.

Another source of sensitivity comes from having to live in the shadow of American technological achievement and with the Americans' quickness to judge the Mexican in that comparison. Stereotypes result of which the Mexican can hardly be unaware.

. . . Since such a large part of American-Mexican negotiation involves technological matters and standards of performance, these images have far-reaching effects.

The Japanese present quite another pattern of self-images and self-perceptions as related to the United States. Actually, to many ordinary Japanese, the very idea of having a "self-image" may be rather abstract, for unlike Americans, they constitute a highly homogeneous society and have little reason, normally, to take outside comparative references into account. For much of Japanese history, foreigners were considered to be so far outside the various recognized categories of social relationships that for all practical purposes they were outside the human universe. Yet at the same time, concern for world opinion did have an appeal and was a strong motivating force for collective performance in rebuilding after World War II and the humiliation of defeat.

Unlike the Mexicans, Japanese have little trouble in coping with the fact that America is a superior power. Perhaps distance helps, but a key factor is said to be a Japanese readiness to extend to the international arena their view of hierarchy and place. There is more inclination to see established hierarchy as affording the security of known position and promoting harmony. The war settled what the order was. So any problem the Japanese have with U.S. power in an unbalanced relationship turns on the way that power is managed in the relationship, and not, as has been suggested, on the slowness of the United States in recognizing Japan's rising status as an *economic* power.

Therefore, when Japan perceives the American position negatively, it is a matter of sensitivity to being ill used, taken for granted, or having their interests ignored by the power on which they depend. Thus their "shock" in not being informed in advance of the opening contact with China was only partly a shock over substance. It was more a reaction to what was perceived to be inappropriate unilateral behavior on the part of a superior power with whom they thought they had a special understanding.

In contrast to the Mexican situation, Japanese do

not necessarily find a dependency relationship undignified or undesirable. Japanese culture provides for this in the *amae* concept in personal relationships, as when a student is dependent on a teacher, a child on its parents, or an employee on his employer. American benevolence in exercising superior power after the war made the *amae* relationship rather natural. The trouble is that as other relationships demand American attention or as Americans see little need to be Japan's patron today, the Japanese request, so often reported by negotiators, that the United States be understanding of special Japanese circumstances, is increasingly resisted. The Japanese reaction to this rejection is cast in a very different psychological mold than that found in American-Mexican negotiation relationships.

Japan's self-image also includes a recognition of racial and cultural uniqueness. Japanese moving for the first time into international circles tend to be inexperienced in carrying this identity outside their homogeneous society, and it is the cause of some anxiety. The possibility of discrimination is a twofold problem: the unpleasantness of discrimination itself when it is, in fact, encountered and the uncertainty as to when it actually is present and the form it might take. When among Westerners, the racial and cultural distinctness is too obvious to easily ignore. Further, in their international dealings, the pressure is usually on *them* to make the social adaptations, not the other way around, and this poses an added burden on both their capabilities for negotiation and on their self-image. All this gives their internationally experienced officers and executives who are comfortable in managing their racial difference a special responsibility and status, a fact not always appreciated in negotiation situations.

Before leaving the discussion of national images as a function of culture and national character, it is well to point out that observers stress the need for Americans to be aware of the psychological baggage they too carry, both their own self-images and those they hold of negotiating opposites. In the cases explored here, it has been obvious that American images of the French, Mexicans, and Japanese have affected the dynamics of negotiation on both formal

and informal levels. When these images were out-of-step, either with reality or the other's image, they not only gave needless offense, but, more important, they clouded judgment of the counterpart's position and intentions. They have led to misattribution of motives and sometimes to misperception of tactics and strategy.

For illustrative purposes, here are just a few items that seem to relate to an American negotiating style. They are presented more to establish this kind of introspection as logical procedure than to delve very far into American self-images.

—American negotiators frequently and necessarily see themselves as basically *multilateral* negotiators; that is, they see American interests and implications of the subject at hand as spread out over a range of countries, of which the counterpart of the moment's country is only one. Thus there is a mathematical standoff in outlook: The counterpart is interested specifically in one-to-one negotiation with the United States; the American sees the other nation as one of many with similar matters pending with the United States. The American's "big picture" is a perspective that most probably will clash with that held by his opposite. In business negotiations, this grand outlook may be less prevalent, though in the case of major industries and American-based multinationals, it no doubt still applies.

—Americans carry a leadership role in their heads and tend to see American objectives as coinciding with those of a larger world community, including the counterpart's country. While this assumption may or may not be accurate, the outlook affects American style. The French and Mexicans, for example, tend to be unimpressed, while the Japanese are more appreciative.

—Americans see themselves as models of modernity and technological success and, therefore, as advisors. This seems to give a license to prescribe, an approach that is taken whether invited or not in many negotiations.

—Among the other kinds of "imperialism," Americans have been accused of "moral imperialism." This may be the identification of a particularly hard-to-take attitude of self-righteousness Americans are perceived as sometimes carrying into negotiations.

—Americans also see themselves playing an international role as problem-solvers working in everyone's best interests. They therefore expect a degree of deference to this role in negotiation and assume that everyone's final position will be arrived at during negotiation. But an American's sense of problem-solving may be interpreted as an attempt to manipulate.

## 2. What specific values and implicit assumptions do negotiators carry with them?

Rarely in communication do two people talk about precisely the same subject, for effective meaning is flavored by the interrelated elements that make up each person's own cognitive world. In international negotiation this, translates into a question of anticipating which culturally related ideas, values, or implicit assumptions tend to explain how the subject at hand is most likely to be understood by a person socialized in a given culture. Such cultural conditioning might not hold each individual in a cognitive straight jacket, but the probability that it will have a basic effect deserves exploration.

Certainly the resources are not available for a full analysis in the cases of Japan, Mexico, and France, but a half dozen samples of conflicting values and assumptions might be useful.

In many instances, implicit assumptions regarding *ethics* and *ethical behavior* lie near or just underneath the surface of discussion. Because these idea patterns carry emotional charge, they are harder to deal with, and, beyond their impact on the substance of discussion, they affect the level of confidence and trust. One sample is what specialists on Japan have cited as an American problem with Japanese "situation ethics." That is, as Japanese appear to take different positions in different settings, the American sees duplicity and lack of individual integrity rather than normal behavior in a consensus society. Japanese, on the other hand, have a problem trying to anticipate the effect of Christian-based ethics and the importance of principles in American positions. They see Americans unnecessarily reject-

ing sound practical ideas simply because they violate principles that are not usual to Japanese ways of thinking.

Americans frequently find their moral fine tuning challenged in deciding what foreign behavior constitutes bribery or corruption. In most societies, including the United States, the lines that divide customary perquisites and expected forms of recompense for services from unacceptable abuse are often defined more by culturally patterned tacit understanding than by the same culture's formal or public codes. This does not eliminate a sense of right and wrong or the subjective feelings that go with ethical issues; it just makes it harder to understand it all cross-culturally. From negotiating gift bottles of Christmas cheer at the customs house to agreeing to special expediters' commissions, finding the formula is rarely an emotionally neutral process. The problem can be seen in mirror image as foreign business or government representatives try to work the gray area in the United States.

Differing values placed on agreements and contracts and differing assumptions as to the way they should be honored are prime examples of the psycho-cultural problem. Americans take them seriously indeed and assume that American credibility in world affairs depends on the strictest adherence. Russian backsliding in this regard is seen as further evidence of the immorality of this system. But Japanese also take a differing view. In fact, traditionally, Japanese have preferred to operate on the basis of understanding and social trust with the need for a more formal contract considered a rather unfortunate circumstance. They even point out that they have an economic advantage in that their system is more efficient with less time and expense wasted on the lawyers and law suits that go with a contract-obsessed society such as the United States.

In any event, they tend to see a contract or formal agreement as the beginning of an adaptive process rather than the end of one. They assume that changes and adjustments will naturally be made in good faith as developments or circumstances indicate. This makes the American assume that the agreement was made in bad faith to begin with. In conducting modern business, the Japanese are adjusting to the world of contractual obligations, of course, but the psychology lingers on.

In Mexico the outlook swings a few degrees in another direction. With some admitted exaggeration, we might say that formal agreements there are works of art and expressions of the ideal, and should be appreciated as such. They, like laws, do not necessarily apply all the time and should not be expected to cover the detailed practical world, which is not a work of art, or situations in which certain human considerations take precedence. Again, Mexicans are very competent in international business and diplomacy, but there is less joy for the Mexican in the cold contract than for the American who finds his security in the exact and impersonal wording.

Any contrasts in the value placed on *compromise* itself certainly would bring cultural relativity to bear on the negotiation process. Americans are among the most enthusiastic proponents of compromise. It was compromise that made America great! It is the natural way to do business; it has a moral aura that helps one live with what might otherwise be a morally ambiguous concession. But the Japanese are not normally prepared to compromise without going back to the drawing board, and the Mexicans and French see less virtue in compromising *per se*. To the French, a well-reasoned position does not call for compromise unless the reasoning is faulty. And that can be discussed. Even when a compromise is pragmatically although reluctantly reached, the French negotiator still gains some satisfaction in recalling the correctness of the preferred uncompromised position. To the Mexican, compromise translates more into a matter of honor—which is held in very high regard. When the American feels that progress has been made with a compromise, the Mexican may feel that something has been lost in his context of values, which stresses a kind of dignity and integrity that is upheld precisely in *not* being compromised. Dueling, it may be recalled, was much more the norm in Latin America than in the United States.

American informality in down-playing status, in using first names, in dress, casualness, impatience with formalities, and so forth, places Americans toward one end of a range of international negotiating behavior. Their egalitarian assumptions have long been a threat to international protocol; typically the American has to rise to the protocol occasion, and relatively few of our negotiators carry it off well. This sometimes contributes to confused signals or disturbing "noise" in the communication background. . . .

Other areas of underlying assumptions relate to the negotiation style as well. For example, should negotiating positions be based on legal precedence, on expert opinion and technical data, on amity, on reciprocal advantage? Is it normal procedure to try to package and sell an argument with visual aids and advertising techniques? How much is deviousness sanctioned in a "buyer beware" approach? Is bargaining a pleasure or a chore? How much value is placed on time and efficiency in the negotiation process versus social amenities and ceremony? Does one prefer privacy and secrecy or openness? Is frankness and directness a virtue? (It is not to Mexicans in formal encounters, apparently, nor to Japanese at any time.) When is humor appropriate, or for that matter, what constitutes humor, especially when directed toward individuals?

More profound areas might reflect differing ideological assumptions and values or different conceptions of social purposes. Is competition "good"? Does the well-being of the individual or that of the group take precedence when property rights, profit, law, or government policy come into discussion? What loyalties are to be honored first in determining how official position is to be used? How is national interest defined and when does it take priority? When are revolutionary goals simply rhetoric and when are they controlling and deeply felt commitments? When is an issue a religious one? When does unthinkably immoral behavior in one society become thinkable in another? Terrorism or the holding of hostages forces one to be analytically responsive to questions of this emotional depth.

### 3. Are there cultural differences in styles of logic and reasoning and therefore in styles of persuasion?

International negotiators frequently find that discussions are impeded because the two sides seem to be pursuing different paths of logic. This breakdown may result from the way that issues are conceptualized, the way evidence and new information are used, or the way one point seems to lead to the next. Here we come to one of the most intriguing but least researched aspects of the cultural dimension in negotiation. Do cultures, and perhaps their languages also, tend to impart to the members of the society distinctive ways of putting ideas together, associating causes and effects, seeking knowledge and understanding, using evidence and reasoning? Could it be that a line of reasoning that would be persuasive in the United States would be ineffective in another culture? In any event, does this impede modern international communication? Generally, thoughtful observers say yes, but in scientific terms the subject is only minimally understood. Because of the potential importance of these questions for understanding the international negotiation process, they are worth posing as a matter of needed inquiry and as a subject for curiosity on the part of the sensitive negotiator. From our sample countries, a few tentative observations can be made.

In this study the matter came up principally in relation to French use of what is popularly referred to as Cartesian logic. Rather imprecisely defined, the idea is that one reasons from a starting point based on what is known, and then pays careful attention to the logical way in which one point leads to the next, and finally reaches a conclusion regarding the issue at hand. The French also assign greater priority than Americans do to establishing the principles on which the reasoning process should be based. Once this reasoning process is under way, it becomes relatively difficult to introduce new evidence or facts, most especially during a negotiation. Hence the appearance of French inflexibility, and the need to introduce new information and considerations early in the game. All this reflects the tradition of French education and becomes the status mark of the educated person. . . . Despite modern management and technical application in the French bureaucracy, some feel that vestiges of this style of deliberation are still encountered.

Consider the case of American versus Mexican logic. The American is persuaded by expert opinion and supporting hard evidence and uses such in presenting a position in negotiation. Mexicans, however, are less likely to be equally impressed. They generally prefer a *deductive* approach as opposed to the American inclination toward the *inductive*. Like other Latin Americans and other nationalities as well—some authorities would include the French and the Russians—the emphasis is placed on starting with the most general aspects by defining issues, categorizing them, and deciding on the main principle. Once this is done, then logic follows along to the conclusion with less attention to supporting evidence. Or new evidence may be interpreted in the light of the main principle already determined.

This contrast in approach is sometimes found in UN debate. Americans become irritated with the time taken in argument over which principle applies, to which UN committee an issue falls, or the exact wording of a title to be assigned to a new issue. The Americans want to concentrate on the facts available, to look for cause and effect, and to get on to problem-solving.

Tentatively, Mexican reasoning may also be more complex because it incorporates some of the Spanish tradition of placing more emphasis on contemplation and intuition. In this regard, Mexican thought is somewhat similar to Japanese in that emotion, drama, and feeling play a larger part as contrasted to American considerations of efficiency, scientific method, and practical application or the colder logic and reasoning of the French. One observer noted that Japanese negotiators tend not to be convinced by hypothetical reasoning, or, as noted above, justification by principles. They do appreciate objective description and data from which conclusions are directly obvious.

These questions in the study of culture pose an inquiry at the most abstract level and are least subject to observation. It is not likely that most negotiators will have occasion to follow their counterpart's thought process through from its base in philosophy, religion, and implicit methodology. But the line of questioning can be placed on our agenda. Much is to be learned by looking for the patterns of reasoning reflected in literature and aesthetics and in the way that discussion is structured and phrased in everyday social situations. The area specialist with time and a bent for philosophy may find this cross-cultural dimension revealing and of practical application in crossing negotiation bridges.

In a study of this scope, it can only be reported that there is a reality here to be taken into account. The negotiator reflects it when he is happily surprised that his counterpart "thinks just like an American." Japanese apparently have this objective in mind when they send their future foreign service officers to such American colleges as Williams or Swarthmore for several years of study. Other countries demonstrate that they have learned something about this when they choose negotiators who can indeed think like Americans when dealing with the United States.

There was the time, for example, when Panama sent a negotiating team to Washington to try to gain American approval for extending their national air route beyond Miami to New York. The team consisted of one man, a graduate of a ranking American business school. He quickly explained that from an economic point of view and by the usual considerations for justifying air traffic routes, he had no case and would not pretend to have one. He said that Panama did, nevertheless, understand the economic importance of Panama to American carriers and did have compelling nationalistic reasons for wanting to see its flag on the big route. He would be at his hotel and would appreciate being informed when it was worked out. This Panamanian was extraordinarily successful as compared with another team in town at the same time with the same purpose, but with a more typically Latin American approach and line of reasoning much less adapted to the American mentality.

# Organizing Courtroom Contexts: Interactional Resolutions to Intercultural Problems

WAYNE A. BEACH

Nearly all English-speaking U.S. citizens have faced difficulties in communicating in courtroom settings. Litigants are often intimidated by the formality of court proceedings, even though they are shown "how" to behave in court (Pollner 1979; Atkinson 1979), and numerous constraints are placed on questioning and answering throughout interrogation and testimony (Atkinson and Drew 1979). As lawyers exert control and witnesses typically defer to their authority, it is not uncommon for witnesses to become frustrated because they cannot "tell their complete story" regarding a past incident (O'Barr 1982, p. 114). Moreover, the presence of "eavesdropping" third parties, such as judges, juries, and observers, is not necessarily conducive to disclosing what may be considered private information in a public setting. Even in more informal plea bargaining sessions, defendants are not always aware of their role in the proceedings or the nature of the plea being negotiated for them (Maynard 1984). For these reasons and more, it becomes obvious that while the U.S. legal system is explicitly designed to aid and protect lay persons, it can nevertheless be a foreign environment for communication, which may make it hard to accomplish social justice and "fair and impartial treatments" for all litigants.

This essay was prepared especially for this fifth edition. All rights reserved. Permission to reprint must be obtained from the publisher and the author. Wayne A. Beach teaches at San Diego State University.

These "normal troubles" (West 1984), however, increase in frequency and become more complex for litigants unable to speak English with enough fluency to comprehend and participate competently in routine court proceedings. The plight of these litigants has not been totally disregarded. Throughout the 1970s, for example, increased attention was given to the communication problems faced by non-English-speaking people in the courts. In 1976 the state of California led the way in trying to solve these problems by commissioning a unique study of the language needs of those who do not speak English. In 1978 the U.S. Congress finally passed a law entitled the Court Interpreters Act, requiring translations for all litigants requesting and/or in need of such a service. At both the state and national levels, it was clear that litigants incapable of understanding the language and the proceedings of the courts were denied a basic American right: to reasonably confront one's accuser and/or adversary *face-to-face* as guaranteed by the Sixth Amendment. Thus it has become customary for courts to provide translators/interpreters in each and every case involving non-English-speaking litigants.

To this date little is known about the emergent *communication* difficulties of routine translations and interpretations. While it has become customary to provide these services, it is by no means sufficient to assume that communication problems are automatically resolved and remedied. The purpose of this article is to address several of these difficulties as displayed in the *interactional organization* of court proceedings. We shall pay attention to the kinds of problems evident when Spanish-speaking defendants interact with judges and lawyers through court interpreters. Data are shown from an ongoing collection of video-recorded court proceedings.[1] Before turning directly to a discussion of these data, however, it may prove useful to address three constituent components of "culture": *language, knowledge, and context*. In so doing, it becomes possible to grasp more fully not only *intercultural* communication processes but also *interactional* resolutions to intercultural problems.

## LANGUAGE, KNOWLEDGE, AND CONTEXT

The communication of cultures may be understood in and through members' methods of assembling social contexts and creating social order. Viewed as context building, the concern is with *how* everyday interactants rely on their social knowledge to get practical activities done *together* (Beach 1982; 1983). In other words, our study of communication and culture should transcend individual (monadic) concerns and focus instead on an understanding of *sequences* of collaboratively produced interactions. As Goffman (1961) repeatedly envisioned, our research efforts should rest *not* with men and their moments but rather with moments and their men— that is, with social occasions and their organizing properties. Thus social occasions may be framed as organized displays of cultural *practices,* used and relied upon to create a "situated condition for adequate, practical comprehension" (Coulter 1979, p. 173). Because language (verbal and nonverbal) is the major vehicle for accomplishing communication, language functions both *in* context and *as* context (Ochs 1979), simultaneously constructing and being constructed by the social occasion. In this sense, the title of Mishler's (1979) article, "Meaning in Context: Is There Any Other Kind?", is more than simply a rhetorical question. Rather, it is a referent for understanding how contexts get "workably built in endless ways" (Sacks, Schegloff, and Jefferson 1974).

Regardless of the contexts within which intercultural communication has been studied, a widely accepted orientation is to provide explanations of such phenomena as misunderstandings, embarrassing moments, and competing perspectives (for example, "reality disjunctures," see Pollner 1975), by invoking differences in "background knowledge" as the reason for certain actions. In most simple terms, when explaining how and why members of different cultures engage in certain communication activities together, one makes reference to the following kinds of phenomena: attitudes, values, beliefs, needs, residual experiences (memory, tradition, and folklore), perceptions, interpretations, morals, and ethics. These features comprise that which counts as knowledge, and there is little doubt as to their importance in connecting thought and culture. But have you ever *seen* any of these phenomena? Do these features hold significance apart from the way they are displayed in and through interaction? More importantly, what features do intercultural interactants *themselves* have available as they encounter one another face-to-face?

The point is that while differences in cultural background and knowledge are normal and inevitable, the problems emerging from such differences are evident in the language practices employed to resolve these problems within intercultural interaction. More specifically, problems that occur when Spanish-speaking defendants appear in an English court emerge *from the interaction itself.* Only by looking at the interactions among judges, lawyers, defendants, and interpreters is it possible to describe and explain if and when problems exist in the process of trials, hearings, and arraignments.

## INTERCULTURAL PROBLEMS IN COURTROOM INTERACTION

Consider a typical sequence where a defendent is called in front of the court to enter a plea of *guilty* or *not guilty* to an alleged criminal activity. For an English-speaking defendant (*ED*) interacting with a judge (*J*), the following sequence is normal:

1. *J:* Question

   *ED:* Answer

The defendant is able to recognize the judge's utterance as a question and respond appropriately; that is, a question projects and receives an answer. If the defendant does not understand the judge, however, the defendant can (and at times does) gain access to the "floor" by initiating a clarification question. The judge can then answer the defendant's clarification question so the defendant can provide an

informed answer. Such a sequence (Schegloff 1972) might be as follows:

2. *J:* Question

   *ED:* Clarification question

   *J:* Answer

   *ED:* Answer

Thus examples 1 and 2 begin to indicate how it is possible for judges and English-speaking defendants to converse and get a plea entered.

In contrast, consider example 3 involving a judge, a court interpreter (*I*), and a Spanish-speaking defendant (*SD*):

3. *J:* Question

   *I:* Question

   *SD:* Answer

   *I:* Answer (to *J*)

In this basic question-answer sequence—the simplest of its kind—the interpreter acts as a mediator and translator between judge and defendant. What took only two turns-at-talk between two interactants in example 1 now requires a minimum of four turns-at-talk among three interactants. Notice also that the Spanish-speaking defendant cannot speak directly to the judge but must instead go through the interpreter. Indeed, the accuracy of the translation must be taken into account. It is reasonable to ask whether the judge's question was "heard" by the Spanish-speaking defendant the way the judge actually asked it, and whether the defendant's answer to the judge was formulated by the interpreter exactly as the defendant said it.

Begin to sound confusing? It is clear that more work is necessary to enter a simple plea when a court interpreter and a Spanish-speaking defendant are involved than it is when the defendant speaks English. For example, a counterpart of example 2 follows, with a clarification sequence through an interpreter added:

4. *J:* Question

   *I:* Repeats question

SD: Clarification question

I: Repeats clarification question

J: Answer (to I)

I: Answer (to SD)

SD: Answer (to I)

I: Answer (to J)

Here eight turns-at-talk are needed to accomplish a basic question-answer sequence (J to SD, SD to J). As noted earlier, SD never speaks directly to J; the court interpreter must do the "bridge work." What problems of interaction and understanding emerge for those who do not speak the same language as the judge compared with those who do?

For a more specific look at the problems that may emerge when court interpreters are necessary, it is useful to look directly at two transcribed pleas; see example 5 involving an English-speaking defendant and example 6 involving a Spanish-speaking defendant. In each case, the judge enacts certain basic steps inherent in a plea sequence: (1) a summary of charges; (2) an understanding check (defendant responds); (3) an option for the defendant to enter a plea or to speak with a lawyer (defendant responds); (4) a question "How do you plea?" (defendant pleas); and (5) a request for the defendant to have a seat in the audience and to study some forms. In examples 5 and 6, the transcripts begin with the judge checking the defendant's understanding:[2]

5. T1/ELAC: D6—26:01:2–26:29:6

J: .

Do you understand the na?ture of the charge and the rights which *we've been discussing*.

ED: ((nods)) I do

J: Are you ready this *morn*ing to enter a plea of guilty or *not*? guilty to that charge or would you like to talk to a *law*yer first. before you de*ci*de how you *might* wish to plea.

ED: (*I'm gonna*) plea

J: How do you plea

ED: Guilty

J: I ask you to study the *same* forms as the first time offense.

(5.1) ((J is doing paper-work))

J: Have a seat in the audi.ence an:d *after* uh: > you've completed that I'll talk to you and others who have filled out that form in ten or fifteen minutes. <

ED: ((begins to leave front court))
[[

J: ((call for next defendant))

6. T1/ELAC: D5—24:36–25:08:8

J:

Do you understand.

SD: ((nodding,    (Espanol, 0.4)
[[

I:              (Espanol, 0.3)

I: Yes I do =
                [ (Espanol)-------------

J: = Were you in a posi*ti*on to understan::d
--------------------------------------------------------
(.) the rights which were summarized a few moments
------------------------------------------------------- )
ago::. (.) through the interpreter. (*Do you understand.)

SD: (Espanol, 0.2)

I: Yes *your honor*
                (Espanol)---

J: Are you *pre*pared? this morning to enter
--------------------------------------------------------
a plea of guilty or not guilty to th- these charges. or
--------------------------------------------------------
would you *like* to talk to a lawyer first. before you decide
((SD shaking head)) -----------)
how you're likely to plea.

*SD:* (Espanol, 1.1)

*I:* (Espanol, 1.7)

*SD:* ((nodding)) S

*I:* ((clearing throat)) (He'd) like to plead *your honor*

*J:* How do you plea.

*I:* (Espanol, 0.5)

　　　　[

*SD:*　　　　　　(Espanol, 0.2)

*I:* Guilty

*J:* There's a form we'd like you to look at ((continues))

In both examples 5 and 6 the plea gets entered, yet some contrasts are apparent. In example 5, one person speaks at a time with little or no gap or overlap occurring between *J*'s and *ED*'s utterances. Answers follow questions directly, each occurring within its appropriate "slot." No clarification sequences emerge in this unproblematic sequence. In example 6, however, *I* and *SD* must essentially listen to and monitor at least two voices at once. Simultaneous interpretation (that is, - - - -) occurs repeatedly, beginning and ending after *J*'s turn. Example 6 also has more insertion sequences, which suggests that additional communicative work is necessary to attain understanding in this courtroom plea.

If you look closely at example 6, you will notice that *SD* is attempting to achieve a desired social order throughout this sequence. For example, notice how *SD* tends to respond to *J* by preempting *I*'s translation, that is, by appearing at times not to need the mediating work of *I*. (How might you account for *SD*'s head shaking as *J*'s utterance is being translated by *I*?) A more detailed analysis of this sequence might reveal that *SD* does, in fact, understand at least *some* English and thus may be attempting to rush this plea through to complete the plea sequence more quickly.

Having looked briefly at two transcribed segments involving an English-speaking and a Spanish-speaking defendant, we can see that the potential for misunderstanding and for routine problems of comprehension is greater when a court interpreter is required. In the most general terms, the problem for both defendants is as follows: How do people cope interactionally with being called into court, accused of wrongdoing, and therefore treated as societal deviants? Being called into court is itself a stigma of sorts; that is, the reputations of the defendants are at least challenged and possibly spoiled by having to defer to court authority in a public setting (Goffman, 1963).

Defendants unable to speak the language of the court are not only unable to speak directly to the judge, they must interact simultaneously with the judge and the interpreter. Several important questions must be raised here:

1. What happens when the judge *and* the defendant speak simultaneously to the interpreter? Does the interpreter give preference to translating the judge's message or respond to (and/or possibly relay) the defendant's query? Several observed instances suggest that preference is given to the judge's message, while the defendant's message is temporarily and/or permanently disregarded.

2. Do defendants requiring interpreters have the same access to the floor, and thus to the judge, as do English-speaking defendants? What evidence would suggest that they do or do not? If they do not, what remedies that would better insure the ability of the legal system to satisfy Sixth Amendment rights for *all* defendants might be implemented?

3. Might court interpreters further intimidate defendants and thus constrain their testimony and responses? Do facts get presented and understood as fully in cases requiring interpreters as they do when the defendants speak English? In short, do the circumstances surrounding alleged criminal activities get reconstructed adequately—and do stories get told completely—in and through court-interpreted interactions?

## CONCLUSION

The questions raised here focus attention on potential problems inherent in the context of the courtroom where intercultural communication encounters are routine. At the very least, it is clear that the answers to these questions reside in the methods by which courtroom interactions are accomplished—turn-by-turn, face-to-face. Because language is the vehicle through which social justice and "fair and impartial treatments" are meted out, we need to pay attention to the way language structures (and is structured by) those constraints inherent in court proceedings. In this sense, language is both the container and the reflection of one's knowledge of the social world. By paying close, analytic attention to talk sequences, we can see how people orient to, make sense of, and construct social realities of the contexts in which they are placed. If and when intercultural encounters create communication problems, the evidence for such problems must ultimately be generated from the collaborative actions of the interacting members—that is, *how* problems emerge interactionally. Such is also the case for remedies to such problems, for language possesses the unique ability to simultaneously create and resolve troubles inherent to intercultural experiences.

## NOTES

1. These data were collected at the East Los Angeles Municipal Court, where nearly 70 percent of the cases require court interpreters.

2. The transcription notation system employed for the trial segments is an adaptation of Gail Jefferson's work in conversation analysis (see Atkinson and Heritage, 1984, pp. ix–xvi). The symbols are described as follows:

*Colon(s)*. An extended sound or syllable is noted by a colon (:). A single colon indicates a short prolongation (e.g., "Uh:h"). Longer sound extensions are indicated by more than one colon (e.g., "de::scribe");

*Underlining*. Vocalic emphasis of syllables, words, or phrases (e.g., "att*ack*ed you was the *eyes*");

*Single Parentheses Enclosing Numbers or Periods within an Utterance*. Speakers often pause during an utterance. If the pause is too short to be timed it is indicated by enclosing a period within parentheses

(e.g., "is the *only* thing that (.) made you believe that (.) the photograph"). Intervals of longer duration are indicated by seconds and tenths of seconds (e.g., "Um:m (1.2) on that occasion (0.4) preliminary hearing (0.2)");

*Single Parentheses Enclosing Numbers between Utterances*. Intervals between same or different speaker's utterance are so noted:

W: Yes.
    (2.6)
P: Uh:h (1.6) did you

*Single Parentheses Enclosing Utterances or Blank Spaces*. Indicates transcriptionist doubt as to words or sounds transcribed as best possible (e.g., "cuz I (left early).",), or when undecipherable and/or when names of interactants are anonymous (e.g., "start work or do ya (    )?").

*Double Parentheses Enclosing Words*. Are employed when providing details of the scene (e.g., "((angered)) When you see somebody").

*Periods*. A falling vocal tone is indicated by a period. Such tones do not necessarily occur at the end of a sentence, though they may (e.g., "I'm not sure.")

*Question Marks*. Indicate a rising inflection, not necessarily a question (e.g., "you saw the suspect's footwear?")

*Asterisk*. A passage of talk noticeably softer and/or quieter than surrounding talk (e.g., "*Yes.")

*Equal Signs*. Suggest latching of adjacent utterances, with no interval and no overlap between utterances:

D: *three* o'clock?=
W: =*Some*time

*Single Brackets*. When overlapping utterances do not start simultaneously, the point at which an ongoing utterance is joined by another is marked with a single left-hand bracket:

P: after they occurred (0.4) or wo ⌈rse.
W. ⌊Worse.

*Exclamation Points*. An animated, though not necessarily exclamatory, tone (e.g., "don't you think you'd recognize 'em!!!").

*Hyphens*. Indicate a halting, abrupt cut off of a word or sound (e.g., "wi- dirty bu- shoes on").

## REFERENCES

Atkinson, J. M. (1979). "Sequencing and Shared Attentiveness to Court Proceedings." In G. Psathas (ed.), *Everyday Language: Studies in Ethnomethodology* (pp. 257–286). New York: Irvington.

Atkinson, J. M., and P. Drew (1979). *Order in Court: The Organization of Verbal Interaction in Judi-*

*cial Settings.* Atlantic Highlands NJ: Humanities Press.

Atkinson, J. M., and M. Heritage (1984). *Structures of Social Action: Studies in Conversation Analysis.* Cambridge: Cambridge University Press.

Beach, W. A. (1982). "Everyday Interaction and Its Practical Accomplishment: Progressive Developments in Ethnomethodological Research." *Quarterly Journal of Speech 68,* 314–327.

Beach, W. A. (1983). "Background Understandings and the Situated Accomplishment of Conversational Telling-Expansions." In R. Craig and K. Tracy (eds.), *Conversational Coherence: Form, Structure, and Strategy* (pp. 196–221). Beverly Hills, CA: Sage Publications.

Beach, W. A. (1985). "Temporal Density in Courtroom Interaction: Constraints on the Recovery of Past Events in Legal Discourse." *Communication Monographs 52,* 1–18.

Coulter, J. (1979). "Beliefs and Practical Understanding." In G. Psathas (ed.), *Everyday Language: Studies in Ethnomethodology* (pp. 163–186). New York: Irvington.

Goffman, E. (1961). *Encounters.* Indianapolis: Bobbs-Merrill.

Goffman, E. (1963). *Stigma: Notes on the Management of Spoiled Identity.* Englewood Cliffs, N.J.: Prentice-Hall, Inc.

Maynard, D. W. (1984). *Inside Plea Bargaining: The Language of Negotiation.* New York: Plenum Press.

Mishler, E. G. (1979). "Meaning in Context: Is There Any Other Kind?" Harvard Educational Review, 49, 1–19.

O'Barr, W. M. (1982). *Linguistic Evidence: Language, Power, and Strategy in the Courtroom.* New York: Academic Press.

Ochs, E. (1979). "Introduction: What Child Language Can Contribute to Pragmatics." In E. Ochs and B. Schiefflen (eds.), *Developmental Pragmatics* (pp. 1–20). New York: Academic Press.

Pollner, M. (1975). "The Very Coinage of Your Brain: The Resolution of Reality Disjunctures." Philosophy of the Social Sciences, 5, 411–430.

Pollner, M. (1979). "Explicative Transactions: Making and Managing Meaning in Traffic Court." In G. Psathas (ed.), *Everyday Language: Studies in Ethnomethodology* (pp. 227–256). New York: Irvington.

Sacks, H., E. Schegloff, and G. Jefferson (1974). "A Simplest Systematics for the Organization of Turn-Taking for Conversation." Language 59, 696–735.

Schegloff, E. (1972). "Notes on a Conversational Practice: Formulating Place." In J. Schenkein (ed.), *Studies in the Organization of Conversational Interaction* (pp. 75–119). New York: The Free Press.

West, C. (1983). *Troubles with Talk between Doctors and Patients.* Bloomington, IN: University Press.

# Cultural Influences on Educational Processes

JANIS F. ANDERSEN
ROBERT POWELL

Nearly two decades ago, anthropologist Edward Hall[1] argued that culture is a hidden dimension. He explained that culture penetrates our perceptual system, thus masking the basic aspects of our existence which are immediately obvious to an outsider. Hall's position is now a basic tenet of intercultural communication,[2] but acknowledging this principle does little to reduce the size of the curtain that masks our culture. One context where the curtain obscures our vision is the classroom environment. In the United States, the role that culture plays in education is becoming particularly salient. At no time in our history has such a culturally diverse population of students participated in our educational system. Students from Asia, Mexico, and Latin America have taken seats in our classrooms. The rules, assumptions, values, customs, practices, and procedures for appropriate classroom behavior may vary for all of these students. Our task in this essay, then, is to try to lift the curtain that is obscuring our culture. By exploring the way in which education functions in other cultures and by describing how culture influences classroom communication, we will uncover some ways that culture influences the instructional context.

Many people tend to think that all classrooms are pretty much the same. When asked to imagine classroom interaction in central Illinois, southern California, northern New York, or even France, Brazil, or the Philippines, they basically picture the classroom with which they are most familiar. They may picture different kinds of people in the different locations, but their overall image does not vary. Maybe they picture wholesome looking, neatly scrubbed, conservatively dressed students sitting at desks in Illinois, while they see blond-haired, informally dressed, suntanned individuals sitting in southern California classrooms, but the rest of the image reflects their own educational experience. The students are probably pictured sitting at desks that look the same and are laid out in the same configuration—whatever location they are imagined to be in. Even the classroom walls are probably visualized as the same color, perhaps a light institutional green or yellow gold.

The point is that people tend to think that the learning environment with which they are most familiar is representative of learning environments in general. Furthermore, even if these culturally based environmental images are not generalized as we suggest, they are often held up as models for what the learning environment should be. Culture provides us with a heritage and a set of expectations about educational settings. If you were asked to create a classroom environment and to structure the interaction to provide the best possible learning situation, chances are you would create something very similar to the classroom in which you are now sitting. This claim may seem remarkable. You may not find your current situation ideal, but your images of a proper learning environment are inextricably linked to your familiarity with and experience in learning environments. Teachers tend to teach the way they were taught; parents treat their children the way they were treated. The entire educational system, together with the rules and procedures for effective classroom interaction, reflects a cultural dictate rather than a universal mandate.

The next section of this essay highlights some intercultural differences in educational practices. These differences are interesting but not very informative. Much systematic, in-depth study of an individual culture, its institutions, and its people

This essay was prepared especially for this fifth edition. All rights reserved. Permission to reprint must be obtained from the publisher and the authors. Janis F. Andersen teaches at San Diego State University. Robert Powell teaches at California State University, Los Angeles.

would be necessary for us to know enough about another culture's educational system to enable us to improve our instructional encounters with someone from that culture. Instead, the discussion that follows is designed to shed insights into our own educational system. Hall[3] believes that we can never really understand another's culture, but being aware of its diversity is a tremendous aid in understanding our own culture better. Furthermore, by studying culture's role in education, we can put our own educational assumptions into perspective and perhaps better understand our educational practices and procedures.

If asked to describe a generic educational system, we might begin by talking about a classroom, a teacher, and some students. However, even these seemingly basic components reflect cultural assumptions. Classrooms are a relatively recent innovation; they are still not used for teaching children in preliterate societies. Socrates, Plato, and Aristotle disseminated their teachings without the benefit of a blackboard and the comfort—or discomfort—of a classroom building. And the students of these classic thinkers learned quite well even though they did not take notes and their teachers did not provide handouts. In the early 1970s, the Metro School in Chicago was a complete high school without walls.[4] The classes met in museums, libraries, bookstores, and other interesting places. Teachers taught a fascinating sociology class by having students walk the length of Halsted Street, through numerous ethnic neighborhoods, where students ate in restaurants, visited the families, and observed street activity.

Teachers, as we think of them, also reflect a cultural bias. In the United States, it was not until around the Civil War period (1860s) that women replaced men as teachers.[5] Today many cultures still refuse to entrust the education of their young to women. One distinguishing characteristic of education in preliterate societies is that kin are responsible for educating the young. Deciding which category of kin will assume which responsibility is highly systematized; being related in a certain way is a teaching credential for a specific content area. Instead of learning art from Mrs. Davis, home economics from

Ms. Young, and woodworking from Mr. Smith, children learn pottery from their father's sister, cooking from their mother, and toolmaking from their mother's father.

Many of us think of teachers as being older than their students. Cultural anthropologist Margaret Mead states that this pattern reflects a culturally determined, postfigurative learning paradigm.[6] In postfigurative societies, older people disseminate their knowledge to younger, less experienced, and less knowledgeable individuals; cofigurative cultures adopt primarily peer learning patterns; and prefigurative societies learn from their younger members who are more up-to-date. The one-room schoolhouses of the early 1900s relied mainly on cofigurative or peer instruction, and cofigurative patterns are prevalent in preliterate and peasant societies. Prefigurative learning patterns emerge in complex, industrial societies where rapid technological and scientific advances quickly outdate previously acquired knowledge. Thus many 50-year-old executives attend special seminars on computer technology that are taught by people 20 or 30 years younger than they are.

Our acceptance of prefigurative learning patterns permits and encourages younger students to inform or even to disagree with older teachers. In many cultures, particularly in traditional Asian ones, students would never disagree with a teacher. In traditional Asian societies, wisdom comes with age, and all important learning is postfigurative. Furthermore, in some societies the teacher is a revered individual who is teaching sacred truth. Teachers in the United States have reported that teaching devices such as "You agree with that, don't you?" often receive a humble yes from young Vietnamese, Korean, and Cambodian immigrants when the question was really intended to spark a lively discussion. The Asian pattern of teacher-student interaction was made evident to one interpersonal communication teacher who was discussing the role of self-disclosure in the development of intimate relationships. He argued that self-disclosure is central to the development of intimacy, and while his observation was met with a great deal of support from the Anglo-American students in the class, the Asian students merely listened politely to the discussion. When the teacher asked one of the Asian students if self-disclosure was used in his culture, he replied no, and he went on to explain that in his country (Korea), feelings of intimacy were understood, not explicitly communicated. The teacher learned two valuable lessons. The first was that self-disclosure may not be a cross-cultural behavior used in the establishment of intimate relationships; the second was that Asian students are unlikely to disagree with a teacher.

The teacher-student relationship is culturally mandated. The primary school system is highly informal in an Israeli kibbutz, with close social relationships between teachers and students.[7] Students move from their desks at will to sharpen pencils or to get drinks. They talk among themselves while writing, readily criticize teachers if they feel the teachers are wrong, and address teachers by their first names.

A typical classroom in the Soviet Union provides a sharp contrast to the one in the kibbutz. Students sit in rows of desks that face the teacher; they rise when a teacher enters the room; they stand at attention when asking or answering a question; and they sit with their arms folded when listening to a lesson.[8] The teacher is in complete control of the classroom.

Rituals and patterns of classroom interaction vary from culture to culture. Obviously we picture students speaking their native languages in classroom interactions throughout the world, and we might picture all students raising their hands to begin an interaction. In fact, mathematics is taught in English in the Philippines since the Filipino language[9] does not have sufficient technical terms for efficient instruction in mathematics. In Jamaica, primary school students flap or snap their fingers to signal that they know the answer. In Trinidad, students put their index and middle fingers on their forehead with the inside facing out to ask permission to be excused.[10] Some cultures do not even have a way for students to signal a desire to talk to a teacher; in these cultures, students speak only after the teacher has spoken to them. There is virtually no classroom interaction in Vietnamese culture, and in Mexican culture all classroom interaction is tightly controlled and directed by the teached.[11]

The classroom in an Israeli kibbutz is very noisy and interaction is spontaneous.[12] In sharp contrast, Chinese classrooms are so quiet that North Americans teaching there often find the silence unnerving.[13] Cultures reflecting a Buddhist tradition hold that knowledge, truth, and wisdom come to those whose quiet silence allows the spirit to enter. Classrooms in the United States tend to reflect more of a Socratic ideal, where teacher and student interact a great deal in pursuit of knowledge.

In the United States, ethnic/cultural differences account for differences in interaction in the educational context. Collier,[14] for example, studied interactions in college advisement contexts, and she found that with Anglo-American advisors, Latinos preferred relational bonding early in the interaction, followed by concrete advice and support. Asian-Americans preferred a more formal, distant relationship, with a small amount of openness and a large amount of concrete advice.

Black children learn to expect an interaction pattern that involves a lot of backchanneling. In the black culture, *backchanneling* is a vocal listener response that is designed to reinforce and encourage the speaker. Vocal utterances such as "yeah," "right on," "go on," "amen," "ahuh," and "tell it" are examples of backchanneling phrases. Anglo-American teachers not used to black interaction patterns are often offended by backchanneling and feel constantly interrupted rather than reinforced.

Social class can also affect student communication behavior. Children reared in middle-class homes are generally taught an elaborate communication code, and their classroom answers tend to be long and involved. Children from lower-class homes tend to learn more restrictive codes for interaction, and they are likely to answer questions with one-word answers.[15] And middle-class teachers often misinterpret short answers from lower-class students; they assume the short answers indicate less knowledge when the answers really reflect a culturally learned interaction pattern.

Many nonverbal behaviors are culturally learned, and the literature on nonverbal behavior is replete with examples of cross-cultural differences in interpreting these behaviors.[16] These differences are also manifest in classroom environments. In the United States we show respect to teachers by looking at them when they talk to us, but in Jamaica looking at teachers is a sign of disrespect, while not looking at them is a sign of respect.[17] Black Americans and many West African cultures also reflect the Jamaican pattern.[18]

In Italian classrooms, teachers and students touch each other frequently, and children greet a teacher with a kiss on both cheeks while putting their arms around the teacher.[19] On the other hand, Chinese and Japanese children show complete emotional restraint in classrooms.[20] In short, our entire communication transaction, with its verbal and nonverbal messages, systematic patterns, and socialized rituals, is a reflection of our culture.

Our use of time and our view of time also reflect a cultural bias that alters our educational process. We value punctuality, often considering students who complete work rapidly to be more intelligent than those who work more slowly, and we designate certain time periods for certain curricular goals. Yet these clock-oriented values reflect a Western "monochronic" view of time. One time-related problem that is often overlooked involves testing. Students are often graded on how many questions they can answer correctly in a designated period of time. This grading philosophy is a disadvantage for students such as those raised in Hispanic cultures, who have not been conditioned to use every moment in a productive, task-oriented manner.[21]

In contrast to the Western "monochronic" view of time, American Indians have a "polychronic" view of time. They do things when they think the time is right, not when the calendar says it's a certain date. In many cultures, classes end when the subject matter has been thoroughly discussed rather than when the clock designates the end of the period. In the United States we measure education itself in time—years spent in school—and it is only recently that our system has allowed credit to be given for knowledge when one has not spent the requisite time in a classroom. However, the entire notion of

education as a timed process is a product of nineteenth-century thought.[22]

Decisions that are central to education, such as deciding what is important and how best to teach it, are closely linked to culture. For example, education is a high national priority in Japan. The Japanese believe that the best way to insure their future is to develop their most valued natural resource— their people. In 1980, more students graduated from the twelfth-grade in Japan than in any country in the world, and this trend continues today.[23] Competition to get into Japanese colleges and universities is especially keen. Almost four applications are submitted for each college opening.[24] The entrance examinations for universities are as important as the World Series or the Super Bowl in our country. With such an attitude about education, it is not surprising that the Japanese are world leaders in technology.

Finally, the methods of teaching are affected by culture. In a thorough outline of cross-cultural education, Jules Henry lists 55 different teaching methods.[25] Teaching by imitation, setting an example, using punishments or rewards, problem solving, guided recall, relevant association, irrelevant association, watching, doing, comparing, and student reports are only a few of Henry's categories. He reports a vivid example of teaching by watching from the writings of Chiang, who states:

*"I do not remember that I ever had any proper lessons in painting from my father. He told me to watch him as closely as possible. . . . I remember that after watching my father painting a few times, I thought I knew just how to paint, but when I actually began I found I was mistaken. . . . I asked my father to help, but he only smiled and told me to watch him again."*[26]

The selection of a particular teaching method reflects cultural values more than it argues for the superiority of the method. Cultures succeed in educating those they choose to educate, and whom they choose to educate also reflects a cultural bias.

In an informative and interesting book on intercultural behavior, Geert Hofstede explores the differences in thinking and action among people from 40 different nations.[27] He argues that people have mental programs based on their cultural experiences that are both developed and reinforced by schools and other social organizations. Many of these patterns are so subtle that people fail to realize that things can be another way. By highlighting intercultural differences in classroom environments, we begin to realize that nothing about the educational process is absolute. Every component reflects a cultural choice, conscious or unconscious, about whom to educate, how, when, in what subjects, for what purpose, and in what manner. Perhaps this realization will not only increase our tolerance for those educated in other systems but also challenge us to improve our own educational processes.

## NOTES

1. Edward T. Hall, *The Hidden Dimensions* (Garden City, N.Y.: Anchor Books, 1969).

2. Larry A. Samovar, Richard E. Porter, and Nemi C. Jain, *Understanding Intercultural Communication* (Belmont, Calif.: Wadsworth, 1981).

3. *Hall* (1969).

4. *Chicago Sun Times*, December 6, 1972.

5. Jules Henry, *"A Cross-Cultural Outline of Education."* In Joan I. Roberts and Sherrie C. Adinsanya, eds. *Educational Patterns and Cultural Configurations* (New York; David McKay, 1976).

6. Margaret Mead, *Culture and Commitment: A Study of the Generation Gap* (Garden City, N.Y.: Natural History Press, Doubleday & Company, 1970).

7. M. Spiro, *Children of the Kibbutz* (Cambridge, Mass.: Harvard University Press, 1958).

8. Nigel Grant, *Soviet Education* (New York: Penguin Books, 1979).

9. Josefine R. Cortes, "The Philippines." In T. Neville Postelethwaite and R. Murray Thomas, eds., *Schooling in the Asian Region* (New York: Pergamon Press, 1980).

10. Aaron Wolfgang, "The Teacher and Nonverbal Behavior in the Multicultural Classroom." In Aaron Wolfgang, ed., *Nonverbal Behavior, Application and Cultural Implications* (New York: Academic Press, 1979).

11. Julie Becker, "A Cross-Cultural Comparison of Interaction Patterns in the Classroom." (Master's Thesis, San Diego State University, 1983).

12. Spiro.

13. Wolfgang, p. 167.

14. Mary Jane Collier, "Rule Violations in Intercultural/Ethnic Advisement Context." (Paper presented at the Western Speech Communication Association, Tucson, 1986).

15. Philip S. Dale, *Language Development: Structure and Function* (New York: Holt Rinehart & Winston, 1976), pp. 315–321.

16. See, for example, Edward Hall *The Silent Language* (Greenwich Conn.: Fawcett Publications, 1959); Loretta Malandro and Larry Barker, *Nonverbal Communication* (Reading Mass.: Addison-Wesley, 1983); Marianne LaFrance and Clara Mavo, *Moving Bodies: Nonverbal Communication in Social Relationships* (Monterey, Calif.: Brooks/Cole, 1978).

17. Wolfgang, p. 167.

18. Wolfgang, p. 167.

19. Wolfgang, p. 169.

20. Wolfgang, p. 170.

21. John Condon, "Cross-Cultural Interferences Affecting Teacher-Pupil Communication in American Schools." *International and Intercultural Annual* 111, 1976, pp. 108–120.

22. James J. Thompson, *Beyond Words: Nonverbal Communication in the Classroom* (New York: Citation Press, 1973).

23. Thomas P. Rohlen, *Japan's High Schools* (Los Angeles: University of California Press, 1983).

24. Rohlen, p. 84.

25. Henry, p. 117.

26. Henry, p. 123–124.

27. Geert Hofstede, *Culture's Consequences: International Differences in Work-Related Values* (Beverly Hills, Calif.: Sage Publications, 1980).

## CONCEPTS AND QUESTIONS FOR CHAPTER 4

**1.** As an employee of a U.S. company, you have just been assigned to the international division and will soon take a position as a department manager at a facility in Saudi Arabia. What differences in the cultural context of the work place might you expect to encounter? How would you prepare yourself for the new assignment?

**2.** How do peer group relations in multinational/multicultural business organizations differ from those in U.S. business organizations?

**3.** What does Stewart mean when she refers to *ringi*?

**4.** How do imported Japanese management techniques affect communication in the conduct of the multinational business organization in the United States?

**5.** Does the Japanese concept of *amae* have any equivalent in the United States?

**6.** How would knowing about *amae* aid you in understanding intercultural communication contexts?

**7.** What does Fisher mean by "national character"? How can an understanding of national character improve intercultural communication?

**8.** How do the specific values and implicit assumptions that negotiators carry with them affect international negotiations? What might a negotiator do to minimize these effects?

**9.** What problems arise when a non-English-speaking person must defend him- or herself in a U.S. courtroom?

**10.** How does the introduction of translators into the courtroom process affect the normal proceedings?

**11.** Does the use of a translator assure that a non-English-speaking defendant will obtain a "fair and impartial" trial?

**12.** What influences does culture have on the context of the classroom?

**13.** How does the culturally defined role of the teacher affect the classroom context? Be specific and give examples.

**14.** Can you think of way in which your culture has shaped the expectations for classroom behavior? Be specific and give examples.

## SUGGESTED READINGS

Bowers, J. R. "A review of small group research in Japan: A communication perspective." *World Communication* 14 (1985), 121–128. Powers addresses the research reported in the Japanese language by Japanese scholars in the fields of social psychology, business administration, and communication on the topic of small groups. He examines studies of group characteristics, interpersonal interaction, group functions, and interaction processes analysis.

Chao, K. and W. I. Gorden. " Culture and communication in the modern Japanese corporate organization." *International and Intercultural Annual* 4 (1977), 23–36. This excellent article concentrates on how to improve communication within the context of the Japanese organization. The authors maintain that we must understand the norms of harmony and group cooperation. These concerns of the Japanese are reflected in "the ambiguities of the Japanese language, the use of face-to-face over written communication, the open-space office setting, the concept of shared leadership and responsibility, and the *ringi* system through which consensus is sought."

Clark, A. "African healing and Western psychotherapy." *International Journal of Intercultural Relations* 6 (1982), 5–15. This study looks at the institutions of traditional healing as practiced in Black Africa and at psychotherapy as practiced in Western culture. These two approaches are compared in terms of their relative positions within the broader health care systems of the respective cultures and in terms of their therapeutic techniques.

Condon, E. C. "Cross-cultural interferences affecting teacher-pupil communication in American schools." *International and Intercultural Annual* 3 (1976), 108–120. This essay looks at the influence of culture on the classroom setting. Specifically Condon examines: (1) the use of language (vocabulary and grammatical structure), (2) language auxiliaries (paralinguistic and kinesic signals), (3) norms of classroom interaction (modes of address, learning style, and classroom roles), and (4) the general context of human interaction (time and space).

Gould, J. W., P. T. McGuire, and C. Tsang Sing. "Adequacy of Hong Kong-California business communication methods." *The Journal of Business Communication* 20 (1983) 33–40. Companies communicating between Hong Kong and California employ seven basic methods: telex, letter, telephone, visit, courier, computer, and telegram. The article discusses the main advantages and disadvantages of these methods and recommends safeguards against their misuse.

Halpern, J. W. "Business communication in China: A second perspective." *The Journal of Business Communication* 20 (1983) 43–56. "To understand the teaching of business communication in China, it is important to have a broad view of the political and educational context in which instruction occurs." The article discusses these areas as observed in China and offers a perspective on English business communication courses in China.

Hofstede, G. *Culture's Consequences: International Differences in Work-Related Values.* Beverly Hills, Calif.: Sage Publications, 1980. Hofstede demonstrates the effects of national cultures by analyzing such countries as France, Belgium, Germany, Japan, and India in terms of organizational behavior and theory.

Hornik, J. "Comparative evaluation of international versus national advertising strategies." *Columbia Journal of World Business* 15 (1980), 36–48. In this paper the author investigates the "standardization dilemma" in international advertising—that is, whether a given concept means to the people of other cultures what it means to the people of the culture in which it was originally developed.

Krarr, L. "The Japanese are coming—with their own style of management." *Fortune* 91 (March 1978), 116–121, 160–161, 164. Krarr, a staff writer for *Fortune*, has written an excellent account of Japanese management techniques in manufacturing plants in the United States. This article describes the stark differences between the roles of management in the United States and in Japan and the effects of Japanese management concepts applied to American workers.

Lin, E. H. "Intraethnic characteristics and the patient-physician interaction: 'Culture blind sports syndrome.'" *Journal of Family Practice* 16 (1983), 91–98. This article uses the case method and a literature review to present a conceptual framework for analyzing patient-physician interaction in any cultural context. The author concludes that a good match of intraethnic factors between patient and physician enhances communication.

Olsson, M. "Meeting styles for intercultural groups." *Occasional Papers in Intercultural Learning* 7 (February 1985), 1–18. The author stresses the dangers of introducing a Western meeting style into other cultures, discusses nine flexible aspects of the structure of meetings, and illustrates five examples using these flexible aspects.

Terpstra, V. *The Cultural Environment of International Business.* Cincinnati: South-Western, 1978. Although this book takes an international business perspective, it nevertheless touches on ideas that are applicable to any intercultural context. Terpstra examines language, religion, values, attitudes toward time, work, change, social organizations, education, and technology, as well as political and legal environments.

Westwood, M. J., A. Bernadelli, and J. Destetano. "Counseling in the culturally diverse society: Some neglected variables in research." *International Journal for the Advancement of Counseling* 4 (1981), 131–137. This paper discusses some of the cultural factors that are relevant to the cross-cultural counseling process, such as differences in perception toward seeking help in a psychological context, perceptions of which type of client-counsel or relation is most helpful, perceptions of counseling as a profession, and expectations of different groups.

Zong, B, and H. W. Hildebrandt. "Business communication in the People's Republic of China." *The Journal of Business Communication* 20 (1983) 25–32. The authors discuss the preeminent position held by business communication in China, as well as historical backgrounds and a review of three courses in business communication and their methods of instruction.

## ADDITIONAL READINGS

Althen, G., ed. *Learning across Cultures: Intercultural Communication and International Education Exchange.* Washington, D.C.: National Association for Foreign Student Affairs, 1981.

Althen, G. *The Handbook of Foreign Student Advising.* Chicago: Intercultural Press, 1983.

Arredondo-Dowd, P. M. and J. Gonsalves. "Preparing culturally effective counselors." *Personnel and Guidance Journal* (1980), 657–661.

Ayman, R. and M. M. Chemers. " Relationship of supervisory behavior rating to work group effectiveness and subordinate satisfaction among Iranian managers." *Journal of Applied Psychology* 68 (1983), 338–341.

Barker, L. L., ed. Communication in the Classroom: Original Essays. Englewood Cliffs, N.J.: Prentice-Hall, 1982.

Bass, B. and F. Burger. Assessment of Managers: An International Comparison. New York: Macmillan, 1979.

Blaylock, J. "The psychological and cultural influences on the reaction to pain. *Nursing Forum* 7 (1985), 262–274.

Castro, F. B., P. Furth, and H. Karlow. "The health beliefs of Mexican, Mexican-American, and Anglo-American Women." *Hispanic Journal of Behavioral Sciences* 6 (1984), 365–383.

Clark, R. R. "African healing and Western psychotherapy." *International Journal of Intercultural Relations* 6 (1982), 5–15.

Delgado, M. "Hispanic cultural values: Implications for groups." *Small Group Behavior* 12 (1981), 69–80.

Dobson, S. "Bringing culture into care." *Nursing Times* 70 (1983), 56–57.

Dyol, J. A. and R. Y. Dyol. "Acculturation, stress and coping: Some implications for research and education." *International Journal of Intercultural Relations* 5 (1981), 301–327.

Endicott, C. "Doing business in Spain." *The Bridge: A Review of Cross-Cultural Affairs and International Training* (Summer 1981), 21–28.

Fishman, R. G. "A note on culture as a variable in providing human services in social service agencies." *Human Organization* 38 (1979), 189–192.

Gritzmacher, K. J. "Multinational companies: Exploring the challenges facing consultants." *The Journal of the Communication Association of the Pacific* 9 (1980), 13–23.

Harris, P. R. and D. L. Harris. "Intercultural education for multinational managers." *International and Intercultural Communication Annual* 3 (1976), 70–85.

Hornik, J. "Contemparative evaluation of international versus national advertising strategies." *Columbia Journal of World Business* (1980), 36–48.

Keys, J. B. and T. R. Miller. "The Japanese management theory jungle." *Academy of Management Review* 9 (1984), 342–353.

Kleinman, A. *Patients and Healers in the Context of Culture*. Berkeley: University of California Press, 1979.

Mangrove, F. *Education and Anthropology: Other Cultures and the Teacher*. New York: John Wiley, 1982.

Nguyen, S. D. "Psychiatric and psychosomatic problems among Southeast Asian refugees." *Psychiatric: Journal of the University of Ottawa* 7 (1982), 163–172.

Nishiyama, K. "Intercultural communication problems in Japanese multinationals." *Communication: The Journal of the Communication Association of the Pacific* 12 (1983), 50–60.

Pedersen, P., W. J. Lonner, and J. G. Draguns, eds. *Counseling Across Cultures*. Honolulu: University Press of Hawaii, 1976.

Philips, S. V. *The Invisible Culture Communication and Community on the Warm Springs Indian Reservation*. New York: Longman, 1983.

Reardon, K. K. "An exploratory study of international business gift giving." *World Communication* 14 (1985), 137–148.

Rome, D. "International training: What is it?" The Bridge: A Review of Cross-Cultural Affairs and Training (Spring 1981), 23–28.

Segal, M. H. "On teaching cross-cultural psychology." *Journal of Cross-Cultural Psychology* 11 (1980), 89–99.

Simpkin, R. and R. Jones. *Business and the Language Barrier*. London: Business Books, Ltd., 1976.

Sue, D. W. and D. Sue. "Barriers to effective cross-cultural counseling." *Journal of Counseling Psychology* 24 (1977), 420–429.

# PART THREE

## Intercultural Interaction: Taking Part in Intercultural Communication

*If we seek to understand a people we have to put ourselves, as far as we can, in that particular historical and cultural background. . . . One has to recognize that countries and people differ in their approach and their ways, in their approach to life and their ways of living and thinking. In order to understand them we have to understand their way of life and approach. If we wish to convince them, we have to use their language as far as we can, not language in the narrow sense of the word, but the language of the mind.*

—*Jawaharlal Nehru*

In this part we are concerned with taking part in intercultural communication. Our interest focuses on both verbal and nonverbal forms of symbolic interaction. As we pointed out in introducing Part Two, meanings reside within people, and symbols serve as stimuli to which these meanings are attributed. Meaning-evoking stimuli consist of both verbal and nonverbal behaviors. Although we consider these forms of symbolic interaction separately for convenience, we hasten to point out their interrelatedness. As nonverbal behavior accompanies verbal behavior, it becomes a unique part of the total symbolic interaction. Verbal messages often rely on their nonverbal accompaniment for cues that aid the receiver in decoding the verbal symbols. Nonverbal behaviors not only serve to amplify and clarify verbal messages but can also serve as forms of symbolic interaction without verbal counterparts.

When we communicate verbally, we use words with seeming ease, because there is a high consensus of agreement about the meanings our words evoke. Our experiential backgrounds are similar enough that we share essentially the same meanings for most of the word symbols we use in everyday communication. But, even within our culture we disagree over the meanings of many word symbols. As words move farther from sense data reality they become more abstract, and there is far less agreement about appropriate meanings. What do highly abstract words such as *love, freedom, equality, democracy,* or *good time* mean to you? Do they mean the same things to everyone? If you are in doubt, ask some friends; take a poll. You will surely find that people have different notions of these concepts and consequently different meanings for these words. Their experiences have been different, and they hold different beliefs, attitudes, values, concepts, and expectations. Yet all, or perhaps most, are from the same culture. Their backgrounds, experiences, and concepts of the universe are really quite uniform. When cultures begin to vary, much larger differences are found.

Culture exerts no small influence over our use of language. In fact, it strongly determines just what our language is and how we use it. In the narrowest sense, language is a set of symbols (vocabulary) that evoke more or less uniform meanings among a particular population and a set of rules (grammar and syntax) for using the symbols. In the broadest sense, language is the symbolic representation of a people, and it includes their historical and cultural backgrounds as well as their approach to life and their ways of living and thinking.

What comes to be symbolized and what the symbols represent are very much functions of culture. Similarly, how we use our verbal symbols is also a function of culture. What we think about or speak with others about must be capable of symbolization, and how we speak or think about things must follow the rules we have for using our language. Because the symbols and rules are culturally determined, how and what we think or talk about are, in effect, a function of our culture. This relation between language and culture is not unidirectional, however. There is an interaction between them—what we think about and how we think about it also affect our culture.

As we can see, language and culture are inseparable. To be effective intercultural communicators requires that we be aware of the relationship between culture and language. It further requires that we learn and know about the culture of the person with whom we communicate so that we can better understand how his or her language represents that person.

Another important aspect of verbal symbols or words is that they can evoke two kinds of meaning: *denotative* and *connotative.* A denotative meaning indicates the referent or the "thing" to which the symbol refers. For example, the denotative meaning of the word *book* is the physical object to which it refers; or, in the case of the set of symbols *"Intercultural Communication: A Reader,"* the referent is the book you are now reading. Not all denotations have a physical correspondence. As we move to higher levels of abstraction, we often deal with words that represent ideas or concepts, which exist only in the mind and do not necessarily have a physical basis. For example, much communication research is directed toward changes in attitude. Yet attitude is only a hypothetical construct used to explain behavior; there is no evidence of any physical correspondence between some group of brain cells and a person's attitudes.

The second type of meaning—connotative—indicates an evaluative dimension. Not only do we identify referents (denotative meaning), we place them along an evaluative dimension that can be described as positive-neutral-negative. Where we place a word on the dimension depends on our prior experiences and how we "feel" about the referent. If we like books, we might place *Intercultural Communication: A Reader* near the positive end of the dimension. When we are dealing with more abstract symbols, we do the same thing. In fact, as the level of abstraction increases, so does our tendency to place more emphasis on connotative meanings. Most will agree that a book is the object you are holding in your hand, but whether books are good or bad or whether this particular book is good or bad or in between is an individual judgment based on prior experience.

Culture affects both denotative and connotative meanings. Consequently, a knowledge of how these meanings vary culturally is essential to effective intercultural communication. To make the assumption that everyone uses the same meanings is to invite communication disaster.

There are other ways in which culture affects language and language use. We tend to believe that our way of using language is both correct and universal and that any deviation is wrong or substandard. This belief can and does elicit many negative responses and judgments when we encounter someone from another culture whose use of language deviates from our own specifications.

What all of these examples are trying to point out should be quite obvious—language and culture are inseparable. In fact, it would be difficult to determine which is the voice and which is the echo. How we learn, employ, and respond to symbols is culturally based. In addition, the sending and the receiving of these culturally grounded symbols are what enable us to interact with people from other cultures. Hence, it is the purpose of this part of the book to highlight these verbal and nonverbal symbols to help you understand some of the complexities, subtleties, and nuances of language.

# 5

# Verbal Interaction

This chapter begins with a general look at the study of language and culture. Stephen W. King in "A Taxonomy for the Classification of Language Studies in Intercultural Communication" brings together and summarizes various approaches to the role of language in intercultural communication. He sets forth a classification scheme that accomplishes two purposes. First, it indicates what is already known about language in intercultural communication. Second, King's taxonomy isolates those issues that scholars have left still unresolved. His overview highlights studies that search for universals (*etic*) as well as those that deal with specific cultural attributes (*emic*). In addition, phonemic, semantic-lexical, syntactic, and pragmatic approaches are reviewed. Although these issues are not examined in detail, they do provide an excellent introduction to the topic of intercultural language.

The second selection, "The Sapir-Whorf Hypothesis" by Harry Hoijer, introduces us to Benjamin Whorf's hypothesis of "linguistic relativity." This classic and sometimes controversial idea postulates that each language both embodies and imposes upon its users and their culture a particular world view that functions not only as a device for reporting experience but also, and more significantly, as a way of defining experience. To help understand this point of view and its ramifications, Hoijer looks at the basic assumptions, usability, and plausibility of "linguistic relativity."

Some people have suggested that it is our ability, as a species, to receive, store, manipulate, and generate symbols that is our most unique feature. All 4.5 billion of us deal with past, present, and future situations by using language; we have sounds and marks on paper that stand for something. In short, language is that special and simple instrument that lets us share our internal states with others.

While all people use the same anatomical and biological tools to communicate, there are vast cultural differences in what these tools produce. These cultural variations are the concern of

Verner C. Bickley's article, "Language as the Bridge." It is Bickley's contention that "Language differences can exacerbate tensions between individuals in the same language community, or in different language communities within a single country, or they can create an intercultural problem which affects individuals from different countries." He also believes that language, with all of its problems, can be a bridge to understanding. To help bring about that understanding, Bickley examines a number of language variables that are in operation during intercultural encounters. Among other factors, he discusses bilingualism, multilingualism, mediation, code-switching, translation, and language used to mediate between societies and cultures. Bickley concludes by offering examples of languages selected by governments to mediate between different cultures of a particular society and between societies.

We have already seen that culture can produce a variety of ways by which people communicate their ideas and feelings. These differences also contribute to how people speak and even argue in public settings. For example, the Chinese and Japanese have a view of dialogue and debate that is contrary to that of North Americans. Many of these cultural distinctions are pointed out by Carl B. Becker in his article, "Reasons for the Lack of Argumentation and Debate in the Far East." Becker does not take the position that one approach to logic, thought patterns, and speech is superior to another, but rather he explains *why* Americans favor discussion and debate while the Chinese and Japanese have a predisposition against these communication forms.

As we noted in the introduction to this part, language involves attaching meanings to word symbols. If those symbols have to be translated, as when a foreign language is dealt with, numerous problems arise. Without accurate translations those trying to communicate often end up simply exchanging noise or meaningless sounds. What usually happens is that the interpretations lack a common vocabulary and familiar referents. For mutual understanding, equivalencies in each culture are needed. A search for this common ground is the main focus of Lee Sechrest, Todd L. Fay, and S. M. Zaidi in their article, "Problems of Translation in Cross-Cultural Communication." They maintain that while equivalence in idiom, grammar, and syntax may be important, equivalence of experience and concepts is probably most important. With this notion as their central thesis, they attempt to point out some of the inherent problems of translation and also suggest some ways for overcoming these problems.

Although Sechrest, Fay, and Zaidi have shown us some of the difficulties encountered in translation, they do not give us a thorough account of the difficulties faced when one individual must transform the thoughts of another individual from one language into another. To overcome many of these problems, a translator is often asked to become part of an intercultural event. This act of introducing a third party often creates another set of problems. Many of these problems are discussed by Jan Carol Berris in her essay, "The Art of Interpreting." Berris makes a distinction between translation and interpreting, and she looks at a host of potential problems that can impede intercultural communication. Among the more serious issues she treats is the problem of not having enough interpreters for long sessions. She also discusses the importance of proper preparation, the differences between precise translations and simple paraphrasing, and nonverbal communication and its role in interpretative events.

# A Taxonomy for the Classification of Language Studies in Intercultural Communication

STEPHEN W. KING

The emerging field of intercultural communication has, apparently, reached consensus on two fundamental propositions:

1. "Intercultural communication occurs whenever a message producer is a member of one culture and a message receiver is a member of another.[1] (Emphasis deleted.)

2. "Culture and language are inseparably intertwined."[2]

These propositions, or ones similar to them, have led researchers from such widely diverse disciplines as cultural anthropology, linguistics, speech communications, and sociology to investigate the complex interrelationships among culture, language, and intercultural communication. However, that research has not been aggregated into a coordinated body of knowledge about the role and nature of language in intercultural communication. Rather, there exists today a variety of disconnected observations, research conclusions, anecdotes, and theoretic speculations on the topic. Two of the causes of the current incoherent situation are (1) the diversity of topics and phenomena justifiably included in the topic of language and intercultural communi-

nication and (2) the numerous objectives and perspectives of the researchers undertaking these studies.

In this article I propose a taxonomy or classification scheme for sorting language studies in intercultural communication into sensible and usable categories. My hope is that this taxonomy will assist both students and scholars in understanding what is currently known about language in intercultural communication and in identifying those areas most in need of additional research. Simply, the taxonomy described in this article is one way to impose coherence on what is now incoherent and to provide direction for research efforts that are currently uncoordinated.

Language studies in intercultural communication can be divided or sorted on three broad dimensions: (1) the type or level of research objective, (2) the level of language investigated, and (3) the level of language community studied. That is, studies can be usefully viewed (1) as searching for language differences or language similarities, (2) by investigating the sounds, words, grammar, or uses of language, (3) within culture(s), subculture(s), or a given group over time. Each of these dimensions, which I will ultimately combine to create an analytic matrix, is discussed in the following pages.

## LEVEL OF RESEARCH OBJECTIVE.

Studies of language are undertaken, generally, to accomplish one of two broad and very different objectives: Research aims at either establishing similarities or discovering differences. Both types of studies are needed for a comprehensive understanding of intercultural communication. As Prosser said, "Central to the study of communication between members of different cultures is the importance of similarities and differences as they affect all intercultural and cross-cultural communication."[3] Clark and Clark echoed the importance of both research objectives when they noted that "if languages are molded in part by the ideas, processing capacities, and social factors all people have in common, they should have certain features in common—linguistic universals. But to the extent that languages are molded by accidental properties of thought, technology, and culture, features will also differ from language to language."[4] Clearly, both objectives will need to be met for a comprehensive understanding of language in intercultural communication.

Studies that search for universal, *etic*, aspects of language take a variety of forms. For example, Osgood and his colleagues established that every one of the 26 languages they investigated employed the dimensions of activity, evaluation, and potency in determining the connotative or affective dimension of meaning.[5] Similarly, Clark and Clark reported that "all languages distinguish at least three characteristics in relatives—generation, blood relationship, and sex."[6] Findings of this type, Prosser argued, cut across cultures and "serve as a primary linkage between communication and culture, and as a base for intercultural communication."[7]

The search for culturally specific, *emic*, attributes of language promotes understanding of the unique relationship between a particular culture and its particular language. For example, Doi's demonstration of "how the psychology of *amae* pervades and actually makes the Japanese patterns of communication" illustrates the connection between Japanese culture and language.[8] On a more particularist level, Folb revealed that for white youth the word *punk* is someone who is disliked, while for black youth *punk* is a male homosexual.[9] Studies of this type highlight the differences between and among language communities and describe the intercultural communication practices involving persons of those communities.

## LEVEL OF LANGUAGE

Language studies in intercultural communication do not, indeed cannot, simultaneously investigate all aspects of language. Rather, researchers must focus attention on one aspect or level of language. A language is, in the simplest terms, a system "of sounds and combinations of sounds in commonly established patterns (words) arranged in commonly understood sequences (word orders, sentences) to communicate."[10] Accordingly, each language is composed of sounds, words, sequences of words, and communicative uses. Studies emphasizing each of these dimensions of a language can be called phonemic, semantic, syntactic, and pragmatic, respectively. To understand the contribution of a given study of language in intercultural communication it is essential that we correctly identify the level of language being investigated.

## Phonemic

Not all languages of the world contain the same set of acceptable or meaningful sounds. The smallest relevant speech sound of a language is a phoneme; for example, in English the phoneme /k/ is common in the words *key* and *cow*. In English there are approximately 45 phonemes.[11] Phonemic theory and research are necessary in intercultural communication because "if we approach other languages naively we will only respond to those cues as different which are significant in our own language. On the other hand, we will attribute significance, and consider an indicative of separate elements, those differences which have a function in our own language, although they may not have such a function, in [another language].[12] For example, "speakers of English have usually never noticed that the sound spelled *t* in 'stop' is unaspirated as contrasted with the *t* in 'top'. Yet this difference is sufficient to differentiate forms in Chinese, Hindustani, and many other languages."[13] Comprehensive understanding of and effective practice in intercultural communication require knowledge of phonemic differences and similarities.

## Semantic/Lexical

Many studies of language in intercultural communication investigate language at the word level. A semantic analysis investigates the nature and evolution of meanings attached to the words of a language. A lexical assessment of a language explores the total stock of words in a language. Numerous lexical and semantic language studies have been undertaken in intercultural communication research.

Obviously, questions of semantics and lexicon are critical to the entire issue of translation.[14] Other general questions at this level of language analysis include investigation of how different cultures have different words with the same meaning, have the same words with different meanings, or have the same words with the same meaning. Less significant is the obvious observation that different cultures have different words with different meanings. Research illustrative of the semantic/lexical type of language study includes the previously mentioned study establishing that connotative meaning is similar in 26 language communities,[15] Clark and Clark's observation that Garo has more names for rice than does Russian,[16] Boas's classic observation that Eskimo has four words for snow while English has only one,[17] and Berlin and Kay's research establishing that every language gets its basic color words from only 11 color names and that those 11 terms are hierarchically arranged.[18] Some languages have as few as only two color terms, but "if a language acquires a new basic color term, it always acquires the next one (in the hierarchy) to the ones it already has."[19] Obviously, intercultural communication, understanding and practice must be based on a solid grounding in the ways languages are different and similar with respect to the total stock of words in a language and the ways meanings are attached to words.

## Syntactic

All languages have rules governing the arrangement of words as elements in sentences; those rules constitute the syntax or grammar of the language. Fundamental issues at the syntactic level of intercultural language analysis include such questions as: How do languages express possession? How do languages resemble or differ from each other with respect to the organization of sentences? For instance, by simply analyzing a sentence as containing a subject (S), a verb (V), and an object (O), we know that English is predominantly an SVO language—for example, George hit the ball. Of the six possible orders for S, V, and O, the world's languages are distributed as follows:[20]

SVO—35 percent
VSO—19 percent
VOS—2 percent
SOV—44 percent
OVS—0 percent
OSV—0 percent

Other illustrative syntactic level studies have reported that the Japanese have a grammatical form, adversative passive, that disclaims responsibility for the reported, and usually unpleasant, event or action.[21] In this case the cultural sensitivity to responsibility among the Japanese apparently resulted in or reflects itself in a grammatical form to avoid responsibility. Price-Williams reported that the Hopi language has no tense system reflecting present, past, and future, as does English.[22]

Knowledge about the syntax of a language and, therefore, the way in which a language community organizes its thought is critical to understanding intercultural communication. The need for syntactic level knowledge for the practice of intercultural communication is self-evident.

## Pragmatic

The pragmatics of a language concern the rules for and consequences of language usage. Questions of interest at this level of analysis include the following: How do users of a language accomplish communicative objectives, such as insulting and paying deference? What are the effects of particular language use patterns? On what basis do language users decide among semantically equivalent utterances? Two research samples will be briefly described here to illustrate studies of the pragmatics of language usage.

Brown and Levinson have comprehensively investigated the ways that various cultures linguistically create and enforce social relationships and accomplish socially defined objectives such as paying respect, thanking, insulting, and complaining.[23] They indicate, among literally hundreds of such conclusions, that persons in especially debt-sensitive cultures, such as India, express thanks by saying something like "I am humiliated, so awful is my debt," which would be heard as anomalous in other cultures.[24] Further, "Tzeltal-speakers use creaking voice to express commiseration and complaint."[25] These conclusions obviously relate not to the structure or phonemics of a language *per se,* but to the use to which language can be put to accomplish particular communicative objectives. Further, knowledge of such conclusions is absolutely essential for understanding and practicing intercultural communication.

Another illustrative area of pragmatics is the extensive research now being conducted on the fact that "the way English is used to make the simplest points can either acknowledge woman's full humanity or relegate the female half of the species to secondary status."[26] Clark and Clark suggested that among the world's languages the bias of male over female is widespread, though not universal.[27] This fact of language in use both reflects and affects soci-ety. Repression of women, socially disadvantaged persons, blacks, Indians, and other minorities occurs, in part, linguistically.

Knowledge of a culture's language use norms, the consequences of alternative language use patterns, and the ways language can be exploited to accomplish various social objectives are all essential for comprehensive understanding of intercultural communication.

## LEVEL OF COMMUNITY

As has been illustrated throughout this essay, studies of language in intercultural communication have taken as their language population both cultures and subcultures. In addition, several language studies have investigated the changes in language use within a particular culture or subculture over time.

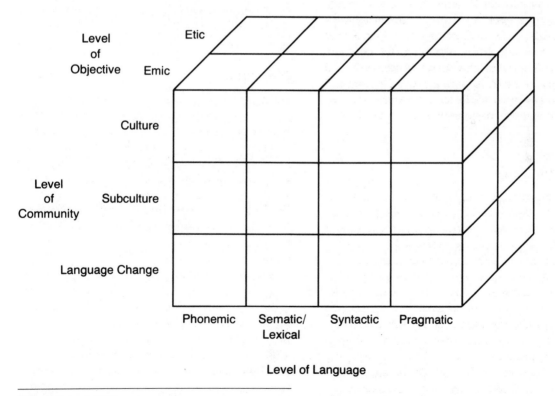

**Figure 1** Analytic Taxonomy

It is useful to distinguish among research conducted on cultures, subcultures, and language change.

Many studies are predominantly concerned with the relationship between a culture and a language. Porter and Samovar suggested both directions of influence when they observed that "to a very great extent our language is a product of our culture. At the same time, our culture is very much a product of our language."[28] Indeed, these authors include language as a defining characteristic of a culture. Other researchers, however, focus on identifiable groups within a culture who ostensibly share a language but are identifiable on the basis of values, experience, socio-economic standing or even linguistic idiosyncrasy. Studies have investigated such subgroups as the socially disadvantaged, homosexuals, and black youth. Finally, some intercultural language studies include a comparison of the same language community at various points of time. For example, as Salus explained, "Given that German, English, Latin, Greek, Russian and Armenian have a common ancestor, how long ago were English and German mutually comprehensible dialects?"[29] The previously cited research on the ways in which a language acquires color terms is also illustrative of the type of research that looks longitudinally at some aspect of a language evolution.

## THE TAXONOMY

The three dimensions described in this essay (level of objective, level of language, and level of community) combine to create a useful matrix for understanding and classifying language studies in intercultural communication. The aggregate analytic grid is presented in Figure 1 on page 223.

The development of knowledge of the nature and role of language in intercultural communication will be facilitated by the use of this, or a similar, taxonomy. The use of this classification scheme assists in (1) understanding what sort of knowledge about language and intercultural communication we now have and (2) identifying areas of needed research.

## NOTES

1. Richard E. Porter and Larry A. Samovar, "Approaching Intercultural Communication," in Larry A. Samovar and Richard E. Porter, eds., *Intercultural Communication: A Reader,* 4th ed. (Belmont, Calif.: Wadsworth, 1982), p. 15.

2. Richard E. Porter and Larry A. Samovar, "Communicating Interculturally," in Larry A. Samovar and Richard E. Porter, eds., *Intercultural Communication: A Reader,* 2nd ed. (Belmont, Calif.: Wadsworth, 1976), p. 18.

3. Michael H. Prosser, "Intercultural Communication Theory and Research: An Overview of Major Constructs," in Brent D. Ruben, ed., *Communication Yearbook* 2 (New Brunswick, N.J.: Transaction Books, 1978), p. 336.

4. Eve V. Clark and Herbert H. Clark, "Universals, Relativity, and Language Processing," in Joseph H. Greenberg, ed., *Universals of Human Language,* Vol. 1 (Stanford, Calif.: Stanford University Press, 1978), p. 227.

5. Charles E. Osgood, W. May, and M. Miron, *Cross-Cultural Universals of Affective Meaning* (Urbana: University of Illinois Press, 1975).

6. Clark and Clark, p. 252.

7. Prosser, p. 340.

8. L. Takeo Doi, "The Japanese Patterns of Communication and the Concept of *Amae,*" in Samovar and Porter, 3rd ed., p. 218.

9. Edith A. Folb, "Vernacular Vocabulary: A View of Interracial Perceptions and Experiences," in Samovar and Porter, 4th ed., p. 232.

10. Thomas Elliott Berry, *The Study of Language* (Encino, Calif.: Dickerson Publishing Co., 1971), pp. 3–4.

11. Berry, p. 224.

12. Joseph H. Greenberg, *Language Universals* (The Hague: Mouton, 1966), p. 123.

13. Ibid.

14. Lee Sechrest, Todd L. Fay, and S. M. Zaidi, "Problems of Translation in Cross-Cultural Communication," in Samovar and Porter, 3rd ed., p. 223.

15. Osgood, May, and Miron.

16. Clark and Clark, p. 228.

17. Franz Boas, "Interaction," in Franz Boas, ed., *Handbook of American Indian Languages, Part 1* (Washington, D.C.: U.S. Government Printing Office, 1911), pp. 1–84.

18. B. Berlin and P. Kaye, *Basic Color Terms: Their University and Evolution* (Berkeley, Calif.: University of California Press, 1969).

19. Clark and Clark, p. 232.

20. Clark and Clark, p. 257.

21. A. M. Niyekawa, *A Study of Second Language Learning* (Washington, D.C.: Department of Health, Education and Welfare, 1968), cited by Tulsi B. Saral, "Intercultural Communication Theory and Research: An Overview," in Brent D. Ruben, ed., *Communication Yearbook I* (New Brunswick, N.J.: Transaction Books, 1977), pp. 389–396.

22. D. Price-Williams, "Cross-Cultural Studies," in Samovar and Porter, 3rd ed., p. 78.

23. Penelope Brown and Stephen Levinson, "Universals in Language Usage: Politeness Phenomena," in Ester N. Goody, ed., *Questions and Politeness: Strategies in Social Interaction* (Cambridge: Cambridge University Press, 1978), pp. 56–289.

24. Brown and Levinson, p. 252.

25. Brown and Levinson, p. 272.

26. Casey Miller and Kate Swift, *Words and Women* (Garden City, N.Y.: Anchor Books, 1977), p. "x."

27. Clark and Clark, p. 253.

28. Porter and Samovar, "Communicating Interculturally," in Samovar and Porter, 2nd ed., p. 18.

29. Peter H. Salus, *Linguistics* (Indianapolis: Bobbs-Merrill, 1969), p. 49.

# The Sapir-Whorf Hypothesis

## HARRY HOIJER

The Sapir-Whorf hypothesis appears to have had its initial formulation in the following two paragraphs, taken from an article of Sapir's, first published in 1929.

*Language is a guide to "social reality." Though language is not ordinarily thought of as of essential interest to the students of social science, it powerfully conditions all of our thinking about social problems and processes. Human beings do not live in the objective world alone, nor alone in the world of social activity as ordinarily understood, but are very much at the mercy of the particular language which has become the medium of expression for their society. It is quite an illusion to imagine that one adjusts to reality essentially without the use of language and that language is merely an incidental means of solving specific problems of communication or reflection. The fact of the matter is that the "real world" is to a large extent unconsciously built up on the language habits of the group. No two languages are ever sufficiently similar to be considered as representing the same social reality. The worlds in which different societies live are distinct worlds, not merely the same world with different labels attached.*

*The understanding of a simple poem, for instance, involves not merely an understanding of the single words in their average significance, but a full comprehension of the whole life of the community as it is mirrored in the words, or as it is suggested by their overtones. Even comparatively simple acts of perception are very much more at the mercy of the social patterns called words than we might suppose. If one draws some dozen lines, for instance, of different shapes, one perceives them as divisible into such categories as "straight," "crooked," "curved," "zigzag" because of the classificatory suggestiveness of the linguistic terms themselves. We see and hear and otherwise experience very largely as we do because the language habits of our community predispose certain choices of interpretation.* [In Mandelbaum 1949: 162]

The notion of language as a "guide to social reality" is not entirely original with Sapir. Somewhat similar ideas, though far less adequately stated, may be found in Boas' writings, at least as early as 1911. Thus we find in Boas' introduction to the *Handbook of American Indian Languages* a number of provocative passages on this theme, to wit:

*It seems, however, that a theoretical study of Indian languages is not less important than a practical knowledge of them; that the purely linguistic inquiry is part and parcel of a thorough investigation of the psychology of the peoples of the world* [p. 63].

*... language seems to be one of the most instructive fields of inquiry in an investigation of the formation of the fundamental ethnic ideas. The great advantage that linguistics offer in this respect is the fact that, on the whole, the categories which are formed always remain unconscious, and that for this reason the processes which lead to their formation can be followed without the misleading and disturbing factors of secondary explanation, which are so common in ethnology, so much so that they generally obscure the real history of the development of ideas entirely* [pp. 70–71].

The Sapir-Whorf hypothesis, however, gains especial significance by virtue of the fact that both these scholars had a major interest in American Indian languages, idioms far removed from any in the Indo-European family and so ideally suited to contrastive studies. It is in the attempt to properly interpret the grammatical categories of an American Indian language, Hopi, that Whorf best illustrates his principle of linguistic relativity, the notion that "users of markedly different grammars are pointed by their grammars toward different types of observations and different evaluations of externally similar acts of observations, and hence are not equivalent as observers but must arrive at somewhat different views of the world" (1952: 11).

The purpose of this paper is twofold: (1) to review and clarify the Sapir-Whorf hypothesis, (2) to illustrate and perhaps add to it by reference to my own work on the Navajo language. . . .

The central idea of the Sapir-Whorf hypothesis is that language functions, not simply as a device for reporting experience, but also, and more significantly, as a way of defining experience for its speakers. Sapir says (1931: 578), for example:

*Language is not merely a more or less systematic inventory of the various items of experience which seem relevant to the individual, as is so often naively assumed, but is also a self-contained, creative symbolic organization, which not only refers to experience largely acquired without its help but actually defines experience for us by reason of its formal completeness and because of our unconscious projection of its implicit expectations into the field of experience. In this respect language is very much like a mathematical system which, also, records experience in the truest sense of the word, only in its crudest beginnings, but, as time goes on, becomes elaborated into a self-contained conceptual system which previsages all possible experience in accordance with certain accepted formal limitations. . . . [Meanings are] not so much discovered in experience as imposed upon it, because of the tyrannical hold that linguistic form has upon our orientation in the world.*

Whorf develops the same thesis when he says (1952: 5):

*... the linguistic system (in other words, the grammar) of each language is not merely a reproducing instrument for voicing ideas but rather is itself the shaper of ideas, the program and guide for the individual's mental activity, for his analysis of impressions, for his synthesis of his mental stock in trade.... We dissect nature along lines laid down by our native languages. The categories and types that we isolate from the world of phenomena we do not find there because they stare every observer in the face; on the contrary, the world is presented in a kaleidoscopic flux of impressions which has to be organized by our minds—and this means largely by the linguistic systems in our minds.*

It is evident from these statements, if they are valid, that language plays a large and significant role in the totality of culture. Far from being simply a technique of communication, it is itself a way of directing the perceptions of its speakers and it provides for them habitual modes of analyzing experience into significant categories. And to the extent that languages differ markedly from each other, so should we expect to find significant and formidable barriers to cross-cultural communication and understanding. These barriers take on even greater importance when it is realized that "the phenomena of a language are to its own speakers largely of a background character and so are outside the critical consciousness and control of the speaker" (Whorf 1952: 4).

It is, however, easy to exaggerate linguistic differences of this nature and the consequent barriers to intercultural understanding. No culture is wholly isolated, self-contained, and unique. There are important resemblances between all known cultures—resemblances that stem in part from diffusion (itself an evidence of successful intercultural communication) and in part from the fact that all cultures are built around biological, psychological, and social characteristics common to all mankind. The languages of human beings do not so much

determine the perceptual and other faculties of their speakers vis-à-vis experience as they influence and direct these faculties into prescribed channels. Intercultural communication, however wide the difference between cultures may be, is not impossible. It is simply more or less difficult, depending on the degree of difference between the cultures concerned.

Some measures of these difficulties is encountered in the process of translating from one language into another language that is divergent and unrelated. Each language has its own peculiar and favorite devices, lexical and grammatical, which are employed in the reporting, analysis, and categorizing of experience. To translate from English into Navaho, or vice versa, frequently involves much circumlocution, since what is easy to express in one language, by virtue of its lexical and grammatical techniques, is often difficult to phrase in the other. A simple illustration is found when we try to translate the English phrases *his horse* and *his horses* into Navaho, which not only lacks a plural category for nouns (Navaho lí·? translates equally English *horse* and *horses*) but lacks as well the English distinction between *his, her, its,* and *their.* (Navaho bìlí·? may be translated, according to context, *his horse* or *horses, her horse* or *horses, its horse* or *horses,* and *their horse* or *horses.*) These Navaho forms lí·?, bìlí·? make difficulties in English also because Navaho makes a distinction between a third person (the bì- in bìlí·?) psychologically close to the speaker (e.g., *his* [that is, a Navajo's] *horse*) as opposed to a third person (the hà- of hàlí·?) psychologically remote (e.g., *his* [that is, a non-Navaho's] *horse*).

Differences of this order, which reflect a people's habitual and favorite modes of reporting, analyzing, and categorizing experience, form the essential data of the Sapir-Whorf hypothesis. According to Whorf (1952: 27), it is in these "constant ways of arranging data and its most ordinary everyday analysis of phenomena that we need to recognize the influence ... [language] has on other activities, cultural and personal."

The Sapir-Whorf hypothesis, it is evident, includes in language both its structural and its semantic aspects. These are held to be inseparable, though it is obvious that we can and do study each more or less independently of the other. The structural aspect of language, which is that most easily analyzed and described, includes its phonology, morphology, and syntax, the numerous but limited frames into which utterances are cast. The semantic aspect consists of a self-contained system of meanings, inextricably bound to the structure but much more difficult to analyze and describe. Meanings, to reiterate, are not in actual fact separable from structure, nor are they, as some have maintained (notably Voegelin 1949: 36), to be equated to the nonlinguistic culture. Our interest lies, not in questions such as "What does this form, or form class, mean?" but, instead, in the question, "In what manner does a language organize, through its structural semantic system, the world of experience in which its speakers live?" The advantage of this approach to the problem of meaning is clear. As Bloomfield long ago pointed out, it appears quite impossible, short of omniscience, to determine precisely the meaning of any single form or form class in a language. But it should be possible to determine the limits of any self-contained structural-semantic system and the ways in which it previsages the experiences of its users.

To illustrate this procedure in brief, let us turn again to Navaho and one of the ways in which it differs from English. The Navaho color vocabulary includes, among others, five terms: lìgài, dìlxìl, lìžìn, lìčí·?, and dò·λìž, to be taken as one way of categorizing certain color impressions. Lìgài is roughly equivalent to English *white*, dìlxìl and lìžìn to English *black,* lìčí·? to English *red* and dò·λìž to English *blue* or *green.* Clearly then, the Navaho five-point system is not the same as English white-black-red-blue-green, which also has five categories. English *black* is divided into two categories in Navaho (dìlxìl and lìžìn), while Navaho has but one category (dò·λìž) for the English *blue* and *green.* We do not, it should be noted, claim either that English speakers cannot perceive the difference between the two "blacks" of Navaho, or that Navaho speakers are unable to differentiate "blue" and "green." The difference between the two systems lies simply in the color categories recognized in ordinary speech, that is, in the ordinary everyday ways in which speakers of English and Navaho analyze color phenomena.

Every language is made up of a large number of such structural-semantic patterns, some of which pertain to lexical sets, as in the case of the Navaho and English color terms, and others of which pertain to sets of grammatical categories, such as the distinction between the singular and plural noun in English. A monolingual speaker, if his reports are to be understood by others in his speech community, is bound to use this apparatus, with all its implications for the analysis and categorization of experience, though he may of course quite often select from a number of alternative expressions in making his report. To quote Sapir again (Mandelbaum 1949: 10–11):

> . . . *as our scientific experience grows we must learn to fight the implications of language. "The grass waves in the wind" is shown by its linguistic form to be a member of the same relational class of experiences as "The man works in the house." As an interim solution of the problem of expressing the experience referred to in this sentence it is clear that the language has proved useful, for it has made significant use of certain symbols of conceptual relations, such as agency and location. If we feel the sentence to be poetic or metaphorical, it is largely because other more complex types of experience with their appropriate symbolisms of reference enable us to reinterpret the situation and to say, for instance, "The grass is waved by the wind" or "The wind causes the grass to wave." The point is that no matter how sophisticated our modes of interpretation become, we never really get beyond the projection and continuous transfer of relations suggested by the forms of our speech. . . . Language is at one and the same time helping and retarding us in our exploration of experience, and the details of these processes of help and hindrance are deposited in the subtler meanings of different cultures.*

It does not necessarily follow that all the structural-semantic patterns of a language are equally important to its speakers in their observation, analysis, and categorizing of experience. In describing a language, we seek to uncover all its structural-semantic patterns, even though many of these exist more as potentialities of the system than in actual usage. For ethnolinguistic analysis we need to know, not only that a particular linguistic pattern exists, but also how frequently it occurs in everyday speech. We also need to know something of the degree of complexity of the pattern of expression. There are numerous patterns of speech, particularly among peoples who have well-developed arts of oratory and writing, that are little used by any except specialists in these pursuits. The patterns of speech significant to ethnolinguistic research fall clearly into the category of habitual, frequently used, and relatively simple structural-semantic devices; those, in short, which are common to the adult speech community as a whole, and are used by its members with the greatest of ease.

Not all the structural patterns of the common speech have the same degree of semantic importance. In English, for example, it is not difficult to ascertain the semantic correlates of the structural distinction between singular and plural nouns; in most cases this is simply a division into the categories of "one" versus "more than one." Similarly, the gender distinction of the English third-person singular pronouns, as between "he," "she," and "it," correlates fairly frequently with the recognition of personality and sex.

In contrast to these, there are structural patterns like that which, in many Indo-European languages, divides nouns into three great classes: masculine, feminine, and neuter. This structural pattern has no discernible semantic correlate; we do not confuse the grammatical terms "masculine," "feminine," and "neuter" with the biological distinctions among male, female, and neuter. Whatever the semantic implications of this structural pattern may have been in origin, and this remains undetermined, it is now quite apparent that the pattern survives only as a grammatical device, important in that function but lacking in semantic value. And it is perhaps significant that the pattern is an old one, going back to

the earliest history of the Indo-European languages and, moreover, that it has disappeared almost completely in some of the modern languages of this family, notably, of course, in English.

In ethnolinguistic research, then, it is necessary to concentrate on those structural patterns of a language which have definable semantic correlates, and to omit those, like the Indo-European gender system, which survive only in a purely grammatical function. The assumption behind this procedure is as follows: every language includes a number of active structural-semantic categories, lexical and grammatical, which by virtue of their active status serve a function in the everyday (nonscientific) analysis and categorizing of experience. It is the study of these categories, distinctive when taken as a whole for each language, that yields, or may yield, significant information concerning the thought world of the speakers of the language.

One further point requires emphasis. Neither Sapir nor Whorf attempted to draw inferences as to the thought world of a people simply from the fact of the presence or absence of specific grammatical categories (e.g., tense, gender, number) in a given language. To quote Whorf (1952: 44) on this point: the concepts of time and matter which he reports for the Hopi

*do not depend so much upon any one system (e.g., tense, or nouns) within the grammar as upon the ways of analyzing and reporting experience which have become fixed in the language as integrated "fashions of speaking" and which cut across the typical grammatical classifications, so that such a "fashion" may include lexical, morphological, syntactic, and otherwise systematically diverse means coordinated in a certain frame of consistency.*

To summarize, ethnolinguistic research requires the investigator to perform, it seems to me, the following steps:

1. To determine the structural patterns of a language (that is, its grammar) as completely as possible. Such determination should include not only

a statement of the modes of utterance but as well a careful indication of the frequency of occurrence of these modes, lexical and grammatical, in the common speech.

2. To determine, as accurately as possible, the semantic patterns, if any, that attach to structural patterns. This is a task neglected by most structural linguists who, as is repeatedly mentioned in the discussions that follow, are frequently content simply to label rather than to define both lexical units and grammatical categories. In this connection it is important to emphasize that the analyst must not be taken in by his own labels; he is to discover, where possible, just how the form, or form class, or grammatical category functions in the utterances available to him.

3. To distinguish between structural categories that are active in the language, and therefore have definable semantic correlates, and those that are not. It goes without saying that such distinction requires a profound knowledge of the language, and possibly even the ability to speak and understand it well. Mark Twain's amusing translation of a German folktale into English, where he regularly translates the gender of German nouns by the English forms "he," "she," and "it," illustrates, though in caricature, the pitfalls of labeling the grammatical categories of one language (in this case, German gender) by terms belonging to an active structural-semantic pattern in another.

4. To examine and compare the active structural-semantic patterns of the language and draw from them the fashions of speaking there evidenced. As in Whorf's analysis of Hopi (1952: 25–45), while clues to a fashion of speaking may be discovered in a particular grammatical category or set of lexical items, its validity and importance cannot be determined until its range and scope within the language as a whole is also known. Whorf's conclusions as to the nature of the concept of time among speakers of English rest not alone on the tense distinctions of the English verb (mixed as these are with many other and diverse distinctions of voice, mode, and aspect) but as well on techniques of numeration,

the treatment of nouns denoting physical quantity and phases of cycles, and a host of other terms and locutions relating to time. He says (1952: 33):

*The three-tense system of SAE verbs colors all our thinking about time. This system is amalgamated with that larger scheme of objectification of the subjective experience of duration already noted in other patterns—in the binomial formula applicable to nouns in general, in temporal nouns, in plurity and numeration.*

5. Taken together, the fashions of speaking found in a language comprise a partial description of the thought world of its speakers. But by the term "thought world" Whorf means

*more than simply language, i.e., than the linguistic patterns themselves. [He includes] . . . all the analogical and suggestive value of the patterns . . . and all the give-and-take between language and the culture as a whole, wherein is a vast amount that is not linguistic yet shows the shaping influence of language. In brief, this "thought world" is the microcosm that each man carries about within himself, by which he measures and understands what he can of the macrocosm* [1952: 36].

It follows then that the thought world, as derived from ethnolinguistic studies, is found reflected as well, though perhaps not as fully, in other aspects of the culture. It is here that we may search for connections between language and the rest of culture. These connections are not direct; we see, instead, in certain patterns of nonlinguistic behavior the same meaningful fashions that are evidenced in the patterns of the language. Whorf summarizes this facet of his reseaches in a discussion of "Habitual Behavior Features of Hopi Culture and Some Impressions of Linguistic Habit in Western Civilization" (1952: 37–52).

It may be helpful to outline briefly some aspects of Navaho culture, including the language, as illustration of the Sapir-Whorf hypothesis. In particular, I shall describe first some of the basic postulates of Navaho religious behavior and attempt to show how these fit in a frame of consistency with certain fashions of speaking evidenced primarily in the morphological patterns of the Navaho verb.

A review of Navaho religious practices, as described by Washington Matthews, Father Berard Haile, as many others, reveals that the Navaho conceive of themselves as in a particular relationship with the environment—physical, social, and supernatural—in which they live. Navaho man lives in a universe of eternal and unchanging forces with which he attempts to maintain an equilibrium, a kind of balancing of powers. The mere fact of living is, however, likely to disturb this balance and throw it out of gear. Any such disturbance, which may result from failure to observe a set rule of behavior or ritual or from the accidental or deliberate committal of some other fault in ritual or the conduct of daily activities, will, the Navaho believe, be revealed in the illness or unexplained death of an individual, in some other personal misfortune or bad luck to an enterprise, or in some community disaster such as a food shortage or an epidemic. Whereupon, a diviner must be consulted, who determines by ritual means the cause of the disturbance and prescribes, in accordance with this knowledge, the appropriate counteracting religious ceremony or ritual.

The underlying purpose of the curing ceremony is to put the maladjusted individual or the community as a whole back into harmony with the universe. Significantly, this is done, not by the shaman or priest acting upon the individual and changing him, nor by any action, by shaman or priest, designed to alter the forces of the universe. It is done by re-enacting one of a complex series of religious dramas which represent, in highly abstract terms, the events, far back in Navaho history, whereby the culture heroes first established harmony between man and nature and so made the world fit for human occupation. By re-enacting these events, or some portion of them, the present disturbance, by a kind of sympathetic magic, is compensated and harmony between man and universe restored. The ill person then gets well, or the community disaster is alleviated, since these misfortunes were but symptoms of a disturbed relation to nature.

From these numerous and very important patterns of Navaho religious behavior, it seems to me

we can abstract a dominant motif belonging to the Navaho thought world. The motif has been well put by Kluckhohn and Leighton, who also illustrate it in many other aspects of Navaho culture. They call it, "Nature is more powerful than man," and amplify this in part by the Navaho premise "that nature will take care of them if they behave as they should and do as she directs" (1946: 227–28). In short, to the Navaho, the way to the good life lies not in modifying nature to man's needs or in changing man's nature but rather in discovering the proper relation of nature to man and in maintaining that relationship intact.

Turning now to the Navaho language, let us look at some aspects of the verb structure, illustrated in the following two forms:

nìńtį́ *you have lain down*
nìšíńłtį́ *you have put, laid me down*

Both these verbs are in the second person of the perfective mode (Hoijer 1946); the ń- marks this inflection. Both also have a prefix nì-, not the same but subtly different in meaning. The nì- of the first means [*movement*] *terminating in a position of rest,* that of the second [*movement*] *ending at a given point*. The second form has the causative prefix t- and incorporates the first person object, expressed in this form by ši-. The stem -tį́, common to both forms, is defined *one animate being moves.*

The theme of the first verb, composed of nì- . . . -tį́, means *one animate being moves to a position of rest,* that is, *one animate being lies down.* In the second verb the meaning of the theme, nì- . . .- ł-tį́, is *cause movement of one animate being to end at a given point* and so, by extension, *put an animate being down* or *lay an animate being down.*

Note now that the first theme includes in its meaning what in English we should call both the actor and the action; these are not, in Navaho, expressed by separate morphemes. The subject pronoun prefix ń- serves then simply to identify a particular being with the class of possible beings already delimited by the theme. It functions, in short, to individuate one belonging to the class *animate being in motion to a position of rest*. The theme of the second verb, by reason of the causative l-, includes in its meaning what in English would be called action and goal. Again the pronoun ši-, as a consequence, simply identifies or individuates one of a class of possible beings defined already in the theme itself. It should be emphasized that the forms used here as illustration are in no sense unusual; this is the regular pattern of the Navaho verb, repeated over and over again in my data.

We are now ready to isolate, from this necessarily brief analysis, a possible fashion of speaking peculiar to Navaho. The Navaho speaks of "actors" and "goals" (the terms are inappropriate to Navaho), not as performers of actions or as ones upon whom actions are performed, as in English, but as entities linked to actions already defined in part as pertaining especially to classes of beings. The form which is glossed *you have lain down* is better understood you [*belong to, equal one of*] *a class of animate beings which has moved to rest*. Similarly the second form, glossed *you have put, laid me down* should read *you, as agent, have set a class of animate beings, to which I belong, in motion to a given point*.

This fashion of speaking, it seems to me, is wholly consistent with the dominant motif we saw in Navaho religious practices. Just as in his religious-curing activities the Navaho sees himself as adjusting to a universe that is given, so in his habits of speaking does he link individuals to actions and movements distinguished, not only as actions and movements, but as well in terms of the entities in action or movement. This division of nature into classes of entity in action or movement is the universe that is given, the behavior of human beings or of any being individuated from the mass is customarily reported by assignment to one or other of these given divisions. . . .

## REFERENCES

Boas, Franz (ed.) (1911). "Introduction," *Handbook of American Indian Languages,* Part I. Washington, D.C.

Hoijer, Harry (1946). "The Apachean Verb, Part III: The Prefixes for Mode and Tense," *International Journal of American Linguistics* 12:1–13—(1953);

"The Relation of Language to Culture." In *Anthropology Today* (by A. L. Kroeber and others), pp. 554–73. Chicago, University of Chicago Press.

Kluckhohn, Clyde, and Dorothea Leighton (1946). *The Navaho*. Cambridge, Harvard University Press.

Mandelbaum, David G. (ed.) (1949). *Selected Writings of Edward Sapir*. Berkeley and Los Angeles, University of California Press.

Sapir, Edward (1931). "Conceptual Categories in Primitive Languages," *Science* 74:578.

Voegelin, C. F. (1949) "Linguistics without Meaning and Culture without Words," *Word* 5:36–42.

Whorf, Benjamin L. (1952). *Collected Papers on Metalinguistics*. Washington, D.C., Department of State, Foreign Service Institute.

# Language as the Bridge

VERNER C. BICKLEY

*What greatly attracts me to the Buddha is the civilized concern which he shows for the temperate use of language.*

*For him a right way of speaking is one of the strands in the eightfold path leading to enlightenment and the end of suffering.*

*To attain this right way all lies, all bitter and double-tongued words, all idle babbling, must be avoided.*

*So equally must harsh abusive speech, arrogant usage heeding only itself, and crude expression tending to corrupt.*

*Style also is important, and bombastic inflated language is condemned no less than gentility and plausible fine words.*

*Above all the Buddha values restraint with words, knowing that silence is often more expressive than the finished poem.*

*Language of the Buddha—Raymond Tong*

## INTRODUCTION

Language is a form of human activity which makes it possible for human beings to think of past, present, and future situations and make plans relating to them. As a mode of thought, it is not simply an instrument which conveys and receives messages. It does, however, enable the individual to communicate with and stimulate responses from persons in his and other speech communities. The messages

From Stephen Bochner (ed.), *Cultures in Contact: Studies in Cross-Cultural Interaction* (Oxford: Pergamon Press, 1982), pp. 99–125. Reprinted by permission of the publisher and author. Verner C. Bickley is Director of the Culture Learning Institute, East-West Center, Honolulu, Hawaii.

which are passed between individuals do not always lead to better understanding. Both cultural and linguistic barriers exist which may sour relations. The fact that everyday things are done differently in different cultures often leads to misunderstanding, and even within an apparently homogeneous language community, varieties of the same language may be culturally divisive.

In some societies linguistic rivalry may be associated with ideas of status and class. For example, the use of the wrong variety of language in a particular situation may create obstacles to social and financial advancement or barriers can be set up through the differences revealed in the use of different linguistic "codes." Geertz (1963) included differences over language issues among the foci around which "primordial discontent" tends to crystallize and considered that several of these foci are usually involved concurrently, sometimes at cross-purposes with one another. Regional conflicts, for example, might stem from differences in language and culture, whilst religion and custom can form a basis for national disunity.

Language differences can exacerbate tensions between individuals in the same language community, or in different language communities within a single country, or they can create an intercultural problem which affects individuals from different countries.

Languages and varieties of languages can, however, provide a "bridge to understanding" when they are used to *mediate* between persons from the same or from different communities. The languages (or language varieties) themselves may function in a mediating way, or the individuals participating in a speech event may employ particular languages or varieties of languages for mediating purposes, as indicated in Table 1.

... What follows in the first part of the article is a description of ways in which language and language varieties are used by individuals, some of whom may have intercultural roles to play as mediators. In the second part, some examples are given of languages which are selected by governments to mediate between different cultures of a particular society and between societies.

**Table 1** Use of Languages and Language Varieties for Purposes of Mediation

| | |
|---|---|
| INDIVIDUALS | Languages and varieties of languages and forms of "linguistic etiquette" used by individuals for mediating purposes in their own cultures and language communities (choices may be habituated as well as subjectively motivated). |
| | Languages and varieties of languages used by individuals for mediating purposes in situations involving persons from cultures and language communities other than their own. Knowledge of aspects of the "other" culture, as well as the person's own culture, is important. |
| | Languages and varieties of languages used by individuals for mediating purposes in situations involving persons from countries other than their own. |
| GOVERNMENTS | Languages and varieties of languages selected by governments for mediating purposes *intra*nationally. |
| | Languages and varieties of languages selected by governments for mediating purposes *inter*nationally. |

## LANGUAGES CHOSEN BY INDIVIDUALS FOR MEDIATING PURPOSES

### Bilingualism, Multilingualism, and Mediation

It is possible for members of a particular cultural group to belong to several language communities, one of which may be common to all of the groups. For example, the increasing number of people in Indonesia who use a form or forms of Bahasa Indonesia (Indonesian language—the national language and the official language) constitute a common language community. Each person in this community, however, will have his own idiolect—his own characteristic usage, which may, of course, change in the course of his life and which may interfere with mutual understanding. He may also belong to two, or more than two, communities, ranging in our example from the Javanese and Sundanese language communities in Java, the most densely populated island and area in the country, to the Christian Batak speech community of Sumatra.

Membership of more than one language community involves degrees of bilingualism and multilingualism which will vary according to the use of the languages concerned. Thus, in many societies, the need to make use of two or more languages is the result of geographical, historical, or political causes. In some countries, for example, the language of two predominant linguistic groups may have national status, and the members of such groups may be required to learn both languages.

Thus, in the Cape, Transvaal, and Orange Free State provinces of South Africa, English and Afrikaans are compulsory for all children. In the Natal province, English is the medium of instruction and Afrikaans is taught as a second language. Proficiency in both languages is a condition of appointment to the civil service and to posts in the school system.

In Canada bilingualism, as defined by the Royal Commission on Bilingualism and Biculturalism (1967), applies only to the nation's two official languages, English and French. There are, therefore, many persons considered unilingual in terms of the two official languages, but who are actually bilingual. Generally there are Canadians of ethnic origins other than French or British, born in Canada or abroad, and who first learned the language of their own group—for example, German, Ukrainian, or Italian. They have subsequently acquired, for mediating purposes between themselves and members of the British and French groups, one of Canada's official languages, most often English.

## Language Varieties Determined According to Their Users

Although the census of Canada listed so many different ethnic origins and "first languages" within the Canadian population that it was impossible for the commission to study the contribution of each group separately, most schools, in practice, provide instruction in English and/or French. The situation is different in Singapore, which has a bilingual policy of providing parity of treatment to four official languages: Malay, Tamil, Chinese, and English. All four languages are available up to the secondary level, so that in each language-medium school there is always a second official language taught and used in instruction. However, the major language (or medium) may not be the "first language" of the students. The second official language used in instruction is often a "third language," and there is also a variety of contacts with other languages.

In the English-medium schools, for example, English is used as a medium for the study of a wide range of subjects geared to the School Certificate examination. The students studying these subjects and the teachers teaching them move in different language communities and use varieties of languages inside these communities. Thus a student of Chinese ethnic background who uses Hokkien at home may be taught history by a teacher of Indian ethnic background who speaks Tamil in his home. Both student and teacher, therefore, leave different language communities in the home for another language community in the school, which they join for educational purposes. The Hokkien student, however, might speak a variety of Chinese which would be unintelligible to a Chinese student living in the same street or studying in the same class as himself, whilst the Indian teacher, although distinguished by

his own characteristic usages of Tamil, would probably be employing a variety of it that would be intelligible to other users of the language in the environment of his home or his school. In other words the student, although still belonging to the Chinese language community, may speak a variety of Chinese which could be classified as a language or a *dialect* not necessarily mutually intelligible with other varieties of Chinese. The teacher, on the other hand, may speak a variety of Tamil which, although it could still be classified as a *dialect,* would have sufficient features similar enough to other varieties to make it intelligible to users of these varieties.

The English language (which has developed its own Singaporean characteristics) serves in such a situation, not only as an educational medium, but also as a language which mediates between two persons and possibly two cultures: the Indian and the Chinese.

English in Singapore, as we shall see, is regarded as an international language which is highly functional to economic progress. There is also increasing evidence (e.g., Chiew 1972; Murray 1971; Tan and Chew 1970) that it is developing into a *lingua franca* which mediates between different ethnic groups, at least among the middle- and upper-class segments of the population, and that it is supporting the emergence of a "Singapore identity."

In the Chinese-medium schools of Singapore, the Pekingese form of Mandarin has been designated as the major language of instruction. Students and teachers in these schools are usually Chinese by ethnic origin but may use different dialects of Mandarin or different Chinese languages in their homes. Thus a student who uses Hokkien at home may be taught geography by a Chinese teacher who speaks Hakka in his own home but teaches through the medium of the Kwangsi form of Mandarin. The kind of Mandarin taught will, of course, depend on the teacher's own idiolect and on whether or not he learned the Mandarin in the People's Republic of China, Taiwan, Hong Kong, or other other areas where the language is current. In this case, teacher and student, although from the same language community and of the same racial background, use different and mutually unintelligible varieties of the language at home but make use of a third variety of the language which, like English in the English-medium schools, may serve a mediating purpose as well as an educational purpose. The mediation here, however, is not between persons from two cultures, rather it is between persons whose ancestors came from one society, but whose "first languages" are mutually unintelligible.

## Language Varieties Determined by Social Functions

The preceding examples show that varieties of language can be determined according to their users. These varieties are determined by the regions of their origin or by social factors. Varieties are, however, also determined by the way each member of a language community employs language for different social purposes. *Medium* distinguishes the different forms of language used for speech and writing. The extent of differentiation between these two forms varies among different speech communities and, in some cases, has historical causes. In the case of classical Chinese, for example, writing and speech were widely separated so that the written language was not affected by dialectal changes and even in its most colloquial form differed from the spoken language. The written language was the carrier of the ancient Confucian culture, and the skillful calligraphy necessary to express this culture was regarded as an art equivalent to the art of printing in the West.

Convergence of the spoken and written forms of language took place as the result of the work of the "May 4 Movement" in 1920. The Cantonese, Fukienese, Swatow, and Amoy communities, each with their own dialects, had to become acquainted with a form of Mandarin which was simpler than the classical medium it replaced, but which was to serve a similar purpose in that it made accessible the content of the classical system; in other words, it served as a link between a number of different ethnic and linguistic groups. Here the medium is the mediator. . . .

## Code-Switching and Mediation

As we have seen, a mediating role may be assumed by an individual who is able to employ more than one language or dialect and is thus able to "switch codes." Bailey (1969) describes how in the Kond hill country of India, persons known as "Digaloos," who were invariably "Untouchables," were employed as middle-men and as mediators between the Konds and the Oriya-speaking persons from the Orissa plains around the Kond hills, who were hired by the East India Company to make trading contacts with the hill people. As bilinguals able to converse with both the Kui-speaking Konds and the Oriya-speaking Orissa peoples, the Digaloos were able to bring both groups together and at the same time to derive a satisfactory profit from the arrangement. . . .

Varieties of language, such as *linguae francae* (or contact languages), which have sprung from metropolitan languages, are used to establish rapport between groups of people who do not have a common language. *Pidgins* are examples of *linguae francae* used for such purposes. Some pidgins were used for centuries as mediating trade languages, for example, Black Portuguese, Black French, and Black English as used on the west coast of Africa, and Swahili on the eastern coastline of the continent. These hybrid languages, based usually on metropolitan languages, but differing as to pronunciation, vocabulary, and syntax, become *creoles* when they are acquired by the children of pidgin speakers as first (native) languages. Creoles may be used in addition to the parent languages to enable two groups to make culture contact. They may, however, eventually displace one of the parent languages and, in consequence, lose something of their value as languages of mediation.

A language used on a large scale for purposes of international communication may be described as a true *lingua franca*. With approximately 500 million users on four continents, a strong claim may be made for English as such a language although, as Quirk and Kachru (1980) point out, there are no intrinsic linguistic characteristics which entitle

English to this status. The users of English differ in the uses they make of it and the ways in which they use it, so that a *distance* is being created between native varieties and non-native varieties which is leading on the one hand to the "nativization" of English[1] while, on the other hand, English has had an effect on a number of major indigenous languages in the Pacific, Asia, and Africa.

Despite the apparent fragility of English in a country such as India, following the achievement of political independence the language began to gain ground after it was adopted as a link (and therefore a *mediating*) language for national and international communication. Kachru (1978) notes that English has become a part of the culture of South Asia and argues that the language has been South Asianized and that it has had a marked effect not only on South Asian languages but also on South Asian literatures. South Asian English literature is a manifestation of what has been called the literature of cross-cultural contact, described by Amirthanayagam (1979) as the artistic expression of the harmonies and discords created by the process of cross-cultural interaction. . . .

## Translation, Translators, and Mediation

Languages and language varieties, as has been indicated, are determined according to their users and according to the different social functions which require their participation. They may be regarded, therefore, as individually differentiated forms of behavior determined specifically by communicative situations.

Bickley (1975) has noted that translation problems provide persuasive evidence that it is difficult to express for one speech community experiences that are rooted in another. He observes that, to some extent because of differences between ethnographical and psychological approaches to the issue, a debate still continues as to whether or not the difficulties occur because language differences predispose cognitive processes to operate in different ways or because of differences in the social structures of such communities.

The links between language and culture and thought, which have concerned scholars for many years, raise difficulties for the translator since the "real linguistic fact" (Malinowski 1935) is the full utterance within its "context of situation," and a translation can never therefore be just a substitution of word for word, but must involve the translation of whole contexts. Misunderstandings caused by inadequate translation run the gamut from laughable to most serious. The *Honolulu Advertiser* newspaper of 13 May 1974, reported that two words and someone who translated them incorrectly from Italian to English were blamed for sensational—but erroneous—statements that Capuchin monks were abandoning their traditional vows of celibacy. According to the superintendent of the Capuchin College in Washington, 29.6 percent of the monks said that they wanted to have "intimo rapporto" (closer friendship) with women. International wire services translated the Italian phrase as "sexual relations."

A grave example of misunderstanding caused by the ambiguity of a Japanese word is the meaning given by different individuals to the word *mokusatsu*—the word used when Japan responded to the Potsdam Declaration. According to Kazuo Kawai (1950), who during the war years was editor of the *Nippon Times,* rough translations of *mokusatsu* are "to be silent," "to withhold comment," or "to ignore." Kawai suggests that "to withhold comment" probably came closest to the true meaning, implying that while something was being held back, there was information that would be forthcoming. Kawai contends that this meaning was what the Japanese government wished to convey. However, Tokyo's newspapers and the Domei Press Agency reported that the government held the Potsdam Declaration in contempt, and that the Suzuki government had rejected it. The Pacific War Research Society in their *Japan's Longest Day* (1968) noted that literally *moku* means "to be silent" and *satsu* means "to kill." They point out that in the *Kenkyusha Dictionary* the word is defined as "take no notice of; treat with silent contempt; ignore by keeping silent." It also means "remain in a wise and masterly inactivity." It is their view that it is this latter definition that Suzuki had in mind. At a news conference a day after the government announcment had appeared in the press, Suzuki called the Potsdam Declaration a "thing of no great value," and used the term *mokusatsu.* According to the foreign minister that was not the intention of the cabinet. Nevertheless, the damage had been done.[2]

Nida (1964) describes one form of translation (intersemiotic) as the transference of a message from one kind of symbolic system to another. For example, in semaphore, the meaning of a flag is rendered as a verbal message. Intersemiotic translation is, of course, necessary across languages and their cultures since not all language is verbal, and communication includes gestures, facial expressions and posture, and features of nonverbal phonology such as loudness, tempo, and pitch. Ekman, Friesen, and Ellsworth (1972) have postulated that persons of different cultures exhibit the same facial expressions when they experience such emotions as anger, disgust, fear, happiness, sadness, and surprise. Brislin (1976) notes that when people speak the same language they know what facial signals go with what words, and so can interpret the *interaction* between these two signals. But when a communicator interacts with a person who speaks a different language, the other person might be able to study the communicator's facial cues but will *not* be able to associate these cues with exact words and sentences. Hence more mistakes of attribution of intent will be made in such a situation, unless there is a good interpreter who can understand and communicate the entire meaning contained in the message. As Boucher (1979) has pointed out, not only does the accuracy of translation affect the comparability of studies across cultures, it also affects the comparability across researchers within the same culture. . . .

Good interpreters in such cases would need to know both languages well and to recognize that a problem exists. They would then be equipped to act as links between persons from two cultures and thus be able to serve as mediators.

## The Law, Lawyers, and Mediation

*Intralingual translation* is defined by Nida (1964) as rewording something within the same language. As such it is of great concern to lawyers and those interested in legal processes. The law, with its verbal apparatus of "rights," "duties," and "wrongs," is a particular application of language as a means of social control. The problem is that, like the cultures of which they are a part, languages are dynamic and therefore raise problems for the lawyer as mediator in his own culture or society (which may contain a number of cultures), or when he plays the mediating role interculturally, on the international scene. Glanville Williams (1945) has remarked on the ambiguities of words, used referentially, which give trouble to lawyers not only in manipulating their own technical language but also in the construction of non-legal language in documents. Many words change their meaning in the course of time, some becoming restricted, some widened, and some transferred by metaphor, the original meaning either remaining or disappearing.

In the English language, for example, "asylum," originally any refuge, now means in particular a refuge for those mentally diseased, but the old meaning has not quite disappeared, for example, "political asylum." "Accident," etymologically, can mean anything that happens, and this meaning is preserved in the judicial determination that murder is an "accident" within the Workmen's Compensation Acts in Britain. The word can, however, also mean damage not caused intentionally, or damage not caused by fault. "Committee" originally meant one individual to whom something was committed, the stress being on the last syllable. Both this meaning and this pronunciation have survived in some contexts, for example, in British Lunacy Law; but generally nowadays a committee is not one person but a body of persons, and in this meaning the stress is shifted to the middle syllable.

In addition to their referential functions, words also have emotive functions which express affective or volitional attitudes or arouse such attitudes in others. As such they produce further headaches for the lawyer, when used either intraculturally or interculturally, since the term "emotive" covers "love, joy, hope, wonder, desire, reverence, obedience, amusement, sympathy, social, moral and religious feeling, rage, fear, grief, horror, disgust, and every other affective–volitional state" (Williams 1945, p. 887).

The commonest type of emotive statement is the value judgment, a statement of approval or disapproval, usually in the form of a generalization. Value judgments need delicate handling by the mediating lawyer when he is involved in intercultural disputes since "rights," "duties," even "justice" itself, have different meanings in different cultures.

## Experts and Immigrants As Mediators

Persons mediating between cultures do so in a variety of social roles. Taft (1981) lists thirteen such roles.[3] One other—the role of *expert*—will be added to the list and discussed here.

## Experts and Counterparts

Development assistance may involve the appointment to a host country of a foreign expert who may be a citizen of the country which is providing the assistance, or a citizen of a "developed" or "developing" country supported by an international organization. Typically, the expert works with a "counterpart," a national of the country in which the project is being carried out. The expert may be an administrator, an adviser to a counterpart who is in an executive, decision-making position, or he may have been recruited to assist with institution-building through, for example, the training of personnel.

In a manual prepared by the World Federation for Mental Health, edited by Margaret Mead and published by UNESCO in 1953, the expert is identified as a person who is immediately concerned, at any level, with purposive technological change, and is sent to bring the benefits of his experience to countries applying for technical assistance.

The manual was intended to be a guide to the kind of thinking and the kind of activity which might be of value in facilitating the technological change itself and in preserving the cultural integrity of those among whom the changes were to be introduced. It acknowledged that each culture was unique, that each particular situation within which a change was occurring or was to be made was unique, that it was not possible to lay down prescriptions for what was to be done in any particular case, and that there must always be specific cooperation with members of the particular community in which a demonstration was to be made or a new practice tried out.

The problem of language was recognized as a serious one. Exact meanings had to be explored; questions of adapting old words to new ideas, as opposed to coining new words, had to be weighed; and choices had to be made among rival dialects and local languages. There was no possible prescription except the insistence upon taking into account the culture and the situation and the individuals involved.

The manual recommended that working groups planning the introduction of technical change should consist of members of more than two cultures. Such groups should include the members of the culture in which the change was being introduced, members of the culture whose developed professional skills and resources were being drawn upon, and members of a third culture, who could maintain a certain objectivity and prevent the consuming group and the resource group from being deadlocked or developing an isolated bit of behavior in which conflicts between, for example, Indonesian and American value systems might become frozen.

What applied to the involvement of members of different cultures and different levels of organization applied equally to the inclusion of different professions; having more than two professions and including one with less involvement would provide steadiness of teamwork.

Such measures were a protection against the intrusion of bias, and a certain guarantee that the programs developed and the steps taken could both embody and be to a degree unhampered by the vested interests, and old and new, conscious and unconscious, prejudices of all those concerned.

*It will be recognized that this recommendation is again based on the principle that culture is mediated through persons, and that a culture, or a profession, or a level of administration, or a point of view cannot be represented by a charter, a diagram, or a printed description, but only by living human beings who themselves embody the position which is to be taken into account (Mead 1953, p. 308).*

The manual contains some perceptive short studies of aspects of technical change. It recognized, as has been indicated, the importance of participation by representatives of the host culture (the counterparts) and envisaged teams which would also include representatives of third cultures. Experts, counterparts, and third-culture representatives would all serve as mediators. . . .

In the first part of this article we have examined some of the ways in which languages are used by individuals for mediating purposes. Participants in a speech event from the same language community may use their common language for mediation. . . . These mediators must serve some of the interests of groups operating on both the community and the national level, and they must also cope with the conflicts raised by the collision of these interests.

Persons from the same country may come from different language communities. The chances of their dialogue being mutually satisfactory may be increased if each is able to make use of a third language, which may be a national language such as Bahasa Indonesia, or an international language such as English which has acquired certain national characteristics as has English in India. But knowledge of a third language alone is not enough. The speakers are more likely to be able to mediate successfully with each other if they also have some knowledge of each other's culture. So, in Indonesia, in the case of a discussion between, say, a Batak speaker from Sumatra and a Javanese speaker from Java, it would be advantageous if both understood the rules of discourse in each other's communities, although it would probably not be necessary to adhere to these rules in the third "mediating" language, which could be Bahasa Indonesia. . . .

If the participants were unable to speak to each other in a third language, then it is possible that the mediating services of a third speaker may be necessary. The mediator in such a case, and also in the case of a situation involving persons from different nations as well as different speech communities, must be familiar not only with the languages of the other two participants, but should also have some knowledge of each other's culture. . . .

## LANGUAGE USED TO MEDIATE BETWEEN SOCIETIES AND CULTURES

This second section of this article notes examples of languages which are selected deliberately by governments for use intraculturally. Such "language planning" may be conducted for political, economic, and social reasons and concomitantly for purposes of mediating between different cultural groups as in, for example, West Malaysia, Singapore, Indonesia, the Philippines, and the United States.

In the case of a relatively "unilingual" country such as Japan, "language planning" may still proceed as, for example, the decision to adopt English as a school subject in a majority of Japanese schools to introduce Japanese students to a language of international communication; or the decision to provide considerable financial and administrative support for the teaching of Japanese in other countries, particularly in Asia.

When individual languages are compared, it is possible to distinguish them along scales in a typological classification. Stewart (1968) divided languages along one axis according to type and along a second axis according to function. The differentiation into types is made in terms of four attributes of which the first is *standardization* (whether or not there exists for the language a codified set of grammatical and lexical norms which are formally accepted and learned by the language's users); the second is *autonomy* (whether or not the linguistic system is "unique and independent" and autonomous in terms of any other linguistic system with which it is not historically related); the third is *historicity* (whether or not the language is the result of a process of development through use over time); and the fourth is *vitality* (whether or not the language has an existing, unisolated community of native speakers).

Stewart notes that in the typology *standardization* is used to indicate *formal* standardization. Few of the world's languages have been codified in this way. However, many languages have been *informally* standardized "when there is a certain amount of normalization of language behavior in the direction of some linguistic usage with high social prestige" (p. 534).

The four attributes can be combined in various ways to produce (in Stewart's typology) seven language types, ranging from standard to pidgin. These are *standard,* combining all four attributes: examples are English, French, and German which are official languages of modern Europe; *classical,* combining the first, second, and third, for example, classical or literary Arabic; *artificial,* marked by the first and second but not by the third and fourth, for example, Esperanto and Voläpuk; *vernacular,* combining the second, third, and fourth, but not the first attribute, for example, most tribal languages of Africa; *dialect,* combining the third and fourth attributes but not the first and second, for example, Schwyzertütsch in Switzerland; *creole,* possessing only the fourth attribute; and *pidgin* possessing none of the four attributes. . . .

## Functional Classification

Languages may also be compared as to *function.* Different languages can have differing functions as media of communication within a state and each may perform several roles. The functional categories suggested by Stewart (1968) are:

1. *Official:* the use of a language as the legally appropriate one for all political and cultural representative purposes on a nationwide basis.

2. *Provincial:* the use of a language provincially or regionally.

3. *Wider communication:* the use of a language, other than an official or a provincial one, across language boundaries within a nation.

4. *International:* the use of a language as a major medium of communication which is international in scope, e.g., for diplomatic relations, foreign trade, et cetera.

5. *Capital:* the use of a language as the primary medium of communication in the vicinity of the national capital.

6. *Group:* the use of a language primarily by the members of a single ethnic or cultural group, or subgroup.

7. *Educational:* the use of a language, other than an official or provincial one, as a medium of instruction, either regionally or nationally.

8. *School subject:* the language which is commonly taught (other than one which already has an official or provincial function) as a subject in secondary and/or higher education.

9. *Literary:* the use of a language primarily for literary or scholarly activities.

10. *Religious:* the use of a language primarily in connection with the practice of a religion.

To Stewart's categories should be added *National,* since national languages are distinguished in some countries from official languages. In Singapore, for example, Mandarin, Chinese, Malay, Tamil, and English are official languages, but Malay has also been given the status of a national language.

These categories can be cross-classified with language types. Thus, in West Malaysia, Malay is a standard language according to type which also functions as a language of wider communication, an international language, a school subject, and, to some extent, a literary language. In Singapore, English is an official language and, in common with Mandarin, Malay, and Tamil, a standard language. In Indonesia, English is a standard language, an international language, and a school subject. . . .

## CONCLUSION

In this article we have examined some of the ways in which languages and varieties of language are used for purposes of mediation, that is, to create "bridges to understanding" for individuals from the same cultures or from different cultures. We have observed that variations within languages and varieties of languages can serve different social contexts and can have different mediating functions, and we have given examples of bilingual and multilingual situations in which mediating roles are assumed by individuals, and of languages that have been selected deliberately by governments as languages of mediation.

Communicative acts are related to aspects of social reality which are determined by cultural norms. Further study is needed of the mediating function of certain speech acts, as those acts are both extrinsically and intrinsically determined.

## NOTES

1. For example, in West African English, *chewing-sponge* or *chewing stick* ("twig used for cleaning teeth"). See Kachru (1980) for other examples.

2. I am indebted to Mr. Norman Geschwind of the East-West Center Culture Learning Institute for drawing my attention to Mr. Kawai's article, and to the publication of the Pacific War Research Society.

3. Interpreter, tourist guide, industrial relations conciliator, marriage counsellor, ombudsman, student counsellor, native welfare officer, representative of ethnic communities on a government board, factory foreman, representative of workers on a management committee, manager of touring sportsmen or entertainers, business agent for a foreign company, intelligence agent.

## REFERENCES

Amirthanayagam, J. G. (1979). *Contact Literature in Cross-National Perspectives*. Honolulu, Hawaii (East–West Center Program Catalogue), p. 23.

Bailey, F. G. (1969). *Stratagems and Spoils*. Oxford, Oxford University Press.

Bickley, V. C. (1975). "Culture, Cognition and the Curriculum." *East–West Center Culture and Language Learning Newsletter* 4 (1), 1–11.

Bochner, S. (ed.) (1981). *The Mediating Person*. Boston, Schenkman.

Boucher, J. (1979). "Culture and Emotion." *Perspectives on Cross-cultural Psychology*. (ed. Marsella, A., R. Tharpe, and T. Ciborowski). New York, Academic Press.

Brislin, R. (1976). "Introduction." *Translation: Applications and Research* (ed. Brislin, R.). New York, Gardner.

Canada (1967). *Report of the Royal Commission on Bilingualism and Biculturalism*. Ottawa, Queen's Printer.

Chiew, S. K. (1972). "Singapore National Identity." Unpublished master's thesis, University of Singapore.

Ekman, P., W. F. Friesen, and P. Ellsworth (1972). *Emotion in the Human Face: Guidelines for Research and an Integration of Findings*. New York, Pergamon.

Ervin-Tripp, S. (1968). "Interaction of Language, Topic and Listener" *Readings in the Sociology of Language* (ed. Fishman, J.). Paris, Mouton.

Frege, G. (1952). "Sense and Reference." *Translations from the Philosophical Writings of Gottlieb Frege* (ed. Geach, P. and M. Black). Oxford, Blackwell.

Geertz, C. (1960). *The Religion of Java*. New York, Free Press of Glencoe.

Geertz, C. (1963). *Old Societies and New States*. New York, Free Press of Glencoe.

Kachru, B. (1978). "English in South Asia." *Advances in the Study of Societal Multilingualism* (ed. Fishman, J.). The Hague, Mouton.

Kachru, B. (1980). "The Pragmatics of Non-Native Varieties of English." *English for Cross-Cultural Communication* (ed. Smith, L.). London, Macmillan.

Kawai, K. (1950). "Mokusatsu, Japan's Response to the Potsdam Declaration." *Pacific Historical Review*, 19, 409–14.

Malinowski, B. (1935). *Coral Gardens and Their Magic*. London, Allen & Unwin.

Marshall, L. (1968). "Sharing, Talking and Giving: Relief of Social Tensions among Kung Bushmen." *Readings in the Sociology of Language* (ed. Fishman, J.). Paris, Mouton.

Mead, M. (1953). *Cultural Patterns and Technical Change*. Paris, UNESCO.

Mühlhäusler, P. (1974). *Pidginization and Simplification of Language*. Canberra, Department of Linguistics, Research School of Pacific Studies, The Australian National University.

Murray, D. (1971). "Multilanguage Education and Bilingualism: The Formation of Social Brokers in Singapore." Unpublished doctoral dissertation, Stanford University.

Nida, E. A. (1964). *Towards a Science of Translating*. Leiden, Brill.

Pacific War Research Society (1968). *Japan's Longest Day*. Tokyo, Kodansha International.

Phillips, H. P. (1965). *Thai Peasant Personality*. Berkeley, Calif., University of California Press.

Quirk, R. and B. Kachru. (1980). "Introduction." *English for Cross-Cultural Communication* (ed. Smith, L.). London, Macmillan.

Richards, I, A. (1953). "Toward a Theory of Translating." *Studies in Chinese Thought* (American Anthropological Association) 55, Memoir 75. Chicago, University of Chicago Press.

Roeming, R. F. (1970). "Bilingualism and the National Interest." *Report of the Twenty-First Annual Round Table Meeting on Linguistics and Language Studies* (ed. Alatis, J.). Washington, D.C., Georgetown University Press.

Stewart, A. W. (1968). "A Sociolinguistic Typology for Describing National Multilingualism." *Readings in the Sociology of Language* (ed. Fishman, J.). Paris, Mouton.

Taft, R. (1981). "The Personality of the Mediating Person." *The Mediating Person* (ed. Bochner, S.). Boston, Schenkman.

Tan, R. and S. F. Chew. (1970). "An Analysis of the Attitudes of Pupils in Chinese Medium, English Medium and Integrated Schools on Selected Variables." Unpublished paper, University of Singapore.

Tong, R. (1975). "Language of the Buddha." *English Language Teaching* 30 (1), 3.

Williams, G. (1945). "Language and the Law." *Law Quarterly Review* 61 (2), 180; 61 (5), 887–8.

Wolf, E. R. (1956). "Aspects of Group Relations in a Complex Society: Mexico." *American Anthropologist* 58 (6), 1065–78.

# Reasons for the Lack of Argumentation and Debate in the Far East

CARL B. BECKER

China and Japan have been much in the spotlight recently, for their political and economic dominance in Asia. Japan is already counted among the world's industrial leaders, and China is also undergoing rapid modernization. Both countries have adopted the forms of Western governments, media, and communications systems. Yet communications on a person-to-person level operate under very different premises than in the West. Western Asia-watchers expect that Asian languages are very different from Western languages, and then try to compensate by careful translation and interpretation techniques. What they often fail to understand until too late, however, is that both the content of the dialogue and the assumptions about what represents acceptable and proper communications are very different in the Orient than in the West.

In particular, the use of public speaking for the debating of conflicting viewpoints, especially popular in election years in the West, has generally been unacceptable in the Orient. This essay will examine the attitudes of Chinese and Japanese towards speech communication in public settings. While there are many differences between China and Japan apparent today, they share common cultural backgrounds and assumptions in the areas which we shall consider as contributing to their common aversion to

From *International Journal of Intercultural Relations* 10 (1986), 75–92. Reprinted by permission of the publisher. Carl B. Becker is Assistant Professor of Asian Curriculum Research and Development at the University of Hawaii.

public debate. We shall focus specifically on three areas of oriental culture which have tended to discourage argumentation: (1) social history, (2) linguistic features, and (3) philosophy and religion. A longer [article] might identify important subtle distinctions between China and Japan on each of these subjects, but for the purposes of our study, we shall argue that the same factors have functioned in both societies to downplay the importance of argumentation and debate.

## SOCIAL HISTORY

China and Japan have been densely populated, labor-intensive rice-growing cultures since ancient times. Their survival depended upon the peaceful cooperation of people in each community for the irrigation and planting of rice. The people were unable or unwilling to change their vocations and residential areas, for both geographic and political reasons, so there was little change in their life-patterns from year to year. The cycles of planting and harvest continued inexorably, and there was little room for radical experimentation with new methods of agriculture, for if a new method failed, some of the populace would likely starve. When travel and change were thus minimized, experience could be accumulated only through the repetitions of years, and the one who had the most experience was naturally the village elder. When a flood or plague threatened the community, the elder was the one consulted about what worked best against such problems when they last occurred some decades previously.

Through such historical evolution, China and Japan developed hierarchical societies in which the very notion of two people being absolutely equal became almost inconceivable. Age became equated with authority, and even twins addressed each other as "older brother" and "younger brother," depending on who emerged a few minutes earlier. Age and rank became the unquestioned basis for distinction of inferior and superior. Once the superior person had been identified by age and rank, his word was taken as law, without further logical examination. ... Such societies left little room for the develop-ment of ideals like "liberty, equality, or individuality" (Nakamura 1964, pp. 205–207). Authority and obligation proceeded not from reason, but from the superior status of the elderly and the superior power of the landed class. ...

Since the individual could not be heard nor recognized on his own, ... there developed the additional tendency towards standardization over individuality. Free thought and individual expression were discouraged, giving way to the safer and surer domain of classical quotation. This attitude can already be seen by the time of Confucius, 2,500 years ago. Throughout Chinese history, there were purges and book-burnings, when all but the few texts approved by officialdom were destroyed, and possession of contraband books carried the death penalty (Goodrich 1935, pp. 39–42). Thus the thought control of Mao's China was nothing new to the Chinese. In such circumstances, safe ritual phrases tend to take over from self-expression. This influence continues to be pervasive even today in both cultures. Speeches at weddings are among the few times that an oriental is ever expected to address a large number of people. Research has shown that these speeches are almost invariably composed of standardized phrases within standardized formulae and structures (Saito 1973). Japanese word processors have prestored a hundred set greetings and phrases from which the operator can compile complete letters without ever thinking up a sentence of his own. Thus there is little self-expression expected even within these most mundane and politically innocent of occasions.

Conversely, in the world of politics, the uses of speech were more frequently *ad hominem* than rational. More than once did outlying states lose favor with or risk invasion from China and Japan by improperly addressing their interlocutors. Jobs could be forfeit by injudicious criticism, while political favors might be curried through flattery. Political friends and enemies were divided along personal rather than ideological lines. One of the greatest intellects of nineteenth century Japan, Yukichi Fukuzawa, wrote that it was hard for him to comprehend the system of Western political parties and amicable argumentation:

*It was beyond my comprehension to understand what these [political enemies] were fighting for, and what was meant, anyway, by "fighting" in peace time ... these "enemies" were to be seen at the same table, eating and drinking with each other. I could not make much sense out of this (Fukuzawa 1934, pp. 142–44).*

In Chinese and Japanese eyes, taking opposite sides of an argument necessarily meant becoming a personal rival and antagonist of the one who held the other side. The more important concomitant of this idea was that if one did not wish to become a lifelong opponent of someone else, he would not venture an opinion contrary to the other person's opinions in public.

Even the legal system was set up in such a way that it avoided direct confrontations and made no demands on logical brief building. While private property rights existed, no freedoms nor personal rights were guaranteed by law, and all power rested with the court (Nakamura 1964, p. 214).

*Chinese court procedure was not characterized by the development of judicial dialogue between the accused and the accuser. The reason is that the Chinese judge was not an arbitrator between two groups, but an official who took evidence from both sides, and then sent out his own underlings to examine the truth of the statements made by both sides (Nakamura 1964, p. 189).*

The danger of "frame-ups" in such a system must be obvious, although they are not unknown to the judicial systems of the West, either. The more important consequence from the viewpoint of communication theory is that there never developed a "spirit of controversial dialogue," nor a "tradition of free public debate."

In this political tradition, *truth* is taken to mean a quality of manhood, not the accuracy of propositions alone. Men could be arrested and imprisoned on the basis of suspicious character; even today, Chinese and Japanese police may detain and interrogate people for "suspicious behavior" in "unsavory neighborhoods." At the same time, few people are convicted on technicalities if their overall character testimony is good. Sino-Japanese thought had no standards for matching propositions with other propositions (coherence) or with other states of affairs in the world ("correspondence tests of truth"). Rather, they maintained the idea that a man whose actions and character followed through on his commitments, and were in line with his way of speaking, was a "true man" or a "man of truth." Instead of the affirmation or negation of particular propositions, Chinese and Japanese thought starts with the "aura," "feeling," or "ring" of truth which is embodied, not in a particular set of hieroglyphs or spoken sounds, but the whole being of the person (Scharfstein 1974, p. 139). ...

## FEATURES OF LANGUAGE

Some of the reasons militating against public argumentation can be traced to social and historical conditions, as we have seen, but other reasons must be sought in the nature of the Chinese and Japanese languages themselves, through which the Chinese and Japanese view and interpret their world.

The Chinese (and thence Japanese) written language was pictographic in origin, like the picture writing on an American Indian tepee, but it was written not on tepees but on tortoise shell fragments. Now a person could fit only a few intelligible pictures—or hieroglyphs derived from pictures—on one tortoise sheel fragment. It became somewhat like composing a telegram: One chose the bare minimum necessary to convey his message, and trusted the other party to decipher it. The length of one line was generally about four pictures; even when paper and other writing surfaces became available, the four-character sentence remained the standard. Thus, a typical written dialogue might run:

*Confucius:* I no desire talk.

*Disciple:* If master no talk, what can disciple(s) learn?

*Confucius:* Does Heaven say anything? ( = Heaven rules without language.) (*Analects,* XVII, 9.)

This excerpt is translated in this literal way, not to mock, but to demonstrate the cryptic and ambiguous style inherent in Chinese. Even the Chinese philosophers were acutely aware of the shortcomings of their own language to reflect anything like the richness of human experience (as we shall examine in greater detail in the section, "Philosophy and Religion").

To this day, the Chinese language remains an efficient but highly ambiguous medium, which makes few distinctions necessary for in-depth debates or discussions. Chinese has no copulas, no plurals, and no tenses unless they are deliberately and awkwardly inserted. Since its contact with Chinese, Japanese language has moved in the same direction (Waley 1958, p. 63). Lacking singulars and plurals, capitalization and tenses, many medieval philosophers got into arguments which Russell could show to be mere pseudo-problems, because neither side was speaking about the same subject. One school would write poems or treatises to show that principles were discernible within temporal events, and the other that Principle was eternal and not instantiated in physical objects. Since Principle and principles are the same word, both schools carried on long and fruitless debates ending only in frustration and embarrassment, unaware that both sides could be right because each was using the same words in very different ways (Ching 1974).

The problem is complicated in Japanese by the fact that the Japanese who originally imitated the Chinese hieroglyphic script and vocabulary were tone deaf. All four Chinese tones of a given phoneme were condensed into the same Japanese sound. Sixteen unique two-syllable Chinese words all came to have the same pronunciation in Japanese. This extreme plethora of homonyms in Japanese handicaps Japanese speech communication further. The more Chinese loan-words the speaker uses, the more he must pause to either verbally or pictorially (on blackboard or palm of his hand) distinguish the word he is using from numerous homonyms. This method, of course, detracts from the elegance and flow of the spoken language. The only alternative is to simply *assume* that the listeners all imagine the same single meaning of the homonym that the speaker intends. In either event, we have a reinforcement of the idea that precision is cumbersome

and inelegant, while ordinary speech is necessarily vague and depends heavily on the cooperative imagination and sympathy of the listener.

Like most other languages, Chinese vocabulary acquires new meanings through a process of accretion and meaning extension. In English, for example, the word *fire* means combustion, then to ignite, then to shoot a gun, then to release from employment. Through the centuries, the Chinese superimposed on a few thousand hieroglyphs some tens of thousands of extended meanings. Indeed, this was the only way to get hieroglyphs for words like "idea" or "unified theory of relativity." The problem with this process is that the pictograph remains the same throughout the centuries, so that in addition to new meanings, the old, more graphic and concrete meanings are still largely preserved. These in turn overlay (or underlie) every more abstract or theoretical expression (Waley 1958, p. 60). Thus Chinese and Japanese develop homonyms in another way, using the same character as well as the same pronunciation in two very different ways, and leaving the interpretation totally open to the reader or listener. Some scholars conclude that written Chinese, read aloud, "was almost too ambiguous to be understood" (Scharfstein 1974; cf. Graham 1964, pp. 54–55).

While these ambiguities enabled many subtle double entendres and poetic turns of phrase, they too reinforced the notion that language was a vehicle for art and not for conveying information; for elegant play, but not for clarifying problems. Nakamura enumerates many specific examples of the confusions in hieroglyphics and syntax, concluding that Chinese has been "an awkward medium for expressing abstract thought" (Nakamura 1964, p. 188). The same can certainly be said of Korean and Japanese. It is no coincidence that, unlike Sanskrit, Greek, and Latin, the Chinese language never produced scholars either conscious enough or interested enough in their own grammar to examine the way syntax and sentences function (Nakamura 1964).

The tremendous ambiguities and difficulties implicit in ancient hieroglyphic languages, reviewed in the previous section, have led over the centuries to language taking on very different functions in the Orient than those it has in the West. This area of scholarship has been all but ignored by Western scholars, although it is painfully obvious to Anglo-American expatriates functioning in oriental languages.

In China and Japan, communication is less of a process of mutually gathering and exchanging information ("How are you? What's happening?") than an affirmation of inevitably shared human conditions ("Sure is hot today. Makes you hot to work in the sun, doesn't it?") A large part of the language activity of any oriental dinner or drinking party consists of the parroting of each others' sentiments in the same words; as the evening wears on, singing and chanting take the place of speech. While the Westerner in such situations tends to feel that such behavior indicates the lack of anything further to talk about, the Oriental feels that in singing and chanting he has achieved true togetherness with his fellows, which in his mind transcends the importance of exchanging ideas. When the oriental climbs staircases, hefts burdens, reaches home, begins to eat, smashes a tennis ball—and in any number of similar situations—he is expected to say or shout words. These words are addressed to no one and communicate nothing; the Japanese will say them even when he is alone or when no one is listening. Some of these words may have psychological functions of demarcating the time of one activity from another; others are little more than animal grunts and cries given phonemic pronunciations. . . . In many situations, then, oriental language is used less to communicate than to commune, congratulate, emote, and to begin and end activities.

One fascinating consequence of the extreme ambiguity and noncommunicative roles of oriental languages is that Chinese and Japanese communication assumes a kind of telepathic intuition which has gone all but ignored in Western studies of communication. Japanese and Chinese languages have many words for their intuitive, nonverbal "stomach-to-stomach" or "heart-to-heart" communication, which serves as the ground for all verbal communication, and can exist independently of words and phrases altogether (Ryu 1974). In addition to leaving off subjects and pronouns, it is not uncommon

for the grammatical objects of sentences (be they ideas or physical things) to be indicated by unreferenced pronouns (like the English "that"). A professor may enter a classroom and ask, "Make it?" Only the person whom the professor has in mind is expected to respond, and he is expected to know exactly what the object of the professor's inquiry is. That oriental languages function in this way is further illustrated by the difficulties that orientals have in learning English—in their omission of subjects, objects, and specific referents until trained to include them. That their cultures function as efficiently as they do is testimony to the well-nigh telepathic sensitivity of each person to the unvoiced intentions of each speaker.

This sensitivity may be due in part to the fact that these cultures have been relatively homogeneous and have possessed single languages for thousands of years. It may be due to the pressures of close-knit families and densely packed societies to preserve harmony through concern with others' feelings. It may be partly due to the fact that hieroglyphic language users sort language into the right hemispheres of their brains (Westerners generally put language in the left, linear-logical hemispheres)—and right hemispheres have been linked to intuition, art, and telepathy (cf. Sasanuma 1980; Sibatani 1980; Tsunoda 1975; Tzeng, 1978; Walker 1981). The intuitive/telepathic abilities of some orientals in communication may strike some Westerners as almost incredible, but are taken for granted as a necessary part of their successful communication process.

Still another problem inherent in Chinese and Japanese is their lack, not only of formal logical systems, but indeed of a principle of noncontradiction. One can add characters to a sentence in order to negate it, but adding two of them does not make a double negation, as a Western observer might wish; nor return the sentence to its unnegated meaning. . . .

Historians of logic might challenge such assertions by pointing out that Sanskrit (Indian) Buddhism had a highly developed mathematical logic by the time of Christ, when Buddhism was just beginning to be introduced to the Chinese. Since

China and Japan adopted Buddhism, should we not also expect them to have adopted many of its logical rules? In fact, however, the Chinese butchering of Indian logical texts almost defies imagination. The dean of Japanese Buddhist historians observes:

*In the history of Buddhist logic in China, we can observe several striking phenomena. First, very few logical works were ever translated. . . . Interest in Buddhist logic was very slight among the Chinese. Secondly, only logical works of the simplest kind were translated. . . . Indian works on epistemology of logical theory were not translated. . . .*

*Indian logic was accepted only in part, and even the part that was accepted was not understood in the sense of the Indian originals. Hsuan-tsang, who introduced Indian logic, seems not to have fully understood it. . . . In developing his arguments, he violated the rules of Indian logic. . . .*

*Ts'u-en's work, which was regarded as the highest authority in China and Japan, contains many fallacies in philosophical and logical analysis. He apparently did not understand the Indian rule that the middle term should be distributed by the major term. . . . He confused* ratio essendi *and* ratio cognoscendi. . . . *in doing this, he simply made a mechanical classification, and his explanation is self-contradictory as well as at odds with the original meaning (Nakamura 1964, p. 192).*

The account could go on and on, but the point should be clear by now. Even the highest authorities on logic in China literally did not know what they were talking about, and frequently contradicted themselves *without being bothered by it!* However, this failure is less to be blamed on the stupidity and mechanical translation methods of the scholars than on the intractable opacity and ambiguity of the Chinese language itself. In Chinese, the fine distinctions and mathematical rules of Sanskrit simply were untranslatable, did not apply, and seemed to make no difference.

From all these features of Chinese and Japanese language: Their telegraphic terseness and consequent ambiguities; their many homonyms; their inabilities to make fine distinctions and abstractions; the use of language in noncommunicative ways and of intuition for communication; and in their lack of logical rules and constraints; we gain further insights as to why public discussion and debate were considered inconclusive if not futile. Unlike Indian and Western traditions, the Chinese had no internal standards for determining when one set of arguments were better than another, so even if debates had occurred, they could neither be governed nor judged by a consistent logic. Thus, these whole languages and cultures tend to frustrate the Western assumptions that reasonable men in free communication can arrive at truer conclusions, either about the natural world or the desirability of a given policy, than can a single man without discussion.

## PHILOSOPHY AND RELIGION

We have already alluded to reasons for oriental respect for age and hence antiquity. Few cultures have so valued the study of classical philosophical and religious texts as have China, Korea, and Japan. In fact, for centuries, examinations on the classical texts constituted the major screening method and stepping stone to political offices in China and Korea. Although there were several antagonistic schools of thought in ancient China, which have dominated the cultural and philosophical scene in the Orient ever since, they each held similarly negative views of speech and language. Let us turn our attention respectively to Confucianism, Taoism, and Buddhism, and finally to an opposition school which favored logic and language, to examine their ideas on speech communication.

Confucius is often known as the father of Chinese philosophy and culture, although he in turn relied heavily upon odes and classics composed centuries before the sixth century B.C. in which he lived. From Confucius' reliance on ancient sources to vindicate his own teachings, we may again observe the recurring theme that it is preferable to copy old solutions to problems rather than inventing and discussing new ones. Confucius' emphasis is continually on being humble and respectful, rather than bold, assertive, or innovative. He sets up a trilemma which virtually precludes the use of persuasive speech:

*To be importunate with one's lord will mean humiliation; to be importunate with friends will mean estrangement (IV, 24).*
*To speak to a man incapable of benefitting is wasting words (XV, 8). (Analects–Lau translation, 1959, standard verse numbering.)*

Even from the format of Confucius' *Analects* themselves, we may observe that Confucius' remarks never run to a paragraph, but usually only to a fleeting fortune-cookie response to a disciple's inquiry. Of course Confucius was aware that there were times when appropriate speech was indispensible, but for the most part, the preceding verses manifest his reticence to speak (cf. *Analects*, XVI, 8). As Confucian biographer Herlee Creel puts it, "Confucius was always markedly contemptuous of eloquence and of ornate language" (Creel 1953, p. 27). This contempt is so often seen that some scholars speculate that Confucius was in fact a poor, tongue-tied speaker, jealous and therefore critical of those with rhetorical eloquence.

Confucius established for China the ideal of the gentleman, or "superior man"—not necessarily someone from the upper classes, but one who has properly cultivated himself in virtue and righteousness. Then how does Confucius envisage the ideal man speaking? Confucius says:

*The superior man is diligent in duty but slow to speak (I, 14).*
*The superior man is slow to speak but quick to act (IV, 24).*
*In antiquity [the ideal time], men were loath to speak (IV, 22).*

. . . Central to Confucius' philosophy was the principle of *hsin*—that one's words should always be in accordance with that which one does, lives, and practices. It is not that the Confucian cannot speak at all, but that he must always speak with discretion only of that which he is prepared to act upon or commit himself to (cf. Lau, "Introduction," *Analects* 1979, p. 25). Naturally, this principle put a damper on bold or persuasive speech.

*The superior man acts before speaking and speaks according to his action (II, 13).*
*Immodest statements are hard to live up to. . . . A superior man is ashamed of his words outstripping his deeds (XIV, 20, 27).*

In Confucius' idea of *hsin*, we can again discern the Chinese idea of the identity of the man and the ideas he voices. Words are not to be treated as sounds, ideas, or propositions which exist independently of their utterers, to be judged by critical linguistic analysis. They are inextricably interrelated to the person who utters them. Their truth depends on his character, and his truth depends on the character of his words. Thus it becomes impossible to scrutinize or criticize an idea without casting aspersions on the character of the person who voices it. Since one of our primary duties is to be respectful to men (*Analects* I, 13), then we should sooner allow their mistakes to pass uncriticized than exhibit a lack of proper respect for their words and hence their selves (*Analects*, XIV, 29). Confucius taught that ordinary men were to learn from the life and deeds of the superior man, and not from his logic or language.

In overview, then, Confucius opposed eloquent and clever speech, advocating hesitancy over brilliance, and he grounded this criticism of speech deeply within his philosophy of the ideal man. This Confucian attitude still persists widely in East Asia.

The ancient Taoist school of Chinese philosophy is best represented by the *Tao-te Ching* of Lao-tzu and by Chuang-tsu. In contrast to the Confucian concerns with public behavior, etiquette, and politics, the Taoists were more interested in man's finding peace within himself and within nature. The Taoists tended to be hermits and recluses whom, even sympathetically, we should have to call quietistic. It is hardly surprising that we find further opposition to speech and rhetoric within the Taoist philosophy. The classic text of the *Tao-te Ching* advocates silence from the beginning:

*The sage spreads doctrines without words (2).*
*Nature says few words, but the whirlwind [windbag] lasts less than a single morning (23).*

It revels in a juxtaposition of opposites:

*The greatest skill seems clumsy and the greatest
eloquence stutters (45).*
*He who knows does not talk; he who talks does
not know.*
*Keep your mouth shut (56).*

Such radical statements are not designed merely
to shock the hearer nor to take issue with all authority. Like Confucius' opposition to speech, the Taoists'
is also grounded in their philosophy, although their
reasons are different from Confucius'. The Taoists
were acutely aware of the artificiality of names and
labels, the inability of their hieroglyphic language
to capture the fullness of experience, and the inap-
propriateness of most linguistic distinctions to the
real world. Thus we are told:

*The Tao that can be named is not the eternal Tao
(1).*
*As soon as there are names, know that it is time to
stop (32).*

The sage, however, remains at peace, because he
does not distinguish good and bad, desirable and
undesirable, proper and improper:

*Common folk make distinctions and are clear
cut. I [the sage] alone make no distinctions (20).*

Thus, within Taoism, language and precision are
thought to be the root of contention and dissatisfaction, therefore a barrier to contentment and
sagehood. . . .

The philosophy of Taoism may appear attractive
to people tired of competition, and to those resigned
in the face of authoritarian administrations. But
Taoism provides no solutions to social problems,
and is thorough going in its rejection of both speech
and communication.

Zen (Chinese: Ch'an) Buddhism first became
known in America for its curious tales about the
sound of one hand, and of monks beating one
another instead of answering questions. In fact, Zen
Buddhism was a uniquely un-Indian Chinese creation, "in persistent and often violent opposition to
words, and then to the intellect which deals exclusively in words" (Suzuki 1953, p. 36). Zen became

the leading school of Chinese Buddhism by the
eleventh century, and the philosophy of the Japanese upper classes by the fourteenth century. Zen
accepted the pervasive relativism of Chuang-tzu, as
can be seen in such statements as "he who drinks
water alone knows if it is cold or warm." It agreed
with the Taoist notions that fundamental principles
are inexpressible in language; and thus that many
questions are also unanswerable (cf. Fung 1948, pp.
257, 262). Zen proclaimed itself in China as a "separate transmission of the *dharma* [true teachings]
outside scriptures and not dependent on words or
phrases" (deBary 1972, p. 208).

The Rinzai school of Zen particularly denounced
eloquent speech:

*Even though your eloquence be like a rushing
torrent, it is nothing but hell-producing* karma
*[activity]. . . . Students become attached to words
and phrases. . . . and cannot gain enlightenment
(deBary 1972, p. 227).*

Rinzai Zen inveighs against studying the words
of the past classics; it calls words "dreams and illu-
sions," and it specifically criticizes those who spend
their days "in idle talk" about rights and wrongs,
landowners and thieves, laws and politics (deBary
1972, p. 230).

In Zen, truth is thought to be intuited only in
silent meditation and incommunicable through language. This is one reason that Zen masters frequently beat their logically minded disciples, or give
them insoluble language-tangles called *koans* to
contemplate until they realize the futility of discur-
sive reason. To their students' logical inquiries, some
masters respond with cries, some with blows. Some
lift tea trays or put their sandals on their heads.
Many simply remain silent to the most serious and
important of questions, or walk out of the room
(Suzuki 1961, pp. 294–296). Hundreds of such
examples have been compiled into the classic literature of Zen, which itself disavows classic literature and scripture. Zen in turn became the model
for *bushido,* the martial code of the Japanese *Samurai,* which was drummed into the heads and hearts
of the educated classes for centuries in Japan. While
Westerners may be fascinated or bemused by Zen

anecdotes of cries and cat-cutting, we must not forget that such tales also represent the deep-seated religious rejection of logic and denial of rational communication in China and Japan.

It is not true that there never existed logicians and debaters in China. The *Ming-chia* (literally, "School of Names") philosophers were a class of lawyers analogous in role and history to the Sophists of Greece. They early became known for their debates about whether white horses were horses and whether criminals were men. In fact, these were very logical arguments designed to demonstrate (1) that there are distinctions within classes of objects, as among horses and among men; (2) that a man sets himself apart from other men by committing criminal deeds; (3) that in so doing, he sacrifices his human right to life and liberty, and therefore (4) capital punishment is justifiable, for taking the life of a criminal is not the same as taking the life of an ordinary man. To the average man, however, the state had the power to kill or free criminals without needing such justifications, and the debates of the *Ming-chia* seemed purest sophistry. As Chuang-tzu criticized: "They can subdue others' mouths but cannot win their hearts" (Chan 1953, p. 233).

Even in their own day, the *Ming-chia* were loathed by other scholars. Historian Ssu-ma T'an wrote (around 110 B.C.):

*The School of Names conducted minute examinations of trifling points in complicated and elaborate statements, which made it impossible for others to refute their ideas (Quoted in Fung 1948, p. 81).*

Some *Ming-chia* lawyers were indeed highly successful in getting their own suspects sentenced or acquitted, and were at the same time accused of turning wrong into right. The typical reaction of both people and government was summarized by philosopher Han Fei-tzu: "When discussion of hardness and whiteness appear [the standard examples of *Ming-chia* logic], then the governmental laws lose their effect" (Fung 1948, p. 82). Popular as well as official opinion militated against the *Ming-chia;* their school was consequently short lived, and their name remained more as an epithet for vacuous language

manipulation than as a respectable title of a school of logicians. Thus the history of Chinese and Japanese thought is dominated by three major philosophico-religious schools: Confucian, Taoist, and Buddhist; and all of them opposed debate, public speech, and even communication. The single small school famous for debate and logical argumentation soon defeated its own purposes; by being too good at argument, it lost the trust of the people and government forever.

## CONCLUSIONS

There are tremendous barriers—socio-historical, linguistic, and philosophical—to the acceptance of argumentation and debate as methods for the consideration of new proposals or as strategies for socio-political change in East Asia. In addition to the many problems reviewed here, there are also the practical problems of education, of martial law, of industrial as well as international rivalries, and of the lack of speech and communication courses in Asian schools and universities. All these factors militate against the rapid rise of public argumentation and debate in the near future.

Many Westerners may be convinced of the importance of logic, and of its superiority to emotive intuition. Yet we need to be careful not to discard those areas of human life and communication in which intuition may be extremely valuable, in our efforts to quantify and mathematize. We may agree with Habermas that an ideal speech situation requires equality of participants, freedom from social coercion, suspension of privilege, and free expression of feeling [rather than self-censorship] (cf. Burleson and Kline 1979, pp. 412–428). But we should realize that this is at best a very Western ideal, both impractical and even theoretically inconceivable to traditionally educated Chinese and Japanese.

We desire to understand our powerful East Asian neighbors, and to do so, we propose to communicate. It is true that they may have many ideas to learn from our forms and modes of argumentation and debate. At the same time, we should not forget the long and relatively peaceful histories they have experienced, entirely without the benefit of our methods of discussion and rhetoric. Before imposing our own models of communication upon them in another gross display of insensitivity and cultural imperialism, let us remind ourselves that our own presuppositions about ideal communications are also culture-bound. In mutual respect, while we make our communications methods and studies available to those in the Far East, let us seek to understand their own respective cultural contexts. It is hoped that this article will have made a start in that direction.

## REFERENCES

*Analects* (1979). (D. C. Lau, Trans.). Harmondsworth, England: Penguin Books.

Becker, C. B. (1983). "The Japanese Way of Debate." *National Forensic Journal* 1 (2), 141–147.

Burleson, B., and S. Kline. (1979). "Habermas' Theory of Communication: A Critical Explanation." *Quarterly Journal of Speech* 65, 412–428.

Chan, W.-T. (1963). *A Sourcebook in Chinese Philosophy*. Princeton: Princeton University Press.

Ching, J. (1974). "The Goose Lake Monastery Debate." *Journal of Chinese Philosophy,* 1 (2), 161–177.

Chuang-Tzu. See Chan, pp. 179–210.

Confucius. See *Analects*.

Creel, H. (1953). *Chinese Thought from Confucius to Mao Tse-tung*. Chicago: The University of Chicago Press.

deBary, W. T. (ed.). (1972). *The Buddhist Tradition in India, China, and Japan*. New York: Random House/Vintage Books.

Fukuzawa, Y. (1934). *Autobiography of Fukuzawa Yukichi*. (E. Kiyooka, Trans.). Tokyo: Hokuseido.

Goodrich, L. C. (1935). *The Literary Inquisition of Ch'ien-lung*. Baltimore: ACLS/Waverly Press.

Graham, A. C. (1964). "The Place of Reason in the Chinese Philosophical Tradition." In R. Dawson (ed.), *The Legacy of China*. London: Oxford University Press.

Nakamura, H. (1964). *Ways of Thinking of Eastern Peoples*. P. Weiner (ed.). Honolulu: East-West Center Press.

Ryu, S. (1974). *A Study of the Concept of* hara *and a Japanese Philosophy of Communication*. Senior Thesis for International Christian University, Tokyo.

Saito, I. (1973). *A Rhetorical Analysis of Japanese Wedding Speeches*. Senior Thesis for International Christian University, Tokyo.

Sasanuma, S. (1980). "The Nature of the Task-Stimulus Interaction in the Tachistoscopic Recognition of *Kanji* and *Kana*." *Brain and Language,* 9, 298–306.

Scharfstein, B.-A. (1974). *The Mind of China*. New York: Delta.

Shigeta, H. (1973). *An Experimental Study of Ambiguity in Japanese and American Speaking Behavior* (Chap. 3). Senior Thesis for International Christian University, Tokyo.

Sibatani, A. (1980). "The Japanese Brain." *Science 80,* 1 (8), 24–27.

Suzuki, D. T. (1953). "Zen: A Reply to Hu Shih." *Philosophy East and West* 3, 36.

Suzuki, D. T. (1953). *Zen Buddhism*. (W. Barrett, ed.). Garden City, N.Y.: Doubleday/Anchor.

Suzuki, D. T. (1961). *Essays in Zen Buddhism* (first series). New York: Grove Press.

*Tao-Te Ching* (1964). (D. C. Lau, Trans.). Harmondsworth, England: Penguin Books.

Tsunoda, T. (1971). "The Difference of Cerebral Dominance of Vowel Sounds among Different Languages." *Journal of Auditory Research* 11, 305.

Tsunoda, T. (1973). "Functional Differences between Right-Cerebral and Left-Cerebral Hemispheres." *Brain and Language* 2, 152–170.

Tzeng, O. J. L. (1978). "Cerebral Lateralization of Function and Bilingual Decision Processes." *Brain and Language* 5 (1), 56–71.

Tzeng. O. J. L. (1979). "Visual lateralization effects in reading Chinese characters." *Nature,* 282, 499–501.

Waley, A. (1958). *The Way and Its Power*. New York: Grove Press.

Walker, L. C. (1981). "The Ontogeny of the Neural Substrate for Language." *Human Evolution* 10, 429–441.

# Problems of Translation in Cross-Cultural Communication

LEE SECHREST
TODD L. FAY
S. M. ZAIDI

To at least some degree every cross-cultural research project must involve the use of language, if only to convey the instructions for a "nonverbal" procedure of some sort. Of course, some projects are far more dependent on linguistic communication than others, and some are exclusively verbal, or linguistic, in nature. We think that there are at least potential communication problems in *all* cross-cultural research, e.g., can one be *sure* that a Pashtun version of "Please do this as quickly as you can" is the same in its meaning as the English? Nonetheless, the problems do vary, and it is worthwhile to note the kinds of problems that are involved and the errors they may produce. We hope in this paper to achieve some clarification of the process of translating from one language into another for purposes of cross-cultural research. We will begin with a discussion of the types of materials which cause translation difficulties, go on to a discussion of the kinds of equivalences which are necessary, and then describe attempts which have been made to over-

From *Journal of Cross-Cultural Psychology*, Vol. 3, No. 1 (March 1972), pp. 41–56 Copyright © 1972. Reprinted by permission of Sage Publications, Inc. and the authors. Professor Sechrest is in the Psychology Department, Northwestern University; Professor Fay is in the Psychology Department, University of Western Ontario; and Professor Zaidi teaches at Karachi University. The preparation of this article was supported in part by the AteneoPenn State Basic Research Program, sponsored by the United States Office of Naval Research, with the Pennsylvania State University as prime contractor (Nonr-656 37).

come translation difficulties. Along the way we will refer to our own work in connection with a comparative study to be carried out in several cultures. It will be evident that we have relied heavily on the work of Werner and Campbell (1970) and Brislin (1970).

## TYPES OF TRANSLATION PROBLEMS IN CROSS-CULTURAL RESEARCH

There are, generally speaking, four types of translation problems in cross-cultural studies although little attention has been paid to but one of them. First, nearly all instances of cross-cultural work require that some orientation to the research be given. Ordinarily those persons who are research subjects or informants must be given some rationale for the tasks set for them, and it would seem obvious that some attention would be paid to the equivalence of such introductions as made in different cultures. However, there are no instances known to us in which an investigator specifically mentions such a problem, let alone a solution to it. In any case, there often will be instances in which an investigator must "explain himself" to members of different language groups, and when that necessity arises, its companion necessity is for precision in translation.

The second type of translation problem involves the translation of instructions specific to different types of tasks or measures being used. Even though the response of a subject may require no verbal component, it is almost always necessary that the nature of the task and of his response be explained in words (Anderson 1967). And those words must be translated from one language to another when one crosses linguistic boundaries. Again, very few investigators seem to have paid much attention to this problem. It seems usually to be *assumed* that translations are adequate. Very few investigators can be described as having been sufficiently wary to make us totally confident in their findings. Rather paradoxically, it is probably the case that the briefer the instructions are, the greater the tendency to assume similarity. However, as Werner and Campbell (1970) make clear, it is, in fact, more difficult to get and to be sure one has gotten a satisfactory translation of a short passage than a longer one. Such phrases as "Do your best," "Guess if you want to," "Take the one you like best," and "Make A the same as B" involve many transitional pitfalls for the unwary. It is the lack of context in short phrases and sentences that makes the problem so difficult. Or, viewed in another way, the redundancy in short messages may be very limited. Recently we have been using the Rod-and-Frame Test to measure field dependence-independence in different cultures, and two of the most difficult problems we encountered were in finding a Tagalog (Philippine) word or phrase for "upright" or an Urdu word for "rod."

The third type of translation problem is the obvious one of phrasing questions or the other verbal stimuli in ways that are comparable in two or more languages. Interview questions, statements on personality inventories or attitude questionnaires, and verbal stimuli on projective tests such as incomplete sentences are all examples of the third type of translation problem. This is a problem to which many investigators have addressed themselves. In fact, the problem is so obvious that it is inescapable, and unlike the first two problems, there are almost no investigators unaware of the problem. However, we might point out that translation problems can and do arise even within cultures when different subcultures are being examined, and many investigators have ignored the likelihood that a particular verbal stimulus may not mean the same to a person in one subculture as to a person in another. Dialect differences, use of scholarly rather than vernacular language, and regional differences in colloquial speech and idiom all contribute to potential subcultural research problems. Odd as it may seem, English may at times need to be translated into English, and Urdu into Urdu.

The fourth type of translation problem involves translation of *responses* from one language or dialect to another so that comparisons may be made. Many questionnaires have limited response alternatives, e.g., true-false, agree-disagree, and the translation is made prior to the response. However,

for open-ended questions, interviews, projective tests, and the like, it may be necessary to translate the responses. When responses must be translated, the same problems exist as in translating other material. In many cases translation and its attendant expense and difficulties can be avoided by coding, categorizing, or scoring responses in the language in which they are given. If the coding system is easily communicated and relatively unambiguous, many difficulties can be obviated. To be sure, the coding system itself must be translated, but that is a decidedly simple task when compared to translation of responses, and especially when one has access to bilingual coders. It should be noted, though, that Ervin (1964) found that language of response could make a difference in the responses of bilinguals, and bilingual coders need to be checked for their consistency also.

## PROBLEMS OF EQUIVALENCE IN TRANSLATION

As we stated earlier the major problem in translation is to determine that the translation is equivalent to the original language. There are, however, a number of different kinds of equivalence that have somewhat different effects and implications. We propose here to discuss several different aspects of equivalence which must be considered in transporting a research instrument from one linguistic area to another. While the problems vary somewhat in importance and are most serious when language and cultures are maximally different we think that all the problems exist in some measure even within cultures; they merely become increasingly troublesome with increasing-decreasing linguistic and cultural similarity.

### Vocabulary Equivalence

Perhaps the most obvious kind of equivalence is in vocabulary, in the words used in two or more translations. For example, an item such as "I am happy most of the time" could be translated rather directly into another language than English with the major vocabulary problem being, in most instances, finding an equivalent term for "happy." Or, in using a Semantic Differential (Osgood, Suci & Tannenbaum, 1957), one would need to find comparable terms for such items as strong-weak, rich-poor, and fast-slow.

While it might seem that vocabulary problems could be solved with a good dictionary, and indeed, that is a valuable resource, the fact of the matter is that the problems are not by any means so simple. In the first place, dictionary language is often not the language of the people. In fact, we could make a parallel comment about the use of translators, who are often chosen from a population of highly educated persons who speak and write somewhat pedantically in both their languages. We have numerous instances of translations made with either dictionary or translator that proved unworkable because they did not have the right meaning to persons for whom the test was intended. Thus, a good first rule in translating is to use translators who have a good acquaintance with the language *as used by the prospective test respondents*.

A second aspect of the problem of vocabulary equivalence in relation to dictionary translations is that most words in the dictionary are defined in a number of ways or by a number of terms. It is not easy to know which terms to select for the translation. The problem is to reflect in the term chosen the obvious meaning and the important nuances of the original term. Such terms as *responsible, suggestible, aloof,* and *tough* are all English terms with nuances that make it difficult to find just the right equivalent in other languages. On the other hand such Urdu terms as *sanjida, pakbaz, ameen,* and *ghairat* (all indicating good and desirable personality traits in Pakistan) are also expressive of delicacies of thought that make the discovery of a vocabulary equivalent difficult.

There may, in fact, be terms in one language for which it is almost impossible to find an equivalent in another language. For example, we found that there is no really good Tagalog term for *feminine,* i.e., a term that makes it possible to say "Maria is more *feminine* than Elena." Similarly, there was no Tagalog equivalent for *domestic* that we might apply in describing people, so as to say, "Mr. Santos is

very *domestic* in his interests." On the other hand, *hiya* (related to shyness, embarrassment, shame, and deference) and *pakikisama* (related to getting along with others, acceding to wishes of one's peer group, and conformity) are Tagalog words difficult to translate into English because there just are not any equivalents. We found it somewhat difficult to find good counterparts for *orderly, conforming,* and *polite* in Urdu, and *moonis, humdum,* and *habeeb* (all indicating differences in degree of friendship and closeness) are Urdu words without ready English equivalents.

A frequent attempted solution to problems of nonequivalence of terms, one recommended by Werner and Campbell (1970), is the use of several words in the target language to try to convey an idea expressible in one word in the source language. Although such a procedure will be discussed later in this paper, we would note here that differences in length of materials should be kept within fairly close limits.

Vocabulary equivalence is not necessarily equally difficult to achieve between all pairs of languages. We have no data on this but there are many reasons such as cultural differences, as well as linguistic traditions, for incomparability between two languages. To illustrate, however, we have been involved in considerable translation from English to Tagalog and back, and from English to Urdu and back. It is our distinct impression that it is easier to translate between English and Urdu than between English and Tagalog. At least a part of the difference in difficulty we attribute to the differential availability of words in the two languages which are comparable to English words. Tagalog does not seem to have very good words for a lot of English terms and vice versa. While there are obvious problems translating from English into Urdu, it seems to be richer in the kinds of words which are used in English texts. Brislin (1970) found substantial differences between languages in translation error rates (while he found Tagalog-English to be relatively easy, it is almost certainly the case that his Tagalogs were more nearly bilingual than his other linguistic assistants).

To the extent that words do not mean the same thing to respondents in different cultures, the responses are uninterpretable with respect to cultural similarities or differences. But, vocabulary equivalence is only part of the problem.

## Idiomatic Equivalence

Frequently in translating one encounters problems that arise because idiomatic speech is employed in one language, and idioms never translate properly, if at all. In fact, one often becomes aware of idiomatic language only when one attempts to translate and realizes that a direct translation would not make sense at all. For example, the direct translation of the Tagalog adjectival expression *hipong-tulog* is "fish sleeping"; yet a more meaningful equivalent in English might be conforming, indecisive, or "following the present current of thought or action."

Although it might seem that one should avoid use of idioms in producing technical research material, and that is what Werner and Campbell recommend, idioms are so firmly embedded in our speech patterns that under most circumstances we are scarcely aware of them. Moreover, to attempt to avoid idioms completely in, for example, writing instructions or writing items, would probably produce a highly stilted, pedantic form of discourse which would be utterly unsuitable for research efforts with the general population in any culture. And, of course, if one is translating the responses of an informant or subject, idiom cannot be avoided. Therefore, the best that can be done is to attempt to ensure that when idioms are used in a translation they are equivalent in meaning to the idioms used in the original, and that the general level of idiomatic speech in the two languages is approximately equivalent so that one does not seem more scholarly, more stilted, or in some other way different from the other. For example, the Tagalog idiom *galitbulkan* is literally translated "angry volcano" and is interpreted to mean a sudden expression of anger. One might be able to use the English slang term "blow up" as an idiomatic equivalent. To "keep your mouth shut" can be translated into Urdu, but a better equivalent in terms of usage would be *tum chup raho,* which back translates as "you keep quiet."

## Grammatical-Syntactical Equivalence

Still another equivalence problem arises from the fact that languages differ widely in their grammars and syntaxes and these differences are often critical to the meanings in various translations. While these problems are probably of somewhat greater importance with longer passages, they do occur even in relation to very short passages, perhaps even for single words. One of the reasons for a grammatical equivalence problem involving single words is that two languages may not have equivalent parts of speech. Thus, for example, if there is no gerund in a particular language there may be some problems in achieving good equivalence for the commonly used gerunds in English. (Urdu has no gerund quite like English.) A fairly ordinary type of test item consists of asking an individual which of a list of activities he enjoys and the list is often couched in terms of such gerunds as singing, dancing, eating, playing, writing, and the like. While it is most certainly possible to develop an equivalent form for such items in most languages, there do arise some difficulties in specifying the exact linguistic form which is to be used in a language which lacks the gerund. Other parts of speech such as adjectives, adverbs, and the like, may be missing in particular languages and may pose some problems for translators.

Nonetheless, the more important problems in attaining grammatical-syntactical equivalence involve longer passages. Probably one of the more common grammatical problems in achieving equivalence is in dealing with verb forms. Not all languages deal with the problems of verb mood, voice, or tense in the same way by any means, and it is sometimes very difficult in a given language to put expressions which have the same verb form or meaning in English. For example, in the Tagalog dialect there is no subjunctive mood. As a result, it becomes impossible to find literal equivalents and difficult to find conceptual equivalents for English conditional subjunctive expressions. The English sentence, "If I had had the money, I would have bought the dress," can be translated in Tagalog to *Kung mayroon sana akong pera, nabili ko sana ang baro.* The literal translation of this Tagalog sentence into English would be, "If I have the money (understood I have not), I bought the dress (understood I did not)." Needless to say, the tense and the conditional sense seem not to be the same as the original English.

The whole area of translation has been so little studied in the context of the field of psychology that it is difficult to cite specific instances of syntactic nonequivalence, although there is no question that they abound and that they can affect the meaning of translations.

The work of Whorf (1956) contains many examples such as the Hopi utilization of what we think of as nouns as verb or action forms. Thus *chair* is *chairing* or the act of sitting. Or, looking elsewhere one finds that in English it is obligatory to specify number in relation to nouns, nearly all of which are either singular or plural. However, in Yoruba (Nigeria) it is not at all obligatory that number be specified. And Arabic obliges that number be specified as singular, dual, or plural. Obviously such syntactical variations can very much affect meaning and the problems of translation.

## Experiential Equivalence

There are two remaining equivalence problems that are of a somewhat different order from the ones we have discussed above, since the remaining two do not involve purely linguistic considerations. Nonetheless, they are important for translators to keep in mind and may constitute severe impediments to the development of adequate materials for studies in societies with different languages. The first of these is experiential equivalence, the second is conceptual equivalence.

By experiential equivalence we mean that in order for translations to be successful from one culture to another they must utilize terms referring to real things and real experiences which are familiar in both cultures, if not exactly equally familiar. Werner and Campbell call this "*cultural* translation" as distinguished from *linguistic* translation. If two cultures differ so greatly in the nature of their objects, in the nature of their social arrangements, in their overall ways of life, or that objects or experiences which are familiar to members of one culture are unfamiliar to members of another, it will be difficult to achieve equivalence in meaning of a variety of linguistic statements no matter how carefully the translation is done from the standpoint of the language involved. Let us take a perhaps trivial, but very obvious example. If the item "I would like to be a florist" appeared on a personality or interest measure for use with Americans it would probably be understood by most of them. That same item, however, would be incomprehensible to most people around the world, no matter how carefully it was explained to them. Flower shops simply are not found in most parts of the world and, in many cases, the idea of a flower shop where one has flowers made into fancy arrangements and the like would be totally foreign to the experience of most people. Consequently, if one wished to achieve experiential equivalence one would have to think about why the item involving doing the work of a florist is used in an American sample and then find an equivalent that is in terms of a local experience type of activity in the other culture being studied. Thus, if in an American test the item is scored for femininity because it is thought to reflect an interest in feminine kinds of activities, then in another culture in which flower shops were missing one would have to look for a similar kind of economic activity primarily identified with females and thought to reflect an effeminate outlook even when it occurred among males. That might not be easy to do but, for example, in the Philippines most market vendors are women, and it is possible that Filipinos might think a male effeminate if he were a market vendor. In that case one could use the item "I would like to be a market vendor" as an experiential equivalent to "I would like to be a florist."

In some cases there may be no alternative but to eliminate items because a counterpart does not exist or would be of too uncertain equivalence in another culture. Animals, household objects, architectural features, terrain features, biological specimens, etc. are all examples of categories of concrete objects where cultures may differ so much in experience that the problem of attaining equivalence is difficult. No translation of "department store" into Urdu is possible because they are unknown in Pakistan, and the closest one could get would be "large shop."

However, it should not be thought that the problems of equivalence pertain only to such concrete aspects of cultures. They may also stem from differences between other cultural arrangements. One good example lies in the kinship patterns and social relations that differ so widely from one culture to another. The term, "cousin," for example, means something very different in the Philippines than it means in the United States, and it means something else again in Pakistani culture. Or, to take another example, the typical school classroom or even university classroom is so very different in its meaning, in the way it is conducted, in the relationship among the students or in the relationship between the students and professors, that it is very difficult to ensure that any items or statements about the university classroom as an experience can possibly be equivalent for members of cultures as diverse as, let us say, Pakistani and American. Such an item as "I seldom speak up in class" would undoubtedly have a different meaning for American and Pakistani students because the experience of being in a class is so very different for the two groups. Again, achieving an adequate translation of the item would involve figuring out what the item was supposed to reflect in the way of a trait or response disposition in an American culture and then finding an equivalent lying within the experience of typical Pakistani students.

The position taken here is much akin to that of Przeworski and Teune (1970), who suggest that in most instances of the kind at issue here the important question concerns the *equivalence of inferences* rather than of stimuli. They indicate that inferences must be validated within rather than across social systems. "An instrument is equivalent across systems to the extent that the *results* provided by the instrument reliably describe with (nearly) the same validity a particular phenomenon in different social systems" (opus cited, p. 108). While we are perhaps somewhat more interested in and sanguine about achieving linguistic equivalence than

Przeworski and Teune, and while we have some reservations about using similarity of factorial structure as the sole criterion of equivalence, we are in general agreement with their propositions.

## Conceptual Equivalence

The final problem in achieving equivalence between measures to be used in two or more cultures is the problem of ensuring that the concepts used in the measures, interview, or other translated materials are equivalent in the two cultures. This is somewhat apart from the previous kinds of equivalence problems for it may very well be that one has in two cultures a word that, when translated, mutually yields high agreement and yet it may not be that the concepts implied by the two words are, in fact, identical or particularly close in nature. For example, the item "I love a parade" might be quite easy to translate into other languages than English and, at least on a word-for-word basis, there would be no problem in equivalence in such things as vocabulary and experience. Nonetheless, the concept "love" as used in that English item is far different in its implications from the concept which might be implicit in words used in other languages. English is, perhaps, not an especially rich language for expressing positive feelings about things and, consequently, the word "love" is used to mean several different things, or at least to connote varying degrees of positive affection toward some object.

A second aspect of the problem of conceptual equivalence is that a concept well understood and frequently employed in one culture may be lacking altogether in another culture, or it may appear at least in such varied different fragmented forms that it is very difficult to construct materials that treat the true concepts equivalently. For example in the Philippines it proved to be very difficult to find even a concept, let alone words, which had the same connotations as the common American concept of homosexual. The available Philippine words are used in a variety of ways which suggests that the concept simply does not exist in the same highly developed form as it does in the American culture (Sechrest & Flores 1969). In fact, it is our feeling that doing translations in both directions in two or more cultures is an excellent way of coming to understand the divergent ways of thinking about problem areas in different cultures.

## The Paradox of Equivalence

We have gone into some detail concerning the problems of achieving equivalence across two or more languages as if equivalences were the fundamental problem. Actually, in certain respects it is not, for there may be a distinct paradox involved in translation for the sake of achieving equivalence. The paradox is that if one demands that a form of a test or other measure yield comparable results in two cultures in order to demonstrate equivalence, then the more equivalent two forms become the less the probability of finding cultural differences. On the other hand, if one looks predominantly for cultural differences and ignores the problem of equivalence, then the less attention that is paid to the problem of equivalence the greater the probability of finding cultural differences. For example, in his work on the comparison of Japanese and American college students' responses to the Edwards Personal Preference Schedule, Barrien (1966) argued that differences found between the two samples stemmed from different concepts of social desirability for the two cultures. If that were done, however, it is entirely possible that important cultural differences would be obliterated, or at least obscured, by the attempt to achieve what is a rather misleading form of equivalence. Obviously, we are not thinking here of the kinds of questions for which prior knowledge can be used to justify expectations either of differences or similarities between cultures, e.g., proportion of Roman Catholics in a culture. The paradox is troublesome for more complex issues for which prior expectations are uncertain or a poor guide, e.g., "What is the true cause of personal misfortune?"

The resolution of the equivalence paradox is not a simple one, but our feeling is that it probably lies in some method of triangulation whereby measures are subjected to increasingly more severe tests of equivalence, and we determine what sort of convergence in the responses of two cultures we may be able to obtain. The more rapidly the findings from two cultures converge in terms of the degree of effort required to achieve equivalence, the smaller the differences between the two cultures probably are. In any case, we can never know for sure what the absolute differences between cultures are and can probably only guess at their relative magnitude. Thus, we may be able to say that the members of two cultures are more similar with respect to one area of functioning than with respect to another, or that they are more or less similar to each other than they are to members of some third culture. There are, of course, some measures for which diminishing returns of equivalence manipulations are likely to be achieved at a very rapid rate. For example, in the case of the Rod-and-Frame Test it seems scarcely likely that any real differences, for example between men and women, are simply a function of equivalence of instructions to the two groups.

Obviously in research the aim of producing versions of some communication which are equivalent in two or more languages has a pragmatic justification. One does not labor over translations for the sake of art. The aim of equivalence is that the specific influence of language on responses may be removed. It is, as we have suggested, difficult to know when equivalence has been achieved, but Werner and Campbell and Brislin have proposed several very useful criteria. However, in his empirical study of translation equivalence Brislin had monolingual raters examine an original English version and one translated back into English in order to detect "errors that might make differences in the meaning people would infer." That process when followed by correction of the errors produced reasonably good translations although pretesting of instruments revealed some additional errors.

## Direct Translation

The most common procedure by which an attempt to achieve equivalent forms of questionnaires, interview, and the like for cross-cultural research has been the direct translation. That is, a translator or translators who are bilingual attempt to translate as best they can from one language into the other. This translation procedure, as a matter of fact, is still characteristic of a great deal of work of a cross-cultural nature and it is particularly likely to be used in relation to brief sets of materials, orientation, instructions, and the like. The method has also been used for the development of adjective check lists and similar materials. However, as Werner and Campbell have pointed out it is exactly for such brief materials that a method of direct translation is likely to be most inadequate. To be sure, it is probably rare that a translator works without any check at all on the adequacies of his efforts, but in a great many instances the checking is likely to be unsystematic and inadequate.

There are several problems with direct translation, the most important of which is that idiosyncracies may be introduced by the translator himself. The translator himself may not be sufficiently skilled on one or the other of the languages in which he is working, he may not be culturally representative of the group for which the materials are to be used, and he may, by reason of his own experience, have peculiarities of word understanding or word use which will not be shared by persons for whom the materials are intended.

Obviously, it would be going beyond the realm of reason to assert that all translations made by a single translator are inadequate, but we feel that the probability of inadequacies of translations may go undetected. Therefore, we believe that the method should be rejected out of hand, particularly when in nearly all instances there are better, if not perfect, alternatives. We would, however, point out that the method of direct translation is still quite common and, in fact, it is probably still characteristic of the large bulk of all anthropological translation.

## Back Translation

Werner and Campbell have described a method of translation which is distinctly superior to the method of direct translation even though it may not be the ideal solution in many instances. In the method of back translation a translation is first made from one language to another, for example, from English to Urdu, by one or more translators. The translated material is then back translated, for example, from Urdu to English, by another translator or set of translators. The two versions of the original can then be checked for the adequacy of the translation. For example, if a statement in English such as "I get tense before examinations," is translated into Urdu and then comes back into English translated from the Urdu as "I get excited before examinations,"[1] the discrepancy between the two versions would suggest to the experimenter that further translation is required. Presumably, by successive translations and back translation a better and better approximation to the original can be obtained, and the final version of the translated material should be satisfactory.

However, we would suggest that not all problems in translation are quite so easily solved as might be suggested by the foregoing. For one thing, when a back translation is accomplished there are almost inevitably some discrepancies between the original English version and the back-translated version. It then requires a judgment on the part of someone whether the two versions are, in fact, equivalent. There may be a number of reasons for nonequivalence which have to be treated quite differently in the process of developing a satisfactory research instrument. For one thing discrepancies may occur because the original translation was inadequate, and if that is true the only solution is improvement of the translation. However, the inadequacy may have stemmed from different sources. It may have been the result of an idiosyncratic translation by the translator. For example, a translator may himself not know the difference between the words "tense" and "excited," or may not regard the distinction as important. A second possibility is that since the translation and back translation are done by different people, the two separate English versions may be more equivalent than they seem because of idiosyncratic habits in the use of English words. Thus, if the word "annoyance" is translated into Urdu and then comes back translated into English as "pain" it is entirely possible that the discrepancy is attributable to faulty knowledge of English rather than to any inadequacies in Urdu. In any case, in such an instance the experimenter would have to make a decision as to whether the translation was inadequate or not, that is, whether "pain" is a reasonable English synonym for "annoyance," e.g., as in "waiting in line is a pain."

A second source of difficulty in producing equivalent back translations is that the lack of equivalence may in fact stem from the absence of a satisfactory word, or at least from the lack of equivalence of concepts in the two languages. Thus, the word "homosexual" when translated into Tagalog usually becomes "bakla" which, when translated back into English might come out as "sissy" or something of that sort. The problem lies not in the idiosyncrasy of the translator or in the failure to use the best term, but simply in the fact that there is no equivalent in Tagalog for the English term "homosexual." Such problems of nonequivalence can only be resolved by having available a number of bilingual speakers who can be consulted with respect to the problems involved. Preferably the bilingual speakers should come from different backgrounds of the subjects who are to respond to the instrument being developed. For example, we have found that many of the persons who are most readily available as translators are persons who are considerably higher in education than the subjects who will be using the instrument and they therefore produce stilted, academic versions of a questionnaire which are not readily understood by the subjects. In fact, an additional problem arose in the Philippines where, since there are many different dialects, many potential translators were not in fact native speakers of the dialect into which they were making translations. Because of the movement toward development of a national language in the Philippines there has been a considerable increase in the number of students who are studying the national language, Pilipino, in school. Such speakers of Pilipino may actually be superior in terms of grammatical knowledge and in terms of formal linguistic knowledge of Pilipino or Tagalog to native speakers, but in fact their language is different from that of the native speaker of Tagalog, and if one is to use a questionnaire with native speakers then the versions produced by the academically trained persons may be quite inadequate. For example, the Tagalog word for science, *agham,* is not familiar to many native speakers who do use the English word. We believe that the only solution is to have available as translators, or at least as informants, persons who are native speakers of the language into which the translation is to be done.

Actually the process of back translation, when properly done, is literative, i.e., an initial translation is made, back translated, examined for errors, corrected, again back translated, etc. At every stage improvement depends upon a rather critical set being taken by the translator working at that stage. Brislin has shown that the pretesting is an important addendum to the back translation process, for he found a number of meaning errors that had previously gone undetected. Errors may well go undetected for any of a number of reasons mentioned above, e.g., translators of different subculture than subjects, conventions in translating that are not completely legitimate (*bakla* = homosexuality), etc. Fortunately, despite the problems with back translation as a technique, Brislin has shown that very good results may be obtained when it is carefully done.

The major advantage of back translation is that it operates as a filter through which nonequivalent terms will not readily pass. If there is not an appropriate word or phrase in a target language for one in the source language, that fact as a high probability of being discovered. For example, if there is no equivalent in a target language for the American expression "take advantage of someone," it will probably be back translated as "boss someone around," "cheat someone," etc. The investigator will be able to decide fairly accurately just what concepts he can employ in the two languages. He need not speculate; he can act on the basis of the back translation results.

### NOTE

1. There is no good Urdu equivalent for *tense,* and the likely substitute, *Tanao,* might be back translated as *excited, upset,* or even *embarrassed.*

## REFERENCES

Anderson, R. B. W. On the comparability of meaningful stimuli in cross-cultural research. *Sociometry,* 1967, *30,* 124–136.

Berrien, F. K. Japanese and American values. *International Journal of Psychology,* 1966, *I,* 129–141.

Brislin, R. W. Back-translation for cross-cultural research. *Journal of Cross-Cultural Psychology,* 1970, *I,* 185–216.

Ervin, S. M. Language and TAT content in bilinguals. *Journal of Abnormal and Social Psychology,* 1964, *68,* 500–507.

Osgood, C. E., Suci, G. J., Tannenbaum, P. H. *The Measurement of meaning.* Urbana, Ill.: Univ. of Illinois Press, 1957.

Sechrest, L., & Flores, L. Homosexuality in the Philippines and the United States: The handwriting on the wall. *Journal of Social Psychology,* 1969, *79,* 3–12.

Werner, O., & Campbell, D. T. Translating, working through interpreters, and the problem of decentering. In R. Naroll & R. Cohen (eds.) *A handbook of method in cultural anthropology.* New York: The Natural History Press, 1970, pp. 398–420.

Whorf, B. L. *Language, thought, and reality.* New York: John Wiley & Sons, 1956.

# The Art of Interpreting

## JAN CAROL BERRIS

Exchanges with the People's Republic of China have proliferated to a degree unimagined just a short time ago. As recently as 1977, fewer than twenty Chinese delegations visited the United States during the whole year; in 1982 delegations were averaging about 100 per month. This enormous increase in contact has necessitated a corresponding increase in the number of Chinese and Americans who can communicate in each other's language. Although many Chinese are learning English (it is by far the most important foreign language in China) and a few Americans know Chinese, interpreters are and will continue to be essential in facilitating communication between both sides.

Interpreting, as I have learned through more than a decade of experience, is a physically exhausting and often emotionally draining art. But those who work with interpreters can do a great deal to help maximize the interpreter's effectiveness and minimize his or her weaknesses.

### WHAT MAKES A GOOD INTERPRETER?

Many people assume that anyone fluent in two languages can function as an interpreter. Indeed, a good command of both languages and alertness to their constant evolution is the foundation of effective interpreting. But that is only the first step. Expressing your own thoughts, choosing your own words,

From Robert A. Kapp (ed.), *Communicating with China* (Chicago: Intercultural Press, 1983), pp. 41–57. Reprinted by permission of the publisher and the author. Jan Berris is Vice President of the National Commission on U.S.-China Relations.

and picking your own sentence patterns in a foreign tongue are very different—and infinitely easier—than precisely reproducing someone else's ideas, phrases, and nuances. At the National Committee on U.S.-China Relations, we interview many people with Chinese language skills ranging from fairly good to excellent. Yet in an interpreting test, nearly all, even those who do quite well in general conversation, fall apart.

A good interpreter is more than a translator of words, since language skills are only a part of the process of communication. Biculturalism—sensitivity to cultural and social differences—is often as important as bilingualism. An interpreter must be sensitive to what is appropriate to the occasion. One of my favorite examples of this concerns a famous Western scientist who was asked to address a large Chinese audience. Before his talk, he was disconcerted to find that a number of children were playing and chattering in the aisles. His impatience increased when he realized that no one was attempting to quiet them down as he was about to begin. He exploded angrily at the interpreter, "Will you tell those little bastards to shut up!" With perfect aplomb the interpreter spoke quietly into the microphone, "Xiao pengyoumen, qing nimen shaowei anjing yidian, hao bu hao!" Which roughly translates, "Little friends, would you please be just a bit more quiet, if you don't mind."

Another important aspect of biculturalism is knowing what makes people laugh in the other culture. Humor is very difficult to translate. In fact, very often American humor just does not work in Chinese. In that case one may have to resort to the tactic of Doonesbury's interpreter Honey (who is actually modeled on one of China's best interpreters, Tang Wensheng) when she tells her audience in one frame, "I think he's about to make a joke. . . ." and in the next, "The joke has been made, and he will be expecting you to laugh at it. Go wild."

Political sensitivity is also an essential aspect of biculturalism. Several times during the past decade we have been spared unhappy incidents when interpreters wisely avoided repeating an American speaker's inadvertent use of "Republic of China" for "People's Republic of China" and translated the lat-ter term into Chinese. No matter how often people are forewarned about this error it is still quite common, whether out of nervousness or habit—especially when one is attempting a phrase like, "the people of the People's Republic of China." Somehow that mouthful usually comes out wrong.

Bilingualism and biculturalism can be learned—though often only by a process of osmosis—during long years of study and/or living in another country. But there are other, more innate characteristics that contribute to the making of a good interpreter.

Good interpreters must have a special kind of personality, in fact, a somewhat schizophrenic one. On the one hand, they must be confident and aggressive enough to be relaxed when speaking in front of audiences large or small, presidents or prime ministers. On the other hand, they must have the ability to submerge their own egos and take on the personalities of the speakers. Frustrated actors probably make some of the best interpreters. They don't mind, in fact they enjoy, mirroring the actions and tones of the speaker or, as is quite often the case, a series of speakers with varying demeanors. Yet sometimes an interpreter can be too much of a ham. This is dangerous because while it makes for an entertaining, lively session, it usually detracts from the speaker, who should be the focus of attention.

Another theatrical talent that comes in handy is projection. Occasionally interpreters have the use of a microphone; more often they have to compete against the whir and rumble of factory machinery or city street noises. Some interpreters have a tendency to look at and speak directly to the leader of a delegation, ignoring the rest of the group. Many times I have found myself in the back of a room, waving my arms or otherwise trying to indicate to the interpreter that the people at the back cannot hear.

These personal traits often compensate for minor language problems. For instance, one interpreter with whom we have worked over the years speaks excellent Chinese, but in a classical, literary style. As an academic interested in traditional China he has not needed to be conversant with contemporary language changes. But since this particular person is also a consummate actor with exaggerated movements and facial expressions, we overlook his literary rather than vernacular language. Although he sometimes interjects too much of himself into the interpreting process, we also like to work with him because he interacts very well with the Chinese. They have great respect for his knowledge of traditional China, and they love to imitate (with great affection) his mannerisms and speech patterns.

On a more practical note, being able to do two (or more) things at one time is important. An interpreter must be listening to what the speaker is saying while thinking about the best way to render it into another language. This is obviously much more critical for simultaneous interpreters, but those who do consecutive interpreting face the problem as well. A few interpreters manage to do four things at the same time: listen; jot down key words to jog their memories; look up unknown words in a small dictionary (which usually appears magically out of a pocket); and, juggling notebook and dictionary, write down the unfamiliar word so if it is repeated later the dictionary will not have to be hauled out again. All this without diverting attention from the speaker.

And speaking of writing things down, interpreters should always carry notebooks—and use them. Even the best of memories sometimes fails. But one should be selective. Only those with super stenographic skills should attempt a verbatim transcript; otherwise they will still be on the third word while the speaker is waiting for the translation. Selected words or phrases should be sufficient to recall the full sentence.

Obviously interpreters should be matched to specific jobs; some will be better at one kind of work while others will excel at another. For technical interpreting someone who not only knows the specific jargon (that, after all, can be looked up in a dictionary) but also is familiar with the concepts behind the words is needed.

There are times when an interpreter who blends into the background is required, perhaps for high-level diplomatic negotiations. At other times, someone with a more forceful personality is required. The National Committee on U.S.-China Relations opts for the latter, since our work generally entails introducing Chinese and American counterparts to one another. Our interpreters must be observant, outgoing, and interested in others, so that in a social situation they can get a group of Americans to stop chatting with their friends and encourage them to interact with the Chinese who, more than likely, have clustered themselves in the corner or at a window to exclaim over the view. We also need interpreters who are lively and knowledgeable about the United States so they can help explain American culture and history to members of Chinese delegations. . . .

## THE INTERPRETING SITUATION

Even if competent interpreters are available, many communication problems can still occur. Insuring that they do not is as much the responsibility of those relying on interpretation as it is of the interpreter. This is particularly true for an American who is conducting negotiations or substantive discussions with the Chinese and who has a clear stake in their success. But everyone involved should be aware of certain pitfalls and try to avoid them. . . .

### Preparation

It is always useful for the interpreter to have some advance knowledge of the material to be translated so that unfamiliar terms can be checked and unclear concepts defined. Providing the interpreter with a copy of the text, promotional brochures about the product that is going to be sold or information about the sites to be visited is always worth the effort. If written material isn't available or if the speaker prefers to talk off-the-cuff, it is a good idea for the speaker to go over the issues that will be addressed in the discussion with the interpreter beforehand. . . .

### Pacing

How long an interpreter can work without losing effectiveness depends very much on the individual. I know a number of Americans and Chinese who can go from 8:00 in the morning until 1:00 the next morning. On the other hand, there are some people who cannot concentrate for more than a two-hour span, and need regular breaks to recharge their batteries. Obviously, knowing the interpreter's capacity in advance is very useful in planning agendas. Once discussions begin, the person in charge should look for clues that the interpreter is tiring.

## Precision Versus Paraphrase

The interpreter should always be given a sense of how precise a translation is expected. For an interpreter to stay up the whole night toiling over an exact, word-for-word translation of a speech is counterproductive if the occasion does not demand it.

Another aspect of this issue is when to translate and when to leave people alone. I am of the school that believes that it is better to overtranslate than to undertranslate. There are those who feel that it is not important to translate everything that is said, especially when the conversation is not a substantive or professional one or when there are visual aids. But I think that interpreters, because they are bilingual, often forget what it is like to be in a strange land with no knowledge whatsoever of the language or culture. The non-English-speaking Chinese do not know that the spiel being given by the trainer at Sea Life Park is not all that relevant. While it might not be necessary to go into great detail in such situations, a quick paraphrase would at least give the Chinese the gist and let them know that they are not missing something really important.

Sometimes we encounter interpreters who feel the need for great precision and will take several seconds (which always seem like eons to listeners) to think of the word or phrase carrying the precise nuance of the situation. This is very commendable and certainly necessary in delicate diplomatic or business negotiations. But for general interpreting, it is more important to keep the flow of speech constant and use the closest approximation so as not to have an awkward silence (during which the speaker is apt to feel compelled to start talking again, thereby throwing the interpreter off balance).

Another kind of interpreter is the paraphraser or editor who tends to give the gist of what the speaker is saying, ignoring the details. If such actions stem from the interpreter's laziness, fatigue, or boredom, it is inexcusable. But if the interpreter "reads" the audience well enough to know that they are indeed tired or not interested, it is forgivable and indeed often desirable to speed things up a bit by omissions or condensations. For instance, before White House and Congressional tours, the National Committee escorts always tell the guides that the Chinese are generally unfamiliar with names of European sculptors, painters, and craftsmen, and with the minutiae of American history. Yet the guides cannot seem to stop themselves from cataloging who painted which portrait of a president's wife and which glass company in what year produced the goblets used by President Hayes! At such times we do not complain if the interpreters leave out some details.

In general, where one strikes a balance depends on the nature of the situation. Usually, only business or diplomatic negotiations demand a precise, word-for-word translation. In other situations, accuracy is the goal but it is permissible to paraphrase on occasion.

## Supplying Background Information

Sometimes, trying to be helpful and fill in gaps in the audience's understanding, interpreters will add background information not supplied by the speaker. This is often quite useful, but the interpreter should indicate to the speaker that this has been done, especially since the speaker may have planned to give the same explanation in the very next sentence.

## Length of Speech Units

Most people are not used to working with interpreters and often talk in long, rambling sentences. Forgetting to pause for translation, they leave the interpreter to scribble madly in a notebook or else to cough discreetly or in some way break into the monologue. Chinese interpreters tend to be more patient and will stand diligently taking notes until the bitter end, perhaps because they are more carefully trained or less aggressive (or more respectful of authority?) than some of their American colleagues. Occasionally the opposite will occur. In an effort to be as helpful as possible, an American speaker will give a phrase at a time, stopping in the middle of sentences and thoughts to allow the interpreter to translate. This may work in some languages, but not in Chinese. Since subject, verb, and object generally occupy different positions in many English and Chinese sentences, interpreters need to have nearly the whole sentence in hand before they set to work. Speakers should always be reminded of this problem.

## Invisibility of Interpreters

Quite a few interpreters tend to speak in the third rather than in the first person. If the speaker is a proud father and wants to regale the listener with stories about his son, the interpreter should say "my son" and should not say "he says his son. . . ."

Interpreters should confine themselves to facilitating communication, and not (except in unusual situations) add their own personal comments. This is a very difficult thing to do; it is even harder when an American looks directly at the interpreter and asks questions that are meant for the delegation member: "What's the next stop on the itinerary?" "How many children do you have?" "What has impressed you most about the United States?" The interpreter knows very well that the next stop is San Francisco, that the delegation member has three children aged 28, 24, and 18 (and even what they all do), and has heard twenty times how impressed the Chinese are with the warmth and friendliness and hospitality of Americans. But that knowledge is no excuse for not turning to the Chinese and asking once again, thus drawing the Chinese into the conversation.

## Direction of Translation

It is always easier to interpret into one's native tongue from the foreign language. Diplomatic practice, however, has made the opposite the rule, based on the theory that as part of a negotiating team, an interpreter is familiar with his or her own side's position and is able to render it better than someone unfamiliar with the background. Thus when interpreters are available from both sides, it is common for American interpreters to go from English to Chinese and for Chinese interpreters to work from Chinese to English even though articulateness would be increased if this were reversed.

## Numbers

Even the best Chinese and American interpreters have problems with large numbers, since the Chinese arrange digits in sets of four, as opposed to sets of three in the West. Numbers should always be checked, especially if the translation seems surprising. Writing figures down and asking the interpreter whether they are correct is the best way of guaranteeing that one hundred thousand has not become one million.

## Translating Substance

It is inevitable that Americans will think and talk in their own categories, which do not necessarily have an analogue in Chinese. This can create problems, especially when the interpreter translates rather mechanistically. One way to compensate is for the Americans to learn as much as possible about China, so that they are more likely to use concepts that Chinese can understand, and, in turn, be able to better comprehend Chinese concepts.

Another dimension of this problem is the American tendency to express ideas in abstract and complex ways, while Chinese are accustomed to more concrete modes of expression. Providing a translation bridge over this gap can often prove very difficult, especially since there is no subjunctive mode in Chinese.

## Questions

The above difference is particularly evident when it comes to questions. Americans often preface questions with statements and then pose their queries in a theoretical fashion. Chinese are more used to questions that are direct, down-to-earth, and pragmatic. Straightforward rather than hypothetical questions will produce better results.

Chinese, especially officials, like to listen to a whole series of questions before giving any answers. They are masters at taking eighteen different questions and then weaving one statement that conveys their message, answers those queries they wish to address, and barely touches those they wish to avoid. Americans can escape this trap by suggesting a question-by-question approach, on the grounds that the answer to one question will spark new and more interesting questions.

## Nonverbal Communication

There are two ways in which body language can affect interpreter-aided communication. The first is in choosing whom one looks at. Most people tend to look at the interpreter when they really should look at the person being addressed. When listening to what is being interpreted one should try to look at the person who first said it. Doing this seems unnatural, and the Chinese are better at it than we are. Second, talking with your hands seems to aid communication. Listeners can pick up a vague idea of what it is being said even before the interpreter translates.

## Helping with Problems

None of us is perfect—including interpreters. But weak points can be minimized. If the interpreter's problem is comprehension, speaking slowly will help. If it is a vocabulary problem, having a good dictionary and paraphrasing creatively are partial remedies. Once when interpreting for a Chinese delegation, I totally blanked on how to say, "The sun set." So I just said, "The sun went to sleep." They got the idea and I got a lot of laughs! Above all, interpreters should receive frequent doses of positive reinforcement and, if necessary, constructive criticism. . . .

## CONCEPTS AND QUESTIONS FOR CHAPTER 5

**1.** Can you think of examples that would demonstrate the validity of linguistic relativity?

**2.** What is meant by the sentence, "Language is a guide to social reality"?

**3.** Can you think of some arguments that would disprove the concept of linguistic relativity?

**4.** What intercultural difficulties could arise as a result of different speaking styles when American and Japanese business persons are engaged in policy development?

**5.** In what manner does culture influence the spoken aspects of decision making in Asian countries?

**6.** What does Verner Bickley mean when he refers to language as a bridge?

**7.** How does the bridge concept help us understand the role of language in intercultural communication?

**8.** How do the types of translation problems discussed by Sechrest, Fay, and Zaidi apply to everyday intercultural encounters?

**9.** Some people have suggested that the problems associated with translation could be solved if everyone spoke the same universal language. Evaluate this view in light of the influence culture has on language.

**10.** What do you consider to be the difference between translating and interpreting?

**11.** What are the advantages of having an interpreter who is aware of nonverbal behaviors as well as verbal behaviors?

**12.** Suggest ways that people might learn about the experiential aspects of other cultures that lead to unique language differences.

## SUGGESTED READINGS

Bosmajian, H. A. "Defining the 'American Indian': A case study in the language of suppression." *The Speech Teacher* 21 (1973), 89–99. Bosmajian shows how language functioned as a force in suppressing the American Indian. He asserts that the first linguistic act of an oppressor is to redefine the victims he intends to suppress (to jail or to eradicate) so that the victims will be seen as deserving suppression.

*The Florida Reporter* (Spring/Summer 1969). This special issue is devoted to the problems of cultural differences in language and language use in the United States. It emphasizes teaching problems and practical methods for improving intercultural understanding.

Folb, E. A. *Runnin' Down Some Lines: The Language and Culture of Black Teenagers*. Cambridge, Mass.: Harvard University Press, 1980. Folb focuses on the special vocabulary, idiomatic usages, and culture of black teenagers who live in the inner city of South Central Los Angeles. Through her study of language, she enables the reader to gain insights into the beliefs, world view, attitudes, and values of this particular group.

Lambert, W. E., and R. G. Tucker. *Tu, Vous, Usted: A Social-Psychological Study of Address Patterns*. Rowley, Mass.: Newbury House, 1976. In this book the authors examine the ways people from different cultures address each other. Lambert and Tucker look at the patterns of distancing relationships through language. The influence of nonreciprocal language patterns was a major area of research.

Lewis, I., ed. *Symbols and Sentiments: Cross-Cultural Studies in Symbolism*. New York: Academic Press, 1977. This collection grew out of an interdisciplinary seminar that focused on the problems of language in a cross-cultural setting. The authors are concerned with the emotional aspects of meaning as well as with the cognitive dimensions of symbols.

Nist, J. *Handicapped English. The Language of the Socially Disadvantaged*. Springfield, Ill.: Charles C. Thomas, 1974. Nist examines the concept of speech and prestige from the perspective of social class as a subculture. He explains how the language and dialect of a subculture can give information about the characteristics of that group. He concentrates on three types of speech to determine the extent to which one finds differences as one moves in and out of various social classes.

Thorne, B., and N. Henley. *Language and Sex: Difference and Dominance*. Rowley, Mass.: Newbury House, 1975. This collection of essays examines the relationship between language and sex. It covers topics such as sexism in language, sex differences in word choice, sex differences in intonation patterns, sex differences in choice of phonetic variants, conversational patterns between the sexes, and the effect of sex on the verbal interaction between teachers and children.

Williamson-Inge, D. K. "Approaches to Black language studies: A cultural critique." *Journal of Black Studies* 15 (1984), 17–29. This article uniquely "represents a cultural critique of approaches to Black language studies." It culturally analyzes various theories surrounding Black language. It also evaluates politically based attitudes and self-determination toward Black communication.

## ADDITIONAL READINGS

Abdulaziz, M. H. "Patterns of language acquisition and use in Kenya: Rural-urban differences." *International Journal of the Sociology of Language* 34 (1982), 95–120.

Angle, J. "Mutual language group accommodation: Can the privileged language group respond to economic incentives too?" *Western Sociological Review,* 12 (1981), 71–89.

Bachman, J. G., and P. M. O'Malley. "Yea-saying, nay-saying, and going to extremes: Black-white differences in response styles." *Public Opinion Quarterly* 48 (1984), 491–509.

Beaujot, R. P. "The decline of official language minorities in Quebec and English Canada." *Canadian Journal of Sociology* 7 (1982), 267–289.

Bond, M. H., and K. Yang. "Ethnic affirmation versus cross-cultural accommodation: The variable impact of questionnaire language on Chinese bilinguals from Hong Kong." *Journal of Cross-Cultural Psychology* 13 (1982), 169–185.

Brasch, W. M. *Black English and the Mass Media*. Amherst, Mass.: University of Massachusetts Press, 1981.

Brislin, R. W., ed. *Translations: Applications and Research*. New York: Halsted, 1976.

Burling, R. *Learning a Field Language*. Ann Arbor, Mich.: The University of Michigan Press, 1984.

Cogdell, R., and S. Wilson. *Black Communication in White Society*. Saratoga, Calif.: Century 21, 1980.

Christensen, K. M. "Conceptual sign language as a bridge between English and Spanish." *American Annals of the Deaf* 130 (1985), 244–249.

Delain, M. T., P. D. Pearson, and R. C. Anderson. "Reading comprehension and creativity in Black language use: You stand to gain by playing the sounding game." *American Education Research Journal* 22 (1985), 155–173.

Dill, B. T. "The dialectics of Black womanhood," *Signs* 4 (1979), 543–555.

Duff, A. *The Third Language: Recurrent Problems of Translation into English*. Oxford: Pergamon Press, 1981.

Fisherman, J. A. "Whorfianism of the third kind: Ethnolinguistic diversity as a worldwide social asset," *Language in Society* 11 (1982), 1–14.

Genzel, R., and M. Graves. *Culturally Speaking*. Rowley, Mass.: Newbury House, 1986.

Graham, J. E., ed. *Difference in Translation*. Ithaca, N.Y.: Cornell University Press, 1985.

Haas, M. *Language, Culture, and History*. Stanford, Calif.: Stanford University Press, 1978.

Hakuta, K. *Mirror of Language: The Debate on Bilingualism*. Rowley, Mass.: Newbury House, 1986.

Hawana, S. A., and J. K. Smith. "Can philosophical meaning cross linguistic/cultural barriers?" *International Journal of Intercultural Relations* 3 (1979), 119–210.

Hoope, R. A., and J. F. Kess. "Differential detection of ambiguity in Japanese." *Journal of Psycholinguistic Research* 3 (1980), 303–318.

Irving, L. A. *The Language of Ethnic Conflict: Social Organization and Lexical Culture*. New York: Columbia University Press, 1983.

Khubchandani, L. M. *Plural Languages, Plural Cultures*. Honolulu: University of Hawaii Press, 1983.

Kirch, M. "Language, communication, and culture." *Modern Language Journal* 57 (1973), 340–343.

Larson, M. *Meaning-Based Translation: A Guide to Cross-Language Equivalence*. New York: University Press of America, 1984.

Lewis, I., ed. *Symbols and Sentiments: Cross-Cultural Studies in Symbolism*. New York: Academic Press, 1977.

Lukens, J. G. "Ethnocentric speech: Its nature and implications." *Ethnic Groups* 2 (1978), 35–53.

Osgood, C. E. et al. *Cross-Cultural Universals of Affective Meaning*. Urbana, Ill.: University of Illinois Press, 1973.

Philipsen, G. "Speaking 'like a man' in Teamsterville: Cultural patterns of role enactment in an urban neighborhood." *Quarterly Journal of Speech* 61 (1975), 13–22.

Simard, L. M. "Cross-cultural interaction: Potential invisible barriers." *Journal of Social Psychology* 2 (1981), 171–182.

Sossman, N. M., and H. M. Rosenfeld. "Influence of culture, language, and sex on conversational distance." *Journal of Personality and Social Psychology* 1 (1982), 66–74.

Stanley, J. P. "Homosexual slang." *American Speech* 45 (1970), 45–59.

Tzeng, O. C., R. Neel, and D. Landis. "Effects of culture and languages on self conceptions." *International Journal of Psychology* 16 (1981), 95–109.

Wilks, W. *The Science of Translation: Problems and Methods*. Tuebinger: Gunter Narr Verlag, 1986.

# 6

# Nonverbal Interaction

Successful participation in intercultural communication requires that we recognize and understand culture's influence not only on verbal interaction but on *nonverbal* interaction as well. Nonverbal behaviors constitute messages to which people attach meaning just as do verbal behaviors. Because nonverbal symbols are derived from such diverse behaviors as body movements, postures, facial expressions, gestures, eye movements, physical appearance, the use and organization of space, and the structuralization of time, these symbolic behaviors often vary from culture to culture. An awareness of the role of nonverbal behaviors is crucial, therefore, if we are to appreciate all aspects of intercultural interaction.

Nonverbal behavior is largely unconscious. We use nonverbal symbols spontaneously, without thinking about what posture, what gesture, or what interpersonal distance is appropriate to the situation. These factors are critically important in intercultural communication because, as with other aspects of the communication process, nonverbal behaviors are subject to cultural variation. These nonverbal behaviors can be categorized in two ways.

In the first, culture tends to determine the specific nonverbal behaviors that represent or symbolize specific thoughts, feelings, or states of the communicator. Thus, what might be a sign of greeting in one culture could very well be an obscene gesture in another. Or what might be a symbol of affirmation in one culture could be meaningless or even signify negation in another. In the second, culture determines when it is appropriate to display or communicate various thoughts, feelings, or internal states; this is particularly evident in the display of emotions. Although there seems to be little cross-cultural difference in the behaviors that represent emotional states, there are great cultural differences in which emotions may be displayed, by whom, and when or where they may be displayed.

As important as verbal language is to a communication event, nonverbal communication is just as, if not more, important. Nonverbal messages tell us how other messages are to be interpreted. They indicate whether verbal messages are true, joking, serious, threatening, and so on. Gregory Bateson has described these "second-order messages" as meta communication, which we use as frames around messages to designate how they are to be interpreted.* The importance of meta communication can be seen from communication research indicating that as much as 90 percent of the social content of a message is transmitted paralinguistically or nonverbally.†

Chapter 6 deals with nonverbal interaction. The readings examine the influence of culture on various aspects of nonverbal behavior in order to demonstrate the variety of culturally derived nonverbal behaviors and the underlying value structures that produce these behaviors.

As in the previous chapter, which dealt with verbal language, we begin this chapter with an overview. Peter Andersen's article "Explaining Intercultural Differences in Nonverbal Communication" begins with an analysis of how culture determines our nonverbal communicative behavior. Andersen goes beyond a mere cataloging of differences in nonverbal communication and offers us insights into cultural explanations for a variety of nonverbal communication differences.

Tom Bruneau in "The Time Dimension in Intercultural Communication" looks at the conscious and unconscious ways different cultures treat the concept of time. He examines such topics as futurism, timing and timekeeping, the pace of life, and cultural tempo.

In Chapter 3 we noted that the experiences of men and women often produce some significant differences in values, attitudes, and communication patterns. One of these major differences is found in the area of nonverbal communication. More specifically, researchers have found sex differences in all the categories normally associated with nonverbal behavior. In "Sex Differences in Nonverbal Communication," Barbara Westbrook Eakins and R. Gene Eakins review these research findings. Male-female comparisons are made for eye contact, facial expressions, posture and bearing, gestures, clothing, grooming and physical appearance, use of space, and touch. Being aware of and knowing how these sex differences in nonverbal behavior operate during interaction should be helpful to both women and men as they attempt to exchange ideas, information, and feelings with one another.

One of the major themes of this volume is that culture touches nearly every phase of the communication process. While seldom viewed in the West as an ingredient of communication, silence also affects communication. The main focus of the next essay is the special link between culture and silence. In "Silence and Silences in Cross-Cultural Perspective: Japan and the United States," Tom Bruneau and Satoshi Ishii discuss the cultural bases of silence, define the concept of silence, and then compare how the East and West use silence as a form of communication. Their analysis of East-West differences in the use of silence goes a long way toward helping us understand the problems that can exist in American-Japanese intercultural communication when the role and function of silence is not understood by both sides.

---

*Gregory Bateson, "A Theory of Play and Fantasy," *Psychiatric Research* 2 (1955), 39–51.

†Albert Mehrabian and Morton Wiener, "Decoding in Inconsistent Messages,"*Journal of Personality and Social Psychology* 6 (1967), 109–114.

# Explaining Intercultural Differences in Nonverbal Communication

## PETER ANDERSEN

Culture has been equated with communication by a number of scholars. Culture and communication are inseparable because culture is both learned and maintained through human interaction (Andersen, Lustig, and Andersen 1986; Prosser 1978; Saral 1977). Moreover, culture is primarily a nonverbal phenomenon because most aspects of one's culture are learned through observation and imitation rather than explicit verbal instruction or expression. The primary level of culture is communicated implicitly, without awareness, by primarily nonverbal means (Hall 1984).

Intercultural communication occurs when two or more individuals with different cultural backgrounds interact. This process is rarely smooth and problem free. In most situations, intercultural interactants do not share the same language, but languages can be learned and larger communication problems occur in the *nonverbal* realm. Nonverbal communication is a subtle, multidimensional, and usually spontaneous process (Andersen 1986). Indeed, individuals are not aware of most of their own nonverbal behavior, which is enacted mindlessly, spontaneously, and unconsciously (Andersen 1986; Burgoon 1985; Samovar and Porter 1985). Since we are not usually aware of our *own* nonverbal behavior, it is extremely difficult to identify and

master the nonverbal behavior of another culture. At times we feel uncomfortable in other cultures because we intuitively know something isn't right. "Because nonverbal behaviors are rarely conscious phenomena, it may be difficult for us to know exactly why we are feeling uncomfortable" (Gudykunst and Kim 1984, p. 149).

This article reviews briefly the codes of nonverbal communication, locates culture as a part of interpersonal behavior, then discusses five main dimensions of cultural variation, including *immediacy, individualism, masculinity, power distance,* and *high* and *low context.* It is argued that each of these dimensions produces differences in a culture's communication, particularly in a culture's nonverbal communication.

## NONVERBAL CODES

Most discussions of nonverbal intercultural communication take an antecdotal approach, where numerous examples of intercultural differences for each nonverbal code are discussed in detail. Recapitulation of the various nonverbal codes of intercultural communication is not a primary purpose of the present article. Thus each code will be discussed only briefly along with references that provide detailed and excellent analyses of how each nonverbal code differs interculturally.

Two of the most fundamental nonverbal differences in intercultural communication involve space and time. *Chronemics*—or the study of meanings, usage, and communication of time—is probably the most discussed and well-researched nonverbal code in the intercultural literature (Bruneau 1979; Burgoon and Saine 1978; Gudykunst and Kim 1984; Hall 1959, 1976, 1984; Malandro and Barker 1983; Merriam 1983). The analyses suggest that the time frames of various cultures differ so dramatically that even if only chronemic differences existed, intercultural misunderstandings would still be abundant. A second nonverbal code that has attracted considerable attention is *proxemics,* the communication of interpersonal space and distance. Research has documented that cultures differ substantially in their use of personal space, the distances they maintain, and their regard for territory, as well as the meanings they assign to proxemic behavior (Burgoon and Saine 1978; Gudykunst and Kim 1984; Hall 1959, 1976; Malandro and Barker 1983; Samovar, Porter, and Jain 1981; Scheflen 1974).

Many intercultural differences have been reported in people's *kinesic* behavior, including their facial expressions, body movements, gestures, and conversational regulators (Burgoon and Saine 1978; Gudykunst and Kim 1984; Hall 1976; Jensen 1985; Malandro and Barker 1983; Rich 1974; Samovar, Porter, and Jain 1981; Scheflen 1974). Interpersonal patterns of tactile communication called *haptics* also reveal substantial intercultural differences (Andersen and Leibowitz 1978; Barker and Malandro 1983; Prosser 1978; Samovar, Porter, and Jain 1981).

Other important codes of nonverbal communication have attracted considerably less space in publications on nonverbal intercultural communication. *Physical appearance,* the most important nonverbal code during initial encounters, is of obvious importance because many intercultural encounters are based on stereotypes and are of short duration. Some discussion of intercultural differences in appearance is provided by Scheflen (1974) and Samovar, Porter, and Jain (1981). *Oculesics*— the study of messages sent by the eyes, including eye contact, blinks, eye movements, and pupil dilation—has received only marginal attention by intercultural communication scholars (Gudykunst and Kim 1984; Jensen 1985; Samovar, Porter, and Jain 1981). Since eye contact has been called an "invitation to communicate," the way it varies cross-culturally is an important communication topic. *Vocalics* or *paralanguage*—the nonverbal elements the voice—also has received comparatively little attention from intercultural researchers (Gudykunst and Kim 1984; LaBarre 1985; Rich 1974; Scheflen 1974; Samovar, Porter, and Jain 1981). Music and singing—a universal form of aesthetic communication— has been almost completely overlooked in intercultural research except for one excellent study (Lomax 1986) that identified several groups of worldwide cultures through differences and similarities in folk songs. Finally, *olfactics*—the study of the interpersonal communication via smell—has

been virtually ignored in intercultural research despite its importance (Samovar, Porter, and Jain 1981).

## LOCATING CULTURE IN INTERPERSONAL BEHAVIOR

Culture is a critical concept to communication scholars because every communicator is a product of her/his culture. Culture, along with traits, situations, and states is one of the four primary sources of interpersonal behavior (Andersen 1987a, 1987b) (see Figure 1). Culture is the enduring influence of the social environment on one's behavior, including one's interpersonal communication behavior. Culture exerts a considerable force on individual behavior through what Geertz (1973) called "control mechanisms—plans, recipes, rules, instructions (what computer engineers call 'programs')— for the governing of behavior" (p. 44). Culture has similar powerful, though not identical, effects on all residents of a cultural system. "Culture can be behaviorally observed by contrasting intragroup homogeneity with intergroup heterogeneity" (Andersen, Lustig, and Andersen 1986, p. 11).

Culture has been confused with personal traits because both are enduring phenomena (Andersen 1987a, 1987b). Traits have multiple causes (Andersen 1987b), only some of which are the result of culture. Culture has also been confused with the situation because both are part of one's social environment. However, culture is an enduring phenomena whereas the situation is a transient one with an observable beginning and end. Culture is one of the most enduring, powerful, and invisible shapers of our behavior.

## DIMENSIONS OF CULTURAL VARIATION

Thousands of anecdotes regarding misunderstandings caused by nonverbal behaviors between persons from different cultures have been reported. While it may be useful to know that Arabs stand closer to one another than do Americans, that the Swiss are more time-conscious than the Italians, and

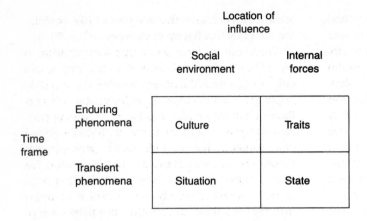

Figure 1 Sources of Influence on Interpersonal Behavior

that Orientals value silence more than Westerners, this anecdotal approach is not sufficient. Because the number of potential pairs of cultures is huge, and because the number of possible misunderstandings based on nonverbal behavior between each pair of cultures is similarly large, millions of potential intercultural anecdotes are possible. What is needed is some way to organize and understand this plethora of potential problems in intercultural communication. Some initial research has shown that cultures can be located along dimensions that help to explain these intercultural differences. Most cultural differences in nonverbal behavior are a result of variations along the dimensions we discuss next.

## Immediacy and Expressiveness

*Immediacy behaviors* are actions that simultaneously communicate warmth, closeness, and availability for communication; they signal approach rather than avoidance and closeness rather than distance (Andersen 1985). Examples of immediacy behaviors are smiling, touching, eye contact, close distances, and vocal animation. Some scholars have labeled these behaviors as "expressive" (Patterson 1983).

Cultures that display considerable interpersonal closeness or immediacy have been labeled "contact

cultures" because people in these countries stand close and touch often (Hall 1966). People in low-contact cultures tend to stand apart and touch less. According to Patterson (1983):

*These habitual patterns of relating to the world permeate all aspects of everyday life, but their effects on social behavior define the manner in which people relate to one another. In the case of contact cultures, this general tendency is manifested in closer approaches so that tactile and olfactory information may be gained easily (p. 145).*

It is interesting that contact cultures are generally located in warm countries and low-contact cultures in cool climates. Considerable research has shown that contact cultures include most Arab countries; the Mediterranean region including France, Greece, and Italy; Jewish people from both Europe and the Middle East; Eastern Europeans and Russians; and Indonesians and Hispanics (Condon and Yousef 1983; Jones and Remland 1982; Mehrabian 1971; Montagu and Matson 1979; Patterson 1983; Samovar, Porter, and Jain 1981; Scheflen 1972). Australians are moderate in their cultural contact level, as are North Americans, although North Americans tend toward low contact (Patterson 1983). Low-contact cultures include most of Northern

Europe, including Scandinavia, Germany, and England; British-Americans; white Anglo-Saxons (the primary culture of the United States); and the Japanese (Andersen, Andersen, and Lustig 1987; Heslin and Alper 1983; Jones and Remland 1982; Mehrabian 1971; Montagu and Matson 1979; Patterson 1983; Samovar, Porter, and Jain 1981; Scheflen 1972).

Explanations for these latitudinal variations have included energy level, climate, and metabolism (Andersen, Lustig, and Andersen 1987). Evidently, cultures in cool climates tend to be task oriented and interpersonally "cool," whereas cultures in warm climates tend to be interpersonally oriented and interpersonally "warm." Even within the United States, people in warm latitudes tend to exhibit more contact than people in cold areas. Andersen, Lustig, and Andersen (1987) found a 0.31 correlation between the latitude of universities and touch avoidance. These data suggest that students at sunbelt universities are more touch-oriented than their counterparts in colder climates.

## Individualism

One of the most fundamental dimensions along which cultures differ is the degree of *individualism* versus *collectivism*. This dimension determines how people live together (alone, in families, or tribes; see Hofstede 1982), their values, and how they communicate. As we shall see, people in the United States are individualists for better or worse. We take individualism for granted and are blind to its impact until travel brings us in contact with less individualistic, more collectivistic cultures.

Individualism has been applauded as a blessing and has been elevated to the status of a national religion in the United States. Indeed, the best and worst features of our culture can be attributed to individualism. Proponents of individualism have argued that it is the basis of liberty, democracy, freedom, and economic incentive and that it serves as a protection against tyranny. On the other hand, individualism has been blamed for our alienation from one another, loneliness, selfishness, and narcissism. Indeed, Hall (1976) claimed that, as an extreme, "Western man has created chaos by denying that part of his self that integrates while enshrining the parts that fragment experience" (p. 9).

There can be little doubt that individualism is one of the fundamental dimensions that distinguish cultures one from the other. Likewise, there is little doubt that Western culture is individualistic, whereas Eastern culture emphasizes harmony among people and between people and nature. Tomkins (1984) demonstrated that an individual's psychological makeup is the result of this cultural dimension. He stated, "Human beings, in Western Civilization, have tended toward self-celebration, positive or negative. In oriental thought another alternative is represented, that of harmony between man and nature" (p. 182). Prosser (1978) suggested that the Western emphasis on individuality finds its culmination in contemporary U.S. cultures, where the chief cultural value is the role of the individual. This idea is verified in the landmark intercultural study of Hofstede (1982). In his study of individualism in 40 noncommunist countries, the nine most individualistic (in order) were the United States, Australia, Great Britain, Canada, the Netherlands, New Zealand, Italy, Belgium, and Denmark—all Western or European cultures. The nine least individualistic (starting with the least) were Venezuela, Colombia, Pakistan, Peru, Taiwan, Thailand, Singapore, Chile, and Hong Kong—all oriental or South American cultures. Similarly, Sitaram and Cogdell (1976) reported individuality to be of primary importance in Western cultures, of secondary importance in black cultures, and of lesser importance in Eastern and Muslim cultures.

While the United States is the most individualistic country on earth (Hofstede 1982), regions of the United States vary in their degree of individualism. Elazar (1972) has shown that the Central Midwest and the mid-Atlantic states have the most individualistic political culture, whereas the Southeast has the most traditionalistic and least individualistic. But these differences are all relative and, by world standards, even Mississippi has an individualistic culture. Bellah et al. (1985) stated:

*Individualism lies at the very core of American culture. . . . Anything that would violate our right* to think for ourselves, judge for ourselves, make our own decisions, live our lives as we see fit, is not only morally wrong, it is sacrilegious (p. 142).

Indeed, our extreme individualism makes it difficult for Americans to interact with and understand people from other cultures. We are unique; all other cultures are less individualistic. As Condon and Yousef (1983) stated:

*The fusion of individualism and equality is so valued and so basic that many Americans find it most difficult to relate to contrasting values in other cultures where interdependence greatly determines a person's sense of self (p. 65).*

The degree to which a culture is individualistic or collectivistic has an impact on the nonverbal behavior of that culture in a variety of ways. First, people from individualistic cultures are comparatively remote and distant proximically. Collectivistic cultures are interdependent and, as a result, they work, play, live, and sleep in close proximity to one another. Hofstede (1972) cites research which suggests that as hunters and gatherers, people lived apart in individualistic nuclear families. As agricultural societies developed, the interdependent extended family began to live in close proximity in large family or tribal units. Urban-industrial societies returned to a norm of individualism, nuclear families, and lack of proximity to one's neighbors, friends, and coworkers.

Kinesic behavior tends to be synchronized in collectivist cultures. Where families work collectively, movements, schedules, and actions need to be highly coordinated (Argyle 1975). In urban cultures, family members often do their "own thing," coming and going, working and playing, eating and sleeping on different schedules. People in individualistic cultures also smile more than people in normatively oriented cultures according to Tomkins (1984). This fact can probably be explained by the fact that individualists are responsible for their relationships and their own happiness, whereas normatively or collectively oriented people regard compliance with norms as a primary value and per-

sonal or interpersonal happiness as a secondary value. Similarly, people in collectivist cultures may suppress both positive and negative emotional displays that are contrary to the mood of the group because maintaining the group is a primary value. People in individualistic cultures are encouraged to express emotions because individual freedom is of paramount value.

Research suggests that people in individualistic cultures are more nonverbally affiliative than people in collectivist cultures. The reason for this is not intuitively obvious because individualism does not require affiliation. However, Hofstede (1982) explained that:

*In less individualistic countries where traditional social ties, like those with extended family members, continue to exist, people have less of a need to make specific friendships. One's friends are predetermined by the social relationships into which one is born. In the more individualistic countries, however, affective relationships are not socially predetermined but must be acquired by each individual personally (p. 163).*

In individualistic countries like the United States, affiliativeness, dating, flirting, small-talk, and initial acquaintance are more important than they are in collectivist countries where the social network is more fixed and less reliant on individual initiative. Bellah et al. (1985) maintain that for centuries in the individualistic and mobile United States, society people could meet very easily and their communication was open. However, their relationships were usually casual and transient.

Finally, in an impressive study of dozens of cultures, Lomax (1968) found that the song-and-dance styles of a country are related to its level of social cohesion and collectivism. Collectivist cultures rate high in stressing groupness and in the cohesion found in their singing styles. Collectivist cultures show both more cohesiveness in singing and more synchrony in their dance style than do individualistic cultures (Lomax 1968). It is not surprising that rock dancing, which emphasizes separateness and "doing your own thing," evolved in individualistic cultures such as those in England and the United

States. These dances may serve as a metaphor for the whole U.S. culture, where individuality is more prevalent than in any other place.

## Masculinity

Masculinity is a neglected dimension of culture. Masculine traits are typically attributes such as strength, assertiveness, competitiveness, and ambitiousness, whereas feminine traits are attributes such as affection, compassion, nurturance, and emotionality (Bem 1974; Hofstede 1982). Cross-cultural research shows that young girls are expected to be more nurturant than boys although there is considerable variation from country to country (Hall 1984). Hofstede (1982) has measured the degree to which people of both sexes in a culture endorse masculine or feminine goals. Masculine cultures regard competition and assertiveness as important, whereas feminine cultures place more importance on nurturance and compassion. Not surprisingly, the masculinity of a culture is negatively correlated with the percentage of women in technical and professional jobs and positively correlated with segregation of the sexes in higher education (Hofstede 1982).

The nine countries with the highest masculinity scores, according to Hofstede (1982) (most masculine first) are Japan, Austria, Venezuela, Italy, Switzerland, Mexico, Ireland, Great Britain, and Germany. With the exception of Japan, these countries all lie in Central Europe and the Caribbean. The nine countries with the lowest masculinity scores (least masculine first) are Sweden, Norway, Netherlands, Denmark, Finland, Chile, Portugal, and Thailand—all Scandinavian or South American cultures with the exception of Thailand. Why don't South American cultures manifest the Latin pattern of machismo? Hofstede (1982) suggests that machismo occurs more often in the Caribbean region than it does in South America itself.

Considerable research suggests that androgynous patterns of behavior (those that are both feminine and masculine) result in a high degree of self-esteem, social competence, success, and intellectual development for both males and females. Nonverbal styles where both men and women are free to express both masculine (e.g., dominance, anger) and feminine (e.g., warmth, emotionality) behavior are likely to be healthy and very effective. Indeed, Buck (1984) has shown that males may harm their health by internalizing emotions rather than externalizing them as women usually do. Internalized emotions that are not expressed result in a high stress level and high blood pressure. Interestingly enough, countries considered very masculine show high levels of stress (Hofstede 1982).

Considerable research has demonstrated significant differences in vocal patterns between egalitarian and nonegalitarian countries. Countries where women are economically important and where sexual standards for women are permissive show more relaxed vocal patterns than other countries (Lomax 1968). Moreover, egalitarian countries show less tension between the sexes, more vocal solidarity and coordination in their songs, and more synchrony in their movement than we see in less egalitarian countries (Lomax 1968).

It is important to note that the United States tends to be a masculine country according to Hofstede (1982) although it is not among the nine most masculine. Intercultural communicators should keep in mind that other countries may be more or less sexually egalitarian than is the United States. Similarly, most countries are more feminine (i.e., nurturant, compassionate), and people of both sexes in the United States frequently seem loud, aggressive, and competitive by world standards.

## Power Distance

A fourth fundamental dimension of intercultural communication is power distance. Power distance—the degree to which power, prestige, and wealth are unequally distributed in a culture—has been measured in a number of cultures using Hofstede's (1982) power distance index (PDI). Cultures with high PDI scores have power and influence concentrated in the hands of a few rather than distributed more or less equally throughout the population. Condon and Yousef (1983) distinguish among three cultural patterns: democratic, authority-centered, and authoritarian. The PDI is highly correlated (0.80) with authoritarianism (as measured by the F-Scale) (Hofstede 1982).

The nine countries with the highest PDI (highest first) are the Philippines, Mexico, Venezuela, India, Singapore, Brazil, Hong Kong, France, and Colombia (Hofstede 1982)—all of which are South Asian or Caribbean countries, with the exception of France. Gudykunst and Kim (1984) report that both African and Asian cultures generally maintain hierarchical role relationships. Asian students are expected to be modest and nonverbally deferent in the presence of their instructors. Likewise, Vietnamese consider employers to be their mentors and will not question orders. The nine countries with the lowest PDI (lowest first) are Austria, Israel, Denmark, New Zealand, Ireland, Sweden, Norway, Finland, and Switzerland (Hofstede 1982)—all of which are European, middle-class democracies located at high latitudes. The United States is slightly lower than the median in power distance. A fundamental determiner of power distance is the latitude of a country. Hofstede (1982) claims that latitude and climate are major forces in shaping cultures. He maintains that the key intervening variable is that technology is needed for survival in colder climates. This need produces a chain of events in which children are less dependent on authority and learn from people other than authority figures. Hofstede (1982) reports a 0.65 correlation between PDI and latitude! In a study conducted at 40 universities throughout the United States, Andersen, Lustig, and Andersen (1987) report a −0.47 correlation between latitude and intolerance for ambiguity and a −0.45 correlation between latitude and authoritarianism. These findings suggest that residents of the northern United States are less authoritarian and more tolerant of ambiguity. Northern cultures may have to be more tolerant and less autocratic to ensure cooperation and survival in harsher climates.

It is obvious that power distance affects the nonverbal behavior of a culture. High PDI countries such as India, with its rigid caste system, may severely limit interaction, as in the case of India's "untouchables." More than 20 percent of India's population are untouchables—those who are at the bottom of India's five-caste system (Chinoy 1967). Any contact

with untouchables by members of other castes is strictly forbidden and considered "polluting." Obviously, tactile communication among castes is greatly curtailed by Indian culture. High PDI countries with less rigid stratification than India may still prohibit interclass dating, marriage, and contact, which are taken for granted in low PDI countries.

Social systems with large power discrepancies also produce different kinesic behavior. According to Andersen and Bowman (1985), subordinates' body tension is more obvious in power-discrepant relationships. Similarly Andersen and Bowman (1985) report that in power-discrepant circumstances, subordinates smile often in an effort to appear polite and to appease superiors. The continual smiles of many orientals may be an effort to appease superiors or to produce smooth social relations; they may be the result of being reared in a high PDI culture.

Vocalic and paralinguistic cues are also affected by the power distance in a culture. People living in low PDI countries are generally less aware that vocal loudness may be offensive to others. The vocal tones of people in the United States are often perceived as noisy, exaggerated, and childlike (Condon and Yousef 1983). Lomax (1968) has shown that in countries where political authority is highly centralized, singing voices are tighter and the voice box is more closed, whereas more permissive societies produce more relaxed, open, and clear sounds.

## High and Low Context

A final essential dimension of intercultural communication is that of context. Hall (1976, 1984) has described high- and low-context cultures in considerable detail. "A high-extent (HC) communication or message is one in which most of the information is either in the physical context or internalized in the person, while very little is in the coded, explicit, transmitted parts of the message"(Hall 1976, p. 91). Lifelong friends often use HC or implicit messages that are nearly impossible for an outsider to understand. The situation, a smile, or a glance provides an implicit meaning that doesn't need to be articulated. In HC situations or cultures, information is integrated from the environment, the context, the situation, and from nonverbal cues that give the message a meaning that is unavailable in the explicit verbal utterance.

Low-context (LC) messages are just the opposite of HC messages; most of the information is in the explicit code (Hall 1976). LC messages must be elaborated, clearly communicated, and highly specific. Unlike personal relationships, which are relatively HC message systems, institutions such as courts of law and formal systems such as mathematics or computer language require explicit, LC systems because nothing can be taken for granted (Hall 1984).

Cultures vary considerably in the degree of context used in communication. The lowest context cultures are probably the Swiss, German, North American (including the United States), and Scandinavian (Hall 1976, 1984; Gudykunst and Kim 1984). These cultures are preoccupied with specifics, details, and precise time schedules at the expense of context. They utilize behavior systems built around Aristotelean logic and linear thinking (Hall 1984). Cultures that have some characteristics of both HC and LC systems include the French, English, and Italian (Gudykunst and Kim 1984), which are somewhat less explicit than Northern European cultures.

The highest context cultures are found in the Orient. China, Japan, and Korea are extremely HC cultures (Elliott, Scott, Jensen, and McDonough 1982; Hall 1976, 1984). Languages are some of the most explicit communication systems, but the Chinese language is an implicit high-context system. To use a Chinese dictionary, one must understand thousands of characters that change meaning when combined with other characters. People from the United States frequently complain that the Japanese never get to the point; they fail to recognize that HC cultures must provide a context and setting and let the point evolve (Hall 1984). American Indian cultures with ancestral migratory roots in East Asia are remarkably like contemporary oriental culture in several ways, especially in their need for high context (Hall 1984). Not surprisingly, most Latin American cultures, a fusion of Iberian (Portuguese-Spanish) and Indian traditions, are also high-context cultures. Southern and eastern Mediterranean people such as Greeks, Turks, and Arabs tend to have HC cultures as well.

Communication is obviously quite different in high- and low-context cultures. First, explicit forms of communication such as verbal codes are more prevalent in low-context cultures such as the United States and Northern Europe. People from LC cultures are often perceived as excessively talkative, belaboring the obvious, and using redundancies. People from HC cultures may be perceived as nondisclosive, sneaky, and mysterious. Second, HC cultures do not value verbal communication the same way as do LC cultures. Elliot et al. (1982) found that people who were more verbal were perceived as more attractive by people in the United States, but people who were less verbal were perceived as more attractive in Korea—a high-context culture. Third, HC cultures are more reliant on and tuned in to nonverbal communication than are LC cultures. LC cultures, and particularly the men in LC cultures, fail to perceive as much nonverbal communication as do members of HC cultures. Nonverbal communication provides the context for all communication (Watzlawick, Beavin, and Jackson 1967), but people from HC cultures are particularly affected by contextual cues. Thus facial expressions, tensions, movements, speed of interaction, location of the interaction, and other subtleties of nonverbal behavior are likely to be perceived by and have more meaning for people from high-context cultures. Finally, people from HC cultures expect more nonverbal communication than do interactants in LC cultures (Hall 1976). People from HC cultures expect communicators to understand unarticulated feelings, subtle gestures, and environmental cues that people from LC cultures simply do not process. What is worse, both cultural extremes fail to recognize these basic differences in behavior, communication, and context, and both are quick to misattribute the causes for the other's behavior.

## CONCLUSION

Reading about these five dimensions of culture cannot ensure competence in intercultural communication. The beauty of international travel, and even travel within the United States, is that it provides a unique perspective on one's own behavior and the behavior of others. Combining cognitive knowledge from articles and courses with actual encounters with people from other cultures is the best way to gain such competence.

A full, practical understanding of the dimensions along which cultures differ, combined with the knowledge of how specific communication acts differ cross-culturally, has several practical benefits. First, First, such knowledge will highlight and challenge assumptions about our own behavior. The structure of our own behavior is invisible and taken for granted until it is exposed and challenged through the study of other cultures and actual intercultural encounters. Indeed, Hall (1976) stated that ethnic diversity in interethnic communication can be a source of strength and an asset from which one can discover oneself.

Second, this discussion should make it clear that our attributions about the nonverbal communication of people from other cultures are often wrong. No dictionary or code of intercultural behavior is available. We cannot read people like books, not even people from our own culture. Understanding that someone is from a masculine, collectivist, or high-context culture will, however, make their behavior less confusing and more interpretable.

Finally, understanding about intercultural differences and actually engaging in intercultural encounters is bound to reduce ethnocentrism and make strangers from other cultures seem less threatening. Fear is often based on ignorance and misunderstanding. The fact of intercultural diversity should produce joy and optimism about the number of possible ways to be human.

## REFERENCES

Andersen, P. A. (1985). "Nonverbal Immediacy in Interpersonal Communication." In A. W. Siegman and S. Feldstein (eds.). *Multichannel Integrations of Nonverbal Behavior* (pp. 1–36). Hillsdale, NJ: Lawrence Erlbaum.

Andersen, P. A. (1986). "Consciousness, Cognition, and Communication." *Western Journal of Speech Communication* 50, 87–101.

Andersen, P. A. (1987a). "Locating the Sources of Interpersonal Behavior." *Distinguishing among Traits, States, Cultures and Situations.* Unpublished paper, San Diego State University, San Diego, CA.

Andersen, P. A. (1987b). "The Trait Debate: A Critical Examination of the Individual Differences Paradigm in Intercultural Communication." In B. Dervin and M. J. Voigt (eds.). *Progress in Communication Sciences* Volume VIII (pp. 47–82). Norwood, NJ: Ablex Publishing.

Andersen, J. F., P. A. Andersen, M. W. Lustig. (February 1987). "Predicting Opposite-Sex Touch Avoidance: A National Replication and Extension." Paper presented at the annual convention of the Western Speech Communication Association, San Diego, CA.

Andersen, P. A. and L. Bowman. (May 1985). "Positions of Power: Nonverbal Cues of Status and Dominance in Organizational Communication." Paper presented at the annual convention of the Interpersonal Communication Association, Honolulu, HI.

Andersen, P. A. and K. Leibowitz. (1978). "The Development and Nature of the Construct Touch Avoidance." *Environmental Psychology and Nonverbal Behavior* 3, 89–106.

Andersen, P. A., M. W. Lustig, and J. F. Andersen. (1986). "Communication Patterns among Cultural Regions of the United States: A Theoretical Perspective." Paper presented at the annual convention of the International Communication Association, Chicago.

Andersen, P. A., R. Lustig, and J. F. Andersen. (1987). "Changes in Latitude, Changes in Attitude: The Relationship between Climate and Interpersonal Communication." Unpublished manuscript, San Diego State University, San Diego, CA.

Argyle, M. (1975). *Bodily Communication.* New York: International Universities Press.

Bellah, R. N., R. Madsen, W. M. Sullivan, A. Swidler, and S. Tipton. (1985). *Habits of the Heart: Individualism and Commitment in American Life.* New York: Harper & Row.

Bem, S. L. (1974). "The Measurement of Psychological Androgyny." *Journal of Consulting and Clinical Psychology* 42, 155–162.

Bruneau, T. (1979). "The Time Dimension in Intercultural Communication." In D. Nimmo (ed.). *Communication Yearbook* 3 (pp. 423–433). New Brunswick, NJ: Transaction Books.

Buck, R. (1984). *The Communication of Emotion.* New York: The Guilford Press.

Burgoon, J. K. (1985). "Nonverbal Signals." In M. L. Knapp and G. R. Miller (eds.). *Handbook of Interpersonal Communication* (pp. 344–390). Beverly Hills, CA: Sage Publications.

Burgoon, J. K. and T. Saine. (1978). *The Unspoken Dialogue: An Introduction to Nonverbal Communication.* Boston: Houghton Mifflin.

Chinoy, E. (1967). *Society.* New York: Random House.

Condon, J. C. and F. Yousef. (1983). *An Introduction to Intercultural Communication.* Indianapolis, IN: Bobbs-Merrill.

Elazar, D. J. (1972). *American Federalism: A View from the States.* New York: Thomas P. Crowell Company.

Elliot, S., M. D. Scott, A. D. Jensen, and M. McDonough. (1982). "Perceptions of Reticence: A Cross-Cultural Investigation." In M. Burgoon (ed.). *Communication Yearbook* 5 (pp. 591–602). New Brunswick, NJ: Transaction Books.

Geertz, C. (1973). *The Interpretation of Cultures.* New York: Basic Books.

Gudykunst, W. B. and Y. Y. Kim. (1984). *Communicating with Strangers: An Approach to Intercultural Communication.* New York: Random House.

Hall, E. T. (1959). *The Silent Language.* New York: Doubleday and Company.

Hall, E. T. (1976). *Beyond Culture.* Garden City, NY: Anchor Books.

Hall, E. T. (1984). *The Dance of Life: The Other Dimension of Time.* Garden City, NY: Anchor Press.

Heslin, R. and T. Alper. (1983). "Touch: A Bonding Gesture." In J. M. Wiemann and R. Harrison (eds.). *Nonverbal Interaction* (pp. 47–75). Beverly Hills, CA: Sage Publications.

Hofstede, G. (1982). *Culture's Consequences* (abridged ed.). Beverly Hills, CA: Sage Publications.

Jensen, J. V. (1985). "Perspective on Nonverbal Intercultural Communication." In L. A. Samovar and R. E. Porter (eds.). *Intercultural Communication: A Reader* (pp. 256–272). Belmont, CA: Wadsworth.

Jones, T. S. and M. S. Remland. (May 1982). "Cross-Cultural Differences in Self-Reported Touch Avoidance." Paper presented at the annual convention of the Eastern Convention Association, Hartford, CT.

LaBarre, W. (1985). "Paralinguistics, Kinesics, and Cultural Anthropology." In L. A. Samovar and R. E. Porter (eds.). *Intercultural Communication: A Reader* (pp. 272–279). Belmont, CA: Wadsworth.

Lomax, A. (1968). *Folk Song Style and Culture.* New Brunswick, NJ: Transaction Books.

Malandro, L. A. and L. Barker. (1983). *Nonverbal Communication.* Reading, MA: Addison-Wesley.

Montagu, A. and F. Matson. (1979). *The Human Connection.* New York: McGraw-Hill.

Mehrabian, A. (1971). *Silent Messages.* Belmont, CA: Wadsworth.

Merriam, A. H. (1983). "Comparative Chronemics and International Communication: American and Iranian Perspectives on Time." In R. N. Bostrom (ed.). *Communication Yearbook* 7, (pp. 35–48). Beverly Hills, CA: Sage Publications.

Patterson, M. L. (1983). *Nonverbal Behavior: A Functional Perspective.* New York: Springer-Verlag.

Prosser, M. H. (1978). *The Culture Dialogue: An Introduction to Intercultural Communication.* Boston, MA.: Houghton Mifflin.

Rich, A. L. (1974). *Interracial Communication.* New York: Harper and Row.

Samovar, L. A. and R. E. Porter. (1985). "Nonverbal Interaction." In L. A. Samovar and R. E. Porter *Intercultural Communication: A Reader.* Belmont, CA.: Wadsworth.

Samovar, L. A., R. E. Porter, and N. C. Jain. (1981). *Understanding Intercultural Communication.* Belmont, CA.: Wadsworth.

Saral, T. (1977). "Intercultural Communication Theory and Research: An Overview." In B. D. Ruben (ed.). *Communication Yearbook* I (pp. 389–396). New Brunswick, NJ: Transaction Books.

Scheflen, A. E. (1972). *Body Language and the Social Order.* Englewood Cliffs, NJ: Prentice Hall.

Scheflen, A. E. (1974). *How Behavior Means.* Garden City, NY: Anchor Press.

Sitaram, K. S. and R. T. Cogdell. (1976). *Foundations of Intercultural Communication.* Columbus, OH: Charles E. Merrill, 1976.

Tomkins, S. S. (1984). "Affect Theory." In K. R. Scherer and P. Ekman (eds.). *Approaches to Emotion* (pp. 163–195). Hillsdale, NJ: Lawrence Erlbaum.

Watzlawick, P., J. H. Beavin, and D. D. Jackson. (1967). *Pragmatics of Human Communication.* New York: W. W. Norton.

# The Time Dimension in Intercultural Communication

TOM BRUNEAU

## INTRODUCTION

At a recent communication conference held in Tokyo, I began a presentation about time concepts, timing behavior, and tempo in organizations with a "time joke." I began by saying that I had just arrived in Tokyo from the island of Guam situated in the Western-Central Pacific. I went on to say that "Guam time" and "Tokyo time" were suddenly contrasted for me and were so very different. "In Guam," I said with naive confidence, "you are never late for a party or fiesta—even if you show up and everyone else has gone home." Well, to my surprise, the audience did not respond in laughing approval. In fact, it was like "no response at all" and I decided to not tell the second part of my joke about "Tokyo time." I had planned to say that "Tokyo time" was monolithic in nature. I was planning to explain that "Tokyo time" may be deriving its power from one large rock and that it was probably that a giant quartz crystal might be buried somewhere near the very heart of Tokyo. In retrospect, I am glad I skipped the second half of my joke. Besides, my talk was being timed to fit a fifteen minute time frame and "being on time" was being stressed.

From *Communication* 3 (August 1979), 169–181. Reprinted by permission of the publisher and the author. Dr. Bruneau teaches at Radford University, Radford, Virginia.

## TIME AND CULTURAL DIFFERENCES: SOME GENERAL CONSIDERATIONS

Oswald Spengler once said that "... it is the meaning that it intuitively attaches to Time that one Culture is differentiated from another..." (1926, p. 130). Accepting this claim by Spengler, however, does not mean that we should also accept his viewpoint that certain temporal orientations are associated with "higher cultures," (pp. 117–60, Chap.: "The Idea of Destiny and the Principle of Causality"). The idea that one culture's temporality is somehow better than another culture's temporality appears to be a major basis for intercultural perceptions of inferiority and superiority. Seldom do people recognize that their perception of peoples from other cultures relates to their elitism or rigidity about their own cultural time orientation. People do compare their time orientations with those of other cultural groups.

Western literature about culture and intercultural perceptions seems to be replete with unconscious assumptions: Western time experiencing is most advanced, most useful, and best for future development. These assumptions seem to be resistant to deep questioning by cultural groupings which have accepted Newtonian and objective forms of temporality as their definition of time. Obviously, when a cultural group assumes that "their time" is superior to the time, timing, and tempo of other cultural groups, a basis is established for preferential judgments about cultural aspects of space, spacing, and motion through space (perhaps *including inner space or subjective, personal time experiencing*). Even languages can then become related to notions of temporal superiority and inferiority. In this regard, the widely respected and accepted symbolic philosophy of Cassirer includes the blunt presumption that "advanced" languages are those which are more elaborate in terms of *zeitworts* (time-words) than other, less developed languages (e.g.: Cassirer, 1953, pp. 215–26). From an intercultural communication perspective which is more temporally open and educated, however, who is to say, for certain, that there

is necessarily more wisdom in a bee than in a butterfly? Is a clock necessarily better or worse than the rhythm of the tides and celestial bodies? Billions of people may believe that clocks are necessary evils at best.

In a splicing statement suggesting that the East and West could be conveniently and arbitrarily divided into time zones, Reyna (1971, p. 228) said "... one cannot constrain the Oriental conceptions of time into the delimiting frames familiar to the West" (1971, p. 228). In terms of traditional notions of time in the Orient (related to Hinduism, Buddhism, and their branches and splinter groups), this statement seems to make much sense. However, a modern viewpoint does not warrant such a dichotomous position. Even though many small, timeless-like temples and pagodas dot many of the urban areas of the Orient, the roar of automobiles and trains, the smell of oil, the crush of politics, and the shattering of jet propulsion shakes the quiet air. In Peking the horns blare, in Shanghai people are beginning to nervously flick their wrists watchward toward their eyes in order to pace their day, throughout China a postponed industrial evolution is beginning to be reconstructed using every workable clock the British left behind. Differences in the time of cultural groups are complex. Examples of differences in time conception, time perspective (past, present, future), and time-experiencing (timekeeping, timing, pacing, and temporal behavior (see taxonomy) between cultural groups are many and varied.[1] It appears that, at every level about the analysis of time, timing, and tempo cultures do differ. For example, one of my students from the Trukese District of Micronesia wrote me a poem recently:

*A snail*
*A mountain*
*Ten thousand years*[2]

He said it does not matter which lines are spoken first or last or in what order.

If we compare this poet's temporal perspective with a British-America (or Western-European) preoccupation with "What came first, the chicken or the egg?" perhaps we will observe two very different orientations toward the nature and importance of causality. From an American or Western-European viewpoint about temporality, when we deal with causality retrospectively and analytically, we can construct a particular kind of past which is based on certain assumptions about memory and memory processing. Indeed, the manner in which certain people imagine historicity or the manner in which cultural groups utilize their memories appears to be grounded in culturally bound time orientations. Various ways of remembering, as well as ways of utilizing nostalgia, incidently, appear to be culturally specific. The various needs to look backward are many and complex. The need to look backward for a certain purpose may vary from cultural group to cultural group. Our example is a case in point. If one sits long enough on white, dry, fossilized coral—with the distant and rhythmic roar of the surf pounding on and under the outer reef—the time-count becomes atemporal. The lush and persistent greens and deep blues in Micronesia seem "always" and "always have been." Even for a visitor or newcomer in such a hypnotic, natural environment, the days can become confused and the hours can be easily forgotten. This seems especially so in some rural areas of Micronesia which are not yet frequented by the noises of modern technology. Acausality appears to be encouraged in such environments. In such a temporal atmosphere, accounting for a sequential accuracy about the past by using retrospective analysis seems to be a futile task. In such an atmosphere, it can become difficult for certain persons to care for minutes, hours, weeks, months, and even years.[3]

## FUTURISM AND INTERCULTURAL COMMUNICATION

Just as concepts about a past perspective of time seem to vary from culture to culture, so does the image of the future. The future is both conceptual and processual—as is the present and the past.

The massive study required to say how cultures differ in their futuristic, temporal orientations has yet to be begun. Futurism is a movement which is multidisciplinary in scope and it is rapidly developing into intensive and sustained efforts of major importance in many academic disciplines. The study of the future should utilize a great deal of scholarly energy on both the near and distant future. This new movement may someday be viewed as a major turning point in the history of the development of human thought. New avenues into unexplored ways of thinking ahead should develop. However, new ways in which to "think ahead" should produce a greater distance between cultures which are rapidly expanding their visions of the future (progressivism) and those cultures in which the image of the future is just beginning to change from traditional visions.

Some cultures seem to have a rigid fixity in their images of the future. The degree of fixity of the image of the future seems to vary between cultural groups. The examples of this are many. For example, some cultural groups have an almost disdainful glimpse of the future. For some cultural groups, the future is feared and hidden from one's reflections. In some cultures, thinking about the future is considered to be: a wasteful activity, a manner of idleness, an unnecessary kind of dreaming, a kind of foolish romantic activity, or even a kind of activity engaged in by strange people or evil people, etc.

In such a temporal environment, a stable and rigid image of a future can develop. When this does occur, the rigid futuristic image appears to function for the purpose of negating other views of the future. For instance, a clear image of "one's own life hereafter" (held by many different cultural groups) may prevent alternative images of the future from developing. The fixity of a cultural group's image of the future may even prevent or hinder members of that culture group from thinking in ways related to planning and alternate avenues of hoping. We do know that individuals within cultural groups can vary widely in their images of their own futures and, still, individuals do tend to develop future images which are similar to members of their culture group. Individuals within cultures seem to vary their images of the future as they grow older, according to their fears of death and the unknown or unpredictable, and according to their particular abilities to think in futuristic modes.[4] There appears to be no reason why we should not begin to assume that each cultural group holds a particular image of the future which can be both similar and different from the images of the future held by members of other cultural groups. In short, the time conceptions and perspectives of different cultures are significant differences between cultural groups and deserve more attention by those studying intercultural communication.

The ability to anticipate consequences and delay gratification seem to be culturally reinforced activities and involve a futuristic perspective. Delay of gratification and the anticipation of consequences are highly related to a group's wealth, economic conditions, and the pace of life. This appears to be the case across most cultural groups. However, cultural groups appear to have traditionally characteristic ways of anticipating consequences as well as delaying gratification. These characteristic ways may interact with changing social and economic conditions and changes in the pace of life in many ways.

In some cultural groups, clear directions for future actions are given by establishing and using various kinds of itinerary, by following the steps provided by custom and practice, or by various ways of creating atmospheres of fate or chance. Sometimes the clash of future perspectives between cultures can be sharply contrasted. An extended example should clarify some of the above ideas:

The Intercultural Traffic Jam

*Let us imagine that a person from one cultural background (Person A) buys his or her first automobile, learns to drive it, and develops a pattern of anticipation for traffic conditions, traffic signs and traffic signals. The pattern of anticipation developed for traffic signs and signals by Person A grew out of particular kinds of conceptions of "thinking ahead" which are positively valued in Culture A. Let us also imagine that Person A belongs to a cultural group which values positive attitudes about the "rewards of thinking ahead."*

*Person B, in buying his or her first automobile, however, comes from a cultural group which is only somewhat familiar with the anticipation of consequences of one's own actions required in terms of a quickened, urban pace of life. Person B happens to come from and is influenced by a cultural group where one operates immediately and in terms of immediately given or perceived conditions. In Culture B, the need to think ahead quickly is not traditionally necessary except for particular cultural customs and activities. It is not that Culture B people cannot think futuristically, it is that most people from Culture B need to do so only infrequently. Their futurism is clearly related to custom and they have developed behavioral patterns to cope with problems or new conditions in a spontaneous fashion. In other words, Person B does not value thinking ahead, has not experienced much positive reinforcement from his cultural group for thinking ahead, and his or her responses to traffic conditions are present-oriented, here-and-now, and immediate.*

*Now, imagine a situation where you are a person driving in traffic behind Person A. If you are from Culture A, you have perhaps begun to anticipate that Person A in the automobile ahead of you will usually give a signal (hand or electronic) indicating that he or she will make a left turn. This signal will often be far enough in advance of the actual turn to give others more than adequate notice of the turning event. In driving behind Person A, one begins to anticipate the anticipatory responses of Person A. This seems to also happen for other persons who are from Culture A. Soon, these anticipatory responses turn into a set of expectations for drivers like Person A. Our expectancy level, if we are from Culture A, begins to be consistent and we can become confident and trustful about the driving of Person A.*

*However, from the viewpoint of a driver from Culture A, who happens to be driving behind an automobile driven by Person B, the "uncertainties of an intercultural traffic situation" become apparent. From a perspective of a Person A driving behind a Person B, Person B appears likely to slow down quickly, slam on his or her brakes, and to turn quickly. These appear to be Person B's turning behaviors. Person B seems to turn when a cue of the "place to turn" appears (arrives in consciousness without expectation) in his or her immediate present. From Person A's perspective, Person B is likely to actually turn his or her vehicle when he or she begins to signal his or her wish to turn. The wish to turn is not a signal requiring a delay of action—from B's perspective. For B, the event and the wish are merged. In other words, Person B will often signal and begin his or her turn upon seeing the place to turn. In such a situation, three functions or aspects of an event seem to share the same moment. In comparison, A seems to divide his or her traffic events into anticipatory units. In contrast to Person A, Person B seems to blend traffic events into unitary action.*

*For Person B, driving behind a vehicle driven by a member of Culture A can be just as confusing. From Person B's perspective, a Person A driver appears to be always ready to turn at any given moment. Person A seems to signal and then, never seems to turn. From B's perspective, some people from Culture A never seem to make up their minds as to when and where they will turn. B may think that people from Culture A confuse a simple act by over-anticipating and making it complex.*

*Imagining a further traffic jam or a complex traffic situation requiring participation and cooperation between people from Cultures A and B, one can now begin to visualize and hear the heat of intercultural conflict. The consternation of red countenances grim with frustration in not being able to predict the temporal behaviors of other drivers would create an interesting image. But, a traffic conflict between persons from Cultures A and B is fairly safe and uncomplicated compared to multicultural*

*situations. A bicultural image is rather uncomplicated and tame compared to a high density traffic situation where people from ten to twenty different cultural groups attempt to survive a drive in the same countryside on the same Sunday afternoon.*

Fred Polak (1961) is a major thinker concerning the development of the image of the future. Polak appears, at first glance, to be extreme about the importance of a futuristic orientation in the shaping of cultures. Polak appears to be claiming that *different future perspectives are highly influential in the actual creation of particular kinds of cultures* (1961). In other words, time perspective is culturally specific, culturally bound, and central to cultural identity and functioning. Polak's major thesis about culture and future perspective is clearly stated:

*Awareness of ideal values is the first step in the conscious creation of images of the future and therefore in the conscious creation of culture. For a value is by definition that which guides toward a "valued" future. . . . It becomes clear now that magic, religion, philosophy, science, and ethics might well owe their origin and further creative development largely to the basic need to get fore-knowledge of the future. In other words, these fundamental fields of culture may have been developed at first mainly as ways and means of visualizing and influencing the future. . . . The images of the future . . . are historic landmarks and cultural mirrors . . . (1961, p. 37).*

Polak's image of the future in cultural perspective appears to be a healthy one. His viewpoints seem to hold deep respect and positive regard for the complexity and challenge of the futurism/culture interface.

## TIMING AND TIMEKEEPING AMONG CULTURES

A major aspect of the time dimension concerns the manner and degree to which objective forms of timekeeping are utilized and how they influence temporal pacing or patterning in particular cultures.[5] Of even greater interest to us is how objective time restraints and constraints may influence people from different cultures with different time orientations differently. In other words, time devices, timekeeping methods, and objective formulations of time are at the core of a modern pace of life. A modern pace of life interacts with a culturally traditional pace of life—at any given decade. The clock may be a machine of all machines. This tiny machine which is carried about on one's wrist may be the most basic and powerful machine in the world. The clock appears to control all other machines and electronic devices.

The idea of an objective time as a true and real form of time is a significant development in the history of human conduct. As Mumford stated, "The clock ... is the key machine of the industrial age [1962, p. 14]. ... The first characteristic of modern machine civilization is its temporal regularity. From the moment of walking, the rhythm of the day is punctuated by the clock. Irrespective of strain or fatigue, despite reluctance or apathy, the household rises close to its set hour" (p. 269).

The widespread use of clocks and timekeeping devices may be growing into irreversible directions during the last half of this century. Such growth in timekeeping expansion is not without dangers to the health of people. Wright (1968, p. 7) states the danger concisely in the introduction of his book about the tyranny of clockworks: "This is the history of an increasing, unchecked, and now intolerable *chronarchy*. That word is not to be found in *The Oxford English Dictionary*. Its coiner should be entitled to define it. [Let chronarchy, then, be not merely 'rule by time,' but regimentation of man by timekeeping.' "] Elsewhere, I expressed the danger to cultural identity posed by the threat of the growth of objective timekeeping throughout the world: the spread of objective time throughout the world has been rapid and is growing. The signification of this movement might best be expressed in two hypotheses: (1) Objective tempo, when largely accepted, tends to destroy cultures which are based in subjective temporality; (2) The widespread adoption of standards of objective temporality tends to neutralize cultural diversity (Bruneau, 1978a).

Clocks imply a standard by which events may be compared and how similar events may be judged to differ. When time is only viewed as timekeeping, timing devices become valued and their functioning becomes associated with activities which are, in turn, valued. In some cultures, certain methods of objective timekeeping are more valued than other forms of objective timekeeping. While reliance on clock time has grown with the rapid growth of intercultural contact and exchange since the beginning of this century, other forms of timekeeping are still popular for millions of people spread throughout the planet. A clock is only one form of "regularized" time and clock time can often clash with other kinds of objective timekeeping which are related to cycles of celestial and natural events or the biological repetitions and periodicities of human beings and other animals. To use a pleasant image about clocks cast forth by Dora Marsden: "The entire universe is weighted toward rhythm ... everywhere, as in a cosmic dance, natural bodies are doing their rounds ... the universe is littered with clocks" (1955, p. 12).

Each natural clock which is replaced with an artificial, objective measure of timekeeping may lose its utility and purpose. One form of timekeeping can replace another. When one form of objective time replaces another form unnecessarily, can the situation be said to have been changed for the better? When highly valued forms of timekeeping associated with customary behaviors of particular cultural groups are replaced, perhaps the behaviors change or become lost to oblivion. When a cultural group changes its timekeeping, it may very well change its more stable characteristics, too.

The manner in which different cultural groups value different kinds of objective timekeeping may establish particular kinds of potential communicative interaction. Cultural groups appear to widely differ in their valuation of the same objective time systems. The differences in the degree to which an objective timekeeping is valued may very well influence the manner in which peoples from different cultures comply with objective time standards or adhere to the dictates of those who control, manipulate, and interpret objective time.

Cultural differences in the valuation of objective time, then, can establish a basis for understanding a number of intercultural communication problems. This is especially so when it is understood that timekeeping and objective time standards can control space and motion through space—and often do so. The imposition of objective time by one or more cultural groups upon another cultural group can be considered as a form of intercultural influence or persuasion.

Media are very time related. Objective timing is highly involved in the structuring of various kinds of media. What is usually not so apparent, however, is that values related to certain forms of timekeeping seem to be unconsciously projected through the media to people from other cultures. People can be influenced to wear wristwatches even if they are not necessary in everyday living. It should not be surprising to find clock time projected as a valued process in all spheres of life which are projected or broadcast by Western and Western-influenced media. Clock time appears to be a *channel of media channels*. Objective forms of time are forms of media controlling other media forms. This fact has not yet seemed to have been recognized for its importance. Western media appear to be hopelessly based in rigid, objective time constraints. With the growth and spread of Western media throughout many non-Western cultural groups, it seems reasonable to assume that these groups will continue to be exposed to massive doses of the value of clock time being projected to them by Westernized media.

## PACE OF LIFE, CULTURAL TEMPO, AND INTERCULTURAL COMMUNICATION

There are many kinds of time which make up an individual's temporal system: biological time, physiological time, perceptual time, objective time, conceptual time, psychological time, social time, and cultural time.[6] The manner in which these interdependent levels of time experiencing interact subsume a "chronemics" of human behavior (Bruneau, 1977, p. 3). Chronemics is a relatively new idea of communication study which can be defined as the meaning of human time experiencing as it influences and is influenced by human communication.[7]

The pace of life of a cultural group concerns the manner in which levels of time experiencing are integrated by individual members and aggregates of individuals in such groups. Further, the pace of life of a cultural group concerns the standards and habits of *temporal behavior* which underscore interaction between members of a cultural group. (It should be noted here that kinds and levels of temporal behavior will be outlined in the "Taxonomy of Temporal Environment.")

Especially important in the pace of life of a cultural group is the manner in which subjective and objective forms of time experiencing interact. In other words, the manner in which highly variable forms of time experiencing in given cultures interact with somewhat constant or consistent forms of time experiencing in given cultures, helps to determine the characteristic tempo of a culture. Some cultural groups are paced by a merging of subjective kinds of time experiencing with cyclic, periodic forms of objective time. Nilsson (1920) has described the importance of such periodic forms of objective time in many "primitive" cultural groups. Periodic, cyclic forms of objective time concern the repetition of biological, natural, and celestial movements. When certain forms of periodic and cyclic objective time interact with personal, social, and cultural activities and events, a particular "cultural tempo" develops and *becomes* the temporal environment of some cultural groups. Certain cultural groups with this particular temporal environment still exist. Fifty years ago, many such cultural groups existed.

Some cultural groups adopt fairly constant forms of objective time (e.g., clocks, timers, bells, daily schedules, etc.). These cultural groups develop characteristic temporal environments by merging such objective forms of time with personal, social, and cultural activities and events. Cultural groups which stress the importance of objective standards of time, the accuracy of such time, and the pacing of life associated with clocks, can become "clock-bound" cultural groups. A clock-bound cultural group seems to stress objective time forms more than it stresses more personal and subjective forms of time experiencing. Often, clock time conformity may be basic to many other kinds of conformity (e.g., proxemic and kinesic habits and customs). The relationship between a chronemics, a proxemics, and a kinesics has yet to be outlined—though such related areas will have to be conjoined eventually. A cultural stress on objective timekeeping may prevent other forms of time experiencing from finding expression. For example, contemplation is a form of subjective time experiencing which appears to be sacrificed in highly clock-bound cultures. As McLuhan once stated, "Clocks are mechanical media that transform tasks and create new work and wealth by accelerating the pace of human association" (1964, p. 143). Such haste is often valued in clock-bound cultures. However, Meerloo, in his analysis of time experiencing, adds a negative note: "Haste is compensation for doubt" (1970, p. 207). Wyndham could very well have been speaking of present-day, clock-bound cultures when he expressed his reservations about "trances of action" long ago:

*Everything in our life to-day conspires to thrust people into prescribed tracks, in what can be called a sort of* trance of action. *Hurrying, without any significant reason, from spot to spot at the maximum speed obtainable, drugged in the mechanical activity, how is the typical individual of this epoch to do some detached thinking for himself? All his life is disposed with a view to banishing reflection. To be alone he finds terrifying (1927, p. vii).*

Cultures which stress clock time and fairly constant forms of objective tempo seem to also extend these forms of tempo into activities and events not traditionally punctuated by clock time. In clock-bound cultures, a tendency seems to develop where temporal conditioning becomes a pervasive style of living. Temporal conditioning develops from the increased use of clocks, time indicators, and time regulators in everyday life (Bruneau, 1974). Highly clock-bound cultures appear to extend the use of clocks into a form of mania which could be called a "chronophilia." In a chronophiliac atmosphere, people value clock time very much, they value accuracy highly, and cherish the order assumed to exist under such standards. In such an atmosphere, temporal conditioning can take place—depending on the degree of chronophilia. In such an atmosphere of temporality, clocks are increasingly extended into pacers which regulate the flow and speed of activities. More and more areas of life-space are regulated and punctuated by clocks and their extensions. Spontaneous activity, creativity, and a number of subjective forms of tempo can quickly lose their credibility and value.[8] Objective time conditioning, when too rigid and pervasive, can evolve into a kind of behavioral puppetry. Under such a puppetry temporal cloaks and robes are placed on as masks to cover traditional and subjective forms of time experiencing. In such an environment, the play unfolds on a fixed stage, the composition and setting of which are predetermined. Behavioral puppetry seems to result in a kind of boredom which finds the actors seeking escape in repetitive compulsions and faster and faster routines. Chronophilia can become, literally, a "chronic" pathology where life can become a constant, dull, grey line of ennui. On such a dull linearity, the players intensify and quicken their dance in a futile effort to expand and enliven the line. However, to use one of Whitehead's more terse statements, the result of more and more intensive activities is clear: "Intensity is the reward of narrowness" (1929, p. 172).

The characteristic tempo of a cultural group can be compared with the range of temporality of each member of that culture group. Each individual must adjust his or her unique, personal temporality to the unique tempo of his or her cultural group. When persons of different cultural tempos attempt to communicate, the temporal environment becomes a merger of both personal and cultural tempos. In the intercultural communication situation, rates of behavior and the expectancies about these rates may vary from person to person. The values held toward different forms of objective and subjective kinds of time can provide a wide range of misunderstandings and misinterpretations in such situations. The temporal behaviors (see taxonomy) of each person in an intercultural communication situation may differ radically and still function unconsciously or out of the awareness of the communicators during intercultural exchanges.

When it is understood that both proxemic and kinesic behaviors appear to be based in the temporal beliefs, attitudes, motives, values, and temporal behaviors of all participants in the intercultural situation, it becomes apparent that the temporal dimension is a most significant factor in intercultural communication. Creative conceptualizing about the manner in which time orientations and perspectives interact with cultural identity, cultural behaviors, and intercultural communication should provide for years of research activity.

The many lines of analysis required for a detailed consideration of the time/intercultural communication interface is beyond the scope of this paper. In lieu of a detailed discussion, a taxonomy is provided. This taxonomy, if used to access intercultural communication situations, should provide images of many probable examples and, hopefully, provide a sounding board for actual intercultural events and situations.

## A TAXONOMY OF TEMPORAL ENVIRONMENT

The taxonomy outlined below was initially developed as a partial attempt to define a "chronemics" of human behavior (Bruneau, 1978a). The taxonomy can be used to analyze and study the temporal behaviors and temporal environments of many forms of human interaction. Hopefully, such a taxonomy can be of benefit by providing a structure in which to help control observations in the complex world of time, timing, and tempo. Such a

tool may provide necessary control for making temporal estimates and judgments (see taxonomy for these terms) in complex intercultural communication situations. It should be understood that the levels of temporality outlined below are highly interrelated and a hierarchy of levels of temporal behaviors is not necessarily advocated:

*Temporal Drives:* involving biorhythmic activity; hormonal and metabolic periodicities; ergic impulses (Cattell 1957; 1965); involving the reduction of physiological need tension, need tension patterning, etc.

*Temporal Cues:* pertaining to the initial sensing and recognition of one's own temporal drives and those of others.

*Temporal Signals:* involving the imposition of perceptual durations and intervals which give rise to individual senses of time; perceptual continuities and discontinuities which give rise to habitual and variable recognition of successions and durations; any durational or processual phenomena giving rise to the formation of perceptual information related to the pacing, control, regulation, or facilitation of human behavior; concerning the recognition of temporal characteristics of nonverbal behavior; etc.

*Temporal Symbols:* pertaining to the symbolic representation of succession and duration, change and permanence, or of temporal perspective and orientation; concepts of subjective and objective tempos; relating to the representation of objective time, timing, and times; concerning linguistic representations and functionings related to levels of time experiencing and all behaviors (including mental) subsumed under the taxonomic items presented here, etc.

*Temporal Beliefs:* pertaining to assumptions held about the nature of time and space; concerning degree of rigidity in the perception and conceptualization of space-time behavior; concerning the validity of temporal cues and estimates; concerning the validity of temporal information arising from temporal drives, temporal signals, and temporal symbolism; pertaining to the validity and nature of temporal judgments (see below); etc.

*Temporal Motives:* relating to psychological intention to influence temporal behavior; concerning the intention to alter personal and objective tempos; concerning the process of altering personal and objective tempos; relating to the influencing of drives, needs, and motivations; intention related to goals and goal behavior; etc.

*Temporal Judgments:* pertaining to the validity of temporal beliefs, temporal motives, and temporal values (below) as exercised by individuals or groups of individuals in sociocultural contexts; etc.

*Temporal Values:* concerning valuation and evaluation of tempo, times (events) and timing as they relate to personal, social, and cultural behaviors.

5. For an excellent account of timekeeping, timekeepers, and objective time, see: Fraser and Lawrence, 1975, pp. 365–485, a special session of the International Society for the Study of Time on timekeeping.

6. Each of these major levels of time experiencing has been outlined elsewhere along with a representative bibliography for each level (Bruneau 1977). It is not in the scope of this article to outline these areas of time experiencing.

7. For a more comprehensive definition of a "Chronemics," see: Bruneau, 1977; 1978a; 1978b. Also see: Poyatos, 1976, p. 61.

8. A model of subjective temporality in terms of different kinds of mental modes of tempo is offered in a theoretically speculative article by Bruneau (1976). In this article, a model of modes of mental relativity is developed which are said to be related to different kinds of sociocultural time perspectives as well as being characteristic of thinking stances.

## NOTES

1. While examples of temporal differences between cultural groups are many, surprisingly little work has been done in this area of study. For those interested in the time/culture interface, two bibliographic sources exist which provide the listing of approximately 2,000 bibliographic items associated with the study of time (Doob 1971; Zelkind and Sprug 1974). Also the proceedings of the International Society for the Study of Time (J. T. Fraser, et al. 1972; 1975; and 1978) can provide a rich source of information for the study of time across cultural groups.

2. I wish to thank one of my students, Jack Sigrah, for writing this poem.

3. The Americans, the British, the French, the Japanese, the Australians, the New Zealanders, the Russians, and others with particular interests in Micronesia do not seem to have such atemporal-acausal orientations. This is especially so with those persons from many countries who seek all forms of modern day "business."

4. I have previously described this mode of thinking as "protension" in an attempt to develop a model of mind-time relativity (Bruneau 1976).

## REFERENCES

Bruneau, Thomas, "Chronemics and the Verbal-Nonverbal Interface," *The Relationship of Verbal and Nonverbal Communication*, ed., Mary Ritchie Key (The Hague: Mouton Press, 1978).

———, "Chronemics: The Study of Time in Human Interaction (with a Glossary of Chronemic Terminology)," *Communication*, CAPUH, 6 (1977), 1–30.

———, "Chronemics: Time and Organizational Communication," paper presented at the Communication Association of the Pacific Conference, Tokyo, Japan, June 1978b.

———, "Silence, Mind-Time Relativity, and Interpersonal Communication," Third Conference, International Society for the Study of Time, Alpbach, Austria, July 1–10, 1976.

———, "Time and Nonverbal Communication," *Journal of Popular Culture* 8 (1974), 658–666.

Cassirer, Ernst, *The Philosophy of Symbolic Forms,*

Vol. 1., *Language* (New Haven, CT.: Yale University Press, 1953).

Cattell, Raymond B., *Personality and Motivation Structure and Measurement* (N.Y.: Harcourt, Brace and World, 1957).

———, *The Scientific Analysis of Personality* (Harmondsworth: Penguin Books, 1965).

Doob, Leonard, *Patterning of Time* (New Haven, CT.: Yale University Press, 1971).

Fraser, J. T., et al., *The Study of Time*, Vol. I (N.Y.: Springer-Verlag, 1972).

Fraser, J. T. and N. Lawrence, *The Study of Time II* (N.Y.: Springer-Verlag, 1975).

Fraser, et al., *The Study of Time III* (N.Y.: Springer-Verlag, 1978).

McLuhan, Marshall, *Understanding Media: The Extensions of Man* (N.Y.: New American Library, 1964).

Marsden, Dora, *The Philosphy of Time* (Oxford: The Holywell Press, 1955).

Meerloo, Joost A. M., *Along the Fourth Dimension* (N.Y.: John Day, 1970).

Mumford, Lewis, *Technics and Civilization* (N.Y.: Harcourt, Brace and World, 1962).

Nilsson, Martin P., *Primitive Time-Reckoning* (Lund, CWK Gleerup, 1920).

Polak, Fred L., *The Image of the Future* (N.Y.: Oceana Publications, 1961).

Poyatos, Fernando, "Language in the Context of Total Body Communication," *Linguistics* 168 (1976), 49–62.

Reyna, Ruth, "Metaphysics of Time in Indian Philosophy and Its Relevance to Particle Science," in J. Zeman, ed. *Time in Science and Philosophy* (Czechoslovak Academy of Sciences, 1971), 227–239.

Spengler, Oswald, *The Decline of the West* Vol. 1, *Form and Actuality* (N.Y.: Alfred A. Knopf, 1926).

Whitehead, Alfred North, *Process and Reality* (N.Y.: Humanities Press, 1929).

Wright, Lawrence, *Clockwork Man* (N.Y.: Horizon Press, 1968).

Wyndham, Lewis, *Time and Western Man* (Boston: Beacon Hill, 1927).

Zelkind, Irving and J. Sprug, *Time Research: 1172 Studies* (Metuchen, N.J.: Scarecrow Press, 1974).

# Sex Differences in Nonverbal Communication

BARBARA WESTBROOK EAKINS
R. GENE EAKINS

*. . . People talking without speaking*
*. . . People hearing without listening*

—*Paul Simon*

In addition to the spoken language that we hear daily, a host of silent messages continually occurs around us. These messages make up a nonverbal code, which is used and responded to by us all. This language is not formally taught. A substantial portion of the nonverbal communication that takes place is not consciously noted. But it is an extremely important aspect of communication, for we make many important decisions on the basis of nonverbal cues.

Ray Birdwhistell estimates that in most two-person conversations the words communicate only about 35 percent of the social meaning of the situation; the nonverbal elements convey more than 65 percent of the meaning. Another estimate is that the nonverbal message carries 4.3 times the weight of the verbal message. This is not so surprising when we consider the many ways in which we communicate information nonverbally: through eye contact, facial expressions, body posture and body tension, hand gestures and body movements, the way we position ourselves in relation to

From Barbara Eakins and R. Gene Eakins, *Sex Differences in Human Communication*. Copyright © 1978 Harper and Row Publishers, Inc. Used with permission of the publisher. Barbara Eakins teaches at the Ohio State University, and R. Gene Eakins teaches at Wright State University. Footnotes have been deleted.

another person, touch, clothing, cosmetics, and possessions.

Some time ago Freud said, "He that has eyes to see and ears to hear may convince himself that no mortal can keep a secret. If his lips are silent, he chatters with his finger tips; betrayal oozes out of him at every pore." To be more skillful communicators, we need to be aware of nonverbal cues and to use what has been learned to improve communication.

Micro-units of nonverbal communication, such as dropping the eyelids, smiling, pointing, lowering the head slightly, or folding the arms are often considered trivia. But some researchers believe these so-called trivia constitute the very core or essence of our communication interactions. They consider them elements in the "micropolitical structure" that help maintain and support the larger political structure. The larger political structure needs these numerous minutiae of human actions and interactions to sustain and reinforce it. These nonverbal cues fall somewhere on a continuum of social control that ranges from socialization or cultivation of minds, at one extreme, to the use of force or physical violence, at the other. There are some significant sex differences in nonverbal communication patterns and, as we shall see, they have important implications in the lives of women and men....

## SEX DIFFERENCES IN NONVERBAL COMMUNICATION

Women seem to be more sensitive than men to social cues. Research has shown that female subjects are more responsive to nonverbal cues, compared with verbal ones, than males. Not only have women been found to be more responsive to nonverbal stimuli, but they apparently read it with greater accuracy than males. One study used the Profile of Nonverbal Sensitivity, a test that utilizes film clips of a series of scenes involving people using body movement and facial expression and showing face, torso, both, or neither. Subjects

heard scrambled voice, content-filtered speech with intonation features preserved, or no sound. They were to select the best of the written interpretations of the nonverbal cues after each scene. Females from fifth grade to adulthood obtained better scores than males, with the exception of men who held jobs involving "nurturant, artistic, or expressive" work. When body cues were included, women did better than men. Sensitivity to nonverbal cues appeared to be independent of general intelligence or test-taking skills.

One could hypothesize that nonverbal awareness is an inborn trait and that females are more sensitive and responsive to nonverbal cues from birth. However, it seems more likely that females learn to become nonverbally sensitive at an early age because of their socialization. Their greater receptivity to nonverbal cues from others may be related to their lower status in society and the necessity of this skill to their survival. Blacks, for example, have been shown to be better than whites at interpreting nonverbal signals.

When a group of teachers took the Profile of Nonverbal Sensitivity, those more sensitive to nonverbal communication scored as less authoritarian and more democratic in teaching orientation. Females were relatively better than males at interpreting negative attitudes. Since females may be placed in subordinate positions or be dependent on others in social situations more often, they may be forced to become adept at reading signs of approbation or displeasure from those on whom they depend. Perhaps more than men, they need to know what expectations for them are. Developing the ability to pick up small nonverbal cues in others quickly may be a defense mechanism or survival technique women unconsciously use. It is much more important to someone in a subordinate position to know the mood, the feelings, or intentions of the dominant one than vice versa. The office worker will immediately note and relay to other office subordinates the information that "the boss is in one of his moods again." Just a look, the manner of walk, or the carriage of the arms and shoulders may provide the clue for that anxious observer. Rare, however, is the authority figure who notices employees' moods or is even aware that they have them.

We are not taught nonverbal communication in school. Our schools emphasize verbal communication. Because we seldom examine how we send and interpret nonverbal messages, the nonverbal channel is a very useful avenue for subtly manipulating people. The manipulation does not have to be consciously perceived.

We are prevented from getting knowledge or understanding of nonverbal communication because a delineation of looks, gait, posture, or facial expression is not legitimate in describing interaction. Such items are surely not accepted as valid data in an argument. ("What do you mean, I look as if I don't approve? I said 'all right,' didn't I?") And yet nonverbal cues have more than four times the impact of verbal messages. Not only are women more sensitive to such cues, but their position in society and their socialization to greater docility and compliance may predispose them to be more vulnerable to manipulation and thus make them ideal targets for this subtle form of social control. It behooves both women and men to learn as much as possible about how nonverbal cues can affect people and can serve to perpetuate status and power relationships in society. With this concern in mind, let us examine the categories of nonverbal behavior.

## Eye Contact

Research in the use of eye contact has shown sharp differences according to sex. In studies involving female and male subjects, women have been found to look more at the other person than men do. In addition, women look at one another more and hold eye contact longer with each other than men do with other men. Women look at one another more while they are speaking, while they are being spoken to, and while they are exchanging simultaneous glances. Whatever the sex of the other, women have been shown to spend more time looking at their partner than men do. What might

account for this asymmetry, or difference, in looking behavior of the sexes? The usual explanation given is that women are more willing to establish and maintain eye contact because they are more inclined toward social and interpersonal relations. The gaze may be an avenue of emotional expression for women.

Another reason has been suggested for sex differences in eye behavior. Some experiments have found that in orienting their bodies in space women are more affected than men by visual cues. In other words, in tests where subjects must make judgments about horizontal and vertical position, women tend to use reference points in the environment rather than internal body cues. This physical characteristic could be generalized to social situations.

Let us consider the paradigm of asymmetrical behavior as an indicator of status. Among unequals the subordinate is the one most likely to want social approval, and it has been shown that people have more eye contact with those from whom they want approval. The kinds of clues or information women may get by observing a male's reactions or behavior are important in helping them gauge the appropriateness of their own behavior. Women may value nonverbal information from males more than males value nonverbal information from females. Furthermore, it has been found that in conversation, the listener tends to look more at the speaker, whereas the speaker often looks away while talking. Since some studies show that men tend to talk more in female-male pairs, women would spend more time listening and, therefore, probably more time looking at the other.

Also it has been shown that the more positive an attitude toward the person being addressed, the more eye contact there is. Increased eye contact with the person being addressed also occurs if that person is of higher status. In some cases males use more positive head nods, but females use more eye contact, when they are seeking approval. In an investigation involving mixed-sex pairs, when women were told their partner's eye contact exceeded normal levels, they had a more favorable evaluation of him. But when men were told their partner looked more than usual, they had a less favorable evaluation of her. These studies suggest that women may be using eye contact to seek approval and that perhaps both women and men perceive women to have less status than men. Perhaps, as one student commented, "They almost *ask* for the subordinate position by their behavior."

In our personal experience, we became acquainted with a graduate student and the woman he had just married. There was a discrepancy in educational background between the man, who was just beginning work on his Ph.D., and the woman, who had a high school education. Not only her uneasiness but her heavy reliance on nonverbal cues to her husband's reaction were evident at social gatherings. During conversation, her eyes would continually stray to his face. When speaking with her, it was difficult to establish eye contact, for during her comments or her answers to questions, her eyes would dart to her husband's face, as if to measure the appropriateness of her remark by his approbation or lack of it.

Some writers have observed that women tend to avert their gaze, especially when stared at by men. Although mutual eye contact between persons can indicate affiliation or liking, prolonged eye contact or staring can signify something quite different. Back in our youth, we sometimes engaged in "double whammy," a game in which we tried to outstare our partner. The first one to break the eyelock by looking away, dropping the eyes, or closing the eyes was the loser. It has been suggested that this kind of competitiveness is involved when two persons' gazes meet, such that "a wordless struggle ensues, until one or the other succeeds in establishing dominance." Dominance is acquiesced to and submissiveness signaled by the person who finally looks away or down. We might ask ourselves, in our last encounter with the boss, someone in very high authority, or a person whom we felt greatly "outclassed" us in position or wealth, who was the first to break the mutual gaze and glance away? Indeed, this is a " 'game' . . . enacted at [subtle] levels thousands of times daily."

Jane van Lawick-Goodall has observed behavior of chimpanzees for a number of years and has noted striking similarities in the behavior of chimpanzees and people, particularly in nonverbal communication patterns. She points out how a greeting between two chimpanzees generally re-establishes the dominance status of the one relative to the other. She describes how one female chimp, "nervous Olly," greets another chimp, "Mike," to whom she may bow to the ground and crouch submissively with downbent head. "She is, in effect, acknowledging Mike's superior rank," says Goodall. This would seem to be the extreme of avoiding eye gaze with one of superior rank. Goodall also indicates that an angry chimpanzee may fixedly stare at an opponent.

Some years ago, when our oldest daughter was quite young, she asked us earnestly, "Why is it baboons don't like you to stare at them?" The family was amused at this, and it became a standing joke at our home for years. But we had been to the zoo and, young as she was, our daughter had apparently noticed that the baboons she saw reacted in a disturbed manner to staring.

Research with humans has shown that staring calls forth the same kinds of responses found in primates and that it serves as threat display. Observations of averted eye behavior in autistic children suggest that the averted glance or downcast eyes may be a gesture of submissiveness in humans. Researchers noted to their surprise that autistic children were rarely attacked by the other children, although they seemed to be "easy targets." They concluded that the autistic child's avoidance of eye contact served as a signal much like the appeasement postures used by certain gulls, for example. That is to say, turning away the gaze and avoiding eye contact seemed to restrain or check aggressive behavior or threat display.

The power of the direct stare and the strength of the message it conveys, as well as the acquiescence that turning the eyes away can signify, was illustrated to us by a humorous incident at a cocktail hour for new faculty. One young couple was eager to please and be accepted because it was the husband's first position after finishing graduate school. The wife was a hearty, direct young woman who had been reared in Iowa. She had a bluff, good-natured sense of humor and an amusing way with idioms that refused to stay tucked under the sedateness she tried in vain to assume for this "important" occasion. She was in a tight little circle with some of the tenured and dignified "old guard," when one of them commented upon the great pleasure of discovering that his young colleague had such a lovely wife. The young woman was pleased and began animatedly telling her elderly admirer she felt "as grateful as the cow who remarked to the farmer, 'Thank you for a warm hand on a cold morning.' " As she spoke, her husband fixed upon her a direct and piercing stare. The young woman then stopped her talk and turned her head slightly as she lowered her eyes and became very intent upon sipping her punch.

There may seem to be a contradiction in reporting that women tend to look at others more than men do and yet claim that they generally follow a pattern of submission in one-sided behavior interactions. But several explanations may be offered. First, more of women's looking consists of mutual eye contact. It is possible that during mutual eye contact women are the first to turn the eyes away, the signal of submission. For example, one observation in which a male stared at 60 females and males showed that females averted their gaze more often. About 40 percent of the females would return the stare, then immediately break eye contact, and then reestablish it—as many as four times in an encounter. Only one male of the group made repetitive eye contact in this way.

Second, it may be useful to identify the nature of the gaze and [to] distinguish between subordinate attentiveness and dominant staring. Women may do more looking or scanning of the other person's face for expressive cues when the other person's gaze is directed elsewhere, just as subordinates in the animal world must stay alert to cues from the powerful. But when that person returns the gaze, a woman may drop hers. Intermittent and repetitive eye contact may be the female's response to two conflicting tendencies: the inclination to avert the eyes in submission and the need to watch for visual cues from the powerful.

Third, people tend to do more looking while they are listening to another speak than when they themselves are speaking; and we have learned that women are listeners more often than talkers. So women may be doing more of their looking while listening (in the submissive role) to the other person talk.

Fourth, looking that is done by subjects in experimental lab situations may function differently from looking that occurs in more natural settings. Some informal studies of eye contact by persons passing one another in public showed 71 percent of the males established eye contact with a female but only 43 percent of the females established eye contact with a male. Other observations have shown a pattern of females averting the eyes from both female and male starers. In contrast, males generally stared back at female starers, although they avoided eye contact with other males.

Apparently two types of eye behavior characterize both dominance and submissiveness, but in different ways.

**1. Dominant staring and looking away.** Staring can be used by a superior in some situations to communicate power and assert dominance. But in other instances staring may not be needed. With subordinates, one can feel comfortable and secure in one's power. A superior need not anxiously scan the inferior's face for approval or feedback, but can instead look away or gaze into space as if the underling were not there.

**2. Submissive watching and averting of the gaze.** Careful watching by an underling can be used to communicate submission and dutiful attentiveness, as well as to gather feedback or attitude cues from the dominant. But in some cases looking is not useful or appropriate. When receiving the fixed stare of a powerful other, for example, a subordinate may signal submission by averting the eyes.

Finally, it is said that while looking directly at a man, a woman will often have her head slightly tilted. This may imply the beginning of a "present-ing" gesture, or enough submission to render the stare ambivalent if not actually submissive.

It is interesting to note that in a "Dear Abby" survey on what women notice first about men and what men notice first about women, the eyes rank third for both sexes. Comments included such sentiments from women as, "The eyes tell everything," or "You can tell more about a man's character from his eyes than from anything else. His mouth can lie, but his eyes can't." Males' comments included explanations such as, "It tells me whether or not she's interested in me," or "The eyes show kindness, cruelty, warmth, trust, friendliness and compassion—or lack of it."

## Facial Expression

Women have been found to be more prone to reveal their emotions in facial expressions than men. A psychologist who conducted an experiment on this subject found that men tended to keep their emotions "all bottled up." Subjects in the experiment (students) were shown slides calculated to arouse strong feelings or emotions. The pictures included scenes that were unpleasant, such as a victim with severe burns; pleasant, such as happy children; unusual, a double-exposed photograph; scenic; or sexual. While the subjects were viewing the slides, their own facial expressions were being picked up over closed-circuit television. The researchers found that it was easier to tell what kind of picture was being shown from viewing the women's facial expressions than from viewing the men's expressions. They concluded that men are "internalizers." Some of the evidence suggesting that men keep their emotions inside were the faster heart beat and greater activity of the sweat glands of males during the experiment.

It is significant to note that while preschool children were found to react differently to pictures, this difference did not seem to occur according to sex but on the basis of individual personality differences. The implication is that while they are grow-ing up males are conditioned by society not to show or express their feelings and females are conditioned to reveal theirs more freely. While perhaps less advantageous in terms of power, it would seem to be healthier to express one's emotions.

Women have been found to be better able to remember names and faces, at least those of high school classmates. A study tested subjects from ages 17 to 47, with men and women put into nine categories, depending on the number of years since they had graduated from high school. In all categories the women's memories were superior to men's in matching names and faces. One would conclude that women are conditioned to associate names with physical characteristics more so than men.

From her study of chimpanzees, Goodall has observed that many of the submissive and aggressive gestures of the chimpanzee closely resemble our own. The chimpanzees have some facial expressions for situations that seem to provide insight when considering the human social environment. One facial expression is the "compressed-lips face" shown by aggressive chimpanzees during a charging display or when attacking others.

Another expression is the "play face" shown during periods of frolicking. The front upper teeth are exposed, and the upper lip is drawn back and up. A "full open grin," with upper and lower front teeth showing and jaws open, is displayed when a chimpanzee is frightened or excited, such as during attack or when a high-ranking male "displays" close to a subordinate. A "low open grin," with the upper lip slightly relaxed to cover the upper front teeth, is shown when the chimpanzee is less frightened or excited.

When the chimpanzee is less frightened or less excited than in the previous situations, "a full closed grin," with upper and lower teeth showing but with jaws closed, may be shown. It is also displayed by a low-ranking chimpanzee, when approaching a superior in silence. Goodall remarked, "If the human nervous or social smile has its equivalent expression in the chimpanzee it is, without doubt, the closed grin." Elsewhere it has been observed that apes use a "rudimentary smile" as an appeasement gesture or to indicate submission. It apparently signals to an aggressor that the subordinate creature intends no harm.

Some writers have pointed out that women smile more than men do, whether or not they are really happy or amused. The smile may be a concomitant of the social status of women and be used as a gesture of submission as a part of their culturally prescribed role. Supposedly the smile is an indicator of submission, particularly from women to men. Silveira indicates two instances in which women are more likely to smile: when a woman and a man greet one another, and when the two are conversing and are only moderately well acquainted. In these situations, rather than indicating friendliness or pleasure, the smile supposedly shows that no aggression or harm is intended. One study found that women tended to smile and laugh more than men during laboratory conversations. Women may have smiled more to cover up uneasiness or nervousness or to meet social expectations. The men who smiled generally did so only after they felt comfortable and to express solidarity or union.

In an investigation of approval seeking, one member in each pair of communicators was instructed to try to either gain or avoid the approval of the other. Those who tried to gain approval used significantly more nonverbal acts, including smiles. There was no difference between the sexes in use of smiles in approval seeking. However, when subjects were instructed to behave so as to avoid the approval of the other, the women avoiding approval tended to smile more often than the men avoiding approval. Perhaps the women were unwilling to withhold this gesture because they believe smiling is expected of them socially, whatever the situation. Or it may be that the forced or ready smile was so much a part of the female subjects' socialization that they used it unconsciously, even when inappropriate for their purposes.

Research has shown that children tend to respond differently to female and male smiles. Children five to eight years old responded to women's smiles, as compared to men's smiles, in a neutral manner. Furthermore, children five to twelve years old tended to react to "kidding" messages, which included a negative statement spoken with a smile, as negative; and the negative interpretation was stronger when the speaker was a woman. Young children's different responses to the smiles of women and men in these studies probably reflect sex differences in the smiling communication patterns of adults.

In another experiment videotapes were made of parents with their children. Half the families in the sample had disturbed children and half had normal children. Ratings were made of the parents' words and smiling during interaction with their children. Results showed that fathers made more positive statements when they smiled than when they did not smile. But mothers' statements were not more positive when they were smiling than when they were not smiling, and sometimes in fact were even slightly more negative when smiling. The pattern was not related to child disturbance.

Mothers in lower-class families smiled considerably less than their middle-class counterparts. Whereas 75 percent of the middle-class mothers smiled more than once, only 13 percent of the lower-class mothers smiled more than once. There was no significant difference between lower- and middle-class fathers in amount of smiling. From the results of this study, it appears that fathers are more sincere when they smile, and they are more likely to be saying something relatively friendlier or more approving when smiling than when they are not smiling. When mothers smile at their children, they may be saying something no more evaluatively positive than when they are not smiling. One may conclude that children are probably "reading" adults accurately when they interpret more friendliness in a male's smile than in a female's smile.

What does the middle-class mother's public smile mean? The researchers suggest that the mother is trying to meet middle-class expectations for a "good" mother, which discourage open expression of negative feelings. Her culturally prescribed role calls for "warm, compliant behavior in public situations." The smile may be used as a kind of softener, or mitigator, of critical statements.

Another explanation is that the woman may use a smile as "socially ingratiating behavior," rather than as an indicator of friendliness or approval. One writer suggests that both women and men are "deeply threatened" by a female who does not smile often enough and who is apparently not unhappy.

A class project by Henley featured a field study in which students smiled at about three hundred persons (half females, half males) in public and recorded whether each individual smiled back or not. Seventy-six percent of the time people returned smiles. But different patterns of smiling could be identified for each sex. Women returned smiles more often, about 89 percent of the time; and they returned smiles more frequently to males (93 percent of the time) than to other females (86 percent). Males returned smiles only 67 percent of the time to females and were even more inhibited in smiling back at other males, which they did only 58 percent of the time. Henley concluded that some short-changing occurs in the tradeoff of smiles between the sexes: "Women are exploited by men—they give 93 percent but receive in return only 67 percent."

Shulamith Firestone represents an extreme but thought-provoking view concerning the smile as a "badge of appeasement." She terms the smile "the child/woman equivalent of the shuffle," since it indicates the acquiescence to power, and she describes her youthful efforts to resocialize herself. "In my own case, I had to train myself out of that phony smile, which is like a nervous tic on every teenage girl. And this meant that I smiled rarely, for in truth, when it came down to real smiling, I had less to smile about." Firestone describes her "'dream' action": "... *a smile boycott*, at which declaration all women would instantly abandon their 'pleasing' smiles, henceforth smiling only when something pleased them."

## Posture and Bearing

It has been observed that among nonequals in status, superordinates can indulge in a casualness and relative unconcern with body comportment that subordinates are not permitted. For example, one researcher observed that doctors in the hospital had the privilege of sitting in undignified positions at staff meetings and could saunter into the nurses' station and lounge on the station's dispensing counter. Other personnel such as attendants and nurses had to be more circumspect in their bearing. We need no handbook to tell us that in most interactions the person whom we observe sprawling out, leaning back, or propping feet up while the other maintains more "proper" bearing probably has the authority or power role.

A number of nonverbal sex differences in bearing and posture seem to parallel this asymmetry between nonequals. Birdwhistell describes some posture differences between the sexes involving leg, arm, and pelvis positioning. He believes these are among the most easily recognizable American gender identification signals. In fact, he indicates that leg angle and arm-body angle can be measured exactly. Women giving off gender signals are said to bring their legs together, sometimes even to the extent that their upper legs cross or they stand knee over knee. The American male, however, tends to keep legs apart by a 10- to 15-degree angle. Anyone who has ever participated in physical fitness exercises and assumed "attention" and "at ease" stances knows that the male stance is a more relaxed one.

As for arm-body carriage, females are said to keep their upper arms close to the trunk, while the male moves the arms 5 to 10 degrees away from the body in giving gender cues. Males may carry the pelvis rolled slightly back and females slightly forward. In movement, females supposedly present the entire body from neck to ankles as a moving whole. Males, in contrast, move the arms independently from the trunk and may subtly wag the hips with a slight right and left movement involving a twist at the rib cage. The male bearing seems the more relaxed of the two. Johnny Carson once said of Dr. Joyce Brothers, "She sits as if her knees were welded together."

That these are socialized positions may be inferred from the fact that often as women and men grow older or become ill, their gender positions may become underemphasized or indistinguishable. An elderly woman may, for example, sit relaxed with her legs apart. Because this is an inappropriate gender signal, such an action appears bizarre or may be the object of humor. Carol Burnett, portraying an old woman in one of her comedy routines, sometimes uses this position to get laughs.

Research indicates that in social situations, men assume a more relaxed posture than women, no matter what the sex of the other partner is. Males have been found to assume more asymmetric leg positions and more reclining postures than females. Generally females tend to position their bodies more directly facing the person with whom they are communicating than male communicators do.

In one study males and females were asked to imagine themselves communicating with different persons and to sit the way they would if addressing those persons. Torso lean proved to be a distinguishing difference in some cases. There is less sideways lean in communications with high-status persons. Torso lean was more relaxed, more backward, when communicators addressed persons they disliked. Torso lean of the males was farther back than that of the females. Women used less arm openness with high-status persons than with low-status persons. Males showed no difference. Leg openness of female communicators was less than that of male communicators.

It appears from these and a number of related studies that males are generally more relaxed than females, just as higher-status persons are more relaxed than those in subordinate roles. Research also shows that communicators in general are more relaxed with females than with males. They show less body tension, more relaxed posture, and more backward lean. By their somewhat tenser postures, women are said to convey submissive attitudes. Their general bodily demeanor and bearing is more restrained and restricted than men's. But society seems to expect this. Greater circumspection in body movement appears to be required of women, even in all-female groups.

It is considered unfeminine or unladylike for a woman to "use her body too forcefully, to sprawl, to stand with her legs widely spread, to sit with her feet up, . . . to cross the ankle of one leg over the knee of the other." And depending on the type of clothing she wears, "she may be expected to sit with her knees together, not to sit cross-legged, or not even to bend over." Although restrictions on women have relaxed recently, these prescriptions of propriety still seem to be in force. Women who break them are not fully accepted.

The public posture, stance, and gait prescribed for and expected of women can be extremely awkward. In an effort to demonstrate to our classes how inconvenient some of the expected behaviors for women are, the authors have borrowed a six-item list of exercises for men for our male students to perform in class. While the result has often led to merriment over the inability of some males to deftly and convincingly perform these actions, the exercises have served to make both the women and the men aware of the extent to which many of our learned behaviors are unexamined.

The following six sets of directions illustrate the inconvenience of the public postures permitted to women:

**1.** Sit down in a straight chair. Cross your legs at the ankles and keep your knees pressed together.

**2.** Bend down to pick up an object from the floor. Each time you bend, remember to bend your knees so that your rear end doesn't stick up, and place one hand on your shirt-front to hold it to your chest.

**3.** Run a short distance, keeping your knees together. You will find you have to take short, high steps.

**4.** Sit comfortably on the floor. . . . Arrange your legs so that no one can see [your underwear]. Sit like this for a long time without changing position.

**5.** Walk down a city street. . . . Look straight ahead. Every time a man walks past you, avert your eyes and make your face expressionless.

6. Walk around with your stomach pulled in tight, your shoulders thrown back, and your chest out. . . . Try to speak loudly and aggressively in this posture.

## Gesture

"Every little gesture has a meaning all its own." So go the lyrics of an old song. And though students of kinesics, like Birdwhistell, hasten to warn us that no position, expression, or movement ever carries meaning in and of itself, research in nonverbal communication seems to indicate that patterns of gesture can tell us a good deal about ourselves and others. An important consideration is this: "The more men and women interact in the way they have been trained to from birth without considering the meaning of what they do, the more they become dulled to the significance of their actions." Outsiders who observe a culture different from their own can sometimes spot behavioral differences, and the significance of these differences, which those engaged in the behaviors are not conscious of. Some observational studies help us get outside ourselves and draw our attention to details we might otherwise not notice.

In viewing nonverbal gestures of preschool children, one investigator discovered that girls exhibited more pronounced bodily behavior when they were with other girls than when they were with boys. When they were paired with boys, they tended to be quieter. She concluded that society's expectations of sex differences in social behavior are evident even in the very young child and that different behavior is expected from boys than from girls.

Hand gestures are generally considered to function as illustrators, and they also serve to reveal our emotional states, intentionally or unintentionally. Hand and foot movements can sometimes signal messages at variance with our words. There seems to be some indication that in approval-seeking situations, women use more gesticulations than do males. Since some studies have shown that males talk more, interrupt more, and in general dominate conversations more than females, perhaps women resort to nonverbal expression more frequently.

Some have concluded that women are molded into more patterns of behavior than are men, for there are more implicit and explicit rules as to how females should act and behave. Although initiative, innovation, boldness, and action are encouraged in males, such qualities are discouraged in women. "Forced to submerge their individual impulses and energies, women tend to express themselves more subtly and covertly." The nonverbal channel may be an outlet for women's covert and more subtle expression.

Peterson did a videotaped study of nonverbal communication that occurred during verbal communication between male-male, female-female, and female-male pairs. Subjects pairs were university students, and each pair held a two-minute conversation on the topic of their choice. She studied number of gestures, kinds of gestures, gestures used primarily be females, and gestures used primarily by males. She focused on hand, leg, and foot movements.

She found that overall, the number of gestures displayed by males exceeded the number exhibited by females, regardless of the sex of the conversation partner. Males displayed about the same number of gestures when conversing with either sex. However, females displayed significantly more gestures with males than with other females.

As for differences between the sexes in the kinds of gestures used, she observed the following:

*Females*

tend to leave both hands down on chair arms more than males do

arrange or play with their hair or ornamentation more

*Males*

use sweeping gestures more than females

use arms to lift or move the body position more

use closed fist more

stroke chin more

sit with ankle of one leg crossing the knee of the other more tend to exhibit greater amount of leg and foot movement

tap their feet more

In addition, certain gestures seemed to be performed exclusively by females and others by males in this study. An asterisk indicates a more frequently performed gesture.

*Female*

hand or hands in lap

tapping hands

legs crossed at knees*

ankles crossed, knees slightly apart

*Male*

stretching hands and cracking knuckles

pointing*

both feet on floor with legs apart

legs stretched out, ankles crossed

knees spread apart when sitting*

General observations that Peterson made in regard to nonverbal gestures and the sexes include the following:

1. Both males and females seemed to be more relaxed with the same sex than with the opposite sex, except in two cases where subjects knew each other previously. Subjects exhibited more nervous gestures with the opposite sex.

2. Exclusively male and exclusively female gestures seemed to be reserved for conversations with the same-sex partner. Pointing generally occurred only between males, and hands in the lap between females.

3. Some traits appeared related to gender display. Females handled their hair and clothing ornamentation a great deal more in front of men than women. Men were significantly more open with their leg position and kept their feet on the floor with legs apart when conversing with other males.

With females, however, the men nearly always crossed one ankle over the other knee.

4. Both males and females tended to display a greater number and greater diversity of gestures with the opposite sex. There seemed to be more foot movement with the same sex.

Peterson believed her study indicated that nonverbal communication fills a dual role in conversation for the sexes. Gesture serves as an illustrator and supplement to the verbal channel, and it acts as a means of gender display. Since certain movements occurred exclusively in same-sex pairs, it is possible that separate nonverbal languages are occurring. There seemed to be a greater display of dominant gestures by males—closed fist, pointing, sweeping gestures. Open and dominant gestures may be signals of power and status.

## Clothing, Grooming, and Physical Appearance

Physical attractiveness and the artifacts that contribute to appearance affect communication and communication responses. One study explored the use of physical attractiveness by females as a means of obtaining higher grades from male college professors. The researcher found no differences in the scores of females and males on a Machiavellian scale, which attempts to get at traits associated with those who use any means (cunning, duplicity, or whatever) to achieve a goal. He hypothesized that cultural and social norms may prevent females from using obvious exploitative or deceptive tactics, so they utilize more socially acceptable, but more covert, means and take advantage of their physical attractiveness.

After comparing faculty ratings of women's pictures with their grade-point averages and position in the family, he found a correlation between physical attractiveness, grade point average, and being firstborn and female. Women who used more exhibiting behavior were probably more memorable to professors and thus fared better on grades. They tended to sit in the front of the room more often or come to see the professor after class or during the instructor's office hours more frequently. Using a series of questions about body measurements, the researcher determined that, as he had hypothesized, the firstborn females did indeed seem more aware of and socially concerned about their looks.

In some respects, claimed the researcher, he found the results "not at all surprising," for "the suggestion that *men* live by their *brains* and *women* by their *bodies* was made as far back as Genesis." He found the implications of these results "rather frightening" since the results suggest that the male college professor is a "rather put-upon creature, *hoodwinked* by the *male* students (later born) and *enticed* by the *female* students (first born)." [Italics added.] Whether the reverse is true for female college professors ought to be the subject for future research. As consolation, however, the writer noticed that when a sample of 22 faculty members was given the Machiavellian scale, their average scores, compared with the scores of students in the study, showed them to be significantly more manipulative.

In another experiment, a girl was made up to look unattractive in one setting and attractive in another. The girl read aloud and explained some questions to listeners. Results showed the attitudes of the male students were modified more by the girl in the attractive condition than in the unattractive condition. However, this result was true for a male audience only.

Several years ago, the authors videotaped two women and two men speakers giving persuasive pro and con speeches about the merits of debate. Each gave his or her speech twice: once when made up to look unattractive with nose putty; subtle, unflattering make-up touches; and poorly styled hair and again when made up to look attractive. Clothing was kept constant. The speeches were such that, in the first set, the pro speech was constructed as a cogent and well-reasoned talk and the con speech was poorly reasoned and dogmatic. In the second set, the pro speech was poorly reasoned and dogmatic, and the con speech was cogent and well-reasoned. Listeners, who were college students, took a pretest concerning their atti-

tudes on the subject and then took a post-test following the talks.

Results showed that physical attractiveness did have a persuasive effect on both sexes in their acceptance of the views of the speakers. Both speakers of the well-reasoned talks had a greater persuasive effect when made up in their attractive state, as was anticipated. An interesting result was a difference in persuasiveness that occurred between the females and males in their unattractive states, whether they gave the poorly reasoned or well-reasoned talk. The males made up unattractively were only slightly less effective than in their attractive state. However, there was considerable difference in the influence of the females, depending on physical state. Unattractiveness in the female caused a decidedly more negative reception of her views. In fact, in one of the videotaped versions the unattractiveness of the female who delivered the cogent pro talk weighed so heavily that the attractive female who answered with the poorly reasoned and ill-constructed con speech had the greater impact on listeners. Both females and males seemed more accepting of arguments or views from an unattractive male than from an unattractive female. Males were most negative toward the unattractive female's stand. Another study showed that regardless of sex, attractive people are rated high on character in credibility scales.

In a "Dear Abby" reader survey mentioned earlier, readers were asked to indicate what they noticed first about the opposite sex. Results indicated that women noticed physique first. Added the columnist: "But nearly every female who wrote that it is the first thing she *notices* about a man also wrote that it was certainly not the most *important*." A close second was grooming, including attire. Most women who wrote that they noticed a man's physical attributes first emphasized that it is "what's on the inside" that counts. Women placed much more importance on behavior than the men did in their survey. Responses from men indicated that men noticed bosoms first. After bosoms, a woman's figure, or whole torso, ranked next in importance, with some male respondents terming themselves "leg men" or "fanny fanciers."

These studies, as well as the casual responses to the "Dear Abby" column, seem to reflect our cultural emphasis on a man's activity—what he does—and on a woman's being—how she appears. This was graphically illustrated last year at Arizona State University, where one of the authors teaches. Several men stationed themselves in front of the student union with signs numbered from 4 to 9. They proceeded to rate women on campus by holding numbered signs over the women's heads as they passed. After the university police were summoned to investigate complaints, one of the self-appointed raters explained lamely, "It seemed to me that everyone in the area enjoyed what we did, except for one woman who asked for a sign so she could rate one of us. Of course I refused."

Perhaps women in our society are expected to be more visible and to reveal more of their bodies than men are. Men are sometimes described as more modest than women. This, at least, was the view of Hollywood dress designer Edith Head during an interview. Head has dressed stars from Cary Grant to Robert Redford, and Carole Lombard to Elizabeth Taylor. "Men for the most part are annoyingly modest in the fitting room if a woman is present," she says. "Women, however, will peel off to their panties and bras with male fitters present without batting an eye." She cited Clark Gable as one who was extremely modest. He could bare his chest, but if he had to unzip his trousers and expose his shorts, "he would bluster and blush and make amusing remarks about what he had to go through for his art." Head mentioned a friend who was the head nurse in a urology clinic. "She faces up to male modesty all day long and it's a bore. Women, for the most part, do not have false modesty about their bodies." The references to modesty in all instances refer to mixed company.

The significance of clothing should be noted in passing. Different clothing types for the sexes is believed by some to have important social ramifications. Of course, pants suits for women have been and are worn extensively today, along with skirts, yet pants remain the symbol of the male and skirts the symbol of the female. Some writers question the notion that skirts should be worn by females.

The roles of both sexes are changing. Women are moving out of old patterns, acquiring more education, exercising control of their childbearing, and getting political power. Yet, say some, they are still dressed in an archaic manner, with hips, thighs, and stomach skirted protectively or defensively hidden. Specialists in the history of dress indicate that the differentiation of pants and skirts goes back many years. Skirts may have been important once to protect the one who bore children because in early ages humans were more at the mercy of the elements, dangerous animals, human enemies, and high infant mortality. Presumably then, men were in awe of women's life-giving power and felt it necessary to "protect women's gateway to birth with skirts."

The division of pants from skirts may have been made originally because men needed freedom of leg movement when hunting and working the soil. Women needed skirts to hide their children under if danger threatened, to protect their own bodies, and to form convenient carrying places to convey children or food. Moira Johnston, a clothing historian, believes that skirts later became a male constriction for females because men feared the power a woman's childbearing ability gave her. So they consigned her sexuality to hiding. Later on the skirt became a form of modesty and an attempt to conceal seductive areas.

According to Johnston, the silhouette loosens when morals are lowered, as for example in the Roaring Twenties with the loose flapper dress. After the Second World War, when women went back to the home and to childbearing, fashions became more constrictive and restrictive. Women wore clothing cinched at the waist, with long, full skirts and high-heeled shoes. In looking at the history of feminism, one writer notes the significance of clothing. Before the 1920s women's clothing was confining and cumbersome. Casting aside the old corsets and long skirts may have had more significance for women's emancipation than women's suffrage had.

Henley notes that women's clothing today is fashioned to be revealing, but it still restricts women's body movement. Women are not supposed to reveal too much, and this required guarded movement in many cases. Another concomitant of clothing designed to reveal physical features is that, unlike more loose-fitting men's clothing, there are not convenient pockets in which to carry belongings—hence women's awkward purses. Some men's clothing styles today are styled for closer fit, and this may account for the carrying bags and purselike cases made and sold for males in some places. A clothing historian hypothesized that women have not freed themselves more from skirts and other restrictive women's clothing styles because they fear "terror of disorientation, and dissolution of identity."

In reflecting upon contemporary feminine clothing styles, the authors of this book would add this thought: The popular pants suit has had a liberating effect upon females. No longer must knees be tightly drawn together when sitting. Pants allow much more freedom of movement when walking, sitting on the floor, or lounging on the arm of a chair. The traditional need to cover and protect the female genital area by posture and apparel has been reduced considerably.

The so-called unisex look in clothing has freed women's bosoms from the protective slouch and the provocative thrust. It would be interesting to do research on how attitudes of the wearer are changed when clothing habits are modified. Perhaps it is true that we are what we wear!

## Use of Space

The way we use space can convey nonverbal messages. It has been observed that dominant animals and dominant human beings keep a larger buffer zone of personal space surrounding them that discourages violation than do subordinate animals and humans. Dominant persons are not approached as closely as persons of lesser status. But research has shown that women are approached by both sexes more closely than men.

In one study, university students carried tape measures with them and when approached by anyone who began a conversation, each student measured the distance nose-to-nose between themselves and each speaker. Distances between pairs varied according to sex, age, and race. It was found that generally women were approached more closely than men by both women and men. Perhaps the envelope of inviolable space surrounding women is generally less than men's, and women are perceived as less dominant. Further, compared with men, women stand more closely to good friends but farther away from those they describe just as friends. It has been suggested that perhaps women are more cautious until they have established close relationships. In addition, it has been found that less distance is maintained between women and members of both sexes when they are sitting. There are indications that compared with men, women perceive their own territory as being smaller and as being more open to influence by others. Both sexes have been found more wary of the approach of males than of females.

Studies on crowding offer some insight on differences in personal space between the sexes. One researcher observed groups of people in crowded and uncrowded rooms during one-hour periods of time. Results showed that generally men had more negative reactions to crowding. They liked others less and considered them less friendly. In general, they found the situation more unpleasant, and they became more contentious and distrustful. In contrast, women found the experience pleasanter, liked others more, and considered them friendlier than men did.

It appears that women's territory is perceived as smaller by both males and females. Women may be more tolerant of, or accustomed to, having their personal space breeched by others. This may also be an indication that they are considered to be of lower status by those with whom they interact.

Certainly control of greater territory and space is a characteristic we associate with dominance and status. Superiors have the prerogative of taking more space. They have larger houses, estates, cars, offices, and desks, as well as more personal space in body spread. Inferiors own less space and take up less space personally with their bodies. Females generally command less space. For example, a study showed that women are less likely to have a special and unviolated room in the home. The male may have his den where "nothing is to be touched." Some will counter that the woman has her territory—her kitchen or sewing room. But this space is often as infinitely invadable for the woman working in it as her time while she is doing so. We are all familiar with Archie Bunker's special chair. While men may have their own chair in a house, women rarely do.

Seating arrangement is another space variable. Research shows that female/male status is evident in the way people seat themselves. At rectangular tables, generally the "head" position (the seat at either end of the table) is associated with higher status. Subjects in a study were shown paper-and-pencil diagrams of rectangular tables and asked how they would locate themselves with regard to a person of higher, lower, or equal status and of either sex. When subjects were asked to choose the seat they would take upon arriving first and then to name the seat the other would then take, approximately twice as many females as males would sit side by side, and this was more frequent in relation to a low-status than a high-status person. When asked to choose which seat the other would take upon arriving first, respondents tended to put others at an "end" chair. This tendency was greater for a high-status male authority figure. Subjects were also told to imagine that either Professor Henry Smith or Professor Susan Smith were there. Twice as many subjects would choose the head chair for themselves when the female professor was there as when the male professor was there.

Students in one of our classes did some observational studies of female and male students walking across the Arizona State University campus during peak class-change times in the heavily trafficked mall areas. They found people of both sexes tend to cut across females' paths more frequently.

When female-male pairs approach each other on the street, apparently women are expected to walk around men, according to the results of one study. Nineteen woman-man pairs were observed, and in 12 out of the 19, the woman moved out of the man's way. In only 3 cases did the man move,

and in the remaining 4 instances both moved. When women approached women or men approached men, however, about half of the time both moved out of each other's way. The rest of the time only one person moved.

Also in regard to space, it has been observed that women's general body comportment is restrained. Often their femininity is judged according to how little space they take up. Women condense or compress; men expand. Whereas males use space expansively, women, by the way they cross their legs, keep their elbows to their sides, and maintain a more erect posture, seem to be trying to take up as little space as possible. Novelist Marge Piercy, describing a character teaching movement to a theater group, put it well:

*Men expanded into available space. They sprawled, or they sat with spread legs. They put their arms on the arms of chairs. They crossed their legs by putting a foot on the other knee. They dominated space expansively. Women condensed. Women crossed their legs by putting one leg over the other and alongside. Women kept their elbows to their sides, taking up as little space as possible. They behaved as if it were their duty not to rub against, not to touch, not to bump a man. If contact occurred, the woman shrank back. If a woman bumped a man, he might choose to interpret it as a come-on. Women sat protectively using elbows not to dominate space, not to mark territory, but to protect their soft tissues.*

## Touch

Touch has been the object of some investigation. Most research seems to show that females are touched by others more than males are. Mothers have been found to touch their female children more than their male children from the age of six months on. In one study of touch, the researcher gave a questionnaire to students concerning which parts of the body are touched most often and by whom. He found that females are considerably more accessible to touch by all persons than males are. Friends of the opposite sex and mothers did the most touching.

Further investigation showed that mothers touched their sons more than fathers did, and fathers touched their daughters more than their sons. Daughters touched their fathers more than sons did, and sons touched their mothers more than they touched their fathers. In other words, fathers and sons tended to refrain from touching each other, but other touching interaction in the family was about equal. As for body regions, mothers touched daughters in more places than they did sons. Fathers touched daughters in more places than they did sons. Fathers also were touched by their daughters in more places than they were by their sons. Males touched their opposite-sex best friends in more regions than females reported touching their opposite-sex friends. So in three of the four comparisons, touch by fathers, touch by mothers, and touch by opposite-sex friends, females were touched more. The mean total being-touched score for women was higher than for men. Also, whereas women's opposite-sex friends touched them the most, men's opposite-sex friends touched them the least.

The pattern of greater touching by males has been interpreted by some as a reflection of sexual interest and greater sexual motivation of men. Henley does not accept this, since she finds research does not support greater sexuality in males than females. Rather, she regards touching as a sign of status or power. Touching is an invasion of one's personal space and involves the deference or lack of deference accorded to the space surrounding the body. Touching between intimates can symbolize friendship and affection. But when the pattern of touching is not reciprocal, and both parties do not take equal touch privileges, it can indicate power and status. An observer of the touch system in a hospital noted that although the doctors might touch other ranks to convey support or comfort, other ranks tended to feel it would be presumptuous to return a doctor's touch, and particularly to initiate it.

One investigation of touching involved some 60 hours of observing incidents of touching in public.

Intentional touch with the hand was recorded, as well as whether the touch was returned. Sex, age, and approximate socioeconomic status of the persons observed was also noted. Results showed that higher-status persons touched lower-status ones significantly more frequently. Comparing touching between the sexes, men touched women at a greater rate, when all else (age and apparent socioeconomic status) was equal. When other things were unequal, for example if women had a socioeconomic status advantage, the women would be the more likely one to initiate touch.

The pattern of sexual status showed up primarily in outdoor settings (shopping plaza, beach, college campus, and so forth) rather than in indoor interaction (bank, store, restaurant, doctor's office, and so on). It was suggested that because outdoor interaction is more public, it may necessitate stricter attention to signals of power. Indoor interaction is more informal and encourages more relaxed power relationships. When people are indoors, power can probably be more easily communicated by other cues than touching. Subtle cues, such as eye movements, gestures, and voice shifts, can convey reminders of status easily. But outdoors gross, larger physical acts, such as touching, seem to be required.

Goodall describes one use of touch among chimpanzees. A chimpanzee, after being threatened or attacked by a superior, may follow the aggressor around, screaming and crouching to the ground or holding out his or her hand. The chimpanzee is begging a reassuring touch from the superior. Sometimes the subordinate chimpanzee will not relax until he or she has been touched or patted and embraced. Greetings also reestablish the dominance status of one chimpanzee in relation to the other. For example, Olly would greet Mike by holding out her hand toward him. By this gesture she was acknowledging his superior rank. Mike would touch, pat, or hold her hand or touch her head in response to her submission. These gestures of dominance and submission observed in primates seem to occur among humans as well. As with apes, the gestures used are probably used by humans to maintain and reinforce the social hierarchy by reminding lower-status persons of their position in the order and by reassuring higher-status people that those of lesser rank accept their place in the pecking order.

An informal test of the significance of touch that is not reciprocated and the authority it symbolizes would be to ask ourselves which person in each of the following pairs would be more likely to touch the other—to lay a hand on the back, put an arm around the shoulder, tap the chest, or grasp the wrist: master and servant; teacher and student; pastor and parishioner; doctor and patient; foreman and worker; executive and secretary; police and accused; lawyer and client. If status can explain touch differences in other groups, it seems reasonable to accept this as a factor in female/male touch differences as well.

A considerable amount of touching of women is so much a part of our culture that it goes virtually unnoticed. It occurs when men guide women through the door, down the stairs, into the car, across the street; when they playfully lift women; when they pat them on the head, or playfully spank them; and in many other instances. Males seem to have greater freedom to touch others. When used with objects, touching seems to connote possession. This may apply to attitudes about women as well. As Henley and Thorne express it: "... the wholesale touching of women carries the message that women are community property. They are tactually accessible just as they are visually and informationally accessible."

It is interesting to consider the difference in interpretation of touch by the sexes. This difference seems to support the idea that touch is used as a sign of status or power among the sexes. The difference in female/male perspective can be shown by an illustration which Henley relates. A woman was at a party one evening and saw a male friend of both her and her husband. At various times in the evening he would come up and sit with his arm around her. This she interpreted as a friendly gesture, and she reciprocated the action with friendly intent. However, later the man approached her in private and made sexual advances. When the woman expressed surprise at his suggestions, he replied, "Wasn't that what you were trying to tell me all evening?" The point is that women do not interpret a man's touch as necessarily a sexual invitation, but men often interpret a woman's touch in that way. Touch, of course, can be either. It can be a gesture of power or of intimacy. But touch as a gesture of power will appear to be inappropriate if it is used by one not having power.

Since women are often subordinate, touching by women will be perceived as a gesture of intimacy or sexual invitation rather than power. One would not anticipate that they would be exercising power. In addition, viewing a woman's gesture as a sexual invitation is not only complimentary to the man, but it can put the woman at a disadvantage. By putting a narrower sexual interpretation on what she does and placing her in the position of a sex object, she is effectively placed outside the arena of primary social interaction.

## STATUS AND NONVERBAL COMMUNICATION

We have looked at a number of nonverbal behavior differences exhibited by females and males. One theoretical thread running through much of the discussion is the concept of asymmetry, or non-reciprocality of behavior, that exists between non-equals in status. Female/male differences have been seen to roughly parallel those between superiors and subordinates in status, suggesting a status and power differential behind the socialization of the sexes, Table 1, which is based on theory and some research cited previously, categorizes behavior cues used by females and males.

To a certain extent we may say that behavior is cued. Perhaps women give gestures of submission because they have been shown gestures of dominance. In some situations some people may use gestures of dominance because they have been shown gestures of acquiescence or ingratiation by the others with whom they interact. One writer had some sobering pronouncements to make concerning many of the so-called womanly gestures. She indicated that submission in women is conveyed by

**Table 1** Asymmetrical Nonverbal Cues

| Cues | Superior [male] | Subordinate [female] |
|---|---|---|
| Eyes | Look or stare aggressively<br>Look elsewhere while speaking | Lower eyes, avert eyes, look away, blink<br>Watch speaker while listening |
| Face | No smile or frown<br>Impassive, not showing emotions | Smile<br>Expressive facial gestures, showing emotions |
| Posture | Relaxed, more body lean | Tense, more erect |
| Bearing | Loose legs, freed arms, non-circumspect positions | Tight, legs together, arms close to body |
| Gestures | Larger, more sweeping, forceful, such as pointing | Smaller, more inhibited |
| Touch | Touches other | Does not touch other or reciprocate touch, cuddles, or yields to touch |
| Use of space | Expands, uses more space | Condenses, contracts, takes as little space as possible |
| Distance | Maintains larger envelope of space<br>Closer<br>Approaches closer, crowds<br>Cuts across other's path<br>Walks into other's path | Maintains smaller envelope of space<br>More distant<br>Approaches more distant, retreats, yields<br>Gives way<br>Moves out of the way |
| Clothing | Loose, comfortable | Constraining, formfitting |

*Source:* Some of the material in this table was suggested by Nancy Henley, "Examples of Some Nonverbal Behaviors with Usage Differing for Status Equals and Nonequals, and for Women and Men," *Siscom '75: Women's (and Men's) Communication,* ed. Barbara Eakins, Gene Eakins, and Barbara Lieb-Brilhart (Falls Church, Va.: Speech Communication Association, 1976), Table 1, p. 39; and Henley, "Gestures of Power and Privilege." Examples of Some Nonverbal Behaviors with Usage Differing for Status Equals and Nonequals, and For Women and Men," *Body Politics Power, Sex and Nonverbal Communication* (Englewood Cliffs, N.J.: Prentice-Hall, 1977), Table 5, p. 181.

such behaviors as smiling, averting the eyes, or lowering or turning the head. Self-improvement specialists would grow pale on hearing her definition of charm: "Charm is nothing more than a series of gestures (including vocalizations) indicating submission!" Staunch feminists would probably add a hearty "amen."

Changing or manipulating the signals and indicators of power or subordination may not go very far toward transforming the inequities of society. But perhaps by becoming aware of what we are signifying or are responding to nonverbally, we can better gain control over our lives and more readily ensure that our actions and responses are more conscious, more voluntary or, at least, less automatic. We may surprise ourselves by the extent to which we can affect the patterns and relationships in our lives.

# Silence and Silences in Cross-Cultural Perspective: Japan and the United States

SATOSHI ISHII

TOM BRUNEAU

## A BRIEF FOCUS

*Every deed and every relationship is surrounded by an atmosphere of silence.... Friendship needs no words—it is solitude delivered from the anguish of loneliness. Silence pervades the world, as do a multitude of kinds of silences and an entire spectrum of silencings. A cultural, social, and political nature. It is certainly not particular to any single cultural tradition. However, different cultural groups seem to stylize their forms of silence according to their own traditional wisdom, beliefs, and attitudes.*

*Hammarskjold (1971, p. 8)*

Most people throughout the world experience some form of silence. However, the manner in which people's attitudes become socially and culturally disposed toward silence is dramatically different in different cultural groups. Northern European and North American societies, for example, are so involved in linear progression that even flashes of silence are filled with action and doing. In these cultures, silence is viewed as dark, negative, and full of "no things"—all of which are considered socially undesirable. In such cultures, silence is ritualized and ceremonialized by authoritative leadership in a wide variety of contexts. In other cultures, however, silence is *often* achieved. Here

This essay was prepared especially for this fifth edition. All rights reserved. Permission to reprint must be obtained from the publisher and the authors. Satoshi Ishii teaches at Otsuma Women's University, Mobara, Chiba-ken, Japan. Tom Bruneau teaches at Radford University, Radford, Virginia.

breaking silence is a necessary evil, at best; speaking is a negative act.

Silence is the mode of communication for the contemplative throughout the world—but it is more practical in some cultural and social groupings than others. For some, Lao Tsu's (1972) simple statement, "To talk little is natural" (No. 23), is obviously and experientially descriptive. Pragmatists and people in action—those mobilized in projects and active planning, in decision making, and the like—seldom experience deep silence. Pragmatists and scientific-minded people shake their heads in utter amazement that what means nothing to them can be significant to others in many different ways.

Silence belongs to the world of being—not to the world of becoming. Silence is stillness—a mental phenomenon of some duration. *Silences*, however, while connected to the deeper level of silence, belong to the world of becoming, or linear progression, of conscious and semiconscious thinking, saying, and doing. Stillness and silence-of-being appear to concern right-brained cortical processes; silence, in its social or asocial manifestations, concerns sitting still, solitude, and inaction. Silences-of-becoming appear to concern left-brained cortical processes.

## Silences

Silences lie on the surface of deeper levels of silence. Silences are like interconnected rivers and lakes; silence is like the sea to which they are connected. Silences are discontinuities; they are breaks in action. Silences are often dynamic variations of processes recognized as having signification. They are stillings of process where we attempt to impose duration (Bruneau 1985). Some cultural groups, many of them Far Eastern, are biased in favor of lengthy silences. These groups create silences more frequently than do those from some Western cultures; they interrupt processual action with long and deep silences.

When we alter continuity significantly, we create silences; when we alter expected succession, we create silences; when we stop to think, we create internal silences.

Silences are not only based in the very comprehensibility of each language of the world but are also the stuff out of which social acts, social actions, social presence, and social events are created and articulated. Thus we can speak of social silences, or interpersonal or group silences. Some lengthy group silences can be viewed as "social silences." These silences are also durational breaks in process, succession, and continuity. Customs, traditions, social mannerisms, social stability, normative actions, and the like can be viewed as they relate to habitual silences.

## Silencing

The process of arresting process is *silencing*. At a basic level, silencing is the imposition of volition or will to give signification or symbolic meaning (Bruneau 1985). At a political or social level, it is a process of using a figure to gain rhetorical import; it is a persuasive act, an exercise in enforcing norms and directing others and one's self; it is many such communicative matters. As far as social and political exigencies, events, situations, and circumstances are concerned, we can speak of those who silence and those who are silenced, those who act and those who observe, those who listen and those who speak.

We silence others to gain attention, to maintain control, to protect, to teach, to attempt to eliminate distractions, to induce reverence for authority or tradition, and to point to something greater than ourselves or our groups. Silencing is also a way of positing a ground of psychological and social neutrality, so that silences and silence can occur positively. Zones of silence, or places where extraneous noise is controlled, are sometimes created as a means of silencing others. These zones can concern authority, expertise, secrecy, thinking, and the like.

Silencing can be the essence of the language of superiority and inferiority, affecting such relationships as teacher-follower, male-female, and expert-client. The definition of much role behavior across many cultural groups concerns the manner of speech and refraining from speech. The process of silencing can have both positive and negative effects. In some situations, quiet is demanded by others and

by those who must themselves be quiet. Being quiet—effecting a self-imposed silence is often valued and rewarded in some social environments. Being quiet is often a sign of respect for the wisdom and expertise of others. The elderly of many Eastern cultural groups expect signs of respect, one of which is the silence of the young, as well as the silence of less authoritative family members. Westerners often do not understand this process: It was common several decades ago but is practiced less and less today.

Contrary to outspoken and often ego-driven Western women (even the milder ones), many women in Eastern cultures view their silent roles as very powerful. Some women see their silent roles as natural (some are unconscious of them) and cannot *imagine* speaking out unless violated personally. There is a power of control in silence and in the outward show of reticence. This power often goes unrecognized by those who value speech-as-power and by those who value assertiveness by all, equally and democratically. It is, without a doubt, a truism that many cultures of the world expect more silences from women and children.

## SILENCES IN CROSS-CULTURAL PERSPECTIVE

Today's communication scholars, who often observe the Western rhetorical tradition uncritically, have been concerned primarily with verbal expressions or speaking out. The Western tradition is relatively negative in its attitude toward silence and ambiguity, especially in social and public relations. People seldom recognize that silences do have linking, affecting revelational, judgmental, and activating communicative functions in Western cultures (Jensen 1973). Also, silences can convey all the various kinds and degrees of messages that may be described as cold, oppressive, defiant, disapproving or condemning, calming, approving, humble, excusing, and consenting (Samovar et al. 1981, p. 184). The intercultural implications of silent behaviors are diverse because the value and use of silence as communication vary markedly from one culture to another. Consequently, communication scholars ought to pay more attention to the cultural values of silence and the interpretations given to silences in communication interactions.

Since the time of ancient Greek philosophers, Western thought has emphasized bipolar values and concepts by opposing terms such as black versus white, good versus bad, and yes versus no. Speech versus silence has been researched and taught from the same bipolarization: Speech has a positive connotation and silence has a negative one. Recently, however, both Eastern and Western scholars have come to advocate relativistic viewpoints on such concepts and values: "A major misconception is. . . . the common, basic assumption that silence is completely other than speech, its foreign opposite, its antagonist" (Bruneau 1973, p. 17). Silence is not the "empty" absence of speech sound; silence creates speech, and speech creates silence; yin and yang are, in this view, counterdependent as well as dynamically concomitant. In Gestalt terms, the two function as the "figure" and the "ground," one being possible because of the other's existence, but dynamically so. Generally, silence is regarded as the ground against which the figures of speech are perceived and valued. The two should sometimes be perceived in the reverse way; silence should be treated as the figure against which the ground of speech functions. Most people, especially in Western cultures, are unconscious of this interdependence between speech and silence.

## Some Pragmatic Comparisons

In intercultural communication, while the basic *form* of silence *may be* universal, its functions and interpretations vary among cultures. For a newcomer to a foreign culture, a general knowledge of when and where to keep silent may be a basic social requirement, just as a little knowledge of verbal communication is. That is, in intercultural communication contexts a deep understanding comes from being sensitive and open-minded to cultural differences in communicative silences. According to Wayne (1974), the U.S. interpretations of silence are: (1) sorrow, (2) critique, (3) obligation, (4) regret, and (5) embarrassment. Australian interpretations proved

to be similar to the U.S. ones. Wayne goes on to conclude, "In every case the fact that the percentage of neutral of uncommitted responses was much higher for the Japanese and thus could be interpreted as a cultural difference" (pp. 127–130).

From the perspective of an ethnography of communication, the notion and significance of silent communication competence should be positively introduced and researched along with verbal communication competence. Humans become communicatively competent by acquiring not only the structure and use of language but also a set of values and patterns of silent interaction. Anthropologically, the relative quantities and values of the silence of children in communicative settings can be said to be related to socialization and child-rearing practices. According to Caudill and Weinstein (1969), for example, Japanese mothers make more efforts than do U.S. mothers to soothe their children with physical, rather than verbal, contact. This effort apparently suggests that Japanese mothers value silence and its association with self-restraint in Japanese society. In contrast to the Western significance of eloquence and self-assertion, the general attitude of Japanese people toward language and verbalization is that fewer words, supported by the *aesthetics of vagueness,* are better than more words.

Socio-cultural impact plays an important role in the characterization of communication patterns. It may be safely said that Japanese culture nurtures silence, reserve, and formality, whereas Western cultures place more value on speech, self-assertion, and informality. Ishii and Klopf (1976) ascertained from their cross-cultural survey results that the average person in the United States devotes about twice the time to conversation (6 hours, 43 minutes) than do the Japanese (3 hours, 31 minutes).

Further evidence to support the idea that the Japanese have negative attitudes toward speaking is in order. Values regarding appropriate communicative behavior are often most clearly reflected in traditional proverbs. Katayama (1982) analyzed 504 Japanese proverbs on the values of language and found: 124 (25 percent) of them had positive values; 320 (63 percent) had negative values; and 59 (12 percent) were neutral. Inagaki (1985) also investigated 3,600 Japanese people's attitudes toward speaking and obtained data indicating that 82 percent of them agreed with the saying *"Kuchi wa wazawai no moto,"* or, in English, "Out of the mouth comes all evil" (p. 6). This finding is not surprising given the many Japanese proverbs expressing negativity toward speech. Ishikawa's (1970) survey results on businessmen and businesswomen in Tokyo revealed that (1) men should or need to be silent to be successful in life and (2) 65 percent of the businesswomen would choose silent males to marry (p. 5).

All these survey results show a contrast between Japanese and U.S. values of speech and silence. Rader and Wunsch (1980) obtained the following results from their survey on oral communication in U.S. businesses: (1) 95 percent responded that the ability to communicate orally and in writing was considered to be important in their jobs and (2) graduates in business were spending the greatest proportion of time in speaking, followed by listening, writing, and reading. Woodstock (1979), who analyzed oral and written communication problems of managerial trainees, secretaries, and immediate supervisors, concluded that oral communication is an area that should be given more emphasis in the business communication classroom.

Not only in business but in everyday social life, people in the United States like to ask questions and force others to talk to fill interpersonal silences. Because silence is not valued and therefore not tolerated socially in U.S. society (and in many European societies), one function of speech is to avoid silence, generally, as well as to fill silences during the transference of messages. Contrary to the U.S. practice, in Japanese society silence and silences are generally considered to be positively meaningful; they are socio-culturally accepted to a much higher degree.

The point here is that the quantity of silences versus the quantity of speech is interpreted and valued differently across cultures. Different norms of appropriate communicative behavior exist, and a variety of intercultural misunderstanding can occur if one does not know when, where, and how to remain silent. To promote natural and effective interaction, especially with Japanese, people in the United States need to learn to feel more comfortable in situations where silence and vagueness prevail. Learning the general rules for silence plays a more important part than generally thought for all people attempting to communicate successfully across cultures.

## Japanese Enryo-Sasshi Versus U.S. Exaggeration-Reduction

Anthropologists, psychologists, sociologists, and communication scholars have often pointed out that Japanese people are oriented to non-confrontational and non-dialectical interpersonal relations. This orientation of the Japanese is unquestionably based on their nonverbal, intuitive communication practices, whereas Americans want to emphasize individualism and self-assertion supported by verbal communication. Barnlund (1975), who compared Japan-U.S. verbal and nonverbal self-disclosure, concluded: "The communicative consequences of cultural emphasis upon 'talkativeness' and 'self assertion' among Americans may cultivate a highly self-oriented person, one who prizes and expresses every inner response no matter how trivial or fleeting." As to Japanese self-disclosure, he goes on to say, "The communicative consequences of cultural encouragement of 'reserve' and 'caution' among Japanese may produce an other-oriented person, who is highly sensitive and receptive to meanings in others" (p. 160). Barnlund's observations are evidentially supported by Ishii, Klopf, and Cambra's (1979, 1984) PVB[1] findings on Japanese and U.S. students' verbal predispositions: The Japanese students were significantly different from the U.S. students, being less dominant, less inclined to initiate and maintain conversations, less apt to speak frequently and long, less inclined to talk, and less fluent than U.S. students (1984). How, then, can these Japan-U.S. communication style differences be explained psychologically in terms of encoding and decoding messages?

In the high-context Japanese culture, most information tends to be in the physical context and internalized into the person. People, therefore, need not participate actively in verbal interaction. Ishii's (1984) study of *enryo-sasshi* communication in such a high-context culture was among the first attempts to analyze and clarify the general process of Japanese interpersonal empathic communication. The speaker, unconsciously depending on the other person and the communicative situation, simplifies and economizes messages rather than elaborating on them. His or her psychological "exit," through which the encoded messages are sent out under the impact of *enryo* (reserve or restraint), is considered to be much smaller than his or her own message-receiving "entrance," called *sasshi*. The sense of *enryo-sasshi* is of utmost importance in high-context Japanese interpersonal relations.

Intrapersonally, the person of good *enyro* considers the active, exaggerated expression of ideas and feelings to be degrading and foreign. Ideas and feelings that might hurt the other person or damage the general atmosphere when expressed are carefully sent back for re-examination in an internal self-feedback process. Only those ideas judged safe and vague are allowed to be sent out through the small exit that functions as a screening filter. This message-screening process in consideration of the other person and the context is *"enryo"*; it makes the Japanese appear silent, vague, and awkward in communicating with superiors, strangers, and people from different cultures. This observation apparently serves to explain the psychological backdrop of Japanese people's communication apprehension: Thirty-five percent of the Japanese considered themselves to be highly apprehensive in communication situations as compared to 20 percent of the Americans.

To make communicative interaction possible in the high-context situation, the Japanese listener is expected to possess good sensitivity and to receive the message through his or her wide entrance. In this message-receiving stage, the restricted and vague information is appropriately "developed" according to the listener's guess competence called *"sasshi."* In Japanese interpersonal relations, a person of good *sasshi*, who is good at mind-reading or perceiving intuitively people's ideas and feelings, is highly appreciated. This process of interaction is *enryo-sasshi* communication, one of the keys to understanding Japanese interpersonal relations.

In the U.S. multi-ethnic low-context culture, a communication process that is in contrast to the Japanese process seems to function. In low-context communication people depend on the active exchange of overt, verbal messages. The speaker is socialized and expected to send out his or her messages through the large exit, in an exaggerated way, rather than simplifying and economizing them. The psychological mechanism of American message-screening and internal self-feedback can be said to be rougher than that of Japanese *enryo-sasshi*. This fact is evidently based upon a *counter-Japanese value* of interpersonal communication that the more speaking, the better—at home, in school, and in business.

The U.S. listener, in receiving and decoding the exaggerated message, subconsciously attempts to reduce the information. The message-receiving entrance seems to be smaller than that of the Japanese; that is, the listener is not expected to guess and develop the message. Clarity and exactitude in decoding are not the norm. This whole process of sending and receiving messages can be called U.S. *exaggeration-reduction communication*.

## CONCLUSION

Whereas verbal communication plays a very important role in promoting intercultural as well as interpersonal understanding, we should recognize that the ultimate goal-stage of communication—interpersonally or interculturally—may be communication through silence. Silence lends substance to speech and gives it tensive direction—being supports becoming. Baker (1955), who constructed a communication model of silence on the basis of "reciprocal identification," claims that silence *is the aim of human communication*. We do not dispute this claim, and although we have been forced here to use words to point to the muted world, we are hopeful that we have shared some of our interior silence and silences with those of the reader.

## NOTE

1. PVB (Predispositions toward Verbal Behavior) is an instrument to measure a person's general feelings of his or her verbal behavior (see Mortensen et al. 1977). For details of the Japan-U.S. cross-cultural surveys, see Ishii et al. 1984.

## REFERENCES

Baker, S. J. (1955). "The Theory of Silence." *Journal of General Psychology* 53, 145–167.

Barnlund, D. C. (1975). *Public and Private Self in Japan and the United States.* Tokyo: Simul Press.

Bruneau, T. J. (1973). "Communicative Silences: Forms and Functions." *Journal of Communication* 23, 1, 17–46.

Bruneau, T. J. (1982). "Communicative Silences in Cross-Cultural Perspective." *Media Development* (London) 29, 4, 6–8.

Bruneau, T. J. (1985). "Silencing and Stilling Process: The Creative and Temporal Bases of Signs." *Semiotica* 56, 3/4, 279–290.

Caudill, W. and H.Weinstein. (1969). "Maternal Care and Infant Behavior in Japan and America." *Psychiatry* 32, 12–43.

Hammarskjold, D. (1971). *Markings* (Transl. L. Sjoberg and W. H. Auden). New York: Alfred A. Knopf.

Inagaki, Y. (1985). *Jiko Hyogen No Gijutsu* ("Skills in Self-Expression"). Tokyo: PHP Institute.

Ishii, S. (1984). "*Enryo-sasshi* Communication: A Key to Understanding Japanese Interpersonal Relations."*Cross Currents* 11, 1, 49–58.

Ishii, S. and D. W. Klopf. (1976). "A Comparison of Communication Activities of Japanese and American Adults." *Eigo Tembo (ELEC Bulletin)* 53, 22–26.

Ishii, S., D. W. Klopf, and R. E. Cambra. (1979). "Oral Communication Apprehension among Students in Japan, Korea and the United States." *Jijieigogaku Kenkyu* ("*Current English Studies*") 18, 12–26.

Ishii, S., D. W. Klopf, and R. E. Cambra. (1984). "The Typical Japanese Student As an Oral Communicator: A Preliminary Profile." *Otsuma Review* 17, 39–63.

Ishikawa, H. (1970). "Chinmoku-gata Wa Shusse Suru" ("The Silent Type Succeeds"). *Mainichi Shimbun.*

Jensen, V. J. (1973). "Communicative Functions of Silence." *ETC: A Review of General Semantics* 30, 259–263.

Katayama, H. (1982). "Kotowaza Ni Hanei Sareta Nipponjin No Gengokan" ("Japaneses views of language as reflected in proverbs"). *Kyoiku Kiyo 8-go* ("*Eighth General Education Annual*"). Matsudo, Chiba-ken: Matsudo Dental School, Nihon University, 1–11.

Mortensen, C. D. et al. (1977). "Measurement of Verbal Predispositions: Scale Development and Application." *Human Communication Research* 3, 146–158.

Rader, M. and A. Wunsch. (1980). "A Survey of Communication Practices of Business School Graduates by Job Category and Undergraduate Major." *Journal of Business Communication* 17, 33–41.

Samovar, L. A., R. E. Porter, and N. C. Jain. (1981). *Understanding Intercultural Communication.* Belmont, Calif.: Wadsworth.

Tsu, Lao. (1972). *Tao Te Ching* (Transl. Gia-Fu-Feng and J. English). New York: Alfred A. Knopf.

Wayne, M. S. (1974). "The Meaning of Silence in Conversations in Three Cultures." In *Patterns of Communication In and Out of Japan.* (International Christian University Communication Student Group, ed.). Tokyo: ICU Communication Department, 127–130.

Woodstock, B. (1979). "Characteristic Oral and Written Business Communication Problems of Selected Managerial Trainees." *Journal of Business Communication* 16, 43–48.

## CONCEPTS AND QUESTIONS
## FOR CHAPTER 6

**1.** From your personal experiences can you think of additional ways that people in various cultures greet, kiss, show contempt, or beckon?

**2.** Are cultural differences that are based on linguistic problems harder or easier to overcome than the problems related to nonverbal actions?

**3.** In what ways do nonverbal behaviors reflect the values, history, and social organization of a culture?

**4.** What are some of the dangers of overgeneralizing from nonverbal communication?

**5.** Have you ever experienced situations where the nonverbal behavior of someone did not meet your expectations? How did you react? Could this have been a cultural problem?

**6.** How can we develop a theory of nonverbal behavior if we go beyond the anecdotal narration of bizarre behaviors?

**7.** Can you think of any cultural examples that would tend to support the notion that a culture's history influences its use of nonverbal communication?

**8.** What are the relationships between verbal and nonverbal forms of communication?

**9.** How might cultural differences in time conceptualization lead to intercultural communication problems?

**10.** What examples can you think of that illustrate differences between the sexes in nonverbal behavior?

**11.** How would you prevent the occurrence of intercultural communication problems that are brought about by the unconscious and unintentional performance of nonverbal behavior and that deeply offend members of another culture?

**12.** Using the Japanese as an example, discuss how differences in nonverbal behavior might frustrate the progress of an intercultural encounter between a Japanese and a North American engaged in a business negotiation.

## SUGGESTED READINGS

Basso, K. H. "To give up on words: Silence in Western Apache culture." *Southwestern Journal of Anthropology.* 26 (1970), 213–230. This article looks at silence as a form of communication among the Western Apache. Basso examines how silence is used when meeting strangers, courting, greeting friends, cursing, and curing someone.

Boucher, J. D. "Display rules and facial affective behavior: A theoretical discussion and suggestions for research" in *Topics for Culture Learning,* vol. 2. Honolulu: East-West Center, 1974. Boucher develops a theory of facial affective behavior in interpersonal intercultural interaction. He defines display rules for facial affective behavior as a set of norms that the individual internalizes during socialization, and he discusses examples of behavior with emphasis on the identification of contextual characteristics of people and settings.

Effron, D. *Gesture, Race and Culture.* The Hague: Mouton, 1972. Here Efron presents the results of his classic study of spatio-temporal and linguistic aspects of the gestural patterns of Eastern Jews and southern Italians in New York City.

Ekman, P. "Communication through nonverbal behavior: A source of information about an interpersonal relationship" in S. S. Tompkins and C. E. Izard, eds. *Affect, Cognition, and Personality.* New York: Springer, 1965, pp. 391–442. This article discusses basic concepts in nonverbal communicative behavior and also explains how nonverbal expressions provide additional information for the interpretation of verbal systems.

Hall, E. T. *The Hidden Dimension.* New York: Doubleday, 1966. People use space to communicate in very much the same way they use words or gestures. In this volume, Hall sets forth his theory of proxemics and describes and discusses cultural variance in proxemic behavior.

Johnson, F. L. and R. White Buttny. "Listener's responses to 'sounding Black' and 'sounding White': The effect of message content on judgments about language." *Communication Monographs* 49 (1982), 33–49. The effects of sounding "black" or "white" are examined in this very interesting study. More specifically, the study asked if white listeners focus their perceptions differently depending on whether a speaker "sounds white" or "sounds black" and depending on whether message content is abstract or experiential. Results suggest that both stereotypic and egocentric filters shape listener response.

LaBarre, W. "The cultural basis of emotions and gestures." *Journal of Personality* 16 (1946), 49–68. Specific emotional expressions and gestures have their bases in culture, both in the appropriateness of the expression and in the manner of expression. In this classic study, LaBarre discusses variations in these forms of nonverbal behaviors that result from cultural differences; he cites numerous examples and describes how different cultures have different nonverbal expressions for the same meaning.

LaFrance, M. and C. Mayo. *Moving Bodies: Nonverbal Communication in Social Relationships*. Monterey, Calif.: Brooks/Cole, 1978. Chapter 13 of this book looks at the role of culture in nonverbal communication. The authors examine cross-cultural similarities and differences in the use of nonverbal cues.

Luce, T. S. "Blacks, whites and yellows: They all look alike to me." *Psychology Today* (November 1974), 105–106, 107. In this article, Luce describes studies that reveal that the stereotype of members of ethnic and racial groups all looking alike to someone from another group is widespread.

Mayo, C. and N. M. Henley, eds. *Gender and Nonverbal Behavior.* New York: Springer-Verlag, 1981. This book explores the relationship between nonverbal cues and gender. The authors maintain that people negotiate their sex roles through the subtle expression of nonverbal cues. Composed of thirteen chapters, this book contains original research reports, state-of-the-art literature reviews, and conceptual essays on new research arenas. Topics discussed include touching, seating arrangements, visual behavior, body movements, facial expressions, and nonverbal signals.

Morris, D. et al. *Gestures, Their Origins and Distribution.* Briarcliff Manor, N.Y.: Stein and Day, 1979. Morris and his associates describe the historical development and use of 20 nonverbal behaviors. Although the research was conducted in Western Europe, it still offers countless specific examples of how gestures and other nonverbal codes shift from culture to culture.

Ramsey, S. "Nonverbal behavior: An intercultural perspective" in M. K. Asante, E. Newmark, and C. A. Blake, eds. *Handbook of Intercultural Communication.* Beverly Hills, Calif.: Sage Publications, 1979, pp. 105–143. Ramsey offers an extensive review and evaluation of research on nonverbal communication and its relationship to culture. She analyzes gestures, bodily contact, spatial behavior, seating, and architecture.

Rich, A. L. "Interracial implications of nonverbal communication" in A. L. Rich. *Interracial Communication.* New York: Harper & Row, 1974. In Chapter 7 of her book, Rich explores the importance of nonverbal communication to interracial interaction. Most dimensions of nonverbal communication are examined in this selection—environment, proxemics, clothing, physical appearance and characteristics, posture, gesture, eye contact, facial expressions, and paralanguage.

Sussman, N. M. and H. M. Rosenfeld. "Influence of culture, language, and sex on conversational distance." *Journal of Personality and Social Psychology* 42 (1982), 66–74. This study assesses interpersonal distance between seated conversants from each of three cultures: Japanese, Venezuelan, and North American.

Watson, M. O. and T. D. Graves. "Quantitative research in proxemic behavior." *American Anthropologist* 68 (1966), 971–985. Watson and Graves report an experimental study between Americans and Arabs that tested the hypothesis that Arabs interact closer physically than do North Americans. This study is important because it not only supports proxemic theory, it also gives insight into cross-cultural research methodologies.

Wolfgang, A., ed. *Nonverbal Behavior: Applications and Cultural Implications.* New York: Academic Press, 1979. This text is a collection of essays on topics such as expressive behavior, emotion and nonverbal behavior, and culture and interracial problems. Contributors include experts such as Scheflen, Argyle, and Hall.

## ADDITIONAL READINGS

Arndt, J., S. Gronms, and D. Hawes. "Allocation of time to leisure activities: Norwegian and American patterns." *Journal of Cross-Cultural Psychology* 11 (1980), 495–511.

Boucher, J. D. and G. E. Carlson. "Recognition of facial expression in three cultures." *Journal of Cross-Cultural Psychology* 11 (1980), 263–280.

Brislin, R. W. "Seating as a measure of behavior: You are where you sit" in *Topics in Culture Learning,* vol. 2. Honolulu: East-West Center, 1974.

Ekman, P., R. Sorenson, and E. Friessen. "Pancultural elements in facial displays of emotion." *Science* 164 (1969), 86–88.

Forston, R. F. and C. U. Larson. "The dynamics of space: An experimental study in proxemic behavior among Latin Americans and North Americans." *Journal of Communication* 18 (1968), 109–116.

Grove, C. L. "Nonverbal behavior: Cross-cultural contact and the urban classroom teacher." *Equal Opportunity Review* (1976), 1–5.

Hall, E. T. *The Dance of Life: The Other Dimension of Time*. New York: Anchor Press/Doubleday, 1983.

Hall, E. T. *The Silent Language*. Garden City, N.Y.: Doubleday, 1959.

Johnson, K. R. "Black kinesics: Some non-verbal communication patterns in the black culture." *Florida FL Reporter* 9 (Spring/Fall 1971), 17–20, 57.

Jones, S. E. and J. R. Aiello. "Proxemic behavior of black and white first-, third-, and fifth-grade children." *Journal of Personality and Social Psychology* 25 (1973), 21–27.

LaFrance, M. and C. Mayo. "Racial differences in gaze behavior during conversations: Two systematic observation studies." *Journal of Personality and Social Psychology* 33 (1976), 574–552.

McCann, L. D. and M. L. Hecht. "Verbal and nonverbal assessment of foreign students' communication apprehension." *The Journal of the Communication Association of the Pacific* 12 (1983), 67–76.

Mehrabian, A. *Silent Messages: Implicit Communication of Emotions and Attitudes*, 2d ed. Belmont, Calif.: Wadsworth, 1981.

Pagan, G. and J. R. Aiello. "Development of personal space among Puerto Ricans." *Journal of Nonverbal Behavior* 7 (1982), 59–68.

Patterson, M. L. *Nonverbal Behavior: A Functional Perspective*. New York: Springer-Verlag, 1983.

Powell, P. "Peacebrokers in the Middle East: The nonverbal dimensions." *World Communication* 15 (1986), 155–167.

Ramsey, S. J. "The kinesics of femininity in Japanese women." *Language Sciences* 3 (1981), 104–123.

Rudden, M. R. and K. D. Frandsen. "An intercultural test of the generality of interpretations of nonverbal cues." *International Journal of Intercultural Relations* 2 (1978), 410–425.

Seward, J. *Japanese in Action*. New York: John Weatherhill, 1968.

Scheflen, A. E. and N. Ashcraft. *Human Territories: How We Behave in Space-Time*. Englewood Cliffs, N.J.: Prentice-Hall, 1976.

Shuter, R. "The gap in the military: Hand-to-hand communication." *Journal of Communication* 29 (1979), 136–142.

Shuter, R. "Gaze behavior in interracial and intraracial interactions." *International and Intercultural Communication Annual* 2 (1979), 48–55.

Shuter, R. "A study of nonverbal communication among Jews and Protestants." *The Journal of Social Psychology* 109 (1979), 31–41.

St. Martin, G. M. "Intercultural differential decoding of nonverbal affective communication." *International and Intercultural Communication Annual* 3 (1976), 44–57.

Wolfgang, A., ed. *Nonverbal Behavior: Perspectives, Applications, Intercultural Insights*. Toronto: C. J. Hogrefe, 1984.

Zanger, V. *Face-to-Face: The Cross-Cultural Workbook*. Newbury House Publishers, 1986.

# PART FOUR

## Intercultural Communication: Becoming More Effective

*Happy are they that hear their detractions and can put them to mending.*

*—Shakespeare*

In a sense, this entire volume has been concerned with the practice of intercultural communication. We have looked at a variety of cultures and a host of communication variables that operate when people from different cultures attempt to interact. However, our analysis thus far has been somewhat theoretical. Previous selections have concentrated primarily on the issue of understanding intercultural communication. We have not, at least up to this point, treated the act of practicing intercultural communication.

We have already pointed out many of the problems that cultural differences can introduce into the communication process. And we have shown how an awareness of not only other cultures but also of one's own culture can help mediate some of the problems. But intercultural communication is not exclusively a single party activity. Like other forms of interpersonal communication, it requires for its highest and most successful practice the complementary participation of all parties to the communication event.

When elevated to its highest level of human activity, intercultural communication becomes what David Berlo in 1960 described as "Interaction: The Goal of Human Communication": the communicative act in which "two individuals make inferences about their own roles and the role of the other at the same time."* Berlo calls this reciprocal role taking: in order for people to achieve the highest level of communication there

---

*David K. Berlo, *The Process of Communication*. New York: Holt, Rinehart & Winston, 1960, p. 130.

must be a mutual reciprocity in achieving an understanding of each other. In intercultural communication, this means that you must not only know about your culture and the culture of the one with whom you are communicating, but that that person must also know about his or her own culture and about your culture as well. Unless there is mutual acknowledgment of each other's cultures and a willingness to accept those cultures as a reality governing communicative interactions, intercultural communication cannot rise to its highest possible level of human interaction.

In this final section we have slightly modified our orientation so that we can include a discussion based on the activity of communication. For although the readings in this portion of the book will increase your understanding, their main purpose is to improve your behavior *during* intercultural communication.

The motivation for this particular section grows out of an important precept found in the study of human communication. It suggests that human interaction is a behavioral act in which people engage for the purpose of changing their environment. Inherent in this notion is the idea that communication is something people *do*—it involves action. Regardless of how much you understand intercultural communication, when you are communicating with someone from another culture you are part of a behavioral situation. You, and your communication counterpart, are doing things to each other. This final part of the book deals with that "doing." In addition, it is intended to help your communication become as effective as possible.

As you might well imagine, personal contact and experience are the most desirable methods for improvement. Knowledge and practice seem to work in tandem. The problem, however, is that we cannot write or select readings that substitute for this personal experience. Therefore, our contribution by necessity must focus on the observations of those who have practiced intercultural communication with some degree of success.

# 7

# Communicating
# Interculturally

The primary purpose of this book is to help you become more effective intercultural communicators. To this end, the articles in this chapter offer advice and counsel aimed at improving the way you communicate when you find yourself in intercultural encounters. To help you achieve this goal, most of the essays discuss problems as well as solutions. Being alert to potential problems is the first step toward understanding. Once problems have been identified it is easier to seek means of improvement.

The first essay looks at both problems and solutions. In "Stumbling Blocks in Intercultural Communication," LaRay M. Barna deals with some specific reasons why intercultural communication often fails to bring about mutual understanding. She has selected six important causes for communication breakdown across cultural boundaries: language problems, nonverbal misunderstanding, the presence of preconceptions and stereotypes, the tendency to evaluate, and the high anxiety that often exists in intercultural encounters.

Brent D. Ruben in "Human Communication and Cross-Cultural Effectiveness" is concerned with ways to increase communication effectiveness in intercultural settings. He examines seven factors that contribute to effective communication behavior: the capacity to communicate respect, the capacity to be nonjudgmental, the capacity to personalize one's knowledge and perceptions, the capacity to display empathy, the capacity to be flexible, the capacity for turn-taking, and the capacity to tolerate ambiguity.

In "Prejudice in Intercultural Communication" Richard W. Brislin examines this problem while looking at the functions and forms of prejudice. He warns of five different forms of prejudice: redneck racism, symbolic racism, tokenism, arms-length prejudice, and the familiar and unfamiliar. Each of these forms must be understood and controlled to achieve successful intercultural communication.

The final article deals with acculturation, a somewhat unique and often overlooked aspect of intercultural communication. Young Yun Kim examines this topic in her article "Communication and Acculturation." With approximately a million refugees immigrating to the United States each year, she is concerned that many of the immigrants' communicative modes, internalized from early childhood, may prove dysfunctional in their new communication environment. She, therefore, presents a discussion of both the problems and the solutions of acculturation. Her thesis is that one learns to communicate by communicating, and that much of that communication takes place between the immigrants and the American people. By understanding the acculturation process, Americans can help with the often difficult transition facing these new arrivals.

# Stumbling Blocks in Intercultural Communication

LARAY M. BARNA

Why is it that contact with persons from other cultures so often is frustrating and fraught with misunderstanding? Good intentions, a friendly approach, and even the possibility of mutual benefits don't seem to be sufficient—to many people's surprise. One answer to the question might be that many of us naively assume there are sufficient similarities among peoples of the world to enable us to successfully exchange information and/or feelings, solve problems of mutual concern, cement business relationships, or just make the kind of impression we wish to make.

The tendency for all people to reproduce, group into families and/or societies, develop a language, and adapt to their environment is particularly deceiving because it leads to the expectation that the forms of these behaviors and the attitudes and values surrounding them will also be similar. It's comforting to believe that "people are people" and "deep down we're all alike," but a determined search for proof of this leads to disappointment.

The major similarities are biological ones, including the need for food, shelter, and safety (with radical variations as to type and amount of each). Eibl-Eibesfeldt lists as cross-cultural similarities the "sucking response, the breast-seeking automatism, smiling, crying and a number of reflexes."[1] There is also Pavlov's "orienting reaction"—the instantaneous bodily changes that occur when threat is

Reprinted by permission of LaRay M. Barna. Professor Barna teaches at Portland State University.

perceived.[2] Such changes include the flow of extra adrenaline and noradrenaline into the system, increased muscle tension, cessation of digestive processes, and other changes that prepare the human animal to "fight or flee." Although this is a universal and a key adaptive mechanism that allowed survival in a hostile environment for early humans, it hinders rather than helps today's intercultural communication process, which calls for calm, considered exchanges.

None of the above universals are much help for purposes of communication. More promising are the cross-cultural studies seeking to support Darwin's theory that facial expressions are universal.[3] Ekman found that "the particular visible pattern on the face, the combination of muscles contracted for anger, fear, surprise, sadness, disgust, happiness (and probably also for interest) is the same for all members of our species."[4] This seems helpful until it is realized that a person's cultural upbringing determines whether or not the emotion will be displayed or suppressed, as well as on which occasions and to what degree.[5] The situations that bring about the emotional feeling also differ from culture to culture; for example, the death of a loved one may be a cause for joy, sorrow, or some other emotion, depending upon the accepted cultural belief.

There seem to be no universals of "human nature" that can be used as a basis for automatic understanding. The aforementioned assumption of similarity might be a common characteristic, however. Each of us seems to be so unconsciously influenced by our own cultural upbringings that we at first assume that the needs, desires, and basic assumptions of others are the same as our own. As expressed by Vinh The Do, "If we realize that we are all culture bound and culturally modified, we will accept the fact that, being unlike, we do not really know what someone else 'is.' This is another way to view the 'people are people' idea. We now have to find a way to sort out the cultural modifiers in each separate encounter to find similarity."[6]

The aura of similarity is a serious stumbling block to successful intercultural communication. A look-alike facade is deceiving when representatives from contrasting cultures meet, each wearing Western dress, speaking English, and using similar greeting rituals. It is like assuming that New York, Tokyo, and Tehran are all alike because each has the appearance of a modern city. Without being alert to possible differences and the need to learn new rules for functioning, persons going from one city to the other will be in immediate trouble, even when acting simple roles such as pedestrian or driver.

Unless a foreigner expects subtle differences it will take a long time of noninsulated living in a new culture (not in an enclave of his or her own kind) before he or she can be jarred into new perceptual and nonevaluative thinking. The confidence that goes with the myth of similarity is much more comfortable than the assumption of differences, the latter requiring tentative assumptions and behaviors and a willingness to accept the anxiety of "not knowing." Only with the assumption of differences, however, can reactions and interpretations be adjusted to fit "what's happening." Otherwise someone is likely to misread signs and judge the scene ethnocentrically.

The stumbling block of assumed similarity is a "trouble," as one English learner expressed it, not only for the foreigner but for the people in the host country (United States or any other) with whom the international visitor comes into contact. The native inhabitants are likely to be lulled into the expectation that, since the foreign person is dressed appropriately and speaks some of the language, he or she will also have similar nonverbal codes, thoughts, and feelings. Thus, nodding, smiling, and affirmative comments will probably be confidently interpreted by straightforward, friendly Americans as meaning that they have informed, helped, and pleased the newcomer. It is likely, however, that the foreigner actually understood very little of the verbal and nonverbal content and was merely indicating polite interest or trying not to embarrass himself or herself or the host with verbalized questions. The conversation may even have confirmed a stereotype that Americans are insensitive and ethnocentric.

Unless there is overt reporting of assumptions made by each party, which seldom happens, there is no chance for comparing impressions and correcting misinterpretations. The university classroom is a convenient laboratory to make such discoveries. For example, U.S. students often complain that international student members of a discussion or project group seem uncooperative or uninterested. One such person who had been judged "guilty" offered the following explanation:

*I was surrounded by Americans with whom I couldn't follow their tempo of discussion half of the time. I have difficulty to listen and speak, but also with the way they handle the group. I felt uncomfortable because sometimes they believe their opinion strongly. I had been very serious about the whole subject but I was afraid I would say something wrong. I had the idea but not the words.*[7]

The classroom is also a good place to test whether one common nonverbal behavior, the smile, is actually the universal people assume it to be. The following enlightening comments came from international students newly arrived in the United States and a U.S. student:[8]

Japanese student: *On my way to and from school I have received a smile by non-acquaintance American girls several times. I have finally learned they have no interest for me; it means only a kind of greeting to a foreigner. If someone smiles at a stranger in Japan, especially a girl, she can assume he is either a sexual maniac or an impolite person.*

Korean student: *An American visited me in my country for one week. His inference was that people in Korea are not very friendly because they didn't smile or want to talk with foreign people. Most Korean people take time to get to be friendly with people. We never talk or smile at strangers.*

Arabian student: *When I walked around the campus my first day many people smiled at me. I was very embarrassed and rushed to the men's room to see if I had made a mistake with my clothes. But I could find nothing for them to smile at. Now I am used to all the smiles.*

U.S. student: *I was waiting for my husband on a downtown corner when a man with a baby and two young children approached. Judging by small quirks of fashion he had not been in the U.S. long. I have a baby about the same age and in appreciation of his family and obvious involvement as a father I smiled at him. Immediately I realized I did the wrong thing as he stopped, looked me over from head to toe and said, "Are you waiting for me? You meet me later?" Apparently I had acted as a prostitute would in his country.*

Vietnamese student: *The reason why certain foreigners may think that Americas are superficial—and they are, some Americans even recognize this—is that they talk and smile too much. For people who come from placid cultures where nonverbal language is more used, and where a silence, a smile, a glance have their own meaning, it is true that Americans speak a lot. The superficiality of Americans can also be detected in their relations with others. Their friendships are, most of the time, so ephemeral compared to the friendships we have at home. Americans make friends very easily and leave their friends almost as quickly, while in my country it takes a long time to find out a possible friend and then she becomes your friend—with a very strong sense of the term.*

Another U.S. student gives her view:

*In general it seems to me that foreign people are not necessarily snobs but are very unfriendly. Some class members have told me that you shouldn't smile at others while passing them by on the street. To me I can't stop smiling. It's just natural to be smiling and friendly. I can see now why so many foreign people stick together. They are impossible to get to know. It's like the Americans are big bad wolves. How do Americans break this barrier? I want friends from all over the world but how do you start to be friends without offending them or scaring them off—like sheep?*[9]

The discussion thus far threatens the popular expectation that increased contact with representatives of diverse cultures through travel, student exchange programs, joint business ventures, and so on will result in better understanding and friendship. Tests of that assumption have indeed been disappointing.[10] Recent research, for example, found that Vietnamese immigrants who speak English well and have the best jobs are suffering the most from psychosomatic complaints and mental problems and are less optimistic about the future than their counterparts who remain in ethnic enclaves without attempts to adjust to their new homeland. One explanation given is that these persons, unlike the less acculturated immigrants, "spend considerable time in the mainstream of society, regularly facing the challenges and stresses of dealing with American attitudes."[11]

After 15 years of listening to conversations between international and U.S. students and professors and seeing the frustrations of both groups as they try to understand each other, this author, for one, is inclined to agree with Charles Frankel, who says, "Tensions exist within nations and between nations that never would have existed were these nations not in such intensive cultural communication with one another."[12] It doesn't have to be that way. Just as more opportunities now exist for cross-cultural contact, so does more information about what will be likely to make the venture more satisfactory. There are more orientation and training programs around the country, more courses in intercultural communication in educational institutions, and more published material.[13] However, until the majority can put aside the euphoria of the expectation of similarity among all people of the world and squarely face the likelihood of difference and misunderstanding, they will not be motivated to take advantage of these resources.

Until recently the method used to improve chances for successful intercultural communica-

tion was just to gather information about the customs of the other country and a smattering of the language. Behaviors and attitudes of its people might be researched, but almost always from a secondhand source. Experts realize that information gained in this fashion is general, seldom sufficient, and may or may not be applicable to the specific situation and area that the traveler visits. Also, knowing "what to expect" often blinds the observer to all but what confirms his or her image. Any contradictory evidence that does filter through the screens of preconception is likely to be treated as an exception and thus discounted.

A better approach is to begin by studying the history, political structure, art, literature, and language of the country if time permits. Even more important, develop an investigative, nonjudgmental attitude and a high tolerance for ambiguity—which means lowered defenses. Margaret Mead suggests sensitizing persons to the kinds of things that need to be taken into account instead of developing behavior and attitude stereotypes. She reasons that there are individual differences in each encounter and that changes occur regularly in culture patterns, which makes researched information obsolete.[14]

Edward Stewart also warns against providing lists of "do's and don't's" for travelers for several reasons, the main one being that behavior is ambiguous. Another reason is that the same action can have different meanings in different situations and no one can be armed with prescriptions for every contingency. Instead Stewart encourages persons to understand the assumptions and values on which their own behavior rests. This can then be compared with what is found in the other culture, and a "third culture" can be adopted based on expanded cross-cultural understanding.[15]

One way to follow Margaret Mead's suggestion of improving sensitivity to what might go wrong is to examine variables in the intercultural communication process. One stumbling block has already been discussed, the hazard of *assuming similarity instead of difference*. A second block is so obvious it hardly needs mentioning—*lan-*

*guage*. Vocabulary, syntax, idioms, slang, dialects, and so on all cause difficulty, but the person struggling with a different language is at least aware of being in this kind of trouble.

A worse language problem is the tenacity with which someone will cling to just one meaning of a word or phrase in the new language, regardless of connotation or context. The infinite variations possible, especially if inflection and tonal qualities are added, are so difficult to cope with that they are often waved aside. The reason this problem is worse than simply struggling to translate foreign words is because each person thinks he or she understands. The nationwide misinterpretation of Khrushchev's sentence "We'll bury you" is a classic example. Even "yes" and "no" cause trouble. When a Japanese hears, "Won't you have some tea?" he or she listens to the literal meaning of the sentence and answers, "No," meaning that he or she wants some. "Yes, I won't" would be a better reply because this tips off the host or hostess that there may be a misunderstanding. Also, in some cultures, it is polite to refuse the first or second offer of refreshment. Many foreign guests have gone hungry because their U.S. host or hostess never presented the third offer—another case of "no" meaning "yes."

Learning the language, which most visitors to foreign countries consider their only barrier to understanding, is actually only the beginning. As Frankel says, "To enter into a culture is to be able to hear, in Lionel Trilling's phrase, its special 'hum and buzz of implication.' "[16] This suggests the third stumbling block, *nonverbal misinterpretations*. People from different cultures inhabit different sensory realities. They see, hear, feel, and smell only that which has some meaning or importance for them. They abstract whatever fits into their personal world of recognition and then interpret it through the frame of reference of their own culture. An example follows.

An Oregon girl in an intercultural communication class asked a young man from Saudi Arabia how he would nonverbally signal that he liked her. His response was to smooth back his hair, which to her was just a common nervous gesture signifying nothing. She repeated her question three times. He smoothed his hair three times, and, realizing that she was not recognizing this movement as his reply to her question, automatically ducked his head and stuck out his tongue slightly in embarrassment. This behavior *was* noticed by the girl and she expressed astonishment that he would show liking for someone by sticking out his tongue.

The lack of comprehension of nonverbal signs and symbols that are easy to observe—such as gestures, postures, and other body movements—is a definite communication barrier. But it is possible to learn the meanings of these messages, usually in informal rather than formal ways. It is more difficult to note correctly the unspoken codes of the other culture that are further from awareness, such as the handling of time and spatial relationships and subtle signs of respect of formality.[17]

The fourth stumbling block is the presence of *preconceptions and stereotypes*. If the label "inscrutable" has preceded the Japanese guest, it is thus we explain the Japanese constant and inappropriate smile. The stereotype that Arabs are "inflammable" causes U.S. students to keep their distance or alert authorities when an animated and noisy group from the Middle East gathers. A professor who expects everyone from Indonesia, Mexico, and many other countries to "bargain" may unfairly interpret a hesitation or request from an international student as a move to manipulate preferential treatment.

Stereotypes help do what Ernest Becker says the anxiety-prone human race must do—reduce the threat of the unknown by making the world predictable.[18] Indeed, this is one of the basic functions of culture: to lay out a predictable world in which the individual is firmly oriented. Stereotypes are overgeneralized beliefs that provide conceptual bases from which to "make sense" out of what goes on around us. In a foreign land their use increases our feeling of security and is psychologically necessary to the degree that we cannot tolerate ambiguity or the sense of helplessness resulting from inability to understand and deal with people and situations beyond our comprehension.

Stereotypes are stumbling blocks for communicators because they interfere with objective viewing of stimuli—the sensitive search for cues to guide the imagination toward the other person's reality. Stereotypes are not easy to overcome in ourselves or to correct in others, even with the presentation of evidence. They persist because they are firmly established as myths or truisms by one's own national culture and because they sometimes rationalize prejudices. They are also sustained and fed by the tendency to perceive selectively only those pieces of new information that correspond to the image held. For example, the Asian or African visitor who is accustomed to privation and the values of self-denial and self-help cannot fail to experience American culture as materialistic and wasteful. The stereotype for the visitor becomes a reality.

The fifth stumbling block and another deterrent to understanding between persons of differing cultures or ethnic groups is the *tendency to evaluate*, to approve or disapprove, the statements and actions of the other person or group rather than to try to comprehend completely the thoughts and feelings expressed from the world view of the other. Each person's culture or way of life always seems right, proper, and natural. This bias prevents the open-minded attention needed to look at the attitudes and behavior patterns from the other's point of view. A mid-day siesta changes from a "lazy habit" to a "pretty good idea" when someone listens long enough to realize the mid-day temperature in that country is 115° F.

The author, fresh from a conference in Tokyo where Japanese professors had emphasized the preference of the people of Japan for simple natural settings of rocks, moss, and water and of muted greens and misty ethereal landscapes, visited the Katsura Imperial Gardens in Kyoto. At the appointed time of the tour a young Japanese guide approached the group of 20 waiting Americans and remarked how fortunate it was that the day was cloudy. This brought hesitant smiles to the group who were less than pleased at the prospect of a shower. The guide's next statement was that the timing of the midsummer visit was particularly appropriate in that the azalea and rhododendron blossoms were gone and the trees had not yet turned to their brilliant fall colors. The group laughed loudly, now convinced that the young man had a fine sense of humor. I winced at his bewildered expression, realizing that had I come before attending the conference I, also evaluating the weather as "not very good," would have shared the group's inference that he could not be serious.

The communication cutoff caused by immediate evaluation is heightened when feelings and emotions are deeply involved; yet this is just the time when listening with understanding is most needed. This can be exemplified by the long deadlock in resolving the issue of the U.S. hostages in Iran. It takes both awareness of the tendency to close our minds and courage to risk change in our own perceptions and values to dare to comprehend why someone thinks and acts differently from us. As stated by Sherif, Sherif, and Nebergall, "A person's commitment to his religion, politics, values of his family, and his stand on the virtue of his way of life are ingredients in his self-picture—intimately felt and cherished."[19]

It is very easy to dismiss strange or different behaviors as "wrong," listen through a thick screen of value judgments, and therefore fail miserably to achieve a fair understanding. The impatience of the American public over the choice of the shape of the conference table at the Paris Peace talks is another example. There are innumerable examples of intercultural value clashes that result in a breach in interpersonal relationships. Two follow:[20]

U.S. student: *A Persian friend got offended because when we got in an argument with a third party, I didn't take his side. He says back home you are supposed to take a friend's or family's side even when they are wrong. When you get home then you can attack the "wrongdoer" but you are never supposed to go against a relative or friend to a stranger. This I found strange because even if it is my mother and I think she is wrong, I say so.*

Korean student: *When I call on my American friend he said through window, "I am sorry. I have no time because of my study." Then he shut the window. I couldn't understand through my cultural background. House owner should have welcome visitor whether he likes or not and whether he is busy or not. Also the owner never speaks without opening his door.*

The sixth stumbling block is *high anxiety*, separately mentioned for the purpose of emphasis. Unlike the other five (assumption of similarity, language, nonverbal misinterpretations, preconceptions and stereotypes, and the practice of immediate evaluation), the stumbling block of high anxiety is not distinct but underlies and compounds the others. Different language and nonverbal patterns are difficult to use or interpret under the best of conditions. The distraction of high anxiety (sometimes called "internal noise") makes mistakes even more likely. As stated by Jack Gibb:

*Defense arousal prevents the listener from concentrating upon the message. Not only do defensive communicators send off multiple value, motive, and affect cues, but also defensive recipients distort what they receive. As a person becomes more and more defensive, he becomes less and less able to perceive accurately the motives, the values, and the emotions of the sender.*[21]

The stumbling blocks other than language and nonverbal are defense mechanisms in themselves, as previously explained, and as such would obviously increase under stress.

The presence of anxiety/tension is common in cross-cultural experiences due to the number of uncertainties present and the personal involvement and risk. Whether or not the reaction will be debilitating depends on the level of activation and whether the feeling is classified as being pleasant (thought of as excitement or anticipation) or un-

pleasant (anxiety). Moderate arousal and positive attitudes prepare one to meet challenges with energy, but high arousal, caused by a buildup of continued moderate stress, depletes the body's energy reserve quickly and defense must be used whether or not the person wills it. If the stay in a foreign country is prolonged and the newcomer cannot let down his or her high alert level, the "culture shock" phenomenon occurs. Illness may result, the body forcing needed rest and recuperation.

Anxious feelings usually permeate both parties in a dialogue. The host national is uncomfortable when talking with a foreigner because he or she cannot maintain the normal flow of verbal and nonverbal interaction. There are language and perception barriers; silences are too long or too short; proxemic and other norms may be violated. He or she is also threatened by the other's unknown knowledge, experience, and evaluation— the visitor's potential for scrutiny and rejection of the host national and his or her country. The inevitable question, "How do you like it here?" which the foreigner abhors, is a quest for reassurance, or at least a "feeler" that reduces the unknown and gives grounds for defense if that seems necessary.

The foreign members of dyads are even more threatened. They feel strange and vulnerable, helpless to cope with messages that swamp them, to which "normal" reactions seem inappropriate. Their self-esteem is often intolerably undermined unless they employ such defenses as withdrawal into their own reference group or into themselves, screening out or misperceiving stimuli, rationalization, overcompensation, "going native," or becoming aggressive or hostile. None of these defenses leads to effective communication.

Fatigue is a natural result of such a continued state of alertness, but, too often, instead of allowing needed rest, the body then tenses even more to keep up its guard in the potentially threatening environment. To relax is to be vulnerable. An international student says it well:

*During those several months after my arrival in the U.S.A., every day I came back from school exhausted so that I had to take a rest for a while, stretching myself on the bed. For, all the time, I strained every nerve in order to understand what the people were saying and make myself understood in my broken English. When I don't understand what American people are talking about and why they are laughing, I sometimes have to pretend to understand by smiling, even though I feel alienated, uneasy and tense.*

*In addition to this, the difference in culture or customs, the way of thinking between two countries, produces more tension because we don't know how we should react to totally foreign customs or attitudes, and sometimes we can't guess how the people from another country react to my saying or behavior. We always have a fear somewhere in the bottom of our hearts that there are much more chances of breakdown in intercultural communication than in communication with our own fellow countrymen.*[22]

Knowing that the aforementioned stumbling blocks are present is certainly an aid in avoiding them, but these particular ones cannot be easily circumvented. For most people it takes insight, training, and sometimes an alteration of long-standing habits or cherished beliefs before progress can be made. But the increasing need for global understanding and cooperation makes the effort vital. To show that it is not impossible a few general suggestions follow.

We can study other languages and learn to expect differences in nonverbal forms and other cultural aspects. It is also possible to train ourselves to meet intercultural encounters with more attention to situational details, using an investigative approach rather than preconceptions and stereotypes. We can gradually expose ourselves to differences so that they become less threatening. By practicing conscious relaxation techniques we can also learn to lower our tension level when needed to avoid triggering defensive reactions. In a relaxed state it is also easier to allow the temporary suspension of our own world view, a necessary step to experience empathy. What the intercultural com-

municator must seek to achieve is summarized by Roger Harrison when he says:

*. . . the communicator cannot stop at knowing that the people he is working with have different customs, goals, and thought patterns from his own. He must be able to feel his way into intimate contact with these alien values, attitudes, and feelings. He must be able to work with them and within them, neither losing his own values in the confrontation nor protecting himself behind a wall of intellectual detachment.*[23]

## NOTES

1. Eibl-Eibesfeldt, Irenaus, "Experimental Criteria for Distinguishing Innate from Culturally Conditioned Behavior," in *Cross-Cultural Understanding: Epistemology in Anthropology*, ed. F. S. C. Northrop and Helen H. Livingston (New York: Harper & Row, 1964), p. 304.

2. Furst, Charles, "Automating Attention," *Psychology Today* (August 1979), p. 112.

3. See Darwin, Charles, *The Expression of Emotions in Man and Animals* (New York: Appleton, 1872); Eibl-Eibesfeldt, Irenaus, *Ethology: The Biology of Behavior* (New York: Holt, Rinehart & Winston, 1970); Ekman, Paul, and Wallace V. Friesan, "Constants Across Cultures in the Face and Emotion," *Journal of Personality and Social Psychology* 17 (1971), pp. 124–129.

4. Ekman, Paul, "Movements with Precise Meanings," *Journal of Communication* 26 (Summer 1976), pp. 19–20.

5. Ekman, Paul, and Wallace Friesen, "The Repertoire of Nonverbal Behavior—Categories, Origins, Usage and Coding," *Semiotica*, 1, 1.

6. Personal correspondence. Mr. Do is a counselor at the Indochinese Center in Portland, Oregon, and a counselor-interpreter at the Indochinese Psychiatry Clinic.

7. Taken from student papers in a course in intercultural communication taught by the author.

8. Ibid.

9. Ibid.

10. See for example: Wedge, Bryant, *Visitors to the United States and How They See Us* (N.J.: D. Van Nostrand Company, 1965); and Miller, Milton, et al., "The Cross-Cultural Student: Lessons in Human Nature, *Bulletin of Menninger Clinic* (March 1971).

11. Horn, Jack D., "Vietnamese Immigrants: Doing Poorly by Doing Well," *Psychology Today* (June 1980), pp. 103–104.

12. Frankel, Charles, *The Neglected Aspect of Foreign Affairs* (Washington, D.C.: Brookings Institution, 1965), p. 1.

13. For information see newsletters and other material prepared by the Society for Intercultural Education, Training and Research (SIETAR), Georgetown Univ., Washington, D.C., 20057. Sources are also listed in the *International and Intercultural Communication Annual*, published by the Speech Communication Association, 5205 Leesburg Pike, Falls Church, Virginia 22041; the *International Journal of Intercultural Relations*, New York: Pergamon Press; and *The Bridge*, 1800 Pontiac, Denver, Colorado 80220.

14. Mead, Margaret, "The Cultural Perspective," in *Communication or Conflict*, ed. Mary Capes (Association Press, 1960).

15. Stewart, Edward C. *American Cultural Patterns: A Cross-Cultural Perspective* (Intercultural Network, Inc., 906 N. Spring Ave., LaGrange Park, Illinois 60525, 1972), p. 20.

16. Frankel, *The Neglected Aspect of Foreign Affairs*, p. 103.

17. For an overview see Ramsey, Sheila J., "Nonverbal Behavior: An Intercultural Perspective," in *Handbook of Intercultural Communication*, ed. Molefi K. Asante, Eileen Newmark, and Cecil A. Blake (Beverly Hills/London: Sage Publications, 1979), pp. 105–143.

18. Becker, Ernest, *The Birth and Death of Meaning* (New York: Free Press, 1962), pp. 84–89.

19. Sherif, Carolyn W., Musafer Sherif, and Roger Nebergall, *Attitude and Attitude Change* (Philadelphia: W. B. Saunders Co., 1965), p. vi.

20. Taken from student papers in a course in intercultural communication taught by the author.

21. Gibb, Jack R., "Defensive Communication," *Journal of Communication* 2 (September 1961), pp. 141–148.

22. Taken from student papers in a course in intercultural communication taught by the author.

23. Harrison, Roger, "The Design of Cross-Cultural Training: An Alternative to the University Model," in *Explorations in Human Relations Training and Research* (Bethesda, Md.: National Training Laboratories, 1966), NEA No. 2, p. 4.

# Human Communication and Cross-Cultural Effectiveness

BRENT D. RUBEN

A great deal has been written about problems so-journers encounter as they strive to adapt to the demands and challenges of a new or different cultural environment.[1] A topic of no less importance to many persons whose professional or technical roles take them to new cultures is the question of how one functions effectively with individuals from other cultures in work and work-related contexts. Especially for the many Western advisors, technical personnel, and sponsoring governmental and private agencies involved in projects in Third World countries, such concerns are of increasing importance. This paper addresses this issue in a very basic manner from the perspective of human communication. To indicate the relevance of communication to problems of skills and knowledge transfer, a prototypical case study is presented. The case highlights some barriers to effective transfer-of-skills, and provides the foundation for a discussion of the professional sojourner as a teacher. Next, a summary of some recent research on the role of particular communication be-havior in cross-cultural effectiveness is presented. Finally, some implications and possible applications of these findings are explored.

## A CASE STUDY

*Mr. S has accepted a position as an advisor in a Third-world country. He will be working directly with Mr. Akwagara, a national. Together they will have administrative responsibility for their project. Mr. S is eager to arrive at his post. His work experience in the U.S. seems exceptionally well suited to the task he must accomplish in his post in the developing country, and his high level of motivation and record of consistently superior achievement reassures him—and those who selected him—that he will encounter little he can't handle in his assignment.*

*After having been on the job for several weeks, Mr. S is experiencing considerable frustration. To S, it appears that Akwagara and most of the subordinates lack both training and motivation. On a number of occasions S has endeavored to point out to Akwagara, tactfully, that his practices are both inefficient and ineffective. Akwagara's responses seemed to S to indicate total indifference. On one occasion, S suggested that he and Akwagara get together one evening for a few drinks, thinking that in an informal setting he might be more successful in making Akwagara aware of some of these problems. The two went out together, but nearly every effort to bring up the work situation by S was followed by Akwagara changing the subject to unrelated chatter about family and friends.*

*The problem became increasingly severe in the weeks that followed. It seemed to S the only way he could get the job done he was sent to do, was to do most of it by himself. Gradually, he assumed more and more of the responsibilities that had been previously performed by Akwagara. Though he feels some concern about this situation from time to time, these feelings are more than compensated for by the knowledge that he is getting the job done that he was sent to do.*

From the *International and Intercultural Communication Annual*, Vol. IV, December 1977, pp. 98–105. Reproduced by permission of the Speech Communication Association and the author. Brent D. Ruben is Associate Professor and Assistant Chairman of the Department of Human Communication at Rutgers University. The author gratefully acknowledges the contributions of Daniel Kealey and Pri Notowidigdo of the Canadian International Development Briefing Centre, and the support and encouragement of Pierre Lortie, Director of the Centre.

Consider the question, is S succeeding or failing? The answer, of course, depends largely upon how one defines the role of the sojourner. If one takes the point of view that the task of the sojourner consists solely of getting the job done, we would probably conclude that S is functioning effectively. Viewed from another perspective, one cannot help but conclude that the advisor has failed sadly. The job is being done at the cost of successful transfer-of-skills. Probable consequences of his approach include the alienation of Akwagara, a loss of credibility for Akwagara among his subordinates he must supervise after S departs, and reinforcement of the view that Western advisors are insensitive, egocentric, and not sincerely interested in the welfare of the host country or nationals.

For S, the sponsoring agency, and the country, the consequence is a failure to be able to share knowledge and skills meaningfully. The ultimate tragedy is that S, with the best of intentions and motives, may in fact spend two years of his life believing that he is functioning as the ideal advisor. All the while, he may actually contribute to forces which retard the process of growth, change, and development in his project and in the country as a whole. As this case, and a number of writings and research well indicate, the ability to satisfactorily understand and relate to others in a cross-cultural setting is probably the single most critical ingredient necessary to an advisor's success, and essential if one is to translate one's own skills and knowledge into the idiom of the culture.

## THE SOJOURNER
## AS TEACHER

In conceptualizing the role of the sojourner or technical advisor in terms of the effective transfer-of-skills, it seems useful to think broadly of the role as one of teacher. A teacher, after all, is a person who possesses particular knowledges and skills he or she wishes to impart to others. There are two distinct components of teaching—at least of effective teaching. First, the teacher must have an appropriate mastery of skills and knowledge in his or her field. Secondly, the teacher must be able to package and deliver those understandings to other persons in such a way that they will be able to accept, utilize, and integrate them. For the sojourner, these same components are crucial.

With regard to most technical advisors selected for overseas postings, the first component is well satisfied. Whether selected for an assignment to assist with the installation of a computer or electronic communication systems, the development of educational, governmental, agricultural, economic, or industrial policy, or any of a number of other less technical positions, job-related competencies are seldom a problem. The second ingredient necessary for effectiveness of the sojourner is a set of skills and knowledge totally unrelated to the job. These skills and understandings have to do with communication, and research and reports from the field indicate that such capabilities are even more critical to the success of an advisor and a project than his or her job skills. For convenience, one can refer to this needed set of skills as *communication competence*.[2] If job or role competence is the ability to complete a task efficiently, communication competence is the ability to effectively relate to other persons in the process. Achieving an integration of the two is important in the short and long run, and from both idealistic and practical points of view.

The importance of communication to effective cross-cultural functioning is well illustrated by the case of Mr. S. As a member of a Western culture, it is likely that to Mr. S time and money are important criteria for success; he may well view wealth and power as essential to the solution of most problems, consider democratic or majority rule as the appropriate form of governance, revere technology, regard competition as good and winning an important goal. He likely values material possessions, the scientific method, efficiency, organization, specialization, and a clear separation between work and leisure. In his communication style, he is likely to be reasonably aggressive, direct, impatient, self-assured, and to regard business as the topic of major importance in most of his interactions, attaching a lesser value to discussion of family and personal matters.

Depending upon Akwagara's cultural background, he is likely to have a quite different communicational framework. For him speech and efficiency may be irrelevant or negative values. Material possessions, competition and winning may be regarded with far less concern, and he may view extended family relationships as the primary source of power and status. The democratic model, technology, progress, and Western development may be viewed with cynicism and suspicion. Conditions of living may be regarded primarily as inevitable consequences of manifest destiny, leaving little room for individual initiative or impact. Work and leisure may well be blended, and he may be little concerned with systematic, or efficient organization, or specialization. In discussions, Akwagara may well be relatively passive, indirect, patient, and will likely place a much higher priority on the topic of family and friends, than upon business. He may also be accustomed to standing or sitting close to persons he is talking to, and to numerous gestures involving frequent physical contact. In such an instance, the two individuals have a great many barriers to overcome if either is to understand with much accuracy the words and actions of the other.

## RELEVANT RESEARCH

There has been considerable research effort directed toward identifying communication behaviors which contribute to effectiveness within one's own culture. Wiemann[3] identified three main schools of thought about face-to-face interaction. The first he characterized as the human relations or T-group approach, typified by the work of Argyris,[4] Bochner and Kelley,[5] and Holland and Baird.[6] The second orientation, the social skill approach, is reflected especially in the work of Argyle and Kendon,[7] and the third is essentially a self-presentation approach suggested in the work of Goffman,[8] Rodnick and Wood,[9] and Weinstein.[10]

Though attempts to consider how these approaches generalize to cross-cultural interpersonal situations have been few, a number of researchers (such as Arensberg and Niehoff;[11] Barna;[12] Brislin and Pedersen;[13] Gudykunst, Hammer, and Wiseman;[14] Bochner;[15] Cleveland and Mangone;[16] and others[17]) have suggested certain personal characteristics and/or skills thought to be crucial to effectiveness in such contexts. A synthesis of findings suggested in intra- and inter-cultural writings yields some consensus. For those concerned particularly with communication, a number of such behaviors seem important. Seven of these are: (1) capacity to communicate respect; (2) capacity to be nonjudgmental; (3) capacity to personalize one's knowledge and perceptions; (4) capacity to display empathy; (5) capacity to be flexible; (6) capacity for turn-taking; and (7) tolerance for ambiguity.

Research was undertaken by Ruben and Kealey[18] to determine the relative importance of these communication behaviors to cross-cultural effectiveness. The findings from in-the-field research suggest that an avoidance of extreme *task, self-centered*, and *judgmental behavior*—in that order—contribute most to effective transfer-of-skills. A *tolerance for ambiguity, the ability to display respect*, and a *personal orientation to knowledge*, are next in importance in cross-cultural effectiveness, followed by *empathy* and *turn-taking*. In the following sections, these communication dimensions will be discussed and their relationship to effective transfer-of-skills briefly explored.

## TASK AND RELATIONAL BEHAVIOR

Roles, how they are enacted, and the impact they have, have been a concern to intra- and inter-cultural researchers alike.[19] Individuals function in a variety of roles within interpersonal, group, and organizational settings. Behaviors that involve the initiation of ideas, requests for information, seeking of clarification, evaluation of ideas, etc., are directly related to the group's task or problem-solving activities. Behaviors that involve harmonizing, mediation, gatekeeping, attempts to regulate the evenness of contribution of group members, compromising, etc., are related to the relationship-building activities of a group.

Some situations seem to call for an intense concern for "getting the job done." Other situations call for building group cohesiveness, encouraging participation, and making certain no one feels excluded from involvement. Westerners seem to learn to focus mostly on the former, and are typically not much concerned about how involved people feel in the process, how much group or organizational solidarity develops, how people value the products of their effort, etc. But as indicated previously, the transfer-of-skills requires not only getting a job done, but also the competence to get it done in such a way that people feel a part of the completed project and have learned something from witnessing the process. Research suggests strongly that too much concern for getting the job done can lead to failure in terms of effectiveness at skills-transfer.[20]

Here, the Akwagara case provides an excellent illustration. Mr. S has apparently mastered the skills often demanded for success in Western occupational roles. His style, appropriate to his own cultural background, is one of fast-paced problem-solving. Yet, in a developmental context, the very skills that were perhaps critical to his selection as a cross-cultural professional, may become a liability in a culture where rapid-fire problem-solving is less valued. From such a cultural perspective, S may well be viewed as impatient, over-zealous, insensitive, and lacking concern for people. The consequences of such a response may well be to foster feelings of resentment toward S, and thereby render his technical skills totally useless, and preclude effectiveness at transfer-of-skills.

## SELF-ORIENTED BEHAVIORS

Other role behaviors sometimes displayed by individuals in an interpersonal context are individualistic or self-centered behaviors that function in negative ways from a group's perspective. Behaviors such as being highly resistant to ideas of others, returning to issues and points of view previously acted upon and/or dismissed by the group, attempting to call attention to oneself, seeking to project a highly positive personal image by noting achieve-

ments and professional qualifications. and attempting to manipulate the group by asserting authority, are dysfunctional in intra-cultural as well as in inter-cultural contexts.

While the S case makes no reference to what might be thought of as self-centered communicative behavior, research conducted by Ruben and Kealey suggests that such behavior patterns toward persons in one's own culture are a good predictor of potential problems at successful interaction with persons from differing cultures.[21]

## NON-JUDGMENTALNESS

People like to feel that what they say is not being judged by someone else without having been given an opportunity to fully explain themselves and be sincerely listened to. When persons find themselves being interrupted before having finished speaking, or notice that someone is nodding in disagreement even before they have finished presenting their thoughts, barriers to effective relating are set in place. The likelihood of teaching or transferring skills in such a setting is greatly lessened.[22] Ideally, one would strive to avoid passing judgments on what others have to say until one has enough information to be fairly certain that his or her evaluations will be based on a reasonably complete understanding of the other's point of view. When persons believe they have been fully and attentively listened to, they are generally much more receptive to hearing reactions—whether positive or negative. In addition to being of use in improving the fidelity of information transmission, nonevaluative postures seem likely to increase the receiver's regard for the source of nonevaluative messages, and thereby improve the quality of the relationship.

Again, with S and Akwagara, it isn't clear from the information presented whether S was nonjudgmental or not. One may infer, however, that had S invested a bit more effort in listening to and trying to understand Akwagara's viewpoint, some of the problems might have been alleviated. Apart from the case, it is interesting to note that persons who are non-judgmental with others in their own culture will often be more effective in cross-cultural skills transfer than persons who are highly judgmental.[23]

## TOLERANCE FOR AMBIGUITY

The ability to react to new and ambiguous situations with little visible discomfort can be an important asset when adapting to a new environment. Although most people probably do react with some degree of personal discomfort to new environments, some seem more able to adjust quickly to those around them. Excessive discomfort resulting from being placed in a new or different environment—or from finding the familiar environment altered in some critical ways—can lead to confusion, frustration, or even hostility. This may well be dysfunctional to the development of effective interpersonal relations within and across cultural boundaries. Colleagues and would-be friends—as with Akwagara—may easily become the unwitting and misplaced targets of verbal hostility during periods of adjustment; and while the frustrations are often short-lived, the feelings about the sojourner that they may have initiated, might not be. Learning to manage the feeling of frustration associated with ambiguity can thus be critical to effective adaptation in a new environment.[24] It is likely that a bit greater tolerance for ambiguity and tolerance for the lack of control one feels in a new environment would have aided S substantially in his efforts to integrate himself successfully into his new situation.

## DISPLAY OF RESPECT

The ability to express respect and positive regard for another person has been suggested as an important component in effective interpersonal relations within and between cultures.[25] The expression of respect can be expected to confer status upon the recipient, contribute to self-esteem, and foster positive regard for the source of the communicated respect. People like to feel that others respect them, their accomplishments, their beliefs, and what they have to say. If one is able, through gestures, eye gaze, smiles, and words of encouragement, to indicate to others that he or she is sincerely interested in them, they are much more likely to respond positively to the person and what he or she has to say. In the case study, listening to Akwagara carefully, attentively, and encouragingly as he discussed family and friends, and reciprocating in kind, would have been an important means for S to have communicated his respect, and to begin to establish a strong foundation for an effective relationship—one that would be productive and satisfying on a day-to-day basis, and one that would facilitate the transfer of S's skills and knowledge, as he has intended.

## PERSONALIZING KNOWLEDGE AND PERCEPTIONS

Different people explain themselves and the world around them in different terms. Some people tend to view their knowledge and perceptions as valid only for them; others tend to assume that their beliefs, values, and perceptions are valid for everyone. Presumably, the more a person recognizes the extent to which knowledge is individual in nature, the more easily he or she will be able to adjust to other people in other cultures whose views of what is "true" or "right" are likely to be quite different.

People who recognize that their values, beliefs, attitudes, knowledge, and opinions are their own—and not necessarily shared by others—often find it easier to form productive relationships, than persons who believe they know *The Truth*, and strive to "sell" their own perceptions, knowledge, skills, and values to others. If a person often begins sentences with phrases like "I think" or "I feel" or "In my own experience . . ." chances are he or she is aware more of the personal nature of their knowledge and values than if they are using introductions like "Africans tend to be . . ." or "Americans are . . ." or "Canadians believe . . ." Among persons whose ideas of what is *True* and *Right* differ dramatically from that to which you've become accustomed, it is useful to keep in mind that one's beliefs, knowledge, and attitudes are products of their own experiences. Remembering also that one's "truths" may bear little in common to those of others—gives one an important advantage as a teacher.

It is in this area where S was perhaps weakest. He unwittingly assumed his job description, his timetable, his mode of operating, his distinctions between work and family, his definitions of "idle chatter," and so on, were in fact *the* understandings—ones which Akwagara *must* certainly share. The results are rather clear in the case study, as in so many other instances of relational problems with persons working within as well as across cultural boundaries.

## DISPLAYING EMPATHY

The capacity to "put oneself in another's shoes," or to behave as if one could, has been often suggested as important to the development and maintenance of positive human relationships within and between cultures.[26] Individuals differ in their ability to display empathy. Some people are able to project an interest in others clearly and seem able to obtain and reflect a reasonably complete and accurate sense of another's thoughts, feelings, and/or experiences. Others may lack interest, or fail to display interest, and may be unable to project even superficial understanding of another's situation.

Many people are attracted to individuals who seem to be able to understand things from "their point of view." Certainly, since each individual has a unique set of past experiences, it is not possible to totally put oneself "in someone else's shoes." Through care in listening and observing, and with a sincere and diligent effort to understand the other person's communicational framework, one can, however, achieve some degree of empathy, a critical ingredient for effective teaching. Had Mr. S devoted more effort to establishing this sort of understanding of Akwagara, and had he been successful in reflecting the resulting awareness in his words

and actions, many of the difficulties he encountered could have been avoided.

## TURN-TAKING

People vary in the manner in which they "manage" (or fail to manage) interactions of which they are a part.[27] Some are skillful at governing their contribution to an interactive situation so that the needs and desires of others play a critical role in defining how the exchange will proceed. Effective management of interaction is displayed through taking turns in discussion and initiating and terminating interaction based on a reasonably accurate assessment of the needs and desires of others. Other individuals are less proficient at these dimensions and proceed in interactions with little or no regard for time sharing, and initiation and termination preferences of others. It is almost too obvious to note that people enjoy having an opportunity to take turns in discussion. This suggests strongly the need to avoid monopolizing conversations, and conversely, to resist the temptation to refuse to share responsibility for even participation. This simple factor is important to how one is perceived in one's own culture, as well as in other cultures, where reciprocity in discussion can serve to indicate interest in, and concern for, the other person.

## SUMMARY

It has been the intention of the foregoing to provide a basic framework for discussing the role of communication in cross-cultural effectiveness. In simplifying these processes for purposes of discussion, there is the risk of neglecting important questions. Perhaps the most crucial of these has to do with the difficulty of generalizing findings from studies of one or two cultures to other cultures. The studies summarized in the last section of this article, for example, were concerned with Canadian technical personnel who worked in various jobs in Kenya. On the basis of these and other studies noted, we can speculate that the findings are likely relevant for "Westerners" working with individuals from the so-called "developing" countries.

Presumably, highly aggressive problem-solving behaviors would carry the same risks of ineffectiveness in many of the countries in Latin America, as in Kenya or other African countries, but further research is needed to verify these relationships.

There is another problem related to generalizing the research findings such as those discussed here. While one can argue that the *importance* of communication behaviors such as empathy, respect, non-judgmentalness, etc., transcends cultural boundaries, the way these are *expressed and interpreted* may vary substantially from one culture (or one subculture) to another. Thus, while prolonged eye contact or head nodding may well be a sign of respect in one culture, it may be interpreted in quite another—perhaps even in an opposite—way in other cultures. A final caution has to do with the difference between *knowing* and *doing*. Even within one's own culture, knowing that one *ought to be* respectful or empathic or non-judgmental does not guarantee that one will be able to perform the behavior, even with good intentions.

For persons who will work in cross-cultural situations, these three issues have a number of implications. The central theme that emerges from studies discussed in this paper is the need to be alert and sensitive to the needs, orientations, values, aspirations, and particularly communication styles of other persons with whom one interacts. One needs to know how respect, empathy, non-judgmentalness, turn-taking, orientation to knowledge, and group and organizational roles are *regarded* and *expressed* in a given culture. Of equal or greater importance to effectiveness at transfer-of-skills is the willingness to be introspective, and committed to see, to examine, and to learn from one's failures and weaknesses as well as one's successes and strengths. Only in this way can one's behavior be brought into congruence with what one believes and intends.

For those persons involved in cross-cultural training and selection, aspects of the studies discussed in this paper have important implications. First, findings underscore the importance of interpersonal communication skills to cross-cultural effectiveness, suggesting a need to attend more closely to interpersonal communication skills in selection and training. Secondly, the research indicates the usefulness of a person's communication behavior in his or her own culture as a predictor of his or her communication behavior in another culture. This seems to suggest a need in effectiveness training and research for relatively more attention to the individual, and perhaps relatively less attention to inherent differences between cultures. Thirdly, the discussion focuses attention on the difference between knowing and doing, underscoring the importance of training which is directed relatively more toward behaviorial effectiveness and relatively less toward theoretical and verbal mastery.

Each of these issues would seem to merit additional attention by researchers, as well. Perhaps most importantly, more study is needed to identify additional communication behaviors which may be significant for cross-cultural effectiveness. Further, research is needed to identify those communication behaviors which best generalize to a large number of cross-cultural situations. Such studies will serve to further strengthen the theoretical and pragmatic link beteen human communication and cross-cultural effectiveness suggested in this article.

## NOTES

1. See C. M. Arensberg and A. H. Niehoff, *Introducting Social Change: A Manual for Community Development* (Chicago: Aldine-Atherton, 1971); R. B. Brislin and P. Pedersen. *Cross-Cultural Orientation Programs* (New York: Gardner Press, 1976); J. Gullahorn and J. Gullahorn, "An Extension of the U-Curve Hypothesis," *Journal of Social Issues* 19, No. 3 (1963), 33–47; E. T. Hall, *The Silent Language* (New York: Doubleday, 1959); and K. Oberg, "Culture Shock: Adjustment to the New Cultural Environments," *Practical Anthropology* 7 (1960), 177–182.

2. Systematic efforts to conceptualize "effective," "successful," or "competent" communication behavior have been relatively few in number. The notion of communication competence—used interchangeably with communication effectiveness—is discussed in this paper as a dyadic concept. For a particular interaction to be termed effective, or a person to be termed competent,

the performance must meet the needs and goals of both the message initiator and the recipient. The term communication competence, as used in this paper, is based on the work of John Wiemann, who credits E. A. Weinstein as the originator of the term. See Brent D. Ruben, "The Machine Gun and the Marshmallow: Some Thoughts on the Concept of Effective Communication." Paper presented at the annual meeting of the Western Speech-Communication Association, Honolulu, Hawaii, 1972; and John M. Wiemann, "An Exploration of Communication Competence in Initial Interactions: An Experimental Study," Unpublished doctoral dissertation, Purdue University (1975).

3. John M. Wiemann (1975) provides an excellent summary and discussion of these orientations.

4. C. Argyris, "Explorations in Interpersonal Competence—1," *Journal of Applied Behavioral Science* (1965), 58–63.

5. A. P. Bochner and C. W. Kelley, "Interpersonal Competence: Rationale, Philosophy, and Implementation of a Conceptual Framework," *Speech Teacher* 23 (1974), 279–301.

6. J. L. Holland and L. L. Baird, "An Interpersonal Competency Scale," *Educational and Psychological Measurement* 28 (1968), 503–510.

7. M. Argyle and A. Kendon, "The Experimental Analysis of Social Performance," *Advances in Experimental Social Psychology* 3 (1967), 55–98.

8. Erving Goffman, *The Presentation of Self in Everyday Life* (Garden City: Doubleday, 1959); *Behavior in Public Places* (New York: Free Press, 1963); *Interaction Ritual* (Garden City: Anchor, 1967).

9. R. Rodnick and B. Wood, "The Communication Strategies of Children," *Speech Teacher* 22 (1973), 114–124.

10. E. A. Weinstein, "Toward a Theory of Interpersonal Tactics," in C. W. Backman and P. F. Secord (eds.), *Problems in Social Psychology* (New York: McGraw-Hill, 1966); "The Development of Interpersonal Competence," in D. A. Goslin (ed.), *Handbook of Socialization and Research* (Chicago: Rand McNally, 1969).

11. Arensberg and Niehoff (1971).

12. L. Barna, "Stumbling Blocks in Interpersonal Intercultural Communication." In David Hoopes (ed.), *Readings in Intercultural Communication*, vol. 1 (1972).

13. R. W. Brislin and P. Pedersen, *Cross-Cultural Orientation Programs* (New York: Gardner Press, 1976).

14. W. B. Gudykunst, M. Hammer, and W. B. Wiseman, "Determinants of the Sojourner's Attitudinal Satisfaction." In *Communication Yearbook* 1, B. Ruben (ed.), (New Brunswick, N.J.: Transaction-International Communication Association, 1977).

15. S. Bochner, "The Meditating Man and Cultural Diversity," *Topics in Cultural Learning* 1 (1973), 23–37.

16. H. Cleveland and G. J. Mangone (eds.), *The Art of Overseasmanship* (Syracuse: Syracuse University Press, 1957); and H. Cleveland, G. J. Mangone, and J. C. Adams, *The Overseas Americans* (New York: McGraw-Hill, 1960).

17. A review of writings on cross-cultural effectiveness is provided by Brent D. Ruben, Lawrence R. Askling, and Daniel J. Kealey in "Cross-Cultural Effectiveness," in *Overview of Intercultural Education, Training and Research*, vol. 1: Theory. David S. Hoopes, Paul B. Pedersen, and George W. Renwick (eds.), (Washington, D.C.: Society for Intercultural Education, Training and Research, 1977), 92–105.

18. The results discussed herein are based on a two-year study conducted in Canda and Kenya by Brent D. Ruben and Daniel J. Kealey, presented in preliminary form at the Third Annual Conference of the Society for Intercultural Education, Training and Research (Chicago: 1977) in a report entitled "Behavioral Assessment and the Prediction of Cross-Cultural Shock, Adjustment, and Effectiveness."

19. K. Benne and P. Sheats, "Functional Roles of Group Members," *Journal of Social Research* 4 (1948).

20. See discussion in Ruben and Kealey (1977).

21. Ruben and Kealey.

22. See Arensberg and Niehoff (1971); Barna (1972); Brislin and Pedersen (1976); and Gudykunst et al. (1977).

23. Ruben, Askling, and Kealey (1977); discussion of the role of this dimensioin in cross-cultural interaction is provided in P. S. Adler, "Beyond Cultural Identity: Reflections Upon Cultura and Multicultural Man," in *Topics in Culture Learning*, vol. 2 (1974), 23–41, and P. S. Adler, "The Transitional Experience: An Alternative View of Culture Shock," *Journal of Humanistic Psychology*, vol. 15. No. 3 (1975).

24. Aitken, T. *The Multinational Man: The Role of the Manager Abroad* (New York: Wiley, 1973) and G. M. Guthrie and I. N. Zektick, "Predicting Performance in the Peace Corps," *Journal of Social Psychology* 71 (1967), 11–21.

25. See R. R. Carkhuff, *Helping and Human Relations* (New York: Holt, Rinehart & Winston, 1969) and Arensberg and Niehoff (1971).

26. See R. R. Carkhuff (1969); Cleveland et al. (1960); Gudykunst et al. (1977).

27. John M. Wiemann and Mark L. Knapp, "Turn-Taking in Conversations," *Journal of Communication* 25, no. 2 (1975).

# Prejudice in Intercultural Communication

## RICHARD W. BRISLIN

### THE FUNCTIONS OF PREJUDICE

When people react negatively to others on an emotional basis, with an absence of direct contact or factual material about the others, the people are said to behave according to prejudice. The concept of prejudice has been subjected to first-rate research investigations by psychologists and sociologists. One of the conclusions of this research is that "prejudice" is a far more complex concept than would be judged from the way the word is used in ordinary, everyday usage. This complexity has to be understood if the problems of prejudice are to be addressed effectively.

An understanding of prejudice can begin if its functions are analyzed. Katz[1] has written the clearest presentation of the functions of various attitudes which people hold, and these can be applied to the more specific case of prejudicial attitudes. In addition, the functions can be applied to the sorts of intercultural contact under scrutiny at this conference. In the past, the majority of research has dealt with interpersonal contact within countries, especially Black-White relations. The four functions that attitudes serve for people are:

1. *The utilitarian or adjustment function.* People

From *Intercultural Theory and Practice: Perspectives on Education, Training, and Research*, December 1979, pp. 28–36. Used with permission of the author. Footnotes have been renumbered. Richard W. Brislin is associated with the Culture Learning Institute, East-West Center, Honolulu, Hawaii.

hold certain prejudices because such attitudes lead to rewards, and lead to the avoidance of punishment, in their culture. For instance, people want to be well liked by others in their culture. If such esteem is dependent upon rejecting members of a certain group, then it is likely that the people will indeed reject members of the outgroup. Or, if jobs are scarce and if people from a certain group want those jobs, it is adjustive to believe that members of a certain group have no responsibility in work settings. Thus there will be less competition for the desired employment.

**2. *The ego-defensive function*.** People hold certain prejudices because they do not want to admit certain things about themselves. Holding the prejudice protects the people from a harsh reality. For instance, if a person is unsuccessful in the business world, (s)he may believe that members of a certain successful group are a scheming bunch of cheaters. This belief protects the individual from the self-admission that (s)he has inadequacies. Another example involves experiences that most people have during childhood, no matter what their culture. People believe, as part of their basic feelings of self-esteem, that they have grown up in a society where proper behavior is practiced. These people may look down upon members of other cultures (or social classes within a culture) who do not behave "correctly." This prejudicial attitude, then, serves the function of protecting people's self-esteem.

**3. *The value-expressive function*.** People hold certain prejudices becuse they want to express the aspects of life which they highly prize. Such aspects include basic values of people concerning religion, government, society, aesthetics, and so forth. Katz[2] emphasizes that this function is related to an individual's "notion of the sort of person he sees himself to be." For example, people who discriminate against members of a certain religious group may do so because they see themselves as standing up for the one true God (as defined by their own religion). As a more intense example,

people have engaged in atrocities toward outgroup members so as to retain the supposed values of a pure racial stock (again, their own).

**4. *The knowledge function*.** People hold certain prejudices because such attitudes allow individuals to organize and structure their world in a way that makes sense to them. People have a need to know about various aspects of their culture so that they can interact effectively in it. But the various aspects are so numerous that various discrete stimuli must be categorized together for efficient organization. People then behave according to the category they have organized, not according to the discrete stimuli.[3] Often these categories are stereotypes that do not allow for variation within a category. For instance, if people believe that members of a certain cultural group are childlike and cannot be given any responsibility, they may employ that stereotype upon meeting a member of that group. Given a set of stereotypes, people do not have to think about each individual they meet. They can then spend time on the many other matters that compete for their attention during an average day. The prejudicial stereotypes thus provide knowledge about the world. The problem, of course, is that the stereotypes are sometimes wrong and always overdrawn.[4]

Certain prejudices can serve several functions, particularly so when an individual's entire life span is considered. Young children develop a prejudice to please their parents (adjustment), continue to hold it because of what they learn in school (knowledge), and behave according to the prejudice since they wish to express their view of themselves (value). Programs to change prejudice often fail because the most important function, or functions, are not recognized. Most change-oriented programs are concerned with presenting well-established facts about the targets of prejudice. But such a program will only change people's attitudes which serve the knowledge function. Much more work has to be done on finding ways to change prejudices that serve the other three functions. This is a research area that should yield very important payoffs to careful investigators.

## THE FORMS OF PREJUDICE

In addition to an understanding of the functions of prejudice, it is also important to consider various forms that prejudice takes in its expression. The range of such expression is large.

1. *Red-neck racism.* Certain people believe that members of a given cultural group are inferior according to some imagined standard and that the group members are not worthy of decent treatment. The term "red-neck" comes from the Southern United States where world attention was focused on the White majority's treatment of Blacks during political demonstrations prior to the Civil Rights Act of 1964. The type of prejudice summarized by the term "red-neck," however, is found all over the world. This extreme form of prejudice has most often been assessed by asking people to agree or disagree with statements like this:[5] "The many faults, and the general inability to get along, of (*insert name of group*), who have recently flooded our community, prove that we ought to send them back where they came from as soon as conditions permit." "(*Insert name of group*) can never advance to the standard of living and civilization of our country due mainly to their innate dirtiness, laziness, and general backwardness."

All of us cringe at the thought of such tasteless, abhorrent sentiments. But we all know that such prejudices exist, and all of us can give many examples from the countries in which we have lived. Formal education has had a tremendous influence on lowering the incidences of red-neck racism. Research has shown that as the number of years of formal education increases, the incidence of racism decreases. However, I do feel that we need accurate figures on the current levels of such prejudice, and only large scale surveys can give us this information. It is possible that attendees at a conference such as this one underestimate the current levels of red-neck racism since they do not normally interact with people who hold such views.

2. *Symbolic racism.* Certain people have negative feelings about a given group because they feel that the group is interfering with aspects of their culture with which they have become familiar. The people do not dislike the group per se, and they do not hold sentiments that are indicative of red-neck racism. Symbolic racism[6] is expressed in terms of threats to people's basic values and to the status quo. When directly questioned, people will assert that members of a certain group are "moving too fast" and are making illegitimate demands in their quest for a place in society. Symbolic racism is expressed by responses to questions like these (the answer indicative of symbolic racism is noted in parentheses):

"Over the past few years, (*insert name of group*) have gotten more economically than they deserve." (agree)

"People in this country should support _____ in their struggle against discrimination and segregation." (disagree)

"_____ are getting too demanding in their push for equal rights." (agree)

Sentiments like these are probably more widespread than red-neck feelings among members of the affluent middle class in various countries. Again, however, exact figures are unavailable, and this lack hampers intelligent planning for programs to deal with this form of prejudice. It is important to understand the differences between red-neck and symbolic racism. People who hold symbolic sentiments do not view themselves as red-necks, and so programs aimed at changing extreme racist views (such programs are presently most common) are doomed to failure. McConahay and Hough[7] are accurate when they state that current change programs seem incomprehensible to holders of symbolic views "and they do not understand what all the fuss is about. This enables racism to be considered 'somebody else's' problem while holders of symbolic views concentrate upon their own private lives."

3. *Tokenism.* Certain people harbor negative feelings about a given group but do not want to admit this fact to themselves. Such people definitely do not view themselves as prejudiced and they do not perceive themselves as discriminatory in their behavior. One way that they reinforce this view of themselves is to engage in unimportant, but positive, intergroup behaviors. By engaging in such unimportant behaviors people can persuade themselves that they are unprejudiced, and thus they can refuse to perform more important intergroup behaviors. For instance, Dutton[8] found that if people gave a small amount of money to an outgroup, they were less willing to later donate a large amount of their time to a "Brotherhood Week" campaign emphasizing intergroup relations and goodwill. Other people in the Dutton study donated time to the Brotherhood Week if they had previously not been asked to give the small sum of money. The small amount of money, then, was a token that allowed some people to persuade themselves that they are unprejudiced and so don't have to prove themselves again by engaging in the more important, time-consuming behavior.

4. *Arms-length prejudice.* Certain people engage in friendly, positive behavior toward outgroup members in certain situations but hold those same outgroup members at an "arm's length" in other situations. The difference across situations seems to be along a dimension of perceived intimacy of behaviors.[9] For semi-formal behaviors such as (1) casual friendships at a place of employment, (2) interactions between speaker and audience at a lecture, or (3) interactions at a catered dinner party, people who harbor an arms-length prejudice will act in a friendly, positive manner. But for more intimate behaviors such as (1) dating, (2) interactions during an informal dinner held at someone's home, or (3) relations between neighbors, people will act in a tense, sometimes hostile manner. Frankly, I have observed this sort of arm's-length prejudice at places where such behavior would

ideally not be expected, as at the East-West Center. I have observed a Caucasian social psychologist (who has long lectured on prejudice), during a visit to my home, become non-communicative and ultimately rude when my Chinese-American neighbor unexpectedly dropped in for a visit. This form of prejudice is hard to detect since people who engage in it seem so tolerant of outgroup members much of the time.

5. *Real likes and dislikes.* Certain people harbor negative feelings about a given group because members of the group engage in behaviors that people dislike. This fifth category is derived from more common sense than scholarly literature, and it represents an expression of my feelings that not all prejudice should be looked upon as an indication of some sickness or flaw. People *do* have real likes and dislikes. No one person is so saintly as to be tolerant and forgiving toward all who engage in behaviors (s)he dislikes. For instance, littering really bothers me, and there are certain groups more likely to leave their trash on the ground after a picnic. Sometimes they are from cultures where servants or laborers are expected to do such cleanup. But my realization of the group's background does not lessen my dislike of litter. Seeing members of a certain group engage in such disliked behaviors, I am less likely to interact pleasantly with other members of the group in the future. My recommendation is to give more attention to this common, but heretofore neglected, type of everyday prejudice.

6. *The familiar and unfamiliar.* People who are socialized into one culture are likely to become familiar and thus comfortable with various aspects of that culture. These people, when interacting with members of another culture, are likely to experience behaviors or ideas that are unfamiliar and hence they are likely to feel uncomfortable. Consequently, the people are likely to prefer to interact with members of their own cultural group. What might seem like prejudice and discrimination to an onlooker, then, may be simply a reflection of people's preference for what is comfortable and non-

stressful. In a study of interaction among members of nine ethnic groups on Guam,[10] I found that informants were able to verbalize this reason for people's choices of friends. An informant from the Marshall Islands wrote:

*Culture makes these groups stick together. Somebody might not get along with one from another country. He likes to find some friends who have the same beliefs he has, and he could only find these characteristics with the people from his own country.*

And a resident of Truk wrote about the type of strained conversation that can arise when members of different groups interact:

*A Trukese who has never experienced the cold winter of the U.S. could not comprehend and intelligently appreciate a Statesider telling him the terrible winter they had in Albany anymore than a person from Albuquerque who has never seen an atoll could visualize the smallness of the islets that make up such an atoll. (Truk, of course, is an atoll.)*

I believe that this sort of mild prejudice based on what is familiar and unfamiliar is the sort of phenomenon recently referred to by the United States Ambassador to the United Nations, Andrew Young.[11] In mid-1977, Young labeled a number of people as "racists,"[12] but in explaining his use of the term he clearly was referring to a lack of understanding and an insensitivity regarding other cultural groups. When questioned by the press, Young had to admit that the insensitivity and misunderstanding stem from unfamiliarity. As with the type of prejudice described under "real likes and dislikes," this everyday type of behavior deserves more attention from behavioral scientists and educators than it has heretofore received.

## NOTES

1. D. Katz, "The functional approach to the study of attitudes," *Public Opinion Quarterly*, 1960, 24, pp. 164–204.

2. Katz, 1960, p. 173.

3. H. Triandis, "Culture training, cognitive complexity and interpersonal attitudes." In R. Brislin, S. Bochner, and W. Lonner (eds). *Cross-Cultural Perspectives on Learning* (New York: Wiley/Halsted Division, 1976) pp. 39–77.

4. The fact that I use the term "prejudicial stereotypes" does not mean that stereotypes and prejudice are isomorphic. *Some* stereotypes stem from prejudicial attitudes, and only these are discussed in this paragraph. More generally, stereotypes refer to any categorization of individual elements that mask differences among those elements. Stereotypes are absolutely necessary for thinking and communicating since people cannot respond individually to the millions of isolated elements they perceive every day. They must group elements together into categories, and then respond to the categories. Stereotypes are a form of generalization that involves names of some group of people and statements about that group. Thus when we speak of "conservatives" or "academics" or "educators," we are using stereotypical categories that mask individual differences within those categories. Stereotypes will always be a factor in any sort of communication, a fact that must be realized in any analysis of communication between individuals from different backgrounds. I mention this because, recently, I have found difficulty in encouraging multicultural groups to discuss stereotypes since the link between prejudice and stereotypes has become so strong. Stereotypes have acquired a distasteful status. Refusal to deal with them, however, means a refusal to deal with one of the most basic aspects of thinking and communication.

5. These statements are adapted from the analysis of such questionnaire items by R. Ashmore, "The problem of intergroup prejudice," in B. Collins, *Social Psychology* (Reading, Mass.: Addison-Wesley, 1970) pp. 245–296.

6. J. McConahay and J. Hough, "Symbolic racism," *Journal of Social Issues*, 1976, 32(2), pp. 23–45.

7. McConahay and Hough, 1976, p. 44.

8. D. Dutton, "Tokenism, reverse discrimination, and egalitarianism in interracial behavior," *Journal of Social Issues*, 1976, 32(2), pp. 93–107.

9. H. Triandis and E. Davis, "Race and belief as determinants of behavioral intentions," *Journal of Personality and Social Psychology*, 1965, 2, pp. 715–725.

**10.** R. Brislin, "Interaction among members of nine ethnic groups and the belief-similarity hypothesis," *Journal of Social Psychology*, 1971, 85, pp. 171–179.

**11.** *Playboy*, July, 1977; also analyzed in *Newsweek*, June 20, 1977, p. 34.

**12.** An "unfortunate" use of the term, Ambassador Young eventually admitted.

# Communication and Acculturation

## YOUNG YUN KIM

### ACCULTURATION

Human beings are sociocultural animals who acquire their social behaviors through learning. What we learn is defined largely by social and cultural forces. Of all aspects of human learning, communication is most central and fundamental. A great deal of our learning consists of communication responses to stimuli from the environment. We must code and decode messages in such a fashion that the messages will be recognized, accepted, and responded to by the individuals with whom we interact. Once acquired, communication activities function as an instrumental, interpretative, and expressive means of coming to terms with our physical and social environment. Communication is our primary means of utilizing the resources of the environment in the service of humanity. Through communication we adapt to and relate to our environment, and acquire membership and a sense of belonging in the various social groups upon which we depend.

Ultimately, it is not only the immigrant but also the host sociocultural system that undergoes changes as a result of the prolonged intercultural contact. The impact of immigrant cultures on the mainstream host culture, however, is relatively insignificant compared to the substantial influence

This original essay appeared in print for the first time in the third edition. All rights reserved. Permission to reprint must be obtained from the publisher and the author. Professor Young Yun Kim teaches at Governor's State University.

of the host culture on the individual immigrant. Clearly, a reason for the essentially unidirectional change in the immigrant is the difference between the number of individuals in the new environment sharing the immigrant's original culture and the size of the host society. Also, the dominant power of the host society in controlling its resources produces more impact on cultural continuity and change in immigrants. The immigrant's need for adaptation to the host sociocultural system, therefore, will be far greater than that of the host society to include elements of an immigrant culture.

Underlying an immigrant's acculturation process is the communication process. Acculturation occurs through the identification and the internalization of the significant symbols of the host society. Just as the natives acquire their cultural patterns through communication, so does an immigrant acquire the host cultural patterns through communication. An immigrant comes to organize himself or herself and to know and be known in relationship within the new culture through communication. The process of trial and error during acculturation can often be frustrating and painful. In many instances, an immigrant's native language is extremely different from that of the host society. Other communication problems fall broadly into a nonverbal category such as differences in the use and organization of space, interpersonal distance, facial expression, eye behavior, other body movement, and in the perceived importance of nonverbal behavior relative to verbal behavior.

Even when an immigrant has acquired a satisfactory blend of using the verbal and nonverbal communication patterns, he or she may still experience a more subtle and profound difficulty in recognizing and responding appropriately to the culturally sanctioned communication rules. The immigrant is rarely aware of the hidden dimensions of the host culture that influence what and how to perceive, how to interpret the observed messages, and how to express thoughts and feelings appropriately in different relational and circumstantial contexts. Cross-cultural differences in these basic aspects of communication are difficult to identify and infrequently discussed in public. They often seriously impede understanding between immigrants and members of the host society.

If we view acculturation as the process of developing communication competence in the host sociocultural system, it is important to emphasize the fact that such communication competence is acquired through communication experiences. *One learns to communicate by communicating.* Through prolonged and varied communication experiences, an immigrant gradually acquires the communication mechanisms necessary for coping with the environment. The acquired host communication competence of an immigrant has a direct bearing upon his or her overall acculturation. The immediate effect lies in the control that the immigrant is able to exercise over his or her own behavior and over the host environment. The immigrant's communication competence will function as a set of adjustive tools assisting the immigrant to satisfy basic needs such as the need for physical survival and the need for a sense of "belonging" and "esteem" (Maslow 1970, p. 47). Recent surveys of Korean and Indochinese immigrants in the United States clearly demonstrate the pivotal role that communication plays in the immigrants' psychological, social, and economic adjustment (Kim 1976, 1980).

The acculturation process, therefore, is an interactive and continuous process that evolves in and through the communication of an immigrant with the new sociocultural environment. The acquired communication competence, in turn, reflects the degree of that immigrant's acculturation. The degree to which an immigrant is acculturated is not only reflected in, but also facilitated by, the degree of consonance between his or her communication patterns and the sanctioned communication patterns of the host society. This does not mean that every detail of an immigrant's communication behavior can be observed in understanding his or her acculturation, nor that all aspects of the acculturation can be understood through his or her communication patterns. However, by focusing on a few key communication variables that are of crucial importance in the acculturation process, we can approximate, with a reasonable degree of accuracy, the reality of acculturation at a point in time, as well as predict the future development of acculturation.

## COMMUNICATION VARIABLES IN ACCULTURATION

One of the most comprehensive and useful conceptual frameworks in analyzing an immigrant's acculturation from the communication perspective is provided by the systems perspective elaborated by Ruben (1975). In the systems perspective, the basic element of a human communication system is viewed as the person who is actively being, seeking, and desiring communication with the environment. As an open communication system, a person interacts with the environment through two interrelated processes—personal communication and social communication.

### Personal Communication

Personal (or intrapersonal) communication refers to the mental processes by which one organizes oneself in and with one's sociocultural milieu, developing ways of seeing, hearing, understanding, and responding to the environment. "Personal communication can be thought of as sensing, making-sense-of, and acting toward the objects and people in one's milieu. It is the process by which the individual informationally fits himself into (adapts to and adopts) his environment" (Ruben 1975, pp. 168–169). In the context of acculturation, an immigrant's personal communication can be viewed as the organization of acculturation experiences into a number of identifiable cognitive and affective response patterns that are consistent with the host culture or that potentially facilitate other aspects of acculturation.

One of the most important variables of personal communication in acculturation is the complexity of an immigrant's *cognitive structure* in perceiving the host environment. During initial phases of acculturation, an immigrant's perception of the host culture is relatively simple; gross stereotypes are salient in the perception of the unfamiliar environment. As the immigrant learns more about the host culture, however, perception becomes more defined and complex, enabling the immigrant to detect variations in the host environment.

Closely related to the cognitive complexity is an immigrant's *knowledge* in patterns and rules of the host communication system. Sufficient empirical evidence supports the critical function of such knowledge (especially knowledge of the host language) in facilitating other aspects of acculturation. The acculturative function of the knowledge in the host communication system has been observed to be particularly important in increasing an immigrant's participation in interpersonal and mass communication networks of the host society (Breton 1964; Chance 1965; Richmond 1967; Kim 1977, 1980).

Another variable of personal communication in acculturation is an immigrant's *self-image* in relation to the immigrant's images of others. The relative position of the immigrant's self-image in relation to his or her images of the host society and the original culture, for example, provides valuable information about the immigrant's subjective reality of acculturation. Feelings of alienation, low self-esteem, and other similar psychological "problems" of immigrants tend to be associated with the greater perceptual distance between self and members of the host society (Kim 1980).

Also, an immigrant's *acculturation motivation* has been observed to be functional in facilitating the acculturation process. Acculturation motivation refers to an immigrant's willingness to learn about, participate in, and be oriented toward the host sociocultural system. Such positive orientation of an immigrant toward the new environment generally promotes participation in communication networks of the host society (Kim 1977, 1980).

### Social Communication

Personal communication is linked to social communication when two or more individuals interact, knowingly or not. "Social communication is the process underlying intersubjectivization, a phenomenon which occurs as a consequence of public symbolization and symbol utilization and diffusion" (Ruben 1975, p. 171). Through social communication, individuals regulate feelings, thoughts, and actions of one another. Social communication can be classified further into interpersonal communication and mass communication. Interpersonal communication occurs through interpersonal relationships, which in turn represent the purpose, function, and product of an individual's interpersonal communication. Mass communication, however, is a more generalized process of social communication, in which individuals interact with their sociocultural environment without involvement in interpersonal relations with specific individuals. An individual's communication experiences through such media as radio, television, newspaper, magazine, movie, theater, and other similar public forms of communication, can be included in this category.

An immigrant's *interpersonal communication* can be observed through the degree of his or her participation in interpersonal relationships with members of the host society. More specifically, we can infer and predict an immigrant's acculturation from the nature of his or her interpersonal networks. An immigrant with a predominantly ethnic interpersonal network can be considered less acculturated and less competent in the host communication system than an immigrant whose associates are primarily members of the host society. In addition, the degree of intimacy in the relationships an immigrant has developed with members of the host society is an important indicator of his or her acquired host communication competence. We may further elaborate on an immigrant's interpersonal communication by observing his or her specific verbal and nonverbal communication patterns in interacting with members of the host society.

The acculturation function of *mass communication* is limited in relation to that of interpersonal communication (Kim 1979a). The immigrant's interpersonal communication experiences have intense and detailed influence over the immigrant's acculturation. Communication involving an interpersonal relationship provides the immigrant with simultaneous feedback, directly controlling and regulating the immigrant's communication

behaviors. Though limited in its relative impact on an immigrant's acculturation, mass communication plays an important role in expanding the immigrant's experiences in the host society beyond the immediate environment. Through mass communication, an immigrant learns about the broader ranges of the various elements of the host sociocultural system. In transmitting messages that reflect the aspirations, myths, work and play, and specific issues and events of the host society, the media explicitly and implicitly convey societal values, norms of behavior, and traditional perspectives for interpreting the environment. Of the immigrant's various mass communication experiences, exposure to the content of information-oriented media such as newspapers, magazines, television news, and other informational programs has been observed to be particularly functional for acculturation when compared to other media that are primarily entertainment oriented (Kim 1977).

The acculturative function of mass communication should be particularly significant during the initial phase of an immigrant's acculturation process. During this phase, the immigrant has not yet developed a sufficient competence to develop satisfactory interpersonal relationships with members of the host society. The communication experiences in direct interpersonal contact with members of the host society can often be frustrating. The immigrant may feel awkward and out of place in relating to others: The direct negative feedback from the other person can be too overwhelming for the immigrant to experience pleasure in the interaction with members of the host society. The immigrant naturally tends to withdraw from such direct interaction and, instead, resorts to mass media as an alternative, pressure-free channel through which elements of the host environment can be absorbed (Ryu 1978).

## Communication Environment

[Immigrants'] personal and social communication and their acculturative function cannot be fully understood in isolation from the communication environment of the host society. Whether the immigrant has resettled in a small rural town or a large metropolitan area, lives in a ghetto area or an affluent suburb, is employed as a factory worker or as an executive—all are environmental conditions that may significantly influence the sociocultural development the immigrant is likely to achieve.

An environmental condition particularly influential in an immigrant's communication and acculturation is the availability of his or her native ethnic community in the local area. The degree to which the ethnic community can influence the immigrant's behavior depends largely upon the degree of "institutional completeness" of the community and its power to maintain the distinctive home culture for its members (Taylor 1979). Available ethnic institutions can ameliorate the stresses of intercultural situations and provide context for acculturation under relatively permissive conditions. In the long run, however, an extensive involvement of an immigrant in the ethnic community without sufficient communication with members of the host society may retard the intensity and rate of the immigrant's acculturation (Broom and Kitsuse 1976).

It is ultimately the host society that permits the degree of freedom, or "plasticity" (Kim 1979b), for minority immigrants to deviate from the dominant cultural patterns of the host society and to develop ethnic institutions. Such permissiveness in the communication environment may vary even within the same country. In a relatively open and pluralistic society such as the contemporary United States, an immigrant may find a difference in the degree of receptivity and openness of the host environment between a large metropolitan area and a small town in a rural area.

## ACCULTURATION POTENTIAL

Individuals respond to the new change in terms of their prior experience, accepting what promises to be rewarding and rejecting what seems unworkable or disadvantageous. Acculturation patterns are not uniform among all individuals but vary depending upon their *acculturation potential* as determined by their preimmigration characteristics. Some are more predisposed toward the host culture than others. Among the multitude of background characteristics, the following characteristics are considered important in contributing to greater acculturation potential.

The *similarity* of the original culture to the host culture is perhaps one of the most important factors of acculturation potential. An immigrant from Canada to the United States, for example, will have a greater acculturation potential than a Vietnamese immigrant from Southeast Asia. Even two immigrants from the same culture may have different subcultural backgrounds. An immigrant from a more cosmopolitan urban center is likely to have a greater acculturation potential than a farmer from a rural area. To the extent that we can understand the similarities and discrepancies between an immigrant's original cultural background and the host culture, we can better understand the immigrant's acculturation potential.

Among demographic characteristics, *age* at the time of immigration and *educational background* have been found to be significantly related to acculturation potential. Older immigrants generally experience greater difficulty in adjusting to the new culture and are slower in acquiring new cultural patterns (Kim 1976). Educational background of an immigrant prior to immigration facilitates acculturation (Kim 1976, 1980). Education, regardless of its cultural context, appears to expand a person's capacity for new learning and the challenges of life. In some cases, an immigrant's educational process in the home country includes training in the language of the host society, which gives the individual a basis for building communication competence after immigration.

On the psychological level, an immigrant's *personality factors*, such as gregariousness, tolerance for ambiguity, risk-taking, cognitive flexibility, open-mindedness, and other related characteristics, are likely to increase acculturation potential. These personality characteristics are likely to help restructure the immigrant's perception, feelings, and behaviors, facilitating acculturation in a new cultural environment.

Similarly, *familiarity* with the host culture prior to immigration through previous travel, interpersonal contacts, and through mass media may also increase the immigrant's acculturation potential.

## FACILITATING ACCULTURATION THROUGH COMMUNICATION

So far, immigrant acculturation has been defined and explained from a communication viewpoint. Just as any native-born person undergoes the enculturation process through communication, so an immigrant is acculturated into the host culture through communication. Much of the acculturation process is to adapt to, and adopt, predominant patterns and rules of communication of the host culture. The acquired host communication competence, in turn, facilitates all other aspects of adjustment in the host society. Communication, therefore, is viewed as the major underlying process as well as an outcome of the acculturation process.

In order to understand an immigrant's acculturation, we must understand his or her communication patterns. Information about the immigrant's communication enables us to predict the degree and pattern of acculturation. As a conceptual framework to analyze the immigrant's communication patterns, the communication systems perspective has been presented. To summarize, the systems perspective recognizes the dynamic interaction processes of personal communication, social communication, and communication environment. Personal communication can be analyzed in terms of cognitive complexity, knowledge of the host communication patterns and rules, self-image, and acculturation motivation. Social communication is conceptualized in interpersonal communication and mass communication. Interpersonal communication is reflected in the nature and pattern of an immigrant's interpersonal networks and specific verbal and nonverbal communication behaviors. Patterns of use and participation in the host mass communication system, particularly the information-oriented contents of the mass media, are also useful indicators of acculturation. The

sociocultural characteristics of the communication environment in which an immigrant carries out day-to-day activities influences the nature of the external communication stimuli that the immigrant is exposed to. Availability and strength of the ethnic community, as well as the plasticity of the host society, slow the acculturation process of an immigrant.

The acculturation potential of an immigrant prior to immigration may contribute to his or her subsequent acculturation in the host society. As discussed previously, acculturation potential is determined by such factors as: (1) similarity between the original culture and the host culture, (2) age at the time of immigration, (3) educational background, (4) some of the personality characteristics such as gregariousness and tolerance for ambiguity, and (5) familiarity with the host culture before immigration.

Once an immigrant enters the host society, the acculturation process is set in motion. The acculturation process will continue as long as the immigrant stays in direct contact with the host sociocultural system. All of the acculturative forces—personal and social communication, communication environment, and preimmigration acculturation potential—interactively influence the course of change in the immigrant's acculturation process. The acculturation process may not be a smooth linear process, but a forward-moving progression toward an ultimate assimilation, the hypothetical state of complete acculturation.

The extensive debate between "assimilationists" (who adhere to the "melting-pot" view) and "cultural pluralists" (proponents of conservation of ethnicity) loses its scientific relevance when we closely examine the inevitable adaptation of humans to their sociocultural environment. No immigrant, as long as livelihood or other needs are functionally dependent upon the host society, can escape acculturation completely. Acculturation, in this sense, is a "natural" phenomenon. A prolonged, direct contact by the immigrant with a new sociocultural environment leads to acculturative change. It is too simplistic to decree that one must be "either A or B," forced to accept or reject one of the two positions. In reality, ethnicity and acculturation can be considered to be two sides of the same coin; they are interrelated and inseparable phenomena. What is important is that both the assimilationist and the pluralist perspectives acknowledge some changes in immigrants over time. When the changes are not complete, it is only natural that there remains a certain degree of ethnicity. Incomplete acculturation, depending on one's point of view, can be interpreted as evidence of (some) assimilation or (some) ethnicity.

Thus, the real issue between the two opposing views—assimilation vs. ethnicity—is not a scientific one, that is to say, whether or not there *is* such a phenomenon as acculturation. Rather, it is an ideological disagreement on the degree to which an individual immigrant *should* maintain (or lose) his or her original culture. Such ideological polarization along a continuum of acculturation among social scientists and social philosophers, however, does not interfere with the natural process of adaptive change or acculturation. Nor should the philosophical disagreement interfere with the ultimate right of an individual immigrant to determine how far to acculturate beyond the minimum, functional level. In reality, most immigrants tend to follow the folk wisdom, "When in Rome, do as the Romans do." They recognize and accept the fact that it is they who are joining an existing sociocultural system, and that the degree of success in building their new lives depends largely on their ability to acculturate into the host society.

Should an immigrant choose to increase his or her acculturative capacity and consciously try to facilitate the acculturation process, then the immigrant must realize the importance of communication as the fundamental mechanism by which such goals may be achieved. To facilitate communication competence in the host culture, the immigrant must develop cognitive, affective, and behavioral competence in dealing with the host environment. By developing a strong acculturation motivation, the immigrant becomes positively oriented to the host society and accepts the norms and rules of the host culture. Through learning the host communication patterns and rules and by being open-minded, the immigrant becomes tolerant of the differences and uncertainties of the intercultural situations. Also, the immigrant must attempt, whenever possible, to maximize participation in the host interpersonal and mass communication systems. Through active participation in the host communication systems, the immigrant will develop a more realistic understanding of, and a more positive outlook on, a new way of life.

The immigrant, however, cannot accomplish his or her acculturative goals alone. The process of acculturation is an interactive process of "push and pull" between an immigrant and the host environment. But members of the host society can facilitate an immigrant's acculturation by accepting the original cultural conditioning of the immigrant, by providing the immigrant with supportive communication situations, and by making themselves patiently available through the often strenuous intercultural encounters. The host society can more actively encourage immigrant acculturation through communication training programs. Such training programs should facilitate the immigrant's acquisition of the host communication competence.

Although prolonged involvement in an ethnic community may ultimately delay the acculturation process, the ethnic community can play a significant acculturative function for the new immigrants in their early stages of acculturation. Ethnic communities can provide support systems to assist new arrivals in coping with the stresses and initial uncertainties and can guide them toward effective acculturation. Studies are beginning to investigate the coping, ego strength, and adaptation mechanisms that are built by natural support systems—family, neighborhood, ethnic associations, and self-help groups (Giordano and Giordano 1977).

All in all, the acculturation process of an immigrant can be facilitated by cooperative effort among the immigrants themselves, the members of the host society, and the ethnic community. At the heart of interactive acculturation lies the communication process linking the individual immigrants to their sociocultural milieu. The importance of communication to acculturation cannot be overemphasized. Acquisition of communication competence by the immigrant is not only instrumental to all other aspects of his or her adjustment, but also vital for the host society if it is to effectively accommodate diverse elements and maintain the necessary societal unity and strength. As long as common channels of communication remain strong, consensus and patterns of concerted action will persist in the host society. As Mendelsohn (1964) describes it, communication makes it possible to merge the minority groups into one democratic social organization of commonly shared ideas and values.

## REFERENCES

Adler, P. S. "Beyond Cultural Identity: Reflections on Cultural and Multicultural Man." In *Intercultural Communication: A Reader*, 2nd ed., ed. L. A. Samovar and R. E. Porter. Belmont, Calif.: Wadsworth, 1976, pp. 363–378.

Breton, R. "Institutional Completeness of Ethnic Communities and the Personal Relations of Immigrants," *American Journal of Sociology* 70 (1964), 193–205.

Broom, L., and J. Kitsuse. "The Validation of Acculturation: A Condition to Ethnic Assimilation." In *Ethnicity: A Conceptual Approach*, ed. D. E. Weinberg. Cleveland: Cleveland Ethnic Heritage Studies, Cleveland State University, 1976, pp. 135–146.

Chance, N. A. "Acculturation, Self-Identification, and Personality Adjustment." *American Anthropologist* 67 (1965), 373–393.

Giordano, J., and G. Giordano. *The Ethno-Cultural Factor in Mental Health: A Literature Review and Bibliography.* New York: Institute on Pluralism and Group Identity of the American Jewish Committee, 1977.

Herskovits, M. J. *Cultural Dynamics.* New York: Alfred A. Knopf, 1966.

Kim, Y. Y. "Communication Patterns of Foreign Immigrants in the Process of Acculturation: A Survey Among the Korean Population in Chicago." Ph.D. Dissertation, Northwestern University, 1976.

——— "Communication Patterns of Foreign Immigrants in the Process of Acculturation."

*Human Communication Research* 4, 1 (1977), 66–77.

———. "Mass Media and Acculturation: Toward Development of an Interactive Theory." Paper presented at the annual conference of the Eastern Communication Association, Philadelphia, Pennsylvania, May 1979a.

———. "Toward an Interactive Theory of Communication-Acculturation." In *Communication Yearbook* 3, ed. D. Nimmo. New Brunswick, N.J.: Transaction Books, 1979b, pp. 435–453.

———. *Indochinese Refugees in the State of Illinois. Volume IV. Psychological, Social and Cultural Adjustment of Indochinese Refugees.* Chicago: Travelers Aid Society of Metropolitan Chicago, 1980.

LeVine, R. A. *Culture, Behavior, and Personality.* Chicago: Aldine, 1973.

Maslow, A. H. *Motivation and Personality*, 2nd ed. New York: Harper & Row, 1970.

Mendelsohn, H. "Sociological Perspectives on the Study of Mass Communication." In *People, Society and Mass Communication*, ed. L. A. Dexter and D. M. White. New York: Free Press of Glencoe, 1964, pp. 29–36.

Peterson, T., J. Jensen, and W. Rivers. *The Mass Media and Modern Society.* New York: Holt, Rinehart & Winston, 1965.

Richmond, A. H. *Post-War Immigrants in Canada.* Toronto: University of Toronto Press, 1967.

Ruben, B. D. "Intrapersonal, Interpersonal, and Mass Communication Process in Individual and Multi-Person Systems." In *General Systems Theory and Human Communication*, ed. B. D. Ruben and J. Y. Kim. Rochelle Park, N.J.: Hayden, 1975.

Ryu, J. S. "Mass Media's Role in the Assimilation Process: A Study of Korean Immigrants in the Los Angeles Area." Paper presented to the annual meeting of the International Communication Association, Chicago, May 1978.

Schutz, A. "The Stranger: An Essay in Social Psychology." In *Identity and Anxiety: Survival of the Person in Mass Society*, ed. M. R. Stein, A. J. Vidich, and D. M. White. New York: Free Press, 1960, pp. 98–109.

Taylor, B. K. "Culture: Whence, Whither and Why?" In *The Future of Cultural Minorities*, ed. A. E. Alcock, B. K. Taylor and J. M. Welton. New York: St. Martin's, 1979.

## CONCEPTS AND QUESTIONS FOR CHAPTER 7

**1.** If you were going to travel abroad, what preparations would you make to ensure the best possible opportunity for effective intercultural communication?

**2.** What specific suggestions can you make that could improve your ability to interact with other ethnic or racial groups in your community? How would you go about gaining the necessary knowledge and experience?

**3.** What are the six stumbling blocks in intercultural communication discussed by LaRay Barna? How can you learn to avoid them?

**4.** Can you think of instances when you have been guilty of assuming similarity instead of difference?

**5.** How would a "non-judgmental attitude and a high tolerance for ambiguity" help intercultural communication? Is there such a thing as "non-judgmental attitude"?

**6.** Can you think of any mannerisms, behaviors, or styles that the U.S. businessperson reflects that are apt to stifle intercultural communication?

**7.** Why is it important to try to locate similarities between cultures as well as differences?

**8.** What current television programs and commercials encourage false media stereotyping?

**9.** Can you think of examples for each of the forms of prejudice discussed by Brislin?

**10.** What specific behaviors can you engage in that will help the immigrant in the acculturation process?

## SUGGESTED READINGS

Abe, H. and R. Wiseman. "Across-cultural confirmation of the dimensions of intercultural effectiveness." *International Journal of Intercultural Relations* 7 (1983), 53–67. This study attempts to examine the topic of "intercultural effectiveness." It compares American sojourners with Japanese sojourners according to 24 personal abilities suggested by a review of literature. Once the authors find similarities and differences between the Americans and the Japanese, they discuss perceptions of intercultural effectiveness.

Amir, Y. "Contact hypothesis in ethnic relations." *Psychological Bulletin* 71 (1969), 319–342. In what has become a classic piece, Amir explores the assumption that ethnic contact will reduce ethnic prejudice and intergroup tension and improve relations among various ethnic groups. His findings suggest that specific conditions are required if contact is to result in tension reduction. Practical applications are also considered.

Kohls, R. L. *Survival Kit for Overseas Living.* LaGrange Park, Ill.: Intercultural Network, 1979. This practical "how-to" book deals with the topics of working and living abroad. Kohls offers a number of suggestions that examine the import of values, stereotyping, cultural shock, and so on.

Stening, B. W. "Problems in cross-cultural contact: A literature review." *International Journal of Intercultural Relations* 3 (1979), 269–313. This excellent article reviews the literature "bearing on the matter of misunderstanding between persons engaged in cross-cultural relationships." The author looks at such factors as stereotyping, ethnocentrism, and prejudice.

Triandis, H. C. "A theoretical framework for the more efficient construction of cultural assimilators." *International Journal of Intercultural Relations* 8 (1984), 301–330. This pertinent article presents dimensions of cultural variations from a theoretical framework. Based on these dimensions, Triandis constructs a theory of cultural differences in social behavior for use in developing cultural assimilators as a shortcut.

Trifonovitch, G. J. "On cross-cultural orientation techniques" in *Topics in Culture Learning* Vol. 1. Honolulu: East-West Center, 1973. This article deals specifically with cross-cultural orientation techniques used by the author with American personnel who were preparing to assume duties and responsibilities in Micronesia. Although the cultural orientation is limited in scope, the techniques and methods can be generalized to training programs for a variety of cultures.

Webb, M. W. "Cross-cultural awareness: A framework for interaction." *Personnel and Guidance Journal* 16 (1983), 498–500. To facilitate cross-cultural understanding, this essay offers a framework for interaction. It focuses on personal experience, attribution theory, and Gullohorn's "W-curve" concept. It suggests that these concepts can be useful in intercultural communication.

## ADDITIONAL READINGS

Bennett, J. "Transition shock: Putting culture shock in perspective." *Intercultural Communication Annual* 4 (1977), 45–52.

Bennett, M. J. "A developmental approach to training for intercultural sensitivity." *International Journal of Intercultural Relations* 10 (1986), 179–196.

Casse, P. *Training for the Cross-Cultural Mind.* Washington, D.C.: Sietar, 1979.

Casse, P. *Training for the Multicultural Manager.* Washington, D.C.: Sietar, 1982.

Church, A. "Sojourner adjustments." *Psychological Bulletin* 91 (1982), 540–592.

Clark, M. L. and W. Pearson, Jr. "Racial Stereotypes revisited." *International Journal of Intercultural Relations* 6 (1982), 381–393.

Close, D. et al. *Interviewing Immigrants.* Melbourne: Clearing House on Migration Issues, 1978.

Dyel, J. A. and R. Y. Dyel. "Acculturation stress and coping." *International Journal of Intercultural Relations* 4 (1981), 301–328.

Graham, J. "Brazilian, Japanese and American Business Negotiations." *Journal of International Business Studies* (Spring-Summer 1983), 44–61.

Gudykunst, W. and M. R. Hammer. "Dimentions of intercultural effectiveness: Culture specific or cultural general?" *International Journal of Intercultural Relations* 8 (1984), 1–10.

Hahn, E. J. "Negotiating with the Japanese." *California Lawyer* 2 (1982), 21–59.

Hwang, J. S., S. J. Chase, and C. W. Kelley. "An intercultural examination of communication competence." *Communication: The Journal of the Communication Association of the Pacific* 9 (1980), 70–79.

Kim, J. K. "Explaining acculturation in a communication framework: An empirical test." *Communication Monographs* 47 (1980), 155–179.

Loveridge, D. "Communication between people." *Hong Kong Psychological Society Bulletin* 9 (1982), 19–26.

Martin, J. N. "Training issues in cross-cultural orientations." *International Journal of Intercultural Relations* 10 (1986), 103–116.

McCrosky, J. C., W. B. Gudykunst, and T. Nishida. "Communication apprehension among Japanese students in native and second language." *Communication Research Reports* 2 (1985), 11–15.

Moran, R. *Getting Your Yen's Worth: How to Negotiate with Japan.* Houston: Gulf Publishing, 1984.

Nann, R. C., ed. *Uprooting and Surviving: Adaptation and Resettlement of Migrant Families and Children.* Boston: D. Reidel Publishing Company, 1984.

Neff, C., ed. *New Directions for Experiential Learning: Cross-Cultural Learning,* No. II. San Francisco: Jossey-Bass, 1981.

Pusch, M. D., ed. *Multicultural Education: A Cross-Cultural Training Approach.* Chicago: Intercultural Press, 1981.

Sell, D. K. "Research on attitude change in U.S. students who participate in foreign study experiences: Past findings and suggestions for future research." *International Journal of Intercultural Relations* 7 (1983), 131–147.

Tseng, W., et al., eds. *Adjustment in Intercultural Marriage.* Honolulu: University of Hawaii Press, 1977.

Wilson, A. "Teachers as short-term international sojourners: Opening windows on the world." *The Social Studies* 75 (1984), 153–158.

# 8

# Ethical Considerations and Prospects for the Future

The goal of this book is to help you understand intercultural communication and to assist you in appreciating the issues and problems inherent in interactions involving people from foreign and alien cultures. To this end we have examined a series of diverse essays that presented a variety of variables operable during intercultural encounters. But what we have looked at up to now is what is already known about intercultural communication. We now shift our emphasis and focus on two issues that are much harder to pin down. These are the ethical considerations that must be inherent in intercultural interactions and the future prospects of this developing field of study. In short, this chapter examines some of the following questions: What do we need to accomplish, what may we expect to accomplish, what philosophical issues must we deal with, and what kinds of personalities must we develop if we are to improve the art and science of intercultural communication during the remainder of this century?

To set the tone for this final chapter we begin with an essay that deals with the ethical questions centering around how we go about judging the actions of people from different cultures. As you would suspect, this issue is indeed a difficult and complex one. In "The Evaluation of Culture," Elvin Hatch tackles this question with a rather optimistic premise. He maintains that "it is possible to arrive at a general principle for evaluating institutions without assuming that ours is a superior way of life." Admittedly, such an idealistic stance is not easy to put into operation. Yet Hatch does offer a framework that can be used to evaluate cultures. His philosophy is predicated on three generalizations: first, that humanistic values seem to be widespread among most human beings; second, that humanistic values are better than ethnocentrism—even though it too is universal; and third, that much of what we evaluate with regard to other cultures falls out of the scope of humanistic philosophy, and therefore we need a way to judge and evaluate such things as sexual mores, kinship relations, styles of leadership and the like. Hatch offers some guidelines to help us make these ethical decisions.

Our next essay by Young Yun Kim is based on one of the basic themes of this book—that today's interconnected and fast-changing world demands that we all change our assumptions about culture and our individual places within that culture. Recognizing these changes, Kim advances a philosophical orientation that she calls *intercultural personhood*. For Kim, intercultural personhood combines the key attributes of Eastern and Western cultural traditions, and she presents a model using these attributes. This model takes into account basic modes of consciousness, cognitive patterns, personal and social values, and communication behavior. The notion of intercultural personhood also leads us into the concept of the multicultural person as set forth in the next article.

The final selection in this chapter is by Rosita D. Albert and Harry C. Triandis. It calls our attention to a topic that is bound to generate a great deal of discussion in the next few years. It is the issue of multicultural education. The concept behind multicultural education is rather simple to state, but very complex and controversial to implement. Advocates of multicultural education maintain that pupils who are culturally different from the majority need multicultural education so that they can learn to function effectively in their own culture as well as in the majority culture. Some educators believe that students of the dominant culture can also benefit from education that asks them to learn about the patterns of perception, values, and behaviors of culturally different classmates. Because this philosophy is not without its critics, Albert and Triandis discuss some of the objections to multicultural education. They also point out three different approaches to teaching multicultural education and some advantages and disadvantages of each. Regardless of your personal feeling about multicultural education, it is a topic that is going to be debated by all people who are interested in the large influx of new minorities seeking an education in the United States educational system.

It might be well to view this exploration of ethics and the future as only a sampling of the many issues that confront those involved in intercultural communication. The field is still so new and the challenges so varied that it is impossible to predict future directions with any degree of assurance. Our intent in this chapter, therefore, is simply to introduce you to a few of the issues and concepts.

One final note. Much of what is offered in this chapter may appear naive and unrealistic. Neither we nor the authors of the articles apologize for suggesting that in intercultural contracts each person should aim for the ideal. What we present here are some challenges to develop new ways of perceiving oneself and others. In so doing we all can help make this complex and shrinking planet a more habitable and peaceful place for its 5 billion residents.

# The Evaluation of Culture

## ELVIN HATCH

If relativism is in such difficulty as a moral philosophy, is there any role at all left for it to play in our thinking? I believe so, and one of my purposes . . . is to indicate what that is. There is another purpose: Given that much of ethical relativism has been nudged aside by recent events, I want to advance a set of principles that will cover much of the ground that relativism has relinquished. These principals constitute a framework that we can use in evaluating cultures, including our own.

The first principle is that there is merit to the criticism that relativism has been accompanied by a conservative bias. What is at issue here is the relativist claim that all cultures or institutions are equally valid or fitting: Anthropologists tended to assume that the mere presence of a cultural trait warrants our valuing it. Elizabeth Colson has put the case quite simply; she wrote, "Ethnographers have usually presented each social group they study as a success story. We have no reason to believe that this is true" (1976, p. 264). A people may get by with inadequate solutions to their problems even judging by their own standards. For example, if the people are genuinely interested in ensuring the productivity of their gardens, they will find innovations like crop rotation and fertilization more effective than human sacrifice—although they will not have the statistical evidence to realize this (cf. Bagish 1981, pp. 12–20).

Second, a general principle is at hand for judging the adequacy of institutions. It may be called the

humanistic principle or standard, by which I mean that the well-being of people ought to be respected. The notion of well-being is a critical aspect of the humanistic principle, and three points can be made with respect to it. For one, I assume that human well-being is not a culture-bound idea. Starvation and violence, for example, are hardly products of Western thought or a function of Western thinking, although they may be conceived in a peculiarly Western idiom. Starvation and violence are phenomena that are recognized as such in the most diverse cultural traditions. Another is that the notion of human well-being is inherently value-laden, and concepts of harm and beneficence are inseparable from it: it seems impossible to imagine the idea of human well-being divorced from moral judgments of approval and disapproval. Whereas such notions as sky or earth may conceivably be held in purely neutral terms in a given culture, such ideas as hunger and torture cannot be. It is even reasonable to argue that the *point* of morality, as a philosophical if not a sociological issue, is to promote the well-being of others (Warnock 1971, esp. pp. 12–26). Finally, the notion of human well-being, when used as the central point of morality, serves to root moral questions in the physical, emotional, and intellectual constitution of people. It may be that any rigorous attempt to work out the content of morality will have to include an analysis of such notions as human wants, needs, interests, and happiness.

The humanistic principle can be divided into two parts. First is Redfield's point about humaneness, that it is good to treat people well, or that we should not do one another harm. We can judge that human sacrifice, torture, and political repression are wrong, whether they occur in our society or some other. Similarly, it is wrong for a person, whatever society he or she may belong to, to be indifferent toward the suffering of others. The matter of coercion, discussed earlier, fits here, in that we may judge it to be wrong when some members of a society deliberately and forcefully interfere in the affairs of other people. Coercion works against the well-being of those toward whom it is directed. Second is the notion that people ought to enjoy a reasonable level of material existence: we may judge that poverty, malnutrition, material discomfort, human suffering, and the like are bad. These two ideas may be brought together to form one standard since both concern the physical well-being of the members of society, and the difference between them is that the former refers to the quality of interpersonal relations, and the latter to the material conditions under which people live.

The humanistic principle may be impossible to define very tightly; it may even be that the best we can do to give it shape is to illustrate it with examples as I have done here. And surely it is difficult to apply in actual situations. Yet these are not good reasons to avoid making judgments about the relative merit of institutions or about the desirability of change. Although we may do harm by expressing judgments across cultural boundaries, we may do as much or more harm by failing to do so.

The orthodox relativist would perhaps argue that there is no humanistic moral principle that we can use for this purpose, in that notions like harm and discomfort are quite variable from one culture to the next. Pain and personal injury may even be highly valued by some people. For example, the Plains Indian willingly engaged in a form of self-torture that a middle-class American could hardly tolerate. The Indians chopped off finger joints and had arrows skewered through their flesh; tied to the arrows were cords, by which the sufferer dragged buffalo skulls around the village. Some American Indians were also reported to have placed a very high value on bravery, and the captive who withstood torture without showing pain was highly regarded by the enemies who tormented him.

Yet cases like these do not make the point that notions of pain and suffering are widely variable. Following this same logic one could say that middle-class Americans value pain since they willingly consent to surgery, and the man or woman who bears up well is complimented for his or her strength of character. The Indian who was tortured to death would surely have preferred a long and respectable life among his people to the honorable death that came to him. The Plains Indian who engaged in self-torture was trying to induce a vision (in our idiom,

a hallucination) for the power and advantages it was believed such an experience would bring. The pain was a means to an end, and surely was not seen as a pleasurable indulgence to look forward to. The difference between middle-class Americans and Plains Indians on this point could be a difference in judgments of reality and not a difference in values—the American would not believe that the vision has the significance attributed to it by the Indian, so he or she would not submit to the pain. Similarly, the plains warrior might not believe in the efficacy of surgery and might refuse to suffer the scalpel.

The widespread trend among non-Western peoples to want such material benefits as steel knives and other labor-saving devices is a clear indication that all is not relative when it comes to hard work, hunger, discomfort, and the like. Cultural values may be widely different in many ways, but in this sphere at least, human beings do seem to have certain preferences in common.

The Yanomamö are an instructive case, for here is a people who do not seem to share the humanistic value I am suggesting. The level of violence and treachery in this society suggests that their regard for pain and suffering is demonstrably different from what I am arguing is the norm among human beings. Yet this is not clearly the case either: Individuals in Yanomamö society are more willing than middle-class Americans to inflict injury on others, yet they want to avoid injury to themselves. Why else would the wife flee in terror when her husband comes at her with a machete, and why else would a village seek refuge from enemies when it is outnumbered and weak? The Yanomamö seem rather to be a case in which we are warranted in making a value judgment across cultural boundaries: They do not exhibit as much regard for the well-being of other persons as they have for themselves, and this can be judged a moral error.

Does this point about the generality of the humanistic principle among human beings not make the same mistake that Herskovits, Benedict, and other relativists were accused of making, which is to derive an "ought" from an "is"? My argument is not quite that simple, for it has two parts. First is the generalization that the humanistic value seems to be widespread among human beings. Second, I am making the moral judgment (quite separately from the empirical generalization) that this is an estimable value to hold, or that it warrants acceptance—in contrast, say, to another widespread value, ethnocentrism, which is not meritorious even if it is universal.

A third principle in the scheme that I propose is that a considerable portion of the cultural inventory of a people falls outside the scope of the humanistic standard mentioned above. In other words, once we have considered those cultural features that we can reasonably judge by this standard, a large portion remains, and it consists of those items which have little if anything to do with the strictly practical affairs of life and which then cannot be appraised by practical considerations. Included are sexual mores, marriage patterns, kinship relations, styles of leadership, forms of etiquette, attitudes toward work and personal advancement, dietary preferences, clothing styles, conceptions of deity, and others. Some of these nonappraisable features are closely linked to others that are, in that there are always nonessential cultural accouterments or trappings associated with institutions that are important on practical grounds. Western medicine provides a surfeit of examples. Health care clearly falls within the orbit of the humanistic principle, yet much of the medical system in the United States is hardly necessary for health's sake, including the rigid social hierarchy among doctors and nurses and the traditional division of labor between them. Successful health care systems can assume different forms from the one exhibited in this country. It is essential (but difficult) to keep in mind this division between what is essential and what is not in such matters as medicine, for otherwise civilization will tend to pack a good deal of unnecessary cultural baggage along with the genuinely useful features when it sets out to share its advantages with others.

Relativism prevails in relation to the institutions that fall outside the orbit of the humanistic principle, for here a genuine diversity of values is found and there are no suitable cross-cultural standards for evaluating them. The finest reasoning that we or anyone else can achieve will not point decisively to the superiority of Western marriage patterns, eating habits, legal institutions, and the like. We ought to show tolerance with respect to these institutions in other societies on the grounds that people ought to be free to live as they choose.

This leads to the fourth principle: Is it possible to identify any areas of culture in which we may speak of improvement? Are there any criteria that will produce a hierarchical ordering of societies that we may say represents a pattern of advance? Or is the distinction between primitive and civilized societies but an expression of our cultural bias?

The first criterion that comes to mind is Redfield's and Kroeber's, according to which civilization has brought a more humane existence, a higher level of morality to mankind, inasmuch as people treat one another better in complex societies. This judgment is very difficult to accept today, however. Recent events have left most of us with considerable ambivalence about Western democracy, to cite one instance. Politicians seem too often to be both incompetent and dishonest, and to be willing to allow private economic interests to influence programs and policies at all levels. Similarly, there is a very strong distrust of the power and intentions of big business, which seems to set its policies chiefly by looking at its margin of profit. The risk of producing a dangerous product is calculated by assessing how much the company is liable to lose in lawsuits relative to its profits, and not by considering the real dangers to human life. Much of the difficulty of assessing moral advance is that this is a highly impressionistic matter. The ledger sheets on which we tote up the pluses and minuses for each culture are so complex that summary calculations of overall moral standing are nearly meaningless. Perhaps the most one can say about whether or not there has been moral advance is that it is impossible to tell—but that it is not very likely.

It is important to distinguish between this conclusion and Herskovits'. According to him, we cannot speak of progress in this sphere because any humanistic principle we might use will necessarily be culture-bound; we have no yardstick to measure with. My point is that we do have a suitable yardstick, but that there are so many measures to take in each culture that the sum total is too complicated to assess.

Another criterion for gauging improvement is the material well-being of people: disregarding whether or not the members of society behave well or ill toward one another, can we say that the material conditions of life have gotten better with civilization? In pursuing this question I need to digress somewhat. The issue of material improvement places the focus on economics and technology, and also on such technical knowledge as that which is provided by medical and agricultural research. So we need first to ask if it is possible to arrive at an objective and meaningful hierarchy of societies based on these features. Herskovits questioned that we can. To him, an ordering of societies according to our criteria of economic production and technological complexity will merely reflect our cultural perspective and not some fundamental principle of general significance to all peoples.

Herskovits' argument is off the mark. On one hand, the criteria of economic complexity and technological sophistication are objective in the sense that they are definable by reference to empirical features that are independent of our culture. For example, the intensity and scale of economic transactions have a physical aspect which is identifiable from other cultural perspectives than ours, and the same is true of such measures as the amount of food produced per farm worker.[1] What is more, the social hierarchy that results from the use of these criteria has historical significance: One would be astonished, say, to discover evidence of complex forms of agricultural production in the Paleolithic. But on the other hand, and even more important, this is a meaningful hierarchy, in that the point of this ordering of societies would not be lost on people from other cultures; it would be meaningful to them because they see the value of increasing agricultural productivity, the use of bicycles (and automobiles), the availability of running water, and the like. It is surely the case that non-Western peoples all over the world are more interested in the products of Western industrial production than they are in the intricacies of Australian kinship, and are more likely to incorporate such Western innovations as fertilizers and matches into their cultures than they are the particulars of the Australian system of marriage and descent. This is an important message we get from the post-World War II drive for economic development among the newly independent nations.

There is a danger in using people's perceptions of the relative superiority of economic and technological systems as a test for the meaningfulness of this social hierarchy, because not all of the world's populations agree about what it is that is good about development and modernization. For example, Burma and Iran are highly selective in the changes they will accept, and at least some very simple societies (like the Andaman Islanders) want little if any change.

There is another way to establish the hierarchy without relying completely and directly on people's opinions. However another society may feel about what they do or do not want with regard to development, the economic and technological relationship between them and Western societies is asymmetrical. It is true that the fully developed nations rely on the less developed ones for natural resources like oil, but processed goods, and both economic and technological innovations, flow chiefly to and not away from the societies that are lower on the scale. To take an extreme case, there is little in the sphere of technology and economics that the Australian aborigines or Andaman Islanders can offer to the developed nations, whereas the reverse is not true. For example, some of the most isolated Andaman Islanders occasionally find empty gasoline drums washed upon their shore. They cut these in half and use them as enormous cooking pots (Cipriani 1966, p. 52). It is unthinkable that this relationship could be reversed—that we would find some technological item from their cultural inventory to be especially useful in our everyday lives. It is true that we may value their pottery or other artifacts as examples of primitive art, but the use we have for such items is esthetic, not practical, and consequently such items are of a different order from the gasoline drums that the Andamanese find so useful.

In noting this asymmetry I do not mean that cultures which are lower in the hierarchy do not have a very sophisticated technical knowledge of their own (they must in order to survive), and in this sense "they have something to teach us," as Brokensha and Riley remark concerning the Mbeere of Kenya. "In fact," these writers continue, "Mbeere and other folk-belief systems contain much that is based on extremely accurate, detailed and thoughtful observations, made over many generations" (1980, p. 115). It is easy to depreciate or ignore the cultural practices and ideas of another society, say, when assisting them in the process of development. In particular, it is tempting to want to replace their traditional practices with "modern" ones in whole-sale fashion, instead of building on or incorporating the indigenous knowledge in helping to bring about change. Nevertheless, the presence of such useful knowledge in indigenous systems of thought does not negate the fundamental asymmetry that exists among societies or the hierarchy which the asymmetry suggests.

The pluralistic notion of development . . . has bearing on the way we should conceive this hierarchy. The idea that Third World countries should become more and more like Western industrial societies is subject to criticism, and it may be preferable to define development differently for each society according to the interests of the people concerned and the nature of their economic and ecological conditions. A people may have achieved as much development as they need and want without embarking on a trajectory of industrial "growth" in the Western sense. In other words, the hierarchy I am suggesting does not represent a set of stages through which all societies will necessarily want to pass. It is simply a ranking of cultural systems according to degrees of economic complexity, technological sophistication, and the like.

Yet this begs a crucial question. Is it not true that to suggest this hierarchy is to imply that the societies higher on the scale are preferable? Does the existence of the hierarchy not mean that the societies that fall below would be better off if only they could manage to come up to a higher level of economic complexity and technological sophistication?

The discussion now comes back to the issue that prompted this digression. Can we say that the social hierarchy we have arrived at represents improvement or advance? The response unfortunately is as indecisive as the one concerning moral progress, and for the same reason. On one hand, civilization has brought a lower infant mortality rate due to better diet, hygiene, and medical care; less vulnerability to infectious disease for the same reasons; greater economic security due to increased economic diversification; less danger from local famine due to improved systems of transportation and economic organization; greater material comfort due to improved housing, and the like. But on the other hand, we have pollution, the horrors of modern warfare, and the boredom and alienation of factory work, to name a few. On one hand we have labor-saving devices like automatic dishwashers, but on the other hand we have to spend our lives on a treadmill to pay for them. The tally sheet is simply too complicated to make an overall judgment. It is not at all clear that other people should want to become like Western civilization.

What we can say about the hierarchy is that the nations that fall toward the upper end of the scale have greater resources than the others. They have better technical knowledge from which the entire world may benefit—knowledge about hygiene, diet, crop rotation, soils, and the like. They also have the physical capacity to undertake programs of assistance when other societies are interested. Yet the higher civilizations also have the capacity to do far greater harm. The industrial system has exploited the powerless, ravaged the environment, meddled in the affairs of other countries, and conducted war in ways that the simpler societies never dreamed of. Even when we set out altruistically to help others we often mismanage the effort or misunderstand what it is we should do. Just as it is not at all clear that industrial civilization provides a happier or more fulfilling life for its members, so it is not clear whether its overall influence on those below it in the hierarchy has been to their detriment or benefit. This is a pessimistic age, and at this point it is difficult to suppress a strong sense of despair on this score.

The place of Western civilization in the hierarchy of human societies is very different from what it was thought to be by Victorian anthropologists, who saw the differences among societies at bottom as a matter of intelligence: Civilization is more thoughtful and shows greater sense than the lower societies, and it provides a happier and more benign mode of living; savages would embrace our way of life if they had the intelligence to understand it, for their institutions are but imperfect specimens of our own. Clearly this is inadequate. Many areas of life cannot be judged by standards that apply across cultural boundaries, for in many respects cultures are oriented in widely different directions. Still, all people desire material comfort and security, and in this sense Western civilization is distinguished from other cultures. The relationship among societies in this respect is one of asymmetry. Just as we may do far more harm to others than they can do to us, so we may do them more good, and we have the obligation to share the material advantages our civilization has to offer. Yet this asymmetry should not be confused with superiority. As a total way of life ours may not be preferable to others, and we need not try to turn them into copies of Western civilization.

An important implication follows from these conclusions: It is possible to arrive at a general principle for evaluating institutions without assuming that ours is a superior way of life. Herskovits for one seems to have believed that this could not be done, and that any general moral principle we might advance would express our own cultural bias and would tacitly make us appear to occupy a position superior to the rest. But this is not so. The matter of arriving at general moral principles and of how we measure up to these principles are two very separate issues.

The idea of ethical relativism in anthropology has had a complicated history. Through the 1930s the discipline expressed an overwhelming confidence in the notion, a confidence that was fortified by the empirical findings about the variability of moral values from culture to culture. And relativism was thought to be an idea of signal importance, for it could be used in world affairs and would contribute to peace and human understanding. But suddenly and with firm conviction, relativism was swept aside. It had all been a mistake.

Was relativism completely mistaken? After we have excised what is unacceptable, is there something left, a residuum of some kind, that still warrants approval? Certainly the relativists' call for tolerance contained an element that is hard to fault. This is the value of freedom: People ought to be free to live as they choose, to be free from the coercion of others more powerful than they. Equally fundamental, perhaps, is the message that relativism contained about the place of Western civilization among human societies. Rejected was the smug belief in Western superiority that dominated anthropological thinking during the 1800s. Just as the universe has not looked the same since the Copernican revolution, so the world and our place in it has not looked the same since ethical relativism appeared at about the turn of the century.

## NOTE

1. The World Bank and other organizations commonly use a number of objective measures in assessing such matters as poverty, physical quality of life, and economic and social development. For example, see Lizer 1977, and World Bank 1979, pp. 117–188.

# Intercultural Personhood: An Integration of Eastern and Western Perspectives

YOUNG YUN KIM

Today we live in a world of global community. Rigid adherence to the culture of our youth is neither feasible nor desirable. The tightly knit communication web has brought cultures of the world together closer than ever before. Strong cultural identity is more a nostalgic conception than a realistic assessment of our attributes. Indeed, we live in an exciting time in which we are challenged to examine ourselves critically. As Toffler (1980) states in *The Third Wave,* "Humanity faces a quantum leap forward. It faces the deepest social upheaval and creative restructuring of all time. Without clearly recognizing it, we are engaged in building a remarkable new civilization from the ground up" (p. 10).

Reflecting the interactive realities of our time, a number of attempts have been made to explore ideologies that are larger than national and cultural interests and that embrace all humanity. As early as 1946, Northrop, in *The Meeting of the East and the West,* proposed an "international cultural ideal" to provide intellectual and emotional foundations for what he envisioned as "partial world sovereignty." Among contemporary critics of culture, Thompson (1973) explored the concept of "planetary culture" in which Eastern mysticism was integrated with Western science and rationalism. Similarly, Elgin (1981) proposed "voluntary simplicity" as an

emerging global "common sense" and a practical lifestyle to reconcile the willful, rational approach to life of the West and the holistic, spiritual orientation of the East.

In this frame of ideas, the present writer has presented the concept "intercultural person" as an image of future human development (Kim 1982; Gudykunst & Kim 1984). The intercultural person represents a type of person whose cognitive, affective, and behavioral characteristics are not limited but are open to growth beyond the psychological parameters of his or her own culture. Other similar terms such as "international" (Lutzker 1960), "universal" (Walsh 1973), and "multicultural" (Adler 1982) person have also been used to project an essentially similar image of personhood with varying degrees of descriptive and explanatory utility.

To envision how we may renew ourselves and grow beyond our own cultural conditioning in this intercultural world, we need to comprehend and to seek meaning and order in the complexity of the fundamental human condition. Our task is to look at both Eastern and Western cultures in their "original form" rather than in their contemporary cultural patterns. The linking back to the origin not only enables us to see the respective foundation of the two cultures clearly, but also creates the possibility of recognizing and bringing into play new lines of development. In this essay, we will examine the basic cultural *a priori* or world view of East and West, concepts deeply rooted in the religious and philosophical traditions of the two cultural groups. Once we rediscover the cultural roots of Eastern and Western worlds, we will then be able to develop a broad perspective on the ground-level human conditions without being restricted by our own cultural "blind spots." Such a pan-human understanding will enable us to construct an image of intercultural personhood—a way of life that is called for by the increasingly intercultural realities of our world.

## EASTERN AND WESTERN WORLD VIEWS

Traditional cultures throughout Asian countries including India, Tibet, Japan, China, Korea, and

Southeast Asia have been profoundly influenced by such religious and philosophical systems as Buddhism, Hinduism, Taoism, and Zen. On the other hand, the Western European nations have historically followed the Greek and the Judaeo-Christian traditions. Of course, any attempt to present the cultural *a priori* of these two broadly categorized civilizations inevitably sacrifices specific details and the uniqueness of variations within each group. No two individuals or groups are identical in their beliefs and behaviors, and whatever we characterize about one culture or cultural group must be thought of as variable rather than as rigidly structured. Nevertheless, there are several key factors in the two perspectives that distinguish each group clearly from the other. To examine these factors is to indicate the equally evident interconnectedness that ties different nations together to constitute the Eastern or Western cultural group.

The characterization of Eastern and Western world views in this section and throughout this article is based on the observations of many authors. Of the existing comparative cultural analyses, Northrop's *The Meeting of the East and the West* (1946/1966), Gulick's *The East and the West* (1963), Nakamura's *Ways of Thought of Eastern Peoples*(1964), Oliver's *Communication and Culture in Ancient India and China* (1971), Capra's *The Tao of Physics (1975),* and Elgin's *Voluntary Simplicity* (1981) have provided a particular influence.

## Universe and Nature

One of the most fundamental ways culture conditions our existence is through explicit and implicit teachings about our relationship to the nature of the universe and to the non-human natural world. Traditional Eastern and Western perspectives diverge significantly in this basic premise. As Needham (1951) observed in his article, "Human laws and the laws of nature in China and the West," people in the West have been dominated by the view that the universe was initially created, and has since been externally controlled, by a divine power.

In this sense, the Western view of the universe is characteristically dualistic, materialistic, and life-less. The Judaeo-Christian tradition sets God apart from this reality; having created it and set it into motion, God could then be viewed as apart from His creation. The fundamental material of the universe is thought to be elementary particles of matter that interact with one another in a predictable fashion. Furthermore, since the foundation of the universe is seen as consisting of matter, it is viewed as essentially non-living. It is seen as an inanimate machine in which humankind occupies a unique and elevated position among the sparse life-forms that exist. Assuming a relatively barren universe, it seems only rational that humans exploit the lifeless material universe (and the lesser life-forms of nature) on behalf of those who live most intensely—humankind itself.

On the other hand, the Eastern view is profoundly holistic, dynamic, and spiritual. From the Eastern perspective, the entirety of the universe is a vast, multidimensional, living organism consisting of many interrelated parts and forces. The universe is conscious and engaged in a continuous dance of creation: the cosmic pattern is viewed as self-contained and self-organizing. It unfolds itself because of its own inner necessity and not because it is "ordered" to by any external volitional power.

What exists in the universe is a manifestation of a divine life force. Beneath the surface appearance of things, an ultimate reality is continuously creating, sustaining, and infusing our worldly experience. The all-sustaining life force that instant by instant creates our manifest universe is not apart from ourselves or our worldly existence. Rather, it is continuously creating and intimately infusing every aspect of the cosmos—from its most minute details to its most grand scale features.

Thus, the Eastern view reveres the common source out of which all things arise, and at the same time recognizes that everything in this dynamic world is fluid, ever-changing, and impermanent. In Hinduism, all static forms are *maya,* that is, they exist only as illusory concepts. This idea of the impermanence of all forms is the starting point of Buddhism. The Buddha taught that "all compounded things are impermanent," and that all suffering in the world arises from our trying to cling to fixed forms—objects, people, or ideas—instead of accepting the world as is moves. This notion of the impermanence of all forms and the appreciation of the aliveness of the universe in the Eastern world view is strongly contrasted with the Western emphasis on the visible forms of physical reality and their improvement through social and material/technological progress.

## Knowledge

Since the East and the West have different cosmic patterns, we can expect a different approach to knowledge. In the East, because the universe is a harmonious organism, there is a lack of any dualism in the cosmic pattern as well as in epistemological patterns. The Eastern view places an emphasis on perceiving and knowing things and events holistically and synthetically, rather than analytically. Furthermore, the ultimate purpose of knowledge is to transcend the apparent contrasts and to "see" the interrelatedness and underlying unity of all things.

When the Eastern mystics tell us they experience all things and events as manifestations of a basic oneness, this does not mean they consider all things equal. They recognize the individuality of things but at the same time are aware that all differences and contrasts are relative within an all-embracing unity. The awareness that all opposites are polar, and thus a unity, is seen as one of the highest aims of knowledge. Suzuki (1968) writes, "The fundamental idea of Buddhism is to pass beyond the world of opposites, a world built up by intellectual distinctions and emotional defilements, and to realize the spiritual world of non-distinction, which involves achieving an absolute point of view" (p. 18).

Since all opposites are interdependent, their conflict can never result in the total victory of one side, but will always be a manifestation of the interplay between the two sides. In the East, therefore, a virtuous person is not one who undertakes the impossible task of striving for the "good" and eliminating the "bad," but rather one who is able to maintain a dynamic balance between the two. Transcending the opposites, one becomes aware of the relativity and polar relationship of all opposites. One

realizes that good and bad, pleasure and pain, life and death, winning and losing, light and dark, are not absolute experiences belonging to different categories, but are merely two sides of the same reality—extreme aspects of a single whole. This point has been emphasized most extensively by the Chinese sages in their symbolism of the archetypal poles, yin and yang. And the opposites cease to be opposites in the very essence of Tao. To know the Tao—the illustrious way of the universe—is the ultimate purpose of human learning.

This holistic approach to knowledge in the East emphasizes understanding concepts and the aesthetic components of things by intuition. A concept by intuition is one of complete meaning and is something immediately experienced, apprehended, and contemplated. Northrop (1946/1966) described it more accurately as the "differentiated aesthetic continuum." Within the total differentiated aesthetic continuum, there is no distinction between subjective and objective. The aesthetic continuum is a single all-embracing continuity. The aesthetic part of the self is also an essential part of the aesthetic object, whether it is a person or a flower. With respect to the immediately apprehended aesthetic nature, the person is identical with the aesthetic object; only with respect to his differentiation is the self other than the aesthetic object.

In this orientation, Taoism pursues the all-embracing, immediately experienced, emotionally moving aesthetic continuum with respect to its manifestations in the differentiated, sensed aesthetic qualities of nature. Confucianism pursues the all-embracing aesthetic continuum with respect to its manifestations in human nature and its moral implications for human society. The Taoist claim is that only by seeing the aesthetic continuity in its all-embracing-ness as ultimate and irreducible will we properly understand the meaning of the universe and nature. The Confucian claim, similarly, is that only if one takes the same standpoint, that of recognizing the all-embracing aesthetic whole to be an ultimate and irreducible part of human nature, will we have a compassionate feeling for human beings other than ourselves.

The ultimate, irreducible, and undifferentiated

aesthetic continuum is the Eastern philosopher's conception of the constituted world. The differentiations within it, such as particular scenes, events, or persons, are not the irreducible atomic identities, but merely arise out of the ultimate undifferentiated reality of the aesthetic continuum. Sooner or later, they fade back into it again and thus are transitory and impermanent. When Eastern sages insist that one must become self-less, they mean that the self consists of two components: one, a differentiated, unique element, distinguishing one person from any other person; and the other, the all-embracing, aesthetically immediate, emotionally moving, compassionate, undifferentiated component. The former is temporary and transitory, and the cherishing of it, the desire for its immortality, is the source of suffering and selfishness. The part of the self that is not transitory but rather immortal is the aesthetic component, and it is identical not merely in all persons, but in all aesthetic objects throughout the universe.

While the East has concentrated its mental processes on the all-embracing, holistic, intuitive, aesthetic continuum, the Western pursuit of knowledge has been based on the doctrine of a dualistic world view. Since in the West the world and its various components came into existence through the individual creative acts of a God, the fundamental question is, how can I reach out to the external inanimate world or to people? In this question, there is a basic dichotomy between the knower and the things to be known.

Along with this epistemological dualism, the West has emphasized rationality in the pursuit of knowledge. Since the Greek philosopher Plato "discovered" reason, virtually all subsequent Western thought—the themes, the questions, and the terms—exists in essence in the writing of Plato (Wei 1980). Even Aristotle, the great hero of all anti-Platonists, was not an exception. Although Aristotle did not have, as Plato did, a realm of eternal essences that were "really real" and that guaranteed the primacy of reason, he was by no means inclined to deny this realm.

Thus, while the East has tended to emphasize the direct experience of oneness via intuitive con-

cepts and contemplation, the West has viewed the faculty of the intellect as the primary instrument of worldly mastery. While thinking in the East tends to conclude in more or less vague, imprecise statements with existential flexibility, Western thinking emphasizes clear and distinct ideas by means of categorization and the linear, analytic logic of syllogism. While the Eastern view expresses its drive for growth in spiritual attainment of oneness with the universe, the Western view expresses its drive for growth in material progress and social change.

## Time

Closely parallel to the differing perception of the nature of knowledge, the perception and experience of time differs significantly between Eastern and Western traditions.

Along with the immediate, undifferentiated experiencing of here and now, Eastern time orientation can be portrayed as a placid, silent pool within which ripples come and go. Historically the East has tended to view material existence as cyclical and has often characterized worldly existence with the metaphor of a wheel. The "wheel of existence" is continually turning but is not seen as going in any predetermined direction. Although individuals in the world may experience a rise or fall in their personal fortunes, the lot of the whole is felt to be fundamentally unchanging. As Northrop (1946/1966) illustrated, "the aesthetic continuum is the great mother of creation, giving birth to the ineffable beauty of the golden yellows on the mountain landscape as the sun drops low in the late afternoon, only a moment later to receive that differentiation back into itself and to put another in its place without any effort" (p. 343).

Because worldly time is not experienced as going anywhere and because in spiritual time there is nowhere to go but to eternity within the now, the future is expected to be virtually the same as the past. Recurrence in both cosmic and psychological realms is very much a part of Eastern thought. Thus, the individual's aim is not to escape from the circular movement into linear and profane time, but to become a part of the eternal through the aesthetic experience of here and now and the conscious evolution of spirituality in knowing the all-embracing, undifferentiated wholeness.

Whereas the East traditionally has perceived time as a dynamic wheel with circular movements and the "now" as a reflection of the eternal, the West has represented time either as an arrow or as a moving river that comes out of a distant place and past (not here and now) and goes into an equally distant place and future (also not here and now). In this linear view of time, history is goal-directed and gradually progressing in a certain direction, such as toward universal salvation and the second coming of Christ or, in a secular form, toward an ideal state such as boundless freedom or a classless society.

Closely corresponding to the above comparison of Eastern and Western time orientations is the recent work of anthropologist Edward Hall in his *Beyond Culture* (1976) and *The Dance of Life: The Other Dimension of Time* (1983). Hall considers Asian cultures "polychronic" and Western cultures "monochronic." The polychronic system is less inclined to adhere rigidly to time as a tangible, discrete, and linear entity; it emphasizes completion of transactions here and now, often carrying out more than one activity simultaneously. On the other hand, the monochronic system emphasizes schedules, segmentation, promptness, and standardization of human activities. The traditional Eastern orientation to time depends on the synchronization of human behavior with the rhythms of nature. The Western orientation to time depends on the synchronization of human behavior with the rhythms of clocks or machines.

## Communication

The historical ideologies examined so far have made the empirical content of the East and West what they are. Eastern and Western perspectives on the universe, nature, knowledge, and time are reflected in many specific activities of individuals as they relate themselves to fellow human beings—how individuals view "self" and the group and how they use verbal and nonverbal symbols in communication.

First, the view of self and identity cultivated in the Eastern view of reality is embedded within an immutable social order. People tend to acquire their sense of identity from an affiliation with, and participation in, a virtually unchanging social order. The sense of "self" that emerges from this social context is not the strongly differentiated "existential ego" of the West, but a more weakly distinct and unchanging "social ego" as pointed out in many contemporary anthropological studies. Thus, individual members of the family tend to be more willing to submit their own self-interest to that of the family. Individuals and families are often expected to submit their views to those of the community or the state.

Also, the Eastern view accepts hierarchy in social order. In a hierarchical structure, individuals are seen as differing in status although all are equally necessary for the total system and its process. A natural result of this orientation is the emphasis on authority—the authority of the parents over the children, of the grandparents over their descendants, and of the official head of the community, the clan, and the state over all its members. Authoritarianism is a distinct feature of Eastern life, not only in government, business, and family, but also in education and beliefs. The more ancient a tradition, the greater its authority.

Furthermore, the Eastern view asserts that who we are is not limited to our physical existence. Consciousness is seen as the bridge between the finite and differentiated (our sense of uniqueness) and the infinite and undifferentiated (the experience of wholeness and eternity). With sufficient training, each person can discover that who we are is correlated with nature and the divine. All are one and the same in the sense that the divine, undifferentiated, aesthetic continuum of the universe is manifested in us in nature. Through this aesthetic connection, we and nature are no other than the Tao, Ultimate Reality, the divine life force, nirvana, God.

On the other hand, the Western view—in which God, nature, and humans are distinctly differentiated—fosters the development of autonomous individuals with strong ego identification. The dualistic world view is manifested in an individual's view of his or her relationship to other persons and nature.

Interpersonal relationships, therefore, are essentially egalitarian—cooperative arrangements between two equal "partners" in which the personal needs and interests of each party are more or less equally respected, negotiated, or "compromised." While the East emphasizes submission (or conformity) of the individual to the group, the West encourages individuality and individual needs to override the group. If the group no longer serves the individual's needs, it—not the individual—must be changed. Thus, the meaning of an interpersonal relationship is decided primarily by what functions each party performs to satisfy the needs of the other. A relationship is considered healthy to the extent that it serves the expected function for all parties involved. As anthropologist Frances Hsu (1981) notes, individualism is a central theme of the Western personality, which distinguishes the Western world from the non-Western.

This functional, pragmatic interpersonal orientation of the West is contrasted with the Eastern tradition—where group membership is a "given" that goes unchallenged—in which individuals must conform to the group in the case of conflicting interest. Members of the group are encouraged to maintain harmony and to minimize competition. Individuality is discouraged while moderation, modesty, and "bending" of one's ego are praised. In some cases, individual and group achievement (in a material sense) must be forsaken to maintain group harmony.

In this social milieu, the primary source of interpersonal understanding is the unwritten and often unspoken norms, values, and ritualized mannerisms relevant to a particular interpersonal context. Rather than relying heavily on verbalized, logical expressions, the Eastern communicator "grasps" the aesthetic "essence" of the communication dynamics by observing the various nonverbal and circumstantial cues. Intuition rather than logical reasoning plays a central role in the Eastern interpersonal understanding of how one talks, how one addresses the other and why, under what circumstances, on what topics, in what varied styles, with what intent, and with what effect. Verbal articulation is less important than nonverbal, contextual sensitivity and

appropriateness. Eastern cultures favor verbal hesitance and ambiguity to avoid disturbing or offending others (Doi 1976; Cathcart & Cathcart 1976). Silence is often preferred to eloquent verbalization even in expressing strong compliments or affection. Sometimes individuals are suspicious of the genuineness of excessive verbal praise or compliments since, to the Eastern view, true feelings are intuitively apparent and therefore do not need to be, nor can be, articulated. In this sense, the burden of communicating effectively is shared equally between all parties involved.

While interpersonal meaning in the Eastern perspective resides primarily in the subtle, implicit, nonverbal, contextual realm and is understood aesthetically and intuitively, the Western communicative mode is primarily a direct, explicit, verbal realm, relying heavily on logical and rational perception, thinking, and articulation. Communicators are seen as distinct individuals, expressing their individuality through verbal articulation and assertiveness. Feelings inside are not to be intuitively "grasped" and understood, but to be clearly verbalized and discussed. In this sense, the burden of communicating effectively lies primarily in the speaker.

The above characterization of communication patterns in the Eastern and the Western traditions parallels the notion of "high-context" and "low-context" communication proposed by Hall (1976). Hall's conceptualization is based on empirical studies of many cultures, and it focuses on the degree to which information is either embedded in physical context or internalized in the person communicating. In this scheme, a low-context communication—more prevalent in the West than in the East—is when most of the interpersonal information is carried in the explicit, verbalized codes.

## A SYNTHESIS

So far, a number of basic dimensions of cultural *a priori* in the Eastern and the Western traditions have been examined. To recapitulate, the many differences between the two civilizations stem fundamentally from their respective premises on the reality of the universe, nature, time, and communication. Based on an organic, holistic, and cyclic perspective, the East has developed an epistemology that emphasizes direct, immediate, and aesthetic components in human nature's experience of the world. The ultimate aim of human learning is to transcend the immediate, differentiated self and to develop an integrative perception of the undifferentiated universe; that is, to be spiritually one with the universe and to find the eternal within the present moment. In this view, the present moment is a reflection of the eternal, and the eternal resides in the present moment.

On the other hand, the West, founded on the cosmology of dualism, determinism, and materialism, encourages an outlook that is rational, analytic, and indirect. History is viewed as a linear progression from the past into the future. The acquisition of knowledge is not so much for spiritual enhancement as for utilization to improve the human condition.

These different world views, in turn, have been reflected in the individual conception of the self, of others, and of the group. While the East has stressed the primacy of the group over the individual, the West has stressed the primacy of the individual over the group. Interpersonally, the Eastern concept of self is less differentiated and more deeply merged in "group ego," while the West encourages distinct and autonomous individuality. Explicit, clear, and logical verbalization has been the most salient feature in the Western communication tradition, compared to the implicit, intuitive, nonverbal messages in the East.

Thus, the mechanistic Western world view has helped to systematically describe and explain the physical phenomena we encounter daily. It has proved extremely successful in technological and scientific development. The West has also learned, however, that the mechanistic world view and the corresponding communication patterns are often inadequate for the subtle, complex phenomena of human relationship—causing alienation from self and others. The West has also learned that its dualistic distinction between humanity and nature has brought about alienation from nature. The analyti-

cal mind of the West has led to modern science and technology, but it has also resulted in knowledge that is departmentalized, specialized, fragmented, and detached from the fuller totality of reality.

The East has not experienced the alienation the West has been experiencing in recent centuries. But, at the same time, the East has not developed as much science and technology since its view of the world does not promote material and social development. It does not encourage worldly activism or promote the empowerment of individuals to fundamentally change the social and material circumstances of life. Furthermore, instead of building greater ego strength and the capacity for more self-determining behavior, the Eastern view tends to work toward ego extinction (transcendence). It also tends to encourage ego dependency and passivity since people feel locked into an unchanging social order.

It should be stressed at this point that the Western emphasis on logical, theoretical, dualistic, and analytic thinking does not suggest that it has been devoid of an intuitive, direct, purely empirical, aesthetic element. Similarly, emphasizing the Western contributions (of worldly dynamism and sociomaterial development) does not suggest that the East has been devoid of learning in these areas. The differences are not in diametric opposition: rather they are differences in emphasis. As a result, the range of sophistication of Western contributions to the sociomaterial process far exceeds the historical learning of the East. Conversely, the aesthetic and holistic view and self-mastery of the East offers a greater depth and range of human experience vis-à-vis other humans, the natural world, and the universe, than the West.

Thus, East and West are not competing views of reality, but are, instead, intensely complementary. It needs to be emphasized that the values, behaviors, and institutions of the West should not be substituted for their Eastern counterparts, and vice versa. The West should no more adopt the world views of the East than the East should adopt the world views of the West. Our task is not to trade one view for another—thereby repeating the excesses of the other—but to integrate. Our task is to find our human unity and simultaneously to express diversity. The purpose of evolution is not to create a homogeneous mass, but to continuously unfold a diverse yet organic whole.

## COMPLEMENTARITY

To explore the possibilities of integrating the two cultural traditions in a limited space, we need to take a one-sided perspective by focusing on significant limitations in either of the two and then projecting the complementary aspects from the other. In the following discussion, then, we will look critically at possible limitations of the Western cultural orientation, and attempt to integrate the complementary Eastern cultural insights.

A growing realization of limitations in the Western world view is expressed by many writers. Using the term "extension transference," Hall (1976) points out the danger of the common intellectual maneuver in which the extensional systems—including language, logic, technology, institutions, and scheduling—are confused with or take the place of the process extended. For instance, the tendency in the West is to assume that the remedy for problems with technology should not be the attempt to minimize our reliance on technology, but the development of even more technology. Burke (1974) calls this tendency of extension transference "technologism":

*There lie the developments whereby "technologism" confronts its inner contradictions, a whole new realm in which the heights of human rationality, as expressed in industrialism, readily become "solutions" that are but the source of new and aggravated problems* (p. 148)

Criticisms have also been directed at the rigid scientific dogmatism that insists on the discovery of "truth" based on mechanistic, linear causality and "objectivity." In this regard, Thayer (1983) comments:

*What the scientific mentality attempts to emulate, mainly, is the presumed method of laboratory science. But laboratory science predicts nothing that it does not control or that is not otherwise fully determined. . . . One cannot successfully study relatively open systems with methods that are appro-*

*priate only for closed systems. Is it possible that this is the kind of mentality that precludes its own success?* (p. 88)

Similarly, Hall (1976) points out that the Western emphasis on logic as synonymous with "truth" denies that part of the human self that integrates. Hall sees logical thinking as only a small fraction of our mental capabilities, and he suggests that there are many different and legitimate ways of thinking that have tended to be less emphasized in Western cultures (p. 9)

The criticisms raised by these and other critics of Western epistemology do not deny the value of rational, inferential knowledge. Instead, they relate to the error in traditional Western philosophy and science, of regarding concepts that do not fit into its mode as not equally valid. It refers to the arrogance or over-confidence of believing that scientific knowledge is the only way to discover "truth," when, in reality, the very process of doing science requires immediate, aesthetic experience of the phenomenon under investigation. Without the immediately apprehended component, the theoretical hypotheses proposed could not be tested empirically with respect to their truth or falsity and, therefore, would lack relevance to the corresponding reality. As Einstein once stated:

*Science is the attempt to make the chaotic diversity of our sense-experience correspond to a logically uniform system of thought. In this system single experiences must be correlated with the theoretic structure in such a way that the resulting coordination is complete and convincing* (Northrop, 1946/1966, p. 443).

In this description of science, Einstein is careful to indicate that the relation between the theoretically postulated component and the immediately experienced aesthetic component is one of correspondence.

In fact, the wide spectrum of our everyday life activities demands both scientific and aesthetic modes of apprehension: from critical analysis to perception of wholes; from doubt and skepticism to unconditional appreciation; from abstraction to concreteness; from the general and regular to the individual and unique; from the literalism of technological terms to the power and richness of poetic language, silence, and art; from casual acquaintances to intimate personal engagement. If we limit ourselves to the traditional Western scientific mode of apprehension, and if we do not value and practice the Eastern aesthetic mode, we are limiting the essential human to only a part of the full span of life activities.

One potential benefit of incorporating the Eastern aesthetic orientation into Western life is a heightened sense of freedom. As discussed earlier, the aesthetic component of human nature is in part indeterminate, and it is this aesthetic component in us that is the basis of our freedom. We would also transcend the clock-bound worldly time to the Eternal Now, the timeless moment embedded in the center of each moment. By withdrawing into the indeterminate aesthetic component of our nature, away from the determinate, transitory circumstances, we may in part overcome the pressures of everyday events and creatively integrate them as a basis for the renewal of our life spirit. The traditional Eastern practice of meditation is designed primarily for the purpose of moving one's consciousness from the determinate to the indeterminate, freer state.

Second, the Eastern view would bring the West to a heightened awareness of the aliveness of the universe. The universe is engaged in a continuous dance of creation at each instant. Everything is intensely alive—brimming with a silent, clear energy that creates, sustains, and infuses all that exists. With the expanded perspective on time, we would increase our sensitivity to rhythms of nature such as the seasons and the cycles of birth and decay.

Third, the holistic, aesthetic component, in human nature and in the nature of all things, is a factor that pacifies us. Because of its all-embracing oneness and unity, the indeterminate aesthetic continuum also tends to make us compassionate and flexible human beings with intuitive sensitivity—not only for other humans but for all of nature's creatures. In this regard, Maslow (1971) refers to Taoistic receptivity or "let-be" as an important attribute of "self-actualizing" persons:

*We may speak of this respectful attention to the matter-in-paradigm as a kind of courtesy or deference (without intrusion of the controlling will) which is akin to 'taking it seriously.' This amounts to treating it as an end, something per se, with its own right to be, rather than as a means to some end other than itself; i.e., as a tool for some extrinsic purpose* (p. 68).

Such aesthetic perception is an instrument of intimate human meeting, a way to bridge the gap between individuals and groups. In dealing with each other aesthetically, we do not subject ourselves to a rigid scheme but do our best in each new situation, listening to the silences as well as to the words of the other, and experiencing the other person or group as a whole living entity without being biased by our own egocentric and ethnocentric demands. A similar attitude can be developed toward the physical world around us, to strengthen our determination to achieve maximum ecological and environmental integrity.

## TOWARD INTERCULTURAL PERSONHOOD

The movement from a cultural to an intercultural perspective in our individual and collective consciousness presents one of the most significant and exciting challenges of our time. As Toffler (1980) convincingly documented and articulated in *The Third Wave,* there are numerous indications today that point clearly to the need for us to actively pursue a new personhood and a culture that integrates Eastern and Western world views. Toffler notes:

*This new culture—oriented to change and growing diversity—attempts to integrate the new view of nature, of evolution and progress, the new, richer conceptions of time and space, and the fusion of reductionism and wholism with a new causality* (p. 309).

Similarly, Gebser's "integral consciousness" (Mickunas 1973) projects an emerging mode of experiencing reality in which "rational," "mythological," and other modes of consciousness are integrated.

If we are to actively participate in this evolutionary process, the dualism inherent in our thinking process, which puts materialism against spiritualism, West against East, must be transcended. The traditional Western emphasis on the intellect and on material progress need not be viewed as "wrong" or "bad." Rather, the Western orientation is a necessary part of an evolutionary stage, out of which yet another birth of higher consciousness—an integration of East and West—might subsequently evolve. We need to acknowledge that both rational and intuitive modes of experiencing life should be cultivated fully. When we realize that both types of concepts are real, ultimate, and meaningful, we also realize that Eastern and Western cultures have given expression to something in part true. The two seemingly incompatible perspectives can be related and reconciled without contradictions in a new, higher-level, intercultural perspective—one that more closely approximates the expression of the whole truth of life.

As Jantsch (1980) observes, "Life, and especially human life, now appears as a process of self-realization" (p. 307). With an openness toward change, a willingness to revise our own cultural premises, and the enthusiasm to work it through, we are on the way to cultivating our fullest human potentialities and to contributing our share in this enormous process of civilizational change. Together, the East and the West are showing each other the way.

## REFERENCES

Adler, P. "Beyond cultural identity: Reflections on cultural and multicultural man." In L. Samovar and R. Porter (eds.), *Intercultural Communication: A Reader,* 3rd ed. Belmont, Calif.: Wadsworth, 1982, pp. 389–408.

Burke, K. "Communication and the human condition." *Communication* 1, 1974, pp. 135–152.

Capra, F. *The Tao of Physics.* Boulder, Colo.: Shambhala, 1975.

Cathcart, D., and Cathcart, R. "Japanese social experience and concept of groups." In L. Samovar and R. Porter (eds.), *Intercultural Communication: A Reader,* 2nd ed. Belmont, Calif.: Wadsworth, 1976, pp. 58–66.

Doi, T., "The Japanese patterns of communication and the concept of amae." In L. Samovar and R. Porter (eds.), *Intercultural Communication: A Reader,* 2nd ed. Belmont, Calif.: Wadsworth, 1976, pp. 188–193.

Elgin, D. *Voluntary Simplicity.* New York: Bantam Books, 1981.

Gudykunst, W., and Kim, Y. *Communicating with Strangers: An Approach to Intercultural Communication.* Reading, Mass.: Addison-Wesley Publishing Company, 1984.

Gulick, S. *The East and the West.* Rutland, Vt.: Charles E. Tuttle, 1963.

Hall, E. *Beyond Culture.* Garden City, New York: Anchor Books, 1976.

Hall, E. *The Dance of Life: The Other Dimension of Time.* Garden City, New York: Anchor Press, 1983.

Hsu, F. *The Challenges of the American Dream.* Belmont, Calif.: Wadsworth, 1981.

Jantsch, E. *The Self-Organizing Universe.* New York: Pergamon, 1980.

Kim, Y. "Becoming intercultural and human development." Paper presented at the annual conference of the International Communication Association, Boston, Mass., May 1982.

Lutzker, D. "Internationalism as a predictor of cooperative behavior." *Journal of Conflict Resolution* 4, 1960, pp. 426–430.

Maslow, A. *The Farther Reaches of Human Nature.* New York: Viking, 1971.

Mickunas, A. "Civilizations as structures of consciousness." *Main Currents* 29, no. 5, 1973, pp. 179–185.

Nakamura, H. *Ways of Thought of Eastern Peoples.* Honolulu: University of Hawaii Press, 1964.

Needham, J. "Human laws and laws of nature in China and the West." *Journal of the History of Ideas* XII, 1951.

Northrop, F. *The Meeting of the East and the West.* New York: Collier Books, 1966 (1946).

Oliver, R. *Communication and Culture in Ancient India and China.* New York: Syracuse University Press, 1971.

Suzuki, D. *The Essence of Buddhism* Kyoto, Japan: Hozokan, 1968.

Thayer, L. "On 'doing' research and 'explaining' things." *Journal of Communication* 33, no. 3, 1983, pp. 80–91.

Thompson, W. *Passages About Earth: An Exploration of the New Planetary Culture*. New York: Harper & Row, 1973.

Toffler, A. *The Third Wave*. New York: Bantam Books, 1980.

Walsh, J. *Intercultural Education in the Community of Man*. Honolulu: University of Hawaii Press, 1973.

Wei, A. "Cultural variations in perception." Paper presented at the Sixth Annual Third World Conference, Chicago, Ill., March 1980.

# Intercultural Education for Multicultural Societies: Critical Issues

ROSITA D. ALBERT
HARRY C. TRIANDIS

This article focuses on the need for intercultural education in multicultural societies. In the first section, we begin by presenting evidence for the notion that individuals from a given cultural group develop behavior patterns and subjective cultures (Triandis 1972) that are functional for their particular environment. We then indicate that when, due to such factors as immigration, colonization, etc., such individuals are forced to function in a different cultural environment, they are likely to experience stress, alienation, and other negative consequences.

In the second section, we propose that an important objective of education should be to prepare such individuals to function effectively in *both* their culture of origin and in their new culture. We further suggest that all children in a multicultural society should have the benefit of intercultural education. We propose that teachers, as well as pupils, should be made aware of cultural differences and should learn something about the patterns of behavior, values, and expectations of persons from other cultures. We present evidence from our own research, as well as that of other researchers, which illustrates the need for this kind of knowledge on the part of teachers.

From the *International Journal of Intercultural Relations* 9 (1985), 391–337. Reprinted by permission of the publisher. Professor Albert teaches at the University of Minnesota and Professor Triandis teaches at the University of Illinois.

In the third part of the article, we present a number of objections which have been raised to intercultural education and propose some refutations based on current work.

In the fourth section, we present three approaches for teaching culture and discuss the advantages and disadvantages of each. The attributional approach (a cognitive approach) is presented in some detail because it is especially suited for use in educational settings. We cite evidence of its effectiveness from evaluation studies done by ourselves and others.

We conclude with a section on the implications of intercultural education.

## ETHNICITY, BEHAVIOR, AND SUBJECTIVE CULTURE

In many countries, the population is polyethnic. This is the case in the United States, where a number of distinct groups (i.e. blacks, Native Americans, Latin Americans, to mention just a few) enjoy cultural traditions that are different from the traditions of the white, Anglo-Saxon or melting-pot-produced majority. A characteristic of any cultural group is that it has a particular way of viewing the social environment, that is, a unique subjective culture (Triandis 1972). Such subjective cultures lead members of a cultural or ethnic group[1] to behave in characteristic ways and to perceive their own behavior and the behaviors of others in a particular manner.

Personality refers to a behavior pattern characteristic of a particular individual. To the extent that ethnic groups have characteristic ways of behaving, they exhibit somewhat different distributions of behavior configurations. Thus, for example, it is widely acknowledged that Latin American individuals tend to be more (overtly) expressive than Anglo-Saxons. An ethnic group, then, may consist of individuals having characteristic behavior patterns and subjective cultures. Behavior patterns comprise patterns of abilities, habits, and predispositions to behave which emerge when individuals interact with their social environments. Subjective cultures can be viewed as consisting of norms, roles, values, and attitudes characteristic of persons in a particular social environment. An important aspect of subjective culture is the language used by an ethnic group, since language is intimately connected with the way in which experience is interpreted and with the cognitive and affective categories which are used to conceptualize the world (Triandis 1964, 1972).

Most of the elements comprising the behavior patterns and subjective cultures of an ethnic group can be shown to be functional for the particular environment in which that cultural group has existed for a long time. For example, in the Arctic, survival requires the development of skills in hunting. Such hunting is usually done most effectively on an individual basis. Studies (e.g., Barry, Child, and Bacon 1959) of peoples who subsist through hunting and fishing (e.g., Berry 1966) have shown that members of these groups develop a highly differentiated perceptual and cognitive style (see Witkin and Berry 1975, for a review), and a personality that is characterized by independence, self-reliance, little affect, and poor interpersonal skills. On the other hand, agricultural societies such as the Temne (Berry 1966) require group action for survival. Tests administered to such groups indicate that their members develop less differentiated perceptual and cognitive styles, and their personality is characterized by much affect, interdependence, reliance on others, and good interpersonal skills. Persons with a less differentiated, or field-dependent, cognitive style are generally more skillful in interpersonally demanding occupations such as selling or entertaining, whereas persons with a highly differentiated, or field-dependent, cognitive style tend to perform well in such tasks as flying airplanes, taking aerial photographs, and doing mechanical work. Thus the ecology determines subsistence patterns, which in turn contribute to distinctive behavioral patterns.

The fact that many cultural elements are functional implies that individuals who have appropriate behavior patterns and personalities for a particular environment will fare well and will receive positive outcomes in that environment. When individuals from one culture are forced to adopt a very different cultural pattern, however, they are likely to experience high levels of stress, a reduction in positive outcomes, lower self-esteem, anomie, and general demoralization. The high rates of alcohol consumption found among Native American (Jessor, Graves, Hanson, and Jessor 1968), and the high incidence of "eco-system distrust" (distrust of people, things, and institutions in one's environment) experienced by the black ghetto unemployed (Triandis 1976) are examples of behavioral and experiential disorientation which can occur when a group is forced to exist in situations for which its culture is not appropriate.

## THE NEED FOR
## INTERCULTURAL EDUCATION

One of the main purposes of education is to prepare an individual to function effectively in his or her environment. Viewed in this manner, education should provide skills, perspectives, and information, and should help develop attitudes which would enable pupils to obtain more positive outcomes than they would have received otherwise. Individuals who belong to an ethnic group which differs from the majority must often be able to function effectively in *two* different social environments. The degree to which such individuals will be part of each environment will, of course, vary, and will be a function of the interaction of a host of complex factors. It would seem, however, that the education of such children should ideally foster the development of skills, perspectives, and attitudes which would enable them to be effective members of both environments. A good model of how this can be done is that of a fully bilingual person. Such a person is able to switch with ease and without interference from one language to the other (Lambert 1967). His or her linguistic skills are suitable not only for one environment, but also for the other. Thus he or she is able to function linguistically in an effective manner in both environments. In a similar manner, a bicultural person should be able to interact effectively with persons from *both* cultures.

In order to enable children who differ in ethnic background from the majority to do this, it is important that educators and teachers take into account the skills, perspectives, and orientations that these children bring with them to school. Ideally, of course,

this should be done for *all* children, and not just for those from a different cultural background. Thus, for example, a child who arrives in school with a field-independent orientation ideally should not be given the same curriculum as a child who arrives with a field-dependent, or field-sensitive, orientation, since for reasons discussed above, a curriculum which emphasizes exposure to many graphic materials would tend to be most helpful to the first child, but not to the second. The latter may well profit more from a curriculum which emphasizes good interpersonal relationships between teachers and students, or group learning as used by Johnson and Johnson (1983).

Ramírez and Castañeda (1974) have argued that our educational system has relied almost exclusively on the use of methods which are appropriate for persons whose cognitive and perceptual style is field-independent. Yet despite intracultural variations, many children form certain cultures (i.e., Mexican-American children) have been found to have a field-dependent or field-sensitive cognitive style. They suggest that to optimize the learning environment of these Mexican-American children, culture-matching teaching strategies, which in this case are field-sensitive strategies, should be utilized as well. Among the strategies that teachers can use, Ramírez and Castañeda mention the following: displaying expressions of approval and warmth, using personalized rewards, expressing confidence in the child's ability to succeed, giving guidance, encouraging cooperation, stressing achievement for the family, eliciting expressions of feelings from the students, emphasizing global aspects of concepts, and encouraging modeling of behaviors. Hale (1982) makes similar suggestions concerning the teaching of black children.

Schools and teachers, then, need to develop diagnostic skills which will lead to different emphases for different pupils. In addition, schools need to utilize culture-sensitization methods to make both teachers and pupils aware of cultural differences to a greater extent than they have so far. Our own research with Latin American or Hispanic pupils and Anglo-American teachers in U.S. schools (Albert 1983b, 1984a, 1984b; Albert and Adamopoulos 1976;

Albert and Triandis 1979) can be used to illustrate the importance of this.

Our objective was to find out if there were significant differences in how Latin American pupils and their Anglo teachers interpreted a wide range of common, naturally occurring school situations and behaviors. Very briefly, the procedure used was the following (see Albert 1983b for a more detailed description): Interviews with samples of teachers ($N = 70$) and pupils ($N = 150$) and detailed observations of classroom interactions were conducted to generate "critical incidents" depicting interactions between a Latin American or Hispanic[2] pupil and an American teacher.

The following is an example of a critical incident or story used in the research:

*Mr. Jones was talking with a group of his students about different kinds of food. Some of the Spanish-speaking students started telling him about a dish from their native country, and Mr. Jones mentioned that he had never tasted it. The next day one of those students brought in a plate of the food they had been talking about for Mr. Jones (Albert 1984a, p. 70).*

These incidents or stories, were then presented to new samples of teachers and pupils from each ethnic group. We asked these persons to provide an interpretation of the behaviors and feelings of pupils and teachers in each of the stories. These interpretations, which were given in the respondents' own words and language, were carefully synthesized by a panel of bicultural judges into four alternative interpretations for each story.

The interpretations provided for the above incident were:
Mr. Jones thought that:

1. The student was very nice.

2. The student wanted him to know more about his country.

3. It would be interesting to try it.

4. The student should not have brought the food (Albert 1984a, p. 70).

These alternative interpretations were paired with each other for each story, and samples of Latin American teachers and pupils, and Anglo teachers and pupils, were asked to choose for each pair of interpretations the one that they preferred. These patterns of preference were then analyzed for significant differences between groups of respondents.

It was found (Albert 1983b) that there were significant differences between groups of respondents in 1,158 out of 5, 922 comparisons made. This is four times the number of significant differences which could be expected by chance alone. Furthermore, there were one or more significant differences in preferences between groups of respondents in 141 out of 176 stories presented to the respondents. As expected, the greatest number of significant differences occurred between American teachers and Hispanic pupils. Some of the differences found between the two groups can be briefly summarized as follows: Latin American pupils tended to favor more personalized, individualized treatment; tended to place greater emphasis on interpersonal aspects of the situation; tended to blame the Hispanic children in the stories, rather than the teacher, for problems; expressed the view that children in several stories felt ashamed and fearful; and tended to feel that reliance on the family was extremely important. American teachers, on the other hand, tended to emphasize fairness and equality, focused more on task-related aspects rather than on interpersonal aspects of the situation, expressed the feeling that the teachers in the stories were uncomfortable with close interpersonal distances and touching, and tended to favor greater independence for the pupils. These are just some of the differences suggested by the data. There are, of course, many others, but we cannot adequately cover them here. (See Albert 1983b, 1984a, and 1984b for a detailed account of the differences found.)

A few examples may illustrate the relevance of these differences to the education of children of Latin American origin (see Albert and Triandis 1979).

The first example concerns the culturally based expectation on the part of many Hispanic children that their teachers will be as physically expressive and affectionate towards them as adults tend to be in their culture. Young Hispanic children, for example, like to cluster around the teacher's desk and touch her and kiss her goodbye. Many American teachers, being used to a different cultural pattern, are not aware of this need for touching; even if they are, they may not feel comfortable with this degree of physical closeness and may avoid these behaviors. The children, in turn, may experience the teacher's behavior as a rejection and may even come to think of their teacher as cold and distant. The Latin American teachers we have observed often reward a child who gives a correct answer with a hug or by touching him gently and with affection. (These teachers, incidentally, have reported that many Anglo kids like this, too.) Clearly here we are dealing with a cultural difference in paralinguistic behavior that has been described as well by Hall (1959) and documented by Sussman and Rosenfeld (1982).

During the interviews we conducted in the preliminary phase of the research (Albert and Triandis 1979), we were told about an instance in which a Hispanic child who did not speak much English was given a workbook and told by the teacher to work on her English lessons for a while, while the rest of the class worked in groups on a different task. The child felt not only isolated, but rejected by the teacher as well. In this particular case the teacher probably intended to help her learn English in the most effective way, but due to both a greater need for personal attention and the more communal nature of her culture, the child experienced the situation in a very negative way.

It is interesting to note that in a number of these situations the teacher is actually doing something which he or she feels is most efficient for teaching purposes (such as, for example, dealing with the class as a whole rather than with each child individually). Because of culturally based differences in expectations and interpretation of behavior, however, some of these actions turn out to have a negative impact on Hispanic children. In fact, in many situations Hispanic children do come to feel that their teacher dislikes them personally, or at least

dislikes Hispanic children. This feeling obviously has a detrimental effect on the child's motivation and is counter-productive for the teachers.

Teachers can help avoid this vicious circle by being aware of the children's culturally based expectations and by providing them, whenever possible, with the kind of personal attention that they need, or by finding other ways of dealing effectively with the problem. At the same time, of course, Hispanic children can be taught that their teachers behave as they do because they have different ways of doing things and not because they do not like them. These students can also be made aware that the teachers do not always have the time to provide individualized attention. (See Albert 1984a and 1984b for examples of one approach to sensitizing Anglo teachers to the perspectives of their Hispanic pupils and vice versa.)

Yet another perspective is provided by a situation in which white middle-class teachers interact with black ghetto children whose parents are unemployed. The parents of such children are likely to view the world with great distrust (Triandis 1976). The establishment, in particular, is distrusted and is often seen as exploitative. Consequently, persons who have "succeeded," such as teachers, are seen as exploitative agents of that establishment. Under these conditions it is not particularly surprising if the children of such parents view the teacher's behavior with considerable skepticism, if not with outright hostility.

Almost any behavior, no matter how positive, can be misinterpreted if the perceiver is strongly inclined to make hostile attributions. For example, if the teacher offers help, this could be viewed as the result of orders received from above and not really as a result of the teacher's good will. Alternatively, the teacher's behavior could be interpreted as ingratiation, the aim of which is to extract valuable information from the students. In short, given a negative perceptual framework on the part of the children, almost any action of the teacher could be seen as a hostile or, at best, a neutral behavior. Conversely, a teacher who is racially prejudiced could interpret any positive behavior of a pupil in a really negative manner. These conditions are obviously ripe for hostility and conflict, no matter how positive the behavior of the actors. In order to extricate teachers and pupils from such a vicious circle, it is necessary to break the perceiver's habit of automatically giving negative interpretations to the behavior of the other person.

The above examples suggest that intercultural education is necessary not only for students from diverse ethnic groups, but also for their teachers. In the course of interviewing teachers for our research, we found that many of these teachers failed to realize that cultural differences do exist and that they probably exert a powerful influence on their own, as well as on their pupils', behaviors. Some teachers, for example, would proffer the view that all children are alike. Others would attribute most, if not all, of the behavior patterns found among Hispanic children to their low socioeconomic status (SES). There is no question that low SES does contribute in important ways to certain behavior patterns. Yet it is also clear from our own research (where the socioeconomic status of the Hispanic pupils in our sample was the same as that of Anglo pupils), as well as from research conducted by other investigators (e.g., Díaz-Guerrero 1975), that cultural factors beyond socioeconomic status affect behavior patterns of members of a group in very important ways.

Albert (1979) has noted, in a different context, that this failure to perceive, or at any rate, to acknowledge, cultural differences has important historical, psychological, and cultural bases. She has identified a number of factors which may contribute to the relative lack of concern with cultural variables on the part of American investigators. These may well apply, perhaps in modified form, to American educators. They are the following: lack of direct experience with other cultures; a psychological need to simplify events, and hence to assume cross-cultural similarities; the realization that differences in test performance can be, and have been, used to discriminate against minority groups; an egalitarian ideology that postulates that teachers should treat every child in the same general manner; the fear of

creating stereotypes; the historical experience of forging a nation out of a multitude of ethnic groups; the dominant economic and political position of the United States in the world; and ethnocentric tendencies which lead us to assume that our patterns of behavior are universal.

Teachers, then, need to develop skills which will enable them to attend to ethnic group *and* individual differences in their students, so that they can understand, and effectively reach, these students. This requires not only a variety of skills, but also flexibility and sensitivity to the cultural background of the students.

Pupils from other ethnic backgrounds need to learn a variety of skills, ideas, and principles which would enable them to function more effectively in both their own and the dominant culture. Thus an understanding of their own culture as well as of the dominant culture would seem to be vitally important for these students.

## OBJECTIONS FREQUENTLY RAISED TO INTERCULTURAL EDUCATION

Having argued for the need for intercultural education, we can reasonably ask whether such education should be provided by our schools, or whether it should be left to other institutions.

For a variety of reasons, the school seems to be the most appropriate setting for intercultural education efforts. A school is often the first institution of the dominant culture which children from a minority group encounter. Their experiences in this setting are, therefore, critical to their subsequent attitudes and feelings about the dominant society. Similarly, it is often in this setting that children from the dominant culture have their first exposure to members of other ethnic and cultural groups. Schools are charged with the function of "educating" students, of teaching them about the physical and social world, as well as giving them some basic skills for functioning as members of society. Thus, while an understanding of different cultural patterns would seem critical for the minority child, it would also seem important and valuable for majority children in a multiethnic society.

A number of objections to the ideas presented here can be anticipated. Some will argue that with limited resources we cannot afford the luxury of multicultural education. The issue of cost is a complicated one, for no one knows how much money various kinds of intercultural education programs would require. Yet there is evidence that minorities drop out from school at higher rates than majority students. To cite but one example, Lucas (1971) found a 70 percent drop-out rate among Puerto Ricans in Chicago. It is well known that dropping out of school lowers a person's earning potential and may be related to higher rates of unemployment and, possibly, to higher rates of welfare payments. Thus the loss of income which results to the minority person who drops out of school, as well as society's loss of well qualified employees, and of the taxes which such employees could contribute—not to mention the human costs—should be entered into the cost equation.

In any case, there is clearly a need for making teachers aware of cultural differences through teacher in-service and pre-service training and by other means as well. Also, many of our schools already have pupils from many cultures and could utilize them as sources of information about other cultures without spending very much money. Either approach would require educational innovations and some effort on the part of teachers and administrators. It seems to us that in a society that spends over $100 billion a year on armaments that become obsolete every few years, there must be mechanisms to accomplish other kinds of goals as well. The crucial question, then, is whether we are willing to spend time, money, and above all, effort, to improve the quality of education in our society.

Another objection is centered around the argument that mainstream culture is "obviously best." This is an ethnocentric argument. As we have discussed previously, a culture produces a particular pattern of assumptions about the way the world is structured. That pattern often appears to be correct to the members of that culture, and the less infor-

mation they have available concerning other patterns, the more totally correct that pattern will appear to be. Ethnocentricism (see LeVine and Campbell 1972) tends to be characteristic of persons who have been exposed to little diverse information and to child-rearing practices which did not allow them to learn about value systems which differ from those of their parents. An ethnocentric person usually considers his or her culture completely correct, better in all respects than other cultures, and obviously suitable for adoption by all others. Yet, as we have previously discussed, there is evidence that forcing members of an ethnic group to adopt the dominant cultural pattern may *not* be the best for these individuals.

Still others may see providing intercultural education as "coddling" some minorities, since in the past other ethnic groups "adjusted" without such help. The implication which underlies this argument is that such "coddling" may be unhealthy and/ or unnecessary. But the discussion presented earlier suggests that for the minority child this may not be the case. In fact, the minority child needs to develop multiple skills in order to function effectively in his or her own environment and also in the environment of the majority.

The case can be made that majority children will also profit from the broad perspectives and the greater cognitive flexibility that are likely to come from intercultural education (Triandis 1976). There is already evidence that multilingual individuals are more creative than their monolingual counterparts (Segalowitz 1981). It is quite likely that *multicultural* individuals will be even more creative. Intercultural education would also probably help children develop a greater appreciation for diversity. In addition, this country is deficient in language skills (United States President's Commission on Foreign Language and International Studies 1979) and mainstream children exposed to other cultures may develop an interest in learning foreign languages.

Finally, some will argue that this is not compatible with American values. This argument is based on historical and cultural assumptions which have been alluded to above. Yet, if there is something unique about this society it is that it permits enough freedom for individuals to actualize their potential in unique ways. The imposition of a particular, limited, ethnocentric perspective limits these freedoms. Hence, it is fundamentally compatible with the American way to move toward multiculturalism and, therefore, toward intercultural education.

## METHODS FOR TEACHING CULTURE IN INTERCULTURAL EDUCATION PROGRAMS

Supposing we wish to provide intercultural education in our schools, the question which arises next is how to do it. We will discuss several ways in which culture has been taught and will point out some of the advantages and disadvantages of each. A broad review of procedures which have been developed for intercultural training can be found in Brislin and Pederson (1976), Landis and Brislin (1983), and Seelye (1975). The three procedures we present below seem to be the most promising. The theoretical underpinnings of these three procedures rest on analyses of social behavior (Triandis 1975, 1977).

The first method is *experiential*. At its best it would entail having the student live in a particular culture for many years. This, however, is not a feasible way to teach a large number of students. Thus, experiential exposure to other cultures utilizing "controlled" or laboratory situations (e.g., setting up a village where trainees interact with their language teachers from the other culture over a period of months) . . . [is] used by some culture-trainers (Trifonovitch 1973). Other experiential activities which can more easily be employed by schools involve tasting foods from different countries, going to ethnic neighborhoods, and participating in relevant parades and festivals.

A second method for teaching culture is *behavioral* (David 1972). This method would entail reinforcing the individual for producing behavioral patterns which are commonly found in another culture, and discouraging behaviors which are inappropriate to that other culture. This approach would probably be most effective when what is desired is

a modification of behaviors which are primarily determined by habits. This method is time-consuming, however, since it requires that each behavior be reinforced. Furthermore, it may be contended that in settings such as schools, where persons from several cultural backgrounds interact, the aim should not be to change behaviors per se, but rather to teach individuals *about* another culture. Since the focus of this approach is changing specific behaviors (e.g., always shaking hands when meeting a person from the other culture), it does not necessarily result in increased knowledge or understanding of diverse aspects of the other culture.

A third method of teaching culture emphasizes *informational* aspects of learning. One way to provide information about another culture is to assign readings about other peoples' customs or history. This alone, however, does not usually teach a person to "see the world" from the perspective of members of the other culture. A special technique designed to do this has been recently derived from social psychological theorizing (Fiedler, Mitchell, and Triandis 1971; Heider 1958; Triandis 1975). This technique, called *attribution training*, aims to teach members of one culture to make attributions commonly made by members of another culture (Triandis 1975). Attributions are *interpretations* of behavior; that is, they are inferences about the causes of a given behavior. Thus teachers commonly make attributions about the causes of their pupils' behaviors. For example, when a pupil performs poorly on a test the teacher will tend to make attributions about the child's performance. The teacher may attribute the poor performance to the pupil's lack of ability, to lack of preparation, to his or her "laziness," to lack of time on the test, or to a myriad of other factors. Pupils similarly make attributions about the actions of their teachers. Attributions are dependent on the norms, role, affects, and consequences of actions seen to be operating in a given situation (Triandis 1975). For this reason, persons from different cultures may make different attributions to the *same* behavior.

When teachers and students come from different cultural backgrounds, they are likely to have some different expectations about what behaviors are appropriate in a given situation and, at least some of the time, they are likely to make different attributions about the same behavior. Misunderstandings can then occur which impede effective interaction between the teacher and the students. It must be noted that people are often not aware of the cause for their difficulty. Thus, for example, a Hispanic student may be doing something "perfectly normal" from his perspective when he spends some time after recess helping a friend look for his lost braces. Consequently, he may be genuinely surprised when his American teacher reacts with anger when he arrives in class ten minutes late.

Attribution training is a technique designed to teach persons from one culture to interpret events as persons from another culture do. It consists of a programmed learning approach in which a person is exposed to an instrument known in the literature as the "intercultural sensitizer" (ICS) or "culture assimilator"(Albert 1983a; Albert and Adamopoulos 1976). The assimilator is an instrument for culture learning which consists of several dozen short episodes depicting a problematic interaction between persons from one culture and persons from another culture. Each episode is followed by several alternative attributions to the behavior of one of the characters in the episode. Some of the attributions provided are those which are typically made by persons from the individual's own culture, while others are attributions commonly made by persons from the other culture. The aim of the training is to teach the individual to choose the attribution typically made by members of the other culture, and thus to expand the trainee's conception of possible attributions in that situation.

At first, the individual will have difficulty doing this, and will select attributions which are made by members of his own culture. With the aid of the feedback which is provided after each choice, the individual gradually learns to select the attributions which tend to be more typical of the members of the other culture. When the individual does this, he is given additional information about the differences between the two cultures. (See Albert 1983a for details about the process of constructing "intercultural sensitizers.")

## SOME IMPLICATIONS OF INTERCULTURAL EDUCATION

Providing intercultural education is one way that schools can add flexibility and richness to each child's experience, and can teach the child that there are many ways of behaving and of perceiving the world. Such an approach could help teachers develop a new appreciation for students from diverse backgrounds, seeing their differences as resources to be explored rather than as sources of difficulty to overcome. As a result of a greater awareness of their students' backgrounds, teachers may develop new modes of teaching which may enhance their effectiveness with particular pupils.

Intercultural education could help children who belong to different ethnic groups to explore and to deal more explicitly with the difficult issue of identity, since such children would learn about their culture of origin as well as about the dominant culture of the society in which they live.

From their inception, the mission of many systems of education has been not only to provide skills and impart information, but also to provide understanding of the society in which the pupils live. Intercultural education would naturally enhance this broader mission.

## NOTES

1. We will use the terms interchangeably following Glazer and Moynihan. Glazer, N., and D. P. Moynihan, (1975) "Introduction." In N. Glazer and D. P. Moynihan (eds.) *Ethnicity: Theory and Experience*. Cambridge, MA: Harvard University Press.

2. We use the terms *Latin American* and *Hispanic* interchangeably, as our samples consisted of immigrant children from Mexico, Puerto Rico, Cuba, and a number of other Latin American countries.

## REFERENCES

Albert, R. D. (September 1979). "The Place of Culture in Modern Social Psychology." Paper presented at the meeting of the American Psychological Association, New York City.

Albert, R. D. (1983). "Mexican American Children in Educational Settings: Research on Children's and Teacher's Perceptions and Interpretations of Behavior." In E. E. García (ed.), *The Mexican American Child: Language, Cognition, and Social Development* (pp. 183–194). Tempe, AZ: Arizona State University.

Albert, R. D. and J. Adamopoulos. (1976). "An Attributional Approach to Culture Learning: The Culture Assimilator. *Topics in Culture Learning* 4, 53–60.

Albert, R. D. and H. C. Triandis. (1979). "Cross-Cultural Learning: A Theoretical Framework and Some Observations." In H. Trueba and C. Barnett-Mizrahi (eds.). *Bilingual Multicultural Education and the Professional: From Theory to Practice* (pp. 181–194). Rowley, MA: Newbury House.

Barry, H., I. Child, and M. Bacon. (1959). "Relation of Child Training to Sustenance Economy." *American Anthropologist* 61, 51–63.

Berry, J. W. (1966). "Temne and Eskimo Perceptual Skills." *International Journal of Psychology* 1, 207–229.

David, K. H. (1972). *Intercultural Adjustment and Application of Reinforcement Theory to Problems of Culture Shock*. Hilo, HI: Center for Cross-Cultural Training.

Díaz-Guerrero, R. (1975). *The Psychology of the Mexican*. Austin: University of Texas Press.

Hale, J. E. (1982). *Black Children: Their Roots, Culture, and Learning Styles*. Provo, UT: Brigham Young University Press.

Hall, E. T. (1959). *The Silent Language*. New York: Doubleday.

Heider, F. (1958). *The Psychology of Interpersonal Behavior*. New York: Wiley.

Jessor, R., T. D. Graves, R. G. Hanson, and S. L. Jessor. (1968). *Society, Personality, and Deviant Behavior*. New York: Holt, Rinehart, and Winston.

Johnson, D. W. and R. T. Johnson. (1983). "The Socialization and Achievement Crises: Are Cooperative Learning Experiences the Solution?" In L. Bickman (ed.) *Applied Social Psychology Annual* 4, (pp. 119–164). Beverly Hills: Sage Publications.

Lambert, W. E. (1967). "The Social Psychology of Bilingualism." *Journal of Social Issues* 23, 91–109.

Landis, D. and R. Brislin. (1983). *Handbook of Intercultural Training*. New York: Pergamon Press.

LeVine, R. A. and D. T. Campbell. (1972). *Ethnocentrism: Theories of Conflict, Ethnic Attitudes, and Group Behavior*. New York: Wiley.

Lucas, I. (1971) *Puerto Rican Dropouts in Chicago: Numbers and Motivation*. Chicago: Council on Urban Education.

Ramírez, M. and A. Castañeda. (1974). *Cultural Democracy, Bicognitive Development, and Education*. New York: Academic Press.

Seelye, H. N. (1975). *Teaching Culture*. Skokie, IL: National Textbook Company, in conjunction with the American Council on the Teaching of Foreign Languages.

Segalowitz, N. (1981). "Issues in the Cross-Cultural Study of Bilingual Development." In H. C. Triandis and A. Hernon (eds.). *Handbook of Cross-Cultural Psychology,* (Vol. 4) (pp. 55–92). Boston: Allyn and Bacon.

Sussman, N. M. and H. M. Rosenfeld. (1982). "Influence of Culture, Language, and Sex on Conversational Distance." *Journal of Personality and Social Psychology* 42, 66–74.

Triandis, H. C. (1964). "Cultural Influences upon Cognitive Processes." In L. Berkowitz (ed.). *Advances in Experimental Social Psychology*. (pp. 1–48). New York: Academic Press.

Triandis, H. C. (1972). *The Analysis of Subjective Culture*. New York: Wiley.

Triandis, H. C. (1975). "Training, Cognitive Complexity, and Interpersonal Attitudes." In R. W. Brislin, S. Bochner, and W. Lonner (eds.). *Cross-Cultural Perspectives on Learning*. (pp. 39–77). New York: Halsted/Wiley/Sage.

Triandis, H. C. (1976). *Variations of Black and White Perceptions of the Social Environment*. Champaign, IL: University of Illinois Press.

Triandis, H. C. (1977). *Interpersonal Behavior*. Monterey, CA: Brooks/ Cole.

Trifonovitch, G. (1973). "On Cross-Cultural Orientation Techniques." *Topics in Culture Learning* 1, 38–47.

United States Presidents Commission on Language

and International Studies. (1979). *Strength through Wisdom: A Critique of U.S. Capability*. Washington, DC: U.S. Government Printing Office.

Witkin, H. A. and J. W. Berry. (1975). "Psychological Differentiation in Cross-Cultural Perspectives." *Journal of Cross-Cultural Psychology* 6, 4–87.

## CONCEPTS AND QUESTIONS FOR CHAPTER 8

**1.** What do you see as most necessary for the improvement of intercultural communication during the next decade?

**2.** How can intercultural communication be improved domestically? Internationally? Is one form more important than the other? Why?

**3.** Given all the complexities associated with intercultural communication, do you think there is really any hope for the future?

**4.** From Hatch's article on the evaluation of culture, what have you discovered that will permit you to evaluate your own culture?

**5.** What does Hatch mean when he differentiates between ethnocentric and humanistic values? Which are best in your opinion? Why?

**6.** What are the important ethical questions that communicators must ask themselves as they engage in intercultural communication?

**7.** What does Kim mean when she refers to a holistic approach to knowledge in the East and how does this approach differ from Western tradition?

**8.** Explain how Kim views Eastern and Western views of reality as complementary rather than competitive.

**9.** How do you believe the educational needs of a multicultural society can best be met?

**10.** What do Albert and Triandis suggest as the best way to achieve intercultural education?

## SUGGESTED READINGS

Asante, M. K. "Intercultural communication: An inquiry into research directions" in D. Nimmo, ed. *Communication Yearbook* 4, New Brunswick, N. J.: Transaction, 1980, pp. 401–410. In this paper Asante explores two prevalent schools of thought in intercultural communication scholarship: the cultural dialogist and the cultural critic. He notes that most intercultural communication theories have a Eurocentric bias, which he explicates along with alternatives to this perspective.

Asuncion-Lang, N. C. *Ethical Perspectives and Critical Issues in Intercultural Communication*. Falls Church, Va.: Speech Communication Association, 1979. This book contains a collection of essays developed at a conference entitled "Ethics, Responsibility, and Standards in Intercultural Communication, Education, Training, and Research." The organizers of the conference and the editor believe that a "new set of ethical questions has attained a new degree of urgency" in the interactions among peoples of different cultures.

Conagelo, N., C. H. Foxley, and D. Dustin, eds. *Multi-Cultural Nonsexist Education: A Human Relations Approach.* Dubuque, Iowa: Kendall Hunt, 1979. Here principles of human relations are applied to teaching. The text contains articles from individual authors on such topics as human emotions and feelings, discovering empathy, mediating cultures, multicultural aspects of human relations, designing multicultural programs, the legal vicissitudes of bilingual communication, and racism. A comprehensive bibliography is included.

Condon, J. "Values and ethics in communication across cultures: Some notes on the North American case." *Communication* 6 (1981), pp. 255–265. The author argues that for an examination of ethics in intercultural communication, one begins not with broad statements of ethical principles, but with a narrower analysis of cultural values and the range of behavior that is permissible in cultures. Within this range it should be possible to identify preferred behaviors and to deduce from them the underlying ethical principles. To illustrate this point, Condon looks at a number of value items in the United States and contrasts them with several other cultures.

Feagin, J. R. *Racial and Ethnic Relations.* Englewood Cliffs, N.J.: Prentice-Hall, 1978. This text contains outlines of the history, education, religion, arts, economy, and so on, of Irish-, Italian-, Jewish-, Mexican-, and Japanese-Americans. It discusses typical conflicts and suggests remedies.

Jervis, R. *Perception and Misperception in International Politics.* Princeton, N. J.: Princeton University Press, 1976. Although this book is concerned primarily with international relations, it nevertheless deals with many issues that are central to any study of cross-cultural relations. Jervis discusses how decision makers perceive information for cultures that are foreign to their own. He also points out some common misperceptions and the various ways these problems can be avoided in international politics.

Rogers, E. M. and F. F. Shoemaker. *Communication of Innovations: A Cross-Cultural Approach,* 2d ed. New York: Free Press, 1971. This book is concerned with the question of how innovations (ideas, products, and practices perceived as new by an individual) diffuse to the members of a social system. The new ideas range from tractors in Turkey to family planning techniques among Hindu housewives.

Samovar, L. A., R. E. Porter, and N. Jain. *Understanding Intercultural Communication.* Belmont, Calif.: Wadsworth, 1980, Chapter 8. The last chapter, entitled "Futurism: What Is Next, and Next, and Next . . . ," focuses on a number of needs and challenges facing intercultural communication and offers the authors' philosophy about how to treat the ethical implications of intercultural communication.

Triandis, H. C. and W. W. Lanbert, eds. *Handbook of Cross-Cultural Psychology,* vol 1. Boston: Allyn & Bacon, 1980. The last chapter deals with the politics and ethics of cross-cultural research, providing guidelines about study design and corroboration, reseachers' responsibilities, and professional responsibility.

Wedge, B. "Communication analysis and comprehensive diplomacy" in A. S. Hoffman, ed. *International Communication and the New Diplomacy.* Bloomington: Indiana University Press, 1968, pp. 22–47. This article stresses the theme that "misunderstandings of the most concrete and literal kind have played a large role in conflicts between nations." It is Wedge's contention that these conflicts are usually based on differing value systems and orientations. To illustrate this point, he examines actual cases in international diplomacy.

## ADDITIONAL READINGS

Allport, G. *The Nature of Prejudice.* New York: Doubleday, 1958.

Banks, J. A. *Multiethnic Education: Theory and Practice.* Boston: Allyn & Bacon, 1981.

Brislin, R. W. "Cross-cultural research in psychology." *Annual Review of Psychology* 34 (1983), 363–400.

Cavalli-Sforza, L. L. and M. M. Feldman. *Cultural Transmission and Education.* Princeton: Princeton University Press, 1981.

Cherry, C. *World Communication: Threat or Promise.* New York: John Wiley, 1971.

Condon, J. C. and S. Mitsuko, eds. *Communication Across Cultures for What? A Symposium on Human Responsibility in Intercultural Communication.* Tokyo: Simual Press, 1976.

Critchfield, T. M. and C. Paik. "Where is the line? Ethics in intercultural translation," *Communication: The Journal of the Communication Association of the Pacific* 9 (1980), 112–116.

Dubois, R. D. *All This and Something More: Pioneering in Intercultural Education.* Bryn Mawr: Dorrance & Company, 1984.

Edelstein, A. C. *Comparative Communication Research.* Beverly Hills, Calif: Sage Publications, 1982.

Fisher, G. *American Communication in a Global Society.* Norwood, N.J.: Ablex, 1979.

Ganley, O. H. and G. D. Ganley. *To Inform or to Control: The New Communication Network.* New York: McGraw-Hill, 1982.

Hanney, R. G. *An Attainable Global Perspective.* New York: Center for Global Perspectives, 1976.

Harwood, K. "Ethical limits of multinational communication." *Communication: The Journal of the Communication Association of the Pacific* 10 (1981), 83–86.

Johnnesen, R. *Ethics in Human Communication.* Manhasset Hills, N. Y.: Avery Publishing Group, 1978.

Lent, J. A. "Western type communications research in the third world: A critical appraisal." *World Communication* 14 (1985), 149–161.

Lovall, O. S., ed. *Cultural Pluralism Versus Assimilation.* Northfield, Minn.: Norwegian American Association, 1977.

Maruyama, M. and A. Harpkins. *Cultures of the Future.* Paris: Mouton, 1978.

Miller, J. *Many Voices: Bilingualism, Culture, and Education.* Boston: Routledge & Kegan Paul, 1983.

Nordenstreng, K. and H. Schiller. *National Sovereignty and International Communication.* Norwood, NJ.: Ablex, 1979.

Pratte, R. *Pluralism in Education: Conflict, Clarity, and Commitment.* Springfield, Ill: Charles C. Thomas, 1979.

Rogers, E. M., ed. *Communication and Development: Critical Perspectives.* Beverly Hills, Calif.: Sage Publications, 1976.

Schramm, W. and D. Lerner, eds. *Communication and Change: The Last Ten Years—and the Next.* Honolulu: University of Hawaii Press, 1976.

Seelye, H. N. *Teaching Culture Strategies for Intercultural Communication.* Lincolnwood, Ill.: National Textbook Co., 1984.

Smith, A. *The Geopolitics of Information: How Western Culture Dominates the World.* New York: Oxford University Press, 1980.

Triandis, H. C. "Reflections on trends in cross-cultural research." *Journal of Cross-Cultural Psychology* 11 (1980), 35–38.

Walsh, J. E. *Humanistic Culture Learning.* Honolulu: University of Hawaii Press, 1979.

Wendt, J. R. "Uncle Sam on the bad news bears: Human rights as intercultural communication" in M. Burgoon, ed. *Communication Yearbook* 5. New Brunswick: N. J.: Transaction Books, 1982, pp. 571–589.

# Epilogue

We introduced the topic of intercultural communication by pointing out both its boundaries and its territory. By looking at what intercultural communication is and is not, we were able to establish some guidelines for our investigation. In general terms, we suggested that intercultural communication occurred whenever a message sender is a member of one culture and a message receiver is of another culture. Once this broad definition was presented we were able to survey some specific refinements. We noted that culture was the sum total of the learned behaviors of a particular group and that these behaviors (attitudes, values, language, and so forth) were transmitted from generation to generation. Differences among international, interracial, and cross-cultural communication also were examined.

Following our general introduction to intercultural communication, we focused on one of the conceptual threads woven through this book. This concept suggests that to understand intercultural communication one must realize the impact and influence of past experience. Anyone who has observed human interaction will have little trouble accepting the notion that where people come from—their cultural histories—is crucial to communication. Your prior experiences, structured by your culture, help to determine what you value, what you see, and how you behave. In short, what your culture has taught you, in both conscious and unconscious ways, will be manifest during intercultural communication. For example, Navajo Indians believe that the universe is full of dangers and that illness is a price to be paid for disorder and disharmony. These particular views are bound to be reflected in Navajo intercultural interactions. In another example, people from some cultures deem men more important than women. These people's behavior toward each sex will be influenced by this orientation. Even one's background colors what is perceived. Judgment of beauty is an example. In the Unites States, the slim, statuesque female represents the cultural stereotype of beauty. Yet in many

Eastern European countries, a heavier, stockier body reflects the ideal. These examples—and there are countless others—point out that your culture gives the framework for your experiences and values. They, in turn, define your view of the world and dictate how you interact within that world.

Because people share cultural experiences in a symbolic manner, we explored the two most common symbol systems—verbal and nonverbal. Representing ideas and feelings by symbols is a complex and complicated procedure at best. When the dimension of culture is added to the encoding and decoding process, however, the act of sharing internal states becomes even more intricate. To help you understand this act, we sought to demonstrate the relationship between three closely related axioms: (1) language helps shape thoughts and perceptions (Whorf's linguistic relativity hypothesis), (2) diverse cultures have *different* words with *similar* meanings (foreign languages), and (3) cultures can have the same words with vastly *different* meanings (subcultural use of vernacular and argot). We noted that the problems of coding systems plague actions as well as words. Even a simple hand motion can convey a host of unrelated meanings and interpretations. The hand gesture used by a hitchhiker in the United States is apt to produce a punch in the nose in Ghana. In short, the symbols used to share cultural experiences may often be subject to confusion and ambiguity.

In the next section of the book we examined ideas and techniques that contribute to successful intercultural communication. We proceeded on the assumption that intercultural communication is, by its very definition and nature, an action and an overt activity. Intercultural communication is, in short, something people do to and with each other. Because of advances in technology, such as improved air travel and communication satellites, all people seem to be engaging in more and more of this activity. In addition to increased communication among foreign cultures, the late 1960s and 1970s revealed that there were a number of subcommunities within the boundaries of the United States. Subcultures such as the blacks, the urban poor, women, gays, the elderly, youth, Chicanos, and Asians wanted and demanded contact and dialogue with the main culture. Consequently, all Americans are engaging in intercultural communication at an accelerating rate. If this interaction is to be significant, and if intercultural communication is to foster increased understanding and cooperation, then potential problems must be avoided.

Finally, we extended our analysis toward the future. This is due, in part, to the fact that most intercultural interactions and meetings lie in the future. The success of your communication experiences may well depend on your philosophy and attitude toward intercultural communication. The way you behave around others is often a reflection of your philosophy toward life and toward yourself. Yet each person is capable of change from day to day and from situation to situation. Individual alterations represent a gift that accompanies personal liberty. As Plutarch noted over two thousand years ago, "All things are daily changing." If intercultural exchanges are to be considered worthy of time and energy, each person must begin to realize that such change is possible.

But change, as everyone knows, is not simple. Many attitudes and behaviors are deeply ingrained. And many of them are subject to ethnocentric influences. By this we mean that as each person learns a cultural pattern of behavior that person is, in both obvious and subtle ways, acquiring a corresponding subjective and normative value judgment associated with that behavior. Many people are guilty of assuming that their cultural group, whatever it may be, is superior to all other groups. Everyone therefore judges other cultures by his or her own standards. How often do people say, "Our way is the right way"? Or they may foolishly assume that their ideas and solutions to problems are the only correct ones. This attitude is often manifest in such ideas as are expressed by the statement, "If you are not part of the solution, you are part of the problem." This shortsighted notion fails to recognize that most social problems are complex and must be solved by many ideas and many approaches. The danger of such a philosophy should be self-evident. It is indeed difficult to achieve mutual understanding if one's culture is placed in a central position of priority or worth. How foolish to assume that because one culture prays on Saturday while another worships on Sunday, one is superior to the other. Or take, for example, the cultural values of competition and winning. Because they are important values to North Americans, many assume that all cultures ought to strive to win and to be first. There are numerous cultures, however, where competition and winning are unimportant. On the contrary, cooperation and sharing are valued highly. To be guilty of ethnocentrism is to doom intercultural communication to failure.

The new mode of communicative behavior should not only be void of ethnocentrism, but it also ought to reflect an attitude of mutual respect and trust. We emphasize that intercultural communication will not be successful if, by actions or words, the communicators appear to be condescending. Every individual and every culture wants to believe it is as worthy as any other. Actions that manifest the opposite will diminish the worth and tend to stifle meaningful interaction.

The changes required are not easy. They require that we all possess a willingness to communicate, have empathy toward foreign and alien cultures, be tolerant of views that differ from our own, and develop a universalistic, relativistic approach to the universe. If we have the resolve to adopt these behaviors and attitudes and the desire to overcome ethnocentrism and feelings of superiority, we can begin to know the feelings of exhilaration that come when we have made contact with someone far removed from our own sphere of experiences. Intercultural communication offers the arena for this interpersonal contact. Our ability to change, to make adjustments in our communication habits, gives us the potential tools to make that contact successful.

# Index of Names

# Index of Subjects